WAYS OF KNOWING

Selected Readings

Second Edition

edited by

Kevin E. Dodson and Jon Avery

KENDALL/HUNT PUBLISHING COMPANY
4050 Westmark Drive   Dubuque, Iowa 52002

Copyright © 1993, 1994 by Kevin E. Dodson, Jon Avery, and Center for Philosophical Studies.

ISBN 0-8403-9464-0

Printed in the United States of America

10   9   8   7   6   5   4   3   2   1

TABLE OF CONTENTS

SECTION VI: THE FINE ARTS AND COMMUNICATION

PREFACE

This text is the product of our experience teaching a course entitled the Philosophy of Knowledge (Philosophy 130) at Lamar University. Philosophy 130 is the centerpiece of Lamar's "Ways of Knowing" core curriculum, hence the title of this book. Our core curriculum seeks to introduce students to the various ways in which we humans acquire and express our knowledge of ourselves and our world. Unfortunately, despite the availability of many fine introductory texts in philosophy, we encountered a dearth of texts that would be appropriate for this type of course. In general, introductory texts tend to focus on the traditional problems of philosophy, which they treat in a piecemeal manner, while we needed a text constructed around our particular theme.

This book employs an integrative approach to philosophy that situates it at the center of our cultural and intellectual life and thus provides an excellent and unique introduction to the field. Given its structure and the range of its coverage, it is also an ideal text for first-year orientation courses seeking to introduce students to college and university life. Every academic department should be able to find some reading here that is applicable to its respective discipline.

So many people played a role in the development of our curriculum, and by extension this text, that it is impossible to do justice to all of their myriad contributions. Nonetheless, at the risk of excluding some, we wish to acknowledge those contributions. Before doing so, however, we would like to express our gratitude to the entire faculty of Lamar University-Beaumont for its support of the Philosophy of Knowledge course and its commitment to an innovative core curriculum.

Lamar's Core Curriculum Council has been central to the development of this program of undergraduate education, and it deserves much of the credit for its success. As members of the Council's Subcommittee on Philosophy, Fred Young, Donna Birdwell-Pheasant, and Mary Alice Baker were especially generous in providing assistance and encouragement to us in our efforts. Arthur Stewart, the Director of Lamar's Center for Philosophical Studies, was instrumental in the evolution of both this text and the course in the philosophy of knowledge, as were our former colleagues Virgil Agnew and George Wall and our current colleague Kevin Daigle.

The final contents of this volume reflect contributions made by numerous members of the Lamar faculty. We would like to express special thanks to Kendall Blanchard, Wayne Carley, Lynne Lokensgard, and Tim Summerlin for the time and effort they devoted to crafting the introductory essays to the various sections of this book. In addition to these contributors, numerous members of the Lamar faculty made suggestions that were pivotal in our selection of the readings contained herein. We would like to thank Cruse Melvin, Dale Ortego, Hugh Peebles, John Sullivan, and Mike Warren from the natural sciences and mathematics. Bruce Drury, James Esser, Charles Hawkins, Don Price, Glen Utter, James Walker, and Stuart Wright generously assisted us with the selections in the social sciences. Lisa Chaisson and Larry King were invaluable as regards the fine arts and communication. We are greatly indebted to Chris Baker, Christine Bridges, Catalina Castillon, Greg Kelley, Robin Latimer, Dale Priest, Ken Rivers, Jim Sanderson, Sallye Sheppeard, JoAnn Stiles, John Storey, and James Vanderholt for their help in the field of the humanities.

No book can ever be completed without the production assistance of dedicated professionals. Kourtney Owens and Linda Jordan are to be commended for their patience and willingness to go above and beyond the call of duty whenever we asked for their aid. In addition to contributing an introductory essay, Tim Summerlin supervised the production of this book. Finally, we owe a very special debt of gratitude to Cindy Colichia, our copy editor for the first edition, without whom this text would not be a reality today.

SECTION I
PHILOSOPHY

THEME QUESTIONS

1. What is philosophy?

2. What is the role of philosophy in our intellectual and cultural life?

3. Why is it important to study philosophy?

Introduction: What is Philosophy?

Kevin E. Dodson

For most of you who are reading these words, this is your first course in philosophy, and you're probably wondering right about now just what philosophy is and why you should be taking a course in it. Well, the easy answer, and the one that probably applies to many of you, is that this course fulfills a requirement. Fair enough. Or is it? If you are an inquisitive sort, that answer wouldn't satisfy you. You want to know why your university or college saw fit to require such a course of you. (Let this be your first lesson in critical thinking: don't accept the easy answer at face value; ask questions.) Well, I can't answer that question without telling you a little about philosophy itself. In the end, you learn about philosophy by doing it, but here is my best shot.

In the history of the western world, systematic inquiry into nature and humanity began in ancient Greece around the sixth century B.C.E. In fact, the word 'philosophy' comes from two Greek words, *philo* (love) and *sophos* (wisdom), and originally meant the love of wisdom. The first western philosophers were a diverse group of thinkers we now call the Presocratics. They asked basic questions about the physical universe: what is it made of? and how does it work? Their answers were simplistic by our standards, but they are the historical starting point of natural science and we wouldn't be where we are today without their pioneering efforts. In the second half of the fifth century B.C.E., a great philosopher named Socrates came onto the scene in ancient Athens. Socrates believed that the most important questions one could ask were not about nature, but about human life and how it should be lived. Thus, the great division between natural philosophy, the study of the physical world or cosmos, and moral philosophy, the study of humanity, was born.

Our modern science comes from these beginnings in natural and moral philosophy. This process took a long time; in fact, it was only completed in the last two hundred years. Before the modern division of intellectual labor into the various social and natural sciences, scientists saw themselves as philosophers. The great Isaac Newton, the father of modern physics, entitled his most important book *The Mathematical Principles of Natural Philosophy*. Today we think of him as a physicist, but he thought of himself as a philosopher. The same is true in the social sciences. Adam Smith, whose book *The Wealth of Nations* started the science of economics, was a philosophy professor and thought of himself as writing a work of moral philosophy, though we consider it to be the first great work of economic thought.

You see philosophy has been like a very successful television series in that it has produced a lot of spinoffs. The same process has been at work over and over again in the history of philosophy. Over time, a field of inquiry within philosophy has developed a well-defined subject matter along with its own unique set of concepts, theories, and techniques of investigation. Once this happens, a child is born. A new science splits off from philosophy and goes its own way.

Now you might think that after having so many fields leave the nest, there wouldn't be that much left for philosophers to do, but that hasn't proven to be the case. There are still lots of questions that philosophers can ask and that need to be asked. We ask questions *about* the sciences, as well as about many other topics. Philosophy is essentially a self-reflective activity and involves all aspects of human life, experience, and activity. Philosophy is the critical reflection on the principles of right thought and right action. Since all human life involves thought and action, all human life has a philosophical dimension, and that leaves philosophers a lot to think about.

In fact, you are something of a philosopher yourself; all human beings are. Every time you asked questions about right and wrong, good and bad, God, and knowledge, to name just a few topics, you were asking philosophical questions. What's more, we cannot seem to avoid such questions because they just come with the territory of being human.

Human life is so rich in science, morality, art, and religion that it provides an inexhaustible store of material for philosophical reflection. In each of these different areas, we can ask questions about the basic concepts we use. For example, when I think about morality, I want to know about the nature of right and wrong, the character of the good life, and where all of this comes from. These are foundational questions or, in other words, the sorts of questions we ask when we want to get to the bottom of things. Further, we can also ask questions about how the various areas of human life that I mentioned are related to each other. When I think about morality, for instance, I eventually get caught up in questions about the relationship between morality, on the one hand, and science, art, and religion, on the other. These are integrative questions, questions about how it all fits or hangs together. In philosophy, we ask and try to answer both of these types of questions, which is what we are about to do with this book. Basically, we are going to try to get to the bottom of things and see how it all fits together.

Philosophy, then, is so fundamental and so central to our intellectual and practical activity as human beings that it is unavoidable. It is merely a question of whether we are going to think clearly, coherently, and critically about philosophical issues, not whether we are going to think about them. By thinking about philosophical issues, you increase your understanding of human intellectual and cultural life (including your own academic major and outside interests), gain new insight into the social and personal issues of the day, and develop your skills of reasoning and communication. And that is why you are required to take a course in philosophy.

Kevin Dodson, What is Philosophy?

1.   The word 'philosophy' comes from the two ancient Greek words,

        _____ and _____, and originally meant

        _____ .

2.   Identify three philosophical questions you have already considered.

3.   Identify your major area of academic interest.

4.   Identify three philosophical questions that relate to your major area of academic interest.

Bertrand Russell*

ON THE VALUE OF PHILOSOPHY

Having now come to the end of our brief and very incomplete review of the problems of philosophy, it will be well to consider, in conclusion, what is the value of philosophy and why it ought to be studied. It is the more necessary to consider this question, in view of the fact that many men, under the influence of science or of practical affairs, are inclined to doubt whether philosophy is anything better than innocent but useless trifling, hair-splitting distinctions, and controversies on matters concerning which knowledge is impossible.

This view of philosophy appears to result, partly from a wrong conception of the ends of life, partly from a wrong conception of the kind of goods which philosophy strives to achieve. Physical science, through the medium of inventions, is useful to innumerable people who are wholly ignorant of it; thus the study of physical science is to be recommended, not only, or primarily, because of the effect on the student, but rather because of the effect on mankind in general. Thus utility does not belong to philosophy. If the study of philosophy has any value at all for others than students of philosophy, it must be only indirectly, through its effects upon the lives of those who study it. It is in these effects, therefore, if anywhere, that the value of philosophy must be primarily sought.

But further, if we are not to fail in our endeavor to determine the value of philosophy, we must first free our minds from the prejudices of what are wrongly called 'practical' men. The 'practical' man, as this word is often used, is one who recognizes only material needs, who realizes that men must have food for the body, but is oblivious of the necessity of providing food for the mind. If all men were well off, if poverty and disease had been reduced to their lowest possible point, there would still remain much to be done to produce a valuable society; and even in the existing world the goods of the mind are at least as important as the goods of the body. It is exclusively among the goods of the mind that the value of philosophy is to be found; and only those who are not indifferent to these goods can be persuaded that the study of philosophy is not a waste of time.

Philosophy, like all other studies, aims primarily at knowledge. The knowledge it aims at is the kind of knowledge which gives unity and system to the body of the sciences, and the kind which results from a critical examination of the grounds of our convictions, prejudices, and beliefs. But it cannot be maintained that philosophy has had any very great measure of success in its attempts to provide answers to its questions. If you ask a mathematician, a mineralogist, a historian, or any other man of learning, what definite body of truths has been ascertained by his science, his answer will last as long as you are willing to listen. But if you put the same question to a philosopher, he will, if he is candid, have to confess that his study has not

*Betrand Russell (1872–1970) was a leading 20th-century British logician, philosopher, and man of letters. Russell and his Cambridge colleague Alfred North Whitehead gained international acclaim in 1910 with the publication of *Principia Mathematica*, in which they attempted to reduce the whole of mathematics to logic. Their systematization of logic formed the basis for later development of modern formal logic. Russell was awarded the Nobel Prize for Literature in 1950 for his over seventy published works, which include *Human Knowledge, its Scope and Limits, Introduction to Mathematical Philosophy,* and *A History of Western Philosophy.* Philosophically, Russell argued for the primacy of logic and science in our understanding of the world and for humanitarianism in politics.

Reprinted from The Problems of Philosophy by Bertrand Russell (1912) by permission of Oxford University Press.

achieved positive results such as have been achieved by other sciences. It is true that this is partly accounted for by the fact that, as soon as definite knowledge concerning any subject becomes possible, this subject ceases to be called philosophy, and becomes a separate science. The whole study of the heavens, which now belongs to astronomy, was once included in philosophy; Newton's great work was called 'the mathematical principles of natural philosophy'. Similarly, the study of the human mind, which was a part of philosophy, has now been separated from philosophy and has become the science of psychology. Thus, to a great extent, the uncertainty of philosophy is more apparent that real: those questions which are already capable of definite answers are placed in the sciences, while those only to which, at present, no definite answer can be given, remain to form the residue which is called philosophy.

This is, however, only a part of the truth concerning the uncertainty of philosophy. There are many question—and among them those that are of the profoundest interest to our spiritual life—which, so far as we can see, must remain insoluble to the human intellect unless its powers become of quite a different order from what they are now. Has the universe any unity of plan or purpose, or is it a fortuitous concourse of atoms? Is consciousness a permanent part of the universe, giving hope of indefinite growth in wisdom, or is it a transitory accident on a small planet on which life must ultimately become impossible? Are good and evil of importance to the universe or only to man? Such questions are asked by philosophy, and variously answered by various philosophers. But it would seem that, whether answers be otherwise discoverable or not, the answers suggested by philosophy are none of them demonstrably true. Yet, however slight may be the hope of discovering an answer, it is part of the business of philosophy to continue the consideration of such questions, to make us aware of their importance, to examine all the approaches to them, and to keep alive that speculative interest in the universe which is apt to be killed by confining ourselves to definitely ascertainable knowledge.

Many philosophers, it is true, have held that philosophy could establish the truth of certain answers to such fundamental questions. They have supposed that what is of most importance in religious beliefs could be proved by strict demonstration to be true. In order to judge of such attempts, it is necessary to take a survey of human knowledge, and to form an opinion as to its methods and its limitations. On such a subject it would be unwise to pronounce dogmatically; but if the investigations of our previous chapters have not led us astray, we shall be compelled to renounce the hope of finding philosophical proofs of religious beliefs. We cannot, therefore, include as part of the value of philosophy any definite set of answers to such questions. Hence, once more, the value of philosophy must not depend upon any supposed body of definitely ascertainable knowledge to be acquired by those who study it.

The value of philosophy is, in fact, to be sought largely in its very uncertainty. The man who has no tincture of philosophy goes through life imprisoned in the prejudices derived from common sense, from the habitual beliefs of his age or his nation, and from convictions which have grown up in his mind without the co-operation or consent of his deliberate reason. To such a man the world tends to become definite, finite, obvious; common objects rouse no questions, and unfamiliar possibilities are contemptuously rejected. As soon as we begin to philosophize, on the contrary, we find, as we saw in our opening chapters, that even the most everyday things lead to problems to which only very incomplete answers can be given. Philosophy, though unable to tell us with certainty what is the true answer to the doubts which it raises, is able to suggest many possibilities which enlarge our thoughts and free them from the tyranny of custom. Thus, while diminishing our feeling of certainty as to what things are, it greatly increases our knowledge as to what they may be; it removes the somewhat arrogant dogmatism of those who have never travelled into the region of liberating doubt, and it keeps alive our sense of wonder by showing familiar things in an unfamiliar aspect.

Apart from its utility in showing unsuspected possibilities, philosophy has a value—perhaps its chief value—through the greatness of the objects which it contemplates, and the freedom from narrow and personal aims resulting from this contemplation. The life of the instinctive man is shut up within the circle of his private interests: family and friends may be included, but the outer world is not regarded except as it may help or hinder what comes within the circle of instinctive wishes. In such a life there is something feverish and confined, in comparison with which the philosophic life is calm and free. The private world of instinctive interests is a small one, set in the midst of a great and powerful world which must, sooner or later, lay our private world in ruins. Unless we can so enlarge our interests as to include the whole outer world, we remain like a garrison in a beleaguered fortress, knowing that the enemy prevents escape and that ultimate surrender is inevitable. In such a life there is no peace, but a constant strife between the insistence of desire and the powerlessness of will. In one way or another, if our life is to be great and free, we must escape this prison and this strife.

One way of escape is by philosophic contemplation. Philosophic contemplation does not, in its widest survey, divide the universe into two hostile camps—friends and foes, helpful and hostile, good and bad—it views the whole impartially. Philosophic contemplation, when it is unalloyed, does not aim at proving that the rest of the universe is akin to man. All acquisition of knowledge is an enlargement of the Self, but this enlargement is best attained when it is not directly sought. It is obtained when the desire for knowledge is alone operative, by a study which does not wish in advance that its objects should have this or that character, but adapts the Self to the characters which it finds in its objects. This enlargement of Self is not obtained when, taking the Self as it is, we try to show that the world is so similar to this Self that knowledge of it is possible without any admission of what seems alien. The desire to prove this is a form of self-assertion and, like all self-assertion, it is an obstacle to the growth of Self which it desires, and of which the Self knows that it is capable. Self-assertion, in philosophic speculation as elsewhere, views the world as a means to its own ends; thus it makes the world of less account than Self, and the Self sets bounds to the greatness of its goods. In contemplation, on the contrary, we start from the not-Self, and through its greatness the boundaries of Self are enlarged; through the infinity of the universe the mind which contemplates it achieves some share in infinity.

For this reason greatness of soul is not fostered by those philosophies which assimilate the universe to Man. Knowledge is a form of union of Self and not-Self; like all union, it is impaired by dominion, and therefore by any attempt to force the universe into conformity with what we find in ourselves. There is a widespread philosophical tendency towards the view which tells us that Man is the measure of all things, that truth is man-made, that space and time and the world of universals are properties of the mind, and that, if there be anything not created by the mind, it is unknowable and of no account for us. This view, if our previous discussions were correct, is untrue; but in addition to being untrue, it has the effect of robbing philosophic contemplation of all that gives it value, since it fetters contemplation to Self. What it calls knowledge is not a union with the not-Self, but a set of prejudices, habits, and desires, making an impenetrable veil between us and the world beyond. The man who finds pleasure in such a theory of knowledge is like the man who never leaves the domestic circle for fear his word might not be law.

The true philosophic contemplation, on the contrary, finds its satisfaction in every enlargement of the not-Self, in everything that magnifies the objects contemplated, and thereby the subject contemplating. Everything, in contemplation, that is personal or private, everything that depends upon habit, self-interest, or desire, distorts the object, and hence impairs the union which the intellect seeks. By thus making a barrier between subject and object, such personal and private things become a prison to the intellect. The free intellect will see as God might see, without a *here* and *now*, without hopes and fears, without the trammels of customary beliefs and traditional prejudices, calmly dispassionately, in the sole and exclusive desire of knowledge—knowledge as impersonal, as purely contemplative, as it is possible for man to attain. Hence also the free intellect will value more the abstract and universal knowledge into which the accidents of private history do not enter, than the knowledge brought by the senses, and dependent, as such knowledge must be, upon an exclusive and personal point of view and a body whose sense-organs distort as much as they reveal.

The mind which has become accustomed to the freedom and impartiality of philosophic contemplation will preserve something of the same freedom and impartiality in the world of action and emotion. It will view its purposes and desires as parts of the whole, with the absence of insistence that results from seeing them as infinitesimal fragments in a world of which all the rest is unaffected by any one man's deeds. The impartiality which, in contemplation, is the unalloyed desire for truth, is the very same quality of mind which, in action, is justice, and in emotion is that universal love which can be given to all, and not only to those who are judged useful or admirable. Thus contemplation enlarges not only the objects of our thoughts, but also the objects of our actions and or affections: it makes us citizens of the universe, not only of one walled city at war with all the rest. In this citizenship of the universe consists man's true freedom, and his liberation from the thraldom of narrow hopes and fears.

Thus, to sum up our discussion of the value of philosophy; Philosophy is to be studied, not for the sake of any definite answers to its questions, since no definite answers can, as a rule, be known to be true, but rather for the sake of the questions themselves; because these questions enlarge our conception of what is possible, enrich our intellectual imagination and diminish the dogmatic assurance which closes the mind against speculation; but above all because, through the greatness of the universe which philosophy contemplates, the mind also is rendered great, and becomes capable of that union with the universe which constitutes its highest good.

Bertrand Russell, On the Value of Philosophy

1.   According to Bertrand Russell, where is the value of philosophy to be found? Explain why Russell thinks this is the case.

2.   Russell maintains that we can include a definite set of answers to philosophical questions as part of the value of philosophy

     a.   True   b.   False

3.   Russell holds that the man who has had some philosophy is bound to go through life imprisoned in the prejudices derived from common sense and the habitual beliefs of his age or nation.

     a.   True   b.   False

4.   According to Russell, which one of the following does philosophy not involve?

     a.   contemplation
     b.   certainty
     c.   freedom of thought
     d.   ennobling of self

Plato*

THE ALLEGORY OF THE CAVE

Next, said I, here is a parable to illustrate the degrees in which our nature may be enlightened or unenlightened. Imagine the condition of men living in a sort of cavernous chamber underground, with an entrance open to the light and a long passage all down the cave. Here they have been from childhood, chained by the leg and also by the neck, so that they cannot move and can see only what is in front of them, because the chains will not let them turn their heads. At some distance higher up is the light of a fire burning behind them; and between the prisoners and the fire is a track with a parapet build along it, like the screen at a puppet-show, which hides the performers while they show their puppets over the top.

I see, said he.

Now behind this parapet imagine persons carrying along various artificial objects, including figures of men and animals in wood or stone or other materials, which project above the parapet. Naturally, some of these persons will be talking, others silent.

It is a strange picture, he said, and a strange sort of prisoners.

Like ourselves, I replied; for in the first place prisoners so confined would have seen nothing of themselves or of one another, except the shadows thrown by the fire-light on the wall of the eave facing them, would they?

Not if all their lives they had been prevented from moving their heads.

And they would have seen as little of the objects carried past.

Of course.

Now, if they could talk to one another, would they not suppose that their words referred only to those passing shadows which they saw?

Necessarily.

And suppose their prison had an echo from the wall facing them? When one of the people crossing behind them spoke, they could only suppose that the sound came from the shadow passing before their eyes.

No doubt.

In every way, then, such prisoners would recognize as reality nothing but the shadows of those artificial objects.

Inevitably.

Now consider what would happen if their release from the chains and the healing of their unwisdom should come about in this way. Suppose one of them set free and forced suddenly to stand up, turn his head, and walk with eyes lifted to the light; all these movements would be painful, and he would be too dazzled to make out the objects whose shadows he had been used to see. What do you think he would say, if someone told him that what he had formerly seen was meaningless illusion, but now, being somewhat nearer to reality and turned towards more real objects, he was getting a truer view? Suppose further that he were shown the various objects being carried by and were made to say,

---

*Plato (427–347 B.C.E.) was one of the founders of the Western philosophical tradition. Born to an influential aristocratic family in Athens, Plato turned from poetry to philosophy under the influence of the philosopher Socrates. Plato's philosophy is a type of metaphysical dualism in which the world is divided between appearance and reality. According to Plato, our senses present us with only the appearances of things, while our intellect reveals what is truly real, the eternal forms. Plato presented his views in the form of dialogues, the main character of which was usually Socrates. The following selection is taken from Plato's most famous work, The Republic. In it, Socrates discourses on the nature and effects of a philosophical education.

in reply to questions, what each of them was. Would he not be perplexed and believe the objects now shown him to be not so real as what he formerly saw?

Yes, not nearly so real.

And if he were forced to look at the fire-light itself, would not his eyes ache, so that he would try to escape and turn back to the things which he could see distinctly, convinced that they really were clearer than these other objects now being show to him?

Yes.

And suppose someone were to drag him away forcibly up the steep and rugged ascent and not let him go until he had hauled him out into the sunlight, would he not suffer pain and vexation at such treatment, and, when he had come out into the light, find his eyes so full of its radiance that he could not see a single one of the things that he was now told were real?

Certainly he would not see them all at once.

He would need, then, to grow accustomed before he could see things in that upper world. At first it would be easiest to make out shadows, and then the images of men and things reflected in water, and later on the things themselves. After that, it would be easier to watch the heavenly bodies and the sky itself by night, looking at the light of the moon and stars rather than the Sun and the Sun's light in the day-time.

Yes, surely.

Last of all, he would be able to look at the Sun and contemplate its nature, not as it appears when reflected in water or any alien medium, but as it is in itself in its own domain.

No doubt.

And now he would begin to draw the conclusion that it is the Sun that produces the seasons and the course of the year and controls everything in the visible world, and moreover is in a way the cause of all that he and his companions used to see.

Clearly he would come at last to that conclusion.

Then if he called to mind his fellow prisoners and what passed for wisdom in his former dwelling-place he would surely think himself happy in the change and be sorry for them. They may have had a practice of honouring and commending one another, with prizes for the man who had the keenest eye for the passing shadows and the best memory for the order in which they followed or accompanied one another, so that he could make a good guess as to which was going to come next. Would our released prisoner be likely to covet those prizes or to envy the men exalted to honour and power in the cave? Would he not feel like Homer's Achilles, that he would far sooner be on earth as a hired servant in the house of a landless man or endure anything rather than go back to his old beliefs and live in the old way?

Yes, he would prefer any fate to such a life.

Now imagine what would happen if he went down again to take his former seat in the Cave. Coming suddenly out of the sunlight, his eyes would be filled with darkness. He might be required once more to deliver his opinion on those shadows, in competition with the prisoners who had never been released, while his eyesight was still dim and unsteady; and it might take some time to become used to the darkness. They would laugh at him and say that he had gone up only to come back with his sign ruined; it was worth no one's while even to attempt the ascent. If they could lay hands on the man who was trying to set them free and lead them up, the would kill him.

Yes, they would.

Every feature in this parable, my dear Glaucon, is meant to fit our earlier analysis. The prison dwelling corresponds to the region revealed to us through the sense of sight, and the fire-light within it to the power of the Sun. The ascent to see the things in the upper world you may take as standing for the upward journey of the soul into the region of the intelligible; then you will be in possession of what I surmise, since that is what you wish to be told. Heaven knows whether it is true; but this, at any rate, is how it appears to me. In the world of knowledge the last thing to be perceived and only with great difficulty is the essential Form of Goodness. Once it is perceived, the conclusion must follow that, for all things, this is the cause of whatever is right and good; in the visible world it gives birth to light and to the lord of light, while it is itself sovereign in the intelligible world and the parent of intelligence and truth. Without having had a vision of this Form no one can act with wisdom, either in his own life or in matters of state.

So far as I can understand, I share your belief.

The you may also agree that it is no wonder if those who have reached this height are reluctant to manage the affairs of men. Their souls long to spend all their time in that upper world—naturally enough, if here once more our parable holds true. Nor, again, is it at all strange that one who comes from the contemplation of divine things to the miseries of human life should appear awkward and ridiculous when, with eyes still dazed and not yet accustomed to the darkness, he is compelled, in a law-court or elsewhere, to dispute about the shadows of justice or the images that cast those shadows, and to wrangle over the notions of what is right in the minds of men who have never beheld Justice itself.

It is not at all strange.

No; a sensible man will remember that the eyes may be confused in two ways—by a change from light to darkness or from darkness to light; and he will recognize that the same thing happens to the soul when he sees it troubled and unable to discern anything clearly, instead of laughing thoughtlessly, he will ask whether, coming from a brighter existence, its unaccustomed vision is obscured by the darkness, in which case he will think its condition enviable and its life a happy one; or whether, emerging from the depths of ignorance, it is dazzled by excess of light. If so, he will rather feel sorry for it; or, if he were inclined to laugh, that would be less ridiculous than to laugh at the soul which has come down from the light.

That is a fair statement.

If this is true, then, we must conclude that education is not what it is said to be by some, who profess to put knowledge into a soul which does not possess it, as if they could put sight into blind eyes. On the contrary, our own account signifies that the soul of every man does possess the power of learning the truth and the organ to see it with; and that, just as one might have to turn the whole body round in order that the eye should see light instead of darkness, so the entire soul must be turned away from this changing world, until its eye can bear to contemplate reality and that supreme splendour which we have called the Good. Hence there may well be an art whose aim would be to effect this very thing, the conversion of the soul, in the readiest way; not to put the power of sight into the soul's eye, which already has it, but to ensure that, instead of looking in the wrong direction, it is turned the way it ought to be.

Yes, it may well be so.

It looks, then, as though wisdom were different from those ordinary virtues, as they are called, which are not far removed from bodily qualities, in that they can be produced by habituation and exercise in a soul which has not possessed them from the first. Wisdom, it seems, is certainly the virtue of some diviner faculty, which never loses its power, though its use for good or harm depends on the direction towards which it is turned. You must have noticed in dishonest men with a reputation for sagacity the shrewd glance of a narrow intelligence piercing the objects to which it is directed. There is nothing wrong with their power of vision, but it has been forced into the service of evil, so that the keener its sight, the more harm it works.

Quite true.

And yet if the growth of a nature like this had been pruned from earliest childhood, cleared of those clinging overgrowths which come of gluttony and all luxurious pleasure and, like leaden weights charged with affinity to this mortal world, hang upon the soul, bending its vision downwards; if, freed from these, the soul were turned round towards true reality, then this same power in these very men would see the truth as keenly as the objects it is turned to now.

Yes, very likely.

Is it not also likely, or indeed certain after what has been said, that a state can never be properly governed either by the uneducated who know nothing of truth or by men who are allowed to spend all their days in the pursuit of culture? The ignorant have no single mark before their eyes at which they must aim in all the conduct of their own lives and of affairs of state; and the others will not engage in action if they can help it, dreaming that, while still alive, they have been translated to the Islands of the Blest.

Quite true.

Plato, The Allegory of the Cave

1.   What is an allegory?

2.   In Plato's allegory of the cave, what do the following symbolize?

    a.   The cave:

    b.   The chains:

    c.   The long arduous trek out of the cave:

3.   Why does Plato think that education is essential for the conduct of one's own life and of public affairs?

I. PHILOSOPHY

LIST OF KEY TERMS

philosophy:

logic:

epistemology:

metaphysics:

ethics:

aesthetics:

integrative questions:

foundational questions:

goods of the mind:

Socratic Method:

allegory:

Editor's Note: A few of the terms on this list and those of the following sections do not appear in any of the readings. In such cases, either the instructor will discuss them in class or the student should endeavor to investigate them on her own.

SECTION II
EPISTEMOLOGY

THEME QUESTIONS

1. What is knowledge?

2. What are the sources of our knowledge?

3. What are the limits of our knowledge?

4. What is the structure of human knowledge?

5. Can we know anything with certainty?

Introduction to Epistemology

Kevin E. Dodson

At one time or another we have all encountered disputes over knowledge. One person claims to know that one thing is true, while another claims to know that it is not. In fact, such disputes are really quite common; one can see them almost everyday on television talk shows. To the philosopher, disputes over what is known provoke reflection on knowledge itself. These reflections belong to a branch of philosophy known as epistemology. Epistemology, or the theory of knowledge, is concerned with the nature, sources, limits, and structure of human knowledge. Epistemologists want to know what knowledge is, what can be known, how we know what we do know, and how all the individual bits and pieces of our knowledge fit together. Since this is an anthology devoted to the different ways of knowing about the world, we will begin by looking at knowledge in general.

In order to talk about knowledge, we need a working definition. Traditionally, philosophers have defined knowledge as justified true belief. In order for someone truthfully to claim that she knows something, she must believe it to be true, it must actually be true, and she must be able to provide an adequate justification for her belief. If you reflect for a moment, you will see that this is really the common sense understanding of knowledge. People have all sorts of opinions, some of which turn out to be true, but we can only claim to know something when we can justify those true opinions.

There are basically two different ways that we can justify our opinions: first, on the basis of what our reason tells us; second, on the basis of our experience of the world. Knowledge that comes from reason alone is called *a priori* knowledge. We say that something is known *a priori* when it is justified on the basis of reason alone without any appeal to our experience of the world. On the other hand, knowledge that comes from the senses is called *a posteriori* knowledge. We say that a statement is known *a posteriori* when it is justified by appealing to our experience.

In the following selections, you will encounter three main theories of knowledge: rationalism, empiricism, and pragmatism. The differences among these theories tend to cluster around the question of how we know what we know. In particular, they diverge over the respective roles of reason and sense experience in human knowledge.

The first selection represents the Rationalist perspective and is by the father of modern rationalism, René Descartes. Rationalism is the doctrine that at least some of our knowledge of the world comes from reason alone, and consequently that our knowledge extends beyond what mere sense experience tells us. Descartes grew up during the first half of the 17th century in a time of intellectual tumult and great uncertainty. The world-view of Europeans was being rocked by the encounter with "the new world" of the Americas, the Protestant Reformation, and the development of modern science. Everything that people thought they knew turned out to be either false or dubious. As a result, some people became skeptics. Epistemological skepticism is the doctrine that no adequate justification for claims to knowledge can be given, and hence we can know nothing except our own ignorance. Descartes decided to rebuild knowledge on a new foundation of bedrock certainties and in so doing began in philosophy what has come to be known as the epistemological turn, the conviction that first and foremost philosophers ought to focus on questions of knowledge before they consider anything else.

The bedrock of certainties forming the foundation of knowledge were to be the "clear and distinct" truths of reason, such as those found in mathematics and in the fundamental principles of science. Descartes believed that these principles were such that no person who considered them with an unbiased, calm, and attentive mind could doubt them, for they were just obviously and self-evidently true. From these basic truths, one could deduce further truths by means of deductive reasoning. Objective certainty in these matters is guaranteed by God. God created both human beings and the world and gave us reason so that we could have knowledge of the way the world really is.

In contrast to the rationalism of Descartes, the second selection is by David Hume, an empiricist who lived in the 18th century. As an empiricist, Hume rejected Descartes's claim that reason alone provided us with knowledge of the world. According to Hume, the only way one knows anything about reality independent of us is by observing it, by basing our knowledge of it on the experiences provided by our senses. Reason is limited to the analysis of our ideas. Thus, mathematics is known *a priori,* but it is purely conceptual and deals with "relations of ideas." However, even ideas in mathematics come from sense experience. Hume maintained that all of our ideas were acquired from sense experience and that none were innate, that is, provided to us by reason prior to experience.

The final selection comes from Charles Sanders Peirce, the founder of the view known as pragmatism in the latter half of the 19th century. Peirce and other pragmatists argue that nothing can truly be known *a priori,* but that all such claims are at root a species of dogmatism. Our real concern in life is the fixation of belief, which should be done in a reasonable manner. According to what is called the belief-doubt model, humans begin with a fixed belief on some given matter. When they encounter experiences contrary to that belief, perhaps in the form of failed actions, doubt sets in. These doubts can be resolved in a variety of ways, but the most reasonable is through application of the experimental method. The experimental method consists in the development of a hypothesis to account for the experiences followed by the rigorous testing of that hypothesis. When an adequate hypothesis is found that survives testing, it becomes the new fixed belief until such time that it is found deficient. Thus all knowledge is provisional in that it is subject to change should the circumstances dictate it.

As you can see, the three selections that follow present a wide range of views on the basic questions in the theory of knowledge. A careful consideration of these readings will get one off on the right foot for the rest of this anthology.

René Descartes*

Meditations

MEDITATION I.

Of the things which may be brought within the sphere of the doubtful.

It is now some years since I detected how many were the false beliefs that I had from my earliest youth admitted as true, and how doubtful was everything I had since constructed on this basis; and from that time I was convinced that I must once for all seriously undertake to rid myself of all the opinions which I had formerly accepted, and commence to build anew from the foundation, if I wanted to establish any firm and permanent structure in the sciences. But as this enterprise appeared to be a very great one, I waited until I had attained an age so mature that I could not hope that at any later date I should be better fitted to execute my design. This reason caused me to delay so long that I should feel that I was doing wrong were I to occupy in deliberation the time that yet remains to me for action. To-day, then, since very opportunely for the plan I have in view I have delivered my mind from every care [and am happily agitated by no passions] and since I have procured for myself an assured leisure in a peaceable retirement, I shall at last seriously and freely address myself to the general upheaval of all my former opinions.

Now for this object it is not necessary that I should show that all of these are false—I shall perhaps never arrive at this end. But inasmuch as reason already persuades me that I ought no less carefully to withhold my assent from matters which are not entirely certain and indubitable than from those which appear to me manifestly to be false, if I am able to find in each one some reason to doubt, this will suffice to justify my rejecting the whole. And for that end it will not be requisite that I should examine each in particular, which would be an endless undertaking; for owing to the fact that the destruction of the foundations of necessity brings with it the downfall of the rest of the edifice, I shall only in the first place attack those principles upon which all my former opinions rested.

All that up to the present time I have accepted as most true and certain I have learned either from the sense or through the senses; but it is sometimes proved to me that these senses are deceptive, and it is wiser not to trust entirely to any thing by which we have once been deceived.

But it may be that although the senses sometimes deceive us concerning things which are hardly perceptible, or very far away, there are yet many others to be met with as to which we cannot reasonably have any doubt, although we recognise them by their means. For example, there is the fact that I am here, seated by the fire, attired in a dressing gown, having this paper in my hands and other similar matters. And how could I deny that these hands and this body are mine, were it not perhaps that I compare myself to certain persons, devoid of sense, whose cerebella are so troubled and clouded by the violent vapours of black bile, that they constantly assure us that they think they are kings when they are really quite poor, or that they are clothed in purple when they are really without covering, or who imagine that they have an earthenware head or are nothing but pumpkins or

*René Descartes (1596–1650) was a French mathematician, scientist, and the first great philosopher of the modern age. In such important works as *Rules for the Regulation of the Mind, The World,* and *Discourse on Method,* Descartes sought to establish science as a purely rational discipline modelled along the lines of geometry. The following selection, which is taken from his most famous work, *Meditations on First Philosophy* (1641), is a classic statement of the rationalist position on knowledge.

are made of glass. But they are mad, and I should not be any the less insane were I to follow examples so extravagant.

At the same time I must remember that I am a man, and that consequently I am in the habit of sleeping, and in my dreams representing to myself the same things or sometimes even less probable things, than do those who are insane in their waking moments. How often has it happened to me that in the night I dreamt that I found myself in this particular place, that I was dressed and seated near the fire, whilst in reality I was lying undressed in bed! At this moment it does indeed seem to me that it is with eyes awake that I am looking at this paper; that this head which I move is not asleep, that it is deliberately and of set purpose that I extend my hand and perceive it; what happens in sleep does not appear so clear nor so distinct as does all this. But in thinking over this I remind myself that on many occasions I have in sleep been deceived by similar illusions, and in dwelling carefully on this rejection I see so manifestly that there are no certain indications by which we may clearly distinguish wakefulness from sleep that I am lost in astonishment. And my astonishment is such that it is almost capable of persuading me that I now dream.

Now let us assume that we are asleep and that all these particulars, e.g. that we open our eyes, shake our head, extend our hands, and so on, are but false delusions; and let us reflect that possibly neither our hands nor our whole body are such as they appear to us to be. At the same time we must at least confess that the things which are represented to us in sleep are like painted representations which can only have been formed as the counterparts of something real and true, and that in this way those general things at least, i.e., eyes, a head, hands, and a whole body, are not imaginary things, but things really existent. For, as a matter of fact, painters, even when they study with the greatest skill to represent sirens and satyrs by forms the most strange and extraordinary, cannot give them natures which are entirely new, but merely make a certain medley of the members of different animals; or if their imagination is extravagant enough to invent something so novel that nothing similar has ever before been seen, and that then their work represents a thing purely fictitious and absolutely false, it is certain all the same that the colours of which this is composed are necessarily real. And for the same reason, although these general things, to wit, [a body], eyes, a head, hands, and such like, may be imaginary, we are bound at the same time to confess that there are at least some other objects yet more simple and more universal, which are real and true;

and of these just in the same way as with certain real colours, all these images of things which dwell in our thoughts, whether true and real or false and fantastic, are formed.

To such a class of things pertains corporeal nature in general, and its extension, the figure of extended things, their quantity or magnitude and number, as also the place in which they are, the time which measures their duration, and so on.

That is possibly why our reasoning is not unjust when we conclude from this that Physics, Astronomy, Medicine and all other sciences which have as their end the consideration of composite things, are very dubious and uncertain; but that Arithmetic, Geometry and other sciences of that kind which only treat of things that are very simple and very general, without taking great trouble to ascertain whether they are actually existent or not, contain some measure of certainty and an element of the indubitable. For whether I am awake or asleep, two and three together always form five, and the square can never have more than four sides, and it does not seem possible that truths so clear and apparent can be suspected of any falsity [or uncertainty].

Nevertheless I have long had fixed in my mind the belief that an all-powerful God existed by whom I have been created such as I am. But how do I know that He has not brought it to pass that there is no earth, no heaven, no extended body, no magnitude, no place, and that nevertheless [I possess the perceptions of all these things and that] they seem to me to exist just exactly as I now see them? And, besides, as I sometimes imagine that others deceive themselves in the things which they think they know best, how do I know that I am not deceived every time that I add two and three, or count the sides of a square, or judge of things yet simpler, if anything simpler can be imagined? But possibly God has not desired that I should be thus deceived, for He is said to be supremely good. If, however, it is contrary to His goodness to have made me such that I constantly deceive myself, it would also appear to be contrary to His goodness to permit me to be sometimes deceived, and nevertheless I cannot doubt that He does permit this.

There may indeed be those who would prefer to deny the existence of a God so powerful rather than believe that all other things are uncertain. But let us not oppose them for the present, and grant that all that is here said of a God is a fable; nevertheless in whatever way they suppose that I have arrived at the state of being that I have reached —whether they attribute it to fate or to accident, or make out that it is by a continual succession of antecedents, or by some other method—since to err and deceive oneself is a defect, it is clear that the greater will be the probability of my being so imperfect as to deceive myself ever, as is the Author to whom they assign my origin the less powerful. To these reasons I have certainly nothing to reply, but at the end I feel constrained to confess that there is nothing in all that I formerly believed to be true, of which I cannot in some measure doubt, and that not merely through want of thought or through levity, but for reasons which are very powerful and maturely considered; so that henceforth I ought not the less carefully to refrain from giving credence to these opinions than to that which is manifestly false, if I desire to arrive at any certainty [in the sciences].

But it is not sufficient to have made these remarks, we must also be careful to keep them in mind. For these ancient and commonly held opinions still revert frequently to my mind, long and familiar custom having given them the right to occupy my mind against my inclination and rendered them almost masters of my belief; nor will I ever lose the habit of deferring to them or of placing my confidence in them, so long as I consider them as they really are, i.e. opinions in some measure doubtful, as I have just shown, and at the same time highly probable, so that there is much more reason to believe in than to deny them. That is why I consider that I shall not be acting amiss, if, taking of set purpose a contrary belief, I allow myself to be deceived, and for a certain time pretend that all these opinions are entirely false and imaginary, until at last, having thus balanced my former prejudices with my latter [so that they cannot divert my opinions more to one side than to the other], my judgment will no longer be dominated by bad usage or turned away from the right knowledge of the truth. For I am assured that there can be neither peril nor error in this course, and that I cannot at present yield too much to distrust, since I am not considering the question of action, but only of knowledge.

I shall then suppose, not that God who is supremely good and the fountain of truth, but some evil genius not less powerful than deceitful, has employed his whole energies in deceiving me; I shall consider that the heavens, the earth, colours, figures, sound, and all other external things are nought but the illusions and dreams of which this genius has availed himself in order to lay traps for my credulity; I shall consider myself as having no hands, no eyes, no flesh, no blood, nor any senses, yet falsely believing myself to possess all these things; I shall remain obstinately attached to this idea, and if by this means it is not in my power to arrive at the knowledge of any truth, I may at least do what is in my power [i.e. suspend my judgment], and with firm purpose avoid giving credence to any false thing, or being imposed upon by this arch deceiver, however powerful and deceptive he may be. But this task is a laborious one, and insensibly a certain lassitude leads me into the course of my ordinary life. And just as a captive who in sleep enjoys an imaginary liberty, when he begins to suspect that his liberty is but a dream, fears to awaken, and conspires with these agreeable illusions that the deception may be prolonged, so insensibly of my own accord I fall back into my former opinions, and I dread awakening from this slumber, lest the laborious wakefulness which would follow the tranquility of this repose should have to be spent not in daylight, but in the excessive darkness of the difficulties which have just been discussed.

MEDITATION II.

Of the Nature of the Human Mind; and that it is more easily known than the Body.

The Meditation of yesterday filled my mind with so many doubts that it is no longer in my power to forget them. And yet I do not see in what manner I can resolve them; and, just as if I had all of a sudden fallen into very deep water, I am so disconcerted that I can neither make certain of setting my feet on the bottom, nor can I swim and so support myself on the surface. I shall nevertheless make an effort and follow anew the same path as that on which I yesterday entered, i.e. I shall proceed by setting aside all that in which the least doubt could be supposed to exist, just as if I had discovered that it was absolutely false; and I shall ever follow in this road until I have met with something which is certain, or at least, if I can do nothing else, until I have learned for certain that there is nothing in the world that is certain. Archimedes, in order that he might draw the terrestrial globe out of its place, and transport it elsewhere, demanded only that one point should be fixed and immoveable; in the same way I shall have the right to conceive high hopes if I am happy enough to discover one thing only which is certain and indubitable.

I suppose, then, that all the things that I see are false; I persuade myself that nothing has ever existed of all that my fallacious memory represents to me. I consider that I possess no senses; I imagine that body, figure, extension, movement and place are but the fictions of my mind. What, then, can be esteemed as true? Perhaps nothing at all, unless that there is nothing in the world that is certain.

But how can I know there is not something different from those things that I have just considered, of which one cannot have the slightest doubt? Is there not some God, or some other being by whatever name we call it, who puts these reflections into my mind? That is not necessary, for is it not possible that I am capable of producing them myself? I myself, am I not at least something? But I have already denied that I had senses and body. Yet I hesitate, for what follows from that? Am I so dependent upon body and senses that I cannot exist without these? But I was persuaded that there was nothing in all the world, that there was no heaven, no earth, that there were no minds, nor any bodies: was I not then likewise persuaded that I did not exist? Not at all; of a surety I myself did exist since I persuaded myself of something [or merely because I thought of something]. But there is some deceiver or other, very powerful and very cunning, who ever employs his ingenuity in deceiving me. Then without doubt I exist also if he deceives me, and let him deceive me as much as he will, he can never cause me to be nothing so long as I think that I am something. So that after having reflected well and carefully examined all things, we must come to the definite conclusion that this proposition: I am, I exist, is necessarily true each time that I pronounce it, or that I mentally conceive it.

But I do not yet know clearly enough what I am, I who am certain that I am; and hence I must be careful to see that I do not imprudently take some other object in place myself, and thus that I do not go astray in respect of this knowledge that I hold to be the most certain and most evident of all that I have formerly learned. That is why I shall now consider anew what I believed myself to be before I embarked upon these last reflections; and of my former opinions I shall withdraw all that might even in a small degree be invalidated by the reasons which I have just brought forward, in order that there may be nothing at all left beyond what is absolutely certain and indubitable.

What then did I formerly believe myself to be? Undoubtedly I believed myself to be a man. But what is a man? Shall I say a reasonable animal? Certainly not; for then I should have to inquire what an animal is, and what is reasonable; and thus from a single question I should insensibly fall into an infinitude of others more difficult; and I should not wish to waste the little time and leisure remaining to me in trying to unravel subtleties like these. But I shall rather stop here to consider the thoughts which of themselves spring up in my mind, and which were not inspired by anything beyond my own nature alone when I applied myself to the consideration of my being. In the first place, then, I considered myself as having a face, hands, arms, and all that system of members composed of bones and flesh as seen in a corpse which I designated by the name of body. In addition to this I considered that I was nourished, that I walked, that I felt, and that I thought, and I referred all these actions to the soul: but I did not stop to consider what the soul was, or if I did stop, I imagined that it was something extremely rare and subtle like a wind, a flame, or an ether, which was spread throughout my grosser parts. As to body I had no manner of doubt about its nature, but thought I had a very clear knowledge of it; and if I had desired to explain it according to the notions that I had then formed of it, I should have described it thus: By the body I understand all that which can be defined by a certain figure: something which can be confined in a certain place, and which can fill a given space in such a way that every other body will be excluded from it: which can be perceived either by touch, or sight, or by hearing, or by taste, or by smell: which can be moved in many ways not, in truth, by itself, but by something which is foreign to it, by which it is touched [and from which it receives impressions]: for to have the power of self-movement, as also of feeling or of thinking, I did not consider to appertain to the nature of body: on the contrary, I was rather astonished to find that faculties similar to them existed in some bodies.

But what am I, now that I suppose that there is a certain genius which is extremely powerful, and, if I may say so, malicious, who employs all his powers in deceiving me? Can I affirm that I possess the least of all those things which I have just said pertain to the nature of body? I pause to consider, I revolve all these things in my mind, and I find none of which I can say that it pertains to me. It would be tedious to stop to enumerate them. Let us pass to the attributes of soul and see if there is any one which is in me? What of nutrition or walking [the first mentioned]? But if it is so that I have no body it is also true that I can neither walk nor take nourishment. Another attribute is sensation. But one cannot feel without body, and besides I have thought I perceived many things during sleep that I recognised in my waking moments as not having been experienced at all. What of thinking? I find here that thought is an attribute that belongs to me; it alone cannot be separated from me. I am, I exist, that is certain. But how often? Just when I think; for it might possibly be the case if I ceased entirely to think, that I should likewise cease altogether to exist. I do not now admit anything which is not necessarily true: to speak accurately I am not more than a thing which thinks, that is to say a mind or a soul, or an understanding, or a reason, which are terms whose significance was formerly unknown to me. I am, however, a real thing and really exist; but what thing? I have answered: a thing which thinks.

And what more? I shall exercise my imagination [in order to see if I am not something more]. I am not a collection of members which we call the human body: I am not a subtle air distributed through these members, I am not a wind, a fire, a vapour, a breath, nor anything at all which I can imagine or conceive; because I have assumed that all these were nothing. Without changing that supposition I find that I only leave myself certain of the fact that I am somewhat. But perhaps it is true that these same things which I supposed were non-existent because they are unknown to me, are really not different from the self which I know. I am not sure about this, I shall not dispute about it now; I can only give judgment on things that are known to me. I know that I exist, and I inquire what I am, I whom I know to exist. But it is very certain that the knowledge of my existence taken in its precise significance does not depend on things whose existence is not yet known to me; consequently it does not depend on those which I can feign in imagination. And indeed the very term *feign* in imagination proves to me my error, for I really do this if I image myself a something, since to imagine is nothing else than to contemplate the figure or image of a corporeal thing. But I already know for certain that I am, and that it may be that all these images, and, speaking generally, all things that relate to the nature of body are nothing but dreams [and chimeras]. For this reason I see clearly that I have as little reason to say, 'I shall stimulate my imagination in order to know more distinctly what I am,' than if I were to say, 'I am now awake, and I perceive somewhat that is real and true: but because I do not yet perceive it distinctly enough, I shall go to sleep of express purpose, so that my dreams may represent the perception with greatest truth and evidence.' And, thus, I know for certain that nothing of all that I can understand by means of my imagination belongs to this knowledge which I have of myself, and that it is necessary to recall the mind from this mode of thought with the utmost diligence in order that it may be able to know its own nature with perfect distinctness.

But what then am I? A thing which thinks. What is a thing which thinks? It is a thing which doubts, understands, [conceives], affirms, denies, wills, refuses, which also imagines and feels.

Certainly it is no small matter if all these things pertain to my nature. But why should they not so pertain? Am I not that being who now doubts nearly everything, who nevertheless understands certain things, who affirms that one only is true, who denies all the others, who desires to know more, is averse from being deceived, who imagines many things, sometimes indeed despite his will, and who perceives many likewise, as by the intervention of the bodily organs? Is there nothing in all this which is as true as it is certain that I exist, even though I should always sleep and though he who has given me being employed all his ingenuity in deceiving me? Is there likewise any one of these attributes which can be distinguished from my thought, or which might be said to be separated from myself? For it is so evident of itself that it is I who doubts, who understands, and who desires, that there is no reason here to add anything to explain it. And I have certainly the power of imagining likewise; for although it may happen (as I formerly supposed) that none of the things which I imagine are true, nevertheless this power of imagining does not cease to be really in use, and it forms part of my thought. Finally, I am the same who feels, that is to say, who perceives certain things, as by the organs of sense, since in truth I see light, I hear noise, I feel heat. But it will be said that these phenomena are false and that I am dreaming. Let it be so; still it is at least quite certain that it seems to me that I see light, that I hear noise and that I feel heat. That cannot be false; properly speaking it is what is in me called feeling; and used in this precise sense that is no other thing than thinking.

From this time I begin to know what I am with a little more clearness and distinction than before; but nevertheless it still seems to me, and I cannot prevent myself from thinking, that corporeal things, whose images are framed by thought, which are tested by the senses, are much more distinctly known than that obscure part of me which does not come under the imagination. Although really it is very strange to say that I know and understand more distinctly these things whose existence seems to me dubious, which are unknown to me and which pertain to my real nature, in a word, than myself. But I see clearly how the case stands: my mind loves to wander, and cannot yet suffer itself to be retained within the just limits of truth. Very good, let us once

22

more give it the freest rein, so that, when afterwards we seize the proper occasion for pulling up, it may the more easily be regulated and controlled.

Let us begin by considering the commonest matters, those which we believe to be the most distinctly comprehended, to wit, the bodies which we touch and see; not indeed bodies in general, for these general ideas are usually a little more confused, but let us consider one body in particular. Let us take, for example, this piece of wax; it has been taken quite freshly from the hive, and it has not yet lost the sweetness of the honey which it contains; it still retains somewhat of the odour of the flowers which it has been culled; its colour, its figure, its size are apparent; it is hard, cold, easily handled, and if you strike it with the finger, it will emit a sound. Finally all the things which are requisite to cause us distinctly to recognise a body, are met with in it. But notice that while I speak and approach the fire what remained of the taste is exhaled, the smell evaporates, the colour alters, the figure is destroyed, the size increases, it becomes liquid, it heats, scarcely can one handle it, and when one strikes it, no sound is emitted. Does the same wax remain after this change? We must confess that it remains; none would judge otherwise. What then did I know so distinctly in this piece of wax? It could certainly be nothing of all that the senses brought to my notice, since all these things which fall under taste, smell, sight, touch, and hearing, are found to be changed, and yet the same wax remains.

Perhaps it was what I now think, viz, that this wax was not that sweetness of honey, nor that agreeable scent of flowers, nor that particular whiteness, nor that figure, not that sound, but simply a body which a little while before appeared to me as perceptible under these forms, and which is now perceptible under others. But what, precisely, is it that I imagine when I form such conceptions? Let us attentively consider this, and, abstracting from all that does not belong to the wax, let us see what remains. Certainly nothing remains excepting a certain extended thing which is flexible and movable. But what is the meaning of flexible and movable? Is it not that I imagine that this piece of wax being round is capable of becoming square and of passing from a square to a triangular figure? No, certainly it is not that, since I imagine it admits of an infinitude of similar changes, and I nevertheless do not know how to compass the infinitude by my imagination, and consequently this conception which I have of the wax is not brought about by the faculty of imagination. What now is this extension? Is it not

also unknown? For it becomes greater when the wax is melted, greater when it is boiled, and greater still when the heat increases; and I should not conceive [clearly] according to truth what wax is, if I did not think that even this piece that we are considering is capable of receiving more variations in extension than I have ever imagined. We must then grant that I could not even understand through the imagination what this piece of wax is, and that it is my mind alone which perceives it. I say this piece of wax in particular, for as to wax in general it is yet clearer. But what is this piece of wax, which cannot be understood excepting by the [understanding or] mind? It is certainly the same that I see, touch, imagine, and finally it is the same which I have always believed it to be from the beginning. But what must particularly be observed is that its perception is neither an act of vision, nor of touch, nor of imagination, and has never been such although it may have appeared formerly to be so, but only an intuition of the mind, which may be imperfect and confused as it was formerly, or clear and distinct as it is at present, according as my attention is more or less directed to the elements which are found in it, and of which it is composed.

Yet in the meantime I am greatly astonished when I consider [the great feebleness of mind] and its proneness to fall [insensibly] into error; for although without giving expression to my thoughts I consider all this in my own mind, words often impede me and I am almost deceived by the terms of ordinary language. For we say that we see the same wax, if it is present, and not that we simply judge that it is the same from its having the same colour and figure. From this I should conclude that I knew the wax by means of vision and not simply by the intuition of the mind; unless by chance I remember that, when looking from a window and saying I see men who pass in the street, I really do not see them, but infer that what I see is men, just as I say that I see wax. And yet what do I see from the window but hats and coats which may cover automatic machines? Yet I judge these to be men. And similarly solely by the faculty of judgment which rests in my mind, I comprehend that which I believed I saw with my eyes.

A man who makes it his aim to raise his knowledge about the common should be ashamed to derive the occasion for doubting from the forms of speech invented by the vulgar; I prefer to pass on and consider whether I had a more evident and perfect conception of what the wax was when I first perceived it, and when I believed I knew it by means of the external senses or at least by the common sense as it is called, that is to say by the imaginative faculty, or whether my present conception is clearer now that I have most carefully examined what it is, and in what way it can be known. It would certainly be absurd to doubt as to this. For what was there in this first perception which was distinct? What was there which might not as well have been perceived by any of the animals? But when I distinguish the wax from its external forms, and when, just as if I had taken from it its vestments, I consider it quite naked, it is certain that although some error may still be found in my judgment, I can nevertheless not perceive it thus without a human mind.

But finally what shall I say of this mind, that is, of myself, for up to this point I do not admit in myself anything but mind? What then, I who seem to perceive this piece of wax so distinctly, do I not know myself, not only with much more truth and certainty, but also with much more distinctness and clearness? For if I judge that the wax is or exists from the fact that I see it, it certainly follows much more clearly that I am or that I exist myself from the fact that I see it. For it may be that what I see is not really wax, it may also be that I do not possess eyes with which to see anything; but it cannot be that when I see, or (for I no longer take account of the distinction) when I think I see, that I myself who think am nought. So if I judge that the wax exists from the fact that I touch it, the same thing will follow, to wit, that I am; and if I judge that my imagination, or some other cause, whatever it is, persuades me that the wax exists, I shall still conclude the same. And what I have here remarked of wax may be applied to all other things which are external to me [and which are met with outside of me]. And further, if the [notion or] perception of wax has seemed to me clearer and more distinct, not only after the sight or the touch, but also after many other causes have rendered it quite manifest to me, with how much more [evidence] and distinctness must it be said that I now know myself, since all the reasons which contribute to the knowledge of wax, or any other body whatever, are yet better proofs of the nature of my mind! And there are so many other things in the mind itself which may contribute to the elucidation of its nature, that those which depend on body such as these just mentioned, hardly merit being taken into account.

But finally here I am, having insensibly reverted to the point I desired, for, since it is now manifest to me that even bodies are not properly speaking known by the senses or by the faculty of imagination, but by the understanding only, and since they are not known from the fact that they are seen or touched, but only because they are understood, I see clearly that there is nothing which is easier for me to know than my mind. But because it is difficult to rid oneself so promptly of an opinion to which one was accustomed for so long, it will be well that I should halt a little at this point, so that by the length of my meditation I may more deeply imprint on my memory this new knowledge.

MEDITATION III.

Of God: that He exists.

I shall now close my eyes, I shall stop my ears, I shall call away all my senses. I shall efface even from my thoughts all the images of corporeal things, or at least (for that is hardly possible) I shall esteem them as vain and false; and thus holding converse only with myself and considering my own nature, I shall try little by little to reach a better knowledge of and a more familiar acquaintanceship with myself. I am a thing that thinks, that is to say, that doubts, affirms, denies, that knows a few things, that is ignorant of many [that loves, that hates], that wills, that desires, that also imagines and perceives; for as I remarked before, although the things which I perceive and imagine are perhaps nothing at all apart from me and in themselves, I am nevertheless assured that these modes of thought that I call perceptions and imaginations, inasmuch only as they are modes of thought, certainly reside [and are met with] in me.

And in the little that I have just said, I think I have summed up all that I really know, or at least all that hitherto I was aware that I knew. I order to try to extend my knowledge further, I shall now look around more carefully and see whether I cannot still discover in myself some other things which I have not hitherto perceived. I am certain I am a thing which thinks; but do I not then likewise know what is requisite to render me certain of a truth? Certainly in this first knowledge there is nothing that assures me of its truth, excepting the clear and distinct perception of that which I state, which would not indeed suffice to assure me that what I say is true, if it could ever happen that a thing which I conceived so clearly and distinctly could be false; and accordingly it seems to me that already I can establish as a general rule that all things which I perceive very clearly and very distinctly are true.

At the same time I have before received and admitted many things to be very certain and manifest, which yet I afterwards recognised as being dubious. What then were these things? They were the earth, sky, stars and all other objects which I apprehended by means of the senses. But what did I clearly [and distinctly] perceive in them? Nothing more than that the ideas or thoughts of these things were presented to my mind. And not even now do I deny that these ideas are met with in me. But there was yet another thing which I affirmed, and which, owing to the habit which I had formed of believing it, I thought I perceived very clearly, although in truth I did not perceive it at all, to wit, that there were objects outside of me from which these ideas proceeded, and to which they were entirely similar. And it was in this that I erred, or, if perchance my judgment was correct, this was not due to any knowledge arising from my perception.

But when I took anything very simple and easy in the sphere of arithmetic or geometry into consideration, e.g. that two and three together made five, and other things of the sort, were not these present to my mind so clearly as to enable me to affirm that they were true? Certainly if I judged that since such matters could be doubted, this would not have been so for any other reason than that it came into my mind that perhaps a God might have endowed me with such a nature that I may have been deceived even concerning things which seemed to me most manifest. But every time that this preconceived opinion of the sovereign power of a God presents itself to my thought, I am constrained to confess that it is easy to Him, if He wishes it, to cause me to err, even in matters in which I believe myself to have the best evidence. And, on the other hand, always when I direct my attention to things which I believe myself to perceive very clearly, I am so persuaded of their truth that I let myself break out into words such as these: Let who will deceive me, He can never cause me to be nothing while I think that I am, or some day cause it to be true to say that I have never been, it being true now to say that I am, or that two and three make more or less than five, or any such thing in which I see a manifest contradiction. And, certainly, since I have no reason to believe that there is a God who is a deceiver, and as I have not yet satisfied myself that there is a God at all, the reason for doubt which depends on this opinion alone is very slight, and so to speak metaphysical. But in order to be able altogether to remove it, I must inquire whether there is a God as soon as the occasion presents itself; and if I find that there is a God, I must also inquire whether He may be a deceiver; for without a knowledge of these two truths I do not see that I can ever be certain of anything.

Descartes, Meditations

1.   What is Descartes's argument in the fifth paragraph of Meditation I? Identify his conclusion and the reasoning offered for it.

2.   In Meditation II, what is the first truth of which Descartes can be certain?

A.   'I exist.'
B.   'I am a thing that thinks.'
C.   'The mind is better known than the body.'
D.   'God exists.'

3.   Why does Descartes think he can be certain of this truth?

4.   In Meditation III, why does Descartes think that he needs to prove the existence of God?

David Hume*

AN ENQUIRY CONCERNING HUMAN UNDERSTANDING

SECTION II

OF THE ORIGIN OF IDEAS

Everyone will readily allow that there is a considerable difference between the perceptions of the mind when a man feels the pain of excessive heat or the pleasure of moderate warmth, and when he afterwards recalls to his memory this sensation or anticipates it by his imagination. These faculties may mimic or copy the perceptions of the senses, but they never can entirely reach the force and vivacity of the original sentiment. The utmost we say of them, even when they operate with greatest vigor, is that they represent their object in so lively a manner that we could *almost* say we feel or see it. But, except the mind be disordered by disease or madness, they never can arrive at such a pitch of vivacity as to render these perceptions altogether undistinguishable. All the colors of poetry, however splendid, can never paint natural objects in such a manner as to make the description be taken for a real landscape. The most lively thought is still inferior to the dullest sensation.

We may observe a like distinction to run through all the other perceptions of the mind. A man in a fit of anger is actuated in a very different manner from one who only thinks of that emotion. If you tell me that any person is in love, I easily understand your meaning and form a just conception of his situation, but never can mistake that conception for the real disorders and agitations of the passion. When we reflect on our past sentiments and affections, our thought is a faithful mirror and copies its objects truly, but the colors which it employs are faint and dull in comparison of those in which our original perceptions were clothed. It requires no nice discernment or metaphysical head to mark the distinction between them.

Here, therefore, we may divide all the perceptions of the mind into two classes or species, which are distinguished by their different degrees of force and vivacity. The less forcible and lively are commonly denominated "thoughts" or "ideas." The other species want a name in our language, and in most others; I suppose, because it was not requisite for any but philosophical purposes to rank them under a general term or appellation. Let us, therefore, use a little freedom and call them "impressions," employing that word in a sense somewhat different from the usual. By the term "impression," then, I mean all our more lively perceptions, when we hear, or see, or feel, or love, or hate, or desire, or will. And impressions are distinguished from ideas, which are the less lively perceptions of which we are conscious when we reflect on any of those sensations or movements above mentioned.

Nothing, at first view, may seem more unbounded than the thought of man, which not only

---

David Hume (1711–76) was the last of the great British empiricists. Born and educated in Scotland, he published *A Treatise on Human Nature,* one of the great works of Western philosophy, while still in his twenties. The following selection is drawn from *An Enquiry Concerning Human Understanding* (1648), a later popularization of the epistemological doctrines of the *Treatise.* In those works, Hume adopted a position of uncompromising empiricism that generates a fundamental critique of the philosophical tradition. Among his many writings, Hume also published a six-volume *History of England* in his lifetime and a set of *Dialogues Concerning Natural Religion* which were released after his death.

escapes all human power and authority, but is not even restrained within the limits of nature and reality. To form monsters and join incongruous shapes and appearances costs the imagination no more trouble than to conceive the most natural and familiar objects. And while the body is confined to one planet, along which it creeps with pain and difficulty, the thought can in an instant transport us into the most distant regions of the universe, or even beyond the universe into the unbounded chaos where nature is supposed to lie in total confusion. What never was seen or heard of, may yet be conceived, nor is anything beyond the power of thought except what implies an absolute contradiction.

But though our thought seems to possess this unbounded liberty, we shall find upon a nearer examination that it is really confined within very narrow limits, and that all this creative power of the mind amounts to no more than the faculty of compounding, transposing, augmenting, or diminishing the materials afforded us by the senses and experience. When we think of a golden mountain, we only join two consistent ideas, "gold" and "mountain," with which we were formerly acquainted. A virtuous horse we can conceive, because, from our own feeling, we can conceive virtue; and this we may unite to the figure and shape of a horse, which is an animal familiar to us. In short, all the materials of thinking are derived either from our outward or inward sentiment; the mixture and composition of these belongs alone to the mind and will, or, to express myself in philosophical language, all our ideas or more feeble perceptions are copies of our impressions or more lively ones.

To prove this, the two following arguments will, I hope, be sufficient. *First,* when we analyze our thoughts or ideas, however compounded or sublime, we always find that they resolve themselves into such simple ideas as were copied from a precedent feeling or sentiment. Even those ideas which at first view seem the most wide of this origin are found, upon a nearer scrutiny, to be derived from it. The idea of God, as meaning an infinitely intelligent, wise, and good Being, arises from reflecting on the operations of our own mind and augmenting, without limit, those qualities of goodness and wisdom. We may prosecute this inquiry to what length we please; where we shall always find that every idea which we examine is copied from a similar impression. Those who would assert that this position is not universally true, nor without exception, have only one, and that an easy, method of refuting it by producing that idea which, in their opinion, is not derived from this source. It will then be incumbent on us, if we would maintain our doctrine, to produce the impression or lively perception which corresponds to it.

Secondly, if it happen, from a defect of the organ, that a man is not susceptible of any species of sensation, we always find that he is as little susceptible of the correspondent idea. A blind man can form no notion of colors, a deaf man of sounds. Restore either of them that sense in which he is deficient by opening this new inlet for his sensations, you also open an inlet for the ideas, and he finds no difficulty in conceiving these objects. The case is the same if the object proper for exciting any sensation has never been applied to the organ. A Laplander or Negro has no notion of the relish of wine. And though there are few or no instances of a like deficiency in the mind where a person has never felt or is wholly incapable of a sentiment or passion that belongs to his species, yet we find the same observation to take place in a less degree. A man of mild manners can form no idea of inveterate revenge or cruelty, nor can a selfish heart easily conceive the heights of friendship and generosity. It is readily allowed that other beings may possess many senses of which we can have no conception, because the ideas of them have never been introduced to us in the only manner by which an idea can have access to the mind, to wit, by the actual feeling and sensation.

There is, however, one contradictory phenomenon which may prove that it is not absolutely impossible for ideas to arise independent of their correspondent impressions. I believe it will readily be allowed that the several distinct ideas of color, which enter by the eye, or those of sound, which are conveyed by the ear, are really different from each other, though at the same time resembling. Now, if this be true of different colors, it must be no less so of the different shades of the same color; and each shade produces a distinct idea, independent of the rest. For if this should be denied, it is possible, by the continual gradation of shades, to run a color insensibly into what is most remote from it; and if you will not allow any of the means to be different, you cannot, without absurdity, deny the extremes to be the same. Suppose, therefore, a person to have enjoyed his sight for thirty years and to have become perfectly acquainted with colors of all kinds, except one particular shade of blue, for instance, which it never has been his fortune to meet with; let all the different shades of that color, except that single one, be placed before him, descending gradually from the deepest to the lightest, it is plain that he will perceive a blank where that shade is wanting, and will be sensible that there is a greater distance in that place between the contiguous colors than in any other. Now I ask whether it be possible for him, from his own imagination, to supply this deficiency and raise up to himself the idea of that particular shade, though it had never been conveyed to him by his senses? I believe there are few but will be of opinion that he can; and this may serve as a proof that the simple ideas are not always, in every instance, derived from the correspondent impressions, though this instance is so singular that it is scarcely worth our observing, and does not merit that for it alone we should alter our general maxim.

Here, therefore, is a proposition which not only seems in itself simple and intelligible, but, if a proper use were made of it, might render every dispute equally intelligible, and banish all that jargon which has so long taken possession of metaphysical reasonings and drawn disgrace upon them. All ideas, especially abstract ones, are naturally faint and obscure. The mind has but a slender hold of them. They are apt to be confounded with other resembling ideas; and when we have often employed any term, though without a distinct meaning, we are apt to imagine it has a determinate idea annexed to it. On the contrary, all impressions, that is, all sensations either outward or inward, are strong and vivid. The limits between them are more exactly determined, nor is it easy to fall into any error or mistake with regard to them. When we entertain, therefore, any suspicion that a philosophical term is employed without any meaning or idea (as is but too frequent), we need but inquire, *from what impression is that supposed idea derived?* And if it be impossible to assign any, this will serve to confirm our suspicion. By bringing ideas in so clear a light, we may reasonably hope to remove all dispute which may arise concerning their nature and reality.[1]

SECTION IV

SKEPTICAL DOUBTS CONCERNING THE OPERATIONS OF THE UNDERSTANDING

PART I

All the objects of human reason or inquiry may naturally be divided into two kinds, to wit, "Relations of Ideas," and "Matters of Fact." Of the first kind are the sciences of Geometry, Algebra, and Arithmetic, and, in short, every affirmation which is either intuitively or demonstratively certain. *That the square of the hypotenuse is equal to the square of the two sides* is a proposition which expresses a relation between these figures. *That three times five is equal to the half of thirty* expresses a relation between these numbers. Propositions of this kind are discoverable by the mere operation of thought, without dependence on what is anywhere existent in the universe. Though there never were a circle or triangle in nature, the truths demonstrated by Euclid would forever retain their certainty and evidence.

Matters of fact, which are the second objects of human reason, are not ascertained in the same manner, nor is our evidence of their truth, however great, of a like nature with the foregoing. The contrary of every matter of fact is still possible, because it can never imply a contradiction and is conceived by the mind with the same facility and distinctness as if ever so conformable to reality. *That the sun will not rise tomorrow* is no less intelligible a proposition and implies no more contradiction than the

---

[1]It is probable that no more was meant by those who denied innate ideas than that all ideas were copies of our impressions, though it must be confessed that the terms which they employed were not chosen with such caution, nor so exactly defined, as to prevent all mistakes about their doctrine. For what is meant by "innate"? If "innate" be equivalent to "natural," then all the perceptions and ideas of the mind must be allowed to be innate or natural, in whatever sense we take the latter word, whether in opposition to what is uncommon, artificial, or miraculous. If by innate be meant contemporary to our birth, the dispute seems to be frivolous, nor is it worth while to inquire at what time thinking begins, whether before, at, or after our birth. Again, the word "idea" seems to be commonly taken in a very loose sense by Locke and others, as standing for any of our perceptions, our sensations and passions, as well as thoughts. Now, in this sense, I should desire to know what can be meant by asserting that self-love, or resentment of injuries, or the passion between the sexes is not innate?

But admitting these terms "impressions" and "ideas" in the sense above explained, and understanding by "innate" what is original or copied from no precedent perception, then may we assert that all our impressions are innate, and our ideas not innate.

To be ingenuous, I must own it to be my opinion that Locke was betrayed into this question by schoolmen, who, making use of undefined terms, draw out their disputes to a tedious length without ever touching the point in question. A like ambiguity and circumlocution seem to run through the philosopher's reasonings, on this as well as most other subjects.

affirmation *that it will rise.* We should in vain, therefore, attempt to demonstrate its falsehood. Were it demonstratively false, it would imply a contradiction and could never be distinctly conceived by the mind.

It may, therefore, be a subject worthy of curiosity to inquire what is the nature of that evidence which assures us of any real existence and matter of fact beyond the present testimony of our senses or the records of our memory. This part of philosophy, it is observable, had been little cultivated either by the ancients or moderns; and, therefore, our doubts and errors in the prosecution of so important an inquiry may be the more excusable while we march through such difficult paths without any guide or direction. They may even prove useful by exciting curiosity and destroying that implicit faith and security which is the bane of all reasoning and free inquiry. The discovery of defects in the common philosophy, if any such there be, will not, I presume, be a discouragement, but rather an incitement, as is usual, to attempt something more full and satisfactory than has yet been proposed to the public.

All reasonings concerning matter of fact seem to be founded on the relation of *cause* and *effect.* By means of that relation alone we can go beyond the evidence of our memory and senses. If you were to ask a man why he believes any matter of fact which is absent, for instance, that his friend is in the country or in France, he would give you a reason, and this reason would be some other fact: as a letter received from him or the knowledge of his former resolutions and promises. A man finding a watch or any other machine in a desert island would conclude that there had once been men in that island. All our reasonings concerning fact are of the same nature. And here it is constantly supposed that there is a connection between the present fact and that which is inferred from it. Were there nothing to bind them together, the inference would be entirely precarious. The hearing of an articulate voice and rational discourse in the dark assures us of the presence of some person. Why? Because these are the effects of the human make and fabric, and closely connected with it. If we anatomize all the other reasonings of this nature, we shall find that they are founded on the relation of cause and effect, and that this relation is either near or remote, direct or collateral. Heat and light are collateral effects of fire, and the one effect may justly be inferred from the other.

If we would satisfy ourselves, therefore, concerning the nature of that evidence which assures us of matters of fact, we must inquire how we arrive at the knowledge of cause and effect.

I shall venture to affirm, as a general proposition which admits of no exception, that the knowledge of this relation is not, in any instance, attained by reasonings *a priori,* but arises entirely from experience, when we find that any particular objects are constantly conjoined with each other. Let an object be presented to a man of ever so strong natural reason and abilities—if that object be entirely new to him, he will not be able, by the most accurate examination of its sensible qualities, to discover any of its causes or effects. Adam, though his rational faculties be supposed, at the very first, entirely perfect, could not have inferred from the fluidity and transparency of water that it would suffocate him, or from the light and warmth of fire that it would consume him. No object ever discovers, by the qualities which appear to the senses, either the causes which produced it or the effects which will arise from it; nor can our reason, unassisted by experience, ever draw any inference concerning real existence and matter of fact.

This proposition, *that causes and effects are discoverable, not by reason, but by experience,* will readily be admitted with regard to such objects as we remember to have once been altogether unknown to us, since we must be conscious of the utter inability which we then lay under of foretelling what would arise from them. Present two smooth pieces of marble to a man who has no tincture of natural philosophy; he will never discover that they will adhere together in such a manner as to require great force to separate them in a direct line, while they make so small a resistance to a lateral pressure. Such events as bear little analogy to the common course of nature are also readily confessed to be known only by experience, nor does any man imagine that the explosion of gunpowder or the attraction of a loadstone could ever be discovered by arguments *a priori.* In like manner, when an effect is supposed to depend upon an intricate machinery or secret structure of parts, we make no difficulty in attributing all our knowledge of it to experience. Who will assert that he can give the ultimate reason why milk or bread is proper nourishment for a man, not for a lion or tiger?

But the same truth may not appear at first sight to have the same evidence with regard to events which have become familiar to us from our first appearance in the world, which bear a close analogy to the whole course of nature, and which are supposed to depend on the simple qualities of objects without any secret structure of parts. We are apt to imagine that we could discover these effects by the mere operation of our reason without experience. We fancy that, were we brought on a sudden into this world, we could at first have inferred that one billiard ball would communicate motion to another upon impulse, and that we needed not to have waited for the event in order to pronounce with certainty concerning it. Such is the influence of custom that where it is strongest it not only covers our natural ignorance but even conceals itself, and seems not to take place, merely because it is found in the highest degree.

But to convince us that all the laws of nature and all the operations of bodies without exception are known only by experience, the following reflections may perhaps suffice. Were any object presented to us, and were we required to pronounce concerning the effect which will result from it without consulting past observation, after what matter, I beseech you, must the mind proceed in this operation? It must invent or imagine some event which it ascribes to the object as its effect; and it is plain that this invention must be entirely arbitrary. The mind can never possibly find the effect in the supposed cause by the most accurate scrutiny and examination. For the effect is totally different from the cause, and consequently can never be discovered in it. Motion in the second billiard ball is a quite distinct event from motion in the first, nor is there anything in the one to suggest the smallest hint of the other. A stone or piece of metal raised into the air and left without any support immediately falls. But to consider the matter *a priori,* is there anything we discover in this situation which can beget the idea of a downward rather than an upward or any other motion in the stone or metal?

And as the first imagination or invention of a particular effect in all natural operations is arbitrary where we consult not experience, so must we also esteem the supposed tie or connection between the cause and effect which binds them together and renders it impossible that any other effect could result from the operation of that cause. When I see, for instance, a billiard ball moving in a straight line toward another, even suppose motion in the second ball should by accident be suggested to me as the result of their contact or impulse, may I not conceive that a hundred different events might as well follow from that cause? May not both these balls remain at absolute rest? May not the first ball return in a straight line or leap off from the second in any line or direction? All these suppositions are consis-

tent and conceivable. Why, then, should we give the preference to one which is no more consistent or conceivable than the rest? All our reasonings *a priori* will never be able to show us any foundation for this preference.

In a word, then, every effect is a distinct event from its cause. It could not, therefore, be discovered in the cause, and the first invention or conception of it, *a priori,* must be entirely arbitrary. And even after it is suggested, the conjunction of it with the cause must appear equally arbitrary, since there are always many other effects which, to reason, must seem fully as consistent and natural. In vain, therefore, should we pretend to determine any single event or infer any cause or effect without the assistance of observation and experience.

Hence we may discover the reason why no philosopher who is rational and modest has ever pretended to assign the ultimate cause of any natural operation, or to show distinctly the action of that power which produces any single effect in the universe. It is confessed that the utmost effort of human reason is to reduce the principles productive of natural phenomena to a greater simplicity, and to resolve the many particular effects into a few general causes, by means of reasonings from analogy, experience, and observation. But as to the causes of these general causes, we should in vain attempt their discovery, nor shall we ever be able to satisfy ourselves by any particular explication of them. These ultimate springs and principles are totally shut up from human curiosity and inquiry. Elasticity, gravity, cohesion of parts, communication of motion by impulse—these are probably the ultimate causes and principles which we shall ever discover in nature; and we may esteem ourselves sufficiently happy if, by accurate inquiry and reasoning, we can trace up the particular phenomena to, or near to, these general principles. The most perfect philosophy of the natural kind only staves off our ignorance a little longer, as perhaps the most perfect philosophy of the moral or metaphysical kind serves only to discover larger portions of it. Thus the observation of human blindness and weakness is the result of all philosophy, and meets us, at every turn, in spite of our endeavors to elude or avoid it.

Nor is geometry, when taken into the assistance of natural philosophy, ever able to remedy this defect or lead us into the knowledge of ultimate causes by all that accuracy of reasoning for which it is so justly celebrated. Every part of mixed mathematics proceeds upon the supposition that certain laws are established by nature in her operations, and abstract reasonings are employed either to assist experience in the discovery of these laws or to determine their influence in particular instances where it depends upon any precise degree of distance and quantity. Thus it is a law of motion, discovered by experience, that the moment or force of any body in motion is in the compound ratio or proportion of its solid contents and its velocity, and, consequently, that a small force may remove the greatest obstacle or raise the greatest weight if by any contrivance or machinery we can increase the velocity of that force so as to make it an overmatch for its antagonist. Geometry assists us in the application of this law by giving us the just dimensions of all the parts and figures which can enter into any species of machine, but still the discovery of the law itself is owing merely to experience, and all the abstract reasonings in the world could never lead us one step toward the knowledge of it. When we reason *a priori* and consider merely any object or cause as it appears to the mind, independent of all observation, it never could suggest to us the notion of any distinct object, such as its effect, much less show us the inseparable and inviolable connection between them. A man must be very sagacious who could discover by reasoning that crystal is the effect of heat, and ice of cold, without being previously acquainted with the operation of these qualities.

PART II

But we have not yet attained any tolerable satisfaction with regard to the question first proposed. Each solution still gives rise to a new question as difficult as the foregoing and leads us on to further inquiries. When it is asked, *What is the nature of all our reasonings concerning matter of fact?* the proper answer seems to be, That they are founded on the relation of cause and effect. When again it is asked, *What is the foundation of all our reasonings and conclusions concerning that relation?* it may be replied in one word, *experience.* But if we still carry on our sifting humor and ask, *What is the foundation of all conclusions from experience?* this implies a new question which may be of more difficult solution and explication. Philosophers that give themselves airs of superior wisdom and sufficiency have a hard task when they encounter persons of inquisitive dispositions, who push them from every corner to which they retreat, and who are sure at last to bring them to some dangerous dilemma. The best expedient to prevent this confusion is to be modest in our pretensions and even to discover the

difficulty ourselves before it is objected to us. By this means we may make a kind of merit of our very ignorance.

I shall content myself in this section with an easy task and shall pretend only to give a negative answer to the question here proposed. I say, then, that even after we have experience of the operations of cause and effect, our conclusions from that experience are *not* founded on reasoning or any process of the understanding. This answer we must endeavor both to explain and to defend.

It must certainly be allowed that nature has kept us at a great distance from all her secrets and has afforded us only the knowledge of a few superficial qualities of objects, while she conceals from us those powers and principles on which the influence of these objects entirely depends. Our senses inform us of the color, weight, and consistency of bread, but neither sense nor reason can ever inform us of those qualities which fit it for the nourishment and support of the human body. Sight or feeling conveys an idea of the actual motion of bodies, but as to that wonderful force or power which would carry on a moving body forever in a continued change of place, and which bodies never lose but by communicating it to others, of this we cannot form the most distant conception. But notwithstanding this ignorance of natural powers and principles, we always presume when we see like sensible qualities that they have like secret powers, and expect that effects similar to those which we have experienced will follow from them. If a body of like color and consistency with that bread which we have formerly eaten be presented to us, we make no scruple of repeating the experiment and foresee with certainty like nourishment and support. Now this is a process of the mind or thought of which I would willingly know the foundation. It is allowed on all hands that there is no known connection between the sensible qualities and the secret powers, and, consequently, that the mind is not led to form such a conclusion concerning their constant and regular conjunction by anything which it knows of their nature. As to past *experience,* it can be allowed to give *direct* and *certain* information of those precise objects only, and that precise period of time which fell under its cognizance: But why this experience should be extended to future times and to other objects which, for aught we know, may be only in appearance similar, this is the main question on which I would insist. The bread which I formerly ate nourished me; that is, a body of such sensible qualities was, at that time, endued with such secret powers. But does it follow that other bread must also nourish me at another time, and that like sensible qualities must always be attended with like secret powers? The consequence seems nowise necessary. At least, it must be acknowledged that there is here a consequence drawn by the mind that there is a certain step taken, a process of thought, and an inference which wants to be explained. These two propositions are far from being the same: *I have found that such an object has always been attended with such an effect*, and *I foresee that other objects which are in appearance similar will be attended with similar effects*. I shall allow, if you please, that the one proposition may justly be inferred from the other: I know, in fact, that it always is inferred. But if you insist that the inference is made by a chain of reasoning, I desire you to produce that reasoning. The connection between these propositions is not intuitive. There is required a medium which may enable the mind to draw such an inference, if indeed it be drawn by reasoning and argument. What that medium is I must confess passes my comprehension; and it is incumbent on those to produce it who assert that it really exists and is the original of all our conclusions concerning matter of fact.

This negative argument must certainly, in process of time, become altogether convincing if many penetrating and able philosophers shall turn their inquiries this way, and no one be ever able to discover any connecting proposition or intermediate step which supports the understanding in this conclusion. But as the question is yet new, every reader may not trust so far to his own penetration as to conclude, because an argument escapes his inquiry, that therefore it does not really exist. For this reason it may be requisite to venture upon a more difficult task, and, enumerating all the branches of human knowledge, endeavor to show that none of them can afford such an argument.

All reasonings may be divided into two kinds, namely, demonstrative reasoning, or that concerning relations of ideas, and moral reasoning, or that concerning matter of fact and existence. That there are no demonstrative arguments in the case seems evident, since it implies no contradiction that the course of nature may change and that an object, seemingly like those which we have experienced, may be attended with different or contrary effects. May I not clearly and distinctly conceive that a body, falling from the clouds and which in all other respects resembles snow, has yet the taste of salt or feeling of fire? Is there any more intelligible proposition than to affirm that all the trees will flourish in December and January, and will decay in May and June? Now, whatever is intelligible and can be distinctly conceived implies no contradiction and can never be proved false by any demonstrative argument or abstract reasoning *a priori*.

If we be, therefore, engaged by arguments to put trust in past experience and make it the standard of our future judgment, these arguments must be probable only, or such as regard matter of fact and real existence, according to the division above mentioned. But that there is no argument of this kind must appear if our explication of that species of reasoning be admitted as solid and satisfactory. We have said that all arguments concerning existence are founded on the relation of cause and effect, that our knowledge of that relation is derived entirely from experience, and that all our experimental conclusions proceed upon the supposition that the future will be conformable to the past. To endeavor, therefore, the proof of this last supposition by probable arguments, or arguments regarding existence, must be evidently going in a circle and taking that for granted which is the very point in question.

In reality, all arguments from experience are founded on the similarity which we discover among natural objects, and by which we are induced to expect effects similar to those which we have found to follow from such objects. And though none but a fool or madman will ever pretend to dispute the authority of experience or to reject that great guide of human life, it may surely be allowed a philosopher to have so much curiosity at least as to examine the principle of human nature which gives this mighty authority to experience and makes us draw advantage from that similarity which nature has placed among different objects. From causes which appear similar, we expect similar effects. This is the sum of all our experimental conclusions. Now it seems evident that, if this conclusion were formed by reason, it would be as perfect at first, and upon one instance, as after ever so long a course of experience; but the case is far otherwise. Nothing so like as eggs, yet no one, on account of this appearing similarity, expects the same taste and relish in all of them. It is only after a long course of uniform experiments in any kind that we attain a firm reliance and security with regard to a particular event. Now, where is that process of reasoning which, from one instance, draws a conclusion so different from that which it infers from a hundred instances that are nowise different from that single one? This question I propose as much for the sake of information as with an intention of raising difficulties. I cannot find, I cannot imagine any such reasoning. But I keep my mind still open to instruction if anyone will vouchsafe to bestow it on me.

Should it be said that, from a number of uniform experiments, we *infer* a connection between the sensible qualities and the secret powers, this, I must confess, seems the same difficulty, couched in different terms. The question still occurs, On what process of argument is this *inference* founded? Where is the medium, the interposing ideas which join propositions so very wide of each other? It is confessed that the color, consistency, and other sensible qualities of bread appear not of themselves to have any connection with the secret powers of nourishment and support; for otherwise we could infer these secret powers from the first appearance of these sensible qualities without the aid of experience, contrary to the sentiment of all philosophers, and contrary to plain matter of fact. Here, then, is our natural state of ignorance with regard to the powers and influence of all objects. How is this remedied by experience? It only shows us a number of uniform effects resulting from certain objects, and teaches us that those particular objects, at that particular time, were endowed with such powers and forces. When a new object endowed with similar sensible qualities is produced, we expect similar powers and forces, and look for a like effect. From a body of like color and consistency with bread, we expect like nourishment and support. But this surely is a step or progress of the mind which wants to be explained. When a man says, *I have found, in all past instances, such sensible qualities, conjoined with such secret powers,* and when he says, *similar sensible qualities will always be conjoined with similar secret powers,* he is not guilty of a tautology, nor are these propositions in any respect the same. You say that the one proposition is an inference from the other; but you must confess that the inference is not intuitive, neither is it demonstrative. Of what nature is it then? To say it is experimental is begging the question. For all inferences from experience suppose, as their foundation, that the future will resemble the past and that similar powers will be conjoined with similar sensible qualities. If there be any suspicion that the course of nature may change, and that the past may be no rule for the future, all experience becomes useless and can give rise to no inference or conclusion. It is impossible, therefore, that any arguments from experience can prove this resemblance of the past to the future, since all these arguments are founded on the supposition of that resemblance. Let the course of things be allowed hitherto ever so regular, that alone, without some new argument or inference, proves not that for the future it will continue so. In vain do you pretend to have learned the nature of bodies from your past experience. Their secret nature, and consequently all their effects and influence, may change without any change in their sensible qualities. This happens sometimes, and with regard to some objects. Why may it not happen always, and with regard to all objects? What logic, what process of argument secures you against this supposition? My practice, you say, refutes my doubts. But you mistake the purport of my question. As an agent, I am quite satisfied in the point; but as a philosopher who has some share of curiosity, I will not say skepticism, I want to learn the foundation of this inference. No reading, no inquiry has yet been able to remove my difficulty or give me satisfaction in a matter of such importance. Can I do better than propose the difficulty to the public, even though, perhaps, I have small hopes of obtaining a solution? We shall at least, by this means, be sensible of our ignorance, if we do not augment our knowledge.

I must confess that a man is guilty of unpardonable arrogance who concludes, because an argument has escaped his own investigation, that therefore it does not really exist. I must also confess that, though all the learned, for several ages, should have employed themselves in fruitless search upon any subject, it may still, perhaps, be rash to conclude positively that the subject must therefore pass all human comprehension. Even though we examine all the sources of our knowledge and conclude them unfit for such a subject, there may still remain a suspicion that the enumeration is not complete or the examination not accurate. But with regard to the present subject, there are some considerations which seem to remove all this accusation of arrogance or suspicion of mistake.

It is certain that the most ignorant and stupid peasants, nay infants, nay even brute beasts, improve by experience and learn the qualities of natural objects by observing the effects which result from them. When a child has felt the sensation of pain from touching the flame of a candle, he will be careful not to put his hand near any candle, but will expect a similar effect from a cause which is similar in its sensible qualities and appearance. If you assert, therefore, that the understanding of the child is led into this conclusion by any process of argument or ratiocination, I may justly require you to produce that argument, nor have you any pretense to refuse so equitable a demand. You cannot say that the argument is abstruse and may possibly escape your inquiry, since you confess that it is obvious to the capacity of a mere infant. If you hesitate, therefore, a moment or if, after reflection, you produce an intricate or profound argument, you, in a manner, give up the question and confess that it is not reasoning which engages us to suppose the past resembling the future, and to expect similar effects from causes which are to appearance similar. This is the proposition which I intended to enforce in the present section. If I be right, I pretend not to have made any mighty discovery. And if I be wrong, I must acknowledge myself to be indeed a very backward scholar, since I cannot now discover an argument which, it seems, was perfectly familiar to me long before I was out of my cradle.

SECTION VII

PART II

But to hasten to a conclusion of this argument, which is already drawn out to too great a length: We have sought in vain for an idea of power or necessary connection in all the sources from which we would suppose it to be derived. It appears that in single instances of the operation of bodies we never can, by our utmost scrutiny, discover anything but one event following another, without being able to comprehend any force or power by which the cause operates or any connection between it and its supposed effect. The same difficulty occurs in contemplating the operations of mind on body, where we observe the motion of the latter to follow upon the volition of the former, but are not able to observe or conceive the tie which binds together the motion and volition, or the energy, by which the mind produces this effect. The authority of the will over its own faculties and ideas is not a whit more comprehensible, so that, upon the whole, there appears not, throughout all nature, any one instance of connection which is conceivable by us. All events seem entirely loose and separate. One event follows another, but we never can observe any tie between them. They seem *conjoined,* but never *connected.* But as we can have no idea of anything which never appeared to our outward sense or inward sentiment, the necessary conclusion *seems* to be that we have no idea of connection or power at all, and that these words are absolutely without any meaning when employed either in philosophical reasonings or common life.

But there still remains one method of avoiding this conclusion, and one source which we have not yet examined. When any natural object or event is presented, it is impossible for us, by any sagacity or penetration, to discover, or even conjecture, without experience, what event will result from it, or to carry our foresight beyond that object which is immediately present to the memory and senses.

Even after one instance or experiment where we have observed a particular event to follow upon another, we are not entitled to form a general rule or foretell what will happen in like cases, it being justly esteemed an unpardonable temerity to judge of the whole course of nature from one single experiment, however accurate or certain. But when one particular species of events has always, in all instances, been conjoined with another, we make no longer any scruple of foretelling one upon the appearance of the other, and of employing that reasoning which can alone assure us of any matter of fact or existence. We then call the one object "cause," the other "effect." We suppose that there is some connection between them, some power in the one by which it infallibly produces the other and operates with the greatest certainty and strongest necessity.

It appears, then, that this idea of a necessary connection among events arises from a number of similar instances which occur, of the constant conjunction of these events; nor can that idea ever be suggested by any one of these instances surveyed in all possible lights and positions. But there is nothing in a number of instances, different from every single instance, which is supposed to be exactly similar, except only that after a repetition of similar instances the mind is carried by habit, upon the appearance of one event, to expect its usual attendant and to believe that it will exist. This connection, therefore, which we *feel* in the mind, this customary transition of the imagination from one object to its usual attendant, is the sentiment or impression from which we form the idea of power or necessary connection. Nothing further is in the case. Contemplate the subjects on all sides, you will never find any other origin of that idea. This is the sole difference between one instance, from which we can never receive the idea of connection, and a number of similar instances by which it is suggested. The first time a man saw the communication of motion by impulse, as by the shock of two billiard balls, he could not pronounce that the one event was *connected,* but only that it was *conjoined* with the other. After he has observed several instances of this nature, he then pronounces them to be *connected.* What alteration has happened to give rise to this new idea of *connection*? Nothing but that he now *feels* these events to be *connected* in his imagination, and can readily foretell the existence of one from the appearance of the other. When we say, therefore, that one object is connected with another, we mean only that they have acquired a connection in our thought and gave rise to this inference by which they become proofs of each other's existence—a conclusion which is somewhat extraordinary, but which seems founded on sufficient evidence. Nor will its evidence be weakened by any general diffidence of the understanding or skeptical suspicion concerning every conclusion which is new and extraordinary. No conclusions can be more agreeable to skepticism than such as make discoveries concerning the weakness and narrow limits of human reason and capacity.

And what stronger instance can be produced of the surprising ignorance and weakness of the understanding than the present? For surely, if there be any relation among objects which it imports us to know perfectly, it is that of cause and effect. On this are founded all our reasonings concerning matter of fact or existence. By means of it alone we attain any assurance concerning objects which are removed from the present testimony of our memory and senses. The only immediate utility of all sciences is to teach us how to control and regulate future events by their causcs. Our thoughts and inquiries are, therefore, every moment employed about this relation; yet so imperfect are the ideas which we form concerning it that it is impossible to give any just definition of cause, except what is drawn from something extraneous and foreign to it. Similar objects are always conjoined with similar. Of this we have experience. Suitably to this experience, therefore, we may define a cause to be *an object followed by another, and where all the objects, similar to the first, are followed by objects similar to the second.* Or, in other words, *where, if the first object had not been, the second never had existed.* The appearance of a cause always conveys the mind, by a customary transition, to the idea of the effect. Of this also we have experience. We may, therefore, suitably to this experience, form another definition of cause and call it *an object followed by another, and whose appearance always conveys the thought to that other.* But though both these definitions be drawn from circumstances foreign to the cause, we cannot remedy this inconvenience or attain any more perfect definition which may point out that circumstance in the cause which gives it a connection with its effect. We have no idea of this connection, nor even any distinct notion what it is we desire to know when we endeavor at a conception of it. We say, for instance, that the vibration of this string is the cause of this particular sound. But what

do we mean by that affirmation? We either mean *that this vibration is followed by this sound, and that all similar vibrations have been followed by similiar sounds;* or, *that this vibration is followed by this sound, and that, upon the appearance of one, the mind anticipates the senses and forms immediately an idea of the other.* We may consider the relation of cause and effect in either of these two lights; but beyond these we have no idea of it.

To recapitulate, therefore, the reasonings of this Section: Every idea is copied from some preceding impression or sentiment; and where we cannot find any impression, we may be certain that there is no idea. In all single instances of the operation of bodies or minds there is nothing that produces any impression, nor consequently can suggest any idea, of power or necessary connection. But when many uniform instances appear, and the same object is always followed by the same event, we then begin to entertain the notion of cause and connection. We then *feel* a new sentiment or impression, to wit, a customary connection in the thought or imagination between one object and its usual attendant; and this sentiment is the original of that idea which we seek for. For as this idea arises from a number of similar instances, and not from any single instance, it must arise from that circumstance in which the number of instances differ from every individual instance. But this customary connection or transition of the imagination is the only circumstance in which they differ. In every other particular they are alike. The first instance which we saw of motion, communicated by the shock of two billiard balls (to return to this obvious illustration), is exactly similar to any instance that may at present occur to us, except only that we could not at first *infer* one event from the other, which we are enabled to do at present, after so long a course of uniform experience. I know not whether the reader will readily apprehend this reasoning. I am afraid that, should I multiply words about it or throw it into a greater variety of lights, it would only become more obscure and intricate. In all abstract reasonings there is one point of view which, if we can happily hit, we shall go further toward illustrating the subject than by all the eloquence and copious expression in the world. This point of view we should endeavor to reach, and reserve the flowers of rhetoric for subjects which are more adapted to them.

David Hume, *An Enquiry Concerning Human Understanding*

1.   According to Hume, how is the mind able to form ideas of things of which it has had no experience? Give an example of this.

2.   According to Hume, if we are in doubt as to the meaningfulness of an idea, what question ought we to ask?

3.   Why does Hume think that our conclusions concerning cause and effect "are not founded on reasoning or any process of the understanding?"

4.   Where does Hume think that the idea of necessity in causation comes from?

C. S. Peirce*

THE FIXATION OF BELIEF

I

Few persons care to study logic, because everybody conceives himself to be proficient enough in the art of reasoning already. But I observe that this satisfaction is limited to one's own ratiocination, and does not extend to that of other men.

We come to the full possession of our power of drawing inferences the last of all our faculties, for it is not so much a natural gift as a long and difficult art. The history of its practice would make a grand subject for a book. The mediæval schoolman, following the Romans, made logic the earliest of a boy's studies after grammar, as being very easy. So it was as they understood it. Its fundamental principles, according to them, was that all knowledge rests on either authority or reason; but that whatever is deduced by reason depends ultimately on a premise derived from authority. Accordingly, as soon as a boy was perfect in the syllogistic procedure, his intellectual kit of tools was held to be complete.

To Roger Bacon, that remarkable mind who in the middle of the thirteenth century was almost a scientific man, the schoolmen's conception of reasoning appeared only an obstacle to truth. He saw that experience alone teaches anything—a proposition which to us seems easy to understand, because a distinct conception of experience has been handed down to us from former generations; which to him also seemed perfectly clear, because its difficulties had not yet unfolded themselves. Of all kinds of experience, the best, be thought, was interior illumination, which teaches many things about nature which the external senses could never discover, such as the transubstantiation of bread.

Four centuries later, the more celebrated Bacon, in the first book of his *Novum Organum*, gave his clear account of experience as something which must be opened to verification and re-examination. But, superior as Lord Bacon's conception is to earlier notions, a modern reader who is not in awe of his grandiloquence is chiefly struck by the inadequacy of his view of scientific procedure. That we have only to make some crude experiments, to draw up briefs of the results in certain blank forms, to go through these by rule, checking off everything disproved and setting down the alternatives, and that thus in a few years physical science would be finished up—what an ideal! "He wrote on science like a Lord Chancellor," indeed, as Harvey, a genuine man of science, said.

The early scientists, Copernicus, Tycho Brahe, Kepler, Gaileo, Harvey, and Gilbert, had methods more like those of their modern brethren. Kepler undertook to draw a curve through the places of Mars;[1] and his greatest service to science was in impressing on men's minds that this was the thing to be done if they wished to improve astronomy; that they were not to content themselves with inquiring whether one system of epicycles was better than another but that they were to sit down by

---

*Charles Sanders Peirce (1839–1914) was a mathematician, scientist, and philosopher. The founder of pragmatism and a prolific writer, he is widely regarded as one of America's most original thinkers. The following article was originally published in *Popular Science Monthly* (1877) as one of a series of articles on the logic of science.

[1]Not quite so, but as nearly as can be told in a few words. [Footnotes are Peirce's throughout drawn from various editions]

the figures and find out what the curve, in truth, was. He accomplished this by his incomparable energy and courage, blundering along in the most inconceivable way (to us), from one irrational hypothesis to another, until, after trying twenty-two of these, he fell by the mere exhaustion of his invention, upon the orbit which a mind well furnished with the weapons of modern logic would have tried almost at the outset.[2]

In the same way, every work of science great enough to be remembered for a few generations affords some exemplification of the defective state of the art of reasoning of the time when it was written; and each chief step in science has been a lesson in logic. It was so when Lavoisier and his contemporaries took up the study of Chemistry. The old chemist's maxim had been *Lege, lege, lege, labora, ora, et relege.* Lavoisier's method was not to read and pray, not to dream that some long and complicated chemical process would have a certain effect, to put it into practice with dull patience, after its inevitable failure to dream that with some modification it would have another result, and to end by publishing the last dream as a fact: his way was to carry his mind into his laboratory, and to make of his alembics and cucurbits instruments of thought, giving a new conception of reasoning as something which was to be done with one's eyes open, by manipulating real things instead of words and fancies.

The Darwinian controversy is, in large part, a question of logic. Mr. Darwin proposed to apply the statistical method to biology.[3] The same thing has been done in a widely different branch of science, the theory of gases. Though unable to say what the movement of any particular molecule of gas would be on a certain hypothesis regarding the constitution of this class of bodies, Clausius and Maxwell were yet able, by the application of the doctrine of probabilities, to predict that in the long run such and such a proportion of the molecules would, under given circumstances, acquire such and such velocities; that there would take place, every second, such and such a number of collisions, etc.; and from

these propositions they were able to deduce certain properties of gases, especially in regard to their heat-relations. In like manner, Darwin, while unable to say what the operation of variation and natural selection in every individual case will be, demonstrates that in the long run they will adapt animals to their circumstances. Whether or not existing animal forms are due to such action, or what position the theory ought to take, forms the subject of a discussion in which questions of fact and questions of logic are curiously interlaced.

II

The object of reasoning is to find out, from the consideration of what we already know, something else which we do not know. Consequently, reasoning is good if it be such[4] as to give a true conclusion from true premises, and not otherwise. Thus, the question of validity is purely one of fact and not of thinking. A being the premises and B being the conclusion, the question is, whether these facts are really so related that if A is B is. If so, the inference is valid; if not, not. It is not in the least the question whether, when the premises are accepted by the mind, we feel an impulse to accept the conclusion also. It is true that we do generally reason correctly by nature. But that is an accident; the true conclusion would remain true if we had no impulse to accept it; and the false one would remain false, though we could not resist the tendency to believe in it.

We are, doubtless, in the main logical animals, but we are not perfectly so. Most of us, for example, are naturally more sanguine and hopeful than logic would justify. We seem to be so constituted that in the absence of any facts to go upon we are happy and self-satisfied; so that the effect of experience is continually to counteract our hopes and aspirations. Yet a lifetime of the application of this corrective does not usually eradicate our sanguine disposition. Where hope is unchecked by any experience, it is likely that our optimism is extravagant. Logicality

[2]—Ed. "I am ashamed at being obliged to confess that this volume contains a very false and foolish remark about Kepler. When I wrote it, I had never studied the original book as I have since. It is now my deliberate opinion that it is the most marvellous piece of inductive reasoning I have been able to find."—1893

[3]"We now know what was authoritatively denied when I first suggested it, that he took a hint from Malthus' book on population."

[4]"I.e., be denominated by such a habit as generally to give."

in regard to practical matters is the most useful quality an animal can possess, and might, therefore, result from the action of natural selection; but outside of these it is probably of more advantage to the animal to have his mind filled with pleasing and encouraging visions, independently of their truth; and thus, upon unpractical subjects, natural selection might occasion a fallacious tendency of thought.[5]

That which determines us, from given premises, to draw one inference rather than another is some habit of mind, whether it be constitutional or acquired. The habit is good or otherwise, according as it produces true conclusions from true premises or not; and an inference is regarded as valid or not, without reference to the truth or falsity of its conclusion specially, but according as the habit which determines it is such as to produce true conclusions in general or not. The particular habit of mind which governs this or that inference may be formulated in a proposition whose truth depends on the validity of the inferences which the habit determines; and such a formula is called a *guiding principle* of inference. Suppose, for example, that we observe that a rotating disk of copper quickly comes to rest when placed between the poles of a magnet, and we infer that this will happen with every disk of copper. The guiding principle is that what is true of one piece of copper is true of another. Such a guiding principle with regard to copper would be much safer than with regard to many other substances—brass, for example.

A book might be written to signalize all the most important of these guiding principles of reasoning. It would probably be, we must confess, of no service to a person whose thought is directed wholly to practical subjects, and whose activity moves along thoroughly beaten paths. The problems which present themselves to such a mind are matters of routine which he has learned once for all to handle in learning his business. But let a man venture into an unfamiliar field, or where his results are not continually checked by experience, and all history shows that the most masculine intellect will ofttimes lose his orientation and waste his efforts in directions which bring him no nearer to his goal or even carry him entirely astray. He is like a ship on the open sea, with no one on board who understands the rules of navigation. And in such a case

some general study of the guiding principles of reasoning would be sure to be found useful.

The subject could hardly be treated, however, without being first limited; since almost any fact may serve as a guiding principle. But it so happens that there exists a division among facts, such that in one class are all those which are absolutely essential as guiding principles, while in the other are all those which have any other interest as objects of research. This division is between those which are necessarily taken for granted in asking whether a certain conclusion follows from certain premises, and those which are not implied in that question. A moment's thought will show that a variety of facts are already assumed when the logical question is first asked. It is implied, for instance, that there are such states of mind as doubt and belief—that a passage from one to the other is possible, the object of thought remaining the same, and that this transition is subject to some rules which all minds are alike bound by. As these are facts which we must already know before we can have any clear conception of reasoning at all, it cannot be supposed to be any longer of much interest to inquire into their truth or falsity. On the other hand, it is easy to believe that those rules of reasoning which are deduced from the very idea of the process are the ones which are the most essential; and, indeed, that so long as it conforms to these it will, at least, not lead to false conclusions from true premises. In point of fact, the importance of what may be deduced from the assumptions involved in the logical question turns out to be greater than might be supposed, and this for reasons which it is difficult to exhibit at the outset. The only one which I shall here mention is that conceptions which are really products of logical reflections, without being readily seen to be so, mingle with our ordinary thoughts, and are frequently the causes of great confusion. This is the case, for example, with the conception of quality. A quality as such is never an object of observation. We can see that a thing is blue or green, but the quality of being blue and the quality of being green are not things which we see; they are products of logical reflections. The truth is that common sense, or thought as it first emerges above the level of the narrowly practical, is deeply imbued with that bad logical quality to which the epithet *metaphysical* is commonly applied; and nothing can clear it up but a severe course of logic.

---

[5]"Let us not, however, be cocksure that natural selection is the only factor of evolution."

III

We generally know when we wish to ask a question and when we wish to pronounce a judgment, for there is a dissimilarity between the sensation of doubting and that of believing.

But this is not all which distinguishes doubt from belief. There is a practical difference. Our beliefs guide our desires and shape our actions. The Assassins, or followers of the Old Man of the Mountain, used to rush into death at his least command, because they believed that obedience to him would insure everlasting felicity. Had they doubted this, they would not have acted as they did. So it is with every belief, according to its degree. The feeling of believing is a more or less sure indication of there being established in our nature some habit which will determine our actions. Doubt never has such an effect.

Nor must we overlook a third point of difference. Doubt is an uneasy and dissatisfied state from which we struggle to free ourselves and pass into the state of belief;[6] while the latter is a calm and satisfactory state which we do not wish to avoid, or to change to a belief in anything else.[7] On the contrary, we cling tenaciously, not merely to believing, but to believing just what we do believe.

Thus, both doubt and belief have positive effects upon us, though very different ones. Belief does not make us act at once, but puts us into such a condition that we shall behave in a certain way, when the occasion arises. Doubt has not the least effect of this sort, but stimulates us to action until it is destroyed. This reminds us of the irritation of a nerve and the reflex action produced thereby; while for the analogue of belief, in the nervous system, we must look to what are called nervous associations—for example, to that habit of the nerves in consequence of which the smell of a peach will make the mouth water.

IV

The irritation of doubt causes a struggle to attain a state of belief.[8] I shall term this struggle *inquiry,* though it must be admitted that this is sometimes not a very apt designation.

The irritation of doubt is the only immediate motive for the struggle to attain belief. It is certainly best for us that our beliefs should be such as may truly guide our actions so as to satisfy our desires; and this reflection will make us reject any belief which does not seem to have been so formed as to insure this result. But it will only do so by creating a doubt in the place of that belief. With the doubt, therefore, the struggle begins, and with the cessation of doubt it ends. Hence, the sole object of inquiry is the settlement of opinion. We may fancy that this is not enough for us, and that we seek not merely an opinion, but a true opinion. But put this fancy to the test, and it proves groundless; for as soon as a firm belief is reached we are entirely satisfied, whether the belief be false or true. And it is clear that nothing out of the sphere of our knowledge can be our object, for nothing which does not affect the mind can be a motive for a mental effort. The most that can be maintained is that we seek for a belief that we shall *think* to be true. But we think each one of our beliefs to be true, and, indeed, it is mere tautology to say so.[9]

That the settlement of opinion is the sole end of inquiry is a very important proposition. It sweeps away, at once, various vague and erroneous conceptions of proof. A few of these may be noticed here.

1. Some philosophers have imagined that to start an inquiry it was only necessary to utter or

---

[6]"In this, it is like any other stimulus. It is true that just as man may, for the sake of the pleasures of the table, like to be hungry and take means to make themselves so, although hunger always involves a desire to fill the stomach, so for the sake of the pleasures of inquiry, men may like to seek out doubts. Yet for all that, doubt essentially involves a struggle to escape it."

[7]I am not speaking of secondary effects occasionally produced by the interference of other impulses.

[8]"Doubt, however, is not usually hestitancy about what is to be done then and there. It is anticipated hesitancy about what I shall do hereafter, or a feigned hesitancy about a fictitious state of things. It is the power of making believe we hesitate, together with the pregnant fact that the decision upon the make-believe dilemma goes toward forming a bona fide habit that will be operative in a real emergency."

[9]"For truth is neither more nor less than that character of a proposition which consists in this, that belief in the proposition would, with sufficient experience and reflection, lead us to such conduct as would tend to satisfy the desires we should then have. To say that truth means more than this is to say that is has no meaning at all."

41

question or set it down on paper, and have even recommended us to begin our studies with questioning everything! But the mere putting of a proposition into the interrogative form does not stimulate the mind to any struggle after belief. There must be a real and living doubt, and without all this, discussion is idle.

2. It is a very common idea that a demonstration must rest on some ultimate and absolutely indubitable propositions. These, according to one school, are first principles of a general nature; according to another, are first sensations. But, in point of fact, an inquiry, to have that completely satisfactory result called demonstration, has only to start with propositions perfectly free from an actual doubt. If the premises are not in fact doubted at all, they cannot be more satisfactory than they are.[10]

3. Some people seem to love to argue a point after all the world is fully convinced of it. But no further advance can be made. When doubt ceases, mental action on the subject comes to an end; and, if it did go on, it would be without a purpose, except that of self-criticism.

V

If the settlement of opinion is the sole object of inquiry, and if belief is of the nature of a habit, why should we not attain the desired end, by taking any answer to a question, which we may fancy, and constantly reiterating it to ourselves, dwelling on all which may conduce to that belief, and learning to turn with contempt and hatred from anything which might disturb it? This simple and direct method is really pursued by many men. I remember once being entreated not to read a certain newspaper lest it might change my opinion upon free-trade. "Lest I might be entrapped by its fallacies and misstatements" was the form of expression. "You are not," my friend said, "a special student of political economy. You might, therefore, easily be deceived by fallacious arguments upon the subject. You might, then, if you read this paper, be led to believe in protection. But you admit that free-trade is the true doctrine; and you do not wish to believe what is not true." I have often known this system to be deliberately adopted. Still oftener, the instinctive dislike of an undecided state of mind, exaggerated into a vague dread of doubt, makes men cling spasmodically to the views they already take. The man feels

that if he only holds to his belief without wavering, it will be entirely satisfactory. Nor can it be denied that a steady and immovable faith yields great peace of mind. It may, indeed, give rise to inconveniences, as if a man should resolutely continue to believe that fire would not burn him, or that he would be eternally damned if he received his *ingesta* otherwise than through a stomach-pump. But then the man who adopts this method will not allow that its inconveniences are greater than its advantages. He will say, "I hold steadfastly to the truth and the truth is always wholesome." And in many cases it may very well be that the pleasure he derives from his calm faith overbalances any inconveniences resulting from its deceptive character. Thus, if it be true that death is annihilation, then the man who believes that he will certainly go straight to heaven when he dies, provided he have fulfilled certain simple observances in this life, has a cheap pleasure which will not be followed by the least disappointment. A similar consideration seems to have weight with many persons in religious topics, for we frequently hear it said, "Oh, I could not believe so-and-so, because I should be wretched if I did." When an ostrich buries its head in the sand as danger approaches, it very likely takes the happiest course. It hides the danger, and then calmly says there is no danger; and, if it feels perfectly sure there is none, why should it raise its head to see? A man may go through life, systematically keeping out of view all that might cause a change in his opinions, and if he only succeeds—basing his method, as he does, on two fundamental psychological laws—I do not see what can be said against his doing so. It would be an egotistical impertinence to object that his procedure is irrational for that only amounts to saying that his method of settling belief is not ours. He does not propose to himself to be rational, and indeed, will often talk with scorn of man's weak and illusive reason. So let him think as he pleases.

But this method of fixing belief, which may be called the method of tenacity, will be unable to hold its ground in practice. The social impulse is against it. The man who adopts it will find that other men think differently from him, and it will be apt to occur to him in some saner moment that their opinions are quite as good as his own, and this will shake his confidence in his belief. This conception, that another man's thought or sentiment may be equivalent to one's own, is a distinctly new step, and

---

[10]"Doubts about them [the premises] may spring up later; but we can find no propositions which are not subject to this contingency."

a highly important one. It arises from an impulse too strong in man to be suppressed, without danger of destroying the human species. Unless we make ourselves hermits, we shall necessarily influence each other's opinions; so that the problem becomes how to fix belief, not in the individual merely, but in the community.

Let the will of the state act, then, instead of that of the individual. Let an institution be created which shall have for its object to keep correct doctrines before the attention of the people, to reiterate them perpetually, and to teach them to the young; having at the same time power to prevent contrary doctrines from being taught, advocated, or expressed. Let all possible causes of a change of mind be removed from men's apprehensions. Let them be kept ignorant, lest they should learn of some reason to think otherwise than they do. Let their passions be enlisted, so that they may regard private and unusual opinions with hatred and horror. Then, let all men who reject the established belief be terrified into silence. Let the people turn out and tar-and-feather such men, or let inquisitions be made into the manner of thinking of suspected persons, and, when they are found guilty of forbidden beliefs, let them be subjected to some signal punishment. When complete agreement could not otherwise be reached, a general massacre of all who have not thought in a certain way has proved a very effective means of settling opinion in a country. If the power to do this be wanting, let a list of opinions be drawn up, to which no man of the least independence of thought can assent, and let the faithful be required to accept all these propositions, in order to segregate them as radically as possible from the influence of the rest of the world.

This method has, from the earliest times, been one of the chief means of upholding correct theological and political doctrines, and of preserving their universal or catholic character. In Rome, especially, it has been practiced from the days of Numa Pompilius to those of Pius Nonus. This is the most perfect example in history; but wherever there is a priesthood—and no religion has been without one—this method has been more or less made use of. Wherever there is aristocracy, or a guild, or any association of a class of men whose interests depend or are supposed to depend on certain propositions, there will be inevitably found some traces of this natural product of social feeling. Cruelties always accompany this system; and when it is consistently carried out, they become atrocities of the most horrible kind in the eyes of any rational man. Nor should this occasion surprise, for the officer of a

society does not feel justified in surrendering the interests of that society for the sake of mercy, as he might his own private interests. It is natural, therefore, that sympathy and fellowship should thus produce a most ruthless power.

In judging this method of fixing belief, which may be called the method of authority, we must, in the first place, allow its immeasurable mental and moral superiority to the method of tenacity. Its success is proportionally greater; and in fact it has over and over again worked the most majestic results. The mere structures of stone which it has caused to be put together—in Siam, for example, in Egypt, and in Europe—have many of them a sublimity hardly more than rivaled by the greatest works of nature. And, except the geological epochs, there are no periods of time so vast as those which are measured by some of these organized faiths. If we scrutinize the matter closely, we shall find that there has not been one of their creeds which has remained always the same; yet the change is so slow as to be imperceptible during one person's life, so that individual belief remains sensibly fixed. For the mass of mankind, then there is perhaps no better method than this. If it is their highest impulse to be intellectual slaves, then slaves they ought to remain.

But no institution can undertake to regulate opinions upon every subject. Only the most important ones can be attended to, and on the rest men's minds must be left to the action of natural causes. This imperfection will be no source of weakness so long as men are in such a state of culture that one opinion does not influence another—that is, so long as they cannot put two and two together. But in the most priest-ridden states some individuals will be found who are raised above that condition. These men possess a wider sort of social feeling; they see that men in other countries and in other ages have held to very different doctrines from those which they themselves have been brought up to believe; and they cannot help seeing that it is the mere accident of their having been taught as they have, and of their having been surrounded with the manners and associations they have, that has caused them to believe as they do and not far differently. And their candor cannot resist the reflection that there is no reason to rate their own views at a higher value than those of other nations and other centuries; and this gives rise to doubts in their minds.

They will further perceive that such doubts as these must exist in their minds with reference to every belief which seems to be determined by the caprice either of themselves or of those who originated the popular opinions. The willful adherence to a belief, and the arbitrary forcing of it upon others, must, therefore, both be given up and a new method of settling opinions must be adopted, which shall not only produce an impulse to believe, but shall also decide what proposition it is which is to be believed. Let the action of natural preferences be unimpeded, then, and under their influence let men conversing together and regarding matters in different lights, gradually develop beliefs in harmony with natural causes. This method resembles that by which conceptions of art have been brought to maturity. The most perfect example of it is to be found in the history of metaphysical philosophy. Systems of this sort have not usually rested upon observed facts, at least not in any great degree. They have been chiefly adopted because their fundamental propositions seemed "agreeable to reason." This is an apt expression; it does not mean that which agrees with experience, but that which we find ourselves inclined to believe. Plato, for example, finds it agreeable to reason that the distances of the celestial spheres from one another should be proportional to the different lengths of strings which produce harmonious chords. Many philosophers have been led to their main conclusions by considerations like this; but this is the lowest and least developed form which the method takes, for it is clear that another man might find Kepler's [earlier] theory, that the celestial spheres are proportional to the inscribed and circumscribed spheres of the different regular solids, more agreeable to *his* reason. But the shock of opinions will soon lead men to rest on preferences of a far more universal nature. Take, for example, the doctrine that man only acts selfishly—that is, from the consideration that acting in one way will afford him more pleasure than acting in another. This rests on no fact in the world, but it has had a wide acceptance as being the only reasonable theory.

This method is far more intellectual and respectable from the point of reason than either of the others which we have noticed. But its failure has been the most manifest. It makes of inquiry something similar to the development of taste; but taste, unfortunately, is always more or less a matter of fashion, and accordingly, metaphysicians have never come to any fixed agreement, but the pendulum has swung backward and forward between a more material and a more spiritual philosophy, from the earliest times to the latest. And so from this, which has been called the *a priori* method, we are driven, in Lord Bacon's phrase, to a true induction. We have examined into this *a priori* method as something which promised to deliver our opinions

from their accidental and capricious element. But development, while it is a process which eliminates the effect of some casual circumstances, only magnifies that of others. This method, therefore, does not differ in a very essential way from that of authority. The government may not have lifted its finger to influence my convictions; I may have been left outwardly quite free to choose, we will say, between monogamy and polygamy, and appealing to my conscience only, I may have concluded that the latter practice is in itself licentious. But when I come to see that the chief obstacle to the spread of Christianity among a people of as high culture as the Hindoos has been a conviction of the immorality of our way of treating women, I cannot help seeing that, though governments do not interfere, sentiments in their development will be very greatly determined by accidental causes. Now, there are some people, among whom I must suppose that my reader is to be found, who, when they see that any belief of theirs is determined by any circumstances extraneous to the facts, will from that moment not merely admit in words that that belief is doubtful, but will experience a real doubt of it, so that it ceases in some degree at least to be a belief.

To satisfy our doubts, therefore, it is necessary that a method should be found by which our beliefs may be caused by nothing human, but by some external permanency—by something upon which our thinking has no effect. Some mystics imagine that they have such a method in a private inspiration from on high. But that is only a form of the method of tenacity, in which the conception of truth as something public is not yet developed. Our external permanency would not be external, in our sense, if it was restricted in its influence to one individual. It must be something which affects, or might affect, every man. And, though these affections are necessary as various as are individual conditions, yet the method must be such that the ultimate conclusion of every man shall be the same, or would be the same if inquiry were sufficiently persisted in. Such is the method of science. Its fundamental hypothesis, restated in more familiar language, is this: There are real things, whose characters are entirely independent of our opinions about them: those realities affect our senses according to regular laws, and, though our sensations are as different as our relations to the objects, yet, by taking advantage of the laws of perception, we can ascertain by reasoning how things really are, and any man, if he have sufficient experience and reason enough about it, will be led to the one true conclusion. The new conception here involved is that of reality. It may be

44

asked how I know that there are any realities. If this hypothesis is the sole support of my method of inquiry, my method of inquiry must not be used to support my hypothesis. The reply is this: (1) If investigation cannot be regarded as proving that there are real things, it at least does not lead to a contrary conclusion; but the method and the conception on which it is based remain ever in harmony. No doubts of the method, therefore, necessarily arise from its practice, as is the case with all the others. (2) The feeling which gives rise to any method of fixing belief is a dissatisfaction at two repugnant propositions. But here already is a vague concession that there is some one thing to which a proposition should conform. Nobody, therefore, can really doubt that there are realities, or, if he did, doubt would not be a source of dissatisfaction. The hypothesis, therefore, is one which every mind admits. So that the social impulse does not cause men to doubt it. (3) Everybody uses the scientific method about a great many things, and only ceases to use it when he does not know how to apply it. (4) Experience of the method has not led us to doubt it, but, on the contrary, scientific investigation has had the most wonderful triumphs in the way of settling opinion. These afford the explanation of my not doubting the method or the hypothesis which is supposes; and not having any doubt, nor believing that anybody else whom I could influence has, it would be the merest babble for me to say more about it. If there be anybody with a living doubt upon the subject, let him consider it.

To describe the method of scientific investigation is the object of this series of papers. At present I have only room to notice some points of contrast between it and other methods of fixing belief.

This is the only one of four methods which presents any distinction of a right and a wrong way. If I adopt the method of tenacity and shut myself out from all influences, whatever I think necessary to doing this is necessary according to that method. So with the method of authority: the state may try to put down heresy by means which, from a scientific point of view, seems very ill-calculated to accomplish its purposes; but the only test *on that method* is what the state thinks, so that it cannot pursue the method wrongly. So with the *a priori* method. The very essence of it is to think as one is inclined to think. All metaphysicians will be sure to do that, however they may be inclined to judge each other to be perversely wrong. The Hegelian system recognizes every natural tendency of thought as logical, although it is certain to be abolished by countertendencies. Hegel thinks there is a regular system in

the succession of these tendencies, in consequence of which, after drifting one way and the other for a long tune, opinion will at last go right. And it is true that metaphysicians get the right ideas at last; Hegel's system of Nature represents tolerably the science of his day; and one may be sure that whatever scientific investigation has put out of doubt will presently receive *a priori* demonstration on the part of the metaphysicians. But with the scientific method the case is different. I may start with known and observed facts to proceed to the unknown; and yet the rules which I follow in doing so may not be such as investigation would approve. The test of whether I am truly following the method is not an immediate appeal to my feelings and purposes, but, on the contrary, itself involves the application of the method. Hence it is that bad reasoning as well as good reasoning is possible; and this fact is the foundation of the practical side of logic.

It is not to be supposed that the first three methods of settling opinion present no advantage whatever over the scientific method. On the contrary, each has some peculiar convenience of its own. The *a priori* method is distinguished for its comfortable conclusions. It is the nature of the process to adopt whatever belief we are inclined to, and there are certain flatteries to one's vanities which we all believe by nature, until we are awakened from our pleasing dream by rough facts. The method of authority will always govern the mass of mankind; and those who wield the various forms of organized force in the state will never be convinced that dangerous reasoning ought not to be suppressed in some way. If liberty of speech is to be untrammeled from the grosser forms of constraint, then uniformity of opinion will be secured by a moral terrorism to which the respectability of society will give its thorough approval. Following the method of authority is the path of peace. Certain non-conformities are permitted; certain others (considered unsafe) are forbidden. These are different in different countries and in different ages; but, wherever you are let it be known that you seriously hold a tabooed belief, and you may be perfectly sure of being treated with a cruelty no less brutal but more refined than hunting you like a wolf. Thus, the greatest intellectual benefactors of mankind have never dared, and dare not now, to utter the whole of their thought; and thus a shade of *prima facie* doubt is cast upon every proposition which is considered essential to the security of society. Singularly enough, the persecution does not all come from without; but a man torments himself and is oftentimes most distressed at finding himself believing propositions which he has been brought up to regard with aversion. The peaceful and sympathetic man will, therefore, find it hard to resist the temptation to submit his opinions to authority. But most of all I admire the method of tenacity for its strength, simplicity, and directness. Men who pursue it are distinguished for their decision of character, which becomes very easy with such a mental rule. They do not waste time in trying to make up their minds to what they want, but, fastening like lightning upon whatever alternative comes first, they hold to it to the end, whatever happens, without an instant's irresolution. This is one of the splendid qualities which generally accompany brilliant, unlasting success. It is impossible not to envy the man who can dismiss reason, although we know how it must turn out at last.

Such are the advantages which the other methods of settling opinions have over scientific investigation. A man should consider well of them; and then he should consider that, after all, he wishes his opinions to coincide with the fact, and that there is no reason why the results of those first three methods should do so. To bring about this effect is the prerogative of the method of science. Upon such considerations he has to make his choice—a choice which is far more than the adoption of any intellectual opinion, which is one of the ruling decisions of his life, to which when once made he is bound to adhere. The force of habit will sometimes cause a man to hold on to old beliefs after he is in a condition to see that they have no sound basis. But reflection upon the state of the case will overcome these habits, and he ought to allow reflection full weight. People sometimes shrink from doing this, having an idea that beliefs are wholesome which they cannot help feeling rest on nothing. But let such persons suppose an analogous though different case from their own. Let them ask themselves what they would say to a reformed Mussulman who should hesitate to give up his old notions in regard to the relations of the sexes; or to a reformed Catholic who should still shrink from the Bible. Would they not say that these persons ought to consider the matter fully, and clearly understand the new doctrine, and then ought to embrace it in its entirety? But, above all, let it be considered that what is more wholesome than any particular belief is integrity of belief; and that to avoid looking into the support of any belief from a fear that it may turn out rotten is quite as immoral as it is disadvantageous. The person who confesses that there is such a thing as truth, which is distinguished from falsehood simply by this, that if acted on it should, on full consideration, carry us to the point we aim at and not astray, and then, though convinced of this, dares not know the truth and seeks to avoid it, is in a sorry state of mind, indeed.

Yes, the other methods do have their merits: a clear logical conscience does cost something—just as any virtue, just as all that we cherish, costs us dear. But, we should not desire it to be otherwise. The genius of a man's logical method should be loved and reverenced as his bride, whom he has chosen from all the world. He need not condemn the others; on the contrary, he may honor them deeply, and in doing so he only honors her the more. But she is the one that he has chosen, and he knows that he was right in making that choice. And having made it, he will work and fight for her, and will not complain that there are blows to take, hoping that there may be as many and as hard to give, and will strive to be the worthy knight and champion of her from the blaze of whose splendors he draws his inspiration and his courage.

C. S. Peirce, "The Fixation of Belief"

1.   According to Peirce, what is the object of reasoning?

2.   What does Peirce think are the three differences between doubt and belief?

3.   In addition to the scientific method, what are the other three methods of fixing belief? State what Peirce sees as the pros and cons of one of these methods.

4.   Why does Peirce think that the scientific or experiemental method is superior to the other three methods of fixing belief?

II. EPISTEMOLOGY

LIST OF KEY TERMS

knowledge:

The Epistemological Turn:

Rationalism:

Empiricism:

Pragmatism:

a priori:

a posteriori:

Foundationalism:

self-evident truth:

Skepticism:

certainty:

The Cogito:

clarity and distinctness:

innate idea:

acquired idea:

impression:

simple/complex ideas:

relations of ideas:

matters of fact:

The experimental method:

The Belief-Doubt Model:

Fallibilism:

SECTION III
MATHEMATICS AND THE NATURAL SCIENCES

THEME QUESTIONS

1. What is Mathematics?

2. What role does mathematics play in our understanding of the world?

3. What is science? What distinguishes the sciences from morality, art, and religion?

4. Is there a scientific method? If so, what is it?

5. What is a scientific theory?

6. What is the relationship between a scientific theory and the evidence for that theory? How are theory and fact related?

7. What constitutes progress in science?

8. What is the purpose of science? What are the social responsibilities of scientists?

9. How has the character of causal explanation changed in the history of science?

Introduction to the Natural Sciences

Wayne W. Carley

Hostility, dislike, mutual incomprehension, but most of all lack of understanding. The English Novelist C. P. Snow used these phrases to describe the relationship between science and the humanities in 1959. I suspect they also mirror the way most nonscientists view science today. Curiously, it has not always been so. In fact, science grew out of the humanities and religion; much early science even was done by the clergy and/or in order to glorify God and explain the meaning and purpose of creation. The readings in this section clearly show the development of science as a field separate from the "natural philosophy" that gave it birth. Even as science matured, its practitioners brought with them prejudices and beliefs that colored both the direction of their work and their interpretations of their results. Sir Francis Bacon eloquently describes these preconceptions we bring to our studies as *idols*. Modern science has its idols as well, many of which include the ethical and social issues of how the knowledge of science impacts the society we live in. We will, then, explore these two themes: (1) The growth of science as a unique field of study with two unique characteristics; and (2) the mutual interactions and effects of science, technology, and society.

The Uniqueness of Science: Testability and Prediction

What do science and the *National Enquirer* have in common? Predictions are important features of both. Of course, the types of predictions differ rather substantially. The predictions of science are special because they are **testable.** In one sense, most of the disciplines you will explore this semester share a common theme. Art, history, music, literature, politics, and science are all ways of describing the world we live in and our place in that world. The artist paints his canvas with oils, the poet paints his words, and the scientist paints his canvas with graphs, tables, and mathematical models. However, science stands apart from all of these other fields; only science can generate predictions about the behavior of systems or bodies or beings. Examples of these predictions, for the motion of the planets and stars, are included in the passages by Galileo and Newton.

Both the predictions of science and their tests arise out of a "scientific method," a series of steps that imposes rigor and logic on science. From an initial set of observations, we generate an hypothesis (the prediction, not an "educated guess" as it is often called). We then conduct experiments to test our predictions. If the experiment supports the hypothesis, we continue to gather evidence to strengthen our position. If we are forced to reject the current hypothesis, we revise the hypothesis and try again. Note that a well done experiment does not fail; rather, the hypothesis it tested fails to be supported. From repeated experiments that support our hypothesis, we gather a body of evidence large enough to turn our hypothesis into a generalization about how the world works. This generalization is a theory, or, if sufficiently broad and useful, a law. Now we can work back down the ladder from general to specific cases. From the generalizations we can assign new evidence as being part of or not part of the group we are studying. For example, if our generalization is that all apples are round and red, we can decide that an orange does not fit these criteria, so it must not be an apple. Of course, this particular generalization is weak because it also excludes the many varieties of green apples.

This scientific method is a direct outgrowth of Francis Bacon's work in the early 1600's. To understand the significance of Bacon's contribution, let us put it into its historical context in the rise of science as a field of study. Modern science might well be said to have begun with Aristotle. Aristotle dominated a wide range of Greek scholarship, contributing everything from the parts of the sentence we use today to ideas on the structure of matter. In Aristotle's time (ca. 345 B.C.E.) science was part of **natural philosophy**, the wide study that included religion, true philosophy, and science. As you will read, Aristotle believed that everything in nature had both a cause and a purpose: "Nature is a cause, a cause that operates for a purpose." The goal of natural philosophy was not to discover *how* things work, but *why* they work. The why and the presence of a purpose strongly suggest belief in a creator and study to understand the creator's purpose. Such a goal stands in sharp contrast to modern science, which actively avoids asking questions about purpose. Aristotle did use one important aspect of modern science: models. He explains mistakes in nature by comparing them to mistakes in human endeavors such as writing or mixing a prescription.

Bacon's work stands in stark contrast to Aristotle's. Bacon emphasized the role of logic and reason in science, and in his idols identified the problems that arise when we fail to apply rigorous objectivity to our science. Compare Bacon's Table of Essence and Presence of Heat to Aristotle's search for cause and purpose. Bacon's list suggests his belief in observation and collection of facts without presuppositions as the basis for growth in scientific knowledge. From his lists of *specific* instances of heat, Bacon derives the *general* properties of heat. This purely theoretical activity is **induction** or **inductive reasoning.** This inductive reasoning is the basis of the scientific method described above. Yet Bacon was not an experimentalist. He believed experiments bring presuppositions and prejudices to the reasoning process. Indeed, he reported that "the mind . . . wearies of experiment." The counterpart to induction is **deduction**, exemplified by the passage by Euclid. In deduction we use general principles, either derived by induction or asserted as universal postulates, to determine the properties of specific items or to assign them to classes.

One of Bacon's most famous contemporaries, Galileo, also asserted the independence of science from religion and natural philosophy. In his letter to Grand Duchess Christina, Galileo argues not only that science should divorce itself from religion, but that religion should divorce itself from science. The purpose of the sacred writings is "the salvation of souls," not the accurate descriptions of the natural sciences. This is not to say that early or modern scientists do not believe in religion or religious forces at work in the world. Almost 100 years after Bacon and Galileo, Sir Isaac Newton derived the formulae to calculate the motions of the planets and the forces that control motions of bodies impelled toward or repelled from each other, i.e., gravity. Although these motions and forces were independent and regular, he clearly saw the hand of a supreme creator in the uniformity of the shapes, motions, and forces. More recently, though, the role of a supreme being or creator has been downplayed. Darwin (1850's–1860's), in the selections reprinted here, makes his case for evolution through the gradual accumulation of changes without the intervention of a creator. And Thomas Kuhn, in one of the most important modern works in the philosophy of science, argues that paradigms cannot change under the control of an unchanging god. A **paradigm** in Kuhn's usage is a scientific concept so global and new that it generates whole new sets of problems and experiments and redefines the way we think about the natural world. The gradual accumulation of evidence against a current paradigm results in the current paradigm being overthrown and replaced with a new paradigm. This shift in world-view is incompatible with a divine creator who endowed everything with fixed properties and revealed these properties through visions and sacred writings.

Science in the World: Idols and Ideals

One often-discussed question is to what extent science can remain "pure." That is, can the search for scientific knowledge be separated from the individual prejudices and preconceptions of scientists and from the social and moral implications of the results. Such questions as, "Should nuclear physicists be held accountable for the devastation caused by atom bombs, or are they justified in their pursuit of knowledge regardless how the knowledge is used?" and "Should we experiment on living animals and cause them pain, even if it saves human lives?" are obvious examples of these issues. But many smaller social, cultural, and personal issues invade everyday science and color the interpretations of our results. For science to progress, we must recognize these problems and either eliminate them or keep them in the forefront of our minds so we can fairly evaluate our knowledge and not inhibit the growth of future knowledge.

Bacon again gives us the guideposts to begin discussion of the issues. Bacon identified four classes of problems that interfered with logical and accurate interpretation of nature. He called these classes of problems Idols. The **Idols of the Tribe** have their roots in human nature and culture. Our senses are not

51

perfect, and we cannot observe nature with complete accuracy. We often, as Bacon points out, place more importance on positive than negative results. A particularly difficult problem is the human tendency to impose order on the universe. We look for generalizations where there may be none, and in our search for ultimate causes we may ignore everything between the beginning and the end. The **Idols of the Cave** come from our individual personalities. Some people hold tightly to out-of-date theories because of a deep reverence for the past or a fear of the future. Others grasp at every new idea, valid or not. Each of us has a unique combination of education, experience, environment, and taste we use in making judgements. When these judgments replace the rational search for true knowledge, we fall prey to the Idols of the Cave. Language is the culprit in the **Idols of the Market Place.** The imprecision in our language clouds our discussions and explanations of phenomena. When one word has many meanings or many words can be used for one concept, it becomes difficult to interpret nature clearly. Finally, Bacon thought the **Idols of the Theater** to be the most dangerous. The Idols of the Theater are the plays that have been produced there in the past: religious beliefs and ancient philosophies. Aristotle's belief in cause and purpose in nature was a prime example of the Idol of the Theater. Galileo's challenge to the Catholic Church illustrates just how hard it is to eliminate the Idols of the Theater. Only in 1992, almost 300 years after his theory was widely accepted and he was placed under house arrest, did the Pope admit that the Catholic Church erred in Galileo's case.

Every age has its idols, and ours is no exception. Scientists may try hard to avoid letting their prejudices affect their science, but Steven Rose and Hilary Rose argue strongly that value-free science is impossible, especially in modern western cultures. The federal government or large corporations fund most of the scientific research in the United States, so both the directions of scientific progress and the nature of the experiments depend upon the idols of the current political powers and the society that supports them. How do scientists balance the need for objective pursuit of the truth, the political and social constraints upon their research, and the desire to improve the human condition? The Roses offer some challenging questions that will fuel debate for some time.

So, science has arrived as a unique, independent field of study characterized by its reliance on stable hypotheses and, when possible, avoidance of idols that cloud understanding. As Polkinghorne points out, quantum mechanics has made science a very uncertain field of study. Even the act of measuring something like an electron makes it impossible to know everything about that object. There may be little certainty in modern science, but there is plenty of excitement. And the selections in this compendium do reflect the strength and excitement both of the science and the scientists who built it through the ages.

Euclid*

THE ELEMENTS

DEFINITIONS

1.   A *point* is that which has no part.

2.   A *line* is breadthless length.

3.   The extremities of a line are points.

4.   A *straight line* is a line which lies evenly with the points on itself.

5.   A *surface* is that which has length and breadth only.

6.   The extremities of a surface are lines.

7.   A *plane surface* is a surface which lies evenly with the straight lines on itself.

8.   A *plane angle* is the inclination to one another of two lines in a plane which meet one another and do not lie in a straight line.

9.   And when the lines containing the angle are straight, the angel is called *rectineal*.

10.   When a straight line set up on a straight line makes the adjacent angles equal to one another, each of the equal angles is *right* and the straight line standing on the other is called a *perpendicular* to that on which it stands.

11.   An *obtuse angle* is an angle greater than a right angle.

12.   An *acute angle* is an angle less than a right angle.

13.   A *boundary* is that which is an extremity of anything.

14.   A *figure* is that which is contained by any boundary or boundaries.

15.   A *circle* is a plane figure contained by one line such that all the straight lines falling upon it from one point among those lying within the figure are equal to one another;

16.   And the point is called the *centre* of the circle.

17.   A *diameter* of the circle is any straight line drawn through the centre and terminated in both directions by the circumference of the circle, and such a straight line also bisects the circle.

18.   A *semicircle* is the figure contained by the diameter and the circumference cut off by it. And the centre of the semicircle is the same as that of the circle.

19.   *Rectilineal figures* are those which are contained by straight lines, *trilateral* figures being those contained by three, *quadrilateral* those contained by four, and *multilateral* those contained by more than four straight lines.

20.   Of trilateral figures, an *equilateral triangle* is that which has its three sides equal, an *isosceles triangle* that which has two of its sides alone equal, and a *scalene triangle* that which has its three sides unequal.

21.   Further, of trilateral figures, a *right-angled triangle* is that which has a right angle, and *obtuse-angled triangle* that which has an obtuse angle, and an *acute-angled triangle* that which has its three angles acute.

22.   Of quadrilateral figures, a *square* is that which is both equilateral and right-angled; an *oblong* that which is right-angled but not equilateral; a *rhombus* that which is equilateral but not right-angled; and a *rhomboid* that which has its opposite sides and angles equal to one another but is neither equilateral nor right-angled. And let quadrilaterals other than these be called *trapezia*.

23.   *Parallel* straight lines are straight lines which, being in the same plane and being produced indefinitely in both directions, do not meet one another in either direction.

---

*Euclid (fl. c. 300 B.C.E.) was an Alexandrian Mathematician who systematized the geometry of his time by showing how each theorem followed with logical necessity from a set of definitions, postulates, and axioms. Euclid's Elements still provides the basis for elementary geometry, though the 19th century mathematicians developed consistent elliptic and hyperbolic geometries by denying his fifth postulate, "the parallel postulate."

POSTULATES

Let the following be postulated:
1. To draw a straight line from any point to any point.
2. To produce a finite straight line continuously in a straight line.
3. To describe a circle with any centre and distance.
4. That all right angles are equal to one another.
5. That, if a straight line falling on two straight lines make the interior angles on the same side less than two right angles, the two straight lines, if produced indefinitely, meet on that side on which are the angles less than the two right angles.

COMMON NOTIONS

1. Things which are equal to the same thing are also equal to one another.
2. If equals be added to equals, the wholes are equal.
3. If equals be subtracted from equals, the remainders are equal.
[7] 4. Things which coincide with one another are equal to one another.
[8] 5. The whole is greater than the part.

BOOK I. PROPOSITIONS

PROPOSITION 1

On a given finite straight line to construct an equilateral triangle.

Let AB be the given finite straight line.

Thus it is required to construct an equilateral triangle on the straight line AB.

With center A and distance AB let the circle BCD be described; [Post. 3] again, with centre B and distance BA let the circle ACE be described;
[Post. 3]
and from the point C, in which the circles cut one another, to the points, A, B let the straight lines CA, CB be joined. [Post. 1]

Now, since the point A is the centre of the circle CDB,

AC is equal to AB. [Def. 15]

Again, since the point B is the centre of the circle CAE,

BC is equal to BA. [Def. 15]

But CA was also proved equal to AB;

therefore, each of the straight lines CA, CB is equal to AB.

And things which are equal to the same thing are also equal to one another; therefore CA is also equal to CB. [C.N. 1]

Therefore the three straight lines CA, AB, BC are equal to one another.

Therefore the triangle ABC is equilateral; and it has been constructed on the given finite straight line AB.

(Being) what it was required to do.

PROPOSITION 2

To place at a given point (as an extremity) a straight line equal to a given straight line.

Let A be the given point, and BC the given straight line.

Thus it is required to place at the point A (as an extremity) a straight line equal to the given straight line BC.

From the point A to the point B let the straight line AB be joined;
[Post. 1]
and on it let the equilateral triangle DAB be constructed. [I.1]

Let the straight lines AE, BF be produced in a straight line with DA, DB;
[Post. 2]

with centre B and distance BC let the circle CGH be described; [Post. 3]

54

and again, with centre D and distance DG let the circle GKL be described. [Post. 3]

Then since the point B is the centre of the circle CGH,
BC is equal to BG.
Again, since the point D is the centre of the circle GKL,
DL is equal to DG.
And in these DA is equal to DB;
therefore the remainder AL is equal to the remainder BG. [C.N. 3]
But BC was also proved equal to BG;
therefore each of the straight lines AL, BC is equal to BG.
And things which are equal to the same thing are also equal to one another; [C.N. 1]
therefore AL is also equal to BC.
Therefore at the given point A the straight line AL is placed equal to the given straight line BC.

(Being) what it was required to do.

PROPOSITION 3

Given two unequal straight lines, to cut off from the greater a straight line equal to the less.

Let AB, C be the two given unequal straight lines, and let AB be the greater of them.

Thus it is required to cut off from AB the greater a straight line equal to C the less.

At the point A let AD be placed equal to the straight line C; [I. 2]
and with centre A and distance AD let the circle DEF be described.[Post. 3]
Now, since the point A is the centre of the circle DEF,
AE is equal to AD [Def. 15]
But C is also equal to AD.
Therefore each of the straight lines AE, C is equal to AD;
so that AE is also equal to C [C.N. 1]
Therefore, given the two straight sides AB, C, from AB the greater AE has been cut off equal to C the less.

(Being) what it was required to do.

NAME _____   DATE _____

EUCLID: THE ELEMENTS

1.   Complete the following statements by matching each term with its appropriate definition.

    a.   A line is _____
    b.   A point is _____
    c.   A surface is _____
    d.   A boundary is _____
    e.   A figure is _____
    f.   An isosceles triangle _____

    1.   that which has no part.
    2.   that which is the extremity of anything.
    3.   a breadthless length.
    4.   that which has length and breadth only.
    5.   that which has two of its sides alone equal.
    6.   that which is contained by any boundary or boundaries.

2.   Axiom of Common Notion 2 states that

    a.   the whole is greater than the part.
    b.   if equals be added to equals, the wholes are equal.
    c.   if equals be subtracted from equals, the remainders are equal.
    d.   the extremities of a surface are lines.
    e.   none of the above.

3.   Which of the following are used in Euclid's proof of Proposition 2?

    a.   Postulate 1.
    b.   Postulate 2.
    c.   Postulate 3.
    d.   All of the above.
    e.   None of the above.

Aristotle*

ON TELEOLOGY IN NATURE

It is clear then that there are causes, and that the number of them is what we have stated. The number is the same as that of the things comprehended under the question 'why'. The 'why' is referred ultimately either, in things which do not involve motion, e.g., in mathematics, to the 'what' (to the definition of straight line or commensurable or the like); or to what initiated a motion, e.g. 'why did they go to war?—because there had been a raid'; or we are inquiring 'for the sake of what?'— 'that they may rule'; or in the case of things that come into being, we are looking for the matter. The causes, therefore, are these and so many in number.

Now, the causes being four, it is the business of the student of nature to know about them all, and if he refers his problems back to all of them, he will assign the 'why' in the way proper to his science— the matter, the form, the mover, that for the sake of which. The last three often coincide; for the what and that for the sake of which are one, while the primary source of motion is the same in species as these. For man generates man—and so too, in general, with all things which cause movement by being themselves moved; and such as are not of this kind are no longer inside the province of natural science, for they cause motion not by possessing motion or a source of motion in themselves, but being themselves incapable of motion. Hence there are three branches of study, one of things which are incapable of motion, the second of things in motion, but indestructible, the third of destructible things.

The question 'why', then, is answered by reference to the matter, to the form, and to the primary moving cause. For in respect of coming to be it is mostly in this last way that causes are investigated—'what comes to be after what? what was the primary agent or patient?' and so at each step of the series.

Now the principles which cause motion in a natural way are two, of which one is not natural, as it has no principle of motion in itself. Of this kind is whatever causes movement, not being itself moved, such as that which is completely unchangeable, the primary reality, and the essence of a thing, i.e. the form; for this is the end or that for the sake of which. Hence since nature is for the sake of something, we must know this cause also. We must explain the 'why' in all the senses of the term, namely, that from this that will necessarily result ('from this' either without qualification or for the most part); that this must be so if that is to be so (as the conclusion presupposes the premises); that this was the essence of the thing; and because it is better thus (not without qualification, but with reference to the substance in each case).

We must explain then first why nature belongs to the class of causes which act for the sake of something; and then about the necessary and its place in nature, for all writers ascribe things to this cause, arguing that since the hot and the cold and the like are of such and such a kind, therefore certain things *necessarily* are and come to be—and if they mention

*Aristotle (384–322 B.C.E.) was a student of Plato's, the tutor of Alexander the Great, and eventually founded his own school in Athens, the Lyceum. Aristotle's works cover the full range of philosophy, to which he made significant contributions. In addition to his strictly philosophical writings, Aristotle engaged in extensive empirical research in biology, astronomy, and politics. Aristotle's didactic writings and empiricism are a striking contrast to Plato's dialogues and rationalism. To this day, he is still one of the most influential figures in the history of Western philosophy.

any other cause (one friendship and strife, another mind), it is only to touch on it, and then good-bye to it.

A difficulty presents itself: why should not nature work, not for the sake of something, nor because it is better so, but just as the sky rains, not in order to make the corn grow, but of necessity? (What is drawn up must cool, and what has been cooled must become water and descend, the result of this being that the corn grows.) Similarly if a man's crop is spoiled on the threshing-floor, the rain did not fall for the sake of this—in order that the crop might be spoiled—but that result just followed. Why then should it not be the same with the parts in nature, e.g. that our teeth should come up of necessity—the front teeth sharp, fitted for tearing, the molars broad and useful for grinding down the food—since they did not arise for this end, but it was merely a coincident result; and so with all other parts in which we suppose that there is purpose? Wherever then all the parts came about just what they would have been if they had come to be for an end, such things survived, being organized spontaneously in a fitting way; whereas those which grew otherwise perished and continue to perish, as Empedocles says his 'man-faced oxprogeny' did.

Such are the arguments (and others of the kind) which may cause difficulty on this point. Yet it is impossible that this should be the true view. For teeth and all other natural things either invariably or for the most part come about in a given way; but of not one of the results of chance or spontaneity is this true. We do not ascribe to chance or mere coincidence the frequency of rain in winter, but frequent rain in summer we do; nor heat in summer but only if we have it in winter. If then, it is agreed that things are either the result of coincidence or for the sake of something, and these cannot be the result of coincidence or spontaneity, it follows that they must be for the sake of something; and that such things are all due to nature even the champions of the theory which is before us would agree. Therefore action for an end is present in things which come to be and are by nature.

Further, where there is an end, all the preceding steps are for the sake of that. Now surely as in action, so in nature; and as in nature, so it is in each action, if nothing interferes. Now action is for the sake of an end; therefore the nature of things also is so. Thus if a house, e.g., had been a thing made by nature, it would have been made in the same way as it is now by art; and if things made by nature were made not only by nature but also by art, they would come to be in the same way as by nature. The one,

then, is for the sake of the other; and generally art in some cases completes what nature cannot bring to a finish, and in others imitates nature. If, therefore, artificial products are for the sake of an end, so clearly also are natural products. The relation of the later to the earlier items is the same in both.

This is most obvious in the animals other than man: they make things neither by art nor after inquiry or deliberation. That is why people wonder whether it is by intelligence or by some other faculty that these creatures work,—spiders, ants, and the like. By gradual advance in this direction we come to see clearly that in plants too that is produced which is conducive to the end—leaves, e.g. grow to provide shade for the fruit. If then it is both by nature and for an end that the swallow makes its nest and the spider its web, and plants grow leaves for the sake of the fruit and send their roots down (not up) for the sake of nourishment, it is plain that this kind of cause is operative in things which come to be and are by nature. And since nature is two-fold, the matter and the form, of which the latter is the end, and since all the rest is for the sake of the end, the form must be the cause in the sense of that for the sake of which.

Now mistakes occur even in the operations of art: the literate man makes a mistake in writing and the doctor pours out the wrong dose. Hence clearly mistakes are possible in the operations of nature also. If then in art there are cases in which what is rightly produced serves a purpose, and if where mistakes occur there was a purpose in what was attempted, only it was not attained, so must it be also in natural products, and monstrosities will be failures in the purposive effect. Thus in the original combinations the 'ox-progeny', if they failed to reach a determinate end must have arisen through the corruption of some principle, as happens now when the seed is defective.

Further, seed must have come into being first, and not straightway the animals: what was 'undifferentiated first' was seed.

Again, in plants too we find that for the sake of which, though the degree of organization is less. Were there then in plants also olive-headed vine-progeny, like the 'man-headed ox-progeny', or not? An absurd suggestion; yet there must have been, if there were such things among animals.

Moreover, among the seeds anything must come to be at random. But the person who asserts this entirely does away with nature and what exists by nature. For those things are natural which, by a continuous movement originated from an internal principle, arrive at some end: the same end is not reached from every principle; nor any chance end, but always the tendency in each is towards the same end, if there is no impediment.

The end and the means towards it may come about by chance. We say, for instance, that a stranger has come by chance, paid the ransom, and gone away, when he does so as if he had come for that purpose, though it was not for that that he came. This is accidental, for chance is an accidental cause, as I remarked before. But when an event takes place always or for the most part, it is not accidental or by chance. In natural products the sequence is invariable, if there is no impediment.

It is absurd to suppose that purpose is not present because we do not observe the agent deliberating. Art does not deliberate. If the ship-building art were in the wood, it would produce the same results by nature. If, therefore, purpose is present in art, it is present also in nature. The best illustration is a doctor doctoring himself: nature is like that.

It is plain then that nature is a cause, a cause that operates for a purpose.

Aristotle, On Teleology in Nature

1.   List Aristotle's four different types of causes.

      a. _____

      b. _____

      c. _____

      d. _____

2.   Which of those four cases corresponds to our modern notion of a cause?

3.   Aristotle compares the operations of nature to _____ .

Francis Bacon*

APHORISMS

i

Man, being the servant and interpreter of nature, can do an understand so much and so much only as he has observed in fact or in thought of the course of nature: beyond this he neither knows anything nor can do anything.

ii

Neither the naked hand nor the understanding left to itself can effect much. It is by instruments and helps that the work is done, which are as much wanted for the understanding as for the hand. And as the instruments of the hand either give motion or guide it, so the instruments of the mind supply either suggestions for the understanding or cautions.

iii

Human knowledge and human power meet in one; for where the cause is not known the effect cannot be produced. Nature to be commanded must be obeyed; and that which in contemplation is as the cause is in operation as the rule.

xix

There are and can be only two ways of searching into and discovering truth. The one flies from the senses and particulars to the most general axioms, and from these principles, the truth of which it takes for settled and immovable, proceeds to judgment and to the discovery of middle axioms. And this way is now in fashion. The other derives axioms from the sense and particulars, rising by a gradual and unbroken ascent, so that it arrives at the most general axioms last of all. This is the true way, but as yet untried.

xxvi

The conclusion of human reason as ordinarily applied in matter of nature, I call for the sake of distinction *Anticipations of Nature* (as a thing rash or premature). That reason which is elicited from facts by a just and methodical process, I call *Interpretation of Nature.*

xxxvi

One method of delivery alone remains to us; which is simply this: we must lead men to the particulars themselves, and their series and order; while men on their side force themselves for awhile to lay their notions by and begin to familiarize themselves with facts.

xxxix

There are four classes of idols which beset men's minds. To these for distinction's sake I have assigned names,—calling the first class *Idols of the Tribe;* the second, *Idols of the Cave;* the third, *Idols of the Marketplace;* the fourth, *Idols of the Theater.*

---

*Sir Francis Bacon (1561–1621) was a distinguished English jurist who rose to become Lord Chancellor under James I. Bacon was not a practicing scientist but a philosopher of science who advocated the use of inductive method to answer questions about the physical universe. He also argued that scentific knowledge should be used to gain control over nature and improve the material conditions of human life. His works include *The Advancement of Learning, The New Atlantis,* and the *Novum Organum* (1620), from which the following has been excerpted.

The formation of ideas and axioms by true induction is no doubt the proper remedy to be applied for the keeping off and clearing away of idols. To point them out, however, is of great use, for the doctrine of idols is to the interpretation of nature what the doctrine of the refutation of sophisms is to common logic.

xli

The Idols of the Tribe have their foundation in human nature itself, and in the tribe or race of men. For it is a false assertion that the sense of man is the measure of things. On the contrary, all perceptions, as well of the sense as of the mind, are according to the measure of the individual and not according to the measure of the universe. And the human understanding is like a false mirror, which, receiving rays irregularly, distorts and discolors the nature of things by mingling its own nature with it.

xlii

The Idols of the Cave are the idols of the individual man. For everyone (besides the errors common to human nature in general) has a cave or den of his own, which refracts and discolors the light of nature; owing either to his own proper and peculiar nature or to his education and conversation with others; or to the reading of books, and the authority of those whom he esteems and admires; or to the differences of impressions, accordingly as they take place in a mind preoccupied and predisposed or in a mind indifferent and settled; or the like. So that the spirit of man (according as it is meted out to different individuals) is in fact a thing variable and full of perturbation, and governed as it were by chance. Whence it was well observed by Heraclitus that men look for sciences in their own lesser worlds, and not in the greater or common world.

xliii

There are also idols formed by the intercourse and association of men with each other, which I call Idols of the Market-place, on account of the commerce and consort of men there. For it is by discourse that men associate; and words are imposed according to the apprehension of the vulgar. And therefore the ill and unfit choice of words wonderfully obstructs the understanding. Nor do the defi-

nitions or explanations wherewith in some things learned men are wont to guard and defend themselves, by any means set the matter right. But words plainly force and overrule the understanding, and throw all into confusion, and lead men away into numberless empty controversies and idle fancies.

xliv

Lastly, there are idols which have immigrated into men's minds from the various dogmas of philosophies, and also from wrong laws of demonstration. These I call Idols of the Theater; because in my judgment all the received systems are but so many stage-plays, representing worlds of their own creation after an unreal and scenic fashion. Nor is it only of the systems now in vogue, or only of the ancient sects and philosophies, that I speak: for many more plays of the same kind may yet be composed and in like artificial manner set forth; seeing that errors the most widely different have nevertheless causes for the most part alike. Neither again do I mean this only of entire systems, but also of many principles and axioms in science, which by tradition, credulity and negligence have come to be received.

But of these several kinds of idols I must speak more largely and exactly, that the understanding may be duly cautioned.

lxxiii

Of all signs there is none more certain or more noble than that taken from fruits. For fruits and works are as it were sponsors and sureties for the truth of philosophies. Now, from all these systems of the Greeks, and their ramifications through particular sciences there can hardly after the lapse of so many years be adduced a single experiment which tends to relieve and benefit the condition of man, and which can with truth be referred to the speculations and theories of philosophy. And Celsus ingenuously and wisely owns as much, when he tells us that the experimental part of medicine was first discovered, and that afterwards men philosophized about it, and hunted for and assigned causes; and not by an inverse process that philosophy and the knowledge of causes led to the discovery and development of the experimental part. And therefore it was not strange that among the Egyptians, who rewarded inventors with divine honors and sacred rites, there were more images of brutes than of men; inasmuch as brutes by their natural instinct have produced many discoveries, whereas men by discussion and the conclusions of reason have given birth to few or none.

Some little has indeed been produced by the industry of chemists; but it has been produced accidentally and in passing, or else by a kind of variation of experiments, such as mechanics use; and not by any art or theory; for the theory which they have devised rather confuses the experiments than aids them. They too who have busied themselves with natural magic, as they call it, have but few discoveries to show, and those trifling and imposture-like. Wherefore, as in religion we are warned to show our faith by works, so in philosophy by the same rule the system should be judged of by its fruits, and pronounced frivolous if it be barren; more especially if, in place of fruits of grape and olive, it bear thorns and briars of dispute and contention.

lxxxi

Again there is another great and powerful cause why the sciences have made but little progress; which is this. It is not possible to run a course aright when the goal itself has not been rightly placed. Now the true and lawful goal of the sciences is none other than this: that human life be endowed with new discoveries and powers. But of this the great majority have no feeling, but are merely hireling and professorial; except when it occasionally happens that some workman of acuter wit and covetous of honor applies himself to a new invention; which he mostly does at the expense of his fortunes. But in general, so far are men from proposing to themselves to augment the mass of arts and sciences, that from the mass already at hand they neither take nor look for anything more than what they may turn to use in their lectures, or to gain, or to reputation, or to some similar advantage. And if any one out of all the multitude court science with honest affection and for her own sake, yet even with him the object will be found to be rather the variety of contemplations and doctrines than the severe and rigid search after truth. And if by chance there be one who seeks after truth in earnest, yet even he will propose to himself such a kind of truth as shall yield satisfaction to the mind and understanding in rendering causes for things long since discovered, and not the truth which shall lead to new assurance of works and new light of axioms. If then the end of the sciences has not yet been well placed, it is not strange that men have erred as to the means.

cxxx

And now it is time for me to propound the art itself of interpreting nature; in which, although I conceive that I have given true and most useful precepts, yet I do not say either that it is absolutely necessary (as if nothing could be done without it) or that it is perfect. For I am of opinion that if men had ready at hand a just history of nature and experience, and labored diligently thereon; and if they could bind themselves to two rules,—the first, to lay aside received opinions and notions; and the second, to refrain the mind for a time from the highest generalizations, and those next to them,—they would be able by the native and genuine force of mind, without any other art, to fall into my form of interpretation. For interpretation is the true and natural work of the mind when freed from impediments. It is true however that by my precepts everything will be in more readiness, and much more sure.

Nor again do I mean to say that no improvement can be made upon these. On the contrary, I that regard the mind not only in its own faculties but in its connection with things, must needs hold that the art of discovery may advance as discoveries advance.

i

On a given body to generate and superinduce a new nature or new natures, is the work and aim of *human power.* Of a given nature to discover the form, or true specific difference, or nature-engendering nature, or source of emanation (for these are the terms which come nearest to a description of the thing), is the work and aim of *human knowledge.* Subordinate to these primary works are two others that are secondary and of inferior mark: to the former, the transformation of concrete bodies, so far as this is possible; to the latter, the discovery, in every case of generation and motion, of the latent process carried on from the manifest efficient and the manifest material to the form which is engendered; and in like manner the discovery of the latent configuration of bodies at rest and not in motion.

x

Having thus set up the mark of knowledge, we must go on to precepts, and that in the most direct and obvious order. Now my directions for the interpretation of nature embrace two generic divisions: the one how to educe and form axioms from experience; the other how to deduce and derive new experiments from axioms. The former again is divided into three ministrations: a ministration to the sense, a ministration to the memory, and a ministration to the mind or reason.

For first of all we must prepare a *Natural and Experimental History,* sufficient and good; and this is the foundation of all; for we are not to imagine or suppose, but to discover, what nature does or may be made to do.

But natural and experimental history is so various and diffuse, that it confounds and distracts the understanding, unless it be ranged and presented to view in a suitable order. We must therefore form *Tables and Arrangements of Instances,* in such a method and order that the understanding may be able to deal with them.

And even when this is done, still the understanding, if left to itself and its own spontaneous movements, is incompetent and unfit to form axioms, unless it be directed and guarded. Therefore in the third place we must use *Induction,* true and legitimate induction, which is the very key of interpretation. But of this, which is the last, I must speak first, and then go back to the other ministrations.

xi

The investigation of Forms proceeds thus: a nature being given, we must first of all have a muster or presentation before the understanding of all known instances which agree in the same nature, though in substances the most unlike. And such collection must be made in the manner of a history, without premature speculation, or any great amount of subtlety. For example, let the investigation be into the Form of heat.

Instances Agreeing in the Nature of Heat.

1. The rays of the sun, especially in summer and at noon.
2. The rays of the sun reflected and condensed, as between mountains, or on walls, and most of all in burning-glasses and mirrors.
3. Fiery meteors.
4. Burning thunderbolts.
5. Eruptions of flame from the cavities of mountains.
6. All flame.
7. Ignited solids.
8. Natural warm-baths.
9. Liquids boiling or heated.
10. Hot vapors and fumes, and the air itself, which conceives the most powerful and glowing heat, if confined; as in reverbatory furnaces.
11. Certain seasons that are fine and cloudless by the constitution of the air itself, without regard to the time of year.
12. Air confined and underground in some caverns, especially in winter.
13. All villous substances, as wool, skins of animals, and down of birds, have heat.
14. All bodies, whether solid or liquid, whether dense or rare (as the air itself is) held for a time near the fire.
15. Sparks struck from flint and steel by strong percussion.
16. All bodies rubbed violently, as stone, wood, cloth, &c., insomuch that poles and axes of wheels sometimes catch fire; and the way they kindled fire in the West Indies was by attrition.

17. Green and moist vegetables confined and bruised together, as roses packed in baskets; insomuch that hay, if damp when stacked, often catches fire.

18. Quick lime sprinkled with water.

19. Iron, when first dissolved by strong waters in glass, and that without being put near the fire. And in like manner tin, &c., but not with equal intensity.

20. Animals, especially and at all times internally; though in insects the heat is not perceptible to the touch by reason of the smallness of their size.

21. Horse-dung and like excrements of animals when fresh.

22. Strong oil of sulphur and vitriol has the effect of heat in burning linen.

23. Oil of marjoram and similar oils have the effect of heat in burning the bones of the teeth.

24. Strong and well rectified spirit of wine has the effect of heat; insomuch that the white of an egg being put into it hardens and whitens almost as if it were boiled; and bread thrown in becomes dry and crusted like toast.

25. Aromatic and hot herbs, as *dracunculus, nasturtium vetus,* &c., although not warm to the hand (either whole or in powder), yet to the tongue and palate, being a little masticated, they feel hot and burning.

26. Strong vinegar, and all acids, on all parts of the body where there is no epidermis, as the eye, tongue, or on any part when wounded and laid bare of the skin; produce a pain but little differing from that which is created by heat.

27. Even keen and intense cold produces a kind of sensation of burning;

Nec Borae penetrabile frigus adurit.[1]

28. Other instances.

This table I call the *Table of Essence and Presence.*

xii

Secondly, we must make a presentation to the understanding of instances in which the given nature is wanting; because the Form, as stated above, ought no less to be absent when the given nature is absent, than present when it is present. But to note all these would be endless.

The negatives should therefore be subjoined to the affirmative, and the absence of the given

nature inquired of in those subjects only that are most akin to the others in which it is present and forthcoming. This I call the *Table of Deviation, or of Absence in Proximity.*

(What follows is a list of instances where heat is absent.—Eds.)

xiii

Thirdly, we must make a presentation to the understanding of instances in which the nature under inquiry is found in different degrees, more or less; which must be done by making a comparison either of its increase and decrease in the same subject, or of its amount in different subjects, as compared one with another. For since the Form of a thing is the very thing itself, and the thing differs from the form no otherwise than as the apparent differs from the real, or the external from the internal, or the thing in reference to man from the thing in reference to the universe; it necessarily follows that no nature can be taken as the true form, unless it always decrease when the nature in question decreases, and in like manner always increase when the nature in question increases. This Table therefore I call the *Table of Degrees* or the *Table of Comparison.*

(What follows is a list of instances where heat varies in degree.—Eds.)

xv

The work and office of these three tables I call the presentation of Instances to the Understanding. Which presentation having been made, Induction itself must be set at work; for the problem is, upon a review of the instances, all and each, to find such a nature as is always present or absent with the given nature, and always increases and decreases with it; and which is, as I have said, a particular case of a more general nature. Now if the mind attempt this affirmatively from the first, when left to itself it is always wont to do, the result will be fancies and guesses and notions ill defined and axioms that must be mended every day; unless like the schoolmen we have a mind to fight for what is false; though doubtless these will be better or worse according to the faculties and strength of the understanding which is at work. To God, truly, the Giver and Architect of

[1]Nor burns the sharp cold of the northern blast.

Forms, and it may be to the angel and higher intelligences, it belongs to have an affirmative knowledge of Forms immediately, and from the first contemplation. But this assuredly is more than man can do, to whom it is granted only to proceed at first by negatives, and at last to end in affirmatives, after exclusion has been exhausted.

xvi

We must make therefore a complete solution and separation of nature; not indeed by fire, but by the mind, which is a kind of divine fire. The first work therefore of true induction (as far as regards the discovery of Forms) is the rejection or exclusion of the several natures which are not found in some instance where the given nature is present, or are found in some instance where the given nature is absent, or are found to increase in some instance when the given nature decreases, or to decrease when the given nature increases. Then indeed after the rejection and exclusion has been duly made, there will remain at the bottom, all light opinions vanishing into smoke, a Form affirmative, solid and true and well defined. This is quickly said; but the way to come at it is winding and intricate. I will endeavor however not to overlook any of the points which may help us towards it.

Francis Bacon, Aphorisms

1.   According to Bacon, what is the appropriate goal of scientific inquiry?

    a. Aesthetic appreciation of the harmony of the divine creation.
    b. The power to control nature.
    c. Contemplative understanding of the order of the cosmos.
    d. Knowledge for its own sake.
    e. None of the above.

2.   Bacon believed that the most important type of reasoning in science was

    a. inductive reasoning.
    b. deductive reasoning.
    c. retroductive reasoning.
    d. fallacious reasoning.
    e. none of the above.

3.   List the three types of tables Bacon thought scientists should construct.

    a. _____

    b. _____

    c. _____

4.   Give four examples of things Bacon considered to be instances of heat.

    a. _____

    b. _____

    c. _____

    d. _____

Galilei Galileo*

LETTER TO THE GRAND DUCHESS CHRISTINA

The reason produced for condemning the opinion that the earth moves and the sun stands still is that in many places in the Bible one may read that the sun moves and the earth stands still. Since the Bible cannot err, it follows as a necessary consequence that anyone takes an erroneous and heretical position who maintains that the sun is inherently motionless and the earth movable.

With regard to this argument, I think in the first place that it is very pious to say and prudent to affirm that the holy Bible can never speak untruth—whenever its true meaning is understood. But I believe nobody will deny that it is often very abstruse, and may say things which are quite different from what its bare words signify. Hence in expounding the Bible if one were always to confine oneself to the unadorned grammatical meaning, one might fall into error. Not only contradictions and propositions far from true might thus be made to appear in the Bible, but even grave heresies and follies. Thus it would be necessary to assign to God feet, hands, and eyes, as well as corporeal and human affections, such as anger, repentance, hatred, and sometimes even the forgetting of things past and ignorance of those to come. These propositions uttered by the Holy Ghost were set down in that manner by the sacred scribes in order to accommodate them to the capacities of the common people, who are rude and unlearned. For the sake of those who deserve to be separated from the herd, it is necessary that wise expositors should produce the true senses of such passages, together with the special reasons for which they were set down in these words. This doctrine is so widespread and so definite with all theologians that it would be superfluous to adduce evidence for it.

Hence I think that I may reasonably conclude that whenever the Bible has occasion to speak of any physical conclusion (especially those which are very abstruse and hard to understand), the rule has been observed of avoiding confusion in the minds of the common people which would render them contumacious toward the higher mysteries. Now the Bible, merely to condescend to popular capacity, has not hesitated to obscure some very important pronouncements, attributing to God himself some qualities extremely remote from (and even contrary to) His essence. Who, then, would positively declare that this principle has been set aside, and the Bible has confined itself rigorously to the bare and restricted sense of its words, when speaking but casually of the earth, of water, of the sun, or of any other created thing? Especially in view of the fact that these things in no way concern the primary purpose of the sacred writings, which is the service of God and the salvation of souls matters infinitely beyond the comprehension of the common people.

This being granted, I think that in discussions of physical problems we ought to begin not from the authority of scriptural passages, but from sense experiences and necessary demonstrations; for the holy Bible and the phenomena of nature proceed

---

*Galileo Galilei (1564–1642) was a famous Italian astronomer and physicist who was one of the founders of modern science. His many works include *The Sidereal Messenger* and the *Dialogue of the Two Great World Systems*. The latter work brought Galileo into conflict with the Vatican for its forceful advocacy of the Copernican, or heliocentric, view of the solar system. Galileo was forced to recant his position and was only exonerated by the Pope in 1992. The following is an excerpt (1615) in which he discusses the relationship of science to religion in connection with the controversy over the Copernican revolution in astronomy.

alike from the divine Word, the former as the dictate of the Holy Ghost and the latter as the observant executrix of God's commands. It is necessary for the Bible, in order to be accommodated to the understanding of every man, to speak many things which appear to differ from the absolute truth so far as the bare meaning of the words is concerned. But Nature, on the other hand, is inexorable and immutable; she never transgresses the laws imposed upon her, or cares a whit whether her abstruse reasons and methods of operation are understandable to man. For that reason it appears that nothing physical which sense-experience sets before our eyes, or which necessary demonstrations prove to us, ought to be called in question (much less condemned) upon the testimony of biblical passages which may have some different meaning beneath their words. For the Bible is not chained in every expression to conditions as strict as those which govern all physical effects; nor is God any less excellently revealed in Nature's actions than in the sacred statements of the Bible. Perhaps this is what Tertullian meant by these words:

"We conclude that God is known first through Nature, and then again, more particularly, by doctrine; by Nature in His works, and by doctrine in His revealed word."[1]

From this I do not mean to infer that we need not have an extraordinary esteem for the passages of holy Scripture. On the contrary, having arrived at any certainties in physics, we ought to utilize these as the most appropriate aids in the true exposition of the Bible and in the investigation of those meanings which are necessarily contained therein, for these must be concordant with demonstrated truths. I should judge that the authority of the Bible was designed to persuade men of those articles and propositions which, surpassing all human reasoning, could not be made credible by science, or by any other means other than through the very mouth of the Holy Spirit.

Yet even in those propositions which are not matters of faith, this authority ought to be preferred over that of any human writings which are supported only by bare assertions or probable arguments, and not set forth in a demonstrative way. This I hold to be necessary and proper to the same extent that divine wisdom surpasses all human judgment and conjecture.

But I do not feel obliged to believe that that same God who has endowed us with senses, reason, and intellect has intended to forgo their use and by some other means to give us knowledge which we can attain by them. He would not require us to deny sense and reason in physical matters which are set before our eyes and minds by direct experience or necessary demonstrations. This must be especially true in those sciences of which but the faintest trace (and that consisting of conclusions) is to be found in the Bible. Of astronomy, for instance, so little is found that none of the planets except Venus are so much as mentioned, and this only once or twice under the name of "Lucifer." If the sacred scribes had had any intention of teaching people certain arrangements and motions of the heavenly bodies, or had they wished us to derive such knowledge from the Bible, then in my opinion they would not have spoken of these matters so sparingly in comparison with the infinite number of admirable conclusions which are demonstrated in that science. Far from pretending to teach us the constitution and motions of the heavens and the stars, with their shapes, magnitudes, and distances, the authors of the Bible intentionally forbore to speak of these things, though all were quite well known to them. . . .

From these things it follows as a necessary consequence that, since the Holy Ghost did not intend to teach us whether heaven moves or stands still, whether its shape is spherical or like a discus or extended in a plane, nor whether the earth is located at its center or off to one side, then so much the less was it intended to settle for us any other conclusion of the same kind. And the motion or rest of the earth and the sun is so closely linked with the things just named, that without a determination of the one, neither side can be taken in the other matters. Now if the Holy Spirit has purposely neglected to teach us propositions of this sort as irrelevant to the highest goal (that is, to our salvation), how can anyone affirm that it is obligatory to take sides on them, and that one belief is required by faith, while the other side is erroneous? Can an opinion be heretical and yet have no concern with the salvation of souls? Can the Holy Ghost be asserted not to have intended teaching us something that does concern our salvation? I would say here something that was heard from an ecclesiastic of the most eminent degree: "That the intention of the Holy Ghost is to teach us how one goes to heaven, not how heaven goes." . . .

---

[1] *Adversus Marcionem, ii, 18.*

Galileo Galilei, Letter to the Grand Duchess Christina

1. Galileo held that in discussions of physical problems we ought to begin with

    a. the authority of scripture.
    b. sense experience.
    c. necessary demonstrations.
    d. b and c.
    e. none of the above.

2. Galileo believed that God gave us sense, reason and intellect and would not require us to deny them in physical matters.

    a. True   b. False

3. According to Galileo, how should we read and interpret scripture? Why did he believe this?

Isaac Newton*

ON CLASSICAL MECHANICS

PREFACE TO THE FIRST EDITION
OF THE *PRINCIPIA*

Since the ancients (as we are told by Pappus) esteemed the science of mechanics of greatest importance in the investigation of natural things, and the moderns, rejecting substantial forms and occult qualities, have endeavored to subject the phenomena of nature to the laws of mathematics, I have in this treatise cultivated mathematics as far as it relates to philosophy. The ancients considered mechanics in a twofold respect: as rational, which proceeds accurately by demonstration, and practical. To practical mechanics all the manual arts belong, from which mechanics took its name. But as artificers do not work with perfect accuracy, it comes to pass that mechanics is so distinguished from geometry that what is perfectly accurate is called geometrical; what is less so is called mechanical. However, the errors are not in the art, but in the artificers. He that works with less accuracy is an imperfect mechanic; and if any could work with perfect accuracy, he would be the most perfect mechanic of all; for the description of right lines and circles, upon which geometry is founded, belongs to mechanics. Geometry does not teach us to draw these lines, but requires them to be drawn; for it requires that the learner should first be taught to describe these accurately before he enters upon geometry, then it shows how by these operations problems may be solved. To describe right lines and circles are problems, but not geometrical problems. The solution of these problems is required from mechanics, and by geometry the use of them, when so solved, is shown; and it is the glory of geometry that from those few principles, brought from without, it is able to produce so many things. Therefore geometry is founded in mechanical practice and is nothing but that part of universal mechanics which accurately proposes and demonstrates the art of measuring. But since the manual arts are chiefly employed in the moving of bodies, it happens that geometry is commonly referred to their magnitude, and mechanics to their motion. In this sense rational mechanics will be the science of motions resulting from any forces whatsoever and of the forces required to produce any motions, accurately proposed and demonstrated. This part of mechanics, as far as it extended to the five powers which relate to manual arts, was cultivated by the ancients, who considered gravity (it not being a manual power) not otherwise than in moving weights by those powers. But I consider philosophy rather than arts, and write not concerning manual but natural powers, and consider chiefly those things which relate to gravity, levity, elastic force, the resistance of fluids, and the like forces, whether attractive or impulsive; and therefore I offer this work as the mathematical principles of philosophy, for the whole burden of philosophy seems to consist in this: from the phenomena of motions to investigate the forces of nature, and then from these forces to demonstrate

*Sir Isaac Newton (1642–1727) was an English mathematician, physicist, and member of Parliament. Newton was appointed Lacasian Professor of Mathematics at the age of 27 for his original contributions to the theories of motion and light. His greatest work was the *Mathematical Principles of Natural Philosophy* (1668) in which he developed the calculus and the theory of gravity. By unifying the work of Galileo on falling bodies and that of Kepler on planetary motion, his theory of universal gravity established the uniformity of nature throughout space and generated a new paradigm of physics that guided scientific research until the development of the theory of relativity and quantum physics in this century.

the other phenomena; and to this end the general propositions in the First and Second Books are directed. In the Third Book I give an example of this in the explication of the System of the World; for by the propositions mathematically demonstrated in the former books, in the third I derive from the celestial phenomena the forces of gravity with which bodies tend to the sun and the several planets. Then from these forces, by other propositions which are also mathematical, I deduce the motions of the planets, the comets, the moon, and the sea. I wish we could derive the rest of the phenomena of Nature by the same kind of reasoning from mechanical principles, for I am induced by many reasons to suspect that they may all depend upon certain forces by which the particles of bodies, by some causes hitherto unknown, are either mutually impelled toward one another and cohere in regular figures, or are repelled and recede from one another. These forces being unknown, philosophers have hitherto attempted the search of Nature in vain; but I hope the principles here laid down will afford some light either to this or some truer method of philosophy.

THE LAWS OF MOTION

LAW I

Every body continues in its state of rest or of uniform motion in a right line unless it is compelled to change that state by forces impressed upon it.

Projectiles continue in their motions, so far as they are not retarded by the resistance of the air or impelled downward by the force of gravity. A top, whose parts by their cohesion are continually drawn aside from rectilinear motions, does not cease its rotation otherwise than as it is retarded by the air. The greater bodies of the planets and comets, meeting with less resistance in freer spaces, preserve their motions both progressive and circular for a much longer time.

LAW II

The change of motion is proportional to the motive force impressed and is made in the direction of the right line in which that force is impressed.

If any force generates a motion, a double force will generate double the motion, a triple force triple the motion, whether that force be impressed altogether and at once or gradually and successively. And this motion (being always directed the same way with the generating force), if the body moved before, is added to or subtracted from the former motion, according as they directly conspire with or are directly contrary to each other; or obliquely joined, when they are oblique, so as to produce a new motion compounded for the determination of both.

LAW III

To every action there is always opposed an equal reaction; or, the mutual actions of two bodies upon each other are always equal and directed to contrary parts.

Whatever draws or presses another is as much drawn or pressed by that other. If you press a stone with your finger, the finger is also pressed by the stone. If a horse draws a stone tied to a rope, the horse (if I may so say) will be equally drawn back toward the stone; for the distended rope, by the same endeavor to relax or unbend itself, will draw the horse as much toward the stone as it does the stone toward the horse and will obstruct the progress of the one as much as it advances that of the other. If a body impinge upon another and by its force change the motion of the other, that body also (because of the quality of the mutual pressure) will undergo an equal change in its own motion, toward the contrary part. The changes made by these actions are equal, not in the velocities but in the motions of the bodies; that is to say, if the bodies are not hindered by any other impediments. For, because the motions are equally changed, the changes of the velocities made toward contrary parts are inversely proportional to the bodies. This law takes place also in attractions, as will be proved in the next scholium.

ON GRAVITY

Hitherto we have explained the phenomena of the heavens and of our sea by the power of gravity, but have not yet assigned the cause of this power. This is certain, that it must proceed from a cause that penetrates to the very centers of the sun and planets, without suffering the least diminution of its force; that operates not according to the quantity of the surfaces of the particles upon which it acts (as mechanical causes used to do), but according to the quantity of the solid matter which they contain, and propagates its virtue on all sides to immense distances, decreasing always as the inverse square of the distances. Gravitation toward the sun is made up out of the gravitations toward the several particles of which the body of the sun is composed, and in receding from the sun decreases accurately as the inverse square of the distances as far as the orbit of Saturn, as evidently appears from the quiescence of the aphelion of the planets; nay, and even to the remotest aphelion of the comets, if those aphelions are also quiescent. But hitherto I have not been able to discover the cause of those properties of gravity from phenomena, and I frame no hypotheses; for whatever is not deduced from the phenomena is to be called a hypothesis, and hypotheses, whether metaphysical or physical, whether of occult qualities or mechanical, have no place in experimental philosophy. In this philosophy particular propositions are inferred from the phenomena and afterward rendered general by induction. Thus it was that the impenetrability, the mobility, and the impulsive force of bodies, and the laws of motion and of gravitation, were discovered. And to us it is enough that gravity does really exist and act according to the laws which we have explained, and abundantly serves to account for all the motions of the celestial bodies and of our sea.

ON UNIVERSAL DESIGN

From a Manuscript

Opposite to godliness is atheism in profession and idolatry in practice. Atheism is so senseless and odious to mankind that it never had many professors. Can it be by accident that all birds, beasts, and men have their right side and left side alike shaped (exception their bowels); and just two eyes, and no more, on either side of the face; and just two ears on either side [of] the head; and a nose with two holes; and other two forelegs or two wings or two arms on the shoulders, and two legs on the hips, and no more. Whence arises this uniformity in all their outward shapes but from the counsel and contrivance of an Author? Whence is it that the eyes of all sorts of living creatures are transparent to the very bottom, and the only transparent members in the body, having on the outside a hard transparent skin and within transparent humors, with a crystalline lens in the middle and a pupil before the lens, all of them so finely shaped and fitted for vision that no artist can mend them? Did blind chance know that there was light and what was its refraction, and fit the eyes of all creatures after the most curious manner to make use of it? These and suchlike considerations always have and ever will prevail with mankind to believe that there is a Being who made all things and has all things in his power, and who is therefore to be feared. . . .

We are, therefore, to acknowledge one God, infinite, eternal, omnipresent, omniscient, omnipotent, the Creator of all things, most wise, most just, most good, most holy. We must love him, fear him, honor him, trust in him, pray to him, give him thanks, praise him, hallow his name, obey his commandments, and set times apart for his service, as we are directed in the Third and Fourth Commandments, for this is the love of God that we keep his commandments, and his commandments are not grievous (I John 5:3). And these things we must do not to any mediators between him and us, but to him alone, that he may give his angels charge over us, who, being our fellow servants, are pleased with the worship which we give to their God. And this is the first and the principal part of religion. This always was and always will be the religion of all God's people, from the beginning to the end of the world.

Isaac Newton, On Classical Mechanics

1.   Newton's goal was to develop

      a.   a science of life.
      b.   a science of the supernatural.
      c.   a science of motion.
      d.   all of the above.
      e.   none of the above.

2.   Newton sought to explain physical phenomena in terms of

      a.   natural purposes.
      b.   forces.
      c.   the supernatural.
      d.   life force.
      e.   none of the above.

3.   Newton's Third Law of Motion states that to every action there is always opposed an equal reaction. Thus, if a horse draws a stone tied to a rope, the horse will be equally drawn back to the stone.

      a.   True   b.   False

J. C. Polkinghorne*

PERPLEXITIES

A layman venturing into the quantum world no doubt expects to encounter some fairly strange phenomena. He is prepared for the paradoxical. Yet the greatest paradox of all is likely to escape his attention unless he has a candid professional friend to point it out to him. It is simply this. Quantum theory is both stupendously successful as an account of the small-scale structure of the world and it is also the subject of unresolved debate and dispute about its interpretation. That sounds rather like being shown an impressively beautiful palace and being told that no one is quite sure whether its foundations rest on bedrock or shifting sand.

Concerning the successfulness of quantum theory there can be no dissent. From the time it reached its fully articulated form in the middle twenties of this century it has been used daily by an army of honest toilers with consistently reliable results. Originally constructed to account for atomic physics it has proved equally applicable to the behaviour of those latest candidates for the role of basic constituents of matter, the quarks and gluons. In going from atoms to quarks there is a change of scale by a factor of at least ten million. It is impressive that quantum mechanics can take that in its stride.

The problems of interpretation cluster around two issues: the nature of reality and the nature of measurement. Philosophers of science have latterly been busy explaining that science is about correlating phenomena or acquiring the power to manipulate them. They stress the theory-laden character of our pictures of the world and the extent to which scientists are said to be influenced in their thinking

by the social factor of the spirit of the age. Such accounts cast doubt on whether an understanding of reality is to be conceived of as the primary goal of science or the actual nature of its achievement. These comments from the touchline may well contain points of value about the scientific game. They should not, however, cause us to neglect the observations of those who are actually players. The overwhelming impression of the participants is that they are investigating the way things are. Discovery is the name of the game. The pay-off for the rigours and *longueurs* of scientific research is the consequent gain in understanding of the way the world is constructed. Contemplating the sweep of the development of some field of science can only reinforce that feeling.

Consider, for example, our understanding of electricity and magnetism and the nature of light. In the nineteenth century, first Thomas Young demonstrated the wave character of light; then Faraday's brilliant experimental researches revealed the interlocking nature of electricity and magnetism; finally the theoretical genius of Maxwell produced an understanding of the electromagnetic field whose oscillations were identifiable with Young's light waves. It all constituted a splendid achievement. Nature, however, proved more subtle than even Maxwell had imagined. The beginning of this century produced phenomena which equally emphatically showed that light was made up of tiny particles. (It is a story which we shall tell in the following chapter.) The resulting wave/particle dilemma was resolved by Dirac in 1928 when he invented quantum field theory, a formalism which succeeds in

---

*J. C. Polkinghorne (1930–) is a physicist interested in explaining quantum physics to the non-specialist. Educated at Cambridge, he was a Professor of Theoretical Elementary Particle Physics there until 1979 when he left to join the ministry. He is currently a vicar in the Church of England.

combining waves and particles without a trace of paradox. Later developments in quantum electrodynamics (as the theory of the interaction of light and electrons is called) have led to the calculation of effects, such as the Lamb shift in hydrogen, which agree with experiment to the limits of available accuracy of a few parts per million. Can one doubt that such a tale is one of a tightening grasp of an actual reality? Of course there is an unusually strong element of corrigibility in this particular story. Quantum electrodynamics contains features completely contrary to the expectations which any nineteenth-century physicist could have entertained. Nevertheless there is also considerable continuity, with the concepts of wave and field playing vital roles throughout. The controlling element in this long development was not the ingenuity of men nor the pressure of society but the nature of the world as it was revealed to increasingly thorough investigation.

Considerations like these make scientists feel that they are right to take a philosophically realist view of the results of their researches; to suppose that they are finding out the way things are. When we are concerned with pre-quantum physics—with classical physics, as we say—that seems a particularly straightforward supposition. The analogy with the 'real' world of everyday experience is direct. In classical physics I can know both where an electron is and what it is doing. In more technical language, its position and momentum can both simultaneously be known. Such an object is not so very different from a table or a cow, concerning which I can have similar information of where they are and what they are doing. The classical electron can be conceived, so to speak, as just a midget brother of everyday things. Of course, philosophers can dispute the reality of the table and the cow too, but common sense is inclined to feel that that is a tiresomely perverse attitude to take to experience.

Heisenberg abolished such cosy picturability for quantum mechanical objects. His uncertainty principle (discussed in detail in Chapter 5) says that if I know where an electron is I have no idea of what it is doing and, conversely, if I know what it is doing I do not know where it is. The existence of such elusive objects clearly modifies our notion of reality. One of the perplexities about the interpretation of quantum mechanics is what, if any, meaning it attaches to the reality of something as protean as an electron. In Chapter 7 we shall find that there is in quantum theory a radical inability to pin things down which goes beyond the simple considerations outlined here.

The second perplexity relates to the act of measurement. It is notorious that there is an inescapable random element in quantum mechanical measurement. Suppose that I am supplied with a sequence of electrons which have been prepared in such a way that they are all in the same state of motion. Every minute, say, I am delivered one of these standard electrons. In classical physics, if I measured each electron's position as it was delivered they would all be found to be in the same place. This is because classically they have a well-defined location at a particular instant whose specification is part of what is involved in saying that they are in the same state of motion. Quantum mechanically, however, Heisenberg will not normally allow the electrons to have a well-determined position (it will usually have to be uncertain). This reflects itself in the fact that when I actually make a measurement I shall find the electron sometimes here and sometimes over there. If I make a large number of such measurements the theory enables me to calculate the proportion of times the electron will be found 'here' and the proportion of times it will be found 'there'. That is to say, the probability of its being found 'here' can be determined. However, I am not able to predict on any particular occasion whether the electron will turn out to be 'here' rather than 'there'. Quantum mechanics puts me in the position of a canny bookmaker who can calculate the odds that a horse may win in the course of the season but not in the position of Our Newmarket Correspondent who claims to be able to forecast the outcome of a particular race.

All that is rather peculiar but it can be digested and lived with. The source of the perplexity is more subtle. Consider what is involved in measuring the position of an electron. It requires the setting up of a chain of correlated consequences linking at one end the position of the microscopic electron and at the other end the registration of the result of that particular measurement. The latter can be thought of either as something like a pointer moving across a scale to a mark labelled 'here', or ultimately as a conscious observer looking at such a pointer and saying 'By Jove, the electron's 'here' on this occasion.' Certainly I cannot perceive the electron directly. There has to be this chain of related consequence blowing-up the position of the microscopic electron into a macroscopically observable signal of its presence 'here'. The puzzle is, where along this chain does it get fixed that on this occasion the answer comes out 'here'? At one end of the chain there is a quantum mechanically uncertain electron; at the other a dependable pointer or equally reliable observer, neither of which exhibits any uncertainty in its behaviour. How do the two enmesh? In Chapter 6 we shall find that it is a matter of perplexity where along the chain the fixity sets in which determines a particular result on a particular occasion. In fact there is a range of different suggestions, none of which appears free from difficulty. The discontinuity involved in the act of measurement is the one really novel feature which sets quantum mechanics apart from all the physics which preceded it.

In what lies ahead I shall try to explain more fully the nature of these problems and the variety of the answers which have been proposed to them. Before attempting that task a short historical excursus will be necessary to explain how it all came about.

J. C. Polkinghorne: "Perplexities"

1.   According to Heisenberg's Uncertainty Principle,

   a.   one can simultaneously know either the position of an electron or its momentum, but not both.
   b.   one can simultaneously know both the position and the momentum of an electron.
   c.   one can know neither the position nor the momentum of an electron.
   d.   one can know only the position of an electron.
   e.   one can know only the momentum of an electron.

2.   There is an inescapably random element in quantum mechanical measurement.

   a.   True   b.   False

3.   Quantum mechanical predictions are

   a.   deterministic.
   b.   impossible.
   c.   probabilistic.
   d.   all of the above.
   e.   none of the above.

Charles Darwin*

Conclusion From THE ORIGIN OF SPECIES

As this whole volume is one long argument, it may be convenient to the reader to have the leading facts and inferences briefly recapitulated.

That many and serious objections may be advanced against the theory of descent with modification through variation and natural selection, I do not deny. I have endeavored to give them their full force. Nothing at first can appear more difficult to believe than that the more complex organs and instincts have been perfected, not by means superior to, though analogous with, human reason, but by the accumulation of innumerable slight variations, each good for the individual possessor. Nevertheless, this difficulty, though appearing to our imagination insuperably great, cannot be considered real if we admit the following propositions, namely, that all parts of the organisation and instincts offer, at least, individual differences—that there is a struggle for existence leading to the preservation of profitable deviations of structure or instinct—and, lastly, that gradations in the state of perfection of each organ may have existed, each good of its kind. The truth of these propositions cannot, I think, be disputed.

It is, no doubt, extremely difficult even to conjecture by what gradations many structures have been perfected, more especially amongst broken and failing groups of organic beings, which have suffered much extinction, but we see so many strange gradations in nature, that we ought to be extremely cautious in saying that any organ or instinct, or any whole structure, could not have arrived at its present state by many graduated steps. There are, it must be admitted, cases of special difficulty opposed to the theory of natural selection; and one of the most curious of these is the existence in the same community of two or three defined castes of workers or sterile female ants; but I have attempted to show how these difficulties can be mastered.

With respect to the almost universal sterility of species when first crossed, which forms so remarkable a contrast with the almost universal fertility of varieties when crossed, I must refer the reader to the recapitulation of the facts given at the end of the ninth chapter, which seem to me conclusively to show that this sterility is no more a special endowment than is the incapacity of two distinct kinds of trees to be grafted together; but that it is incidental on differences confined to the reproductive systems of the intercrossed species. We see the truth of this conclusion in the vast difference in the results of crossing the same two species reciprocally,—that is, when one species is first used as the father and then as the mother. Analogy from the consideration of dimorphic and trimorphic plants clearly leads to the same conclusion, for when the forms are illegitimately united, they yield few or no seed, and

---

*Charles Darwin (1809–1882) was an English naturalist who changed the face of biology with his theory of evolution. As a young naturalist serving aboard the H.M.S. Beagle for a five year voyage around the globe (1831–6), Darwin began searching for an explanation of the wide diversity of life that he observed. This work culminated in his publication of *On the Origin of the Species* (1859) and *The Descent of Man*. In these books, Darwin argued that all species are the result of a process of evolution in which complex life forms develop out of simpler ones by means of a gradual accumulation of changes. While his work generated storms of controversy for many years after its publication, the concept of evolution is now central to modern biology.

their offspring are more or less sterile; and these forms belong to the same undoubted species, and differ from each other in no respect except in their reproductive organs and functions.

Although the fertility of varieties when intercrossed and of their mongrel offspring has been asserted by so many authors to be universal, this cannot be considered as quite correct after the facts given on the high authority of Gärtner and Kölreuter. Most of the varieties which have been experimented on have been produced under domestication; and as domestication (I do not mean mere confinement) almost certainly tends to eliminate that sterility which, judging from analogy, would have affected the parent-species if intercrossed, we ought not to expect that domestication would likewise induce sterility in their modified descendants when crossed. This elimination of sterility apparently follows from the same cause which allows our domestic animals to breed freely under diversified circumstances; and this again apparently follows from their having been gradually accustomed to frequent changes in their conditions of life.

A double and parallel series of facts seems to throw much light on the sterility of species, when first crossed, and of their hybrid offspring. On the one side, there is good reason to believe that slight changes in the conditions of life give vigour and fertility to all organic beings. We know also that a cross between the distinct individuals of the same variety, and between distinct varieties, increases the number of their offspring, and certainly gives to them increased size and vigour. This is chiefly owing to the forms which are crossed having been exposed to somewhat different conditions of life; for I have ascertained by a laborious series of experiments that if all the individuals of the same variety be subjected during several generations to the same conditions, the good derived from crossing is often much diminished or wholly disappears. This is one side of the case. On the other side, we know that species which have long been exposed to nearly uniform conditions, when they are subjected under confinement to new and greatly changed conditions, either perish, or if they survive, are rendered sterile, though retaining perfect health. This does not occur, or only in a very slight degree, with our domesticated productions, which have long been exposed to fluctuating conditions. Hence when we find that hybrids produced by a cross between two distinct species are few in number, owing to their perishing soon after conception or at a very early age, or if surviving that they are rendered more or less sterile, it seems highly probable that this result is due to their having been in fact subjected to a great change in their conditions of life, from being compounded of two distinct organisations. He who will explain in a definite manner why, for instance, an elephant or a fox will not breed under confinement in its native country, whilst the domestic pig or dog will breed freely under the most diversified conditions, will at the same time be able to give a definite answer to the question why two distinct species, when crossed, as well as their hybrid offspring, are generally rendered more or less sterile, whilst two domesticated varieties when crossed and their mongrel offspring are perfectly fertile.

Turning to geographical distribution, the difficulties encountered on the theory of descent with modification are serious enough. All the individuals of the same species, and all the species of the same genus, or even higher group, are descended from common parents; and therefore, in however distant and isolated parts of the world they may now be found, they must in the course of successive generations have travelled from some one point to all the others. We are often wholly unable even to conjecture how this could have been effected. Yet, as we have reason to believe that some species have retained the same specific form for very long periods of time, immensely long as measured by years, too much stress ought not to be laid on the occasional wide diffusion of the same species; for during very long periods there will always have been a good chance for wide migration by many means. A broken or interrupted range may often be accounted for by the extinction of the species in the intermediate regions. It cannot be denied that we are as yet very ignorant as to the full extent of the various climatal and geographical changes which have affected the earth during modern periods; and such changes will often have facilitated migration. As an example, I have attempted to show how potent has been the influence of the Glacial period on the distribution of the same and of allied species throughout the world. We are as yet profoundly ignorant of the many occasional means of transport. With respect to distinct species of the same genus inhabiting distant and isolated regions, as the process of modification has necessarily been slow, all the means of migration will have been possible during a very long period; and consequently the difficulty of the wide diffusion of the species of the same genus is in some degree lessened.

As according to the theory of natural selection an interminable number of intermediate forms must have existed, linking together all the species in each group by gradations as fine as are our existing varieties, it may be asked: Why do we not see these linking forms all around us? Why are not all organic beings blended together in an inextricable chaos? With respect to existing forms, we should remember that we have no right to expect (excepting in rare cases) to discover *directly* connecting links between them, but only between each and some extinct and supplanted form. Even on a wide area, which has during a long period remained continuous, and of which the climatic and other conditions of life change insensibly in proceeding from a district occupied by one species into another district occupied by a closely allied species, we have no just right to expect often to find intermediate varieties in the intermediate zones. For we have reason to believe that only a few species of a genus ever undergo change; the other species becoming utterly extinct and leaving no modified progeny. Of the species which do change, only a few within the same country change at the same time; and all modifications are slowly effected. I have also shown that the intermediate varieties which probably at first existed in the intermediate zones, would be liable to be supplanted by the allied forms on either hand; for the latter, from existing in greater numbers, would generally be modified and improved at a quicker rate than the intermediate varieties, which existed in lesser numbers; so that the intermediate varieties would, in the long run, be supplanted and exterminated.

On this doctrine of the extermination of an infinitude of connecting links, between the living and extinct inhabitants of the world, and at each successive period between the extinct and still older species, why is not every geological formation charged with such links? Why does not every collection of fossil remains afford plain evidence of the gradation and mutation of the forms of life? Although geological research has undoubtedly revealed the former existence of many links, bringing numerous forms of life much closer together, it does not yield the infinitely many fine gradations between past and present species required on the theory; and this is the most obvious of the many objections which may be urged against it. Why, again, do whole groups of allied species appear, though this appearance is often false, to have come in suddenly on the successive geological stages? Although we now know that organic beings appeared on this globe, at a period incalculably remote, long before the lowest bed of the Cambrian system was deposited, why do we not find beneath this system great piles of strata stored with the remains of the progenitors of the Cambrian fossils? For on the theory, such strata must somewhere have been deposited at these ancient and utterly unknown epochs of the worlds' history.

I can answer these questions and objections only on the supposition that the geological record is far more imperfect than most geologists believe. The number of specimens in all our museums is absolutely as nothing compared with the countless generations of countless species which have certainly existed. The parent-form of any two or more species would not be in all its characters directly intermediate between its modified offspring, any more than the rock-pigeon is directly intermediate in crop and tail between its descendants, the pouter and fantail pigeons. We should not be able to recognise a species as the parent of another and modified species, if we were to examine the two ever so closely, unless we possessed most of the intermediate links; and owing to the imperfection of the geological record, we have no just right to expect to find so many links. If two or three, or even more linking forms were discovered, they would simply be ranked by many naturalists as so many new species, more especially if found in different geological sub-stages, let their differences be ever so slight. Numerous existing doubtful forms could be named which are probably varieties; but who will pretend that in future ages so many fossil links will be discovered, that naturalists will be able to decide whether or not these doubtful forms ought to be called varieties? Only a small portion of the world has been geologically explored. Only organic beings of certain classes can be preserved in a fossil condition, at least in any great number. Many species when once formed never undergo any further change but become extinct without leaving modified descendants; and the periods, during which species have undergone modification, though long as measured by years, have probably been short in comparison with the periods during which they retain the same form. It is the dominant and widely ranging species which vary most frequently and vary most, and varieties are often at first local—both causes rendering the discovery of intermediate links in any one formation less likely. Local varieties will not spread into other and distant regions until they are considerably modified and improved; and when they have spread, and are discovered in a geological formation, they appear as if suddenly created there, and will be simply classed as new species. Most formations have been intermittent in their accumulation; and their duration has probably been shorter than the average duration of specific forms. Successive formations are in most cases separated from each other by blank intervals of time of great length; for fossiliferous formations thick enough to resist future degradations can as a general rule be accumulated only where much sediment is deposited on the subsiding bed of the sea. During the alternate period of elevation and of stationary level the record will generally be blank. During these latter periods there will probably be more variability in the forms of life; during periods of subsidence, more extinction.

With respect to the absence of strata rich in fossils beneath the Cambrian formation, I can recur only to the hypothesis given in the tenth chapter; namely, that though our continents and oceans have endured for an enormous period in nearly their present relative positions, we have no reason to assume that this has always been the case; consequently formations much older than any now known may lie buried beneath the great oceans. With respect to the lapse of time not having been sufficient since our planet was consolidated for the assumed amount of organic change, and this objection, as urged by Sir William Thompson, is probably one of the gravest as yet advanced, I can only say, firstly, that we do not know at what rate species change as measured by years, and secondly, that many philosophers are not as yet willing to admit that we know enough of the constitution of the universe and of the interior of our globe to speculate with safety on its past duration.

That the geological record is imperfect all will admit; but that it is imperfect to the degree required by our theory, few will be inclined to admit. If we look to long enough intervals of time, geology plainly declares that species have all changed; and they have changed in the manner required by the theory, for they have changed slowly and in a graduated manner. We clearly see this in the fossil remains from consecutive formations invariably being much more closely related to each other, than are the fossils from widely separated formations.

Such is the sum of the several chief objections and difficulties which may be justly urged against the theory; and I have now briefly recapitulated the answer and explanations which, as far as I can see, may be given. I have felt these difficulties far too heavily during many years to doubt their weight. But it deserves especial notice that the more important objections relate to questions on which we are confessedly ignorant; nor do we know how ignorant we are. We do not know all the possible transitional gradations between the simplest and the most perfect organs; it cannot be pretended that we know all the varied means of Distribution during the long

lapse of years, or that we know how imperfect is the Geological Record. Serious as these several objections are, in my judgment they are by no means sufficient to overthrow the theory of descent with subsequent modification.

Now let us turn to the other side of the argument. Under domestication we see much variability, caused, or at least excited, by changed conditions of life; but often in so obscure a manner, that we are tempted to consider the variations as spontaneous. Variability is governed by many complex laws,—by correlated growth, compensation, the increased use and disuse of parts, and the definite action of the surrounding conditions. There is much difficulty in ascertaining how largely our domestic productions have been modified; but we may safely infer that the amount has been large, and that modifications can be inherited for long periods. As long as the conditions of life remain the same, we have reason to believe that a modification, which has already been inherited for many generations, may continue to be inherited for an almost infinite number of generations. On the other hand, we have evidence that variability when it has once come into play, does not cease under domestication for a very long period; nor do we know that it ever ceases, for new varieties are still occasionally produced by our oldest domesticated productions.

Variability is not actually caused by man; he only unintentionally exposes organic beings to new conditions of life, and then nature acts on the organisation and causes it to vary. But man can and does select the variations given to him by nature, and thus accumulates them in any desired manner. He thus adapts animals and plants for his own benefit or pleasure. He may do this methodically, or he may do it unconsciously by preserving the individuals most useful or pleasing to him without any intention of altering the breed. It is certain that he can largely influence the character of a breed by selecting, in each successive generation, individual differences so slight as to be inappreciable except by an educated eye. This unconscious process of selection has been the great agency in the formation of the most distinct and useful domestic breeds. That many breeds produced by man have to a large extent the character of natural species, is shown by the inextricable doubts whether many of them are varieties or aboriginally distinct species.

There is no reason why the principles which have acted so efficiently under domestication should not have acted under nature. In the survival of favoured individuals and races, during the constantly-recurrent Struggle for Existence, we see a powerful and ever-acting form of Selection. The struggle for existence inevitably follows from the high geometrical ratio of increase which is common to all organic beings. This high rate of increase is proved by calculation,—by the rapid increase of many animals and plants during a succession of peculiar seasons, and when naturalised in new countries. More individuals are born than can possibly survive. A grain in the balance may determine which individuals shall live and which shall die,—which variety or species shall increase in number, and which shall decrease, or finally become extinct. As the individuals of the same species come in all respects into the closest competition with each other, the struggle will generally be most severe between them; it will be almost equally severe between the varieties of the same species, and next in severity between the species of the same genus. On the other hand the struggle will often be severe between beings remote in the scale of nature. The slightest advantage in certain individuals, at any age or during any season, over those with which they come into competition, or better adaptation in however slight a degree to the surrounding physical conditions, will, in the long run, turn the balance.

With animals having separated sexes, there will be in most cases a struggle between the males for the possession of the females. The most vigorous males, or those which have most successfully struggled with their conditions of life, will generally leave most progeny. But success will often depend on the males having special weapons, or means of defence, or charms; and a slight advantage will lead to victory.

As geology plainly proclaims that each land has undergone great physical changes, we might have expected to find that organic beings have varied under nature, in the same way as they have varied under domestication. And if there has been any variability under nature, it would be an unaccountable fact if natural selection had not come into play. It has often been asserted, but the assertion is incapable of proof, that the amount of variation under nature is strictly limited quantity. Man, though acting on external characters alone and often capriciously, can produce within a short period a great result by adding up mere individual differences in his domestic productions; and every one admits that species present individual differences. But, besides such differences, all naturalists admit that natural varieties exist, which are considered sufficiently distinct to be worthy of record in systematic works. No one has drawn any clear distinc-

tion between individual differences and slight varieties; or between more plainly marked varieties and sub-species, and species. On separate continents, and on different parts of the same continent when divided by barriers of any kind, and on outlying islands, what a multitude of forms exist, which some experienced naturalists rank as varieties, others as geographical races or sub-species, and others as distinct, though closely allied species!

If, then, animals and plants do vary, let it be every so slightly or slowly, why should not variations or individual differences, which are in any way beneficial, be preserved and accumulated through natural selection, or the survival of the fittest? If man can by patience select variations useful to him, why, under changing and complex conditions of life, should not variations useful to nature's living products often arise, and be preserved or selected? What limit can be put to this power, acting during long ages and rigidly scrutinising the whole constitution, structure, and habits of each creature,—favouring the good and rejecting the bad? I can see no limit to this power, in slowly and beautifully adapting each form to the most complex relations of life. The theory of natural selection, even if we look no farther than this, seems to be in the highest degree probable. I have already recapitulated, as fairly as I could, the opposed difficulties and objections; now let us turn to the special facts and arguments in favour of the theory.

On the view that species are only strongly marked and permanent varieties, and that each species first existed as a variety, we can see why it is that no line of demarcation can be drawn between species, commonly supposed to have been produced by special acts of creation, and varieties which are acknowledged to have been produced by secondary laws. On this same view we can understand how it is that in a region where many species of a genus have been produced, and where they now flourish, these same species should present many varieties; for where the manufactory of species has been active, we might expect, as a general rule, to find it still in action; and this is the case if varieties be incipient species. Moreover, the species of the larger genera, which afford the greater number of varieties or incipient species, retain to a certain degree the character of varieties; for they differ from each other by a less amount of difference than do the species of smaller genera. The closely allied species also of the larger genera apparently have restricted ranges, and in their affinities they are clustered in little groups round other species—in both respects resembling varieties. These are strange relations on the view that each species was independently created, but are intelligible if each existed first as a variety.

As each species tends by its geometrical rate of reproduction to increase inordinately in number; and as the modified descendants of each species will be enabled to increase by as much as they become more diversified in habits and structure, so as to be able to seize on many and widely different places in the economy of nature, three will be a constant tendency in natural selection to preserve the most divergent offspring of any one species. Hence, during a long-continued course of modification, the slight differences characteristic of varieties of the same species, tend to be augmented into the greater differences characteristic of the species of the same genus. New and improved varieties will inevitably supplant and exterminate the older, less improved, and intermediate varieties; and thus species are rendered to a large extent defined and distinct objects. Dominant species belonging to the larger groups within each class tend to give birth to new and dominant forms; so that each large group tends to become still larger, and at the same time more divergent in character. But as all groups cannot thus go in increasing in size, for the world would not hold them, the more dominant groups beat the less dominant. This tendency in the large groups to go on increasing in size and diverging in character, together with the inevitable contingency of much extinction, explains the arrangement of all the forms of life in groups subordinate to groups, all within a few great classes, which has prevailed throughout all time. This grand fact of the grouping of all organic beings under what is called the Natural System, is utterly inexplicable on the theory of creation.

As natural selection acts solely by accumulating slight, successive, favourable variations, it can produce no great or sudden modifications; it can act only by short and slow steps. Hence, the canon of *"Natura non facit saltum,"* which every fresh addition to our knowledge tends to confirm, is on this theory intelligible. We can see why throughout nature the same general end is gained by an almost infinite diversity of means, for every peculiarity when once acquired is long inherited, and structures already modified in many different ways have to be adapted from the same general purpose. We can, in short, see why nature is prodigal in variety, though niggard in innovation. But why this should be a law of nature if each species has been independently created no man can explain.

Many other facts are, as it seems to me, explicable on this theory. How strange it is that a bird, under the form of woodpecker, should prey on insects on the ground; that upland geese which rarely or never swim, should possess webbed feet; that a thrushlike bird should dive and feed on sub-aquatic insects; and that a petrel should have the habits and structure fitting it for the life of an auk! and so in endless other cases. But on the view of each species constantly trying to increase in number, with natural selection always ready to adapt the slowly varying descendants of each to any unoccupied or ill-occupied place in nature, these facts cease to be strange, or might even have been anticipated.

We can to a certain extent understand how it is that there is so much beauty throughout nature; for this may be largely attributed to the agency of selection. That beauty, according to our sense of it, is not universal, must be admitted by every one who will look at some venomous snakes, at some fishes, and at certain hideous bats with a distorted resemblance to the human face. Sexual selection has given the most brilliant colours, elegant patterns, and other ornaments to the males, and sometimes to both sexes of many birds, butterflies, and other animals. With birds it has often rendered the voice of the male musical to the female, as well as to our ears. Flowers and fruit have been rendered conspicuous by brilliant colours in contrast with the green foliage, in order that the flowers may be readily seen, visited and fertilised by insects, and the seeds disseminated by birds. How it comes that certain colours, sounds, and forms should give pleasure to man and the lower animals,—that is, how the sense of beauty in its simplest form was first acquired, —we do not know any more than how certain odours and flavours were first rendered agreeable.

As natural selection acts by competition, it adapts and improves the inhabitants of each country only in relation to their co-inhabitants; so that we need feel no surprise at the species of any one country, although on the ordinary view supposed to have been created and specially adapted for that country, being beaten and supplanted by the naturalised productions from another land. Nor ought we to marvel if all the contrivances in nature be not, as far as we can judge, absolutely perfect, as in the case even of the human eye; or if some of them be abhorrent to our ideas of fitness. We need not marvel at the sting of the bee, when used against an enemy, causing the bee's own death; at drones being produced in such great numbers for one single act, and being then slaughtered by their sterile

84

sisters; at the astonishing waste of pollen by our fir-trees; at the instinctive hatred of the queen-bee for her own fertile daughters; at the Ichneumonidæ feeding within the living bodies of caterpillars; or at other such cases. The wonder indeed is, on the theory of natural selection, that more cases of the want of absolute perfection have not been detected.

The complex and little known laws governing the production of varieties are the same, as far as we can judge, with the laws which have governed the production of distinct species. In both cases physical conditions seem to have produced some direct and definite effect, but how much we cannot say. Thus, when varieties enter any new station, they occasionally assume some of the characters proper to the species of that station. With both varieties and species, use and disuse seem to have produced a considerable effect; for it is impossible to resist this conclusion when we look, for instance, at the logger-headed duck, which has wings incapable of flight, in nearly the same condition as in the domestic duck; or when we look at the burrowing tucu-tucu, which is occasionally blind, and then at certain moles, which are habitually blind and have their eyes covered with skin; or when we look at the blind animals inhabiting the dark caves of America and Europe. With varieties and species, correlated variation seems to have played an important part, so that when one part has been modified other parts have been necessarily modified. With both parties and species, reversions to long-lost characters occasionally occur. How inexplicable on the theory of creation is the occasional appearance of stripes on the shoulders and legs of the several species of the horsegenus and of their hybrids! How simply is this fact explained if we believe that these species are all descended from a striped progenitor, in the same manner as the several domestic breeds of the pigeon are descended from the blue and barred rock-pigeon!

On the ordinary view of each species having been independently created, why should specific characters, or those by which the species of the same genus differ from each other, be more variable than generic characters in which they all agree? Why, for instance, should the colour of a flower be more likely to vary in any one species of a genus, if the other species possess differently coloured flowers, than if all possessed the same coloured flowers? If species are only well-marked varieties, of which the characters have become in a high degree permanent, we can understand this fact; for they have already varied since they branched off from a common progenitor in certain characters, by which they have come to be specifically distinct from each other; therefore these same characters would be more likely again to vary than the generic characters which have been inherited without change for an immense period. It is inexplicable on the theory of creation why a part developed in a very unusual manner in one species alone of a genus, and therefore, as we may naturally infer, of great importance to that species, should be eminently liable to variation; but, on our view, this part has undergone, since the several species branched off from a common progenitor, an unusual amount of variability and modification, and therefore we might expect the part generally to be still variable. But a part may be developed in the most unusual manner, like the wing of a bat, and yet not be more variable than any other structure, if the part be common to many subordinate forms, that is, if it has been inherited for a very long period; for in this case, it will have been rendered constant by long-continued natural selection.

Glancing at instincts, marvelous as some are, they offer no greater difficulty than do corporeal structures on the theory of the natural selection of successive slight, but profitable modifications. We can thus understand why nature moves by graduate steps in endowing different animals of the same class with their several instincts. I have attempted to show how much light the principle of gradation throws on the admirable architectural powers of the hive-bee. Habit no doubt often comes into play in modifying instincts; but it certainly is not indispensable, as we see in the case of neuter insects, which leave no progeny to inherit the effects of long-continued habit. On the view of all the species of the same genus having descended from the common parent, and having inherited much in common, we can understand how it is that allied species, when placed under widely different conditions of life, yet follow nearly the same instincts; why the thrushes of tropical and temperate South America, for instance, line their nests with mud like our British species. On the view of instincts having been slowly acquired through natural selection, we need not marvel at some instincts being not perfect and liable to mistakes, and at many instincts causing other animals to suffer.

If species be only well-marked and permanent varieties, we can at once see why their crossed offspring should follow the same complex laws in their degrees and kinds of resemblance to their parents, —in being absorbed into each other by successive crosses, and in other such points,—as do the crossed offspring of acknowledged varieties. This similarity would be a strange fact, if species had been independently created and varieties had been produced through secondary laws.

If we admit that the geological record is imperfect to an extreme degree, then the facts, which the record does give, strongly support the theory of descent with modification. New species have come on the stage slowly and at successive intervals; and the amount of change, after equal intervals of time, is widely different in different groups. The extinction of species and of whole groups of species which has played so conspicuous a part in the history of the organic world, almost inevitably follows from the principle of natural selection; for old forms are supplanted by new and improved forms. Neither single species nor groups of species reappear when the chain of ordinary generation is once broken. The gradual diffusion of dominant forms, with the slow modification of their descendants, causes the forms of life, after long intervals of time, to appear as if they had changed simultaneously throughout the world. The fact of the fossil remains of each formation being in some degree intermediate in character between the fossils in the formations above and below, is simply explained by their intermediate position in the chain of descent. The grand fact that all extinct beings can be classed with all recent beings, naturally follows from the living and the extinct being the offspring of common parents. As species have generally diverged in character during their long course of descent and modification, we can understand why it is that the more ancient forms, or early progenitors of each group, so often occupy a position in some degree intermediate between existing groups. Recent forms are generally looked upon as being, on the whole, higher in the scale of organisation than ancient forms; and they must be higher, in so far as the later and more improved forms have conquered the older and less improved forms in the struggle for life; they have also generally had their organs more specialised for different functions. This fact is perfectly compatible with numerous beings still retaining simple and but little improved structures, fitted for simple conditions of life; it is likewise compatible with some forms having retrograded in organisation, by having become at each stage of descent better fitted for new and degraded habits of life. Lastly, the wonderful law of the long endurance of allied forms on the same continent,—of marsupials in Australia, of Edentata in America, and other such cases,—is intelligible, for within the same

country the existing and the extinct will be closely allied by descent.

Looking to geographical distribution, if we admit that there has been during the long course of ages much migration from one part of the world to another, owing to former climatal and geographical changes and to the many occasional and unknown means of dispersal, then we can understand, on the theory of descent with modification, most of the great leading facts in Distribution. We can see why there should be so striking a parallelism in the distribution of organic beings throughout space, and in their geological succession throughout time; for in both cases the beings have been connected by the bond of ordinary generation, and the means of modification have been the same. We see the full meaning of the wonderful fact, which has struck every traveller, namely, that on the same continent, under the most diverse conditions, under heat and cold, on mountain and lowland, on deserts and marshes, most of the inhabitants within each great class are plainly related; for they are the descendants of the same progenitors and early colonists. On this same principle of former migration, combined in most cases with modification, we can understand, by the aid of the Glacial period, the identity of some few plants, and the close alliance of many others, on the most distant mountains, and in the northern and southern temperate zones; and likewise the close alliance of some of the inhabitants of the sea in the northern and southern temperate latitudes, though separated by the whole intertropical ocean. Although two countries may present physical conditions as closely similar as the same species ever require, we need feel no surprise at their inhabitants being widely different, if they have been for a long period completely sundered from each other; for as the relation of organism to organism is the most important of all relations, and as the two countries will have received colonists at various periods and in different proportions, from some other country or from each other, the course of modification in the two areas will inevitably have been different.

On this view of migration with subsequent modification, we see why oceanic islands are inhabited by only few species, but of these, why many are peculiar or endemic forms. We clearly see why species belonging to those groups of animals which cannot cross wide spaces of the ocean, as frogs and terrestrial mammals, do not inhabit oceanic islands; and why, on the other hand, new and peculiar species of bats, animals which can traverse the ocean, are found on islands far distant from any continent. Such cases as the presence of peculiar species of bats on oceanic islands and the absence of all other terrestrial mammals, are facts utterly inexplicable on the theory of independent acts of creation.

The existence of closely allied or representative species in any two areas, implies, on the theory of descent with modification, that the same parent-forms formerly inhabited both areas; and we almost invariably find that wherever many closely allied species inhabit two areas, some identical species are still common to both. Wherever many closely allied yet distinct species occur, doubtful forms and varieties belonging to the same groups likewise occur. It is a rule of high generality that the inhabitants of each area are related to the inhabitants of the nearest source whence immigrants might have been derived. We see this in the striking relation of nearly all plants and animals of the Galapagos Archipelago, of Juan Fernandez, and of the other American islands, to the plants and animals of the neighbouring American mainland; and of those of the Cape de Verde Archipelago, and of the other African islands to the African mainland. It must be admitted that these facts receive no explanation on the theory of creation.

The fact, as we have seen, that all past and present organic beings can be arranged within a few great classes, in groups subordinate to groups, and with the extinct groups often falling in between the recent groups, is intelligible on the theory of natural selection with its contingencies of extinction and divergence of character. On these same principles we see how it is, that the mutual affinities of the forms within each class are so complex and circuitous. We see why certain characters are far more serviceable than others for classification;—why adaptive characters, though of paramount importance other beings, are of hardly any importance in classification; why characters derived from rudimentary parts, though of no service to the beings, are often of high classificatory value; and why embryological characters are often the most valuable of all. The real affinities of all organic beings, in contradistinction to their adaptive resemblances, are due to inheritance or community of descent. The Natural System is a genealogical arrangement, with the acquired grades of difference, marked by the terms, varieties, species, genera, families, &c.; and we have to discover the lines of descent by the most permanent characters whatever they may be and of however slight vital importance.

The similar framework of bones in the hand of a man, wing of a bat, fin of the porpoise, and leg of the horse,—the same number of vertebræ forming the neck of the giraffe and of the elephant,—and innumerable other such facts, at once explain themselves on the theory of descent with slow and slight successive modifications. The similarity of pattern in the wing and in the leg of a bat, though used for such different purpose,—in the jaws and legs of a crab, —in the petals, stamens, and pistils of a flower, is likewise, to a large extent, intelligible on the view of the gradual modification of parts or organs, which were aboriginally alike in an early progenitor in each of these classes. On the principle of successive variations not always supervening at an early age, and being inherited at a corresponding not early period of life, we clearly see why the embryos of mammals, birds, reptiles, and fishes should be so closely similar, and so unlike the adult forms. We may cease marvelling at the embryo of an airbreathing mammal or bird having branchial slits and arteries running in loops, like those of a fish which has to breathe the air dissolved in water by the aid of well-developed branchiæ.

Disuse, aided sometimes by natural selection, will often have reduced organs when rendered useless under changed habits of conditions of life; and we can understand on this view the meaning of rudimentary organs. But disuse and selection will generally act on each creature, when it has come to maturity and has to play its full part in the struggle for existence, and will thus have little power on an organ during early life; hence the organ will not be reduced or rendered rudimentary at this early age. The calf, for instance, has inherited teeth, which never cut through the gums of the upper jaw, from an early progenitor having well-developed teeth; and we may believe, that the teeth in the mature animal were formerly reduced by disuse, owing to the tongue and palate, or lips, having become excellently fitted through natural selection to browse without their aid; whereas in the calf, the teeth have been left unaffected, and on the principle of inheritance at corresponding ages have been inherited from a remote period to the present day. On the view of each organism with all its separate parts having been specially created, how utterly inexplicable is it that organs bearing the plain stamp of inutility, such as the teeth in the embryonic calf or the shrivelled wings under the soldered wing-covers of many beetles, should so frequently occur. Nature may be said to have taken pains to reveal her scheme of modification, by means of rudimentary organs, of embryological and homologous structures, but we are too blind to understand her meaning.

I have now recapitulated the facts and considerations which have thoroughly convinced me that species have been modified, during a long course of descent. This has been effected chiefly through the natural selection of numerous successive, slight, favourable variations; aided in an important manner by the inherited effects of the use and disuse of parts; and in an unimportant manner, that is in relation to adaptive structures, whether past or present, by the direct action of external conditions, and by variations which seem to us in our ignorance to arise spontaneously. It appears that I formerly underrated the frequency and value of these latter forms of variation, as leading to permanent modifications of structure independently of natural selection. But as my conclusions have lately been much misrepresented, and it has been stated that I attribute the modification of species exclusively to natural selection, I may be permitted to remark that in the first edition of this work, and subsequently, I placed in a most conspicuous position—namely, at the close of the Introduction—the following words: "I am convinced that natural selection has been the main but not the exclusive means of modification." This has been of no avail. Great is the power of steady misrepresentation; but the history of science shows that fortunately this power does not long endure.

It can hardly be supposed that a false theory would explain, in so satisfactory a manner as does the theory of natural selection, the several large classes of facts above specified. It has recently been objected that this is an unsafe method of arguing; but it is a method used in judging of the common events of life, and has often been used by the greatest natural philosophers. The undulatory theory of light has thus been arrived at; and the belief in the revolution of the earth on its own axis was until lately supported by hardly any direct evidence. It is no valid objection that science as yet throws no light on the far higher problem of the essence or origin of life. Who can explain what is the essence of the attraction of gravity? No one now objects to following out the results consequent on this unknown element of attraction; notwithstanding that Leibnitz formerly accused Newton of introducing "occult qualities and miracles into philosophy."

I see no good reason why the views given in this volume should shock the religious feelings of any one. It is satisfactory, as showing how transient such impressions are, to remember that the greatest discovery ever made by man, namely, the law of the attraction of gravity, was also attacked by Leibnitz, "as subversive of natural, and inferentially of revealed, religion." A celebrated author and divine has written to me that "he has gradually learnt to see that it is just as noble a conception of the Deity to believe that He created a few original forms capable of self-development into other and needful forms, as to believe that He required a fresh act of creation to supply the voids caused by the action of His laws."

Why, it may be asked, until recently did nearly all the most eminent living naturalists and geologists disbelieve in the mutability of species? It cannot be asserted that organic beings in a state of nature are subject to no variation; it cannot be proved that the amount of variation in the course of long ages is a limited quality; no clear distinction has been, or can be, drawn between species and well-marked varieties. It cannot be maintained that species when intercrossed are invariably sterile, and varieties invariably fertile; or that sterility is a special endowment and sign of creation. The belief that species were immutable productions was almost unavoidable as long as the history of the world was thought to be of short duration; and now that we have acquired some idea of the lapse of time, we are too apt to assume, without proof, that the geological record is so perfect that it would have afforded us plain evidence of the mutation of species, if they had undergone mutation.

But the chief cause of our natural unwillingness to admit that one species has given birth to clear and distinct species, is that we are always slow in admitting great changes of which we do not see the steps. The difficulty is the same as that felt by so many geologists, when Lyell first insisted that long lines of inland cliffs had been formed, the great valleys excavated, by the agencies which we see still at work. The mind cannot possibly grasp the full meaning of the term of even a million years; it cannot add up and perceive the full effects of many slight variations, accumulated during an almost infinite number of generations.

Although I am fully convinced of the truth of the views given in this volume under the form of an abstract, I by no means expect to convince experienced naturalists whose minds are stocked with a multitude of facts all viewed, during a long course of years, from a point of view directly opposite to mine. It is so easy to hide our ignorance under such expressions as the "plan of creation," "unity of design," &c., and to think that we give an explanation when we only re-state a fact. Any one whose disposition leads him to attach more weight to unexplained difficulties than the explanation of a certain number of facts will certainly reject the theory. A few naturalists, endowed with much flexibility of mind, and who have already begun to doubt the immutability of species, may be influenced by this volume; but I look with confidence to the future, to young and rising naturalists, who will be able to view both sides of the question with impartiality. Whoever is led to believe that species are mutable will do good service by conscientiously expressing his conviction; for thus only can the load of prejudice by which this subject is overwhelmed be removed.

Several eminent naturalists have of late published their belief that a multitude of reputed species in each genus are not real species; but that other species are real, that is, have been independently created. This seems to me a strange conclusion to arrive at. They admit that a multitude of forms, which till lately they themselves thought were special creations, and which are still thus looked at by the majority of naturalists, and which consequently have all the external characteristic features of true species,—they admit that these have been produced by variation, but they refuse to extend the same view to other and slightly different forms. Nevertheless they do not pretend that they can define, or even conjecture, which are the created forms of life, and which are those produced by secondary laws. They admit variation as a *vera causa* in one case, they arbitrarily reject it in another, without assigning any distinction in the two cases. The day will come when this will be given as a curious illustration of the blindness of preconceived opinion. These authors seem no more startled at a miraculous act of creation than at an ordinary birth. But do they really believe that at innumerable periods in the earth's history certain elemental atoms have been commanded suddenly to flash into living tissues? Do they believe that at each supposed act of creation one individual or many were produced? Were all the infinitely numerous kinds of animals and plants created as eggs or seed, or as full grown? and in the case of mammals, were they created bearing the false marks of nourishment from the mother's womb? Undoubtedly some of these same questions cannot be answered by those who believe in the appearance or creation of only a few forms of life, or of some one form alone. It has been maintained by several authors that it is as easy to believe in the creation of a million beings as of one; but Maupertuis' philosophical axiom "of least action" leads the mind more willingly to admit the smaller number;

and certainly we ought not to believe that innumerable beings within each great class have been created with plain, but deceptive, marks of descent from a single parent.

As a record of a former state of things, I have retained in the foregoing paragraphs, and elsewhere, several sentences which imply that naturalists believe in the separate creation of each species and I have been much censured for having thus expressed myself. But undoubtedly this was the general belief when the first edition of the present work appeared. I formerly spoke to very many naturalists on the subject of evolution, and never once met with any sympathetic agreement. It is probable that some did then believe in evolution, but they were either silent, or expressed themselves so ambiguously that it was not easy to understand their meaning. Now things are wholly changed, and almost every naturalist admits the great principle of evolution. There are, however, some who still think that species have suddenly given birth, through quite unexplained means, to new and totally different forms: but, as I have attempted to show, weighty evidence can be opposed to the admission of great and abrupt modifications. Under a scientific point of view, and as leading to further investigation, but little advantage is gained by believing that new forms are suddenly developed in an inexplicable manner from old and widely different forms, over the old belief in the creation of species from the dust of the earth.

It may be asked how far I extend the doctrine of the modification of species. The question is difficult to answer, because the more distinct the forms are which we consider, by so much the arguments in favour of community of descent become fewer in number and less in force. But some arguments of the greatest weight extend very far. All the members of whole classes are connected together by a chain of affinities, and all can be classed on the same principle, in groups subordinate to groups. Fossil remains sometimes tend to fill up very wide intervals between existing orders.

Organs in a rudimentary condition plainly show that an early progenitor had the organ in a fully developed condition; and this in some cases implies an enormous amount of modification in the descendants. Throughout whole classes various structures are formed on the same pattern, and at a very early age the embryos closely resemble each other. Therefore I cannot doubt that the theory of descent with modification embraces all the members of the same great class or kingdom. I believe that animals are descended from at most only four or five progenitors, and plants from an equal or lesser number.

Analogy would lead me one step farther, namely, to the belief that all animals and plants are descended from some one prototype. But analogy may be a deceitful guide. Nevertheless all living things have much in common, in their chemical composition, their cellular structure, their laws of growth, and their liability to injurious influences. We see this even in so trifling a fact as that the same poison often similarly affects plants and animals; or that the poison secreted by the gall-fly produces monstrous growths on the wild rose or oak-tree. With all organic beings excepting perhaps some of the very lowest, sexual production seems to be essentially similar. With all, as far as is at present known the germinal vesicle is the same; so that all organisms start from a common origin. If we look even to the two main divisions—namely, to the animal and vegetable kingdoms—certain low forms are so far intermediate in character that naturalists have disputed to which kingdom they should be referred. As Professor Asa Gray has remarked, "The spores and other reproductive bodies of many of the lower algæ may claim to have first a characteristically animal, and then an unequivocally vegetable existence." Therefore, on the principle of natural selection with divergence of character, it does not seem incredible that, from such low and intermediate form, both animals and plants may have been developed; and, if we admit this, we must likewise admit that all the organic beings which have ever lived on this earth may be descended from some one primordial form. But this inference is chiefly grounded on analogy and it is immaterial whether or not it be accepted. No doubt it is possible, as Mr. G. H. Lewes has urged, that at the first commencement of life many different forms were evolved; but if so we may conclude that only a very few have left modified descendants. For, as I have recently remarked in regard to the members of each great kingdom, such as the Vertebrata, Articulata &c., we have distinct evidence in their embryological homologous and rudimentary structures that within each kingdom all the members are descended from a single progenitor.

When the views advanced by me in this volume, and by Mr. Wallace, or when analogous views on the origin of species are generally admitted, we can dimly foresee that there will be a considerable revolution in natural history. Systematists will be able to pursue their labours as at present; but they will not be incessantly haunted by the shadowy doubt whether this or that form be a true species. This, I feel sure and I speak after experience, will be no slight relief. The endless disputes whether or not some fifty species of British brambles are good species will cease. Systematists will have only to decide (not that this will be easy) whether any form be sufficiently constant and distinct from other forms, to be capable of definition; and if definable, whether the differences be sufficiently important to deserve a specific name. This latter point will become a far more essential consideration than it is at present; for differences, however, slight, between any two forms if not blended by intermediate gradations, are looked at by most naturalists as sufficient to raise both forms to the rank of species.

Hereafter we shall be compelled to acknowledge that the only distinction between species and well-marked varieties is, that the latter are known, or believed, to be connected at the present day by intermediate gradations, whereas species were formerly thus connected. Hence, without rejecting the consideration of the present existence of intermediate gradations between any two forms we shall be led to weigh more carefully and to value higher the actual amount of difference between them. It is quite possible that forms now generally acknowledged to be merely varieties may hereafter be thought worthy of specific names; and in this case scientific and common language will come into accordance. In short, we shall have to treat species in the same manner as those naturalists treat genera, who admit that genera are merely artificial combinations made for convenience. This may not be a cheering prospect; but we shall at least be free from the vain search for the undiscovered and undiscoverable essence of the term species.

The other and more general departments of natural history will rise greatly in interest. The terms used by naturalists, of affinity, relationship, community of type, paternity, morphology, adaptive characters, rudimentary and aborted organs, &c., will cease to be metaphorical, and will have a plain signification. When we no longer look at an organic being as a savage looks at a ship, as something wholly beyond his comprehension; when we regard every production of nature as one which has had a long history; when we contemplate every complex structure and instinct as the summing up of many contrivances, each useful to the possessor, in the same way as any great mechanical invention is the summing up of the labour, the experience, the reason, and even the blunders of numerous workmen; when we thus view each organic being, how far more interesting—I speak from experience—does the study of natural history become!

A grand and almost untrodden field of inquiry will be opened, on the causes and laws of variation, on correlation, on the effects of use and disuse, on the direct action of external conditions, and so forth. The study of domestic productions will rise immensely in value. A new variety raised by man will be a more important and interesting subject for study than one more species added to the infinitude of already recorded species. Our classifications will come to be, as far as they can be so made, genealogies; and will then truly give what may be called the plan of creation. The rules for classifying will no doubt become simpler when we have a definite object in view. We possess no pedigrees or armorial bearings; and we have to discover and trace the many diverging lines of descent in our natural genealogies, by characters of any kind which have long been inherited. Rudimentary organs will speak infallibly with respect to the nature of long-lost structures. Species and groups of species which are called aberrant, and which may fancifully be called living fossils, will aid us in forming a picture of the ancient forms of life. Embryology will often reveal to us the structure, in some degree obscured, of the prototype of each great class.

When we feel assured that all the individuals of the same species, and all the closely allied species of most genera, have within a not very remote period descended from one parent, and have migrated from some one birth-place; and when we better know the many means of migration, then, by the light which geology now throws, and will continue to throw, on former changes of climate and of the level of the land, we shall surely be enabled to trace in an admirable manner the former migrations of the inhabitants of the whole world. Even at present, by comparing the differences between the inhabitants of the sea on the opposite sides of a continent, and the nature of the various inhabitants on that continent, in relation to their apparent means of immigration, some light can be thrown on ancient geography.

The noble science of Geology loses glory from the extreme imperfection of the record. The crust of the earth with its imbedded remains must not be looked at as a well-filled museum, but as a poor collection made at hazard and at rare intervals. The accumulation of each great fossiliferous formation will be recognised as having depended on an unusual concurrence of favourable circumstances, and the blank intervals between the successive stages as having been of vast duration. But we shall be able to gauge with some security the duration of these intervals by a comparison of the preceding and succeeding organic forms. We must be cautious in attempting to correlate as strictly contemporaneous two formations, which do not include many identical species, by the general succession of the forms of life. As species are produced and exterminated by slowly acting and still existing causes, and not by miraculous acts of creation; and as the most important of all causes of organic change is one which is almost independent of altered and perhaps suddenly altered physical conditions, namely, the mutual relation of organism to organism,—the improvement of one organism entailing the improvement or the extermination of others; it follows, that the amount of organic change in the fossil of consecutive formations probably serves as a fair measure of the relative though not actual lapse of time. A number of species, however, keeping in a body might remain for a long period unchanged, whilst within the same period several of these species by migrating into new countries and coming into competition with foreign associates, might become modified; so that we must not overrate the accuracy of organic change as a measure of time.

In the future I see open fields for far more important researches. Psychology will be securely based on the foundation already well laid by Mr. Herbert Spencer, that of the necessary acquirement of each mental power and capacity by gradation. Much light will be thrown on the origin of man and his history.

Authors of the highest eminence seem to be fully satisfied with the view that each species has been independently created. To my mind it accords better with what we know of the laws impressed on matter by the Creator, that the production and extinction of the past and present inhabitants of the world should have been due to secondary causes, like those determining the birth and death of the individual. When I view all beings not as special creations, but as the lineal descendants of some few beings which lived long before the first bed of the Cambrian system was deposited, they seem to me to become ennobled. Judging from the past, we may safely infer that not one living species will transmit its unaltered likeness to a distant futurity. And of the species now living very few will transmit progeny of any kind to a far distant futurity; for the manner in which all organic beings are grouped, shows that the greater number of species in each genus, and all the species in many genera, have left no descendants, but have become utterly extinct. We can so far take a prophetic glance into futurity as to foretell that it will be the common and widely-spread species, belonging to the larger and dominant groups within each class, which will ultimately prevail and procreate new and dominant species. As all the living forms of life are the lineal descendants of those which lived long before the Cambrian epoch, we may feel certain that the ordinary succession by generation has never once been broken, and that no cataclysm has desolated the whole world. Hence we may look with some confidence to a secure future of great length. And as natural selection works solely by and for the good of each being, all corporeal and mental endowments will tend to progress towards perfection.

It is interesting to contemplate a tangled bank, clothed with many plants of many kinds, with birds singing on the bushes, with various insects flitting about, and with worms crawling through the damp earth, and to reflect that these elaborately con-structed forms so different from each other, and dependent upon each other in so complex a manner, have all been produced by laws acting around us. These laws, taken in the largest sense, being Growth with Reproduction; Inheritance which is almost implied by reproduction; Variability from the indirect and direct action of the conditions of life and from use and disuse: a Ratio of Increase so high as to lead to a Struggle for Life, and as a consequence to Natural Selection, entailing Divergence of Character and the Extinction of less-improved forms. Thus, from the war of nature, from famine and death, the most exalted object which we are capable of conceiving, namely, the production of the higher animals, directly follows. There is grandeur in this view of life, with its several powers, having been originally breathed by the Creator into a few forms or into one; and that, whilst this planet has gone cycling on according to the fixed law of gravity, from so simple a beginning endless forms most beautiful and most wonderful have been, and are being evolved.

Charles Darwin, Conclusion from The Origin of the Species

1.   How did Darwin define evolution?

2.   Darwin maintained that the domestication and selective breeding of plants and animals by humans was similar to the processes that operated in nature.

a. True   b. False

3.   Darwin believed that the theory of evolution was incompatible with belief in the existence of God.

a. True   b. False

4.   Explain how natural selection works.

Thomas Kuhn*

ON THE STRUCTURE OF SCIENTIFIC REVOLUTIONS

I. Introduction: A Role for History

History, if viewed as a repository for more than anecdote or chronology, could produce a decisive transformation in the image of science by which we are now possessed. That image has previously been drawn, even by scientists themselves, mainly from the study of finished scientific achievements as these are recorded in the classics and, more recently, in the textbooks from which each new scientific generation learns to practice its trade. Inevitably, however, the aim of such books is persuasive and pedagogic; a concept of science drawn from them is no more likely to fit the enterprise that produced them than an image of a national culture drawn from a tourist brochure or a language text. This essay attempts to show that we have been misled by them in fundamental ways. Its aim is a sketch of the quite different concept of science that can emerge from the historical record of the research activity itself.

Even from history, however, that new concept will not be forthcoming if historical data continue to be sought and scrutinized mainly to answer questions posed by the unhistorical stereotype drawn from science texts. Those texts have, for example, often seemed to imply that the content of science is uniquely exemplified by the observations, laws, and theories described in their pages. Almost as regularly, the same books have been read as saying that scientific methods are simply the ones illustrated by the manipulative techniques used in gathering textbook data, together with the logical operations employed when relating those data to the textbook's theoretical generalizations. The result has been a concept of science with profound implications about its nature and development.

If science is the constellation of facts, theories, and methods collected in current texts, then scientists are the men who, successfully or not, have striven to contribute one or another element to that particular constellation. Scientific development becomes the piecemeal process by which these items have been added, singly and in combination, to the ever growing stockpile that constitutes scientific technique and knowledge. And history of science becomes the discipline that chronicles both these successive increments and the obstacles that have inhibited their accumulation. Concerned with scientific development, the historian then appears to have two main tasks. On the one hand, he must determine by what man and at what point in time each contemporary scientific fact, law, and theory was discovered or invented. On the other, he must describe and explain the congeries of error, myth, and superstition that have inhibited the more rapid accumulation of the constituents of the modern science text. Much research has been directed to these ends, and some still is.

In recent years, however, a few historians of science have been finding it more and more difficult to fulfil the functions that the concept of develop-

*Thomas Kuhn (1922–   ) earned his Ph.D. in Physics at Harvard. He has taught at Princeton, Harvard, Berkeley, and the Massachusetts Institute of Technology. He is the author of *The Copernican Revolution: Planetary Astronomy in the Development of Western Thought, Black-Body Theory and Quantum Discontinuity,* and *The Essential Tension.* The following selection is taken from his seminal work, *The Structure of Scientific Revolutions* (1962), in which he argued for a historical and sociological understanding of the practice of science.

ment-by-accumulation assigns to them. As chroniclers of an incremental process, they discover that additional research makes it harder, not easier, to answer questions like: When was oxygen discovered? Who first conceived of energy conservation? Increasingly, a few of them suspect that these are simply the wrong sorts of questions to ask. Perhaps science does not develop by the accumulation of individual discoveries and inventions. Simultaneously, these same historians confront growing difficulties in distinguishing the "scientific" component of past observation and belief from what their predecessors had readily labeled "error" and "superstition." The more carefully they study, say, Aristotelian dynamics, phlogistic chemistry, or caloric thermodynamics, the more certain they feel that those once current views of nature were, as a whole, neither less scientific nor more the product of human idiosyncrasy than those current today. If these out-of-date beliefs are to be called myths, then myths can be produced by the same sorts of methods and held for the same sorts of reasons that now lead to scientific knowledge. If, on the other hand, they are to be called science, then science has included bodies of belief quite incompatible with the ones we hold today. Given these alternatives, the historian must choose the latter. Out-of-date theories are not in principle unscientific because they have been discarded. That choice, however, makes it difficult to see scientific development as a process of accretion. The same historical research that displays the difficulties in isolating individual inventions and discoveries gives ground for profound doubts about the cumulative process through which these individual contributions to science were thought to have been compounded.

The result of all these doubts and difficulties is a historiographic revolution in the study of science, though one that is still in its early stage. Gradually, and often without entirely realizing they are doing so, historians of science have begun to ask new sorts of questions and to trace different, and often less than cumulative, developmental lines for the sciences. Rather than seeking the permanent contributions of an older science to our present vantage, they attempt to display the historical integrity of that science in its own time. They ask, for example, not about the relation of Galileo's views to those of modern science, but rather about the relationship between his views and those of his group, i.e., his teachers, contemporaries, and immediate successors in the sciences. Furthermore, they insist upon studying the opinions of that group and other similar ones from the viewpoint—usually very different

from that of modern science—that gives those opinions the maximum internal coherence and the closest possible fit to nature. Seen through the works that result, works perhaps best exemplified in the writings of Alexandre Koyré, science does not seem altogether the same enterprise as the one discussed by writers in the older historiographic tradition. By implication, at least, these historical studies suggest the possibility of a new image of science. This essay aims to delineate that image by making explicit some of the new historiography's implications.

What aspects of science will emerge to prominence in the course of this effort? First, at least in order of presentation, is the insufficiency of methodological directives, by themselves, to dictate a unique substantive conclusion to many sorts of scientific questions. Instructed to examine electrical or chemical phenomena, the man who is ignorant of these fields but who knows what it is to be scientific may legitimately reach any one of a number of incompatible conclusions. Among those legitimate possibilities, the particular conclusions he does arrive at are probably determined by his prior experience in other fields, by the accidents of his investigation, and by his own individual makeup. What beliefs about the stars, for example, does he bring to the study of chemistry or electricity? Which of the many conceivable experiments relevant to the new field does he elect to perform first? And what aspects of the complex phenomenon that then results strike him as particularly relevant to an elucidation of the nature of chemical change or of electrical affinity? For the individual, at least, and sometimes for the scientific community as well, answers to questions like these are often essential determinants of scientific development. We shall note, for example, that the early developmental stages of most sciences have been characterized by continual competition between a number of distinct views of nature, each partially derived from, and all roughly compatible with, the dictates of scientific observation and method. What differentiated these various schools was not one or another failure of method—they were all "scientific"—but what we shall come to call their incommensurable ways of seeing the world and of practicing science in it. Observation and experience can and must drastically restrict the range of admissible scientific belief, else there would be no science. But they cannot alone determine a particular body of such belief. An apparently arbitrary element, compounded of personal and historical accident, is always a formative ingredient of the beliefs espoused by a given scientific community at a given time.

That element of arbitrariness does not, however, indicate that any scientific group could practice its trade without some set of received beliefs. Nor does it make less consequential the particular constellation to which the group, at a given time, is in fact committed. Effective research scarcely begins before a scientific community thinks it has acquired firm answers to questions like the following: What are the fundamental entities of which the universe is composed? How do these interact with each other and with the senses? What questions may legitimately be asked about such entities and what techniques employed in seeking solutions? At least in the mature sciences, answers (or full substitutes for answers) to questions like these are firmly embedded in the educational initiation that prepares and licenses the student for professional practice. Because that education is both rigorous and rigid, these answers come to exert a deep hold on the scientific mind. That they can do so does much to account both for the peculiar efficiency of the normal research activity and for the direction in which it proceeds at any given time. When examining normal science we shall want finally to describe that research as a strenuous and devoted attempt to force nature into the conceptual boxes supplied by professional education. Simultaneously, we shall wonder whether research could proceed without such boxes, whatever the element of arbitrariness in their historic origins and, occasionally, in their subsequent development.

Yet that element of arbitrariness is present, and it too has an important effect on scientific development. Normal science, the activity in which most scientists inevitably spend almost all their time, is predicated on the assumption that the scientific community knows what the world is like. Much of the success of the enterprise derives from the community's willingness to defend that assumption, if necessary at considerable cost. Normal science, for example, often suppresses fundamental novelties because they are necessarily subversive of its basic commitments. Nevertheless, so long as those commitments retain an element of the arbitrary, the very nature of normal research ensures that novelty shall not be suppressed for very long. Sometimes a normal problem, one that ought to be solvable by known rules and procedures, resists the reiterated onslaught of the ablest members of the group within whose competence it falls. On other occasions a piece of equipment designed and constructed for the purpose of normal research fails to perform in the anticipated manner, revealing an anomaly that cannot, despite repeated effort, be

aligned with professional expectation. In these and other ways besides, normal science repeatedly goes astray. And when it does—when, that is, the profession can no longer evade anomalies that subvert the existing tradition of scientific practice—then begin the extraordinary investigations that lead the profession at last to a new set of commitments, a new basis for the practice of science. The extraordinary episodes in which that shift of professional commitments occurs are the ones known in this essay as scientific revolutions. They are the tradition-shattering complements to the tradition-bound activity of normal science.

The most obvious examples of scientific revolutions are those famous episodes in scientific development that have often been labeled revolutions before. Therefore, where the nature of scientific revolutions is first directly scrutinized, we shall deal repeatedly with the major turning points in scientific development associated with the names of Copernicus, Newton, Lavoisier, and Einstein. More clearly than most other episodes in the history of at least the physical sciences, these display what all scientific revolutions are about. Each of them necessitated the community's rejection of one time-honored scientific theory in favor of another incompatible with it. Each produced a consequent shift in the problems available for scientific scrutiny and in the standards by which the profession determined what should count as an admissible problem or as a legitimate problem-solution. And each transformed the scientific imagination in ways that we shall ultimately need to describe as a transformation of the world within which scientific work was done. Such changes, together with the controversies that almost always accompany them, are the defining characteristics of scientific revolutions.

These characteristics emerge with particular clarity from a study of, say, the Newtonian or the chemical revolution. It is, however, a fundamental thesis of this essay that they can also be retrieved from the study of many other episodes that were not so obviously revolutionary. For the far smaller professional group affected by them, Maxwell's equations were as revolutionary as Einstein's, and they were resisted accordingly. The invention of other new theories regularly, and appropriately, evokes the same response from some of the specialists on whose area of special competence they impinge. For these men the new theory implies a change in the rules governing the prior practice of normal science. Inevitably, therefore, it reflects upon much scientific work they have already successfully completed. That is why a new theory, however special its range of application, is seldom or never just an increment to what is already known. Its assimilation requires the reconstruction of prior theory and the re-evaluation of prior fact, an intrinsically revolutionary process that is seldom completed by a single man and never overnight. No wonder historians have had difficulty in dating precisely this extended process that their vocabulary impels them to view as an isolated event.

Nor are new inventions of theory the only scientific events that have revolutionary impact upon the specialists in whose domain they occur. The commitments that govern normal science specify not only what sorts of entities the universe does contain, but also, by implication, those it does not. It follows, though the point will require extended discussion, that a discovery like that of oxygen or X-rays does not simply add one more item to the population of the scientist's world. Ultimately it has that effect, but not until the professional community has re-evaluated traditional experimental procedures, altered its conception of entities with which it has long been familiar, and, in the process, shifted the network of theory through which it deals with the world. Scientific fact and theory are not categorically separable, except perhaps within a single tradition of normal-scientific practice. That is why the unexpected discovery is not simply factual in its import and why the scientist's world is qualitatively transformed as well as quantitatively enriched by fundamental novelties of either fact or theory.

Undoubtedly, some readers will already have wondered whether historical study can possibly effect the sort of conceptual transformation aimed at here. An entire arsenal of dichotomies is available to suggest that it cannot properly do so. History, we too often say, is a purely descriptive discipline. The theses suggested above are, however, often interpretive and some sometimes normative. Again, many of my generalizations are about the sociology or social psychology of scientists; yet at least a few of my conclusions belong traditionally to logic or epistemology. In the preceding paragraph I may even seem to have violated the very influential contemporary distinction between "the context of discovery needed" and "the context of justification." Can anything more than profound confusion be indicated by this admixture of diverse fields and concerns?

Having been weaned intellectually on these distinctions and others like them, I could scarcely be more aware of their import and force. For many years I took them to be about the nature of knowledge, and I still suppose that, appropriately recast, they have something important to tell us. Yet my attempts to apply them, even *grosso modo,* to the actual situations in which knowledge is gained, accepted, and assimilated have made them seem extraordinarily problematic. Rather than being elementary logical or methodological distinctions, which would thus be prior to the analysis of scientific knowledge, they now seem integral parts of a traditional set of substantive answers to the very questions upon which they have been deployed. That circularity does not at all invalidate them. But it does make them parts of a theory and, by doing so, subjects them to the same scrutiny regularly applied to theories in other fields. If they are to have more than pure abstraction as their content, then that content must be discovered by observing them in application to the data they are meant to elucidate. How could history of science fail to be a source of phenomena to which theories about knowledge may legitimately be asked to apply?

II. The Route to Normal Science

In this essay, 'normal science' means research firmly based upon one or more past scientific achievements, achievements that some particular scientific community acknowledges for a time as supplying the foundation for its further practice. Today such achievements are recounted, though seldom in their original form, by science textbooks, elementary and advanced. These textbooks expound the body of accepted theory, illustrate many of all of its successful applications, and compare these applications with exemplary observations and experiments. Before such books became popular early in the nineteenth century (and until even more recently in the newly matured sciences), many of the famous classics of science fulfilled a similar function. Aristotle's *Physica,* Ptolemy's *Almagest,* Newton's *Principia* and *Opticks,* Franklin's *Electricity,* Lavoisier's *Chemistry,* and Lyell's *Geology—* these and many other works served for a time implicitly to define the legitimate problems and methods of a research field for succeeding generations of practitioners. They were able to do so because they shared two essential characteristics. Their achievement was sufficiently unprecedented to attract an enduring group of adherents away from competing modes of scientific activity. Simultaneously, it was sufficiently open-ended to leave all sorts of problems for the redefined group of practitioners to resolve.

Achievements that share these two characteristics I shall henceforth refer to as 'paradigms,' a term that relates closely to 'normal science.' By choosing it, I mean to suggest that some accepted examples of actual scientific practice—examples which include law, theory, application, and instrumentation together—provide models from which spring particular coherent traditions of scientific research. These are the traditions which the historian describes under such rubrics as 'Ptolemaic astronomy' (or 'Copernican'), 'Aristotelian dynamics' (or 'Newtonian'), 'corpuscular optics' (or 'wave optics'), and so on. The study of paradigms, including many that are far more specialized than those named illustratively above, is what mainly prepares the student for membership in the particular scientific community with which he will later practice. Because he there joins men who learned the bases of their field from the same concrete models, his subsequent practice will seldom evoke overt disagreement over fundamentals. Men whose research is based on shared paradigms are committed to the same rules and standards for scientific practice. That commitment and the apparent consensus it produces are prerequisites for normal science, i.e., for the genesis and continuation of a particular research tradition.

If the historian traces the scientific knowledge of any selected group of related phenomena backward in time, he is likely to encounter some minor variant of a pattern here illustrated from the history of physical optics. Today's physics textbooks tell the student that light is photons, i.e., quantum-mechanical entities that exhibit some characteristics of waves and some of particles. Research proceeds accordingly, or rather according to the more elaborate and mathematical characterization from which this usual verbalization is derived. That characterization of light is, however, scarcely half a century old. Before it was developed by Planck, Einstein, and others early in this century, physics texts taught that light was transverse wave motion, a conception rooted in a paradigm that derived ultimately from the optical writings of Young and Frensel in the early nineteenth century. Nor was the wave theory the first to be embraced by almost all practitioners of optical science. During the eighteenth century the paradigm for this field was provided by Newton's *Opticks,* which taught that light was material corpuscles. At that time physicists sought evidence, as the early wave theorists had not, of the pressure exerted by light particles impinging on solid bodies.[1]

These transformations of the paradigms of physical optics are scientific revolutions, and the successive transition from one paradigm to another via revolution is the usual developmental pattern of mature science. It is not, however, the pattern characteristic of the period before Newton's work, and that is the contrast that concerns us here. No period between remote antiquity and the end of the seventeenth century exhibited a single generally accepted view about the nature of light. Instead there were a number of competing schools and sub schools, most of them espousing one variant or another of Epicurean, Aristotelian, or Platonic theory. One group took light to be particles emanating from material bodies; for another it was a modification of the medium that intervened between the body and the eye; still another explained light in terms of an interaction of the medium with an emanation from the eye; and there were other combinations and modifications besides. Each of the corresponding schools derived strength from its relation to some particular metaphysic, and each emphasized, as paradigmatic observations, the particular cluster of optical phenomena that its own theory could do most to explain. Other observations were dealt with by *ad hoc* elaborations, or they remained as outstanding problems for further research.[2]

At various times all these schools made significant contributions to the body of concepts, phenomena, and techniques from which Newton drew the first nearly uniformly accepted paradigm for physical optics. Any definition of the scientist that excludes at least the more creative members of these various schools will exclude their modern successors as well. Those men were scientists. Yet anyone examining a survey of physical optics before Newton may well conclude that, though the field's practitioners were scientists, the net result of their activity was something less than science. Being able to take no common body of belief for granted, each writer on physical optics felt forced to build his field anew from its foundations. In doing so, his choice of supporting observation and experiment was relatively free, for there was no standard set of methods or of phenomena that every optical writer felt forced to employ and explain. Under these circumstances, the dialogue of the resulting books was often directed as much to the members of other

---

[1] Joseph Priestly, *The History and Present State of Discoveries Relating to Vision, Light, and Colours* (London, 1772), pp. 385–90.

[2] Vasco Ronchi, *Historie de la lumière,* trans. Jean Taton (Paris, 1956), chaps. i–iv.

schools as it was to nature. That pattern is not unfamiliar in a number of creative fields today, nor is it incompatible with significant discovery and invention. It is not, however, the pattern of development that physical optics acquired after Newton and that other natural sciences make familiar today.

The history of electrical research in the first half of the eighteenth century provides a more concrete and better known example of the way a science develops before it acquires its first universally received paradigm. During that period there were almost as many views about the nature of electricity as there were important electrical experimenters, men like Hauksbee, Gray, Desaguliers, Du Fay, Nollett, Watson, Franklin, and others. All their numerous concepts of electricity had something in common—they were partially derived from one or an other version of the mechanico-corpuscular philosophy that guided all scientific research of the day. In addition, all were components of real scientific theories, of theories that had been drawn in part from experiment and observation and that partially determined the choice and interpretation of additional problems undertaken in research. Yet though all the experiments were electrical and though most of the experimenters read each other's works, their theories had no more than a family resemblance.[3]

One early group of theories, following seventeenth-century practice, regarded attraction and frictional generation as the fundamental electrical phenomena. This group tended to treat repulsion as a secondary effect due to some sort of mechanical rebounding and also to postpone for as long as possible both discussion and systematic research on Gray's newly discovered effect, electrical conduction. Other "electricians" (the term is their own) took attraction and repulsion to be equally elementary manifestations of electricity and modified their theories and research accordingly. (Actually, this group is remarkably small—even Franklin's theory never quite accounted for the mutual repulsion of two negatively charged bodies.) But they had as much difficulty as the first group in accounting simultaneously for any but the simplest conduction

effects. Those effects, however, provided the starting point for still a third group, one which tended to speak of electricity as a "fluid" that could run through conductors rather than as an "effluvium" that emanated from non-conductors. This group, in its turn, had difficulty reconciling its theory with a number of attractive and repulsive effects. Only through the work of Franklin and his immediate successors did a theory arise that could account with something like equal facility for very nearly all these effects and that therefore could and did provide a subsequent generation of "electricians" with a common paradigm for its research.

Excluding those fields, like mathematics and astronomy, in which the first firm paradigms date from prehistory and also those, like biochemistry, that arose by division and recombination of specialties already matured, the situations outlined above are historically typical. Though it involves my continuing to employ the unfortunate simplification that tags an extended historical episode with a single and somewhat arbitrarily chosen name (e.g., Newton or Franklin), I suggest that similar fundamental disagreements characterized, for example, the study of motion before Aristotle and of statics before Archimedes, the study of heat before Black, of chemistry before Boyle and Boerhaave, and of historical geology before Hutton. In parts of biology—the study of heredity, for example—the first universally received paradigms are still more recent; and it remains an open question what parts of social science have yet acquired such paradigms at all. History suggests that the road to a firm research consensus is extraordinarily arduous.

History also suggests, however, some reason for the difficulties encountered on that road. In the absence of a paradigm or some candidate for paradigm, all of the facts that could possibly pertain to the development of a given science are likely to seem equally relevant. As a result, early fact-gathering is a far more nearly random activity than the one that subsequent scientific development makes familiar. Furthermore, in the absence of a reason for seeking some particular form of more recondite information, early fact-gathering is usu-

---

[3]Duane Roller and Duane H. D. Roller, *The Development of the Concept of Electric Charge: Electricity from the Greeks to Coulomb* ("Harvard Case Histories in Experimental Science," Case 8; Cambridge, Mass., 1954); and I. B. Cohen, *Franklin and Newton: An Inquiry into Speculative Newtonian Experimental Science and Franklin's Work in Electricity as an Example Thereof* (Philadelphia, 1956), chaps vii–xii. For some of the analytic detail in the paragraph that follows in the text, I am indebted to a still unpublished paper by my student John L. Heilbron. Pending its publication, a somewhat more extended and more precise account of the emergence of Franklin's paradigm is included in T. S. Kuhn, "The Function of Dogma in Scientific Research," in A. C. Crombie (ed.), "Symposium on the History of Science, University of Oxford, July 9–15, 1961," to be published by Heinemann Educational Books, Ltd.

ally restricted to the wealth of data that lie ready to hand. The resulting pool of facts contains those accessible to casual observation and experiment together with some of the more esoteric data retrievable from established crafts like medicine, calendar making, and metallurgy. Because the crafts are one readily accessible source of facts that could not have been casually discovered, technology has often played a vital role in the emergence of new sciences.

But though this sort of fact-collecting has been essential to the origin of many significant sciences, anyone who examines, for example, Pliny's encyclopedic writings or the Baconian natural histories of the seventeenth century will discover that it produces a morass. One somehow hesitates to call the literature that results scientific. The Baconian "histories" of heat, color, wind, mining, and so on, are filled with information, some of it recondite. But they juxtapose facts that will later prove revealing (e.g., heating by mixture) with others (e.g., the warmth of dung heaps) that will for some time remain too complex to be integrated with theory at all.[4] In addition, since any description must be partial the typical natural history often omits from its immensely circumstantial accounts just those details that later scientists will find sources of important illumination. Almost none of the early "histories" of electricity, for example, mention that chaff, attracted to a rubbed glass rod, bounces off again. That effect seemed mechanical, not electrical.[5] Moreover, since the casual fact-gatherer seldom possesses the time or the tools to be critical the natural histories often juxtapose descriptions like the above with others, say, heating by antiperistasis (or by cooling), that we are now quite unable to confirm.[6] Only very occasionally, as in the cases of ancient statics, dynamics, and geometrical optics, do facts collected with so little guidance from preestablished theory speak with sufficient clarity to permit the emergence of a first paradigm.

This is the situation that creates the schools characteristic of the early states of a science's development. No natural history can be interpreted in the absence of at least some implicit body of intertwined theoretical and methodological belief that permits selection, evaluation, and criticism. If that body of belief is not already implicit in the collection of facts—in which case more than "mere facts" are at hand—it must be externally supplied, perhaps by a current metaphysic, by another science, or by personal and historical accident. No wonder, then, that in the early stages of the development of any science different men confronting the same range of phenomena, but not usually all the same particular phenomena, describe and interpret them in different ways. What is surprising, and perhaps also unique in its degree to the fields we call science, is that such initial divergences should ever largely disappear.

For they do disappear to a very considerable extent and then apparently once and for all. Furthermore, their disappearance is usually caused by the triumph of one of the pre-paradigm schools, which, because of its own characteristic beliefs and preconceptions, emphasized only some special part of the too sizable and inchoate pool of information. Those electricians who thought electricity a fluid and therefore gave particular emphasis to conduction provide an excellent case in point. Led by this belief, which could scarcely cope with the known multiplicity of attractive and repulsive effects, several of them conceived the idea of bottling the electrical fluid. The immediate fruit of their efforts was the Leyden jar, a device which might never have been discovered by a man exploring nature casually or at random, but which was in fact independently developed by at least two investigators in the early 1740's.[7] Almost from the start of his electrical researches, Franklin was particularly concerned to explain that strange and, in the event, particularly revealing piece of special apparatus. His success in doing so provided the most effective of the arguments that made his theory a paradigm, though one that was still unable to account for quite

---

[4]Compare the ketch for a natural history of heat in Bacon's *Novum Organun,* Vol. VIII of *The Works of Francis Bacon,* ed. J. Spedding, R. L. Ellis, and D. D. Heath (New York, 1869), pp. 179–203.

[5]Roller and Roller, *op. cit.,* pp. 14, 22, 28, 43. Only after the work recorded in the last of these citations do repulsive effects gain general recognition as unequivocally electrical.

[6]Bacon, *op. cit.,* pp. 235, 337, says "Water slightly warm is more easily frozen than quite cold." For a partial account of the earlier history of this strange observation, see Marshall Clagett, *Giovanni Marliani and Late Medieval Physics* (New York, 1941), chap. iv.

[7]Roller and Roller, *op. cit.,* pp. 51–54.

all the known cases of electrical repulsion.[8] To be be accepted as a paradigm, a theory must seem better than its competitors, but it need not, and in fact never does, explain all the facts with which it can be confronted.

What the fluid theory of electricity did for the subgroup that held it, the Franklinian paradigm later did for the entire group of electricians. It suggested which experiments would be worth performing and which, because directed to secondary or to overly complex manifestations of electricity, would not. Only the paradigm did the job far more effectively, partly because the end of interschool debate ended the constant reiteration of fundamentals and partly because the confidence that they were on the right track encouraged scientists to undertake more precise, esoteric, and consuming sorts of work.[9] Freed from the concern with any and all electrical phenomena, the united group of electricians could pursue selected phenomena in far more detail, designing much special equipment for the task and employing it more stubbornly and systematically than electricians had ever done before. Both fact collection and theory articulation became highly directed activities. The effectiveness and efficiency of electrical research increased accordingly, providing evidence for a social version of Francis Bacon's acute methodological dictum: "Truth emerges more readily from error than from confusion."[10]

We shall be examining the nature of this highly directed or paradigm-based research in the next section, but must first note briefly how the emergence of a paradigm affects the structure of the group that practices the field. When, in the development of a natural science, an individual or group first produces a synthesis able to attract most of the next generation's practitioners, the older schools gradually disappear. In part their disappearance is caused by their members' conversion to the new paradigm. But there are always some men who cling to one or another of the older views, and they are simply read out of the profession, which thereafter ignores their work. The new paradigm implies a new and more rigid definition of the field. Those unwilling or unable to accommodate their work to it must proceed in isolation or attach themselves to some other group.[11] Historically, they have often simply stayed in the departments of philosophy from which so many of the special sciences have been spawned. As these indications hint, it is sometimes just its reception of a paradigm that transforms a group previously interested merely in the study of nature into a profession or, at least, a discipline. In the sciences (though not in fields like medicine, technology, and law, of which the principal *raison d'être* is an external social need), the formation of specialized journals, the foundation of specialists' societies, and the claim for a special place in the curriculum have usually been associated with a group's first reception of a single paradigm. At least this was the case between the time, a century and a half ago, when the institutional pattern of scientific specialization first developed and the very recent time when the paraphernalia of specialization acquired a prestige of their own.

---

[8]The troublesome case was the mutual repulsion of negatively charged bodies, for which see Cohen, *op. cit.*, pp. 491–94, 531–43.

[9]It should be noted that the acceptance of Franklin's theory did not end quite all debate. In 1759 Robert Symmer proposed a two-fluid version of that theory, and for many years thereafter electricians were divided about whether electricity was a single fluid or two. But the debates on this subject only confirm what has been said above about the manner in which a universally recognized achievement unites the profession. Electricians, though they continued divided on this point, rapidly concluded that no experimental tests could distinguish the two versions of the theory and that they were therefore equivalent. After that, both schools could and did exploit all the benefits that the Franklinian theory provided (*ibid.*, pp. 543–46, 548–54).

[10]Bacon, *op. cit.*, p. 210.

[11]The history of electricity provides an excellent example which could be duplicated from the careers of Priestley, Kelvin, and others. Franklin reports that Nollet, who at mid-century was the most influential of the Continental electricians, "lived to see himself the last of his Sect, except Mr. B.—his Eleve and immediate Disciple" (Max Farrand [ed.], *Benjamine Franklin's Memoirs* [Berkeley, Calif., 1949], pp. 384–86). More interesting, however, is the endurance of whole schools in increasing isolation from professional science. Consider, for example, the case of astrology, which was once an integral part of astronomy. Or consider the continuation of the late eighteenth and early nineteenth centuries of a previously respected tradition of "romantic" chemistry. This is the tradition discussed by Charles C. Gillispie in "The *Encyclopédie* and the Jacobin Philosophy of Science: A Study in Ideas and Consequences," *Critical Problems in the History of Science*, ed. Marshall Clagett (Madison, Wis., 1959), pp. 255–89; and "The Formation of Lamarck's Evolutionary Theory," *Archives internationales d'historie des sciences*, XXXVII (1956), 323–38.

The more rigid definition of the scientific group has other consequences. When the individual scientist can take a paradigm for granted, he need no longer, in his major works, attempt to build his field anew, starting from first principles and justifying the use of each concept introduced. That can be left to the writer of textbooks. Given a textbook, however, the creative scientist can begin his research where it leaves off and thus concentrate exclusively upon the subtlest and most esoteric aspects of the natural phenomena that concern his group. And as he does this, his research communiqués will begin to change in ways whose evolution has been too little studied but whose modern end products are obvious to all and oppressive to many. No longer will his researches usually be embodied in books addressed, like Franklin's *Experiments . . . on Electricity* or Darwin's *Origin of Species,* to anyone who might be interested in the subject matter of the field. Instead they will usually appear as brief articles addressed only to professional colleagues, the men whose knowledge of a shared paradigm can be assumed and who prove to be the only ones able to read the papers addressed to them.

Today in the sciences, books are usually either texts or retrospective reflections upon one aspect or another of the scientific life. The scientist who writes one is more likely to find his professional reputation impaired than enhanced. Only in the earlier, pre-paradigm, stages of the development of the various sciences did the book ordinarily possess the same relation to professional achievement that it still retains in other creative fields. And only in those fields that still retain the book, with or without the article, as a vehicle for research communication are the lines of professionalization still so loosely drawn that the layman may hope to follow progress by reading the practitioner's original reports. Both in mathematics and astronomy, research reports had ceased already in antiquity to be intelligible to a generally educated audience. In dynamics, research became similarly esoteric in the later Middle Ages, and it recaptured general intelligibility only briefly during the early seventeenth century when a new paradigm replaced the one that had guided medieval research. Electrical research began to require translation for the layman before the end of the eighteenth century, and most other fields of physical science ceased to be generally accessible in the nineteenth. During the same two centuries similar transitions can be isolated in the various parts of the biological sciences. In parts of the social sciences they may well be occurring today. Although it has become customary, and is surely proper, to deplore the widening gulf that separates the professional scientist from his colleagues in other fields, too little attention is paid to the essential relationship between that gulf and the mechanisms intrinsic to scientific advance.

Ever since prehistoric antiquity one field of study after another has crossed the divide between what the historian might call its prehistory as a science and its history proper. These transitions to maturity have seldom been so sudden or so unequivocal as my necessarily schematic discussion may have implied. But neither have they been historically gradual, coextensive, that is to say, with the entire development of the fields within which they occurred. Writers on electricity during the first four decades of the eighteenth century possessed far more information about electrical phenomena than had their sixteenth-century predecessors. During the half-century after 1740, few new sorts of electrical phenomena were added to their lists. Nevertheless, in important respects, the electrical writings of Cavendish, Coulomb, and Volta in the last third of the eighteenth century seem further removed from those of Gray, Du Fay, and even Franklin than are the writings of these early eighteenth century electrical discoverers from those of the sixteenth century.[12] Sometime between 1740 and 1780, electricians were for the first time enabled to take the foundations of their field for granted. From that point they pushed on to more concrete and recondite problems, and increasingly they then reported their results in articles addressed to other electricians rather than in books addressed to the learned world at large. As a group they achieved what had been gained by astronomers in antiquity and by students of motion in the Middle Ages, of physical optics in the late seventeenth century, and of historical geology in the early nineteenth. They had, that is, achieved a paradigm that proved able to guide the whole group's research. Except with the advantage of hindsight, it is hard to find another criterion that so clearly proclaims a field a science.

---

[12]The post-Franklinian developments include an immense increase in the sensitivity of charge detectors, the first reliable and generally diffused techniques for measuring charge, the evolution of the concept of capacity and its relation to a newly refined notion of electric tension, and the quantification of electrostatic force. On all of these see Roller and Roller, *op. cit.,* pp. 66–81; W. C. Walker, "The Detection and Estimation of Electric Charges in the Eighteenth Century," *Annals of Science,* I (1936), 66–100; and Edmund Hoppe, *Geschichte der Elektrizität* (Leipzig, 1884), Part I, chaps. iii–iv.

Thomas Kuhn, On The Structure of Scientific Revolutions

1.   According to Kuhn, historical research has revealed that

    a.   out-of date theories are not in principle unscientific.
    b.   science does not develop by individual discoveries and inventions.
    c.   the development of science is not just a process of accumulation facts, theories, and methods.
    d.   all of the above.
    e.   none of the above.

2.   In the absence of a paradigm, all scientific work is impossible.

    a.   True   b.   False

3.   Identify three different paradigms in the history of science.

    a. _____

    b. _____

    c. _____

4.   Why is the establishment of a paradigm so important in the development of a science?

Steven and Hilary Rose*

THE MYTH OF THE NEUTRALITY OF SCIENCE

One of the key items of intellectual baggage which most practicing scientists carry over from their training—there are not many such, for few scientific training programs have more than a passing reference to theory—is one labelled "the neutrality of science." Briefly stated the phrase may be explained thus: "The activities of science are morally and socially value-free. Science is the pursuit of natural laws, laws which are valid irrespective of the nation, race, politics, religion or class position of their discoverer. Although science proceeds by a series of approximations to a never-attained objective truth, the laws and facts of science have an immutable quality. The velocity of light is the same whoever makes the experiment which measures it. Because this is the case, although the uses to which society may put science may be good or evil, the scientist carries no special responsibility for those uses, save as a normal citizen. The two-edged sword of science is fashioned for whomsoever will pick it up and wield it."

Thus, a recent analysis of the social responsibility of the scientist by a Nobel laureate, E. B. Chain, italicized the statement that "science, as long as it limits itself to the descriptive study of the laws of nature, has no moral or ethical quality and this applies to the physical as well as the biological sciences."[1]

It is this set of beliefs and ideas concerning the neutrality of science which has begun to wear the aspect of a myth, which while at present ubiquitous in socialist and capitalist, industrialized and non-industrialized societies, none the less is of relatively recent origin. Our purpose here is to challenge this myth, to reveal it for what it is, for it is our feeling that the unthinking, unquestioning acceptance of it as gospel has been to a large degree responsible for the anti-social applications—the non-human or inhuman uses—of science, which have strongly contributed to many of the world's major problems.

If we treat the neutrality of science as a myth, we are then committed to attempting to discuss a series of questions: How has the myth emerged? What role has it played? How has the myth been challenged? How far does the future of science and of human survival itself depend on our ability to transcend and refashion such myths of science? These are dauntingly large questions, yet it is inescapably clear that they form the agenda of increasing numbers of socially aware scientists, and that they reflect the intellectual and moral crisis of contemporary science.

The Emergence of the Myth of Pure Science

It is widely accepted that the modern activity of science emerged and began to find its social and philosophical articulation in post-Renaissance Europe, and rather specifically in seventeenth-century Britain. That science was seen as a progressive

---

*Steven Rose is Professor of Biology at London's Open University. Hilary Rose is Professor of Applied Social Studies at the University of Bradford in England. In the following selection, which was published in 1971, the Roses challenge the claim that scientific research is independent of moral and political values.

[1]E. B. Chain, "The Social Responsibility of the Scientist," *New Scientist,* October 22, 1970.

From SCIENCE AND LIBERATION by Steven and Hilary Rose. South End Press. Reprinted by permission.

force, closely linked to the enhancement of human welfare, is clear from the writings of Francis Bacon and the founders of the Royal Society. For Bacon, knowledge for knowledge's sake, or for power's sake, was subordinate to knowledge for charity's sake, for "of charity there can be no excess." And for the chemist, Sir Robert Boyle, science was for "the greater glory of God and for the good of mankind."

But this clarity of purpose did not survive into the eighteenth century in Britain, where science became an activity for a cultured, moneyed and leisured class. It is no accident that the term "scientist" did not exist in Britain until the mid-nineteenth century; the phrase actually used was "a cultivator of science." In France, too, rigid social stratification made the Academie des Sciences a cultured gentlemen inventor's club until its degeneration and transformation following the 1789 Revolution. And the discrepancy between "aristocratic" and "citizen's" science even then contributed to the death of Lavoisier.

The Industrial Revolution in the nineteenth century saw the continuation and hardening of this gulf. The rigid amateurism of the Royal Society precipitated the formation of alternative institutions more clearly integrated with the needs of burgeoning capitalism, such as the Midland industrialists' Lunar Society, which embraced Wedgwood, Boulton, Watt and Dalton, and later Babbage's British Association for the Advancement of Science. Yet such was the forward thrust of the scientific temper that Lunar Society members were attacked for their radical political views and sympathy to the French Revolution, while the debates at the early British Association raised such fundamental questions as to convince a magistrate that "science and learning, if universally diffused, would speedily overturn the best-constituted government on earth." The movement in Britain towards working-class scientific education in the mid-nineteenth century reflected a constant tension between Establishment fears of the revolutionary potential of scientific thought and recognition of the needs of capitalist society for a more skilled worker.

The conflicts were equally in evidence in the rest of Europe. France saw the emergence of the strange scientific religion of St. Simonism, whilst in Germany the *naturphilosophen,* with their speculative attempts to synthesize science and natural knowledge into an all-embracing scheme of the world, conflicted with the more arid traditions of the university scholar. Eventually, the universities digested this development; "pure" science emerged as a university discipline uncontaminated with relevance to anything, and the *Technische Hochschulen* concentrated on the practical side of science and industry's needs, contributing to the success of the German science-based industries, which served the nation so well right into the First World War.

The development of socialist materialist ideas in the later nineteenth century, and particularly those of Marxism, set these tensions into a new frame; Marxism claimed to be a scientific socialism. It applied the techniques and dialectical methods of the natural sciences to the disordered world of human affairs. Socialism was seen to be on the side of history, and science was on the side of socialism. Major theoretical scientific advances contributed to the interpretation of society; Marx, like the conservative Herbert Spencer, saw the value of a biological metaphor for human activities. It is well known that Marx wished to dedicate one of the volumes of *Das Kapital* to Darwin, who declined the honor. At the same time Darwinism found itself recruited to service the needs of racists and eugenicists.

Nor was it just biology which was seen as both deriving impetus from, and contributing to, social analysis. The inmost heart of science itself—fundamental physics—could be interpreted in terms of dialectical materialism and in the *Dialectics of Nature* Engels attempts precisely this major task: a theoretical re-interpretation of the whole of science, as then perceived, as exemplifying the workings of the dialectic—a degree of grand theorizing which has daunted most later Marxists.

Engels' attempt to interpret the activities of science as conforming to the workings of the dialectic was extended by later Marxists, but could only expect to achieve recognition in practical policies subsequent to the Soviet Revolution of 1917. But even in the Soviet Union, it was not until ten years after the revolution, when the at times uneasy truce of experts and professionals with the Party which typified the period of the New Economic Policy was coming to an end, that a specific attempt was made to break with the ideology of pure science which still dominated the Academy of Sciences. The period of Five-Year Plans and the march towards socialism was typified, as Joravsky has documented, by a fresh attempt to define a "socialist physics," "socialist biology," and so forth.[2]

The form of such a socialist science was uncertain and open to debate. What was clear was that

---

[2]D. Joravsky, *Soviet Marxism and National Science,* London, Routledge & Kegan Paul, 1961.

it ought to be different from "capitalist" science, and that in this scheme of things, there was no such thing as "pure" science.

"Pure" science was simultaneously under ideological attack not only from the left, but from the right, for the emergent Nazism of Germany was beginning to talk of "Aryan" and "non-Aryan" (i.e. Jewish) science. Some branches of physics, notably Einsteinian relativity and quantum theory, were under attack for their non-Aryan quality, and there were cases when the same type of physics was attached both for its non-Aryanism and for its non-socialist, "idealist" nature.

The reaction to these attacks upon its self-perceived integrity by the majority of the scientific community was predictable. In Germany and the Soviet Union, the response was one which Haberer has characterized as the politics of "prudential acquiescence."[3] This acquiescence led in Germany to the dismissal of Jewish university scientists and the official acceptance of an openly racialist biology, justifying the organized and monstrous slaughter of the concentration camps. In the Soviet Union, it took the milder form of prudential acquiescence in the systematic destruction of a particular field of science, genetics, and the exile or silencing of its protagonists.

In pre-war Britain, the debate took a different turn. Traditional empiricism reduced a discussion of whether the internal logic of science itself was ideologically determined to one concerning the harnessing of science to human welfare. Radical and Marxist scientists generated a wave of optimism about the prospects and significance of science as a factor in the liberation of humankind. This opinion is typified by Bernal, writing just before the Second World War.

> Science puts into our hands the means of satisfying our material needs. It gives us also the ideas which will enable us to understand, to co-ordinate and to satisfy our needs in the social sphere. Beyond this, science has something important to offer: a reasonable hope in the unexplored possibilities of the future, an inspiration which is slowly but surely becoming the dominant driving force of modern thought and action.[4]

To achieve this effect science must be rationally planned and organized. In an appropriate social structure, science would inevitably proceed so as to enhance human welfare. Even this proposition, however, resulted in much of the academic community closing ranks against the onslaught, proclaiming its self-interested purity with virginal fastidiousness. Polanyi provided the philosophical rationale and Baker the organizational steam for a Society for Freedom in Science, whose exponents demanded independence of the Republic of Science. This claim found voice in the complaint that the Bernalians proposed to direct science to such an extent that a microscopist would not even be allowed to choose what color to stain his preparations.

War, and the mobilization of the scientific community in the prosecution of war, made the debate meaningless. Even the most prudential of the German scientists found themselves involved in the war effort—some Jewish scientists even managed to survive the war in their laboratories. In Britain, the purest of academics were registered and drafted into war research. And in the United States, the biggest scientific mobilization the world had ever seen, the Manhattan Project, took place. The Republic of Science became a dream of peace which science, even when the peace at length came, was never really to recover.

By the end of the war, the era of Big Science had arrived, ushered in by the explosions at Hiroshima and Nagasaki, and the debates of the 1930s seemed strangely irrelevant. Science was paid for by the government; the largest part of this payment was for war (defense) science, but governmental and industrial research contracts permeated the universities, too. At first opposed, at least in Britain, by the end of the 1950s such a permeation was being actively welcomed. In the United States, of course, it always has been, for there the concept of academic freedom was one of freedom for the scientific entrepreneur, typified by the archetypal Dr. Grant Swinger, the mythical money-hunting scientist created by Dan Greenberg, of *Science* magazine. The key to American economic and scientific success was seen in precisely this articulation by university, industry and government. Its devotees urged the creation, in Britain and elsewhere in Europe, of

[3]J. Haberer, *Politics and the Community of Science,* New York, Van Nostrand-Reinhold, 1969.

[4]J. D. Bernal, *The Social Function of Science,* London, Routledge & Kegan, Paul, 1939; also Cambridge, Massachusetts, MIT Press, 1967.

local versions of the impressive "Route 128," the highway which is lined with science-based industries which have sprung out of research at the mighty Massachusetts Institute of Technology.

The acceptance and rationalization of this new conventional wisdom may be plotted as a function of the emergence in many nations, over the late 1950s and through the 1960s, of science policy-making committees and Ministers of Science—an inconceivable prospect in the 1930s, except amongst the Bernalians, though advocated by some prescient individuals as far back as the 1850s. By 1970, indeed, something like an academic discipline (meta-discipline) of "science policy" has emerged. For such policymakers, the suggestion that science should *not* be locked into the national economy, making its appropriate contribution to national goals, is risible. National goals may even be specifically technological, such as the commitment of Kennedy to put an American on the moon by 1970. And in a technologically based society, the preservation of the scientocracy and technocracy's neutrality and independence from governmental process has become impossible.

Meanwhile science and technology are judged by their economic and political pay-off for the nation. British participation in the proposed 300 GeV particle accelerator at CERN was ruled out by the Labor Government in 1968 precisely on the grounds that no economic pay-off in the short or middle term could be perceived from it; a cheaper version was ruled in again by the Conservative Government in 1970 on the grounds of the national advantage to be gained politically by close scientific links with Europe.

The Present Status of the Myth

What then of the present status of the myth of the neutrality of science? Surprisingly, it has not withered *pari passu* with the emergence of Big Science. The reasons for this seem to relate back in part to the debate of the 1930s and 1940s on neutrality. For many scientists the debate effectively ended during a confrontation in Moscow between the agronomist Lysenko and his critics. Lysenko, defending his own "Michurinist" (or modified Lamarckian) biology, against the "idealist" and "quasi-fascist" genetics attributed to Mendel, Morgan and Weissman, and against the rump of Soviet geneticists, finally clinched his argument by reveal-

ing that his views had the approval of Stalin himself. The revelation of the distortions introduced by the imposition of Lysenkoism in Soviet biology threw Marxist Western scientists into a state of intellectual disarray. Some left the Party, like Haldane. Most retreated from an outspoken defense of the prospects of a socialist science into a more neutralist position.

A second, and perhaps still more important factor in strengthening the neutrality of science idea arose from the dilemma faced by many physicists who had taken part, many with the noblest of intentions, in the Manhattan Project. Believing that Hitler was developing the Bomb and that Hitler must be stopped and Fascism destroyed, what choice was there but to attempt to provide a Bomb for the Allies?

The fact that Hitler was not on the way to getting an atomic bomb, and that the ones that the physicists had made were used on Hiroshima and Nagasaki, provoked a crisis of conscience. If their profession was to be saved, and their consciences salved, they needed to discriminate between the effects of this use of their physics, and the physics itself: the physics has to be neutral, only the use to which it is put need be condemned. And as more and more it became apparent that, in the West, science was being applied to evil ends, the need to maintain the distinction between the subject and its use became sharper. For precisely those who in the past had argued that the link between science and human progress was inevitable, the retreat back to the laboratory and its neutrality became a necessity *if they were not to stop doing science altogether.*

An interesting parallel evolution seems to have taken place in the Soviet Union. Again, it may be related both to the failure of Lysenkoism and to the success of the Bomb. It is exemplified by the changing Soviet view on nuclear weapons. In the early 1950s the official view still reflected a belief that technology could be made to serve man's ends. The Bomb was seen as an adjunct to, but not a transformation of, the class war, which by definition must be victorious. The language of nuclear holocaust, the Doomsday machine, and the jargon of the United States arms control experts was repugnant. But by 1970, this view was no longer held in the Soviet Union. The Bomb is now seen as transforming war.[5]

The jargon of the two super powers is a mutual one, the language of the strategic arms limitation

---

[5]N. Moss, *Men Who Play God,* Harmondsworth, Middlesex, The Penguin Press, 1970.

talks (SALT). Technology is seen to be just as sweetly inevitable to the Soviets as it was to Oppenheimer, when asked his views on the American H-bomb. And the corollary of technological inevitability is neutrality. "Science," a distinguished Soviet physicist assured one of us recently, "is neutral; it is how one uses it which determines its good or evil potential."

The Reaction Against Science

It is only in the last few years that this ubiquitous acceptance of a science simultaneously closely articulated into the bureaucratic, military and industrial machine of contemporary society, and yet freed from responsibility, of the ethos of the god-given right of the scientist to ask for the money he wants from the government, and to do research on what the government and he like when he gets it, has been effectively challenged. Partly, the challenge has taken the form of a wave of anti-science and the deliberate advocacy of non-rational forms of truth, of a refusal by many young people to do science—a phenomenon anxiously analyzed as the "swing from science" by governmental committees in several nation. Partly, it has been a rediscovery of the ideological issues by science and engineering students, who have become increasingly politicized by the general ferment in the universities which is occurring as practically a world-wide phenomenon.

And partly, it has undoubtedly been catalyzed by the repercussions of events following the Cultural Revolution in China in the late 1960s. For the Maoists in China resuscitated old arguments about the relationship of science and scientists to the people. With their insistence on egalitarianism, the down-grading of the expert, and the demand that his/her work should "serve the people," they made a demand whose echoes were those of the populist scientist artisans of the French Revolution, who closed the Academie des Sciences and helped send Lavoisier to the guillotine.

For Western Maoists, science is valid—and correct—only in so far as it is ideologically sound; its internal logic is totally subordinated to the ideological demands made upon it. It is scarcely surprising that virtually the only overt defenders of Lysenko to be found today, in or out of the Soviet Union, are the Maoist students.

For the less ideologically coherent, the rejection of neutral science has been enlarged to embrace a rejection of all science as irrevocably linked with the instruments of State oppression. The relationship perceived by Marcuse between the products of contemporary physics and the needs of IBM and the U.S. Atomic Energy Commission has, we have argued elsewhere, resulted in a specific rejection, not only of the sciences of the Establishment, but of the whole methodological apparatus and rationality of science itself.[6]

It is against this background, the re-opened questions of the continuance of science itself and of its ideological inputs, that the 1960s and 1970s have seen the emergence in several countries of Societies for Social Responsibility in Science. These groups have disparate views, but they are all linked in a common attempt to restate the values and the methods of science and the possibilities of harnessing it for constructive purposes, to recognize the ideological inputs inherent in science which the consensus politics of West and East of the last fifteen years have obscured, and to recreate a critical science. The objectives of such groups must be to use the critical methods of science to analyze and where necessary combat the social implications of particular kinds of science. This means taking issue with certain bits of science itself.

The Philosophical Issues

This compressed discussion of more than three centuries of philosophical, methodological and ideological debate has of necessity had to make a number of sweeping generalizations. Having both chronicled and asserted the validity of a particular point of view in this debate we now attempt to state more clearly what we mean when we question the validity of the claim that science is neutral.

One way of doing this is to document the nature of the constraints that operate on the activity of science within the present system. But, if we recognize that Big Science is State financed and that there is always more possible science than actual science, as well as more ideas about what to do than people or money to do them, the debate is, in a sense, short-circuited. Science policy means making choices about what science to do. Whoever makes these choices, by definition they cannot be ideology- or value-free, they imply an acceptance of certain directions for science and not others. Putting a man on the moon means not doing other sorts of things. Such choices are inherent in any system. And as

---

[6]H. Rose and S. Rose, *Science and Society,* London, The Penguin Press, 1969.

they are clearly not neutral choices, the science they generate cannot be neutral.

This is easiest to see, of course, in such obviously applied fields as space technology. But it can be seen in other fields as well. In biology, for example, when an American woman scientist was awarded the United States Army's highest civilian award for the development of a more effective form of rice-blast fungus, specifically suited to Southeast Asian conditions, this award was clearly not given for neutral science.

But what about the basic science that led up to this work, which may not have been done under military contract or in a defense establishment? Take the development of the tear-gas CS, now extensively used in Vietnam, for example. This gas was developed in the mid-1950s by Britain's chemical defense establishment at Porton Down, as a result of a recognition of the inadequacies of the then-used tear gas, CN, on a number of technical criteria. Researchers at Porton began their search for a new agent as a result of a specific directive from the British Ministry of Defense. In the course of screening a number of possible agents they came across CS. Bulk production followed. Thus the work was done for a specific objective; it was clearly not value-free, by definition not neutral. Porton work was plainly mission-oriented. As a mission cannot be neutral, the science done in achieving it cannot either.

But what about the work from which the Porton studies were derived? Are we to indict Corson and Stoughton, back in the 1920s, for the initial observation that ortho-chlorobenzylidene-malonitrile was a lacrymator, just because thirty years later Porton picked it up and used it for a new purpose?

If this is the case, we should indict not only Corson and Stoughton but also all the other hundreds or thousands or academic researchers doing their "pure" research in the laboratories of the 1920s, churning out their three papers a year on the properties of odd chemicals and the behaviour of model systems, simply because they were working in the ambience of a society whose structure imposes a consequence not in harmony with human welfare. We would have to indict not merely Rutherford and Einstein for the atomic bomb, but practically all the chemists, physicists, mathematicians and biologists who have published research in the present century. Plainly, this is a *reductio ad absurdum*.

It might then be argued that there is a cut-off point in the neutrality debate: non-mission-oriented basic research, whose immediate application is not apparent, might seem excluded from it. At a pragmatic level, such a common sense idea might seem acceptable, provided the research was not sponsored by a fund-giving agency or organization with a mission other than the support of basic science for its own sake, such as a Department of Defense or industry. Particle physics and molecular biology might seem to come into this category.

While such a view might appear sound enough as a rule of thumb for everyday practical purposes, it avoids recognition of the possible interconnections between science as a cognitive system and the social system. That is, it assumes that, whatever the goal choices made by funding agencies, within those financial constraints the actual content of the science which is done depends only on the objective accretion of data, facts and theories. It thus implies a purely "internalist" view of the nature of scientific knowledge, as a set of ever-advancing and self-consistent absolute approaches to a statement of "truth" about the universe.

This view of science, though, is one that has come under serious challenge recently from the philosophers of science. Thus, the activity of scientists can be divided, according to the illuminating insight of Kuhn, into "normal" science and "revolutionary" science.[7] Normal science is what most scientists do all the time, and all scientists do most of the time; it is solving a set of puzzles about the natural world. The puzzles are designed and solved in terms of a paradigm, a gestalt view of the world, which provides a framework for normal science. At certain periods in science, and for a variety of only partially understood reasons, Kuhn argues, there occurs a paradigm switch, a change in the gestalt view of the world among working scientists which alters the puzzles they set themselves. This paradigm-switching is what Kuhn calls revolutionary science: problem-solving instead of puzzle-solving.

Kuhn's concept of revolutionary science may be suspect; what is sure is that his view of normal puzzle-solving science strikes an answering chord from many working scientists who recognize it as an accurate description of their activity, so different from the pompous proposals of verification, falsification and hypothesis-making which they were always supposed to be doing by philosophers in the past.

[7]T. S. Kuhn, *The Structure of Scientific Revolutions*, Chicago, IL, University of Chicago Press, 1970.

Corson and Stoughton's work, like that of the great majority of scientists, is essentially of the puzzle-solving kind. What we wish to propose here is that, while it is not possible to ascribe a "value," a measurement of non-neutrality, to all single pieces of puzzle-solving basic science of this type, it is possible to ascribe a value to the paradigm within which they are conducted. Puzzle-solving basic science of itself, unlike mission-oriented science or development, cannot have either neutrality or non-neutrality ascribed to it; the concepts are irrelevant. They are relevant only to the paradigm within which the puzzle-solving activity is being conducted.

But a paradigm is never value-free. A paradigm is never neutral. Hence while we do not have to search for non-neutrality, or its moral congener, responsibility, in the work of a particular puzzle-solving scientist, we find it without difficulty in the paradigm within which s/he is working. To put it in other terms, and to answer the question which we raised earlier, while we cannot indict Corson and Stoughton and other puzzle-solving basic scientists for their "pure" research because of the uses to which their results are put independently of them, we assert that their work is non-neutral because the paradigm within which it is done is non-neutral.

Let us take some perhaps obvious examples of the non-neutrality of some biological paradigms. The framework of evolutionary biology set by the Darwinian revolution of the 1850s was one in which the central metaphors, drawn from society, and in their turn interacting with society, were of the competition of species, the struggle for existence, the ecological niche, and the survival of the fittest—a set of metaphors which closely reflected the norms of the society in which they arose, and contributed to the subsequent development of its ideology by giving it a seemingly "inevitable" biological base. The metaphors replaced earlier ones which located biology firmly into an explanation of a god-designed universe. Using these metaphors, a vast amount of puzzle-solving research has been conducted.

Today's central biological metaphors are framed in a different language system; they refer to control, communication and community, feedback and interaction, metaphors certainly more appropriate to the managed society in which we move today—and indeed, by virtue of a group of determined ethological extrapolators such as Morris and Lorenz, going some way to provide it with a biological rationale as well. And once again, today's puzzle-solving science is conducted within the framework provided by the metaphors.

The paradigm—the metaphor—sets the questions we ask of our subject, and hence the answers we seek from our materials. If a behaviour geneticist asks the question, "How much does heredity determine intelligence?" the person has limited the answers to the question before beginning the empirical research—that is, s/he has located the answer within a particular paradigm. It is the question and its framework, not so much the answer, which are non-neutral, their historical antecedents belonging in the line of eugenics stretching back to Galton and beyond. And we should not be surprised to find this type of research providing certain types of answers, which are then clearly related to certain social and political purposes.

It is not that the question should not be asked, but that we need to be very clear about the nature of the paradigm which sponsors it and which, within the limits of the data, specifies the answer, as it must for all puzzle-solving research. For much of science, the analysis of possible non-neutral components in specific paradigms is very difficult. It may well be that it is only in periods of social and intellectual crisis that we can glimpse the interconnections between science and the social system.

To suggest the non-neutrality of science is, we realize, not merely to recognize the passing of a myth—a myth which has nurtured academic science, and its considerable achievements, for more than a hundred years. To reject the myth also comes close to taking away another leg from the already wobbling basic tenet of scientific philosophy—that of the objectivity of the natural sciences. Admittedly this is a tenet that the philosopher-physicists of the Copenhagen School have in their time taken a healthy crack at and been attacked as idealists in consequence. It is a tenet, too, which has been under attack in contemporary biology, for the seeming success of the reductionist, objective techniques in such fields as molecular biology has begun to generate a counter-attack, an anti-reductionism which again poses the central problems of the relationship, in biology, between observer and observed.[8]

None the less, this is not to deny the validity of science's inner logic, that the advance of science, despite the shifting perspective of its paradigms, presents successively more accurate approximations to comprehensive statements about the nature of

[8]D. McKay, "The Bankruptcy of Determinism," *New Scientist,* July 2, 1970.

the universe. The way in which people see the world may vary with their viewpoint, but the variation will be confined within the crucial limitation that, for all of us, our viewpoint is human; there is a finite specification to the way in which our brains function, and to the relationship of this functioning to the environment.

Hence, in so far as objectivity specifies a public viewpoint that is more or less common to all people, there is an objective internal logic to science, which new techniques, experimentation and paradigms help refine. The universe may be (can be?) solved in this sense, granted time—and a paradigm which does not precipitate disaster. But the language in which the solution will be framed will depend upon the paradigm; of the infinity of questions we can ask about the universe, we will choose some of them and not others from within the ideological framework set by the paradigm.

When, as they now are, issues of human survival are on the agenda, it means that the time has come when it is right to assert, as a necessary counter-myth, that it is possible to use the techniques and methods of science for people-centered and not people-destroying purposes; that we must build human relevance into the paradigms of science itself.

From Abstraction to Action

How do we even begin to translate those abstractions into a concrete program for action? There are four distinct areas of activity possible.

First, scientists themselves have to become aware of the social, political and economic pressures affecting the development of science. They must learn the significance of the old saying, "he who pays the piper calls the tune," for all science in general and for their own science in particular. They have to find out how decisions are made, in and for science, and, where these decisions are concealed and undemocratic, expose them, working with the community at large to open the decision-making processes and make them democratically accountable.

At the same time, scientists will be wise to recognize that their criticisms will not necessarily endear them to those who pay for their research. They cannot afford to be as naive as those mathematicians in the United States who publicly deplored the massive abuse of science and technology in Vietnam and were then surprised when the Department of Defense threatened to cut off their research funds.

Second, scientists must learn to communicate not only with the community at large but also with their colleagues. They must be willing—and able—to explain what work they are doing, and why, and to speak out plainly if they feel that the social implications of their work are ambiguous or dangerous. They cannot afford to leave this communication task to the professional communicators alone; communication is not merely a matter of professional expertise but of moral responsibility. It is no longer adequate for the scientists to retire to their ivory-towered laboratories, emerging only to share the mutually congratulatory blandnesses of the scientific establishment. They have to learn to speak out.

But speaking out does not mean cheap sensationalism or wild prophesy of doom. To preach a sort of technological fatalism, of the inevitability of scientific and technological advance in this or that direction, is not merely irresponsible, it is to misunderstand the nature of science and its links with the social order. It is to subscribe to the myth of the scientific and technological imperative.

Nor does speaking out imply the carrying of apparently bulky but in reality lightweight burdens of specious moral responsibility about potential future abuses, the sort of attitudinizing morality of several biologists who have become concerned at prospects of "genetic engineering" for example. It is not the scientists' responsibility to carry this burden—if indeed it is a real one—and it distracts attention from the real issues of survival that are on today's agenda.

Third, the problem of science education and course content must be tackled. We cannot continue to educate as scientists individuals who are not taught to be aware of the pressures on, and real value of the activity by which they will subsequently earn their living. Science must cease to be taught; as it is in almost all countries of the world, in a sort of moral and social vacuum, as if there were no relations between the activities of the laboratory and the "real world" outside. Present experiments in which ways of introducing social relevance into science education are being attempted, need to be evaluated, improved and extended.

Finally, and most important, even having done all this, the scientists cannot merely sigh with relief, return to the laboratories with a "business as usual" sign up and get back to their favored research topics. They must instead ask themselves the question, "How can my scientific skills best be used to serve the people; to expose and correct the role of science and technology in wreaking genocide in wars, in oppressing individuals and minorities by acting as an agency of civil power, and in permitting malnutrition and disease both throughout the world at large, and even in rich societies?''

We are not facing a single once-and-for-all crisis in science but rather a chronic condition where the world, made one by massive science and technology, lurches either towards barbarism or progress. Survival itself demands revolutionary changes in society, and a precondition of this in a scientific society is the mobilization of the scientific community.

Where once revolutionary activity was argued for as a guarantor of progress, we now have to argue for its necessity as a guarantor against barbarism.

Steven and Hilary Rose, The Myth of the Neutrality of Science

1.   Some scientists believe that science is value-neutral because

    a.   scientists aim to discover the laws of nature.
    b.   the laws of nature are valid for all peoples at all times.
    c.   scientific knowledge can be used for either good or evil.
    d.   all of the above.
    e.   none of the above.

2.   What is mission oriented research? Why do the Roses believe that it can never be value-free and politically neutral?

3.   The Roses maintain that paradigms are never value-free or neutral.

    a.   True   b.   False

4.   Which of the following is *not* a component of the Roses' proposed program of action?

    a.   Scientists themselves have to become aware of the pressures affecting the development of science.
    b.   Scientists must learn to communicate with the community and their colleagues about their work.
    c.   Science must cease to be taught in a moral and social vacuum.
    d.   Scientists must ask themselves how their skills can best be used to serve the people.
    e.   None of the above.

III. MATHEMATICS AND THE NATURAL SCIENCES

LIST OF KEY TERMS

geometry:

definition:

postulate:

common notion or axiom:

theorem:

teleological explanation:

mechanistic explanation:

determinism:

law of nature:

Ptolemaic Theory:

Copernican Theory:

indeterminism:

probability:

Heisenberg's Principle of Uncertainty:

natural selection:

evolution:

idols:

inductivism:

theory:

prediction:

evidence:

normal science:

paradigm:

anomaly:

scientific revolution:

mission-oriented research:

basic research:

SECTION IV
THE SOCIAL SCIENCES

THEME QUESTIONS

1. What distinguishes the social sciences from the natural sciences? Is there a distinctive methodology and mode of explanation that social scientists employ?

2. Should social phenomena be investigated and explained in terms of the individuals who compose society or must they be explained in terms of society as a whole?

3. Is value neutrality possible in the social sciences? Should social scientists be morally and politically neutral in the conduct of their work?

4. What distinguishes the social sciences from the humanities?

Introduction to the Social Sciences

Kendall Blanchard

A story is told about a group of clerics in a 13th-century monastic order in Europe that was trying to determine the number of teeth contained in the mouth of a horse. The group searched through the scriptures and the writings of the church fathers at great length. But the answer to their question was nowhere to be found. Recognizing the limitations of the group's approach to the problem, one of the younger less experienced monks suggested that perhaps the best way to determine how many teeth were in the mouth of a horse would be to open the horse's mouth and count them. The story has it that he was subsequently stoned to death for his audacity.

The story may be apocryphal, but it illustrates the way in which values, moral norms, and traditions influence and shape the approach to truth. It also illustrates how in the era before the European Renaissance truth by revelation took precedence over truth by experience. In other words, knowing was the result of revealed evidence or truth by authority. It was from within this context of an intellectual world governed by the canons of Christian scripture and theology that modern science ultimately emerged.

The physical or natural sciences were the first to establish themselves. People like Roger Bacon with his inventions, Copernicus and Galileo with their discoveries regarding interplanetary relationships, and Leonardo da Vinci with his careful attention to the details of anatomy, helped to establish the theoretical foundations of science. Gradually the scientific way of knowing, with its emphasis on objective reality, experimentation, and inductive reasoning became a legitimate alternative to knowing by revelation.

The social sciences grew out of the physical sciences and predominantly the work of 16th, 17th, and 18th-century philosophers such as Hobbes, Hume, Locke, More, Machiavelli, Rousseau, and others. Rene Descartes, in particular, was instrumental in the development of principles that made legitimate the application of scientific procedures to the study of human behavior. And this is what the social sciences are about: the study of human beings and human institutions. As one writer has suggested, the social sciences are "those mental or cultural sciences which deal with the activities of the individual as a member of a group" (Seligman, 1930:3).

In one sense, then, the social scientific way of knowing has its roots in the Renaissance and in the writings of many of the great thinkers of the post-Renaissance era. However, the scientific study of human society did not actually emerge as a set of distinct disciplines until well into the 19th century. A variety of historical circumstances led to the emergence of these disciplines and the distinctive ways of knowing they represent. Perhaps the most important of these historical circumstances were the French Revolution and the Industrial Revolution; the former for the form of democracy it created and the latter for the major economic and social changes it wrought. Specifically, these events led to massive population growth, urbanization, new technology, and novel forms of labor, and innovative means of production (e.g., the factory). The conditions begged for analysis, and in many ways the emergence of the social sciences can be seen as a response to that need.

During the mid-19th century the social sciences began to take shape as individual disciplines, yet sharing common concerns and responding to similar theoretical influences. The major ideological themes of the period were positivism, humanitarianism, evolutionism, and comparativism. Positivism is the idea that the only truth is that which can be experienced directly by the senses (i.e., the basis for scientific truth). Humanitarianism is the concern for the welfare of the disadvantaged. Evolutionism is the idea that change of all types, social, biological, cultural, is a part of a larger systematic process of evolution. Comparativism is a method that assumes that the comparison of similar categories of behavior (e.g., burial customs, kinships

118

systems) leads to a better understanding of human nature in general. These themes run through the writings of the major social thinkers of the 19th and early 20th centuries: Auguste Comte, Emile Durkheim, Karl Marx, Max Weber, Herbert Spencer, Jean-Baptiste Say, Jeremy Bentham, John Austin, Edward Tylor, Lewis Henry Morgan, and others.

Social thought in the 18th century envisaged a single social science, a unified approach to the study of human behavior. However, the trend toward specialization led to a splintering of social thought so that eventually what might have been "social science" became by the mid-19th century the "social sciences." Today, the social sciences encompass a wide range of academic enterprises, specializations, and disciplines. These disciplines include economics, sociology, political science, social statistics, anthropology, geography, and psychology.

The social sciences of today share many paradigms, theoretical models, and methods of data collection and analysis. All have as their most important objective the understanding of human behavior. In this sense they are all formal responses to the question "What makes people tick?" They represent a distinctive way of knowing: knowing by observing, describing, and analyzing human behavior from a scientific perspective. At the same time, the social sciences are different from the natural sciences. Human behavior is in many ways a more complex, elusive, and unpredictable subject than those things studied by astronomers, physicists, geologists, and chemists. The social sciences are also different from each other. Each has its own special way or ways of knowing.

Economics, considered by some to be the oldest of the social sciences, is likewise a special way of knowing. Economists study the way goods and services are produced, distributed, and consumed. More specifically, those who study modern economic systems focus on economic choices that people make in the effort to satisfy what are virtually insatiable wants with scarce or limited resources. Knowing from an economic perspective, according to John Kenneth Galbraith in the article on economics included in this section, focuses on "what we earn and what we can get for it." The economist understands human beings as laborers, managers, and consumers. Human behavior is most likely to be explained by the economist in economic terms. Knowing like an economist means looking below the surface of ordinary behavior to such causative factors as subsistence needs, acquisitiveness, maximization of assets, market forces, and consumer preferences. For the economist, these are the types of things that make human beings tick.

Sociology is the social science that studies human behavior in the context of social relations and group life. Sociologists tend to focus on the concept of "society," defined as a collection of people who interact on a regular basis, share a common culture, and think of themselves as a self-perpetuating group that will exist well beyond the lives of its current membership. The sociologist knows by understanding human behavior as a product of one's participation in society. Emile Durkheim, in the selections from his *Rules of Sociological Method* that are included in this section, argues that the basic data of sociology, "social facts," have an objective reality. In other words, they are to be viewed as "things" not unlike oak trees, fire hydrants, and elbows. Durkheim illustrates how "social facts" can have a constraining effect on behavior. He also provides a list of principles that one should use in the isolation, description, and analysis of social facts. The sociological perspective, then, is one that explains by reference to social context. For example, a sociologist, in trying to understand why a particular individual has committed a crime, will in most cases attempt to sort out the root social causes of that crime: the criminal's socioeconomic class, family life, living conditions, peer groups, and other social facts. In sum, social reality is for the sociologist a perspective and a principal way of understanding or knowing human behavior.

Psychology is similar to the other social sciences in that its principal focus is on human behavior. However, it is different in that it looks at that behavior as though its explanation were internal to the individual. Durkheim refers to the data of psychology as "psychical facts" and suggests that contrary to social facts these data are "internal by definition." Psychologists tend to focus on such concepts as self, personality, mind, and consciousness. This is the distinctive nature of psychology's way of knowing. The psychologist who is trying to understand the same criminal that the sociologist above is studying, in contrast to that sociologist, would most likely ask questions about mental health, intelligence, cognitive frame of reference, value system, sense of self, and other aspects of the criminal's inner life. Knowing is penetrating, understanding, and analyzing the mind.

However, not all psychologists study behavior from this internal perspective. Behavioral psychologists in particular see behavior as external to the individual. John B. Watson, one of the principal forces behind the development of behaviorism in psychology, argues in the article included in this section that one understands what people do by observing stimulus and response. So objective is the methodology proposed by Watson he concludes that behaviorism is "a true natural science." It should be noted, however, that behaviorists from Watson to B. F. Skinner have tended to be overly ambitious in their judgement of behavioral psychology's importance and must be viewed as only one of many forces which shape modern academic psychology.

Carol Gilligan, in her article "Woman's Place in Man's Life Cycle," is a bit less ambitious than Watson. Gilligan suggests that even in science, "categories of knowledge are human constructions" and that observations can be significantly affected by the gender or theoretical bias of the observer. Citing various life-cycle studies, she calls into question the value of such studies that analyze female behavior from the perspective of male standards.

Political Science is the study of government, its structure and its function. The discipline is typically divided into several independent fields of study that include international politics, comparative politics, home-country politics, and political philosophy. For the political scientist, knowing is a process of understanding the way governments work, people engage in and are affected by politics, and governmental systems change.

The article by Gabriel Almond illustrates the complex nature of theory and method in political science and the way in which a single discipline can comprehend many different ways of knowing. Almond begins by suggesting that political science in the 1980s was a lonely discipline, marked by an "uneasy separateness." He then divides the discipline into five major groups (soft left, hard right, soft right, hard left, and center) and describes in some detail the variables that lend themselves to that separateness. But this separateness is basic to the discipline's vitality. The author eventually concludes that there is merit in the complexity of perspectives or ways of knowing that characterize political science, suggesting the discipline is well-served by "all methods that illuminate the world of politics and public policy."

Practically everyone has heard the story of the blind men who were asked to describe an elephant subsequent to touching some part of its anatomy (e.g., trunk, tail, belly, leg). Predictably, each of the men got a different impression of what an elephant was like. Picking up on that same theme, if the elephant were to be thought of as the complex totality of human behavior and the blind men as social scientists, the end result would be much the same. What the economist perceived about this gargantuan beast called human behavior would be different than what the anthropologist perceived, though both perceptions would share some traits in common. In similar fashion, the sociologist, political scientist, and psychologist would come away with impressions quite different than those of the other social scientists. These different impressions, taken by themselves, would be important but in some ways incomplete. However, if all of the social scientific perceptions of that animal we have labeled "human behavior" were put together, we would have a reasonably comprehensive and complete understanding.

Knowing in the social sciences is about understanding human behavior in general, other people, social systems, cultures, and self in particular. It is about asking certain types of questions. It is about the interpretation of the responses to those questions.

Social science, as a collection of specialized disciplines, can be viewed as a systematic method for knowing and understanding the human experience, a vital component of the academic enterprise, and an important part of an undergraduate education. The social sciences contribute to the knowledge and skills of the educated person. They also are important to one's preparation for life and leadership in a democratic society where decisions made by the individual must be educated decisions. Understandings of the economy, the political process, other ethnic and religious groups, social statistics, and mental health are just a few of the many contributions that a social science education makes to such preparation. In this sense, the social sciences lend themselves to openness, freedom of expression, and the objective search for truth. They also protect a civil society from retreating to the intellectual tyranny of a world in which human beings, whether miner, model, or monk, can be punished for asking inappropriate questions.

For more information about the social sciences see the *International Encyclopedia of the Social Sciences* (1968), and Ernest Schusky, *Introduction to Social Sciences* (1981; New York: Prentice Hall).

REFERENCE CITED

Seligman, Edwin A. 1930 What are the Social Sciences? In *Encyclopedia of the Social Sciences,* Vol. I, pp. 3–7.

John Watson*

What is Behaviorism?

THE OLD AND NEW PSYCHOLOGY CONTRASTED

Two opposed points of view are still dominant in American psychological thinking—introspective or subjective psychology, and behaviorism or objective psychology.[1] Until the advent of behaviorism in 1912, introspective psychology completely dominated American university psychological life.

The conspicuous leaders of introspective psychology in the first decade of the twentieth century were E. B. Titchener of Cornell and William James of Harvard. The death of James in 1910 and the death of Titchener in 1927 left introspective psychology without emotional leadership. Although Titchener's psychology differed in many points from that William James, their fundamental assumptions were the same. In the first place both were of German origin. In the second place, and of more importance, both claimed that *consciousness is the subject matter of psychology.*

Behaviorism, on the contrary, holds that the subject matter of human psychology *is the behavior of the human being.* Behaviorism claims that consciousness is neither a definite not a usable concept. The behaviorist, who has been trained always as an experimentalist, holds, further, that belief in the existence of consciousness goes back to the ancient days of superstition and magic.

The great mass of the people even today has not yet progressed very far away from savagery—it wants to believe in magic. The savage believes that incantations can bring rain, good crops, good hunting, that an unfriendly voodoo doctor can bring disaster to a person or to a whole tribe; that an enemy who has obtained a nail paring or a lock of your hair can cast a harmful spell over you and control your actions. There is always interest and

---

*John B. Watson (1878–1958) was a prominent American psychologist and the foremost proponent of behaviorism during the first half of this century. Educated at the University of Chicago, he taught at Johns Hopkins University. His works include *Behavior: An Introduction to Commparative Psychology, Psychology from the Standpoint of a Behaviorist,* and *Behaviorism* (1913), of which the following selection is the first chapter. Watson advocated treating psychology as a natural science and the restriction of psychology to observable stimulus/response relationships.

[1]In the last few decades there have been two other more or less prominent but temporary points of view—the so-called functional psychology of Dewey, Angell and Judd and the Gestalt Psychologie of Wertheimer, Koffka and Köhler. In my opinion both of these points of view are, as it were, illegitimate children of introspective psychology. Functional psychology, which one rarely hears of now, owed its vogue to considerable patter about the physiologically adaptive functions of the mind. The mind with them is a kind of adjusting "guardian angel." The philosophy behind it smacks very much of the good old Christian philosophy of Berkeley (interaction or control of the body by the deity).

Gestalt psychology makes its patter about "configurational response (really inborn!)." As a psychological theory it cannot gain very much headway. It is as obscure as Kant's treatment of imagination, which it resembles quite a little. The kernel of truth behind it has been very much better and more clearly expressed by William James in his *Principles* in the chapters on Sensation and Perception. Those chapters could be read with profit by the sponsors of Gestalt. Gestalt is still a part of introspective psychology. Incidentally a bit of collateral reading for any student who works on Gestalt is Hobhouse's *Mind in Evolution.*

---

news in magic. Almost every era has its new magic, black or white, and its new magician. Moses had his magic: he smote the rock and water gushed out. Christ had his magic: he turned water into wine and raised the dead to life. Coué had his magic word formula. Mrs. Eddy had a similar one.

Magic lives forever. As time goes on, all of these critically undigested, innumerably told tales get woven into the folk lore of the people. Folk lore in turn gets organized into religions. Religions get caught up into the political and economic network of the country. Then they are used as tools. The public is forced to accept all of the old wives' tales, and it passes them on as gospel to its children's children.

The extent to which most of us are shot through with a savage background is almost unbelievable. Few of us escape it. Not even a college education seems to correct it. If anything, it seems to strengthen it, since the colleges themselves are filled with instructors who have the same background. Some of our greatest biologists, physicists, and chemists, when outside of their laboratories, fall back upon folk lore which has become crystallized into religious concepts. These concepts—these heritages of a timid savage past—have made the emergence and growth of scientific psychology extremely difficult.

AN EXAMPLE OF SUCH CONCEPTS

One example of such a religious concept is that every individual has a *soul* which is separate and distinct from the *body*. This soul is really a part of a supreme being. This ancient view led to the philosophical platform called "dualism." This dogma has been present in human psychology from earliest antiquity. No one has ever touched a soul, or seen one in a test tube, or has in any way come into relationship with it as he has with the other objects of his daily experience. Nevertheless, to doubt its existence is to become a heretic and once might possibly even have led to the loss of one's head. Even today the man holding a public position dare not question it.

With the development of the physical sciences which came with the renaissance, a certain release from this stifling soul cloud was obtained. A man could think of astronomy, of the celestial bodies and their motions, of gravitation and the like, without involving soul. Although the early scientists were as a rule devout Christians, nevertheless they began to leave soul out of their test tubes.

Psychology and philosophy, however, in dealing as they thought with non-material objects, found it difficult to escape the language of the church, and hence the concept of mind or soul as distinct from the body came down almost unchanged in essence to the latter part of the nineteenth century.

Wundt, the real father of experimental psychology, unquestionably wanted in 1879 a scientific psychology. He grew up in the midst of a dualistic philosophy of the most pronounced type. He could not see his way clear to a solution of the mind-body problem. His psychology, which has reigned supreme to the present day, is necessarily a compromise. He substituted the term *consciousness* for the term soul. Consciousness is not quite so unobservable as soul. We observe it by peeking in suddenly and catching it unawares as it were *(introspection)*.

Wundt had an immense following. Just as now it is fashionable to go to Vienna to study psychoanalysis under Freud, just so was it fashionable some 40 years ago to study at Leipzig with Wundt. The men who returned founded the laboratories at Johns Hopkins University, the University of Pennsylvania, Columbia, Clark and Cornell. All were equipped to do battle with the elusive (almost soullike) thing called consciousness.

To show how unscientific is the main concept behind this great German-American school of psychology, look for a moment at William James' definition of psychology. "Psychology is the description and explanation of states of consciousness as such." Starting with a definition which *assumes* what he starts out to prove, he escapes his difficulty by an *argumentum ad hominem*. Consciousness—Oh, yes everybody must know what this "consciousness" is. When we have a sensation of red, a perception, a thought, when we *will* to do something, or when we *purpose* to do something, or when we desire to do something, we are being *conscious*.

All other introspectionists are equally illogical. In other words, they do not tell us what consciousness is, but merely begin to put things into it by assumption; and then when they come to analyze consciousness, naturally they find in it just what they put into it. Consequently, in the analyses of consciousness made by certain of the psychologists you find such elements as *sensations* and their ghosts, the *images*. With others you find not only sensations, but so-called *affective elements;* in still others you find such elements as *will*—the so-called *conative element* in consciousness. With some psychologists you find many hundreds of sensations of a certain type; others maintain that only a few of that type exist. And so it goes. Literally hundreds of thousands of printed pages have been published on the minute analysis of this intangible something called "consciousness." And how do we begin to work upon it? Not by analyzing it as we would a chemical compound, or the way a plant grows. No, those things are material things. This thing we call consciousness can be analyzed only by *introspection*—a looking in on what takes place inside of us.

As a result of this major assumption that there is such a thing as consciousness and that we can analyze it by introspection, we find as many analyses as there are individual psychologists. There is no way of experimentally attacking and solving psychological problems and standardizing methods.

THE ADVENT OF THE BEHAVIORISTS

In 1912 the objective psychologists or behaviorists reached the conclusion that they could no longer be content to work with Wundt's formulations. They felt that the 30 odd barren years since the establishment of Wundt's laboratory had proved conclusively that the so called introspective psychology of Germany was founded upon wrong hypotheses—that no psychology which included the religious mind-body problem could ever arrive at verifiable conclusions. They decided either to give up psychology or else make it a natural science. They saw their brother-scientists making progress in medicine, in chemistry, in physics. Every new discovery in those fields was of prime importance; every new element isolated in one laboratory could be isolated in some other laboratory; each new element was immediately taken up in the warp and woof of science as a whole. One need only mention wireless, radium, insulin, thyroxin, to verify this. Elements so isolated and methods so formulated immediately began to function in human achievement.

In his first efforts to get uniformity in subject matter and in methods the behaviorist began his own formulation of the problem of psychology by sweeping aside all medieval conceptions. He dropped from his scientific vocabulary all subjective terms such as sensation, perception, image, desire, purpose, and even thinking and emotion as they were subjectively defined.

THE BEHAVIORISTS PLATFORM

The behaviorist asks: Why don't we make what we can *observe* the real field of psychology? Let us limit ourselves to things that can be observed, and formulate laws concerning only those things. Now what can we observe? We can observe *behavior—what the organism does or says*. And let us point out at once: that *saying* is doing—that is, *behaving*. Speaking overtly or to ourselves (thinking) is just as objective a type of behavior as baseball.

The rule, or measuring rod, which the behaviorist puts in front of him always is: Can I describe this bit of behavior I see in terms of "stimulus and response?" By stimulus we mean any object in the general environment or any change in the tissues themselves due to the physiological condition of the animal, such as the change we get when we keep an animal from sex activity, when we keep it from feeding, when we keep it from building a nest. By response we mean anything the animal does—such as turning toward or away from a light, jumping at a sound, and more highly organized activities such as building a skyscraper, drawing plans, having babies, writing books, and the like.

SOME SPECIFIC PROBLEMS OF THE BEHAVIORISTS

You will find, then, the behaviorist working like any other scientist. His sole object is to gather facts about behavior—verify his data—subject them both to logic and to mathematics (the tools of every scientist). He brings the new-born individual *into his experimental nursery* and begins to set problems: What is the baby doing now? What is the stimulus that makes him behave this way? He finds that the stimulus of tickling the cheek brings the response of turning the mouth to the side stimulated. The stimulus of the nipple brings out the sucking response. The stimulus of a rod placed on the palm of the hand brings closure of the hand and the suspension of the whole body by that hand and arm if the rod is raised. Stimulating the infant with a rapidly moving shadow across the eye will not produce blinking until the individual is sixty-five days of age. Stimulating the infant with an apple or stick of candy or any other object will not call out attempts at reaching until the baby is around 120 days of age. Stimulating a properly brought up infant at any age with snakes, fish, darkness, burning paper, birds, cats, dogs, monkeys, will not bring out that type of response which we call "fear" (which to be objective we might call reaction "X") which is a catching of breath, a stiffening of the whole body, a turning away of the body from the source of stimulation, a running or crawling away from it. (See page 152.)

On the other hand, there are just two things which will call out a fear response, namely, a loud sound, and loss of support.

Now the behaviorist finds from observing children brought up *outside of his nursery* that hundreds of these objects will call out fear responses. Consequently, the scientific question arises: If at birth only two stimuli will call out fear, how do all these other things ever finally come to call it out? Please note that the question is not a speculative one. It can be answered by experiments, and the experiments can be reproduced and the same findings can be had in very other laboratory if the original observation is sound. Convince yourself of this by making a simple test.

If you take a snake, mouse or dog and show it to a baby who has never seen these objects or been frightened in other ways, he begins to manipulate it, poking at this, that or the other part. Do this for ten days until you are logically certain that the child will always go toward the dog and never run away from it (positive reaction) and that it does not call out a fear response at any time. In contrast to this, pick up a steel bar and strike upon it loudly behind the infant's head. Immediately the fear response is called forth. Now try this: At the instant you show him the animal and just as he begins to reach for it, strike the steel bar behind his head. Repeat the experiment three or four times. A new and important change is apparent. The animal now calls out the same response as the steel bar, namely a fear response. We call this, in behavioristic psychology, the *conditioned emotional response*—a form of *conditioned reflex.*

Our studies of conditioned reflexes make it easy for us to account for the child's fear of the dog on a thoroughly natural science basis without lugging in consciousness or any other so called mental process. A dog comes toward the child rapidly, jumps upon him, pushes him down and at the same time barks loudly. Oftentimes one such combined stimulation is all that is necessary to make the baby run away from the dog the moment it comes within his range of vision.

There are many other types of conditioned emotional responses, such as those connected with *love,* where the mother by petting the child, rocking it, stimulating its sex organs in bathing, and the like, calls out the embrace, gurgling and crowing as an unlearned original response. Soon this response becomes conditioned. The mere sight of the mother calls out the same kind of response as actual bodily contacts. In *rage* we get a similar set of facts. The stimulus of holding the infant's moving members

brings out the original unlearned response we call rage. Soon the mere sight of a nurse who handles a child badly throws the child into a fit. Thus we see how relatively simple our emotional responses are in the beginning and how terribly complicated home life soon makes them.

The behaviorist has his problems with the adult as well. What methods shall we use systematically to condition the adult? For example, to teach him business habits, scientific habits? Both manual habits (technique and skill) and laryngeal habits (habits of speech and thought) must be formed and tied together before the task of learning is complete. After these work habits are formed, what system of changing stimuli shall we surround him with in order to keep his level of efficiency high and constantly rising?

In addition to vocational habits, there comes the problem of his emotional life. How much of it is carried over from childhood? What part of it interferes with his present adjustment? How can we make him lose this part of it; that is, uncondition him where unconditioning is necessary, and condition him where conditioning is necessary? Indeed we know all too little about the amount and kind of emotional or, better, visceral habits (by this term we mean that our stomach, intestines, breathing, and circulation become conditioned—form habits) that should be formed. We do know that they are formed in large numbers and that they are important.

Probably more adults in this universe of ours suffer vicissitudes in family life and in business activities because of poor and insufficient visceral habits than through the lack of technique and skill in manual and verbal accomplishments. One of the large problems in big organizations today is that of personality adjustments. The young men and young women entering business organizations have plenty of skill to do their work but they fail because they do not know how to get along with other people.

DOES THIS BEHAVIORISTIC APPROACH LEAVE ANYTHING OUT OF PSYCHOLOGY?

After so brief a survey of the behavioristic approach to the problems of psychology, one is inclined to say: "Why, yes it is worth while to study human behavior in this way, but the study of behavior is not the whole of psychology. It leaves out too much. Don't I have sensations, perceptions, conceptions? Do I not forget things and remember things, imagine things, have visual images and auditory images of things I once have seen and heard?

Can I not see and hear things that I have never seen or heard in nature? Can I not be attentive or inattentive? Can I not will to do a thing or will not to do it, as the case may be? Do not certain things arouse pleasure in me, and others displeasure? Behaviorism is trying to rob us of everything we have believed in since earliest childhood."

Having been brought up on introspective psychology, as most of us have, you naturally ask these questions and you will find it hard to put away the old terminology and begin to formulate your psychological life in terms of behaviorism. Behaviorism is new wine and it will not go into old bottles. It is advisable for the time being to allay your natural antagonism and accept the behavioristic platform at least until you get more deeply into it. Later you will find that you have progressed so far with behaviorism that the questions you now raise will answer themselves in a perfectly satisfactory natural science way. Let me hasten to add that if the behaviorist were to ask you what you mean by the subjective terms you have been in the habit of using he could soon make you tongue-tied with contradictions. He could even convince you that you do not know what you mean by them. You have been using them uncritically as a part of your social and literary tradition.

TO UNDERSTAND BEHAVIORISM BEGIN TO OBSERVE PEOPLE

This is the fundamental starting point of behaviorism. You will soon find that instead of self-observation being the easiest and most natural way of studying psychology, it is an impossible one; you can observe in yourselves only the most elementary forms of response. You will find, on the other hand, that when you begin to study what your neighbor is doing, you will rapidly become proficient in giving a reason for his behavior and in setting situations (presenting stimuli) that will make him behave in a predictable manner.

DEFINITION OF BEHAVIORISM

Definitions are not as popular today as they once were. The definition of any one science, physics, for example, would necessarily include the definition of all other sciences. And the same is true of behaviorism. About all that we can do in the way of defining a science at the present time is to mark a ring around that part of the whole or natural science that we claim particularly as our own.

Behaviorism, as you have already grasped from our preliminary discussion, is, then, a natural science that takes the whole field of human adjustments as its own. Its closest scientific companion is physiology. Indeed you may wonder, as we proceed, whether behaviorism can be differentiated from that science. It is different from physiology only in the grouping of its problems, not in fundamentals or in central viewpoint. Physiology is particularly interested in the functioning of parts of the animal—for example, its digestive system, the circulatory system, the nervous system, the excretory systems, the mechanics of neural and muscular response. Behaviorism, on the other hand, while it is intensely interested in all of the functioning of these parts, is intrinsically interested in what the whole animal will do from morning to night and from night to morning.

The interest of the behaviorist in man's doings is more than the interest of the spectator—he wants to control man's reactions as physical scientists want to control and manipulate other natural phenomena. It is the business of behavioristic psychology to be able to predict and control human activity. To do this it must gather scientific data by experimental methods. Only then can the trained behaviorist predict, given the stimulus, what reaction will take place; or, given the reaction, state what the situation or stimulus is that has caused the reaction.

Let us look for a moment more closely at the two terms—stimulus and response.

WHAT IS A STIMULUS?

If I suddenly flash a strong light in your eye, your pupil will contract rapidly. If I were suddenly to shut off all light in the room in which you are sitting, the pupil would begin to widen. If a pistol shot were suddenly fired behind you you would jump and possibly turn your head around. If hydrogen sulphide were suddenly released in your sitting room you would begin to hold your nose and possibly even seek to leave the room. If I suddenly made the room very warm, you would begin to unbutton your coat and perspire. If I suddenly made it cold, another response would take place.

Again, on the inside of us we have an equally large realm in which stimuli can exert their effect. For example, just before dinner the muscles of your stomach begin to contract and expand rhythmically because of the absence of food. As soon as food is eaten those contractions cease. By swallowing a small balloon and attaching it to a recording instrument we can easily register the response of the stomach to lack of food and note the lack of response when food is present. In the male, at any rate, the pressure of certain fluids (semen) may lead to sex activity. In the case of the female possibly the presence of certain chemical bodies can lead in a similar way to overt sex behavior. The muscles of our arms and legs and trunk are not only subject to stimuli coming from the blood; they are also stimulated by their own responses—that is, the muscle is under constant tension; any increase in that tension, as when a movement is made, gives rise to a stimulus which leads to another response in that same muscle or in one in some distant part of the body; any decrease in that tension, as when the muscle is relaxed, similarly gives rise to a stimulus.

So we see that the organism is constantly assailed by stimuli—which come through the eye, the ear, the nose and the mouth—the so called objects of our environment; at the same time the inside of our body is likewise assailed at every movement by stimuli arising from changes in the tissues themselves. Don't get the idea, please, that the inside of your body is different from or any more mysterious than the outside of your body.

Through the process of evolution human beings have put on sense organs—specialized areas where special types of stimuli are most effective—such as the eye, the ear, the nose, the tongue, the skin and semi-circular canals.[2] To these must be added the whole muscular system, both the striped muscles (for example, the large red muscles of arms, legs and trunks) and the unstriped muscles (those, for example, which make up the hollow tube-like structures of the stomach and intestines and blood vessels). The muscles are thus not only organs of response—they are sense organs as well. You will see as we proceed that the last two systems play a tremendous rôle in the behavior of the human being. Many of our most intimate and personal reactions are due to stimuli set up by tissue changes in our striped muscles and in our viscera.

HOW TRAINING ENLARGES THE RANGE OF STIMULI

One of the problems of behaviorism is what might be called the ever-increasing range of stimuli to which an individual responds. Indeed so marked is this that you might be tempted at first sight to doubt the formulation we gave above, namely, that response can be predicted. If you will watch the growth and development of behavior in the human being, you will find that while a great many stimuli will produce a response in the new-born, many other stimuli will not. At any rate they do not call out the same response they later call out. For example you don't get very far by showing a new-born infant a crayon, a piece of paper, or the printed score of a Beethoven symphony. In other words, habit formation has to come in before certain stimuli can become effective. Later we shall take up the procedure by means of which we can get stimuli which do not ordinarily call out responses to call them out. The general term we use to describe this is "conditioning." Conditioned responses will be more fully gone into in chapter II.

It is conditioning from earliest childhood on that makes the problem of the behaviorist in predicting what a given response will be so difficult. The sight of a horse does not ordinarily produce the fear response, and yet among almost every group of thirty to forty people there is one person who will walk a block to avoid coming near a horse. While the study of behaviorism will never enable its students to look at you and predict that such a state of affairs exists, nevertheless if the behaviorist sees the reaction taking place, it is very easy for him to state approximately what the situation was in the early experience of such a one that brought about this unusual type of adult response. In spite of the difficulty of predicting responses in detail we live in general upon the theory that we can predict what our neighbor will do. There is no other basis upon which we can live with our fellow men.

WHAT THE BEHAVIORIST MEANS BY RESPONSE

We have already brought out the fact that from birth to death the organism is being assailed by stimuli on the outside of the body and by stimuli arising in the body itself. Now the organism does something when it is assailed by stimuli. It responds. It moves. The response may be so slight that it can be observed only by the use of instruments. The response may confine itself merely to a change in respiration, or to an increase or decrease in blood pressure. It may call out merely a movement of the eye. The more commonly observed responses, however, are movements of the whole body, movements of the arm, leg, trunk, or combinations of all the moving parts.

---

[2]In chapter III we shall see how sense organs are made up and what their general relation is to the rest of the body.

Usually the response that the organism makes to a stimulus brings about an adjustment, though not always. By an adjustment we mean merely that the organism by moving so alters its physiological state that the stimulus no longer arouses reaction. This may sound a bit complicated, but examples will clear it up. If I am hungry, stomach contractions begin to drive me ceaselessly to and fro. If, in these restless seeking movements, I spy apples on a tree, I immediately climb the tree and pluck the apples and begin to eat. When surfeited, the stomach contractions cease. Although there are apples still hanging round about me, I no longer pluck and eat them. Again, the cold air stimulates me. I move around about until I am out of the wind. In the open I may even dig a hole. Having escaped the wind, it no longer stimulates me to further action. Under sex excitement the male may go to any length to capture a willing female. Once sex activity has been completed the restless seeking movements disappear. The female no longer stimulates the male to sex activity.

The behaviorist has often been criticized for this emphasis upon response. Some psychologists seem to have the notion that the behaviorist is interested only in the recording of minute muscular responses. Nothing could be further from the truth. Let me emphasize again that the behaviorist is primarily interested in the behavior of the whole man. From morning to night he watches him perform his daily round of duties. If it is brick-laying, we would like to measure the number of bricks he can lay under different conditions, how long he can do without dropping from fatigue, how long it takes him to learn his trade, whether we can improve his efficiency or get him to do the same amount of work in a less period of time. In other words, the response the behaviorist is interested in is the commonsense answer to the question "what is he doing and why is he doing it?" Surely with this as a general statement, no one can distort the behaviorist's platform to such an extent that it can be claimed that the behaviorist is merely a muscle physiologist.

The behaviorist claims that there is a response to every effective stimulus and that the response is immediate. By effective stimulus we mean that it must be strong enough to overcome the normal resistance to the passage of the sensory impulse from sense organs to muscles. Don't get confused at this point by what the psychologist and the psychoanalyst sometimes tell you. If you read their statements, you are likely to believe that the stimulus can be applied today and produce its effect maybe the next day, maybe within the next few months, or

years. The behaviorist doesn't believe in any such mythological conception. It is true that I can give the verbal stimulus to you "Meet me at the Ritz tomorrow for lunch at one o'clock." Your immediate response is "All right, I'll be there." Now what happens after that? We will not cross this difficult bridge now, but may I point out that we have in our verbal habits a mechanism by means of which the stimulus is reapplied from moment to moment until the final reaction occurs, namely going to the Ritz at one o'clock the next day.

GENERAL CLASSIFICATION OF RESPONSE

The two commonsense classifications of response are "external" and "internal"—or possibly the terms "overt" (explicit) and "implicit" are better. By external or overt responses we mean the ordinary doings of the human being: he stoops to pick up a tennis ball, he writes a letter, he enters an automobile and starts driving, he digs a hole in the ground, he sits down to write a lecture, or dances, or flirts with a woman, or makes love to his wife. We do not need instruments to make these observations. On the other hand, responses may be wholly confined to the muscular and glandular systems inside the body. A child or hungry adult may be standing stock still in front of a window filled with pastry. Your first exclamation may be "He isn't doing anything" or "he is just looking at the pastry." An instrument would show that his salivary glands are pouring out secretions, that his stomach is rhythmically contracting and expanding, and that marked changes in blood pressure are taking place—that the endocrine glands are pouring substances into the blood. The internal or implicit responses are difficult to observe not because they are inherently different from the external or overt responses, but merely because they are hidden from the eye.

Another general classification is that of *learned* and *unlearned* responses. I brought out the fact above that the range of stimuli to which we react is ever increasing. The behaviorist has found by his study that most of the things we see the adult doing are really learned. We used to think that a lot of them were instinctive, that is, "unlearned." But we are now almost at the point of throwing away the word "instinct." Still there are a lot of things we do that we do not have to learn—to perspire, to breathe, to have our heart beat, to have digestion take place, to have our eyes turn toward a source of light, to have our pupils contract, to show a fear response when a loud sound is given. Let us keep as our second classification then "learned responses," and make it include all of our complicated habits and all of our conditioned responses; and "unlearned" responses, and mean by that all of the things that we do in earliest infancy before the processes of conditioning and habit formation get the upper hand.

Another purely logical way to classify responses is to designate them by the sense organ which initiates them. We could thus have a *visual unlearned response*—for example, the turning of the eye of the youngster at birth toward a source of light. Contrast this with a *visual learned response,* the response, for example, to a printed score of music or a word. Again, we could have a *kinaesthetic[3] unlearned response* when the infant reacts by crying to a long-sustained twisted position of the arm. We could have a *kinaesthetic learned response* when we manipulate a delicate object in the dark or, for example tread a tortuous maze. Again, we can have a visceral *unlearned response* as, for example, when stomach contractions due to the absence of food in the 3 day old infant will produce crying. Contrast this with the learned or visceral *conditioned* response where the sight of pastry in a baker's window will cause the mouth of the hungry schoolboy to water.

The discussion of stimulus and response shows what material we have to work with in behavioristic psychology and why behavioristic psychology has as its goal *to be able, given the stimulus, to predict the response*—or, *seeing the reaction take place to state what the stimulus is that has called out the reaction.*

IS BEHAVIORISM MERELY A METHODOLOGICAL APPROACH TO THE STUDY OF PSYCHOLOGICAL PROBLEMS, OR IS IT AN ACTUAL SYSTEM OF PSYCHOLOGY?

If psychology can do without the terms "mind" and "consciousness," indeed it can find no objective evidence for their existence, what is going to become of philosophy and the so-called social sciences which today are built around the concept of mind and consciousness? Almost every day the behaviorist is asked this question, sometimes in a friendly inquiring way, and sometimes not so kindly. While behaviorism was fighting for its existence it was afraid to answer this question. Its contentions were too new; its field too unworked for it to allow itself even to think that some day it might be able to stand up and tell philosophy and the social sciences that they, too, must scrutinize anew their own premises. Hence the behaviorist's one answer when approached in this way was to say, "I can't let myself worry about such questions now. Behaviorism is at present a satisfactory way of going at the solution of psychological problems—it is really a methodological approach to psychological problems." Today behaviorism is strongly entrenched. It finds its way of going at the study of psychological problems and its formulation of its results growing more and more adequate.

It may never make a pretense of being a *system.* Indeed systems in every scientific field are out of date. We collect our facts from observation. Now and then we select a group of facts and draw certain general conclusions about them. In a few years as new experimental data are gathered by better methods, even these tentative general conclusions have to be modified. Every scientific field, zoölogy, physiology, chemistry and physics, is more or less in a state of flux. Experimental technique, the accumulation of facts by that technique, occasional tentative consolidation of these facts into a theory or an hypothesis describe our procedure in science. Judged upon this basis, behaviorism is a true natural science.

---

[3]By kinaesthetic we mean the muscle sense. Our muscles are supplied with sensory nerve endings. When we move the muscles these sensory nerve endings are stimulated. Thus, the stimulus to the kinaesthetic or muscle sense is a *movement of the muscle itself.*

NAME _____   DATE _____

John B. Watson, What is Behaviorism?

1.   Behaviorists believe that psychology is a natural science.

        A. True   B. False

2.   What is introspection?

3.   What is behavior? Why does Watson believe that psychologists should study it?

4.   According to Watson, psychologists should frame their explanations of behavior in terms of

        a. the id, the superego, and the ego
        b. the will to power.
        c. cognitive processes.
        d. stimulus and response.
        e. none of the above.

Emile Durkheim*

WHAT IS A SOCIAL FACT?

Before beginning the search for the method appropriate to the study of social facts it is important to know what are the facts termed 'social'.

The question is all the more necessary because the term is used without much precision. It is commonly used to designate almost all the phenomena that occur within society, however little social interest of some generality they present. Yet under this heading there is, so to speak, no human occurrence that cannot be called social. Every individual drinks, sleeps, eats, or employs his reason, and society has every interest in seeing that these functions are regularly exercised. If therefore these facts were social ones, sociology would possess no subject matter peculiarly its own, and its domain would be confused with that of biology and psychology.

However, in reality there is in every society a clearly determined group of phenomena separable, because of their distinct characteristics, from those that form the subject matter of other sciences of nature.

When I perform my duties as a brother, a husband or a citizen and carry out the commitments I have entered into, I fulfil obligations which are defined in law and custom and which are external to myself and my actions. Even when they conform to my own sentiments and when I feel their reality within me, that reality does not cease to be objective, for it is not I who have prescribed these duties; I have received them through education. Moreover, how often does it happen that we are ignorant of the details of the obligations that we must assume, and that, to know them, we must consult the legal code and its authorised interpreters! Similarly the believer has discovered from birth, ready fashioned, the beliefs and practices of his religious life; if they existed before he did, it follows that they exist outside him. The system of signs that I employ to express my thoughts, the monetary system I use to pay my debts, the credit instruments I utilise in my commercial relationships, the practices I follow in my profession, etc., all function independently of the use I make of them. Considering in turn each member of society, the foregoing remarks can be repeated for each single one of them. Thus there are ways of acting, thinking and feeling which possess the remarkable property of existing outside the consciousness of the individual.

Not only are these types of behaviour and thinking external to the individual, but they are endued with a compelling and coercive power by virtue of which, whether he wishes it or not, they impose themselves upon him. Undoubtedly when I conform to them of my own free will, this coercion is not felt or felt hardly at all, since it is unnecessary. None the less it is intrinsically a characteristic of these facts; the proof of this is that it asserts itself as soon as I try to resist. If I attempt to violate the rules of law they react against me so as to forestall my action, if there is still time. Alternatively, they annul it or make my action conform to the norm if it is already accomplished by capable of being

---

*Emile Durkheim (1958–1917) was a French sociologist who taught at the University of Paris. As a founder and leading figure of modern sociology, he was an uncompromising proponent of its scientific character. His most famous works are *The Division of Labor in Society*, *The Elementary Forms of Religious Life*, and *Suicide*. In the following selection (1917), Durkheim lays out his conception of a social fact. The existence of social facts led Durkheim to advocate methodological collectivism—the view that social phenomena must be studied as a whole and cannot be reduced to the thought and actions of individuals.

reversed; or they cause me to pay the penalty for it if it is irreparable. If purely moral rules are at stake, the public conscience restricts any ct which infringes them by the surveillance it exercises over the conduct of citizens and by the special punishments it has at its disposal. In other cases the constraint is less violent; nevertheless, it does not cease to exist. If I do not conform to ordinary conventions, if in my mode of dress I pay no heed to what is customary in my country and in my social class, the laughter I provoke, the social distance at which I am kept, produce, although in a more mitigated form, the same results as any real penalty. In other cases, although it may be indirect, constraint is no less effective. I am not forced to speak French with my compatriots, nor to use the legal currency, but it is impossible for me to do otherwise. If I tried to escape the necessity, my attempt would fail miserably. As an industrialist nothing prevents me from working with the processes and methods of the previous century, but if I do I will most certainly ruin myself. Even when in fact I can struggle free from these rules and successfully break them, it is never without being forced to fight against them. Even if in the end they are overcome, they make their constraining power sufficiently felt in the resistance that they afford. There is no innovator, even a fortunate one, whose ventures do not encounter opposition of this kind.

Here, then is a category of facts which present very special characteristics: they consist of manners of acting, thinking and feeling external to the individual, which are invested with a coercive power by virtue of which they exercise control over him. Consequently, since they consist of representations and actions, they cannot be confused with organic phenomena, nor with physical phenomena, which have no existence save in and through the individual consciousness. Thus they constitute a new species and to them must be exclusively assigned the term *social*. It is appropriate, since it is clear that, not having the individual as their substratum, they can have none other than society, either political society in its entirety or one of the partial groups that it includes—religious denominations, political and literary schools, occupational corporations, etc. Moreover, it is for such as these alone that the term is fitting, for the word 'social' has the sole meaning of designating those phenomena which fall into none of the categories of facts already constituted and labelled. They are consequently the proper field of sociology. It is true that this word 'constraint', in terms of which we define them, is in danger of infuriating those who zealously uphold out-and-out individualism. Since they maintain that the individual is completely autonomous, it seems to them that he is diminished every time he is made aware that he is not dependent on himself alone. Yet since it is indisputable today that most of our ideas and tendencies are not developed by ourselves, but come to us from outside, they can only penetrate us by imposing themselves upon us. This is all that our definition implies. Moreover, we know that all social constraints do not necessarily exclude the individual personality.[1]

Yet since the examples just cited (legal and moral rules, religious dogmas, financial systems, etc.) consist wholly of beliefs and practices already well established, in view of what has been said it might be maintained that no social fact can exist except where there is a well defined social organisation. But there are other facts which do not present themselves in this already crystallised form but which also possess the same objectivity and ascendancy over the individual. These are what are called social 'currents.' Thus in a public gathering the great waves of enthusiasm, indignation and pity that are produced have their seat in no one individual consciousness. They come to each one of us from outside and can sweep us along in spite of ourselves. If perhaps I abandon myself to them I may not be conscious of the pressure that they are exerting upon me, but that pressure makes its presence felt immediately I attempt to struggle against them. If an individual tries to pit himself against one of these collective manifestations, the sentiments that he is rejecting will be turned against him. Now if this external coercive power asserts itself so acutely in cases of resistance, it must be because it exists in the other instances cited above without our being conscious of it. Hence we are the victims of an illusion which leads us to believe we have ourselves produced what has been imposed upon us externally. But if the willingness with which we let ourselves be carried along disguises the pressure we have undergone, it does not eradicate it. Thus air does not cease to have weight, although we no longer feel that weight. Even when we have indi-

---

[1]Moreover, this is not to say that all constraint is normal. We shall return to this point later.

vidually and spontaneously shared in the common emotion, the impression we have experienced is utterly different from what we would have felt if we had been alone. Once the assembly has broken up and these social influences have ceased to act upon us, and we are once more on our own, the emotions we have felt seem an alien phenomenon, one in which we no longer recognise ourselves. It is then we perceive that we have undergone the emotions much more than generated them. These emotions may even perhaps fill us with horror, so much do they go against the grain. Thus individuals who are normally perfectly harmless may, when gathered together in a crowd, let themselves be drawn into acts of atrocity. And what we assert about these transitory outbreaks likewise applies to those more lasting movements of opinion which relate to religious, political, literary and artistic matters, etc., and which are constantly being produced around us, whether throughout society or in a more limited sphere.

Moreover, this definition of a social fact can be verified by examining an experience that is characteristic. It is sufficient to observe how children are brought up. If one views the facts as they are and indeed as they have always been, it is patently obvious that all education consists of a continual effort to impose upon the child ways of seeing, thinking and acting which he himself would not have arrived at spontaneously. From his earliest years we oblige him to eat, drink and sleep at regular hours, and to observe cleanliness, calm and obedience; later we force him to learn how to be mindful of others, to respect customs and conventions, and to work, etc. If this constraint in time ceases to be felt it is because it gradually gives rise to habits, to inner tendencies which render it superfluous; but they supplant the constraint only because they are derived from it. It is true that, in Spencer's view, a rational education should shun such means and allow the child complete freedom to do what he will. Yet as this educational theory has never been put into practice among any known people, it can only be the personal expression of a *desideratum* and not a fact which can be established in contradiction to the other facts given above. What renders these latter facts particularly illuminating is that education sets out precisely with the object of creating a social being. Thus there can be seen, as in an abbreviated form, how the social being has been fashioned historically. The pressure to which the child is subjected unremittingly is the same pressure of the social environment which seeks to shape him in its own image, and in which parents and teachers are only the representatives and intermediaries.

Thus it is not the fact that they are general which can serve to characterise sociological phenomena. Thoughts to be found in the consciousness of each individual and movements which are repeated by all individuals are not for this reason social facts. If some have been content with using this characteristic in order to define them it is because they have been confused, wrongly, with what might be termed their individual incarnations. What constitutes social facts are the beliefs, tendencies and practices of the group taken collectively. But the forms that these collective states may assume when they are 'refracted' through individuals are things of a different kind. What irrefutably demonstrates this duality of kind is that these two categories of facts frequently are manifested dissociated from each other. Indeed some of these ways of acting or thinking acquire, by dint of repetition, a sort of consistency which, so to speak, separates them out, isolating them from the particular events which reflect them. Thus they assume a shape, a tangible form peculiar to them and constitute a reality *sui generis* vastly distinct from the individual facts which manifest that reality. Collective custom does not exist only in a state of immanence in the successive actions which it determines, but, by a privilege without example in the biological kingdom, expresses itself once and for all in a formula repeated by word of mouth, transmitted by education and even enshrined in the written word. Such are the origins and nature of legal and moral rules, aphorisms and popular sayings, articles of faith in which religious or political sects epitomise their beliefs, and standards of taste drawn up by literary schools, etc. None of these modes of acting and thinking are go be found wholly in the application made of them by individuals, since they can even exist without being applied at the time.

Undoubtedly this state of dissociation does not always present itself with equal distinctiveness. It is sufficient for dissociation to exist unquestionably in the numerous important instances cited, for us to prove that the social fact exists separately from its individual effects. Moreover, even when the dissociation is not immediately observable, it can often be made so with the help of certain methodological devices. Indeed it is essential to embark on such procedures if one wishes to refine out the social fact from any amalgam and so observe it in its pure state. Thus certain currents of opinion, whose intensity varies according to the time and country in which they occur, impel us, for example, towards marriage or suicide, towards higher or lower birth-rates, etc. Such currents are plainly social facts. At first sight they seem inseparable from the forms they assume in individual cases. But statistics afford us a means of isolating them. They are indeed not inaccurately represented by rates of births, marriages and suicides, that is, by the result obtained after dividing the average annual total of marriages, births, and voluntary homicides by the number of persons of an age to marry, produce children, or commit suicide.[2] Since each one of these statistics includes without distinction all individual cases, the individual circumstances which may have played some part in producing the phenomenon cancel each other out and consequently do not contribute to determining the nature of the phenomenon. What it expresses is a certain state of the collective mind.

That is what social phenomena are when stripped of all extraneous elements. As regards their private manifestations, these do indeed having something social about them, since in part they reproduce the collective model. But to a large extent each one depends also upon the psychical and organic constitution of the individual, and on the particular circumstances in which he is placed. Therefore they are not phenomena which are in the strict sense sociological. They depend on both domains at the same time, and could be termed socio-psychical. They are of interest to the sociologist without constituting the immediate content of sociology. The same characteristic is to be found in the organisms of those mixed phenomena of nature studied in the combined sciences such as bio-chemistry.

It may be objected that a phenomenon can only be collective if it is common to all the members of society, or at the very least to a majority, and consequently, if it is general. This is doubtless the case, but if it is general it is because it is collective (that is, more or less obligatory); but it is very far from being collective because it is general. It is a condition of the group repeated in individuals because it imposes itself upon them. It is in each part because it is in the whole, but far from being in the whole because it is in the parts. This is supremely evident in those beliefs and practices which are handed down to us ready fashioned by previous generations. We accept and adopt them because, since they are the work of the collectivity and one that is centuries old, they are invested with a special authority that our education has taught us to recognise and respect. It is worthy of note that the vast majority of social phenomena come to us in this way. But even when the social fact is partly due to our direct co-operation, it is no different in nature. An outburst of collective emotion in a gathering does not merely express the sum total of what individual feelings share in common, but is something of a very different order, as we have demonstrated. It is a product of shared existence, of actions and reactions called into play between the consciousnesses of individuals. If it is echoed in each one of them it is precisely by virtue of the special energy derived from its collective origins. If all hearts beat in unison, this is not as a consequence of a spontaneous, pre-established harmony; it is because one and the same force is propelling them in the same direction. Each one is borne along by the rest.

We have therefore succeeded in delineating for ourselves the exact field of sociology. It embraces one single, well defined group of phenomena. A social fact is identifiable through the power of external coercion which it exerts or is capable of exerting upon individuals. The presence of this power is in turn recognisable because of the existence of some pre-determined sanction, or through the resistance that the fact opposes to any individual action that may threaten it. However, it can also be defined by ascertaining how widespread it is within the group, provided that, as noted above, one is careful to add a second essential characteristic; this is, that it exists independently of the particular forms that it may assume in the process of spreading itself within the group. In certain cases this latter criterion can even be more easily applied than the former one. The presence of constraint is easily ascertainable when it is manifested externally through some direct reaction of society, as in the case of law, morality, beliefs, customs and even fashions. But when constraint is merely indirect, as with that exerted by an economic organisation, it is not always so clearly discernible. Generality combined with objectivity may then be easier to establish. Moreover, this second definition is simply another formulation of the first one: if a mode of

---

[2]Suicides do not occur at any age, nor do they occur at all ages of life with the same frequency.

behaviour existing outside the consciousnesses of individuals becomes general, it can only do so by exerting pressure upon them.[3]

However, one may well ask whether this definition is complete. Indeed the facts which have provided us with its basis are all *ways of functioning:* they are 'physiological' in nature. But there are also collective *ways of being,* namely, social facts of an 'anatomical' or morphological nature. Sociology cannot dissociate itself from what concerns the substratum of collective life. Yet the number and nature of the elementary parts which constitute society, the way in which they are articulated, the degree of coalescence they have attained, the distribution of population over the earth's surface, the extent and nature of the network of communications, the design of dwellings, etc., do not at first sight seem relatable to ways of acting, feeling or thinking.

Yet, first and foremost, these various phenomena present the same characteristic which has served us in defining the others. These ways of being impose themselves upon the individual just as do the ways of acting we have dealt with. In fact, when we wish to learn how a society is divided up politically, in what its divisions consist and the degree of solidarity that exists between them, it is not through physical inspection and geographical observation that we may come to find this out: such divisions are social, although they may have some physical basis. It is only through public law that we can study such political organisation, because this law is what determines its nature, just as it determines our domestic and civic relationships. The organisation is no less a form of compulsion. If the population clusters together in our cities instead of being scattered over the rural areas, it is because there exists a trend of opinion, a collective drive which imposes this concentration upon individuals. We can no more choose the design of our houses than the cut of our clothes—at least, the one is as much obligatory as the other. The communication network forcibly prescribes the direction of internal migrations or commercial exchanges, etc., and even their intensity. Consequently, at the most there are grounds for adding one further category to the list of phenomena already enumerated as bearing the distinctive stamp of a social fact. But as that enumeration was in no wise strictly exhaustive, this addition would not be indispensable.

Moreover, it does not even serve a purpose, for these ways of being are only ways of acting that have been consolidated. A society's political structure is only the way in which its various component segments have become accustomed to living with each other. If relationships between them are traditionally close, the segments tend to merge together; if the contrary, they tend to remain distinct. The type of dwelling imposed upon us is merely the way in which everyone around us and, in part, previous generations, have customarily built their houses. The communication network is only the channel which has been cut by the regular current of commerce and migrations, etc., flowing in the same direction. Doubtless if phenomena of a morphological kind were the only ones that displayed this rigidity, it might be thought that they constituted a separate species. But a legal rule is no less permanent an arrangement than an architectural style, and yet it is a 'physiological' fact. A simple moral maxim is certainly more malleable, yet it is cast in forms much more rigid than a mere professional custom or fashion. Thus there exists a whole range of gradations which, without any break in continuity, join the most clearly delineated structural facts to those free currents of social life which are not yet caught in any definite mould. This therefore signifies that the differences between them concern only the degree to which they have become consolidated. Both are forms of life at varying stages of crystallisation. It would undoubtedly be advantageous to reserve the term 'morphological' for those social facts which

---

[3]It can be seen how far removed this definition of the social fact is from that which serves as the basis for the ingenious system of Tarde. We must first state that our research has nowhere led us to corroboration of the preponderant influence that Tarde attributes to imitation in the genesis of collective facts. Moreover, from this definition, which is not a theory but a mere résumé of the immediate data observed, it seems clearly to follow that imitation does not always express, indeed never expresses, what is essential and characteristic in the social fact. Doubtless every social fact is imitated and has, as we have just shown, a tendency to become generalised, but this is because it is social, i.e., obligatory. Its capacity for expansion is not the cause but the consequence of its sociological character. If social facts were unique in bringing about this effect, imitation might serve, if not to explain them, at least to define them. But an individual state which impacts on others none the less remains individual. Moreover, one may speculate whether the term 'limitation' is indeed appropriate to designate a proliferation which occurs through some coercive influence. In such a single term very different phenomena, which need to be distinguished, are confused.

relate to the social substratum, but only on condition that one is aware that they are of the same nature as the others. Our definition will therefore subsume all that has to be defined if it states:

A social fact is any way of acting, whether fixed or not, capable of exerting over the individual an external constraint;

or:

which is general over the whole of a given society whilst having an existence of its own, independent of its individual manifestations.[4]

---

[4]This close affinity of life and structure, organ and function, can be readily established in sociology because there exists between these two extremes a whole series of intermediate stages, immediately observable, which reveal the link between them. Biology lacks this methodological resource. But one may believe legitimately that sociological inductions on this subject are applicable to biology and that, in organisms as in societies, between these two categories of facts only differences in degree exist.

Emile Durkheim, What is a Social Fact?

1.   State Durkheim's definition of a social fact.

2.   Give three examples of social facts.

       a.

       b.

       c.

3.   What experience does Durkheim use to verify his definition of a social fact?

4.   Durkheim argues that social phenomena are general because they are collective.

       a. True   b. False

Gabriel A. Almond*

SEPARATE TABLES: SCHOOLS AND SECTS IN POLITICAL SCIENCE

Miss Cooper: Loneliness is a terrible thing
don't you agree?
Anne: Yes, I do agree. A terrible thing . . .
Miss Meacham: She's not an "alone" type.
Miss Cooper: Is any type an "alone" type,
Miss Meacham . . . ?

(From Terence Rattigan's *Separate Tables*, 1955, 78, 92)

In *Separate Tables,* the hit of the 1955 New York theatrical season, the Irish playwright, Terence Rattigan, used the metaphor of solitary diners in a second-rate residential hotel in Cornwall to convey the loneliness of the human condition. It may be a bit farfetched to use this metaphor to describe the condition of political science in the 1980s. But in some sense the various schools and sects of political science now sit at separate tables, each with its own conception of proper political science, but each protecting some secret island of vulnerability.

It was not always so. If we recall the state of the profession a quarter of a century ago, let us say in the early 1960s, David Easton's (1953) and David Truman's (1955) scoldings of the profession for its backwardness among the social science disciplines had been taken to heart by a substantial and productive cadre of young political scientists. In 1961 David Dahl wrote his *Epitaph for a Monument to a Successful Protest,* reflecting the sure confidence of a successful movement, whose leaders were rapidly becoming the most visible figures in the profession. Neither Dahl nor Heinz Eulau, whose *Behavioral Persuasion* appeared in 1963, made exaggerated or

exclusive claims for the new political science. They expressed the view that the scientific approach to the study of political phenomena had proven itself, and that it could take its place alongside political philosophy, public law, and institutional history and description, as an important approach to the study of politics. As the part of the discipline "on the move," so to speak, it created some worry among the older subdisciplines. An appropriate metaphor for the state of political science at that time perhaps would be the "young Turk-old Turk" model, with the young Turks already beginning to gray at the temples. But we were all Turks.

Now there is this uneasy separateness. The public choice people seek an anchorage in reality, a "new institutionalism," to house their powerful deductive apparatus; the political econometricians want to relate to historical and institutional processes; the humanists cringe at the avoidance of political values by "scientism," and suffer from feelings of inadequacy in a world dominated by statistics and technology; and the radical and "critical" political theorists, like the ancient prophets, lay about them with anathemas against the behaviorists and positivists, and the very notion of a political science professionalism that would separate knowledge from action. But their anti-professionalism must leave them in doubt as to whether they are scholars or politicians.

The uneasiness in the political science profession is not of the body but of the soul. In the last several decades the profession has more than

*Gabriel Almond is Professor of Political Science at Stanford University. He is the author *Political Development, The Civic Culture Revisited* (with Sidney Verba), and *Comparative Politics* (with G. B. Powell), among other works. In the following article (1990), Almond defends what he sees as the broad, eclectic center within political science against attacks from the right and the left.

"Separate Tables: Schools and Sects in American Political Science," *PS,* 21:4, 1988. Reprinted by permission of American Political Science Association.

doubled in numbers. American-type political science has spread to Europe, Latin America, Japan, and more interestingly to China and the USSR. Political science has taken on the organizational and methodological attributes of science-research institutes, large-scale budgets, the use of statistical and mathematical methods, and the like. Political science has prospered materially, but it is not a happy profession.

We are separated along two dimensions: an ideological one, and a methodological one (see Figure 1.1). On the methodological dimension there are the extremes of soft and hard. At the soft extreme are Clifford Geertz (1972) types of "thickly descriptive" clinical studies. As an example of this kind of scholarship, Albert Hirschman (1970) celebrated the John Womack (1969) biography of the Mexican guerrilla hero, Emiliano Zapata, with its almost complete lack of conceptualization, hypothesizing, efforts to prove propositions, and the like. Despite this lack of self-conscious social science, Hirschman argues, the Zapata study was full of theoretical implications of the greatest importance. Leo Strauss (1959) and his followers in political philosophy with their exegetical approach to the evocation of the ideas of political philosophers come pretty close to this soft extreme as well, but while Womack's kind of work leaves everything but narrative and description to implication, Straussian exegesis involves the discipline of the explication of the great texts, ascertaining their "true" meaning through the analysis of their language.

Somewhat away from the soft extreme, but still on the soft side of the continuum, would be political philosophical studies more open to empirical evidence and logical analysis. Recent work such as that of Michael Walzer on justice (1983) and obligation (1970), Carole Pateman on participation (1970) and obligation (1979) would be illustrative. Here there is more than a simple, rich evocation of an event or personality, or precise exegesis of the ideas of political philosophers. A logical argument is advanced, often tested through the examination of evidence, and developed more or less rigorously.

At the other extreme of the methodological continuum are the quantitative, econometric, and mathematical modeling studies; and the most extreme would be the combination of mathematical modeling, statistical analysis, experiment, and computer simulation in the public choice literature. Theories of voting, coalition making, decision-making in committees, and in bureaucracies, involving the testing of hypotheses generated by formal, mathematical models would exemplify this hard extreme.

| | | Ideological Dimension | |
		Left	Right
Methodological	Hard	HL	HR
Dimension	Soft	SL	SR

Figure 1.1.

On the ideological continuum on the left we have four groups in the Marxist tradition—the Marxists properly speaking, the "critical political theorists," the *dependencistas,* and the world system theorists, all of whom deny the possibility of separating knowledge from action, and who subordinate political science to the struggle for socialism. At the conservative end of the continuum are the neoconservatives, who favor among other things a free market economy and limits on the power of the state, as well as an aggressive anti-communist foreign policy.

If we combine these two dimensions we end up with four schools of political science, four separate tables—the soft-left, the hard-left, the soft-right, and the hard-right tables. Reality, of course, is not quite this neat. The ideological and methodological shadings are more complex, more subtle. To elaborate our metaphor a bit but still within the refectoral realm, since the overwhelming majority of political scientists are somewhere in the center— "liberal" and moderate in ideology, and eclectic and open to conviction in methodology—we might speak of the great cafeteria of the center, from which most of us select our intellectual food, and where we are seated at large tables with mixed and changing table companions.

The outlying tables in this disciplinary refectory are strongly lit and visible, while the large center lies in shade. It is unfortunate that the mood and reputation of the political science discipline is so heavily influenced by these extreme views. This is in part because the extremes make themselves highly audible and visible—the soft left providing a pervasive flagellant background noise, and the hard right providing virtuoso mathematical and statistical displays appearing in the pages of our learned journals.

THE SOFT LEFT

Suppose we begin with the soft left. All of the subgroups of the soft left share in the meta-methodological assumption that the empirical world cannot be understood in terms of separate spheres and dimensions, but has to be understood as a time-space totality. "Critical theory," as developed by Horkheimer, Adorno, Marcuse, and others of the

"Frankfurt School," rejects the alleged detachment and disaggregating strategy of mainstream social science. The various parts of the social process must be seen "as aspects of a total situation caught up the process of historical change" (Lukacs, quoted in David Held, 1980, 164). The student as well as that which he studies is involved in struggle. Hence objectivity is inappropriate. "Positivists fail to comprehend that the process of knowing cannot be severed from the historical struggle between humans and the world. Theory and theoretical labor are intertwined in social life processes. The theorist cannot remain detached, passively contemplating, reflecting and describing 'society' or 'nature'" (Held, 165). To understand and explain one must have a commitment to an outcome. There is no political *science* in the positivist sense, that is, a political science separable from ideological commitment. To seek to separate it is a commitment to support the existing, historically obsolescent order.

The more orthodox Marxists such as Perry Anderson (1976), Goran Therborn (1977), Philip Slater (1977), and others, while sharing the meta-methodology of the "Critical school," go further and argue that unless one accepts historical materialism in the fullest reductionist sense of explaining the political realm in class struggle terms, one ends up failing to appreciate the relationship between theory and "praxis."

As we consider the composition of the soft left our fourfold metaphor of separate tables begins to break down. The Marxist theorists of several persuasions—the "critical theorists," the "dependency" writers, and "world system" theorists—make quarrelsome table companions. What they all share is a common belief in the unity of theory and praxis, in the impossibility of separating science and politics. As a logical consequence, positivist political science, which believes in the necessity of separating scientific activity from political activity, loses contact with the overriding unity of the historical process and is mindlessly linked to the status quo. Positivist political science fails to take into account the historical dialectic which makes the shift from capitalism to socialism inevitable.

Fernando Cardoso, the leading theorist of the dependency school, contrasts the methodology of dependency theory with the North American social science tradition in the following language:

We attempt to reestablish the intellectual tradition based on a comprehensive social science. We seek a global and dynamic understanding of social structures instead of looking only at specific dimensions of the social process. We oppose the academic tradition which conceived of domination and social-cultural relations as "dimensions" analytically independent of one another and together independent of the economy, as if each one of these dimensions corresponded to separate features of reality . . . . We use a dialectical approach to study society, its structures and processes of change . . . . In the end what has to be discussed as an alternative is not the consolidation of the state and the fulfillment of "autonomous capitalism," but how to supersede them. The important question, then, is how to construct paths toward socialism. (Cardoso and Faletto, 1979, ix and xxiv)

Political science can be science, then, only if it is fully committed to the attainment of socialism.

One of the leading American expositors of the "dependency" approach, Richard Fagen, draws the implications of Cardoso's views for the academic community concerned with development issues. Real progress in development scholarship has to be associated with a restructuring of asymmetric international power relations and "a much more difficult and historically significant assault on capitalist forms of development themselves. . . . Only when this crucial understanding infuses the nascent academic critique of the global capitalist system will we be able to say that the paradigm shift in mainstream U.S. social science is gathering steam and moving scholarship closer to what really matters" (1978, 80).

Two recent interpretations of the history of American political science show that this "soft-left" critique of mainstream work in the discipline has taken on some momentum. David Ricci in *The Tragedy of Political Science* (1984) traces the emergence of a liberal scientific school of political science in post-World War II America, a movement dedicated, according to Ricci, to proving the superior virtue of liberal pluralistic values and assumptions by the most precise methods. The validity of this complacent "empirical political theory" constructed by such political scientists as David Truman, Robert Dahl, C. E. Lindblom, the University of Michigan group of voting specialists, and others, was undermined in the disorders of the late 1960s and early 1970s, and in the associated discrediting of American politics and public policy. Ricci draws the implication of this behavioral-postbehavioral episode, as demonstrating that political science as empirical science without the systematic inclusion of moral and ethical values and alternatives, and a commitment to political action, is doomed to disillusion.

Political science has to chose sides; failing to do so results in its withdrawal into specialized preciosity, and futility.

Ricci's soft leftism is of the humanist moderate left variety. That of Raymond Seidelman (1985) is a more sharply radical treatment of the history of American political science. In a book entitled *Disenchanted Realists: Political Science and the American Crisis, 1884–1984,* Seidelman develops the thesis in detail that there have been three trends in American political theory—an institutionalist trend, a democratic populist trend, and a relatively short-lived "liberal political science" trend, initiated in the 1920s and 1930s by the University of Chicago school, and flowering in the United States in the post-World War II years roughly until the 1970s. The institutionalist trend is the Hamiltonian-Madisonian tradition embodied in the constitutional system, so constructed that it would frustrate the will of majorities. Separation of powers theory is based on a distrust of popular propensities. Contrasted with this tradition of American political theory is the democratic populist trend manifested in early agrarian egalitarianism, abolitionism, populism, and the like. This second Thomas Paine tradition is anti-statist, anti-government and was discredited by the rise of industrial-urban society and the necessity for strong central government.

The third tradition was based on a belief in the possibility of a science of politics which would help produce a powerful national state, manned by trained experts pursuing constructive and coherent public policies, and supported by virtuous popular majorities. This third tradition dream of a great constructive political science has been dispelled on both the political and the science sides. Political reality has turned into a disarticulated set of elite-dominated "issue networks" and "iron triangles," incapable of pursuing consistent and effective public policies; and the science has turned into a set of disembodied specialties lacking in linkage to politics and public policy. Seidelman concludes:

Historically, political science professionalism has only obscured fundamental conflicts and choices in American public life, for it has treated citizens as objects of study or clients of a benign political paternalism . . . . Until political scientists realize that their democratic politics cannot be realized through a barren professionalism, intellectual life will remain cleaved from the genuine if heretofore subterranean dreams of American citizens. Political science history has confirmed this separation

even as it has tried to bridge it. Modern political science must bridge it, if delusions are to be transformed into new democratic realities. (241)

The burden of the soft left, thus, is an attack on political science professionalism. It is a call to the academy to join the political fray, to orient its teaching and research around left ideological commitments—in particular, moderate or revolutionary socialism.

THE HARD RIGHT

The hard right, on the other hand, is ultra-professional at the methodological level, deploying a formidable array of scientific methodologies—deductive, statistical, and experimental. There is a tendency to view softer historical, descriptive, and unsophisticated quantitative analysis as preprofessional, as inferior breeds of political science, although in recent years there has been a notable rediscovery of political institutions, and an effort to relate formal deductive work to the empirical tradition pioneered by Gosnell, Herring, and V. O. Key.

William Mitchell (1988), in a recent review of the public choice movement in political science, distinguishes between the two principal centers, which he calls the Virginia and Rochester schools. The Virginia school, influential mainly among economists, was founded by James Buchanan and Gordon Tullock. The founder of the Rochester school, more influential among political scientists, was William Riker. Both schools tend to be skeptical of politics and bureaucracy and are fiscally conservative. But the Virginia school views the market unambiguously as the benchmark of efficient allocation. The Virginians according to Mitchell display a "firm conviction that the private economy is far more robust, efficient, and perhaps equitable than other economies, and much more successful than political processes in efficiently allocating resources. . . . Much of what has been produced by the [Virginian] Center for Study of Public Choice, can best be described as contributions to a theory of the failure of political processes . . . inequity, inefficiency, and coercion are the most general results of democratic policy formation" (106–107). Buchanan proposed an automatic deficit reduction plan years before the adoption of the Gramm-Rudman-Hollings proposal; and he was the author of an early version of the proposed constitutional budget-balancing amendment. Buchanan, in two books—*Democracy in Deficit: The Political Legacy of Lord*

Keynes (Buchanan and Wagner, 1977), and *The Economics of Politics* (1978)—presents a view of democratic politics in which voters act in terms of their short-run interests, that is to say, oppose taxes and favor material benefits for themselves; politicians naturally play into these propensities by favoring spending and opposing taxing; and bureaucrats seek to extend their power and resources without regard to the public interest.

These theorists differ in the extent to which they believe that the short-run utility-maximizer model captures human reality. Some scholars employ the model only as a way of generating hypotheses. Thus Robert Axelrod, using deductive modeling, experimentation, and computer simulation, has made important contributions to our understanding of how cooperative norms emerge, and in particular how norms of international cooperation might develop from an original short-run utility-maximizing perspective (1984). Douglass North (1981), Samuel Popkin (1979), Robert Bates (1988), and others combine rational choice modeling with sociological analysis in their studies of Third World development and historical process.

That this view is on the defensive is reflected in recent comments of scholars with unquestionable scientific credentials. Thus Herbert Simon challenges the rational choice assumption of this literature:

It makes a difference to research, a very large difference, to our research strategy whether we are studying the nearly omniscient *homo economics* of rational choice theory or the boundedly rational *homo psychologicus* of cognitive psychology. It makes a difference for research, but it also makes a difference for the proper design of political institutions. James Madison was well aware of that, and in the pages of the *Federalist Papers,* he opted for this view of the human condition; "As there is a degree of depravity in mankind which requires a certain degree of circumspection and distrust, so there are other qualities in human nature which justify a certain portion of esteem and confidence:"—a balanced and realistic view we may concede, of bounded human rationality and its accompanying frailties of motive and reason. (303)

James March and Johan Olsen attack the formalism of the public choice literature: "The new institutionalism is an empirically based prejudice, an assertion that what we observe in the world is inconsistent with the ways in which contemporary theories ask us to talk. . . . The bureaucratic agency, the legislative committee, and the appellate court are arenas for contending social forces, but they are also collections of standard operating procedures and structures that define and defend interest" (1984, 738). They similarly question the rational self-interest assumption of the public choice literature, arguing,

Although self-interest undoubtedly permeates politics, action is often based more on discovering the normatively appropriate behavior than on calculating the return expected from alternative choices. As a result, political behavior, like other behavior, can be described in terms of duties, obligations, roles, and rules. (744)

THE SOFT RIGHT

In the soft-right cell there are miscellaneous conservatives of an old and a "neo" variety, who tend to be traditional in their methodologies and on the right side of the ideological spectrum. But the followers of Leo Strauss in political theory are a distinctive breed indeed. Their methodological conservatism is unambiguous. The enlightenment and the scientific revolution are the archenemy. High on their list of targets is the value-free and ethically neutral political science of Max Weber. As Leo Strauss put it, "Moral obtuseness is the necessary condition for scientific analysis. The more serious we are as social scientists the more completely we develop within ourselves a state of indifference to any goal, or to aimlessness and drifting, a state of what may be called nihilism" (1959, 19). But political *science* is not only amoral, it is not really productive of knowledge. Again Leo Strauss, "Generally speaking, one may wonder whether the new political science has brought to light anything of political importance which intelligent political practitioners with a deep knowledge of history, nay intelligent and educated journalists, to say nothing of the old political scientists, did not know at least as well beforehand" (in Storing, 1962, 312).

The Straussians reject all "historicist" and "sociology of knowledge" interpretations of political theory. The true meaning of philosophical texts is contained in what has been written. The political philosopher must have the skill and insight necessary to explicate this original meaning. The ultimate truth can be located in the writings of the original classic philosophers, and particularly in the writings of Plato—in his Socratic rationalism shorn of all contingency. Truths transcend time, place, and context. Post-Machiavellian political philosophy has led to moral relativism and the decay of civic virtue; "behavioral" political science is the debased product of this moral decline.

In the recent celebrations of the 200th anniversary of the Constitution, the Straussians, as one might expect, were in the vanguard of the "original intent" school of constitutional interpretation. Gordon Wood, in a recent review of the Straussian literature on the Constitution (1988), points out that for such Straussians as Gary McDowell and Walter Berns the whole truth about the Constitution is contained in the constitutional text, and perhaps the record of the debates, and the Federalist Papers. Wood points out that the Straussian commitment to "natural right" leads them to distrust of all historically derived rights, "particularly those recently discovered by the Supreme Court" (1988, 39). For some Straussians the natural right to property postulated by the Founders may be grounds for rolling back the modern welfare state. The moral model regime for many Straussians is the Platonic aristocracy, or as second-best, Aristotelian "mixed government." Their program of action is a call for an intellectual elite which will bring us back to first principles.

THE HARD LEFT

There is finally a hard-left school, which employs scientific methodology in testing propositions derived from socialist and dependency theories. However, the moment one makes explicit and testable the assumptions and beliefs of left ideologies, one has gone part of the way toward rejecting the anti-professionalism of the left. And this is reflected in the nervousness of leading socialist and dependency theorists over quantification and the testing of hypotheses. Thus Christopher Chase-Dunn, one of the leading world system quantifiers, pleads with his colleagues, "My concern is that we not become bogged down in a sterile debate between 'historicists' and 'social scientists,' or between quantitative and qualitative researchers. The 'ethnic' boundaries may provide us with much material for spirited dialogue, but a real understanding of the world system will require that we transcend methodological sectarianism" (1982, 181). The leading dependency theorists such as Cardoso and Fagen raise serious questions regarding the validity of "scientific type, quantitative" studies of dependency propositions. For reasons not clearly specified such research

is "premature," or misses the point. Thus they probably would not accept as valid the findings of the Sylvan, Snidal, Russett, Jackson, and Duvall (1983) group, which tested a formal model of "dependencia" on a worldwide set of dependent countries in the 1970–75 period, and came up with mixed and inconclusive results. Nevertheless, the dependency and world system quantifiers and econometricians, including political scientists and sociologists such as Chase-Dunn (1982), Richard Rubinson (see Rubinson and Chase-Dunn, 1979), Albert Bergesen (1980), Volker Bornischier and J. P. Hoby (1981), and others, are carrying on quantitative studies oriented toward the demonstration of the validity of world system and dependency propositions.

GETTING OUR PROFESSIONAL HISTORY STRAIGHT

Most political scientists would find themselves uncomfortable seated at these outlying tables. Having become a major academic profession only in the last two or three generations, we are not about to cast off our badges of professional integrity by turning our research and teaching into political advocacy. This is reflected in the partial defection from anti-professionalism by the hard left, who insist that assertions about society and politics can be tested by formulating them explicitly and precisely, and using statistical methods where appropriate.

Similarly, most of us are troubled at the preemption by the public choice and statistical political scientists of the badge of professionalism, and their demotion of the rest of us to a prescientific status. And this concern is shared by some of the most reputable and sophisticated of our more rigorous political scientists, who are currently engaged in relating to and rehabilitating the older political science methodologies, such as philosophical, legal, and historical analysis, and institutional description.

And there are few political scientists indeed who would share the view that all political science since the sixteenth century is a deviation from the true path, and that the sole route to professionalism is through the exegesis of the classical texts of political theory.

It is noteworthy that each of these schools or sects presents us with a particular version of the history of the political science discipline. Whoever controls the interpretation of the past in our professional history writing has gone a long way toward controlling the future. The soft left has almost preempted the writing of professional political science history in recent years. I believe they may have succeeded in convincing some of us that we have deviated from the true path. Both Ricci and Seidelman would have us believe that modern political science with its stress on methodology and objectivity could only develop in the United States, where for a brief interval it appeared that liberal democracy and an objective professionalism were possible. As this American optimism abates, and as party and class antagonism sharpens inevitably, they argue, a politically neutral political science becomes untenable. According to this view political science must again become an active part of a political and, for some, a revolutionary movement.

The view of professional history presented by the hard right is a very foreshortened one. According to this view, prior to the introduction of mathematical, statistical, and experimental methodologies there was no political science and theory in the proper sense.

But the large methodologically eclectic majority of political scientists, and those who are committed to the control of ideological bias in the conduct of professional work—what I call the "cafeteria of the center"—ought not to concede the writing of disciplinary history to any one of these schools. The history of political science does not lead to any one of these separate tables, but rather to the methodologically mixed and objectivity-aspiring scholarship of the center.

It is not correct to argue that political science deviated from classical political philosophy in the sixteenth and seventeenth centuries, and that it has been on the wrong path ever since. Nor is it correct to attribute to American political science the effort to separate political theory from political action. The Straussians cannot legitimately claim exclusive origin in classical Greek philosophy. The scientific impulse in political studies had its beginnings among the classical Greek philosophers. Robert Dahl, for my money, is a more legitimate follower of Aristotle than is Leo Strauss.

There is a political sociological tradition going all the way back to Plato and Aristotle, continuing through Polybius, Cicero, Machiavelli, Hobbes, Locke, Montesquieu, Hume, Rousseau, Tocqueville, Comte, Marx, Pareto, Durkheim, Weber and continuing up to Dahl, Lipset, Rokkan, Sartori, Moore, and Lijphart, which sought, and seeks, to relate socioeconomic conditions to political constitutions and institutional arrangements, and to relate these structural characteristics to policy propensities in war and peace.

Our founding fathers belonged to this tradition. Alexander Hamilton observed in *Federalist 9,* "The science of politics . . . like most other sciences, has received great improvement. The efficacy of various principles is now well understood, which were either not known at all, or imperfectly known to the ancients" (1937). And in *Federalist 31* Hamilton deals with the perennial question of just how scientific moral and political studies could be. He concludes,

Though it cannot be pretended that the principles of moral and political knowledge have, in general, the same degree of certainty with those of the mathematics, yet they have much better claims in this respect than . . . we should be disposed to allow them. (189)

It is worth noting that the hard science-soft science polarity, which we have been led to assume is a recent phenomenon attributable to the heresy of the American behavioral movement, has in fact been endemic to the discipline since its origins.

In the nineteenth and early twentieth centuries, Auguste Comte, Marx and Engels and their followers, Max Weber, Emile Durkheim, Vilfredo Pareto, and others treated politics in larger social science perspectives, with lawlike regularities and necessary relationships. At the turn of the twentieth century John Robert Seeley and Otto Hintze, Moissaye Ostrogorski, and Roberto Michels all produced what they considered to be "scientific laws" of politics—Seeley and Hintze on the relationship between external pressure and internal freedom in the development of the nation states of Western Europe; Ostrogorski, on the incompatibility of the mass-bureaucratic political party and democracy which has derived from a comparative study of the rise of the British and American party systems; and Michels, on the "iron law of oligarchy," the propensity in large bureaucratic organizations for power to gravitate to the top leadership, which he derived from his "critical" case study of the Social Democratic party of Germany. More recently, Duverger's "law" of the relationship between the electoral and party systems also came from Europe.

Among the early pioneers of modern professional political science it was common practice to speak of this branch of scholarship as a "science" from the very beginning. Thus Sir Frederick Pollock and John Robert Seeley, the first lecturing from Oxford and the Royal Institution, the second from Cambridge, entitled their books *The History of the Science of Politics* (1890) and *An Introduction to*

Political Science (1896), respectively. What these early writers meant by "science" varied from case to case. Pollock distinguishes between the natural and moral sciences:

> The comparative inexactness of the moral sciences is not the fault of the men who have devoted their abilities to them, but depends, as Aristotle already saw, on the nature of their subject matter. (5)

For John Robert Seeley political science was to be a body of propositions drawn from historical knowledge. He expected a takeoff in the development of political science because of the development of historiography in the nineteenth century. If the moderns were to do so much better than Locke, Hobbes, and Montesquieu, it was because their historical data base was much richer.

For Seeley, who introduced political science into the Cambridge Tripos, it meant learning to "reason, generalize, define, and distinguish . . . as well as collecting, authenticating, and investigating facts." These two processes constituted political science. "If we neglect the first process, we shall accumulate facts to little purpose, because we shall have not test by which to distinguish facts which are important from those which are unimportant; and of course, if we neglect the second process, our reasonings will be baseless, and we shall but weave scholastic cobwebs" (1896, 27–28).

There were two schools of thought in the nineteenth and early twentieth century social sciences regarding the degree or kind of science that was possible. The work of August Comte, Karl Marx, and Vilfredo Pareto makes no distinction between the social and the "natural" sciences. Both groups of sciences sought uniformities, regularities, laws. On the other hand, the notion of a social science which would consist of "a closed system of concepts, in which reality is synthesized in some sort of permanently and universally valid classification, and from which it can again be deduced" was viewed as entirely meaningless by Max Weber:

> The stream of immeasurable events flows unendingly towards eternity. The cultural problems which move men form themselves ever anew and in different colors, and the boundaries of that area in the infinite stream of concrete events which acquires meaning and significance for us, i.e., which becomes an "historical individual" are constantly subject

to change. The intellectual contexts from which it is viewed and scientifically analyzed shift. (1949, 80)

The "lawfulness" of human interactions is of a different order for Max Weber. The subject matter of the social sciences—human action—involves value orientation, memory and learning, which can only yield "soft" regularities, "objective possibilities," and probabilities. Cultural change may attenuate or even dissolve these relationships. Similarly, Durkheim viewed cultural phenomena as too complex and open to human creativity to lend themselves to the same degree of causal certainty as the natural sciences.

During the first decades of professional political science in the United States—from 1900 to the 1930s—two scholars, Merriam and Catlin, the first as American as apple pie, the second a temporarily transplanted Englishman—took the lead in advocating the introduction of scientific methods and standards in the study of politics. Merriam's contribution was primarily programmatic, and promotional. He advocated, recruited personnel, and funded a particular research program at the University of Chicago. He also was a founder of the Social Science Research Council. Catlin wrote on methodological questions, differentiating between history and political science, and locating political science among the social sciences.

In his 1921 manifesto, "The Present State of the Study of Politics," Merriam advocated the introduction of psychological insights into the study of political institutions and processes, and of the introduction of statistical methods in an effort to enhance the rigor of political analysis. Nowhere in this early call to professional growth and improvement is there anything approximating a discussion of scientific methodology. He proposed to *do* political science rather than talk abut it. And indeed, in the decades following at the University of Chicago, a research program unfolded exemplifying Merriam's stress on empirical research, quantification, and social-psychological interpretation. The scholars produced by this program constituted a substantial part of the nucleus of the post-World War "behavioral movement."

George Catlin may have been the first to speak of a "behaviorist treatment of politics" (1927, xi), and in his argument about a science of politics seems to dispose of all of those objections which would differentiate social and human subject matters from those of natural science. But he is hardly sanguine about the prospects of science.

Politics must for the present confine itself to the humble task of collecting, where possible measuring, and sorting the historical material, past and contemporary; and following up probable clues to the discover of permanent forms and general principles of action. . . . It is reasonable to expect that political science will prove to be more than this, that it will give us some insight into the possibility of controlling the social situation, and will show us, if not what it is wise to do, at least what, human nature being what it is, it is unwise to do, because such action will cut across the grain of the social structure and athwart the lines of activity of the deeper forces which have built up this structure. (1927, 142–43)

Thus Bernard Crick's (1959) argument that it was the behavioral movement in American political science, and particularly the Chicago school that was responsible for leading political science down the garden path of scientism cannot bear careful examination of the sources. In both Europe and America meta-methodological opinion has been divided on this question. It would be hard to find more hard-science-oriented scholars than Comte, Marx, Pareto, and Freud. Durkheim and Weber, while fully committed to the pursuit of science, clearly recognized that the social scientist dealt with a subject matter less tractable to covering-law hard-science forms of explanation. This polemic diffused to the United States in the course of the twentieth century.

Crick's attribution of this scientific orientation to Chicago populists does not hold up when we examine the evidence. One has to read the Tocqueville correspondence (1962) to appreciate how close that brilliant interpreter of American democracy, a century before the Chicago school saw the light of day, came to doing an opinion survey in his travels around the country. As he talked to a steamboat captain on the Mississippi, to farmers in the interior, to bourgeois dinner companions on the eastern seaboard, and to officeholders in Washington, D.C., sampling the American population was clearly on his mind. Karl Marx drew up a six-page questionnaire for the study of the living conditions, working conditions, attitudes, and beliefs of the French working class in the early 1880s. A large number of copies were distributed to socialists and working-class organizations. The data gathered were to be used in the forthcoming general election (1880). In Max Weber's working papers for his study of the peasantry in East Prussia there is evi-dence that he planned and partially executed a survey of Polish and German peasant attitudes. And in his study of comparative religion he used a formal two-by-two table—worldliness-unworldliness, asceticism-mysticism—as a way of generating hypotheses about the relationship between religious ethics and economic attitudes.

Most of the important discoveries in the development of statistics were made by Europeans. La Place and Condorcet were Frenchmen; the Bernoulli family were Swiss; Bayes, Galton, Pearson, and Fisher were Englishmen; Pareto was an Italian; Markov a Russian. The first "public choice" theorist was the Scotsman, Duncan Black (1958). The view that the quantitative approach to social science analysis was peculiarly American doesn't stand up to the historical record. What was peculiarly American was the improvement in, and the application of, quantitative methods as in survey research, content analysis, aggregate statistical analysis, mathematical modeling, and the like, and the pursuit in empirical depth of psychological and sociological hypotheses largely generated in the European social science literature.

At the darkest moment in European history —in the 1930s—there was a strong infusion of European social science into the United States through refugees such as Paul Lazarsfeld, Kurt Lewin, Marie Jahoda, Wolfgang Kohler, Hans Speier, Erich Fromm, Franz Neumann, Otto Kircheimer, Leo Lowenthal, Franz Alexander, Hannah Arendt, Hans Morgenthau, Leo Strauss, and many others. It should be quite clear from this litany of names that this emigration carried the various social science polemics within it, and that the counterposition of a European and an American approach to social science around the issue of humanist vs. scientific scholarship will simply not bear the light of day. There is clear continuity from the European background to the growth of the social sciences and political science in the United States.

This broad tradition of political science, beginning with the Greeks and continuing up to the creative scholars of our own generation, is the historically correct version of our disciplinary history. The critical and Marxist schools throw in the professional sponge. Confronting this simplistic temptation we need to have a deep-rooted and unshakable firmness in our commitment to the search for objectivity. The call for "relevance" associated with "postbehavioralism" implies a greater concern for policy implications in our scholarly work, but it cannot imply a commitment to a particular course of political action. A political scientist is not necessarily a socialist, and surely not a socialist of a particular kind.

The version of disciplinary history presented to us in Straussian political philosophy cannot be taken seriously. The hard-nosed public choice version of our history mistakes technique for substance. Mainstream political science is open to all methods that illuminate the world of politics and public policy. It will not turn its back on the illumination we get from our older methodologies just because it now can employ the powerful tools of statistics and mathematics.

We have good grounds for professional pride in the development of political science in the last decades. And as Americans we have made important contributions to an age-old, worldwide effort to bring the power of knowledge to bear on the tragic dilemmas of the world of politics.

REFERENCES

Anderson, Perry. 1976. *Considerations on Western Marxism*. London: New Left Books.

Axelrod, Robert. 1984. *The Evolution of Cooperation*. New York: Basic Books.

Bates, Robert. 1988. *Macro-Political Economy in the Field of Development*. Duke University Program in International Political Economy, Working Paper No. 40 (June).

Bergesen, Albert. 1980. "The Class Structure of the World System." In *Contending Approaches to World System Analysis*, ed. William R. Thompson. Beverly Hills, CA: Sage Publications.

Black, Duncan. 1958. *The Theory of Committees and Elections*. Cambridge: Cambridge University Press.

Bornschier, Volker, and J. P. Hoby. 1981. "Economic Policy and Multi-National Corporations in Development: The Measurable Impacts in Cross National Perspective." *Social Problems*, 28: 363–377.

Bornschier, Volker, C. Chase-Dunn, and R. Rubinson. 1978. "Cross-national Evidence of Effects of Foreign Aid and Investment on Development." *American Journal of Sociology*, 84(3): 207–222.

Buchanan, James. 1978. *The Economics of Politics*. Lancing, West Sussex: Institute of Economic Affairs.

Buchanan, James and Richard Wagner. 1977. *Democracy in Deficit: The Political Legacy of Lord Keynes*. New York: Academic Press.

Cardoso, Fernando, and Enzo Faletto. 1979. *Dependency and Development in Latin America*. Berkeley: University of California Press.

Catlin, George E. G. 1927. *The Science and Method of Politics*. Hamden, CT: Anchor Books.

Chase-Dunn, Christopher. 1982. "Commentary." In *World System Analysis: Theory and Methodology*, ed. Terence Hopkins and Immanuel Wallerstein. Beverly Hills, CA: Sage Publications.

Crick, Bernard. 1959. *The American Science of Politics*. Berkeley: University of California Press.

Dahl, Robert A. 1961. "The Behavioral Approach in Political Science: Epitaph for a Monument to a Successful Protest." *American Political Science Review*, 55(Dec.): 763–772.

Easton, David. 1953. *The Political System*. New York. A. A. Knopf.

Eulau, Heinz. 1963. *The Behavioral Persuasion in Politics*. New York: Random House.

Fagen, Richard. 1978. "A Funny Thing Happened on the Way to the Market: Thoughts on Extending Dependency Ideas." *International Organization*, 32(1): 287–300.

Geertz, Clifford. 1972. *The Interpretation of Cultures*. New York: Basic Books.

Hamilton, Alexander. 1937. *The Federalist*. Washington, DC: National Home Library Foundation.

Held, David. 1980. *Introduction to Critical Theory: Horkheimer to Habermas*. Berkeley: University of California Press.

Hirschman, Albert. 1970. "The Search for Paradigms as a Hindrance to Understanding." *World Politics*. 22(3, March): 329–343.

March, James, and Johan Olsen. 1984. "The New Institutionalism: Organizational Factors in Political Life." *American Political Science Review*, 78(3 Sept.): 734–750.

Marx, Karl. 1880. "Enquiete Ouvriere." *La Revue Socialiste* (20 April).

Merriam, Charles E. 1921. "The Present State of the Study of Politics." *American Political Science Review,* 15(May): 173–185.

Mitchell, William. 1988. "Virginia, Rochester, and Bloomington: Twenty-five Years of Public Choice and Political Science." *Political Choice,* 56: 101–119.

North, Douglass. 1981. *Structure and Change in Economic History.* New York: W. W. Norton.

Pateman, Carole. 1970. *Participation and Democratic Theory.* Cambridge: Cambridge University Press.

Pateman, Carole. 1979. *The Problem of Political Obligation.* Chichester: Wiley.

Pollock, Frederick. 1890. *The History of Politics.* London: Macmillan.

Popkin, Samuel. 1979. *The Rational Peasant.* Berkeley: University of California Press.

Rattigan, Terence. 1955. *Separate Tables.* New York: Random House.

Ricci, David. 1984. *The Tragedy of Political Science.* New Haven, CT: Yale University Press.

Riker, William. 1982. *Liberalism Against Populism.* San Francisco: Freeman.

Rubinson, Richard, and C. Chase-Dunn. 1979. "Cycles, Trends, and New Departures in World System Development." In *National Development and World Systems,* ed. J. W. Meyer and M. T. Hannan. Chicago: University of Chicago Press.

Seeley, John Robert. 1896. *An Introduction to Political Science.* London: Macmillan.

Seidelman, Raymond. 1985. *Disenchanted Realists: Political Science and the American Crisis, 1884–1984.* Albany: State University of New York Press.

Simon, Herbert. 1985. "Human Nature in Politics: The Dialogue of Psychology with Political Science." *American Political Science Review,* 79(2 June): 293–304.

Slater, Philip. 1977. *Origin and Significance of the Frankfurt School: A Marxist Perspective.* London: Routledge & Kegan Paul.

Strauss, Leo. 1959. *What Is Political Philosophy?* Glencoe, IL: Free Press.

Strauss, Leo. 1972. "Political Philosophy and the Crisis of Our Time." In *The Post Behavioral Era,* ed. George Graham and George Carey. New York: Holt, Rinehart & Winston, pp. 217–242.

Sylvan, David, Duncan Snidal, Bruce M. Russett, Steven Jackson, and Raymond Duvall. 1983. "The Peripheral Economies: Penetration and Economic Distortion, 1970–1975." In *Contending Approaches to World System Analysis,* ed. William Thompson, Beverly Hills, CA: Sage Publications.

Therborn, Goran. 1977. *The Frankfurt School in Western Marxism: A Critical Reader.* London: New Left Books.

Tocqueville, Alexis de. 1962. *Journey to America.* New Haven, CT: Yale University Press.

Truman, David. 1955. "The Impact of the Revolution in Behavior Science on Political Science." *Brookings Lectures.* Washington, DC: Brookings Institution, pp. 202–231.

Walzer, Michael. 1970. *Obligations.* Cambridge, MA: Harvard University Press.

Walzer, Michael. 1983. *Spheres of Justice.* New York: Basic Books.

Weber, Max. 1949. *The Methodology of the Social Sciences* (translated by E. A. Shils and H. A. Finch). Glencoe, IL: Free Press.

Womack, John. 1969. *Zapata and the Mexican Revolution.* New York: A. A. Knopf.

Wood, Gordon S. 1988. "The Fundamentalists and the Constitution." *New York Review of Books* (18 Feb.).

Gabriel Almond, Separate Tables: A Discipline Divided

1.   Identify the two dimensions Almond uses to classify the different positions he discusses.

        a. _____

        b. _____

2.   Explain the nature of these two dimensions.

        a.

        b.

3.   According to Almond, where are the majority of political scientists located in his scheme of classification? Explain why.

John Kenneth Galbraith
and Nicole Salinger*

WHAT IS ECONOMICS ANYWAY?

NICOLE SALINGER: *Winston Churchill said he could understand almost anything else but could not get his mind around economics. And yet obviously it is very important. What is economics exactly? And can I get my mind around it?*

JOHN KENNETH GALBRAITH: As to the last, certainly. And on essentials Churchill could, too. Let me remind you of the rest of his statement. He said he couldn't get his mind around economics, but he did know that shooting Montagu Norman would be a good thing. Montagu Norman was then the head of the Bank of England.

Alfred Marshall, the great Cambridge economist who dominated the accepted British—and American—economic teaching from the 1880s to the 1920s, said that economics is merely the study of mankind in the ordinary business of life. I would now add a reference to organization—to the study of the way people are organized for economic tasks by corporations, by trade unions and by government. Also of how and when and to what extent organizations serve their own purposes as opposed to those of the people at large. And of how the public purposes can be made to prevail.

NICOLE: *When I understand economics, what can it do for me? Anything?*

JKG: To have a working understanding of economics is to understand the largest part of life. We pass our years, most of us, contemplating the relationship between the money we earn and the money we need, our thoughts suspended, as it were, between the two. Economics is about what we earn and what we can get for it. So an understanding of economics is an understanding of life's principal preoccupation.

There is another thing it can do for you. The newspaper headlines, when they escape from sex and the Middle East, are largely concerned with the economic decisions of governments. If people make no effort to understand these decisions, do not have an intelligent position and do not make that position known, they obviously surrender all power to those who do understand, pretend to understand or believe they understand. And you can be sure that the decisions so made will rarely be damaging to those who make them or to the people they represent.

NICOLE: *Valéry Giscard d'Estaing said in his recent book that economics is like the human body, an automatic regulatory mechanism and a further decision taken by the brain. Is that so?*

JKG: All similes for economic life should be resisted, but this is better than most. There are aspects of economic life which are still self-regulating, although they are diminishing in relation to the whole. And there are aspects which require guidance. It's the issues in this guidance—who is favored and who isn't—that the citizen and voter must understand.

*John Kenneth Galbraith is one of America's most distinguished economists and is currently Professor Emeritus at Harvard. His many published works include *The Affluent Society, The New Industrial State* and *Economics and the Public Purpose.* Professor Galbraith advocates an historical approach that focuses on the study of the character and role of economic institutions within society. Nicole Salinger is a writer. The following interview was published in 1978.

Do you think we've now persuaded all susceptible people that they should have a working knowledge of economics?

NICOLE: *I'm persuaded, all right. But why don't more people try?*

JKG: Partly they are put off by the terminology. We economists protect ourselves from outsiders by resort to a language of our own. People in all professions do it to some extent. Physicians have their own language, as do lawyers and psychiatrists and burglars, I'm told. All like to see themselves as a priestly class with a knowledge, a mystique, that isn't available to the everyday citizen.

And some people, maybe many, are deterred by the feeling that current economic explanations are at odds with everyday reality. They hear an economist say, in describing how prices are set, that he assumes pure competition—the competition of many small firms in the market. And in the real world they see only a few vast enterprises supplying the gasoline, automobiles, chemicals, pharmaceuticals, electricity, telephone services or what have you. So they say to hell with it—economics isn't my world.

NICOLE: *Economists don't all agree; many totally disagree. Why do they disagree? How do I tell whom I should believe?*

JKG: You should believe me, of course. As to the disagreement, there are several reasons. There is self-interest, something we all recognize and are usually too polite to mention. An economist who works for a large New York bank rarely comes up with a conclusion that is adverse to the interest of his bank as that is understood by his employers. His public truth is what gains their approval. There has always been in the United States a healthy suspicion of the views of the economics professor who has a remunerative consulting relationship with corporations. Certainly his view will be different from that of an economist who is employed by a trade union.

Political identification also makes for disagreement. In the United States we have Republican economists and Democratic economists. Their personal politics controls or shapes their conclusions. That has been true in my case; over the years I've found virtue, at election time, in the views of some Democrats of exceptional illiteracy, economically speaking.

Quite a few economists measure their truth by the applause it evokes; they adjust their position,

perhaps unconsciously, to what their audience will think agreeable.

Then, more important and perhaps more to be forgiven, there is the problem of change. The ultimate subject matter of the physical sciences is fixed. That of economics, in contrast, is always in the process of change—the corporation, the labor force, the behavior of the consumer, the role of government, are all always in transition. This means that economics, if it to avoid obsolescence, must adapt in two ways. It must change as new information is added or interpretation is improved. And it must change as basic institutions change. Disagreement then comes because different economists have different reactions to change. Some yearn to believe that the basic subject matter, like that of the hard sciences, is given for all time. Some accept that economic institutions are in a process of continual alteration—that what was true of corporate, trade union, consumer or government behavior yesterday will not be true today and certainly not tomorrow.

There are still other reasons for disagreement. Some economists are very economical of thought and bring the lessons of their profession into their personal lives. They seek, accordingly, to make any ideas, once acquired, last a lifetime. A measure of disagreement comes, I suppose, from some being more intelligent that other, although that, too, is a thought that all decent and modest scholars suppress.

There isn't much difficulty in telling who has an ax to grind; our oldest instinct is to ask who is paying. Also, if an economist gets too much applause from the affluent, you should always be suspicious. The rich in all countries combine a fairly acute self-interest with an ever-present feeling of anxiety and guilt. Anyone who relieves that anxiety and guilt is assured of applause, and seeking that applause, not the truth, easily becomes a habit. Beyond that, the only test is to ask for the fullest possible explanation, then ask yourself whether the explanation is truly complete and makes sense. If an economist ever suggests that you take something on faith because of his or her professional knowledge, dismiss him or her forthwith from your thoughts.

NICOLE: *There is reference to "economics" and also to "political economy." Does it become political economy when the government assumes a critical function and role?*

JKG: That would be logical, as you French require. In fact, political economy is the older term. In the early professional discussion of the subject in Britain—that started by Adam Smith with *Wealth of Nations* in 1776 and continued by David Ricardo, Thomas Robert Malthus and John Stuart Mill in the first half of the last century—the reference was to political economy. No sharp line was drawn between the role of the consumer and business firm on the one hand and that of the state on the other. All were seen as part of one great system.

Then, toward the end of the last century, the term "economics" came into use. It reflected a more virginal view of the subject, from which the government was largely excluded, Producers and consumers came together in the market; the market was the all-powerful regulatory force in society. All important needs were so supplied. The state had only a minor and often rather derogatory role. Economics was political economy cleansed of politics.

In very recent times there has been an effort to revive the older term and bring the reference to political economy back into use. This, as you might suppose, is on the grounds that the distinction between economics and politics is now an artificial one, that government has a necessary and powerful influence on economic behavior and performance. Even the term "political economy" is now misleadingly narrow in its connotations.

NICOLE; *If you can't separate economics from politics, can you separate it from philosophy, history, sociology, demography, geography—I suppose not from pornography. Don't they all bear on economic understanding?*

JKG: All distinction—all lines of separation—are artificial. If something influences economic behavior, then it is important for economics. You mentioned demography—the dynamics of population growth. It's a vital matter, especially for understanding economic life in the poor countries. And demography leads on to biology, family structure, social preferences and compulsions. All bear upon the rate of population increase and the economic result. An economist can't know everything. But neither can he exclude anything.

NICOLE: *Coming back to economics: is it the same for all countries—the United States, France, Britain, India, Algeria? Do the same rules hold in the Soviet Union, Poland, Yugoslavia? Or is there a different economics—or political economy—for each country?*

JKG: Certainly there are differences. But there is a broad resemblance between countries at the same stage in development. Certainly as between the United States, Britain and France the similarities are very much greater that the differences. All make steel, automobiles, chemicals, numerous other products, on a large scale. For such manufacture, inevitably, you have very large corporations. And in all large corporations the structure of organization is much the same. Also all bring trade unions into existence; given the power of the corporation as a buyer and user of labor, it occurs to workers that they must, of necessity, have unions as a form of countervailing power.

In addition, large corporations make similar demands on government for essential services, qualified manpower, research and development, financial rescue when they get in trouble. And as some industries lend themselves only to large-scale organization, others—agriculture, consumer services, artistic effort—operate best with smaller units. What is necessary in France is required also in the United States. So there is a basic structural similarity as between the developed industrial economies. And this similarity extends in a general way to the socialist countries—to the Soviet Union and Eastern Europe. There, too, the large-scale production of steel, automobiles or chemicals requires large organizations. Agriculture woks best in smaller units. Artists work by themselves. These differences in organization shape the character of the society.

NICOLE: *What about planning?*

JKG: The socialist economies are planned. The need for materials and components is foreseen and related to the intended production of finished goods. The aggregate of income is related, if imperfectly, to what there will be to buy, none of this being as simple as it sounds. But there is also much planning in the nonsocialist countries—by corporations to ensure the supply of steel and components for the automobiles they will produce; by their marketing men to ensure that consumers will want the new automobile design when it appears; and by the government to provide highways on which the cars can be driven, to ensure gasoline to propel them and also the purchasing power to buy them. Though devout free-enterprisers suppress the thought, all modern industrial economies are extensively planned. They must be.

NICOLE: *What about the Third World countries?*

JKG: The great difference in economic organization is between the rich countries and the poor countries. The poor countries, because they are poor, are primarily concerned with the necessaries of life: food, clothing, shelter. These are mostly produced by small firms with a simple structure—one man, a family. Being small, the individual producer is without power. The firms being numerous, he is much more subject to the impersonal forces of the market. Producers in the poor countries also have fewer needs from the state, and government services play a smaller part in living standards. In all everyday discussion we exaggerate the differences in economic structure of the United States and the Soviet Union. And we greatly underestimate the differences between the economic systems of, say, the United States and India or of France and her former African colonies.

NICOLE: *Aren't there countries in between, countries which still are considered undeveloped in the general character of their production and consumption but which have some highly technical or mass production industry, sometimes based on a primary resource? I think of Iran, for instance.*

JKG: Yes. This is a needed correction of my generalization. Even in the poorest countries, such as Iran or India, there are highly developed islands of industry—petrochemicals in Iran, steel in India. And the structure there, in turn, is very similar to that of the same industries in the developed countries. There is no difference that need detain us between Aramco in Saudi Arabia and Texaco in the United States.

NICOLE: *Let me go on to another subject. Can economists tell what will happen in the future? Did they predict the oil crisis?*

JKG: Maybe someone did. But no one paid attention. And rightly, for there was no way of knowing he was prescient. In fact, there are very great limits to what economists can predict. We must be judged by what we explain and what results from the policies we urge, not by what we foretell as to the stock market or the price of oil. You must always remember that prediction itself derives from the fact that no one knows. If something can be known, as for example that the sun will rise tomorrow morning and at exactly 6:24.24, then no one predicts it, not even on television.

Remember, too, that official economic prediction is not meant to be right; it only tells what governments need to have happen. A high government economist never predicts that unemployment will continue and get worse, that inflation will continue and accelerate and that the budget deficit will eventually be the highest on record. Any chairman of the Council of Economic Advisers in Washington who unleashed that kind of news would get an urgent message from the Oval Office. Yet, sadly enough, unemployment, inflation and the deficit do very often increase.

I should add that many economists make predictions, especially around Christmastime for the new year, not because they know what will happen but because they get asked. It's a ritual.

The safe rule for the citizen on economic predictions is to ignore them.

NICOLE: *I want to ask you later on about inflation and unemployment. But should we have a definition of them now?*

JKG: There is no mystery. Inflation is steadily rising prices—not some going up, others going down, but all or most going up together. This, needless to say, includes wages and salaries, at least of the fortunate. Our great definition of unemployment comes down to us from Calvin Coolidge. He said, "When a great many people are out of work, unemployment results." You got similar wisdom, I believe, from Monsieur de la Palisse.

NICOLE: *What is the definition of Economic growth? Why do people talk about it so much? Why does every politician praise himself for the growth he has achieved—or will achieve?*

JKG: Economic growth is merely an increase—a more than momentary increase—in the output of all the things we consume, use, invest in or otherwise produce. Economic growth and increasing production are the same thing.

NICOLE: *Is that the same as increasing Gross National Product—GNP?*

JKG: Yes, the Gross National Product is the value, in current prices or those of some past time, of everything that is produced and sold in the course of the year. It includes, of course, the value at cost of all public services.

NICOLE: *And what is the National Income?*

JKG: Nearly the same thing, in practice. Everything that is produced and sold returns income to some-

154

body. From the sale somebody gets a profit, a wage, a salary or, if no profit, a loss that is a gain to someone else. The value of the product is one side of the account, the income the other side of the same account. Gross National Product and National Income are not, in fact, quite equal; some things go into the value of the product that don't come out as income. That needn't bother us, at least today.

NICOLE: *Why are the GNP and National Income so important, both of them?*

JKG: In the years following World War II, economic growth, meaning the increase in Gross National Product, became the test of national economic performance and to some extent of national virtue. A country was known to be doing well or badly in accordance with its percentage rate of annual increase in GNP.

I never tire of my own aphorisms: eventually it came to pass that when economists and politicians presented themselves at the Holy Gate, Saint Peter asked only what they had done to increase the GNP. Japan was the greatest success in this period because it had the greatest increase in Gross National Product. The British were the wretched of the earth because of their low annual increase in GNP.

You ask why it is important. In fact Gross National Product has been oversold.

NICOLE: *That is because not everything is included?*

JKG: Partly. Only things that are readily measurable are included in the Gross National Product. I work in a very leisurely way as befits a Harvard professor, but my production, measured by my salary, is included in the Gross National Product of the United States. My wife works very hard managing our family and household, but, since she doesn't get a wage, she doesn't get included. Economists could get a very sudden increase in the GNP by discovering and including the unpaid labor of women.

There is another oddity having to do with sex. A woman of the street, since she charges for her affection, contributes to Gross National Product, at least in principle. A lovely and loving mistress does not.

More seriously, a city that plans its growth properly, manages its parks well and has clean, safe streets can have a lower contribution to the GNP than a city that does none of these things but produces and sells a lot of goods. You brought up pornography. A busy shop selling dirty pictures does more for the GNP than the absence of air pollution.

NICOLE: *Is it because the enjoyment from good city planning, pleasant parks, safe streets, cannot be measured? They are like true love?*

JKG: That is why they are excluded. And it's quite arbitrary. Many unmeasurable things have a greater human reward than measurable things.

NICOLE: *Including the arts?*

JKG: Arts, love, enjoyment of one's surroundings, nice highways that wind through the countryside without a great clutter of advertising. All these things give a great deal of pleasure but aren't included in the Gross National Product.

NICOLE: *I've heard it said that rather than talk about a Gross National Product we should talk about a Gross National Happiness. Should we not have a measure of the quality of life rather than the quantity of goods?*

JKG: There have been efforts in that direction—to include values associated with social contentment and enjoyment. They haven't been very successful —again, the problem of measurement. One reason the British have had a low increase in Gross National Product is that they take a larger part of their return in the unmeasurable rewards. They have the best maintained countryside in Europe, much better certainly that the United States has, better even than that in France. They have good public services. It is much easier and more pleasant to commute into London than into New York. Recreational facilities, parks, playing fields, are far better arranged and looked after in London than in New York. So one can easily argue that the average Londoner has a lower per capita GNP but a high standard of well-being than the average New Yorker.

Still, there is a beloved economic cliche; do not throw out the baby with the bath water unless it's a very dirty baby indeed. The Gross National Product does not measure the quality of life. But it does tell us something useful about the trend in the production of goods and services. We should use it for what it tells us so long as we know what it doesn't tell us.

NICOLE: *May I become more technical? Economists talk about microeconomics and macroeconomics. Could you explain?*

JKG: You are not becoming all that technical—nothing that would impress Professor Samuelson or your Professor Malinvaud.

Microeconomics is the branch of economics that deals with the firm and the household, the ultimate cellular structure; thus the overtones of microscope and microbiology. It then goes on to deal with the market—to tell, or anyhow imagine, how consumers, given their income and preferences, interact through the market with business firms to determine what is produced, in what amount, at what profit and at what price.

Macroeconomics became a separate topic of discussion and was so named in the aftermath of John Maynard Keynes and the Great Depression. It then came generally to be realized that consumers and business firms might not have enough spendable income or might not spend or invest enough from their income to buy all the goods and services that could be produced. There would, as a consequence, be idle plant capacity and unemployment. Or, though it was not a problem during the Depression, people and governments might spend in excess of the productive capacity of the economy. Then there would be inflation—one kind of inflation.

So it became a function of government to regulate the overall or aggregate relationships between all buyers and all sellers. This meant providing more purchasing power and more demand when that was indicated, restricting purchasing power and demand when that was called for. The expansion was accomplished by lowering taxes or increasing public expenditures or encouraging borrowing from the banks and consequent spending for business investment, housing or automobiles. Restriction was achieved by putting all these actions in reverse. Such is macroeconomic policy.

I might add that the distinction between microeconomics and macroeconomics, though still greatly cherished by economists in setting up courses and examining doctoral candidates, is no longer useful in real life. More likely it is now a barrier to understanding. That is because the line between microeconomics and macroeconomics becomes very blurred in a time when corporations can raise their prices and trade unions can increase their wages. These actions, as much as an excess of purchasing power, have become a cause of inflation. And unemployment is now the normal consequence of the effort to keep corporations, trade unions and other from increasing their prices and wages by cutting back on demand. So both inflation and unemployment are now as much or more a consequence of microeconomic phenomena as of macroeconomic policy. In economics artificial divisions of the subject matter—specialization—can be a prime source of error. Economic truth only emerges when things are examined whole.

NICOLE: *Inflation and unemployment are surely the paramount issues of our time. Every country is struggling with them. Why?*

JKG: We talked of change. Before I can answer your question, we must see how underlying conditions have changed and how the ideas that interpret those conditions have lagged behind.

NICOLE: *One final question for today. Is this combination of inflation and unemployment what some economists call stagflation?*

JKG: Yes. But it's a term I do not use. One has to draw the line. There are some additions to the English language that are too wretched.

J. K. Galbraith and Nicole Salinger, What is Economics Anyway?

1.   According to Galbraith, one needs to understand economics in order to

    a.   understand the principal preoccupation of life.
    b.   exercise political power as a citizen.
    c.   run for political office.
    d.   make millions of dollars.
    e.   a and b.

2.   What does Galbraith believe is the difference between the subject matter of the physical sciences and that of economics?

3.   The two branches of economics are

    a.   microeconomics and macroeconomics.
    b.   communism and capitalism.
    c.   econometrics and humanist economics.
    d.   rich and poor
    e.   none of the above.

4.   Why does Galbraith believe that Gross National Product has been oversold as an economic indicator.

Carol Gilligan*

Woman's Place in Man's Life Cycle

In the second act of *The Cherry Orchard*, Lopahin, a young merchant, describes his life of had work and success. Failing to convince Madame Ranevskaya to cut down the cherry orchard to save her estate, he will go on in the next act to buy it himself. He is the self-made man who, in purchasing the estate where his father and grandfather were slaves, seeks to eradicate the "awkward, unhappy life" of the past, replacing the cherry orchard with summer cottages where coming generations "will see a new life." In elaborating this developmental vision, he reveals the image of man that underlies and supports his activity: "At times when I can't go to sleep, I think: Lord, thou gavest us immense forests, unbounded fields and the widest horizons, and living in the midst of them we should indeed be giants"—at which point, Madame Ranevskaya interrupts him, saying, "You feel the need for giants—They are good only in fairy tales, anywhere else they only frighten us."

Conceptions of the human life cycle represent attempts to order and make coherent the unfolding experiences and perceptions, the changing wishes and realities of everyday life. But the nature of such conceptions depends in part on the position of the observer. The brief excerpt from Chekhov's play suggests that when the observer is a woman, the perspective may be of a different sort. Different judgments of the image of man as giant imply different ideas about human development, different

ways of imagining the human condition, different notions of what is of value in life.

At a time when efforts are being made to eradicate discrimination between the sexes in the search for social equality and justice, the differences between the sexes are being rediscovered in the social sciences. This discovery occurs when theories formerly considered to be sexually neutral in their scientific objectivity are found instead to reflect a consistent observational and evaluative bias. Then the presumed neutrality of science, like that of language itself, gives way to the recognition that the categories of knowledge are human constructions. The fascination with point of view that has informed the fiction of the twentieth century and the corresponding recognition of the relativity of judgement infuse our scientific understanding as well when we begin to notice how accustomed we have become to seeing life through men's eyes.

A recent discovery of this sort pertains to the apparently innocent classic *The Elements of Style* by William Strunk and E. B. White. A Supreme Court ruling on the subject of sex discrimination led one teacher of English to notice that the elementary rules of English usage were being taught through examples which counterposed the birth of Napoleon, the writings of Coleridge, and statements such as "He was an interesting talker. A man who had traveled all over the world and lived in half a dozen countries," with "Well, Susan, this is a fine mess

*Carol Gilligan is Professor of Education at Harvard University and a leading feminist voice in moral psychology. The following selection is taken from her influential book *In A Different Voice* (1979). In that work, she critiques the masculine bias of previous theories of moral development and proposes an alternative sequence of developmental stages to account for the distinctive moral perspective of women.

you are in" or, less drastically, "He saw a woman, accompanied by two children, walking slowly down the road."

Psychological theorists have fallen as innocently as Strunk and White into the same observational bias. Implicitly adopting the male life as the norm, they have tried to fashion women out of a masculine cloth. It all goes back, of course, to Adam and Eve—a story which shows, among other things, that if you make a woman out of a man, you are bound to get into trouble. In the life cycle, as in the Garden of Eden, the woman has been the deviant.

The penchant of developmental theorists to project a masculine image, and one that appears frightening to women, goes back at least to Freud (1905), who built his theory of psychosexual development around the experiences of the male child that culminate in the Oedipus complex. In the 1920s, Freud struggled to resolve the contradictions posed for his theory by the differences in female anatomy and the different configuration of the young girl's early family relationships. After trying to fit women into his masculine conception, seeing them as envying that which they missed, he came instead to acknowledge, in the strength and persistence of women's pre-Oedipal attachments to their mothers, a developmental difference. He considered this difference in women's development to be responsible for what he saw as women's developmental failure.

Having tied the formation of the superego or conscience to castration anxiety, Freud considered women to be deprived by nature of the impetus for a clear-cut Oedipal resolution. Consequently, women's superego—the heir to the Oedipus complex—was compromised; it was never "so inexorable, so impersonal, so independent of its emotional origins as we require it to be in men." From this observation of difference, that "for women the level of what is ethically normal is different from what it is in men," Freud concluded that women "show less sense of justice than men, that they are less ready to submit to the great exigencies of life, that they are more often influenced in their judgements by feeling of affection or hostility" (1925, pp. 257–258).

Thus a problem in theory became cast as a problem in women's development, and the problem in women's development was located in their experience of relationships. Nancy Chodorow (1974), attempting to account for "the reproduction within each generation of certain general and nearly universal differences that characterize masculine and feminine personality and roles," attributes these differences between the sexes not to anatomy but rather to "the fact that women, universally, are largely responsible for early child care." Because this early social environment differs for and is experienced differently by male and female children, basic sex differences recur in personality development. As a result, "in any given society, feminine personality comes to define itself in relation and connection to other people more than masculine personality does" (pp. 43–44).

In her analysis, Chodorow relies primarily on Robert Stoller's studies which indicate that gender identity, the unchanging core of personality formation, is "with rare exception firmly and irreversibly established for both sexes by the time a child is around three." Given that for both sexes the primary caretaker in the first three years of life is typically female, the interpersonal dynamics of gender identity formation are different for boys and girls. Female identity formation takes place in a context of ongoing relationship since "mothers tend to experience their daughters as more like, and continuous with, themselves." Correspondingly, girls, in identifying themselves as female, experience themselves as like their mothers, thus fusing the experience of attachment with the process of identity formation. In contrast, "mothers experience their sons as a male opposite," and boys, in defining themselves as masculine, separate their mothers from themselves, thus curtailing "their primary love and sense of empathic tie." Consequently, male development entails a "more emphatic individuation and a more defensive firming of experienced ego boundaries." For boys, but not girls, "issues of differentiation have become intertwined with sexual issues" (1978, pp. 150, 166–167).

Writing against the masculine bias of psychoanalytic theory, Chodorow argues that the existence of sex differences in the early experiences of individuation and relationship "does not mean that women have 'weaker' ego boundaries than men or are more prone to psychosis." It means instead that "girls emerge from this period with a basis for 'empathy' built into their primary definition of self in a way that boys do not." Chodorow thus replaces Freud's negative and derivative description of female psychology with a positive and direct account of her own: "Girls emerge with a stronger basis for experiencing another's needs or feelings as one's own (or of thinking that one is so experiencing another's needs and feeling). Furthermore, girls do not define themselves in terms of the denial of preoedipal relational modes to the same extent as do boys. Therefore, regression to these modes tends not to feel as much a basic threat to their ego. From very early, then, because they are parented by a person of the same gender . . . girls come to experience themselves as less differentiated than boys, as more continuous with and related to the external object-world, and as differently oriented to their inner object-world as well" (p. 167)

Consequently, relationships, and particularly issues of dependency, are experienced differently by women and men. For boys and men, separation and individuation are critically tied to gender identity since separation from the mother is essential for the development of masculinity. For girls and women, issues of femininity or feminine identity do not depend on the achievement of separation from the mother or on the progress of individuation. Since masculinity is defined through separation while femininity is defined through attachment, male gender identity is threatened by intimacy while female gender identity is threatened by separation. Thus males tend to have difficulty with relationships, while females tend to have problems with individuation. The quality of embeddedness in social interaction and personal relationships that characterizes women's lives in contrast to men's, however, becomes not only a descriptive difference but also a developmental liability when the milestones of childhood and adolescent development in the psychological literature are markers of increasing separation. Women's failure to separate then becomes by definition a failure to develop.

The sex differences in personality formation that Chodorow describes in early childhood appear during the middle childhood years in studies of children's games. Children's games are considered by George Herbert Mead (1934) and Jean Piaget (1932) as the crucible of social development during the school years. In games, children learn to take the role of the other and come to seem themselves through another's eyes. In games, they learn respect for rules and come to understand the ways rules can be made and changed.

Janet Lever (1976), considering the peer group to be the agent of socialization during the elementary school years and play to be a major activity of socialization at that time, set out to discover whether there are sex differences in the games that children play. Studying 181 fifth-grade, white, middle-class children, ages ten and eleven, she observed the organization and structure of their playtime activities. She watched the children as they played at school during recess and in physical edu-cation class, and in addition kept diaries of their accounts as to how they spent their out-of-school time. From this study, Lever reports sex differences: boys play out of doors more often than girls do; boys play more often in large and age-heterogeneous groups; they play competitive games more often, and their games last longer than girls' games. The last is in some ways the most interesting finding. Boys' games appeared to last longer not only because they required a higher level of skill and were thus less likely to become boring, but also because, when disputes arose in the course of a game, boys were able to resolve the disputes more effectively than girls: "During the course of this study, boys were seen quarrelling all the time, but not once was a game terminated because of a quarrel and no game was interrupted for more than seven minutes. In the gravest debates, the final word was always, to 'repeat the play,' generally followed by a chorus of 'cheater's proof' " (p. 482). In fact, it seemed that the boys enjoyed the legal debates as much as they did the game itself, and even marginal players of lesser size or skill participated equally in these recurrent squabbles. In contrast, the eruption of disputes among girls tended to end the game.

Thus Lever extends and corroborates the observations of Piaget in his study of the rules of the game, where he finds boys becoming through childhood increasingly fascinated with the legal elaboration of rules and the development of fair procedures for adjudicating conflicts, a fascination that, he notes, does not hold for girls. Girls, Piaget observes, have a more "pragmatic" attitude toward rules, "regarding a rule as good as long as the game repaid it" (p. 83) Girls are more tolerant in their attitudes toward rules, more willing to make exceptions, and more easily reconciled to innovations. As a result, the legal sense, which Piaget considers essential to moral development, "is far less developed in little girls than in boys" (p. 77).

The bias that leads Piaget to equate male development with child development also colors Lever's work. The assumption that shapes her discussion of results is that the male model is the better one since it fits the requirements for modern corporate success. In contrast, the sensitivity and care for the feelings of others that girls develop through their play have little market value and can even impede professional success. Lever implies that, given the realities of adult life, if a girl does not want to be left dependent on men, she will have to learn to play like a boy.

To Piaget's argument that children learn the respect for rules necessary for moral development by playing rule-bound games, Lawrence Kohlberg (1969) adds that these lessons are most effectively learned through the opportunities for role-taking that arise in the course of resolving disputes. Consequently, the moral lessons inherent in girls' play appear to be fewer than in boys'. Traditional girls' games like jump rope and hopscotch are turn-taking games, where competition is indirect since one person's success does not necessarily signify another's failure. Consequently, disputes requiring adjudication are less likely to occur. In fact, most of the girls whom Lever interviewed claimed that when a quarrel broke out, they ended the game. Rather than elaborating a system of rules for resolving disputes, girls subordinated the continuation of the game to the continuation of relationships.

Lever concludes that from the games they play, boys learn both the independence and the organizational skills necessary for coordinating the activities of large and diverse groups of people. By participating in controlled and socially approved competitive situations, they learn to deal with competition in a relatively forthright manner—to play with their enemies and to compete with their friends—all in accordance with the rules of the game. In contrast, girls' play tends to occur in smaller, more intimate groups, often the best-friend dyad, and in private places. This play replicates the social pattern of primary human relationships in that its organization is more cooperative. Thus, it points less, in Mead's terms, toward learning to take the role of "the generalized other," less toward the abstraction of human relationships. But it fosters the development of the empathy and sensitivity necessary for taking the role of "the particular other" and points more toward knowing the other as different from the self.

The sex differences in personality formation in early childhood that Chodorow derives from her analysis of the mother-child relationship are thus extended by Lever's observations of sex differences in the play activities of middle childhood. Together these accounts suggest that boys and girls arrive at puberty with a different interpersonal orientation and a different range of social experiences. Yet, since adolescence is considered a crucial time for separation, the period of "the second individuation process" (Blos, 1967), female development has appeared most divergent and thus most problematic at this time.

"Puberty," Freud says, "which brings about so great an accession of libido in boys, is marked in girls by a fresh wave of *repression*," necessary for the transformation of the young girl's "masculine sexuality" into the specifically feminine sexuality of her adulthood (1905, pp. 220–221). Freud posits this transformation on the girl's acknowledgement and acceptance of "the fact of her castration" (1931, p. 229). To the girl, Freud explains, puberty brings a new awareness of "the wound to her narcissism" and leads her to develop, "like a scar, a sense of inferiority" (1925, p. 253). Since in Erik Erikson's expansion of Freud's psychoanalytic account, adolescence is the time when development hinges on identity, the girl arrives at this juncture either psychologically at risk or with a different agenda.

The problem that female adolescence presents for theorists of human development is apparent in Erikson's scheme. Erikson (1950) charts eight stages of psychosocial development, of which adolescence is the fifth. The task at this stage is to forge a coherent sense of self, to verify an identity that can span the discontinuity of puberty and make possible the adult capacity to love and work. The preparation for the successful resolution of the adolescent identity crisis is delineated in Erikson's description of the crises that characterize the preceding four stages. Although the initial crisis in infancy of "trust versus mistrust" anchors development in the experience of relationship, the task then clearly becomes one of individuation. Erikson's second stage centers on the crisis of "autonomy versus shame and doubt," which marks the walking child's emerging sense of separateness and agency. From there, development goes on through the crisis of "initiative versus guilt," successful resolution of which represents a further move in the direction of autonomy. Next, following the inevitable disappointment of the magical wishes of the Oedipal period, children realize that to compete with their parents, they must first join them and learn to do what they do so well. Thus in the middle childhood years, development turns on the crisis of "industry versus inferiority," as the demonstration of competence becomes critical to the child's developing self-esteem. This is the time when children strive to learn and master the technology of their culture, in order to recognize themselves and to be recognized by others as capable of becoming adults. Next comes adolescence, the celebration of the autonomous, initiating, industrious self through the forging of an identity based on an ideology that can support and justify adult commitments. But about whom is Erickson talking?

Once again it turns out to be the male child. For the female, Erikson (1968) says, the sequence is a bit different. She holds her identity in abeyance as she prepares to attract the man by whose name she will be known, by whose status she will be defined, the man who will rescue her from emptiness and loneliness by filling "the inner space." While for men, identity precedes intimacy and generativity in the optimal cycle of human separation and attachment, for women these tasks seem instead to be fused. Intimacy goes along with identity, as the female comes to know herself as she is known, through her relationships with others.

Yet despite Erikson's observations of sex differences, his chart of life-cycle stages remains unchanged: identity continues to precede intimacy as male experience continues to define his life-cycle conception. But in this male life cycle there is little preparation for the intimacy of the first adult stage. Only the initial stage of trust versus mistrust suggests the type of mutuality that Erikson means by intimacy and generativity and Freud means by genitality. The rest is separateness, with the result that development itself comes to be identified with separation, and attachments appear to be developmental impediments, as is repeatedly the case in the assessment of women.

Erikson's description of male identity as forged in relation to the world and of female identity as awakened in the relationship of intimacy with another person is hardly new. In the fairy tales that Bruno Bettelheim (1976) describes an identical portrayal appears. The dynamics of male adolescence are illustrated archetypically by the conflict between father and son in "The Three Languages." Here a son, considered hopelessly stupid by his father, is given one last chance at education and sent for a year to study with a master. But when he returns, all he has learned is "what the dogs bark." After two further attempts of this sort, the father gives up in disgust and orders his servants to take the child into the forest and kill him. But the servants, those perpetual rescuers of disowned and abandoned children, take pity on the child and decide simply to leave him in the forest. From there, his wanderings take him to a land beset by furious dogs whose barking permits nobody to rest and who periodically devour one of the inhabitants. Now it turns out that our hero has learned just the right thing: he can talk with the dogs and is able to quiet them, thus restoring peace to the land. Since the other knowledge he acquires serves him equally well, he emerges triumphant from his adolescent confrontation with his father, a giant of the life-cycle conception.

In contrast, the dynamics of female adolescence are depicted through the telling of a very different story. In the world of the fairy tale, the girl's first bleeding is followed by a period of intense passivity in which nothing seems to be happening. Yet in the deep sleeps of Snow White and Sleeping Beauty, Bettelheim sees that inner concentration which he considers to be the necessary counterpart to the activity of adventure. Since the adolescent heroines awake from their sleep, not to conquer the world, but to marry the prince, their identity is inwardly and interpersonally defined. For women, in Bettelheim's as in Erikson's account, identity and intimacy are intricately conjoined. The sex differences depicted in the world of fairy tales, like the fantasy of the woman warrior in Maxine Hong Kingston's (1977) recent autobiographical novel which echoes the old stories of Troilus and Cressida and Tancred and Chlorinda, indicate repeatedly that active adventure is a male activity, and that if a woman is to embark on such endeavors, she must at least dress like a man.

These observations about sex difference support the conclusion reached by David McClelland (1975) that "sex role turns out to be one of the most important determinants of human behavior; psychologists have found sex differences in their studies from the moment they started doing empirical research." But since it is difficult to say "different" without saying "better" or "worse," since there is a tendency to construct a single scale of measurement, and since that scale has generally been derived from and standardized on the basis of men's interpretations of research data drawn predominantly or exclusively from studies of males, psychologists "have tended to regard male behavior as the 'norm' and female behavior as some kind of deviation from that norm" (p. 81). Thus, when women do not conform to the standards of psychological expectation, the conclusion has generally been that something is wrong with women.

What Matina Horner (1972) found to be wrong with women was the anxiety they showed about competitive achievement. From the beginning, research on human motivation using the Thematic Apperception Test (TAT) was plagued by evidence of sex differences which appeared to confuse and complicate data analysis. The TAT presents for interpretation an ambiguous cue—a picture about which a story is to be written or a segment of a story that is to be completed. Such stories, in reflecting projective imagination, are considered by psychologists to reveal the ways in which people construe what they perceive, that is, the concepts and interpretations they bring to their experience and thus presumably the kind of sense that they make of their lives. Prior to Horner's work it was clear that women made a different kind of sense than men of situations of competitive achievement, that in some way they saw the situations differently or the situations aroused in them some different response.

On the basis of his studies of men, McClelland divided the concept of achievement motivation into what appeared to be its two logical components, a motive to approach success ("hope success") and a motive to avoid failure ("fear failure"). From her studies of women, Horner identified as a third category the unlikely motivation to avoid success ("fear success"). Women appeared to have a problem with competitive achievement, and that problem seemed to emanate from a perceived conflict between femininity and success, the dilemma of the female adolescent who struggles to integrate her feminine aspirations and the identifications of her early childhood with the more masculine competence she has acquired at school. From her analysis of women's completions of a story that began "after first term finals, Anne finds herself at the top of her medical school class," and from her observations of women's performance in competitive achievement situations, Horner reports that, "when success is likely or possible, threatened by the negative consequences they expect to follow success, young women become anxious and their positive achievement strivings become thwarted" (p. 171). She concludes that this fear "exists because for most women, the anticipation of success in competitive achievement activity, especially against men, produces anticipation of certain negative consequences, for example, threat of social rejection and loss of femininity" (1968, p. 125).

Such conflicts about success, however, may be viewed in a different light. Georgia Sassen (1980) suggests that the conflicts expressed by the women might instead indicate "a heightened perception of the 'other side' of competitive success, that is, the great emotional costs at which success achieved through competition is often gained—an understanding which, though confused, indicates some underlying sense that something is rotten in the state in which success is defined as having better grades than everyone else" (p. 15). Sassen points out that Horner found success anxiety to be present in women only when achievement was directly competitive, that is, when one person's success was at the expense of another's failure.

In his elaboration of the identity crisis, Erikson (1968) cites the life of George Bernard Shaw to illustrate the young person's sense of being co-opted prematurely by success in a career he cannot wholeheartedly endorse. Shaw at seventy, reflecting upon his life, described his crisis at the age of twenty as having been caused not by the lack of success or the absence of recognition, but by too much of both: "I made good in spite of myself, and found, to my dismay, that Business, instead of expelling me as the worthless imposter I was, was fastening upon me with no intention of letting me go. Behold me, therefore, in my twentieth year, with a business training, in an occupation which I detested as cordially as any sane person lets himself detest anything he cannot escape from. In March 1876 I broke loose" (p. 143). At this point Shaw settled down to study and write as he pleased. Hardly interpreted as evidence of neurotic anxiety about achievement and competition, Shaw's refusal suggests to Erikson "the extraordinary workings of an extraordinary personality [coming] to the fore" (p. 144).

We might on these grounds begin to ask, not why women have conflicts about competitive success, but why men show such readiness to adopt and celebrate a rather narrow vision of success. Remembering Piaget's observation, corroborated by Lever, that boys in their games are more concerned with rules while girls are more concerned with relationships, often at the expense of the game itself—and given Chodorow's conclusion that men's social orientation is positional while women's is personal—we begin to understand why, when "Anne" becomes "John" in Horner's tale of competitive success and the story is completed by men, fear of success tends to disappear. John is considered to have played by the rules and won. He has the *right* to feel good about his success. Confirmed in the sense of his own identity as separate from those who, compared to him, are less competent, his positional sense of self is affirmed. For Anne, it is possible that the position she could obtain by being at the top of her medical school class may not, in fact, be what she wants.

"It is obvious," Virginia Woolf says, "that the values of women differ very often from the values which have been made by the other sex" (1929, p. 76). Yet, she adds, "it is the masculine values that prevail." As a result, women come to question the normality of their feelings and to alter their judgments in deference to the opinion of others. In the nineteenth century novels written by women, Woolf sees at work "a mind which was slightly pulled from the straight and made to alter its clear vision in deference to external authority." The same deference to the values and opinions of others can be seen in the judgments of twentieth century women. The difficulty women experience in finding or speaking publicly in their own voices emerges repeatedly in the form of qualification and self-doubt, but also in intimations of a divided judgment, a public assessment and private assessment which are fundamentally at odds.

Yet the deference and confusion that Woolf criticizes in women derive from the values she sees as their strengths. Women's deference is rooted not only in their social subordination but also in the substance of their moral concern. Sensitivity to the needs of others and the assumption of responsibility for taking care lead women to attend to voices other than their own and to include in their judgment other points of view. Women's moral weakness, manifest in an apparent diffusion and confusion of judgment, is thus inseparable from women's moral strength, an overriding concern with relationships and responsibilities. The reluctance to judge may itself be indicative of the care and concern for others that infuse the psychology of women's development and are responsible for what is generally seen as problematic in its nature.

Thus women not only define themselves in a context of human relationship but also judge themselves in terms of their ability to care. Women's place in man's life cycle has been that of nurturer, caretaker, and helpmate, the weaver of those networks of relationships on which she in turn relies. But while women have thus taken care of men, men have, in their theories of psychological development, as in their economic arrangements, tended to assume or devalue that care. When the focus on individuation and individual achievement extends into adulthood and maturity is equated with personal autonomy, concern with relationships appears as a weakness of women rather than as a human strength (Miller, 1976).

The discrepancy between womanhood and adulthood is nowhere more evident than in the studies on sex-role stereotypes reported by Broverman, Vogel, Broverman, Clarkson, and Rosenkrantz (1972). The repeated finding of these studies is that the qualities deemed necessary for adulthood—the capacity for autonomous thinking, clear decision-making, and responsible action—are those associated with masculinity and considered undesirable as attributes of the feminine self. The stereotypes suggest a splitting of love and work that relegates expressive capacities to women while placing instrumental abilities in the masculine domain. Yet looked at from a different perspective, these stereotypes reflect a conception of adulthood that is itself out of balance, favoring the separateness of the individual self over connection to others, and leaning more toward an autonomous life of work than toward the interdependence of love and care.

The discovery now being celebrated by men in mid-life of the importance of intimacy, relationships, and care is something that women have known from the beginning. However, because that knowledge in women has been considered "intuitive" or "instinctive," a function of anatomy coupled with destiny, psychologists have neglected to describe its development. In my research, I have found that women's moral development centers on the elaboration of that knowledge and thus delineates a critical line of psychological development in the lives of both sexes. The subject of moral development not only provides the final illustration of the reiterative pattern in the observation and assessment of sex differences in the literature on human development, but also indicates more particularly why the nature and significance of women's development has been for so long obscured and shrouded in mystery.

The criticism that Freud makes of women's sense of justice, seeing it as compromised in its refusal of blind impartiality, reappears not only in the work of Piaget but also in that of Kohlberg. While in Piaget's account (1932) of the moral judgment of the child, girls are an aside, a curiosity to whom he devotes four brief entries in an index that omits "boys" altogether because "the child" is assumed to be male, in the research from which Kohlberg derives his theory, females simply do not exist. Kohlberg's (1958, 1981) six stages that describe the development of moral judgment from childhood to adulthood are based empirically on a study of eighty-four boys whose development Kohlberg has followed for a period of over twenty years. Although Kohlberg claims universality for his stage sequence, those groups not included in his original sample rarely reach his higher stages (Edwards, 1975; Holstein, 1976; Simpson, 1974). Prominent among those who thus appear to be deficient in moral development when measured by Kohlberg's scale are women, whose judgments seem to exemplify the third stage of his six-stage sequence. At this stage morality is conceived in interpersonal terms and goodness is equated with helping and pleasing others. This conception of goodness is considered by Kohlberg and Kramer (1969) to be functional in the lives of mature women insofar as their lives take place in the home. Kohlberg and Kramer imply that only if women enter the traditional arena of male activity will they recognize the inadequacy of this moral perspective and progress like men toward higher stages where relationships are subordinated to rules (stage four) and rules to universal principles of justice (stages five and six).

Yet herein lies a paradox, for the very traits

that traditionally have defined the "goodness" of women, their care for and sensitivity to the needs of others, are those that mark them as deficient in moral development. In this version of moral development, however, the conception of maturity is derived from the study of men's lives and reflects the importance of individuation in their development. Piaget (1970), challenging the common impression that a developmental theory is built like a pyramid from its base in infancy, points out that a conception of development instead hangs from its vertex of maturity, the point toward which progress is traced. Thus a change in the definition of maturity does not simply alter the description of the highest stage but recasts the understanding of development, changing the entire account.

When one begins with the study of women and derives developmental constructs from their lives, the outline of a moral conception different from that described by Freud, Piaget, or Kohlberg begins to emerge and informs a different description of development. In this conception, the moral problem arises from conflicting responsibilities rather than from competing rights and requires for its resolution a mode of thinking that is contextual and narrative rather than formal and abstract. This conception of morality as concerned with the activity of care centers moral development around the understanding of responsibility and relationships, just as the conception of morality as fairness ties moral development to the understanding of rights and rules.

This different construction of the moral problem by women may be seen as the critical reason for their failure to develop within the constraints of Kohlberg's system. Regarding all constructions of responsibility as evidence of a conventional moral understanding, Kohlberg defines the highest stages of moral development as deriving from a reflective understanding of human rights. That the morality of rights differs from the morality of responsibility in its emphasis on separation rather than connection, in its consideration of the individual rather than the relationship as primary, is illustrated by two responses to interview questions about the nature of morality. The first comes from a twenty-five-year-old man, one of the participants in Kohlberg's study:

[*What does the word morality mean to you?*] Nobody in the world knows the answer. I think it is recognizing the right of the individual, the rights of other individuals, not interfering with those rights. Act as fairly as you would have them treat you. I think it is basically to preserve the human being's right to

existence. I think that is the most important. Secondly, the human being's right to do as he pleases, again without interfering with somebody else's rights.

[*How have your views on morality changed since the last interview?*] I think I am more aware of an individual's rights now. I used to be looking at it strictly from my point of view, just for me. Now I think I am more aware of what the individual has a right to.

Kohlberg (1973) cites this man's response as illustrative of the principled conception of human rights that exemplifies his fifth and sixth stages. Commenting on the response, Kohlberg says: "Moving to a perspective outside of that of his society, he identifies morality with justice (fairness, rights, the Golden Rule), with recognition of the rights of others as these defined naturally or intrinsically. The human being's right to do as he pleases without interfering with somebody else's rights is a formula defining rights prior to social legislation" (p. 29–30).

The second response comes from a woman who participated in the rights and responsibilities study. She also was twenty-five and, at the time, a third-year law student:

[*Is there really some correct solution to moral problems, or is everybody's opinion equally right?*] No, I don't think everybody's opinion is equally right. I think that in some situations there may be opinions that are equally valid, and one could conscientiously adopt one of several courses of action. But there are other situations in which I think there are right and wrong answers, that sort of adhere in the nature of existence, of all individuals here who need to live with each other to live. We need to depend on each other, and hopefully it is not only a physical need but a need of fulfillment in ourselves, that a person's life is enriched by cooperating with other people and striving to live in harmony with everybody else, and to that end, there are right and wrong, there are things which promote that end and that move away from it, and in that way it is possible to choose in certain cases among different courses of action that obviously promote or harm that goal.

[*Is there a time in the past when you would have thought about these things differently?*] Oh, yeah, I think that I went through a time when I thought that things were pretty relative, that I can't tell you what to do and you can't tell me what to do, because you've got your conscience and I've got mine.

165

[When was that?] When I was in high school. I guess that it just sort of dawned on me that my own ideas changed, and because my own judgment changed, I felt I couldn't judge another person's judgment. But now I think even when it is only the person himself who is going to be affected, I say it is wrong to the extent it doesn't cohere with what I know about human nature and what I know about you, and just from what I think is true about the operations of the universe, I could say I think you are making a mistake.

[What led you to change, do you think?] Just seeing more of life, just recognizing that there are an awful lot of things that are common among people. There are certain things that you come to learn promote a better life and better relationships and more personal fulfillment than other things that in general tend to do the opposite, and the things that promote these things, you would call morally right.

This response also represents a personal reconstruction of morality following a period of questioning and doubt, but the reconstruction of moral understanding is based not on the primacy and universality of individual rights, but rather on what she describes as a "very strong sense of being responsible to the world." Within this construction, the moral dilemma changes from how to exercise one's rights without interfering with the rights of others to how "to lead a moral life which includes obligations to myself and my family and people in general." The problem then becomes one of limiting responsibilities without abandoning moral concern. When asked to describe herself, this woman says that she values "having other people that I am tied to, and also having people that I am responsible to. I have a very strong sense of being responsible to the world, that I can't just live for my enjoyment, but just the fact of being in the world gives me an obligation to do what I can to make the world a better place to live in, no matter how small a scale that may be on." Thus while Kohlberg's subject worries about people interfering with each other's rights, this woman worries about "the possibility of omission, of your not helping others when you could help them."

The issue that this woman raises is addressed by Jane Loevinger's fifth "autonomous" stage of ego development, where autonomy, placed in a context of relationships, is defined as modulating an excessive sense of responsibility through the recognition

that other people have responsibility for their own destiny. The autonomous stage in Loevinger's account (1970) witnesses a relinquishing of moral dichotomies and their replacement with "a feeling for the complexity and multifaceted character of real people in real situations" (p. 6). Whereas the rights conception of morality that informs Kohlberg's principled level (stages five and six) is geared to arriving at an objectively fair or just resolution to moral dilemmas upon which all rational persons could agree, the responsibility conception focuses instead on the limitations of any particular resolution and describes the conflicts that remain.

Thus it becomes clear why a morality of rights and noninterference may appear frightening to women in its potential justification of indifference and unconcern. At the same time, it becomes clear why, from a male perspective, a morality of responsibility appears inconclusive and diffuse, given its insistent contextual relativism. Women's moral judgments thus elucidate the pattern observed in the description of the developmental differences between the sexes, but they also provide an alternative conception of maturity by which these differences can be assessed and their implications traced. The psychology of women that has consistently been described as distinctive in its greater orientation toward relationships and interdependence implies a more contextual mode of judgment and a different moral understanding. Given the differences in women's conceptions of self and morality, women bring to the life cycle a different point of view and order human experience in terms of different priorities.

The myth of Demeter and Persephone, which McClelland (1975) cites as exemplifying the feminine attitude toward power, was associated with the Eleusinian Mysteries celebrated in ancient Greece for over two thousand years. As told in the Homeric *Hymn to Demeter*, the story of Persephone indicates the strengths of interdependence, building up resources and giving, that McClelland found in his research on power motivation to characterize the mature feminine style. Although, McClelland says, "it is fashionable to conclude that no one knows what went on in the Mysteries, it is known that they were probably the most important religious ceremonies, even partly on the historical record, which were organized by and for women, especially at the onset before men by means of the cult of Dionysos began to take them over." Thus McClelland regards the myth as "a special presentation of feminine psychology" (p. 96). It is, as well, a life-cycle story par excellence.

166

Persephone, the daughter of Demeter, while playing in a meadow with her girlfriends, sees a beautiful narcissus which she runs to pick. As she does so, the earth opens and she is snatched away by Hades, who takes her to his underworld kingdom. Demeter, goddess of the earth, so mourns the loss of her daughter that she refuses to allow anything to grow. The crops that sustain life on earth shrivel up, killing men and animals alike, until Zeus takes pity on man's suffering and persuades his brother to return Persephone to her mother. But before she leaves, Persephone eats some pomegranate seeds, which ensures that she will spend part of every year with Hades in the underworld.

The elusive mystery of women's development lies in its recognition of the continuing importance of attachment in the human life cycle. Woman's place in man's life cycle is to protect this recognition while the developmental litany intones the celebration of separation, autonomy, individuation, and natural rights. The myth of Persephone speaks directly to the distortion in this view by reminding us that narcissism leads to death, that the fertility of the earth is in some mysterious way tied to the continuation of the mother-daughter relationship, and that the life cycle itself arises from an alternation between the world of women and that of men. Only when life-cycle theorists divide their attention and begin to live with women as they have lived with men will their vision encompass the experience of both sexes and their theories become correspondingly more fertile.

Carol Gilligan, Woman's Place in Man's Life Cycle

1.   Conceptions of the human life cycle represent attempts to order and make coherent the unfolding experiences and perceptions of everyday life.

        a. True   b. False

2.   Gilligan believes that psychological theorists have

        a. been unbiased observers.
        b. implicitly adopted male life as the norm.
        c. turned a problem with their theory into a problem with women.
        d. b and c
        e. none of the above

3.   What does Gilligan think is the source of gender identity?

4.   Compare the masculine moral perspective with the feminine moral perspective.

IV. THE SOCIAL SCIENCES

LIST OF KEY TERMS

consciousness:

behavior:

stimulus/response:

conditioning:

social fact:

methodological individualism:

methodological collectivism:

cultural relativism:

positivism:

interpretivism:

objectivity:

ideology:

theory/praxis:

ethical neutrality:

law-like generalization (regularity):

political economy:

developmental psychology:

theoretical and observational bias:

stage sequence:

ethic of caring vs. ethic of justice:

SECTION V
THE HUMANITIES

THEME QUESTIONS

1. What is the source of the humanities?

2. What is the common thread that runs throughout the humanities?

3. What are the similarities and differences among the various humanistic disciplines?

4. How are interpretation and imagination used as methods of inquiry in the humanities?

5. What are the criteria for truth and value in the different humanistic disciplines? Where do these criteria come from?

6. What is the proper role of the humanities within society?

7. What distinguishes the humanities from the fine arts?

Introduction to the Humanities

Charles Timothy Summerlin

To some extent the categories (history, ethics, religion, aesthetics and literature) included in this section of your anthology are, of necessity, arbitrarily grouped. The humanities are variously defined, and those disciplines traditionally so designated vary considerably among themselves. In general, the humanities are those disciplines which comprise the intellectual, ethical, and aesthetic dimensions of human experience. They attempt to answer the question, what does it mean to be human?

Our effort to study ourselves as creatures in time, what we call history, is the first discipline whose ways of knowing you will be introduced to in this section of the book. Not surprisingly, philosophical inquiry, fundamental to what this course is all about, is a division of the humanities. Ethics, the attempt to define the good and its expression in human conduct, is a branch of philosophy. The efforts of a finite creature to probe the eternal—religion—is another dimension of the humanities. Religious inquiry necessarily involves the exercise of imagination; that branch of philosophy concerned with the imagination and its creations is called aesthetics. Literature, our means of articulating our imaginations in words, is the final humanities discipline you will encounter.

In ancient times Aristotle distinguished between poetry's attention to "what may happen" and history's record of "what has happened." In this sense, history inquires into the *particular,* rather than the *general.* In a very simple sense history may mean to us 1066, 1492 and 1863, lists of kings and presidents or generals and battles. Historians know that the meanings of the past—and our efforts to understand them—are far more complex. But only in comparatively recent times, the last 200 years or so, has mankind addressed itself to the basis on which a philosophy of history, or a historical "way of knowing," can be established. Analyzing that process is a central concern of R. G. Collingwood in the selection provided from his *The Idea of History.* As Collingwood demonstrates, what we call history is a kind of intellectual inquiry based on certain premises regarding methodology and purpose. Knowing history is more subtle than knowing facts, even a great many facts. Central to Collingwood's argument is his conception of the historical imagination, the evidence it must consider, and the ongoing nature of its work. Observe the affinities that history has with the arts, on the one hand, and the sciences, on the other. In addition, you will find Collingwood tracing similarities between the logic and use of evidence of the historian and those of mathematical reasoning and the natural sciences. His work offers a reminder of how education enables us to integrate kinds of knowledge.

In Fernand Braudel's essay "History and the Social Sciences," you will encounter a contrast between history that concerns itself with events, or brief moments of time, and history as expressed over the *longue durée.* Like Collingwood, Braudel is conscious of the variety of ways we may productively try to understand the past, and he argues that "these expanses of slow-moving history" can enable us to recognize structures of the past that endure even as more superficial political and social circumstances change. But Braudel is not addressing historians alone, because it is precisely here that he believes historical study relates to the social sciences—economics, sociology, geography,and anthropology. How does he apply his concept of the "model" as instrument for understanding all of these disciplines? You may be interested to note that Braudel is not dealing with a merely theoretical question, but is practically concerned with "border disputes" between academicians who are determined to differentiate themselves from one another.

Few, if any, modern philosophers can compare with Immanuel Kant, an eighteenth century German, in breadth of insight or complexity of thought. His inquiry into a rational basis for human morality produced concepts that remain influential today. While acknowledging the obvious fact that our morality is thoroughly intertwined with our selfishness, Kant believed that a universal, rational moral law existed and could be articulated. Be aware of this critical concept of a "categorical" law and how it differs from a hypothetical one. Does Kant make the case that ethical knowledge can be rationally determined rather than merely a matter of what feels good? John Stuart Mill directs his energy toward stripping a familiar term, "utilitarianism," of what he considers unfair negative baggage and toward defining that ethical principle justly and accurately. The ethical principle he affirms is perhaps more socially oriented than is Kant's, but is it any more or less universal? Both ethicists are determined to arrive at their conception of the good objectively, in rational terms. But the good is also intimately related to religion, and religious knowledge is often conveyed by other than rational means and rooted in subjective experience.

The search for the divine is an enduring element of human experience and hence properly considered within the category of the humanities. Call it by whatever name we choose—God, the transcendent, the ground of our being—the object of religious knowledge is particularly elusive and subject to intense debate. John Hick offers a sketch of how consciousness of the divine or "Eternal One" can be understood in historical and cultural contexts, although he does not regard the religious experience itself as fully determined by those contexts. At the heart of Hick's thesis is a proposition of the medieval theologian Thomas Aquinas: "The thing known is in the knower according to the mode of the knower." In other words, who I am and what my life circumstances are shape what I know. The distinction between religious knowledge expressed in propositional statements and actual religious experience is the beginning point of Sally McFague's "Toward a Metaphorical Theology." She wrestles with the place of religious language in a positivist age, examining the twin threats she calls "idolatry" and "irrelevance." Although McFague questions whether the "symbolic sacramentalism" of former times is recoverable, she argues for the relevance of metaphor in conveying valid religious insight and explores its relationship to culture and conceptualizing.

Metaphor, which equates two things otherwise different ("God is our father," "life is a bowl of cherries"), raises the subject of literature and the meaning of aesthetic experience. Since at least the time of Plato, humans have debated the value of literature. Interestingly, Plato was apparently divided on the subject, since on the one hand he appreciated the Greek notion that a "rhapsode" or poet was inspired by the gods into a divine frenzy, but on the other he regarded poets as threats to the order of society because of their power over the emotions. In our selection from *The Republic,* you will find a rigorous defense of the latter position. What is the relationship here between equating the rational with the good and the final dismissal of the poet from the ideal state? Or is poetry dismissed entirely?

Like Plato, Aristotle has some things to say about the effect of poetry (his essay examines the poetry of the tragic drama) on its audience, but you will notice that his main concern lies elsewhere. Aristotle is interested in tragedy's *form,* in the characteristics that make it a particular literary genre (we have lost his similar analysis of comedy). In this essay, Aristotle offers an early example of the formal analysis of literature. What distinguishes this kind of writing from others is its "significant form"; that is, *how* it is written as well as *what* it conveys is part of its meaning. Indeed, many students of literature would say that finally one cannot separate, in a great poem, *how* (form) from *what* (content). The notion of significant form has implications, naturally, for what it means to "know" a piece of literature. Simply being able to summarize the events of a narrative or to paraphrase what a poem is about is only the beginning of such knowledge.

In William Wordsworth's 1800 "Preface" to poems he and S. T. Coleridge had written, we find one of the grand assertions of the "truth" of poetic insight. Although Wordsworth's essay touches on several themes (what kind of language a poem should use, what subjects it should deal with, what sort of person a poet is), at the heart of his thesis is a revolutionary conception of what poetry is, the passionate expression of the sympathetic imagination and the essence of what it means to be human. You may see similarities between his and Plato's concept of poetry's origin, but you will also note a radical difference between how they *value* it. In a word, Wordsworth claims a fundamental authority for the imagination in how we know and engage our world.

Knowing through our imagination and knowing the products of the imagination are two separate, though related, activities. One is the work of the poet; the other the work of the critic. We have already seen in Aristotle, Plato and Wordsworth theories about what the artist is like, what the work of art contains, and how art affects audiences. Northrop Frye insists that criticism also has an important role to play: "it can talk, and all the arts are dumb." Do you see a similarity between what Frye is trying to do for the term "literary critic" and what J. S. Mill was doing for "utilitarian"? Frye's central thesis is that legitimate criticism must be "an examination of literature in terms of a conceptual framework derivable from an inductive survey of the literary field." Criticism, then is a science, a social science, not an art. Annette Kolodny argues a very different thesis in her survey of feminist contributions to literary interpretation. She echoes the thoughts of many in a "postmodern" world in seeing both literature and criticism as shot through with ideology. In other words, she raises the question of whether a literature that transcends race, gender and other power issues can even exist. If not, traditional notions about objectivity and even rationality come under question. Is Kolodny merely supporting the dictum "The thing known is in the knower according to the mode of the knower"? Or does our definition of what it means to be human alter if we view our intellectual and imaginative creations as inevitably compromised by conditions of race, gender, and class?

R. G. Collingwood*

HISTORICAL IMAGINATION AND HISTORICAL EVIDENCE

This brings me back to the question what this criterion is. And at this point a partial and provisional answer can be given. The web of imaginative construction is something far more solid and powerful than we have hitherto realized. So far from relying for its validity upon the support of given facts, it actually serves as the touchstone by which we decide whether alleged facts are genuine. Suetonius tells me that Nero at one time intended to evacuate Britain. I reject his statement, not because any better authority flatly contradicts it, for of course none does; but because my reconstruction of Nero's policy based on Tacitus will not allow me to think that Suetonius is right. And if I am told that this is merely to say I prefer Tacitus to Suetonius, I confess that I do: but I do so just because I find myself able to incorporate what Tacitus tells me into a coherent and continuous picture of my own, and cannot do this for Suetonius.

It is thus the historian's picture of the past, the product of his own *a priori* imagination, that has to justify the sources used in its construction. These sources are sources, that is to say, credence is given to them, only because they are in this way justified. For any source may be tainted: this writer prejudiced, that misinformed; this inscription misread by a bad epigraphist, that blundered by a careless stonemason; this potsherd placed out of its context by an incompetent excavator, that by a blameless rabbit. The critical historian has to discover and correct all these and many other kinds of falsification. He does it, and can only do it, by considering whether the picture of the past to which the evidence leads him is a coherent and continuous picture, one which makes sense. The *a priori* imagination which does the work of historical construction supplies the means of historical criticism as well.

Freed from its dependence on fixed point supplied from without, the historian's picture of the past is thus in every detail an imaginary picture, and its necessity is at every point the necessity of the *a priori* imagination. Whatever goes into it, goes into it not because his imagination passively accepts it, but because it actively demands it.

The resemblance between the historian and the novelist, to which I have already referred, here reaches its culmination. Each of them makes it his business to construct a picture which is partly a narrative of events, partly a description of situations, exhibition of motives, analysis of characters. Each aims at making his picture a coherent whole, where every character and every situation is so bound up with the rest that this character in this situation cannot but act in this way, and we cannot imagine him as acting otherwise. The novel and the history must both of them make sense; nothing is admissible in either except what is necessary, and the judge of this necessity is in both cases the imagination. Both the novel and the history are self-explanatory, self-justifying, the product of an autonomous or self-authorizing activity; and in both cases this activity is the *a priori* imagination.

*Robin George Collingwood (1889–1943) was a prominent philosopher and historian who taught at Oxford University. His books include *Speculum Mentis, The Principles of Art, The Idea of Nature,* and *The Idea of History* (1946), from which this selection is drawn. In general, Collingwood maintained that all forms of knowledge are creations of the human mind and must be studied historically. In the following piece, Collingwood considers the similarities between historical and literary narratives.

Reprinted from The Idea of History by R. G. Collingwood (1946) by permission of Oxford University Press.

As works of imagination, the historians work and the novelist's do not differ. Where they do differ is that the historian's picture is meant to be true. The novelist has a single task only: to construct a coherent picture, one that makes sense. The historian has a double task: he has both to do this, and to construct a picture of things as they really were and of events as they really happened. This further necessity imposes upon him obedience to three rules of method, from which the novelist or artist in general is free.

First, his picture must be localized in space and tune. The artist's need not; essentially, the things that he imagines are imagined as happening at no place and at no date. Of Wuthering Heights it has been well said that the scene is laid in Hell, though the place-names are English; and it was a sure instinct that led another great novelist to replace Oxford by Christminster, Wantage by Alfredston, and Fawley by Marychurch, recoiling against the discord of topographical fact in what should be a purely imaginary world.

Secondly, all history must be consistent with itself. Purely imaginary worlds cannot clash and need not agree; each is a world to itself. But there is only one historical world, and everything in it must stand in some relation to everything else, even if that relation is only topographical and chronological.

Thirdly, and most important, the historian's picture stands in a peculiar relation to something called evidence. The only way in which the historian or any one else can judge, even tentatively, of its truth is by considering this relation; and, in practice, what we mean by asking whether an historical statement is true is whether it can be justified by an appeal to the evidence: for a truth unable to be so justified is to the historian a thing of no interest. What is this thing called evidence, and what is its relation to the finished historical work?

We already know what evidence is not. It is not ready-made historical knowledge, to be swallowed and regurgitated by the historian's mind. Everything is evidence which the historian can use as evidence. But what can he so use? It must be something here and now perceptible to him: this written page, this spoken utterance, this building, this finger-print. And of all the things perceptible to him there is not one which he might not conceivably use as evidence on some question, if he came to it with the right question in mind. The enlargement of historical knowledge comes about mainly through finding how to use as evidence this or that kind of perceived fact which historians have hitherto thought useless to them.

The whole perceptible world, then, is potentially and in principle evidence to the historian. It becomes actual evidence in so far as he can use it. And he cannot use it unless he comes to it with the right kind of historical knowledge. The more historical knowledge we have, the more we can learn from any given piece of evidence; if we had none, we could learn nothing. Evidence is evidence only when some one contemplates it historically. Otherwise it is merely perceived fact, historically dumb. It follows that historical knowledge can only grow out of historical knowledge; in other words, that historical thinking is an original and fundamental activity of the human mind, or, as Descartes might have said, that the idea of the past is an 'innate' idea.

Historical thinking is that activity of the imagination by which we endeavour to provide this innate idea with detailed content. And this we do by using the present as evidence for its own past. Every present has a past of its own, and any imaginative reconstruction of the past aims at reconstructing the past of this present, the present in which the act of imagination is going on, as here and now perceived. In principle the aim of any such act is to use the entire perceptible here-and-now as evidence for the entire past through whose process it has come into being. In practice, this aim can never by achieved. The perceptible here-and-now can never be perceived, still less interpreted, in its entirety; and the infinite process of past time can never be envisaged as a whole. But this separation between what is attempted in principle and what is achieved in practice is the lot of mankind, not a peculiarity of historical thinking. The fact that it is found there only shows that herein history is like art, science, philosophy, the pursuit of virtue, and the search for happiness.

It is for the same reason that in history, as in all serious matters, no achievement is final. The evidence available for solving any given problem changes with every change of historical method and with every variation in the competence of historians. The principles by which this evidence is interpreted change too; since the interpreting of evidence is a task to which a man must bring everything he knows: historical knowledge, knowledge of nature and man, mathematical knowledge, philosophical knowledge; and not knowledge only, but mental habits and possessions of every kind: and none of these is unchanging. Because of these changes, which never cease, however slow they may appear to observers who take a short view, every new generation must rewrite history in its own way; every new historian, not content with giving new answers to old questions, must revise the questions themselves; and—since historical thought is a river into which none can step twice—even a single historian, working at a single subject for a certain length of time, finds when he tries to reopen an old question that the question has changed.

This is not an argument for historical scepticism. It is only the discovery of a second dimension of historical thought, the history of history: the discovery that the historian himself, together with the here-and-now which forms the total body of evidence available to him, is a part of the process he is studying, has his own place in that process, and can see it only from the point of view which at this present moment he occupies within it.

But neither the raw material of historical knowledge, the detail of the here-and-now as given him in perception, nor the various endowments that serve him as aids to interpreting this evidence, can give the historian his criterion of historical truth. That criterion is the idea of history itself: the idea of an imaginary picture of the past. That idea is, in Cartesian language, innate; in Kantian language, *a priori*. It is not a chance product of psychological causes; it is an idea which every man possesses as part of the furniture of his mind, and discovers himself to possess in so far as he becomes conscious of what it is to have a mind. Like other ideas of the same sort, it is one to which no fact of experience exactly corresponds. The historian, however long and faithfully he works, can never say that his work, even in crudest outline or in this or that smallest detail, is done once for all. He can never say that his picture of the past is at any point adequate to his idea of what it ought to be. But, however, fragmentary and faulty the results of his work may be, the idea which governed its course is clear, rational, and universal. It is the idea of the historical imagination as a self-dependent, self-determining, and self justifying form of thought.

Historical Evidence

'History,' said Bury, 'is a science; no less, and no more.'

Perhaps it is no less: that depends on what you mean by a science. There is a slang usage, like that for which 'hall' means a music-hall or 'pictures' moving pictures, according to which 'science' means natural science. Whether history is a science in that sense of the word, however, need not be asked; for in the tradition of European speech, going back to the time when Latin speakers translated the Greek ἐπιστήμη by their own word *scientia,* and continuing unbroken down to the present day, the word 'science' means any organized body of knowledge. If that is what the word means Bury is so far incontestably right, that history is a science, nothing less.

But if it is no less, it is certainly more. For anything that is a science at all must be more than merely a science, it must be a science of some special kind. A body of knowledge is never merely organized, it is always organized in some particular way. Some bodies of knowledge, like meteorology, are organized by collecting observations concerned with events of a certain kind which the scientist can watch as they happen, though he cannot produce them at will. Others, like chemistry, are organized not only by observing events as they happen, but by making them happen under strictly controlled conditions. Others again are organized not by observing events at all, but by making certain assumptions and proceeding with the utmost exactitude to argue out their consequences.

History is organized in none of these ways. Wars and revolutions, and the other events with which it deals, are not deliberately produced by historians under laboratory conditions in order to be studied with scientific precision. Nor are they even observed by historians, in the sense in which events are observed by natural scientists. Meteorologists and astronomers will make arduous and expensive journeys in order to observe for themselves events of the kinds in which they are interested, because their standard of observation is such that they cannot be satisfied with descriptions by inexpert witnesses; but historians do not fit out expeditions to countries where wars and revolutions are going on. And this is not because historians are less energetic or courageous than natural scientists, or less able to obtain the money such expeditions would cost. It is because the facts which might be learned through such expeditions, like the facts which might be learned through the deliberate fomenting of a war or a revolution at home, would not teach historians anything they want to know.

The sciences of observation and experiment are alike in this, that their aim is to detect the constant or recurring features in all events of a certain kind. A meteorologist studies one cyclone in order to compare it with others; and by studying a number of them he hopes to find out what features in them are constant, that is, to find out what cyclones as such are like. But the historian has no such aim. If you find him on a certain occasion studying the Hundred Years War or the Revolution of 1688, you cannot infer that he is in the preliminary stages of an inquiry whose ultimate aim is to reach conclusions about wars or revolutions as such. If he is in the preliminary stages of any inquiry, it is more likely to be a general study of the Middle Ages or the seventeenth century. This is because the sciences of observation and experiment are organized in one way and history is organized in another. In the organization of meteorology, the ulterior value of what has been observed about one cyclone is conditioned by its relation to what has been observed about other cyclones. In the organization of history, the ulterior value of what is known about the Hundred Years War is conditioned, not by its relation to what is known about other wars, but by its relation to what is known about other things that people did in the Middle Ages.

Equally obvious is the difference between the organization of history and that of the 'exact' sciences. It is true that in history, as in exact science, the normal process of thought is inferential; that is to say, it begins by asserting this or that, and goes on to ask what it proves. But the starting-points are of very different kinds. In exact science they are assumptions, and the traditional way of expressing them is in sentences beginning with a word of command prescribing that a certain assumption be made: 'Let ABC be a triangle, and let AB = AC.' In history they are not assumptions, they are facts, and facts coming under the historian's observation, such as, that on the page open before him there is printed what purports to be a charter by which a certain king grants certain lands to a certain monastery. The conclusions, too, are of different kinds. In exact science, they are conclusions about things which have no special habitation in space or time: if they are anywhere, they are everywhere, and if they are at any time they are at all times. In history, they are conclusions about events, each having a place and date of its own. The exactitude with which place and date are known to the historian is variable; but he always knows that there were both a place and a date, and within limits he always knows what they were; this knowledge being part of the conclusion to which he is led by arguing from the facts before him.

These differences in starting-point and conclusion imply a difference in the entire organization of the respective sciences. When a mathematician has made up his mind what the problem is which he desires to solve, the next step before him is to make assumptions which will enable him to solve it; and this involves an appeal to his powers of invention. When an historian has similarly made up his mind, his next business is to place himself in a position where he can say: 'The facts which I am now observing are the facts from which I can infer the solution of my problem.' His business is not to invent anything, it is to discover something. And the finished products, too, are differently organized. The scheme upon which exact sciences have been traditionally arranged depends on relations of logical priority and posteriority: one proposition is placed before a second, if understanding of the first is needed in order that the second should be understood; the traditional scheme of arrangement in history is a chronological scheme, in which one event is placed before a second if it happened at an earlier time.

History, then, is a science, but a science of a special kind. It is a science whose business is to study events not accessible to our observation, and to study these events inferentially, arguing to them from something else which is accessible to our observation, and which the historian calls 'evidence' for the events in which he is interested.

(i) History as inferential

History has this in common with every other science: that the historian is not allowed to claim any single piece of knowledge, except where he can justify his claim by exhibiting to himself in the first place, and secondly to anyone else who is both able and willing to follow his demonstration, the grounds upon which it is based. This is what was meant, above, by describing history as inferential. The knowledge in virtue of which a man is an historian is a knowledge of what the evidence at his disposal proves about certain events. If he or somebody else could have the very same knowledge of the very same events by way of memory, or second sight, or some Wellsian machine for looking backwards through time, this would not be historical knowledge; and the proof would be that he could not produce, either to himself or to any other critic of his claims, the evidence from which he had derived it. Critic, not sceptic; for a critic is a person able and willing to go over somebody else's thoughts for himself to see if they have been well done; whereas a sceptic is a person who will not do this; and because you cannot make a man think, any more than you can make a horse drink, there is no way of proving to a sceptic that a certain piece of thinking is sound, and no reason for taking his denials to heart. It is only by his peers that any claimant to knowledge is judged.

This necessity of justifying any claim to knowledge by exhibiting the grounds upon which it is based is a universal characteristic of science because it arises from the fact that a science is an organized body of knowledge. To say that knowledge is inferential is only another way of saying that it is organized. What memory is, and whether it is a kind of knowledge or not, are questions that need not be considered in a book about history: for this at least is clear, in spite of what Bacon and others have said, that memory is not history, because history is a certain kind of organized or inferential knowledge, and memory is not organized, not inferential, at all. If I say 'I remember writing a letter to So and-so last week', that is a statement of memory, but it is not an historical statement. But if I can add 'and my memory is not deceiving me; because here is his reply', then I am basing a statement about the past on evidence; I am talking history. For the same reason, there is no need in an essay like this to consider the claims of people who say that when they are in a place where a certain event has recurred they can in some way see the event going on before their eyes. What actually happens on occasions like this, and whether the people to whom it happens thereby obtain knowledge of the past, are certainly interesting questions, but this is not the right place to discuss them; for even if these people do obtain knowledge of the past, it is not organized or inferential knowledge; not scientific knowledge; not history.

(ii) Different kinds of inference

Different kinds of science are organized in different ways and it should follow (indeed, this would seem to be only the same thing in other words) that different kinds of science are characterized by different kinds of inference. The way in which knowledge is related to the grounds upon which it is based is in fact not one and the same for all kinds of knowledge. That this is so, and that therefore a person who has studied the nature of

inference as such—let us call him a logician—can correctly judge the validity of an inference purely by attending to its form, although he has no special knowledge of its subject-matter, is a doctrine of Aristotle; but it is a delusion, although it is still believed by many very able persons who have been trained too exclusively in the Aristotelian logic and the logics that depend upon it for their chief doctrines.[1]

The main scientific achievement of the ancient Greeks lay in mathematics; their main work on the logic of inference was naturally, therefore, devoted to that form of inference which occurs in exact science. When at the end of the Middle Ages the modern natural sciences of observation and experiment began to take shape, a revolt against Aristotelian logic was inevitable; in particular, a revolt against the Aristotelian theory of demonstration, which could by no manner of means be made to cover the technique actually used in the new sciences. Thus, by degrees, there came into existence a new logic of inference, based on analysis of the procedure used in the new natural sciences. The text-books of logic in use to-day still bear the marks of this revolt in the distinction they draw between two kinds of inference, 'deductive' and 'inductive'. It was not until late in the nineteenth century that historical thought reached a state of development comparable with that reached by natural science about the beginning of the seventeenth; but this event has not yet begun to interest those philosophers who write text-books of logic.

The chief characteristic of difference in the exact sciences, the characteristic of which Greek logicians tried to give a theoretical account when they formulated the rules of the syllogism, is a kind of logical compulsion where by a person who makes certain assumptions is forced, simply by so doing, to make others. He has freedom of choice in two ways: he is not compelled to make the initial assumption (a fact technically expressed by saying that 'the starting-points of demonstrative reason are not themselves demonstrable'), and when once he has done so he is still at liberty, whenever he likes, to stop thinking. What he cannot do is to make the initial assumption, to go on thinking, and to arrive

---

[1]The reader will perhaps forgive me a personal reminiscence here. I was still a young man when a very distinguished visitor addressed an academic society on an archaeological subject that came within my special field of studies. The point he made was new and revolutionary, and it was easy for me to see that he had proved it up to the hilt. I imagined, foolishly enough, that so lucid and cogent a piece of reasoning must convince any hearer, even one who previously knew nothing about its subject-matter. I was at first much disconcerted, but in the long run greatly instructed, by finding that the demonstration had quite failed to convince the (very learned and acute) logicians in the audience.   .

at a conclusion different from that which is scientifically correct.

In what is called 'inductive' thinking there is not such compulsion. The essence of the process, here, is that having put certain observations together, and having found that they make a pattern, we extrapolate this pattern indefinitely, just as a man who has plotted a few points on squared paper and says to himself 'the points I have plotted suggest a parabola', proceeds to draw as much of the parabola as he likes in either direction. This is technically described as 'proceeding from the known to the unknown' or 'from the particular to the universal'. It is essential to 'inductive' thinking, though the logicians who have tried to construct a theory of such thinking have not always realized this, that the step so described is never taken under any kind of logical compulsion. The thinker who takes it is logically free to take it or not to take it, just as he pleases. There is nothing in the pattern formed by the observations he or someone else has actually made which can oblige him to extrapolate in that particular way, or indeed to extrapolate at all. The reason why this very obvious truth has been so often overlooked is that people have been hypnotized by the prestige of Aristotelian logic into thinking that they see a closer resemblance than actually existed between 'deductive' and "inductive' thinking, that is, between exact science and the sciences of observation and experiment. In both cases there are, for any given piece of thinking, certain starting-points, traditionally called premisses, and a certain terminal point, traditionally called a conclusion; and in both cases the premisses 'prove' the conclusion. But whereas in exact science this means that they enforce the conclusion, or make it logically obligatory, in the sciences of observation and experiment it means only that they justify it, that is, authorize anybody to think it who wishes to do so. What they provide, when they are said to 'prove' a certain conclusion, is not compulsion to embrace it, but only permission; a perfectly legitimate sense of the word 'prove' (*approuver, probare*), as there should be no need to show.

If in practice this permission, like so many permissions, amounts to virtual compulsion, that is only because the thinker who avails himself of it does not regard himself as free to extrapolate or not, just as he pleases. He regards himself as under an obligation to do so, and to do it in certain ways; obligations which, when we inquire into their history, we find to have their roots in certain religious beliefs about nature and its creator God. It would

be out of place to develop this statement more fully here—but not, perhaps, to add that if to-day it seems to some readers paradoxical, that is only because the facts have been obscured by a smoke-screen of propagandist literature, beginning with the 'illuminist' movement of the eighteenth century and prolonged by the 'conflict between religion and science' in the nineteenth, whose purpose was to attack Christian theology in the supposed interests of a 'scientific view of the world' which in fact is based upon it and could not for a moment survive its destruction. Take away Christian theology, and the scientist has no longer any motive for doing what inductive thought gives him permission to do. If he goes on doing it at all, that is only because he is blindly following the conventions of the professional society to which he belongs.

(iii) Testimony

Before trying to describe the special characteristics of historical inference positively, we shall find it useful to describe them negatively: to describe something that is very often, but mistakenly, identified with it. Like every science, history is autonomous. The historian has the right, and is under an obligation, to make up his own mind by the methods proper to his own science as to the correct solution of every problem that arises for him in the pursuit of that science. He can never be under any obligation, or have any right, to let someone else make up his mind for him. If anyone else, no matter who, even a very learned historian, or an eyewitness, or a person in the confidence of the man who did the thing he is inquiring into, or even the man who did it himself, hands him on a plate a ready-made answer to his question, all he can do is to reject it: not because he thinks his informant is trying to deceive him, or is himself deceived, but because if he accepts it he is giving up his autonomy as an historian and allowing someone else to do for him what, if he is a scientific thinker, he can only do for himself. There is no need for me to offer the reader any proof of this statement. If he knows anything of historical work, he already knows of his own experience that it is true. If he does not already know that it is true, he does not know enough about history to read this essay with any profit, and the best thing he can do is to stop here and now.

When the historian accepts a ready-made answer to some question he has asked, given him by another person, this other person is called his 'authority', and the statement made by such an authority and accepted by the historian is called 'testimony'. In so far as an historian accepts the testimony of an authority and treats it as historical truth, he obviously forfeits the name of historian; but we have no other name by which to call him.

Now, I am not for a moment suggesting that testimony ought never to be accepted. In the practical life of every day, we constantly and rightly accept the information that other people offer us, believing them to be both well informed and truthful, and having, sometimes, grounds for this belief. I do not even deny, though I do not assert it, that there may be cases in which, as perhaps in some cases of memory, our acceptance of such testimony may go beyond mere belief and deserve the name of knowledge. What I assert is that it can never be historical knowledge, because it can never be scientific knowledge. It is not scientific knowledge because it cannot be vindicated by appeal to the grounds on which it is based. As soon as there are such grounds, the case is no longer one of testimony. When testimony is reinforced by evidence, our acceptance of it is no longer the acceptance of testimony as such; it is the affirmation of something based upon evidence, that is, historical knowledge.

R. G. Collingwood, Historical Imagination and Historical Evidence

1.   According to Collingwood, history is an imaginative reconstruction of the past.

   a. True   b. False

2.   The idea of history is not an a priori idea.

   a. True   b. False

3.   Collingwood maintains that the method of inquiry in history is

   a. to speculate about the past from present evidence.
   b. to draw logical inferences about the past from present evidence.
   c. to interpret the past in terms of a politically-correct position.
   d. simply to chronicle the sequence of events in the past.

4. Explain the similarities and differences that Collingwood sees between historian and the novelist.

Fernand Braudel*

HISTORY AND THE SOCIAL SCIENCES: THE *LONGUE DURÉE*

There is a general crisis in the human sciences: they are all overwhelmed by their own progress, if only because of the accumulation of new knowledge and the need to work together in a way which is yet to be properly organized. Directly or indirectly, willingly or unwillingly, none of them can remain unaffected by the progress of the more active among them. But they remain in the grip of an insidious and retrograde humanism no longer capable of providing them with a valid framework for their studies. With varying degrees of clear-sightedness, all the sciences are preoccupied with their own position in the whole monstrous agglomeration of past and present researches, researches whose necessary convergence can now clearly be seen.

Will the human sciences solve these difficulties by an extra effort at definition or by an increase in ill temper? They certainly seem to think so, for (at the risk of going over some very well trodden ground and of raising a few red herrings), today they are engaged more busily than ever in defining their aims, their methods, and their superiorities. You can see them vying with each other, skirmishing along the frontiers separating them, or not separating them, or barely separating them from their neighbors. For each of them, in fact, persists in a dream of staying in, or returning to, its home. A few isolated scholars have managed to bring things together: Claude Lévi-Strauss[1] has pushed "structural" anthropology toward the procedures of linguistics, the horizons of "unconscious" history, and the youthful imperialism of "qualitative" mathematics. He leans toward a science which would unite, under the title of communications science, anthropology, political economy, linguistics . . . But is there in fact anyone who is prepared to cross the frontiers like this, and to realign things in this way? Given half a chance, geography would even like to split off from history!

But we must not be unfair. These squabbles and denials have a certain significance. The wish to affirm one's own existence in the face of others is necessarily the basis for new knowledge: to deny someone is already to know him. Moreover, without explicitly wishing it, the social sciences force themselves on each other, each trying to capture society as a whole, in its "totality." Each science encroaches on its neighbors, all the while believing it is staying in its own domain. Economics finds sociology closing in on it, history—perhaps the least

---

*Fernand Braudel (1902–1985) was one of the foremost historians of this century. His works include the three-volume study *Capitalism and Civilization* and the two-volume *The Mediterranean and the Mediterranean World in the Age of Phillip II*. Braudel sought to shift the focus of historiography from narrative history to a concern with enduring social, economic, and geographical structures that persist over long periods of time.

Annales E.S.C., no. 4 (October–December 1958), Débats et combats, pp. 725–53.

[1]Claude Lévi-Strauss, *Structural Anthropology*, trans. Claire Jacobson and Brooke Grundfest Schoepf (London: Allen Lane, The Penguin Press, 1968), 1:300 and passim.

structured of all the human sciences—is open to all the lessons learned by its many neighbors, and is then at pains to reflect them back again. So, despite all the reluctance, opposition, and blissful ignorance, the beginnings of a "common market" are being sketched out. This would be well worth a trial during the coming years, even if each science might later be better off readopting, for a while, some more strictly personal approach.

But the crucial thing now is to get together in the first place. In the United States this coming together has taken the form of collective research on the cultures of different areas of the modern world, "area studies" being, above all, the study by a team of social scientists of those political Leviathans of our time: China, India, Russia, Latin America, the United States. Understanding them is a question of life and death! But at the same time as sharing techniques and knowledge, it is essential that each of the participants should not remain buried in his private research, as deaf and blind as before to what the others are saying, writing, or thinking! Equally, it is essential that this gathering of the social sciences should make no omissions, that they should all be there, that the older ones should not be neglected in favor of the younger ones that seem to promise so much, even if they do not always deliver it. For instance, the position allotted to geography in these American exercises is almost nil, and that allowed to history extremely meager. Not to mention the sort of history it is!

The other social sciences are fairly ill informed as to the crisis which our discipline has gone through in the past twenty or thirty years, and they tend to misunderstand not only the work of historians, but also that aspect of social reality for which history has always been a faithful servant, if not always a good salesman: social time, the multifarious, contradictory times of the life of men, which not only make up the past, but also the social life of the present. Yet history, or rather the dialectic of duration as it arises in the exercise of our profession, from our repeated observations, is important in the coming debate among all the human sciences. For nothing is more important, nothing comes closer to the crux of social reality than this living, intimate, infinitely repeated opposition between the instant of time and that time which flows only slowly. Whether it is a question of the past or of the present, a clear awareness of this plurality of social time is indispensable to the communal methodology of the human sciences.

So I propose to deal at length with history and with time in history. Less for the sake of present readers of this journal, who are already specialists in our field, than for that of those who work in the neighboring human sciences: economists, ethnographers, ethnologists (or anthropologists), sociologists, psychologists, linguists, demographers, geographers, even social mathematicians or statisticians —all neighbors of ours whose experiments and whose researches we have been following for these many years because it seemed to us (and seems so still) that we would thus see history itself in a new light. And perhaps we in our turn have something to offer them. From the recent experiments and efforts of history, an increasingly clear idea has emerged— whether consciously or not, whether excepted or not—of the multiplicity of time, and of the exceptional value of the long time span. It is this last idea which even more than history itself—history of a hundred aspects—should engage the attention and interest of our neighbors, the social sciences.

History and Time Spans

All historical work is concerned with breaking down time past, choosing among its chronological realities according to more or less conscious preferences and exclusions. Traditional history, with its concern for the short time span, for the individual and the event, has long accustomed us to the headlong, dramatic, breathless rush of its narrative.

The new economic and social history puts cyclical movement in the forefront of its research and is committed to that time span: it has been captivated by the mirage and the reality of the cyclic rise and fall of prices. So today, side by side with traditional narrative history, there is an account of conjunctures which lays open large sections of the past, ten, twenty, fifty years at a stretch ready for for examination.

Far beyond this second account we find a history capable of traversing even greater distances, a history to be measured in centuries this time: the history of the long, even of the very long time span, of the *longue durée*. This is a phrase which I have become accustomed to for good or ill, in order to distinguish the opposite of what François Simiand, not long after Paul Lacombe, christened "*l'histoire événementielle*," the history of events. The phrases matter little; what matters is the fact that our discussion will move between these two poles of time, the instant and the *longue durée*.

Not that these words are absolutely reliable. Take the word *event:* for myself I would limit it, and imprison it within the short time span: an event is explosive, a *"nouvelle sonnante"* ("a matter of moment") as they said in the sixteenth century. Its delusive smoke fills the minds of its contemporaries, but it does not last, and its flame can scarcely ever be discerned.

Doubtless philosophers would tell us that to treat the word thus is to empty it of a great part of its meaning. An event can if necessary take on a whole range of meanings and associations. It can occasionally bear witness to very profound movements, and by making play, factitiously or not, with those "causes" and "effects" so dear to the hearts of the historians of yore, it can appropriate a time far greater than its own time span. Infinitely extensible, it becomes wedded, either freely or not, to a whole chain of events, of underlying realities which are then, it seems, impossible to separate. It was by adding things together like this that Benedetto Croce could claim that within any event all history, all of man is embodied, to be rediscovered at will. Though this, of course, is on condition of adding to that fragment whatever it did not at first sight appear to contain, which in turn entails knowing what is appropriate—or not appropriate—to add. It is the clever and perilous process which some of Jean-Paul Sartre's recent thinking seems to propose.[2]

So, to put things more clearly, let us say that instead of a history of events, we would speak of a short time span, proportionate to individuals, to daily life, to our illusions, to our hasty awareness—above all the time of the chronicle and the journalist. Now, it is worth noticing that side by side with great and, so to speak, historic events, the chronicle or the daily paper offers us all the mediocre accidents of ordinary life: a fire, a railway crash, the price of wheat, a crime, a theatrical production, a flood. It is clear, then, that there is a short time span which plays a part in all forms of life, economic, social, literary, institutional, religious, even geographical (a gust of wind, a storm), just as much as political.

At first sight, the past seems to consist in just this mass of diverse facts, some of which catch the eye, and some of which are dim and repeat themselves indefinitely. The very facts, that is, which go to make up the daily booty of microsociology or of sociometry (there is microhistory too). But this mass does not make up all of reality, all the depth of history on which scientific thought is free to work. Social science has almost what amounts to a horror of the event. And not without some justification, for the short time span is the most capricious and the most delusive of all.

Thus there is among some of us, as historians, a lively distrust of traditional history, the history of events—a label which tends to become confused, rather inexactly, with political history. Political history is not necessarily bound to events, nor is it forced to be. Yet except for the factitious panoramas almost without substance in time which break up its narrative,[3] except for the overviews inserted for the sake of variety, on the whole the history of the past hundred years, almost always political history centered on the drama of "great events," has worked on and in the short time span. Perhaps that was the price which had to be paid for the progress made during this same period in the scientific mastery of particular tools and rigorous methods. The momentous discovery of the document led historians to believe that documentary authenticity was the repository of the whole truth. "All we need to do," Louis Halphen wrote only yesterday,[4] is allow ourselves to be borne along by the documents, one after another, just as they offer themselves to us, in order to see the chain of facts and events reconstitute themselves almost automatically before our eyes." Toward the end of the nineteenth century, this ideal of history "in the raw," led to a new style of chronicle, which in its desire for exactitude followed the history of events step by step as it emerged from ambassadorial letters or parliamentary debates. The historians of the eighteenth and early nineteenth centuries had been attentive to the perspectives of the *longue durée* in a way in which, afterwards, only a few great spirits—Michelet, Ranke, Jacob Burckhardt, Fustel—were able to recapture. If one accepts that this going beyond the short span has been the most precious, because the most rare, of historiographical achievements during the past hundred years, then one understand the

---

[2] Jean-Paul Sartre, "Questions de méthode," *Les Temps Modernes* nos. 139 and 140 (1957).

[3] "Europe in 1500," "The World in 1880," "Germany on the Eve of the Reformation," and so on.

[4] Louis Halphen, *Introduction à l'historie* (Paris: P.U.F., 1946), p. 50.

185

preeminent role of the history of institutions, of religions, of civilizations, and (thanks to archeology with its need for vast chronological expanses) the ground-breaking role of the studies devoted to classical antiquities. It was only yesterday that they proved the saviours of our profession.

The recent break with the traditional forms of nineteenth-century history has not meant a complete break with the short time span. It has worked, as we know, in favor of economic and social history, and against the interests of political history. This has entailed upheavals and an undeniable renewal, and also, inevitably, changes in method, the shifting of centers of interest with the advent of a quantitative history that has certainly not exhausted all it has to offer.

But above all, there has been an alteration in traditional historical time. A day, a year once seemed useful gauges. Time, after all, was made up of an accumulation of days. But a price curve, a demographic progression, the movement of wages, the variations in interest rates, the study (as yet more dreamed of than achieved) of productivity, a rigorous analysis of money supply all demand much wider terms of reference.

A new kind of historical narrative has appeared, that of the conjuncture, of the cycle, and even of the "intercycle," covering a decade, a quarter of a century and, at the outside, the half-century of Kondratiev's classic cycle. For instance, if we disregard any brief and superficial fluctuations, prices in Europe went up between 1791 and 1817, and went down between 1817 and 1852. This unhurried double movement of increase and decrease represents an entire intercycle measured by the time of Europe, and more or less by that of the whole world. Of course these chronological periods have no absolute value. François Perroux[5] would offer us other, perhaps more valid, dividing lines, measured with other barometers, those of economic growth, income, or the gross national product. But what do all these current debates matter! What is quite clear is that the historian can make use of a new notion of time, a time raised to the level of explication, and that history can attempt to explain itself by dividing

itself at new points of reference in response to these curves and to the very way they breathe.

Thus Ernest Labrousse and his students, after their manifesto at the last Rome Historical Congress (1955), set up a vast inquiry into social history in quantitative terms. I do not think I am misrepresenting their intention when I say that this inquiry must necessarily lead to the determination of social conjunctures (and even of structure) that may not share the same rate of progress, fast or slow, as the economic conjuncture. Besides, these two distinguished gentlemen—the economic conjuncture and the social conjuncture,—must not make us lose sight of other actors, though their progress will be difficult if not impossible to track, for lack of a precise way of measuring it. Science, technology, political institutions, conceptual changes, civilizations (to fall back on that useful word) all have their own rhythms of life and growth, and the new history of conjunctures will be complete only when it has made up a whole orchestra of them all.

In all logic, this orchestration of conjunctures, by transcending itself, should have led us straight to the *longue durée*. But for a thousand reasons this transcendence has not been the rule, and a return to the short term is being accomplished even now before our very eyes. Perhaps this is because it seems more necessary (or more urgent) to knit together "cyclical" history and short-term traditional history than to go forward, toward the unknown. In military terms, it has been a question of consolidating newly secured positions. Ernest Labrousse's first great book, published in 1933, was thus a study of the general movement of prices in France during the eighteenth century,[6] a movement lasting a good hundred years. In 1943, in the most important work of history to have appeared in France in twenty-five years, this very same Ernest Labrousse succumbed to this need to return to a less cumbersome measure of time when he pinpointed the depression of 1774 to 1791 as being one of the most compelling sources, one of the prime launching pads of the French Revolution. He was still employing a demi-intercycle, a large measure. In his address to the International Congress in Paris, in 1948, *Comment naissent les révolutions?* ("How are

[5]See his *Théorie générale du progrès économique*, Cahiers de l'I.S.E.A., 1957.

[6]*Esquisse du mouvement des prix et des revenus en France au XVIIIᵉ siècle*, 2 vols. (Paris: Dalloz, 1933).

revolutions born?''), he attempted this time to link a new-style pathetic fallacy (short-term economic) to a very old style pathetic fallacy (political, "revolutionary days"). And behold us back up to our ears in the short time span. Of course, this is a perfectly fair and justifiable procedure, but how very revealing! The historian is naturally only too willing to act as theatrical producer. How could he be expected to renounce the drama of the short time span, and all the best tricks of a very old trade?

Over and above cycles and intercycles, there is what the economists without always having studied it call the secular tendency. But so far only a few economists have proved interested in it, and their deliberations on structural crises, based only on the recent past, as far back as 1929, or 1870 at the very most,[7] not having had to withstand the test of historical verification, are more in the nature of sketches and hypotheses. They offer nonetheless a useful introduction to the history of the *longue durée*. They provide a first key.

The second and far more useful key consists in the word *structure*. For good or ill, this word dominates the problems of the *longue durée*. By *structure*, observers of social questions mean an organization, a coherent and fairly fixed series of relationships between realities and social masses. For us historians, a structure is of course a construct, an architecture, but over and above that it is a reality which time uses and abuses over long periods. Some structures, because of their long life, become stable elements for an infinite number of generations: they get in the way of history, hinder its flow, and in hindering it shape it. Others wear themselves out more quickly. But all of them provide both support and hindrance. As hindrances they stand as limits ("envelopes," in the mathematical sense) beyond which man and his experiences cannot go. Just think of the difficulties of breaking out of certain geographical frameworks, certain biological realities, certain limits of productivity, even

particular spiritual constraints: mental frameworks too can form prisons of the *longue durée*.

The example which comes most readily to mind is once again that of the geographical constraint. For centuries, man has been a prisoner of climate, of vegetation, of the animal population, of a particular agriculture, of a whole slowly established balance from which he cannot escape without the risk of everything's being upset. Look at the position held by the movement of flocks in the lives of mountain people, the permanence of certain sectors of maritime life, rooted in the favorable conditions wrought by particular coastal configurations, look at the way the sites of cities endure, the persistence of routes and trade, and all the amazing fixity of the geographical setting of civilizations.

There is the same element of permanence or survival in the vast domain of cultural affairs. Ernst Robert Curtius's magnificent book,[8] which has at long last appeared in a French translation, is a study of a cultural system which prolonged the Latin civilization of the Byzantine Empire, even while it distorted it through selections and omissions. This civilization was itself weighted down by its own ponderous inheritance. Right up to the thirteenth and fourteenth centuries, right up to the birth of national literatures, the civilization of the intellectual élite fed on the same subjects, the same comparisons, the same commonplaces and catchwords. Pursuing an analogous line of thought, Lucien Febvre's study *Rabelais et le problème de l'incroyance au XVIe siècle*,[9] is an attempt to specify the mental tools available to French thought at the time of Rabelais. Febvre was concerned to define the whole body of concepts which regulated the arts of living, thinking, and believing well before Rabelais and long after him and which profoundly limited the intellectual endeavors of the freest spirits from the very outset. Alphonse Dupront's subject[10] too appears as one of the freshest lines of research

---

[7]Considered in René Clémens, *Prolégomènes d'une théorie de la structure économique* (Paris: Domat-Montchrestien, 1952); see also Johann Akerman, "Cycle et struture," *Revue économique*, no. 1 (1952).

[8]Ernst Robert Curtius, *Europaïsche Literatur und lateinisches Mittelalter* (Berne, 1948).

[9]Paris, Albin Michel, 1943; 3d ed., 1969.

[10]"Le mythe de croisade: Essai de sociologie religieuse," thesis, Sorbonne.

within the French school of history. In it the idea of the crusade is examined in the West after the fourteenth century, that is, well after the age of the "true" crusade, in the continuity of an attitude endlessly repeated over the *longue durée,* which cut across the most diverse societies, worlds, and psyches, and touched the men of the nineteenth century with one last ray. In another, related field, Pierre Francastel's book *Peinture et société,*[11] demonstrates the permanence of "geometric" pictorial space from the beginnings of the Florentine Renaissance until cubism and the emergence of intellectual painting at the beginning of our own century. In the history of science, too, all the many model universes are just as many incomplete explanations, but they also regularly last for centuries. They are cast aside only when they have served their turn over a long period. The Aristotelian concept of the universe persisted unchallenged, or virtually unchallenged, right up to the time of Galileo, Descartes, and Newton; then it disappeared before the advent of a geometrized universe which in turn collapsed, though much later, in the face of the Einsteinian revolution.[12]

In a seeming paradox, the main problem lies in discerning the *longue durée* in the sphere in which historical research has just achieved its most notable successes: that is, the economic sphere. All the cycles and intercycles and structural crises tend to mask the regularities, the permanence of particular systems that some have gone so far as to call civilizations[13]—that is to say, all the old habits of thinking and acting, the set patterns which do not break down easily and which, however illogical, are a long time dying.

But let us base our argument on an example, and one which can be swiftly analyzed. Close at hand, within the European sphere, there is an economic system which can be set down in a few lines:

it preserved its position pretty well intact from the fourteenth to the eighteenth century or, to be quite sure of our ground, until about 1750. For whole centuries, economic activity was dependent on demographically fragile populations, as was demonstrated by the great decline in population from 1350 to 1450, and of course from 1630 to 1730.[14] For whole centuries, all movement was dominated by the primacy of water and ships, any inland location being an obstacle and a source of inferiority. The great European points of growth, except for a few exceptions which go only to prove the role (such as the fairs in Champagne which were already on the decline at the beginning of the period, and the Leipzig fairs in the eighteenth century), were situated along the coastal fringes. As for other characteristics of this system, one might cite the primacy of merchants; the prominent role of precious metals, gold, silver, even copper, whose endless vicissitudes would only be damped down, if then, by the decisive development of credit at the end of the sixteenth century; the repeated sharp difficulties caused by seasonal agricultural crises; let us say the fragility of the very basis of economic life; and finally the at first sight utterly disproportionate role accorded to one or two external trade routes: the trade with the Levant from the twelfth to the sixteenth century and the colonial trade in the eighteenth century.

These are what I would define, or rather suggest in my turn following many others, as being the major characteristics of mercantile capitalism in Western Europe, a stage which lasted over the *longue durée.* Despite all the obvious changes which run through them, these four or five centuries of economic life had a certain coherence, right up to the upheavals of the eighteenth century and the industrial revolution from which we have yet to emerge. These shared characteristics persisted de-

---

[11]Pierre Francastel, *Peinture et société: Naissance et destruction d'un espace plastique, de la Renaissance au cubisme* (Lyon: Audin, 1951).

[12]Other arguments: I would like to suggest those forceful articles which all of them advance a similar thesis, such as Otto Brunner's (*Historische Zeitshrift,* vol. 177, no. 3) on the social history of Europe; R. Bultmann's (ibid., vol. 176, no. 1), on humanism; Georges Lefebvre's (*Annales historiques de la Révolution française,* no. 114 [1949]) and F. Hartung's (*Historische Zeitschrift,* vol. 180, no. 1), on enlightened despotism.

[13]René Courtin, *La Civilisation économique du Brésil* (Paris: Librairie de Médicis. 1941).

[14]As far as France is concerned. In Spain, the demographic decline was visible from the end of the sixteenth century.

188

spite the fact that all around them, amid other continuities, a thousand reversals and ruptures totally altered the face of the world.

Among the different kinds of historical time, the *longue durée* often seems a troublesome character, full of complications, and all too frequently lacking in any sort of organization. To give it a place in the heart of our profession would entail more than a routine expansion of our studies and our curiosities. Nor would it be a question of making a simple choice in its favor. For the historian, accepting the *longue durée* entails a readiness to change his style, his attitudes, a whole reversal in his thinking, a whole new way of conceiving of social affairs. It means becoming used to a slower tempo, which sometimes almost borders on the motionless. At that stage, though not at any other—this is a point to which I will return—it is proper to free oneself from the demanding time scheme of history, to get out of it and return later with a fresh view, burdened with other anxieties and other questions. In any case, it is in relation to these expanses of slow-moving history that the whole of history is to be rethought, as if on the basis of an infrastructure. All the stages, all the thousands of stages, all the thousand explosions of historical time can be understood on the basis of these depths, this semistillness. Everything gravitates around it.

I make no claim to have defined the historian's profession in the preceding lines—merely one conception of that profession. After the storms we have been through during recent years, happy not to say naïf the man who could believe that we have hit upon true principles, clear limits, the Right School. In fact, all the social sciences find their tasks shifting all the time, both because of their own developments and because of the active development of them all as a body. History is no exception. There is no rest in view, the time for disciples has not yet come. It is a long way from Charles-Victor Langlois and Charles Seignobos to Marc Bloch. But since Marc Bloch, the wheel has not stopped turning. For me, history is the total of all possible histories—an assemblage of professions and points of view, from yesterday, today, and tomorrow.

The only error, in my view, would be to choose one of these histories to the exclusion of all others. That was, and always will be, the cardinal error of historicizing. It will not be easy, we know, to convince all historians of the truth of this. Still less, to convince all the social sciences, with their burning desire to get us back to history as we used to know it yesterday. It will take us a good deal of time and trouble to accommodate all these changes and innovations beneath the old heading of history. And yet a new historical "science" has been born, and goes on questioning and transforming itself. It revealed itself as early as 1900, with the *Revue de synthèse historique,* and with *Annales* which started to come out in 1929. The historian felt the desire to concentrate his attention on *all* the human sciences. It is this which has given our profession its strange frontiers, and its strange preoccupations. So it must not be imagined that the same barriers and differences exist between the historian and the social scientist as existed yesterday. All the human sciences, history included, are affected by one another. They speak the same language, or could if they wanted to.

Whether you take 1558 or this year of grace 1958, the problem for anyone tackling the world scene is to define a hierarchy of forces, of currents, of particular movements, and then tackle them as an entire constellation. At each moment of this research, one has to distinguish between long-lasting movements and short bursts, the latter detected from the moment they originate, the former over the course of a distant time. The world of 1558, which appeared so gloomy in France, was not born at the beginning of that charmless year. The same with our own troubled year of 1958. Each "current event" brings together movements of different origins, of a different rhythm: today's time dates from yesterday, the day before yesterday, and all former times.

Communication and Social Mathematics

Perhaps we were wrong to linger on the tempestuous borders of the short time span. In actual fact, that debate proceeds without any great interest, certainly without any useful revelations. The crucial debate is elsewhere, among our neighbors who are being carried away by the newest experiment in the social sciences, under the double heading of "communications" and mathematics.

But this will be no easy brief to argue. I mean it will be by no means easy to prove that there is no sort of social study which can avoid historical time, when here is one which, ostensibly at least, has its being entirely outside it.

In any case, the reader who wishes to follow our argument (either to agree or to dissociate himself from our point of view) would do well to weigh for himself, one after another, the terms of a vocabulary which, though certainly not entirely new, have been taken up afresh and rejuvenated for the purposes of these new debates. There is nothing more to be said here, obviously, about events, or the *longue durée*. Nor a great deal about *structures,* though the word—and the thing—is by no means entirely free from uncertainty and debate.[15] Nor would there be any point in dwelling on the words *synchronous* and *diachronous:* they are self-defining, though their function in the actual study of social questions might be less easy to make out than it appears. In fact, as far as the language of history is concerned (insofar as I conceive it) there can be no question of perfect synchrony: a sudden halt, in which all time spans would be suspended, is almost an absurdity in itself, or, and this comes to the same thing, is highly factitious. In the same way, a descent following the onward stream of time is conceivable only in terms of a multiplicity of descents, following the innumerable different rivers of time.

These brief summaries and warnings must suffice for now. But one must be more explicit when dealing with *unconscious history, models,* and *social mathematics.* Besides, these commentaries will, I hope, without too much delay, link together what is problematic in all the social sciences.

Unconscious history, is, of course, the history of the unconscious elements in social development. "Men make their own history, but they do not know that they are making it."[16] Marx's formula pinpoints the problem, but does not explain it. In fact it is the same old problem of short time span, of "micro-time," of the event, that we find ourselves confronted with under a new name. Men have always had the impression, in living out their time, of being able to grasp its passage from day to day. But is this clear, conscious history delusory, as many historians have agreed? Yesterday linguistics believed that it could derive everything from words. History was under the illusion that it could derive everything from events. More than one of our contemporaries would be happy to believe that everything is the result of the agreements at Yalta or Potsdam, the incidents at Dien Bien Phu or Sakhiet-Sidi-Youssef, or again from that other event, important in a different way it is true, the launching of the sput-

niks. Unconscious history proceeds beyond the reach of these illuminations and their brief flashes. One has, then to concede that there does exist, at some distance, a social unconscious. And concede, too, that this unconscious might well be thought more rich, scientifically speaking, than the glittering surface to which our eyes are accustomed. More rich scientifically, meaning simpler, easier to exploit—not easier to discover. But the step from bright surface to murky depths—from noise to silence—is difficult and dangerous. Equally let it be said that "unconscious" history, belonging half to the time of conjunctures and wholly to structural time, is clearly visible more frequently than one would willingly admit. Each one of us can sense, over and above his own life, a mass history, though it is true he is more conscious of its power and impetus than of its laws or direction. And this consciousness is not only of recent date (like the concerns of economic history), although today it may be increasingly sharp. The revolution, for it is an intellectual revolution, consisted in confronting this half darkness head on, and giving it a greater and greater place next to, and even to the detriment of, a history purely of events.

History is not alone in this prospecting (quite the reverse, all it has done has been to follow others into the area, and adapt the perspectives of the new social sciences for its own use), and new instruments of knowledge and research have had to be created: hence *models,* some more or less perfected, some still rather rough and ready. Models are only hypotheses, systems of explanations tied solidly together in the form of an equation, or a function: this equals that, or determines the other. Such and such a reality never appears without that one, and constant and close links are revealed between the one and the other. The carefully constructed model will thus allow us to inquire, throughout time and space, into other social environments similar to the observed social environment on the basis of which it was originally constructed. That is its constant value.

These systems of explanation vary infinitely according to the temperament, calculations, and aims of those using them: simple or complex, qualitative or quantitative, static or dynamic, mechani-

---

[15]See the Colloquium on Structures, 6th section of the École Pratique des Hautes Études, typed summary, 1958.

[16]Quoted by Claude Lévi-Strauss, *Structural Anthropology,* vol. 1, p. 23.

cal or statistical. I am indebted to Lévi-Strauss for this last distinction. A mechanical model would be of the same dimensions as directly observed reality, a reality of limited dimensions, of interest only to very small groups of people (this is how ethnologists proceed when dealing with primitive societies). When dealing with large societies, where great numbers come in, the calculation of the average becomes necessary: this leads to the construction of statistical models. But what do these sometimes debatable distinctions really matter!

In my opinion, before establishing a common program for the social sciences, the crucial thing is to define the function and limits of models, the scope of which some undertakings seem to be in danger of enlarging inordinately. Whence the need to confront models, too, with the notion of the time span; for the meaning and the value of their explanations depend fairly heavily, it seems to me, on their implied duration.

To be more clear, let us select our examples from among historical models,[17] by which I mean those constructed by historians. They are fairly rough and ready as models go, not often driven to the rigor of an authentic scientific law, and never worried about coming out with some revolutionary mathematical language—but models nonetheless, in their own way.

Above we have discussed mercantile capitalism between the fourteenth and the eighteenth centuries: one model which, among others, can be drawn from Marx's work. It can be applied in full only to one particular family of societies at one particular given time, even if it leaves the door open to every extrapolation.

There is already a difference between this and the model which I sketched out in an earlier book,[18]

of the cycle of economic development in Italian cities between the sixteenth and eighteenth centuries. These cities became in turn mercantile, "industrial," and finally specialists in banking, this last development being the slowest to grow and the slowest to die away. Though in fact less all-embracing than the structure of mercantile capitalism, this sketch would be much the more easily extended in time and space. It records a phenomenon (some would say a dynamic structure, but all structures in history have at least an elementary dynamism) capable of recurring under a number of common circumstances. Perhaps the same could be said of the model sketched out by Frank Spooner and myself[19] which dealt with the history of precious metals before, during, and after the sixteenth century: gold, silver, copper—and credit, that agile substitute for metal—all play their part too. The "strategy" of one weighs on the "strategy" of another. It would not be particularly difficult to remove this model from the special and particularly turbulent world of the sixteenth century, which happened to be the one we selected for our observations. Have not economists dealing with the particular case of underdeveloped countries attempted to verify the old quantitative theory of money, which was, after all, a model too in its own fashion.[20]

But the time spans possible to all these models are brief compared with those of the model conceived by the young American social historian Sigmund Diamond.[21] Diamond was struck by the double language of the dominant class of great American financier contemporaries of Pierpont Morgan, consisting of a language internal to their class, and an eternal language. This last, truth to tell, was a brand of special pleading with public

---

[17]It would be tempting to make room here for the "models" created by economists, which have, in fact, been a source of inspiration to us.

[18]*The Mediterranean and the Mediterranean World in the Age of Philip II,* trans. Sian Reynolds, 2 vols. (New York: Harper & Row, 1972–74).

[19]Fernand Braudel and Frank Spooner, *Les Métaux monétaires et l'économie au XVIᵉ siècle, Rapports au Congrès international de Rome* 4 (1955): 233–64.

[20]Alexandre Chabert, *Structure économique et théorie monétaire,* Publications du Centre d'Études économiques (Paris: Armand Colin, 1956).

[21]Sigmund Diamond, *The Reputation of the American Businessman* (Cambridge, Mass., 1955).

opinion to whom the success of the financier is presented as the typical triumph of the *self-made man,* the condition necessary for the nation's prosperity. Struck by this double language, Diamond saw in it the customary reaction of any dominant class which feels its prestige waning and its privileges threatened. In order to camouflage itself, it is necessary for it to confuse its own fate with that of the City or the Nation, its own private interests with the public interest. Sigmund Diamond would willingly explain the evolution of the idea of dynasty or of empire, the English dynasty or the Roman empire, in the same way. The model thus conceived clearly has the run of the centuries. It presupposes certain conditions, but these are conditions with which history is abundantly supplied: it follows that it is valid for a much longer time span than either of the preceding models, but at the same time it puts into question much more precise and exact aspects of reality.

At the limit, as the mathematicians would say, this kind of model is kin to the favorite, almost timeless models of sociological mathematicians. Almost timeless, in actual fact, traveling the dark, untended byways of the extreme *longue durée.*

But let us get back to the question of time spans. I have said that models are of varying duration: they are valid for as long as the reality with which they are dealing. And for the social observer, that length of time is fundamental, for even more significant than the deep-rooted structures of life are their points of rupture, their swift or slow deterioration under the effect of contradictory pressures.

I have sometime compared models to ships. What interests me, once the boat is built, is to put it in the water to see if it will float, and then to make it ascend and descend the waters of time, at my will. The significant moment is when it can keep afloat no longer, and sinks. Thus the explanation which Frank Spooner and I proposed for the interplay of precious metals seems to me to have little validity before the fifteenth century. Earlier than that, the competition between metals was of a violence quite unparalleled in previous observations. It was up to us then to find out why. Just as, going downstream this time, we had to find out why the navigation of our over-simple craft became first difficult and then impossible in the eighteenth century with the unprecedented growth of credit. It seems to me that

research is a question of endlessly proceeding from the social reality to the model, and then back again, and so on, in a series of readjustments and patiently renewed trips. In this way the model is, in turn, an attempt at an explanation of the structure, and an instrument of control and comparison, able to verify the solidity and the very life of a given structure. If I were to construct a model on the basis of the present, I would immediately relocate it in its context in reality, and then take it back in time, as far back as its origins, if possible. After which, I would project its probable life, right up to the next break, in accordance with the corresponding movement of other social realities. Unless I should decide to use it as an element of comparison, and take it off through time and space, in search of other aspects of reality on which it might shed new light.

I do not know whether this rather excessively cut and dried article, relying overmuch, as historians have a tendency to do, on the use of examples, will meet with the agreement of sociologists and of our other neighbors. I rather doubt it. Anyway, it is never a good thing, when writing a conclusion, simply to repeat some insistently recurrent leitmotif. Should history by its very nature be called upon to pay special attention to the span of time and to *all* the movements of which it may be made up, the *longue durée* appears to us, within this array, as the most useful line to take toward a way of observing and thinking common to all the social sciences. Is it too much to ask our neighbors that, at some stage in their reasoning, they might locate their findings and their research along this axis?

For historians, not all of whom would share my views, it would be a case of reversing engines. Their preference goes instinctively toward the short term. It is an attitude aided and abetted by the sacrosanct university course. Jean-Paul Sartre, in recent articles,[22] strengthens their point of view, when he protests against that which is both oversimplified and too ponderous in Marxism in the name of the biographical, of the teeming reality of events. You have not said everything when you have "situated" Flaubert as bourgeois, or Tintoretto as petty bourgeois. I entirely agree. But in every case a study of the concrete situation—whether Flaubert, Valéry, or the foreign policies of the Gironde—ends up by bringing Sartre back to its deep-seated structural context. His research moves from the surface

---

[22]Ibid. See also Jean-Paul Sartre, "Fragment d'un livre à paraître sur le Tintoret," *Les Temps Modernes* (November 1957).

to the depths, and so links up with my own preoccupations. It would link up even better if the hourglass could be turned over both ways—from event to structure, and then from structure and model back to the event.

Marxism is peopled with models. Sartre would rebel against the rigidity, the schematic nature, the insufficiency of the model, in the name of the particular and the individual. I would rebel with him (with certain slight differences in emphasis) not against the model, though, but against the use which has been made of it, the use which it has been felt proper to make. Marx's genius, the secret of his long sway, lies in the fact that he was the first to construct true social models, on the basis of a historical *longue durée*. These models have been frozen in all their simplicity by being given the status of laws, of a preordained and automatic explanation, valid in all places and to any society. Whereas if they were put back within the ever-changing stream of time, they would constantly reappear, but with changes of emphasis, sometimes overshadowed, sometimes thrown into relief by the presence of other structures which would themselves be susceptible to definition by other rules and thus by other models. In this way, the creative potential of the most powerful social analysis of the last century has been stymied. It cannot regain its youth and vigor except in the *longue durée*. Should I add that contemporary Marxism appears to me to be the very image of the danger lying in wait for any social science wholly taken up with the model in its pure state, with models for models' sake?

What I would like to emphasize in conclusion is that the *longue durée* is but one possibility of a common language arising from a confrontation among the social sciences. There are others. I have indicated, adequately, the experiments being made by the new social mathematics. The new mathematics draws me, but the old mathematics, whose triumph is obvious in economics—perhaps the most advanced of the human sciences—does not deserve to be dismissed with a cynical aside. Huge calculations await us in this classic field, but there are squads of calculators and of calculating machines ready too, being rendered daily yet more perfect. I am a great believer in the usefulness of long sequences of statistics, and in the necessity of taking calculations and research further and further back in time. The whole of the eighteenth century in Europe is riddled with our workings, but they crop up even in the seventeenth, and even more in the sixteenth century. Statistics going back an unbelievably long way reveal the depths of the Chinese past to us through their universal language.[23] No doubt statistics simplify the better to come to grips with their subject. But all science is a movement from the complex to the simple.

And yet, let us not forget one last language, one last family of models, in fact: the necessary reduction of any social reality to the place in which it occurs. Let us call it either geography or ecology, without dwelling too long on these differences in terminology. Geography too often conceives of itself as a world on its own, and that is a pity. It has need of a Vidal de la Blache who would consider not time and place this time, but place and social reality. If that happened, geographical research would put the problems of all the human sciences first on its agenda. For sociologists, not that they would always admit it to themselves, the word ecology is a way of not saying geography, and by the same token of dodging all the problems posed by place and revealed by place to careful observation. Spatial models are the charts upon which social reality is projected, and through which it may become at least partially clear; they are truly models for all the different movements of time (and especially for the *longue durée*), and for all the categories of social life. But, amazingly, social science chooses to ignore them. I have often thought that one of the French superiorities in the social sciences was precisely that school of geography founded by Vidal de la Blache, the betrayal of whose thought and teachings is an inconsolable loss. All the social sciences must make room "for an increasingly geographical conception of mankind."[24] This is what Vidal de la Blache was asking for as early as 1903.

On the practical level—for this article does have a practical aim—I would hope that the social sciences, at least provisionally, would suspend their

---

[23]Otto Berkelbach, Van der Sprenkel, "Population Statistics of Ming China," B.S.O.A.S., 1953; Marianne Rieger, "Zur Finanz- und Agrargeschichte der Ming Dynastie, 1368–1643," *Sinica*, 1932.

[24]P. Vidal de la Blache, *Revue de synthèse historique* (1903), p. 239.

constant border disputes over what is or is not a social science, what is or is not a structure . . . Rather let them try to trace those lines across our research which if they exist would serve to orient some kind of collective research, and make possible the first stages of some sort of coming together. I would personally call such lines mathematization, a concentration on place, the *longue durée* . . . But I would be very interested to know what other specialists would suggest. For it goes without saying that this article has not been placed under the rubric *Débats et Combats*[25] by pure chance. It claims to pose, but not resolve, the obvious problems to which, unhappily, each one of us, when he ventures outside his own specialty, finds himself exposed. These pages are a call to discussion.

---

[25]Well-known rubric of *Annales E.S.C.*

Fernand Braudel, History and the Social Sciences: The *Longue Durée*

1.   Identify three different kinds of historical time.

      a. _____

      b. _____

      c. _____

2.   For Braudel, history is the total of all possible histories.

      a. True   b. False

3.   Why does Braudel think it is important to pay attention to *longue durée?*

4.   According to Braudel, how should historians study the *longue durée?*

Immanuel Kant*

ON PRACTICAL REASON

Although we have derived our earlier concept of duty from the ordinary use of our practical reason, it is by no means to be inferred that we have treated it as an empirical concept. On the contrary, if we attend to our experience of the way men act, we meet frequent and, as we must confess, justified complaints that we cannot cite a single sure example of the disposition to act from pure duty. There are also justified complaints that, though much may be done that accords with what duty commands, it is nevertheless always doubtful whether it is done from duty and thus whether it has moral worth. There have always been philosophers who for this reason have absolutely denied the reality of this disposition in human actions, attributing everything to more or less refined self-love. They have done so without questioning the correctness of the concept of morality. Rather they spoke with sincere regret of the frailty and corruption of human nature, which is noble enough to take as its precept an Idea so worthy of respect but which at the same time is too weak to follow it, employing reason, which should give laws for human nature, only to provide for the interest of the inclinations either singly or, at best, in their greatest possible harmony with one another.

It is, in fact, absolutely impossible by experience to discern with complete certainty a single case in which the maxim of an action, however much it might conform to duty, rested solely on moral grounds and on the conception of one's duty. It sometimes happens that in the most searching self-examination we can find nothing except the moral ground of duty which could have been powerful enough to move us to this or that good action and to such great sacrifice. But from this we cannot by any means conclude with certainty that a secret impulse of self-love, falsely appearing as the Idea of duty, was not actually the true determining cause of the will. For we like to flatter ourselves with a pretended nobler motive, while in fact even the strictest examination can never lead us entirely behind the secret incentives, for when moral worth is in question it is not a matter of actions which one sees but of their inner principles which one does not see.

Moreover, one cannot better serve the wishes of those who ridicule all morality as a mere phantom of human imagination overreaching itself through self-conceit than by conceding that the concepts of duty must be derived only from experience (for they are ready, from indolence, to believe that this is true of all other concepts too). For, by this concession, a sure triumph is prepared for them. Out of love for humanity I am willing to admit that most of our actions are in accord with duty; but if we look more closely at our thoughts and aspirations, we come everywhere upon the dear self, which is always turning up, and it is this instead of the stern command of duty (which would often require self-denial) which supports our plans. One need not be an enemy of virtue, but only a cool observer who does not confuse even the liveliest aspiration for the good with its actuality, to be sometimes doubtful whether true virtue can really be found anywhere in the world. This is especially true as one's years

---

*Immanuel Kant (1724–1804) was born and lived his whole life in Königsberg, Prussia. Despite the geographical limitations of his horizons, he made major contributions to every field of philosophy, as well as astronomy. His greatest work came later in life and includes *The Critique of Pure Reason, The Critique of Practical Reason, The Critique of Judgment,* and *Religion within the Limits of Reason Alone.* The following selection is taken from his *Foundations of the Metaphysics of Morals* (1785), one of the most influential works of moral theory in the Western tradition. In it, he argues that reason alone can determine action through the concept of law.

increase and the power of judgment is made wiser by experience and more acute in observation. This being so, nothing can secure us against the complete abandonment of our ideas of duty and preserve in us a well-founded respect for its law except the conviction that, even if there never were actions springing from such pure sources, our concern is not whether this or that was done, but that reason of itself and independently of all appearances commanded what ought to be done. Our concern is with actions of which perhaps the world has never had an example, with actions whose feasibility might be seriously doubted by those who base everything on experience, and yet with actions inexorably commanded by reason. For example, pure sincerity in friendship can be demanded of every man, and this demand is not in the least diminished if a sincere friend has never existed, because this duty, as duty in general, prior to all experience lies in the Idea of reason which determines the will on a priori grounds.

No experience, it is clear, can give occasion for inferring the possibility of such apodictic laws. This is especially clear when we add that, unless we wish to deny all truth to the concept of morality and renounce its application to any possible object, we cannot refuse to admit that the law is of such broad significance that it holds not merely for men but for all rational beings as such; we must grant that it must be valid with absolute necessity, and not merely under contingent conditions and with exceptions. For with what right could we bring into unlimited respect something that might be valid only under contingent human conditions? And how could laws of the determination of our will be held to be laws of the determination of the will of any rational being whatever and of ourselves in so far as we are rational beings, if they were merely empirical and did not have their origin completely a priori in pure, but practical, reason?

Nor could one given poorer counsel to morality than to attempt to derive it from examples. For each example of morality which is exhibited must itself have been previously judged according to principles of morality to see whether it was worthy to serve as an original example or model. By no means could it authoritatively furnish the concept of morality. Even the Holy One of the Gospel must be compared with our ideal of moral perfection before He is recognized as such; even He says of Himself, "Why call ye Me (Whom you see) good? None is good (the archetype of the good) except God only (Whom you do not see)." But whence do we have the concept of God as the highest good? Solely from the Idea of moral perfection which reason formulates a priori and which it inseparably connects with the concept of a free will. Imitation has no place in moral matters, and examples serve only for encouragement. That is, they put beyond question the possibility for performing what the law commands, and they make visible that which the practical rule expresses more generally. But they can never justify our guiding ourselves by examples and our setting aside their true original, which lies in reason.

From what has been said it is clear that all moral concepts have their seat and origin entirely a priori in reason. This is just as much the case in the most ordinary reason as in the reason which is speculative to the highest degree. It is obvious that they can be abstracted for no empirical and hence merely contingent cognitions. In the purity of origin lies their worthiness to serve us as supreme practical principles, and to the extent that something empirical is added to them, just this much is subtracted from their genuine influence and for the unqualified worth of actions. Furthermore, it is evident that it is not only of the greatest necessity from a theoretical point of view when it is a question of speculation but also of the utmost practical importance to derive the concepts and laws of morals from pure reason and to present them pure and unmixed, and to determine the scope of this entire practical but pure rational knowledge (the entire faculty of pure practical reason) without making the principles depend upon the particular nature of human reason, as speculative philosophy may permit and even find necessary. But since moral laws should hold for every rational being as such, the principles must be derived from the universal concept of a rational being in general. In this manner all morals, which need anthropology for their application to men, must be completely developed first as pure philosophy (i.e., metaphysics), independently of anthropology (a thing feasibly done in such distinct fields of knowledge). For we know well that if we are not in possession of such a metaphysics, it is not merely futile [to try to] define accurately for the purposes of speculative judgment the moral element of duty in all actions which accord with duty, but impossible to base morals on legitimate principles for even ordinary practical use, especially in moral instruction; and it is only in this manner that pure moral dispositions can be produced and engrafted on men's minds for the purpose of the highest good in the world.

In this study we do not advance merely from the common moral judgment (which here is very worthy of respect) to the philosophical, as this has already been done; but we advance by natural stages from popular philosophy (which goes no farther than it can grope by means of examples to metaphysics (which is not held back by anything empirical and which, as it must measure out the entire scope of rational knowledge of this kind, reaches even Ideas, where examples fail us). In order to make this advance, we must follow and clearly present the practical faculty of reason from its universal rules of determination to the point where the concept of duty arises from it.

Everything in nature works according to laws. Only a rational being has the capacity of acting according to the *conception* of laws (i.e., according to principles). This capacity is the will. Since reason is required for the derivation of actions from laws, will is nothing less than practical reason. If reason infallibly determines the will, the actions which such a being recognizes as objectively necessary are also subjectively necessary. That is, the will is a faculty of choosing only that which reason, independently of inclination, recognizes as practically necessary (i.e., as good). But if reason of itself does not sufficiently determine the will, and if the will is subjugated to subjective conditions (certain incentives) which do not always agree with the objective conditions—in a word, if the will is not of itself in complete accord with reason (which is the actual case with men), then the actions which are recognized as objectively necessary are subjectively contingent, and the determination of such a will according to objective laws is a constraint. That is, the relation of objective laws to a will which is not completely good is conceived as the determination of the will of a rational being by principles of reason to which this will is not by its nature necessarily obedient.

The conception of an objective principle, so far as it constrains a will, is a command (of reason), and the formula of this command is called an *imperative.*

All imperatives are expressed by an "ought" and thereby indicate the relation of an objective law of reason to a will which is not in its subjective constitution necessarily determined by this law. This relation is that of constraint. Imperatives say that it would be good to do or to refrain from doing something, but they say it to a will which does not always do something simply because the thing is presented to it as good to do. Practical good is what determines the will by means of the conception of reason and hence not by subjective causes but objectively, on grounds which are valid for every rational being as such. It is distinguished from the pleasant, as that which has an influence on the will only by means of a sensation from purely subjective causes, which hold for the senses only of this or that person and not as a principle of reason which holds for everyone.

A perfectly good will, therefore, would be equally subject to objective laws of the good, but it could not be conceived as constrained by them to accord with them, because it can be determined to act by its own subjective constitution only through the conception of the good. Thus no imperatives hold for the divine will or, more generally, for a holy will. The "ought" here is out of place, for the volition of itself is necessarily in unison with the law. Therefore imperatives are only formulas expressing the relation of objective laws of volition in general to the subjective imperfection of the will of this or that rational being, for example, the human will.

All imperatives command either *hypothetically* or *categorically.* The former present the practical necessity of a possible action as a means to achieving something else which one desires (or which one may possibly desire). The categorical imperative would be one which presented an action as of itself objectively necessary, without regard to any other end.

Since every practical law presents a possible action as good and thus as necessary for a subject practically determinable by reason, all imperatives are formulas of the determination of action which is necessary by the principle of a will which is in any way good. If the action is good only as a means to something else, the imperative is hypothetical; but if it is thought of as good in itself, and hence as necessary in a will which of itself conforms to reason as the principle of this will, the imperative is categorical.

The imperative thus says what action possible for me would be good, and it presents the practical rule in relation to a will which does not forthwith perform an action simply because it is good, in part because the subject does not always know that the action is good, and in part (when he does know it) because his maxims can still be opposed to the objective principles of a practical reason.

The hypothetical imperative, therefore, says only that the action is good to some purpose, possible or actual. In the former case, it is a problematical, in the latter an assertorical, practical principle. The categorical imperative, which declares the action to be of itself objectively necessary without making any reference to any end in view (i.e., without having any other purpose), holds as an apodictical practical principle.

We can think of what is possible only through the powers of some rational being as a possible end in view of any will. As a consequence, the principles of action thought of as necessary to attain a possible end in view which can be achieved by them, are in reality infinitely numerous. All sciences have some practical part consisting of problems which presuppose some purpose as well as imperatives directing how it can be reached. These imperatives can therefore be called, generally, imperatives of skill. Whether the purpose is reasonable and good is not in question at all, for the questions concerns only what must be done in order to attain it. The precepts to be followed by a physician in order to cure his patient and by a poisoner to bring about certain death are of equal value in so far as each does that which will perfectly accomplish his purpose. Since in early youth we do not know what purposes we may have in the course of our life, parents seek to let their children learn a great many things and provide for skill in the use of means to all sorts of ends which they might choose, among which they cannot determine whether any one of them will become their child's actual purpose, though it may be that someday he may have it as his actual purpose. And this anxiety is so great that they commonly neglect to form and correct their children's judgment on the worth of the things which they may make their ends.

There is one end, however, which we may presuppose as actual in all rational beings so far as imperatives apply to them, that is, so far as they are dependent beings. There is one purpose which they not only *can* have but which we can presuppose that they all *do* have by a necessity of nature. This purpose is happiness. The hypothetical imperative which represents the practical necessity of an action as means to the promotion of happiness is an assertorical imperative. We may not expound it as necessary to a merely uncertain and merely possible purpose, but as necessary to a purpose which we can a priori and with assurance assume for everyone because it belongs to his essence. Skill in the choice of means to one's own highest well-being can be

called prudence in the narrowest sense. Thus the imperative which refers to the choice of means to one's own happiness (i.e., the precept of prudence) is still only hypothetical, and the action is not commanded absolutely but commanded only as a means to another end in view.

Finally, there is one imperative which directly commands certain conduct without making its condition some purpose to be reached by it. This imperative is categorical. It concerns not the material of the action and its intended result, but the form and principle from which it originates. What is essentially good in it consists in the mental disposition, the result being what it may. This imperative may be called the imperative of morality.

If I think of a hypothetical imperative as such, I do not know what it will contain until the condition is stated [under which it is an imperative]. But if I think of a categorical imperative, I know immediately what it will contain. For since the imperative contains, besides the law, only the necessity of the maxim[1] of acting in accordance with the law, while the law contains no condition to which it is restricted, nothing remains except the universality of law as such to which the maxim of the action should conform; and this conformity alone is what is represented as necessary by the imperative.

There is, therefore, only one categorical imperative. It is: Act only according to that maxim by which you can at the same time will that it should become a universal law.

Now if all imperatives of duty can be derived from this one imperative as a principle, we can at least show what we understand by the concept of duty and what it means, even though it remain undecided whether that which is called duty is an empty concept or not.

The universality of law according to which effects are produced constitutes what is properly called nature in the most general sense (as to form) (i.e., the existence of things so far as it is determined by universal laws). [By analogy], then, the universal imperative of duty can be expressed as follows: Act as though the maxim of your action were by your will to become a universal law of nature.

---

[1]A maxim is the subjective principle of acting and must be distinguished from the objective principle (i.e., the practical law). The former contains the practical rule which reason determines according to the conditions of the subject (often his ignorance or inclinations) and is thus the principle according to which the subject acts. The law, on the other hand, is the objective principle valid for every rational being, and the principle by which it ought to act, i.e., an imperative.

When we observe ourselves in any transgression of a duty, we find that we do not actually will that our maxim should become a universal law. That is impossible for us; rather, the contrary of this maxim should remain as a law generally, and we only take the liberty of making an exception to it for ourselves or for the sake of our inclination, and for this one occasion. Consequently, if we weighed everything from one and the same standpoint, namely, reason, we would come upon a contradiction in our own will, viz., that a certain principle is objectively necessary as a universal law and yet subjectively does not hold universally but rather admits exceptions. However, since we regard our action at one time from the point of view of a will wholly conformable to reason and then from that of a will affected by inclinations, there is actually no contradiction, but rather an opposition of inclination to the precept of reason (*antagonismus*). In this the universality of the principle (*universalitas*) is changed into mere generality (*generalitas*), whereby the practical principle of reason meets the maxim halfway. Although this cannot be justified in our own impartial judgment, it does show that we actually acknowledge the validity of the categorical imperative and allow ourselves (with all respect to it) only a few exceptions which seem to us to be unimportant and forced upon us.

The will is thought of as a faculty of determining itself to action in accordance with the conception of certain laws. Such a faculty can be found only in rational beings. That which serves the will as the objective ground of its self-determination is a purpose, and if it is given by reason alone it must hold alike for all rational beings. On the other hand, that which contains the ground of the possibility of the action, whose result is an end, is called the means. The subjective ground of desire is the incentive (*Triebfeder*) while the objective ground of volition is the motive (*Bewegungsgrund*). Thus arises the distinction between subjective purposes, which rest on incentives, and objective purposes, which depend on motives valid for every rational being. Practical principles are formal when they disregard all subjective purposes; they are material when they have subjective purposes and thus certain incentives as their basis. The purposes that a rational being holds before himself by choice as consequences of his action are material purposes and are without exception only relative, for only their relation to a particularly constituted faculty of desire in the subject gives them their worth. And this worth cannot afford any universal principles for all rational beings or any principles valid and necessary for every vo-

lition. That is, they cannot give rise to any practical laws. All these relative purposes, therefore, are grounds for hypothetical imperatives only.

But suppose that there were something the existence of which in itself had absolute worth, something which, as an end in itself, could be a ground of definite laws. In it and only in it could lie the ground of a possible categorical imperative (i.e., of a practical law).

Now, I say, man, and in general, every rational being exists as an end in himself and not merely as a means to be arbitrarily used by this or that will. In all his actions, whether they are directed toward himself or toward other rational beings, he must always be regarded at the same time as an end. All objects of inclination have only conditional worth, for if the inclinations and needs founded on them did not exist, their object would be worthless. The inclinations themselves as the sources of needs, however, are so lacking in absolute worth that the universal wish of every rational being must be indeed to free himself completely from them. Therefore, the worth of any objects to be obtained by our actions is at times conditional. Beings whose existence does not depend on our will but on nature, if they are not rational beings, have only relative worth as means, and are therefore called "things"; rational beings, on the other hand, are designated "persons" because their nature indicates that they are ends in themselves (i.e., things which may not be used merely as means). Such a being is thus an object of respect, and as such restricts all [arbitrary] choice. Such beings are not merely subjective ends whose existence as a result of our action has a worth for us, but are objective ends (i.e., beings whose existence is an end in itself). Such an end is one in the place of which no other end, to which these beings should serve merely as means, can be put. Without them, nothing of absolute worth could be found, and if all worth is conditional and thus contingent, no supreme practical principle for reason could be found anywhere.

Thus if there is to be a supreme practical principle and a categorical imperative for the human will, it must be one that forms an objective principle of the will from the conception of that which is necessarily an end for everyone because it is an end in itself. Hence this objective principle can serve as a universal law. The ground of this principle is: rational nature exists as an end in itself. Man necessarily thinks of his own existence in this way, and thus far it is a subjective principle of human actions. Also every other rational being thinks of his existence on the same rational ground which holds also for myself;[2] thus it is at the same time an objective principle from which, as a supreme practical ground, it must be possible to derive all laws of the will. The practical imperative, therefore, is the following: Act so that you treat humanity, whether in your own person or in that of another, always as an end and never as a means only.

This principle of humanity, and in general of every rational creature an end in itself, is the supreme limiting condition on the freedom of action of each man. It is not borrowed from experience, first, because of its universality, since it applies to all rational beings generally, and experience does not suffice to determine anything about them; and secondly, because in experience humanity is not thought of (subjectively) as the purpose of men (i.e., as an object which we of ourselves really make our purpose). Rather it is thought of as the objective end which ought to constitute the supreme limiting condition of all subjective ends whatever they may be. Thus this principle must arise from pure reason. Objectively the ground of all practical legislation lies (according to the first principle) in the rule and form of universality, which makes it capable of being a law (at least a natural law); subjectively it lies in the end. But the subject of all ends is every rational being as an end in itself (by the second principle); from this there follows the third practical principle of the will as the supreme condition of its harmony with universal practical reason, viz, the Idea of the will of every rational being as making universal law.

By this principle all maxims are rejected which are not consistent with the will's giving universal law. The will is not only subject to the law, but subject in such a way that it must be conceived also as itself prescribing the law, of which reason can hold itself to be the author; it is on this ground alone that the will is regarded as subject to the law.

If now we look back upon all previous attempts which have ever been undertaken to discover the principle of morality, it is not to be wondered at that they all had to fail. Man was seen to be bound to laws by his duty, but it was not seen that he is subject to his own, but still universal, legislation, and that he is bound to act only in accordance with his own will, which is, however, designed by nature to be a will giving universal law. For if one thought of him as only subject to a law (whatever it may be), this necessarily implied some interest as a stimulus or compulsion to obedience because the law did not arise from his will. Rather, his will had to be constrained by something else to act in a certain way. By this strictly necessary consequence, however, all the labor of finding a supreme ground for duty was irrevocably lost, and one never arrived at duty but only at the necessity of acting from a certain interest. This might be his own interest or that of another, but in either case the imperative always had to be conditional, and could not at all serve as a moral command. The moral principle I will call the principle of *autonomy* of the will in contrast to all other principles which I accordingly count under *heteronomy*.

The concept of any rational being as a being that must regard itself as giving universal law through all the maxims of its will, so that it may judge itself and its actions from this standpoint, leads to a very fruitful concept, namely that of a *realm of ends*.

By *realm* I understand the systematic union of different rational beings though common laws. Because laws determine which ends have universal validity, if we abstract from personal differences of rational beings, and thus from all content of their private purposes, we can think of a whole of all ends in systematic connection, a whole of rational beings as ends in themselves as well as a whole of particular purposes which each may set for himself. This is a realm of ends, which is possible on the principles stated above. For all rational beings stand under the law that each of them should treat himself and all others never merely as means, but in every case at the same time as an end in himself. Thus there arises a systematic union of rational beings through common objective laws. This is a realm which may be called a realm of ends (certainly only an ideal) because what these laws have in view is just the relation of these beings to each other as ends and means.

A rational being belongs to the realm of ends as a member when he gives universal laws in it while also himself subject to these laws. He belongs to it as sovereign when, as legislating, he is subject to the will of no other. The rational being must regard himself always as legislative in a realm of ends possible through the freedom of the will whether he belongs to it as member or as sovereign. He cannot maintain his position as sovereign merely through the maxims of his will, but only when he is a completely independent being without need and with unlimited power adequate to his will.

---

[2]Here I present this proposition as a postulate, but in the last Section grounds for it will be found.

Morality, therefore, consists in the relation of every action to the legislation through which alone a realm of ends is possible. This legislation must be found in every rational being. It must be able to arise from his will, whose principle then is to do no action according to any maxim which would be inconsistent with its being a universal law, and thus to act only so that the will through its maxims could regard itself at the same time as giving universal law. If the maxims do not by their nature already necessarily conform to this objective principle of rational beings as giving universal law, the necessity of acting according to that principle is called practical constraint, which is to say: duty. Duty pertains not to the sovereign of the realm of ends, but rather to each member and to each in the same degree.

The practical necessity of acting according to this principle (duty) does not rest at all on feelings, impulses, and inclinations; it rests solely on the relation of rational beings to one another, in which the will of a rational being must always be regarded as legislative, for otherwise it could not be thought of as an end in itself. Reason, therefore, relates every maxim of the will as giving universal laws to every other will and also to every action towards itself; it does not do so for the sake of any other practical motive or future advantage but rather from the Idea of the dignity of a rational being who obeys no law except one which he himself also gives.

In the realm of ends everything has either a *price* or a *dignity*. Whatever has a price can be replaced by something else as its equivalent; on the other hand, whatever is above all price and therefore admits of no equivalent, has dignity.

That which is related to general human inclinations and needs has a *market price*. That which, without presupposing any need, accords with a certain taste (i.e., with pleasure in the purposeless play of our faculties) has a *fancy price*. But that which constitutes the condition under which alone something can be an end in itself does not have mere relative worth (price) but an intrinsic worth (*dignity*).

Morality is the condition under which alone a rational being can be an end in himself, because only through it is it possible to be a lawgiving member in the realm of ends. Thus morality, and humanity so far as it is capable of morality, alone have dignity. Skill and diligence in work have a market value; wit, lively imagination, and humor have a fancy price; but fidelity in promises and benevolence on principle (not benevolence from instinct) have intrinsic worth. Nature and likewise art contain nothing which could make up for their lack, for their worth consists not in the effects which flow from them nor in any advantage and utility which they procure; it consists only in mental dispositions, maxims of the will, which are ready to reveal themselves in this manner through actions even though success does not favor them. These actions need no recommendation from my subjective disposition or taste in order that they may be looked upon with immediate favor and satisfaction, nor do they have need of any direct propensity or feeling directed to them. They exhibit the will which performs them as the object of an immediate respect, since nothing but reason is required in order to impose them upon the will. The will is not to be cajoled into them, for this, in the case of duties, would be a contradiction. This esteem lets the worth of such a turn of mind be recognized as dignity and puts it infinitely beyond any price; with things of price it cannot in the least be brought into any competition or comparison without, as it were, violating its holiness.

And what is it that justifies the morally good disposition or virtue in making such lofty claims? It is nothing less that the participation it affords the rational being in giving universal laws. He is thus fitted to be a member in a possible realm of ends, to which his own nature already destined him. For, as an end in himself, he is destined to be a lawgiver in the realm of ends, free from all laws of nature and obedient only to those laws which he himself gives. Accordingly, his maxims can belong to a universal legislation to which he is at the same time subject. A thing has no worth other than that determined for it by the law. The lawgiving which determines all worth must therefore have a dignity (i.e., an unconditional and incomparable worth). For the esteem which a rational being must have for it, only the word "respect"[3] is suitable. Autonomy is thus the basis of the dignity of both human nature and every rational nature.

The three aforementioned ways of presenting the principle of morality are fundamentally only so many formulas of the very same law, and each of them unites the others in itself. There is, nevertheless, a difference between them, but the difference is more subjectively than objectively practical, for the difference is intended to bring an Idea of reason

---

[3]H. J. Paton, in his translation of this text, prefers to translate the German word *Achtung* as *reverence*. There are religious overtones of awe before the sublimity of the the moral law which speak in favor of Paton's choice.

closer to intuition (by means of a certain analogy) and thus nearer to feeling. All maxims have:

1. A form which consists in universality, and in this respect the formula of the moral imperative requires that maxims be chosen as though they should hold as universal laws of nature.
2. A material (i.e., an end), and in this respect the formula says that the rational being, as by its nature an end and thus as an end in itself, must serve in every maxim as the condition restricting all merely relative and arbitrary ends.
3. A complete determination of all maxims by the formula that all maxims which stem from autonomous legislation ought to harmonize with a possible realm of ends as with a realm of nature.

Immanuel Kant, On Practical Reason

1.   According to Kant, we can never be sure if we are acting purely from duty.

      a. True   b. False

2.   Why does Kant believe that morality cannot be derived from experience and the examples
      it provides, but must come from our reason?

3.   What is the difference between a hypothetical and a categorical imperative?

4.   A maxim is

      a. a recipe.
      b. a rule of conduct.
      c. a restaurant.
      d. the greatest amount of something.
      e. none of the above.

5.   Autonomy is the condition of being

      a. self-taught.
      b. self-centered.
      c. self-motivated.
      d. self-legislating.
      e. selfish

John Stuart Mill*

WHAT UTILITARIANISM IS

A passing remark is all that needs be given to the ignorant blunder of supposing that those who stand up for utility as the test of right and wrong use the term in that restricted and merely colloquial sense in which utility is opposed to pleasure. An apology is due to the philosophical opponents of utilitarianism for even the momentary appearance of confounding them with anyone capable of so absurd a misconception; which is the more extraordinary, inasmuch as the contrary accusation, of referring everything to pleasure, and that, too, in its grossest form, is another of the common charges against utilitarianism: and, as has been pointedly remarked by an able writer, the same sort of persons, and often the very same persons, denounce the theory "as impracticably dry when the word 'utility' precedes the word 'pleasure,' and as too practically voluptuous when the word 'pleasure' precedes the word 'utility.' " Those who know anything about the matter are aware that every writer, from Epicurus to Bentham, who maintained the theory of utility meant by it, not something to be contradistinguished from pleasure, but pleasure itself, together with exemption from pain; and instead of opposing the useful to the agreeable or the ornamental, have always declared that the useful means these, among other things. Yet the common herd, including the herd of writers, not only in newspapers and periodicals, but in books of weight and pretension, are perpetually falling into this shallow mistake. Having caught up the word "utilitarian," while knowing nothing whatever about it but its sound, they habitually express by it the rejection or the neglect of pleasure in some of its forms: of beauty, of ornament, or of amusement. Nor is the term thus ignorantly misapplied solely in disparagement, but occasionally in compliment, as though it implied superiority to frivolity and the mere pleasures of the moment And this perverted use is the only one in which the word is popularly known, and the one from which the new generation are acquiring their sole notion of its meaning. Those who introduced the word, but who had for many years discontinued it as a distinctive appellation, may well feel themselves called upon to resume it if by doing so they can hope to contribute anything toward rescuing it from this utter degradation.[1]

The creed which accepts as the foundation of morals "utility" or the "greatest happiness principle" holds that actions are right in proportion as they tend to promote happiness; wrong as they tend to produce the reverse of happiness. By happiness is

---

*John Stuart Mill (1806–1873) was an English philosopher, economist, and one-term member of Parliament who was educated by his father, James Mill, to be a social reformer and the leader of the philosophical movement known as Utilitarianism. Mill was a liberal who sought to reform the institutions of British society in order to make them promote the general happiness. His many writings include *Logic, The Principles of Political Economy,* and *On Liberty.* The following selection is taken from his book *Utilitarianism* (1863).

[1]The author of this essay has reason for believing himself to the first person who brought the word "utilitarian" into use. He did not invent it, but adopted it from a passing expression in Mr. Galt's *Annals of the Parish.* After using it as a designation for several years, he and others abandoned it from a growing dislike to anything resembling a badge or watchword of sectarian distinction. But as a name for one single opinion, not a set of opinions—to denote the recognition of utility as a standard, not any particular way of applying it—the term supplies a want in the language, and offers, in many cases, a convenient mode of avoiding tiresome circumlocution.

intended pleasure and the absence of pain; by unhappiness, pain and the privation of pleasure. To give a clear view of the moral standard set up by the theory, much more requires to be said; in particular, what things it includes in the ideas of pain and pleasure, and to what extent this is left an open question. But these supplementary explanations do not affect the theory of life on which this theory of morality is grounded—namely, that pleasure and freedom from pain are the only things desirable as ends; and that all desirable things (which are as numerous in the utilitarian as in any other scheme) are desirable either for pleasure inherent in themselves or as means to the promotion of pleasure and the prevention of pain.

Now such a theory of life excites in many minds, and among them in some of the most estimable in feeling and purpose, inveterate dislike. To suppose that life has (as they express it) no higher end than pleasure—no better and nobler object of desire and pursuit—they designate as utterly mean and groveling & as a doctrine worthy only of swine, to whom the followers of Epicurus were, at a very early period, contemptuously likened; and modern holders of the doctrine are occasionally made the subject of equally polite comparisons by its German, French, and English assailants.

When thus attacked, the Epicureans have always answered that it is not they, but their accusers, who represent human nature in a degrading light, since the accusation supposes human beings to be capable of no pleasures except those of which swine are capable. If this supposition were true, the charge could not be gainsaid, but would then be no longer an imputation; for if the sources of pleasure were precisely the same to human beings and to swine, the rule of life which is good enough for the one would be good enough for the other. The comparison of the Epicurean life to that of beasts is felt as degrading, precisely because a beast's pleasures do not satisfy a human beings' conceptions of happiness. Human beings have faculties more elevated than the animal appetites and, when once made conscious of them, do not regard anything as happiness which does not include their gratification. I do not, indeed, consider the Epicureans to have been by any means faultless in drawing out their scheme of consequences from the utilitarian principle. To do this in any sufficient manner, many Stoic, as well as Christian, elements require to be included. But there is no known Epicurean theory of life which does not assign to the pleasures of the intellect, of the feelings and imagination, and of the moral sentiments a much higher value as pleasures than to those of mere sensation. It must be admitted, however, that utilitarian writers in general have placed the superiority of mental over bodily pleasures chiefly in the greater permanency, safety, uncostliness, etc., of the former—that is, in their circumstantial advantages rather than in their intrinsic nature. And on all these points utilitarians have fully proved their case; but they might have taken the other and, as it may be called, higher ground with entire consistency. It is quite compatible with the principle of utility to recognize the fact that some kinds of pleasure are more desirable and more valuable than others. It would be absurd that, while in estimating all other things quality is considered as well as quantity, the estimation of pleasure should be supposed to depend on quantity alone.

If I am asked what I mean by difference of quality in pleasures, or what makes one pleasure more valuable than another, merely as a pleasure, except its being greater in amount, there is but one possible answer. Of two pleasures, if there be one to which all or almost all who have experience of both give a decided preference, irrespective of any feeling of moral obligation to prefer it, that is the more desirable pleasure. If one of the two is, by those who are competently acquainted with both, placed so far above the other that they prefer it, even though knowing it to be attended with a greater amount of discontent, and would not resign it for any quantity of the other pleasure which their nature is capable of, we are justified in ascribing to the preferred enjoyment a superiority in quality so far outweighing quantity as to render it, in comparison, of small account.

Now it is an unquestionable fact that those who are equally acquainted with and equally capable of appreciating and enjoying both do give a most marked preference to the manner of existence which employs their higher faculties. Few human creatures would consent to be changed into any of the lower animals for a promise of the fullest allowance of a beast's pleasures; no intelligent human being would consent to be a fool, no instructed person would be an ignoramus, no person of feeling and conscience would be selfish and base, even though they should be persuaded that the fool, the dunce, or the rascal is better satisfied with his lot than they are with theirs. They would not resign what they possess more than he for the most complete satisfaction of all these desires which they have in common with him. If they ever fancy they would, it is only in cases of unhappiness so extreme that to escape from it they would exchange their lot for almost any other, however undesirable in their own eyes. A being of higher faculties requires more to make him happy, is capable probably of more acute suffering and certainly accessible to it at more points, than one of an inferior type; but in spite of these liabilities, he can never really wish to sink into what he feels to be a lower grade of existence. We may give what explanation we please of this unwillingness; we may attribute it to pride, a name which is given indiscriminately to some of the most and to some of the least estimable feelings of which mankind are capable; we may refer it to the love of liberty and personal independence, an appeal to which was with the Stoics one of the most effective means for the inculcation of it; to the love of power or to the love of excitement, both of which do really enter into and contribute to it; but its most appropriate appellation is a sense of dignity, which all human beings possess in one form or other, and in some, though by no means in exact, proportion to their higher faculties, and which is so essential a part of the happiness of those in whom it is strong that nothing which conflicts with it could be otherwise than momentarily an object of desire to them. Whoever supposes that this preference takes place at a sacrifice of happiness—that the superior being, in anything like equal circumstances, is not happier than the inferior—confounds the two very different ideas of happiness and content. It is indisputable that the being whose capacities of enjoyment are low has the greatest chance of having them fully satisfied; and a highly endowed being will always feel that any happiness which he can look for, as the world is constituted, is imperfect. But he can learn to bear its imperfections, if they are at all bearable; and they will not make him envy the being who is indeed unconscious of the imperfections, but only because he feels not at all the good which those imperfections qualify. It is better to be a human being dissatisfied than a pig satisfied; better to be Socrates dissatisfied than a fool satisfied. And if the fool, or the pig, are of a different opinion, it is because they only know their own side of the question. The other party to the comparison knows both sides.

It may be objected that many who are capable of the higher pleasures occasionally, under the influence of temptation, postpone them to the lower. But this is quite compatible with a full appreciation of the intrinsic superiority of the higher. Men often, from infirmity of character, make their election for the nearer good, though they know it to be the less valuable; and this no less when the choice is between two bodily pleasures than when it is between bodily and mental. They pursue sensual indulgences

to the injury of health, though perfectly aware that health is the greater good. It may be further objected that many who begin with youthful enthusiasm for everything noble, as they advance in years, sink into indolence and selfishness. But I do not believe that those who undergo this very common change voluntarily choose the lower description of pleasures in preference to the higher. I believe that, before they devote themselves exclusively to the one, they have already become incapable of the other. Capacity for the nobler feelings is in most natures a very tender plant, easily killed, not only by hostile influences, but by mere want of sustenance; and in the majority of young persons it speedily dies away if the occupations to which their position in life has devoted them, and the society into which it has thrown them, are not favorable to keeping that higher capacity in exercise. Men lose their light aspirations as they lose their intellectual tastes, because they have not time or opportunity for indulging them; and they addict themselves to inferior pleasures, not because they deliberately prefer them, but because they are either the only ones to which they have access or the only ones which they are any longer capable of enjoying. It may be questioned whether anyone who has remained equally susceptible to both classes of pleasures ever knowingly and calmly preferred the lower, though many, in all ages, have broken down in an ineffectual attempt to combine both.

From this verdict of the only competent judges, I apprehend there can be no appeal. On a question which is the best worth having of two pleasures, or which of two modes of existence is the most grateful to the feelings, apart from its moral attributes and from its consequences, the judgment of those who are qualified by knowledge of both, or, if they differ, that of the majority among them, must be admitted as final. And there needs to be the less hesitation to accept this judgment respecting the quality of pleasures, since there is no other tribunal to be referred to even on the question of quantity. What means are there of determining which is the acutest of two pains, or the intensest of two pleasurable sensations, except the general suffrage of those who are familiar with both? Neither pains nor pleasures are homogeneous, and pain is always heterogeneous with pleasure. What is there to decide whether a particular pleasure is worth purchasing at the cost of a particular pain, except the feelings and judgment of the experienced? When, therefore, those feelings and judgment declare the pleasures derived from the higher faculties to be preferable *in kind,* apart from the question of intensity, to those of which the animal nature, disjoined from the higher faculties, is susceptible, they are entitled on this subject to the same regard.

I have dwelt on this point as being a necessary part of a perfectly just conception of utility or happiness considered as the directive rule of human conduct. But it is by no means an indispensable condition to the acceptance of the utilitarian standard; for that standard is not the agent's own greatest happiness, but the greatest amount of happiness altogether; and if it may possibly be doubted whether a noble character is always the happier for its nobleness, there can be no doubt that it makes other people happier, and that the world in general is immensely a gainer by it. Utilitarianism, therefore, could only attain its end by the general cultivation of nobleness of character, even if each individual were only benefited by the nobleness of others, and his own, so far as happiness is concerned, were a sheer deduction from the benefit. But the bare enunciation of such an absurdity as this last renders refutation superfluous.

According to the greatest happiness principle, as above explained, the ultimate end, with reference to and for the sake of which all other things are desirable—whether we are considering our own good or that of other people—is an existence exempt as far as possible from pain, and as rich as possible in enjoyments, both in point of quantity and quality; the test of quality and the rule for measuring it against quantity being the preference felt by those who, in their opportunities of experience, to which must be added their habits of self-consciousness and self-observation, are best furnished with the means of comparison. This, being according to the utilitarian opinion the end of human action, is necessarily also the standard of morality, which may accordingly be defined "the rules and precepts for human conduct," by the observance of which an existence such as has been described might be, to the greatest extent possible, secured to all mankind; and not to them only, but, so far as the nature of things admits, to the whole sentient creation.

Against this doctrine, however, arises another class of objectors who say that happiness, in any form, cannot be the rational purpose of human life and action; because, in the first place, it is unattainable; and they contemptuously ask, What right hast thou to be happy?—a question which Mr. Carlyle clinches by the addition, What right, a short time ago, hadst thou even *to be?* Next they say that men can do *without* happiness; that all noble human beings have felt this, and could not have become noble but by learning the lesson of *Entsagen,* or renunciation; which lesson, thoroughly learned and submitted to, they affirm to be the beginning and necessary condition of all virtue.

The first of these objections would go to the root of the matter were it well founded; for if no happiness is to be had at all by human beings, the attainment of it cannot be the end of morality or of any rational conduct. Though, even in that case, something might still be said for the utilitarian theory, since utility includes not solely the pursuit of happiness, but the prevention or mitigation of unhappiness; and if the former aim be chimerical, there will be all the greater scope and more imperative need for the latter so long at least as mankind think fit to live and do not take refuge in the simultaneous act of suicide recommended under certain conditions by Novalis.[2] When, however, it is thus positively asserted to be impossible that human life should be happy, the assertion, if not something like a verbal quibble, is at least an exaggeration. If by happiness be meant a continuity of highly pleasurable excitement, it is evident enough that this is impossible. A state of exalted pleasure lasts only moments or in some cases, and with some intermissions, hours or days, and is the occasional brilliant flash of enjoyment, not its permanent and steady flame. Of this the philosophers who have taught that happiness is the end of life were as fully aware as those who taunt them. The happiness which they meant was not a life of rapture, but moments of such, in an existence made up of few and transitory pains, many and various pleasures, with a decided predominance of the active over the passive, and having as the foundation of the whole not to expect more from life than it is capable of bestowing. A life thus composed, to those who have been fortunate enough to obtain it, has always appeared worthy of the name of happiness. And such an existence is even now the lot of many during some considerable portion of their lives. The present wretched education and wretched social arrangements are the only real hindrance to its being attainable by almost all.

The objectors perhaps may doubt whether human beings, if taught to consider happiness as the end of life, would be satisfied with such a moderate

---

[2][Pseudonym of Friedrich Leopold Freiherr von Hardenberg (1772–1801). German poet and leader of early German Romanticism.]

share of it. But great numbers of mankind have been satisfied with much less. The main constituents of a satisfied life appear to be two, either of which by itself is often found sufficient for the purpose: tranquility and excitement. With much tranquility, many find that they can be content with very little pleasure; with much excitement, many can reconcile themselves to a considerable quantity of pain. There is assuredly no inherent impossibility of enabling even the mass of mankind to unite both, since the two are so far from being incompatible that they are in natural alliance, the prolongation of either being a preparation for, and exciting a wish for, the other. It is only those in whom indolence amounts to a vice that do not desire excitement after an interval of repose; it is only those in whom the need of excitement is a disease that feel the tranquility which follows excitement dull and insipid, instead of pleasurable in direct proportion to the excitement which preceded it. When people who are tolerably fortunate in their outward lot do not find in life sufficient enjoyment to make it valuable to them, the cause generally is caring for nobody but themselves. To those who have neither public nor private affections, the excitements of life are much curtailed, and in any case dwindle in value as the time approaches when all selfish interests must be terminated by death; while those who leave after them objects of personal affection, and especially those who have also cultivated a fellow-feeling with the collective interests of mankind, retain as lively an interest in life on the eve of death as in the vigor of youth and health. Next to selfishness, the principal cause which makes life unsatisfactory is want of mental cultivation. A cultivated mind—I do not mean that of a philosopher, but any mind to which the fountains of knowledge have been opened, and which has been taught, in any tolerable degree, to exercise its faculties—finds sources of inexhaustible interest in all that surrounds it: in the objects of nature, the achievements of art, the imaginations of poetry, the incidents of history, the ways of mankind, past and present, and their prospects in the future. It is possible, indeed, to become indifferent to all this, and that too without having exhausted a thousandth part of it, but only when one has had from the beginning no moral or human interest in these things and has sought in them only the gratification of curiosity.

Now there is absolutely no reason in the nature of things why an amount of mental culture sufficient to give an intelligent interest in these objects of contemplation should not be the inheritance of everyone born in a civilized country. As little is there an inherent necessity that any human being should be a selfish egotist, devoid of every feeling or care but those which center in his own miserable individuality. Something far superior to this is sufficiently common even now, to give ample earnest of what the human species may be made. Genuine private affections and a sincere interest in the public good are possible, though in unequal degrees, to every rightly brought up human being In a world in which there is so much to interest, so much to enjoy, and so much also to correct and improve, everyone who has this moderate amount of moral and intellectual requisites is capable of an existence which may be called enviable; and unless such a person, through bad laws or subjection to the will of others, is denied the liberty to use the sources of happiness within his reach, he will not fail to find this enviable existence, if he escape the positive evils of life, the great sources of physical and mental suffering—such as indigence, disease, and the unkindness, worthlessness, or premature loss of objects of affection. The main stress of the problem lies, therefore, in the contest with these calamities from which it is a rare good fortune entirely to escape; which, as things now are, cannot be obviated, and often cannot be in any material degree mitigated. Yet no one whose opinion deserves a moment's consideration can doubt that most of the great positive evils of the world are in themselves removable, and will, if human affairs continue to improve, be in the end reduced within narrow limits. Poverty, in any sense implying suffering, may be completely extinguished by the wisdom of society combined with the good sense and providence of individuals. Even that most intractable of enemies, disease, may be indefinitely reduced in dimensions by good physical and moral education and proper control of noxious influences, while the progress of science holds out a promise for the future of still more direct conquests over this detestable foe. And every advance in that direction relieves us from some, not only of the chances which cut short our own lives, but, what concerns us still more, which deprive us of those in whom our happiness is wrapt up. As for vicissitudes of fortune and other disappointments connected with worldly circumstances, these are principally the effect either of gross imprudence, of ill-regulated desires, or of bad or imperfect social institutions. All the grand sources, in short, of human suffering are in a great degree, many of them almost entirely, conquerable by human care and effort; and though their removal is grievously slow—though a long succession of generations will perish in the breach before the conquest is completed, and this world becomes all that, if will and knowledge were not wanting, it might easily be made—yet every mind sufficiently intelligent and generous to bear a part, however small and inconspicuous, in the endeavor will draw a noble enjoyment from the contest itself, which he would not for any bribe in the form of selfish indulgence consent to be without.

And this leads to the true estimation of what is said by the objectors concerning the possibility and the obligation of learning to do without happiness. Unquestionably it is possible to do without happiness; it is done involuntarily by nineteen-twentieths of mankind, even in those parts of our present world which are least deep in barbarism; and it often has to be done voluntarily by the hero or the martyr, for the sake of something which he prizes more than his individual happiness. But this something, what is it, unless the happiness of others or some of the requisites of happiness? It is noble to be capable of resigning entirely one's own portion of happiness, or chances of it; but, after all, this self-sacrifice must be for some end; it is not its own end; and if we are told that its end is not happiness but virtue, which is better than happiness, I ask, would the sacrifice be made if the hero or martyr did not believe that it would earn for others immunity from similar sacrifices? Would it be made if he thought that his renunciation of happiness for himself would produce no fruit for any of his fellow creatures, but to make their lot like his and place them also in the condition of persons who have renounced happiness? All honor to those who can abnegate for themselves the personal enjoyment of life when by such renunciation they contribute worthily to increase the amount of happiness in the world; but he who does it or professes to do it for any other purpose is no more deserving of admiration than the ascetic mounted on his pillar. He may be an inspiriting proof of what men *can* do, but assuredly not an example of what they *should.*

Though it is only in a very imperfect state of the world's arrangements that anyone can best serve the happiness of others by the absolute sacrifice of his own, yet, so long as the world is in that imperfect state, I fully acknowledge that the readiness to make such a sacrifice is the highest virtue which can be found in man. I will add that in this condition of the world, paradoxical as the assertion may be, the conscious ability to do without happiness gives the best prospect of realizing such happiness as is attainable. For nothing except that consciousness can raise a person above the chances of life by making him feel that, let fate and fortune do their worst,

they have not power to subdue him; which, once felt, frees him from excess of anxiety concerning the evils of life and enables him, like many a Stoic in the worst times of the Roman Empire, to cultivate in tranquility the sources of satisfaction accessible to him, without concerning himself about the uncertainty of their duration any more than about their inevitable end.

Meanwhile, let utilitarians never cease to claim the morality of self-devotion as a possession which belongs by as good a right to them as either to the Stoic or to the Transcendentalist. The utilitarian morality does recognize in human beings the power of sacrificing their own greatest good for the good of others. It only refuses to admit that the sacrifice is itself a good. A sacrifice which does not increase or tend to increase the sum total of happiness, it considers as wasted. The only self-renunciation which it applauds is devotion to the happiness, or to some of the means of happiness, of others, either of mankind collectively or of individuals within the limits imposed by the collective interests of mankind.

I must again repeat what the assailants of utilitarianism seldom have the justice to acknowledge, that the happiness which forms the utilitarian standard of what is right in conduct is not the agent's own happiness but that of all concerned. As between his own happiness and that of others, utilitarianism requires him to be as strictly impartial as a disinterested and benevolent spectator. In the golden rule of Jesus of Nazareth, we read the complete spirit of the ethics of utility. "To do as you would be done by," and "to love your neighbor as yourself," constitute the ideal perfection of utilitarian morality. As the means of making the nearest approach to this ideal, utility would enjoin, first, that laws and social arrangements should place the happiness or (as, speaking practically, it may be called) the interest of every individual as nearly as possible in harmony with the interest of the whole; and, secondly, that education and opinion, which have so vast a power over human character, should so use that power as to establish in the mind of every individual an indissoluble association between his own happiness and the good of the whole, especially between his own happiness and the practice of such modes of conduct, negative and positive, as regard for the universal happiness prescribes; so that not only he may be unable to conceive the possibility of happiness to himself, consistently with conduct opposed to the general good, but also that a direct impulse to promote the general good may be in every individual one of the habitual motives of action, and the sentiments connected therewith may fill a large and prominent place in every human being's sentient existence. If the impugners of the utilitarian morality represented it to their own minds in this its true character, I know not what recommendation possessed by any other morality they could possibly affirm to be wanting to it; what more beautiful or more exalted developments of human nature any other ethical system can be supposed to foster, or what springs of action, not accessible to the utilitarian, such systems rely on for giving effect to their mandates.

The objectors to utilitarianism cannot always be charged with representing it in a discreditable light. On the contrary, those among them who entertain anything like a just idea of its disinterested character sometimes find fault with its standard as being too high for humanity. They say it is exacting too much to require that people shall always act from the inducement of promoting the general interests of society. But this is to mistake the very meaning of a standard of morals and confound the rule of action with the motive of it. It is the business of ethics to tell us what are our duties, or by what test we may know them; but no system of ethics requires that the sole motive of all we do shall be a feeling of duty; on the contrary, ninety-nine hundredths of all our actions are done from other motives, and rightly so done if the rule of duty does not condemn them. It is the more unjust to utilitarianism that this particular misapprehension should be made a ground of objection to it, inasmuch as utilitarian moralists have gone beyond almost all others in affirming that the motive has nothing to do with the morality of the action, though much with the worth of the agent. He who saves a fellow creature from drowning does what is morally right, whether his motive be duty or the hope of being paid for his trouble; he who betrays the friend that trusts him is guilty of a crime, even if his object be to serve another friend to whom he is under greater obligations.[3] But to speak only of actions done for the motive of duty, and in direct obedience to principle: it is a misapprehension of the utilitarian mode of thought to conceive it as implying that people should fix their minds upon so wide a generality as the world, or society at large. The great majority of good actions are intended not for the benefit of the world, but for that of individuals, of which the good of the world is made up; and the thoughts of the most virtuous man need not on these occasions travel beyond the particular persons concerned, except so far as is necessary to assure himself that in benefiting them he is not violating the rights, that is, the legitimate and authorized expectations, of anyone else. The multiplication of happiness is, according to the utilitarian ethics, the object of virtue: the occasions on which any person (except one in a thousand) has it in his power to do this on an extended scale—in other words, to be a public benefactor—are but exceptional; and on these occasions alone is he called on to consider public utility; in every other case, private utility, the interest or happiness of some few persons, is all he has to attend to. Those alone the influence of whose actions extends to society in general need concern themselves habitually about so large an object. In the case of abstinences indeed—of things which people forbear to do from moral considerations, though the consequences in the particular case might be beneficial—it would be unworthy of an

---

[3]As opponent, whose intellectual and moral fairness it is a pleasure to acknowledge (the Rev. J. Llewellyn Davies), has objected to this passage, saying, "surely the rightness of wrongness of saving a man from drowning does depend very much upon the motive with which it is done. Suppose that a tyrant, when his enemy jumped into the sea to escape from him, saved him from drowning simply in order that he might inflict upon him more exquisite tortures, would it tend to clearness to speak of the rescue as 'a morally right action'? Or suppose again, according to one of the stock illustrations of ethical inquiries, that a man betrayed a trust received from a friend, because the discharge of it would fatally injure that friend himself or someone belonging to him, would utilitarianism compel one to call the betrayal 'a crime' as much as if it had been done from the meanest motive?"

I submit that he who saves another from drowning in order to kill him by torture afterwards does not differ only in motive from him who does the same thing from duty or benevolence; the act itself is different. The rescue of the man is, in the case supposed, only the necessary first step of an act far more atrocious than leaving him to drown would have been. Had Mr. Davies said "the rightness or wrongness of saving a man from drowning does depend very much"—not upon the motive, but—"upon the *intention*," no utilitarian would have differed from him. Mr. Davies, by an oversight too common not to be quite venial, has in this case confounded the very different ideas of Motive and Intention. There is no point which utilitarian thinkers (and Bentham preeminently) have taken more pains to illustrate that this. The morality of the action depends entirely upon the intention—that is, upon what the agent *wills to do*. But the motive, that is, the feeling which makes him will so to do, if it makes no difference in the act, makes none in the morality: though it makes a great difference in our moral estimation of the agent, especially if it indicates a good or a bad habitual *disposition*—a bent of character from which useful, or from which hurtful actions are likely to arise.

[The foregoing note appeared in the second (1864) edition of *Utilitarianism* but was dropped in succeeding ones.]

intelligent agent not to be consciously aware that the action is of a class which, if practiced generally, would be generally injurious, and that this is the ground of the obligation to abstain from it. The amount of regard for the public interest implied in this recognition is no greater than is demanded by every system of morals, for they all enjoin to abstain from whatever is manifestly pernicious to society.

The same considerations dispose of another reproach against the doctrine of utility, founded on a still grosser misconception of the purpose of a standard of morality and of the very meaning of the words "right" and "wrong." It is often affirmed that utilitarianism renders men cold and unsympathizing; that it chills their moral feelings toward individuals; that it makes them regard only the dry hard consideration of the consequences of actions, not taking into their moral estimate the qualities from which those actions emanate. If the assertion means that they do not allow their judgment respecting the rightness or wrongness of an action to be influenced by their opinion of the qualities of the person who does it, this is a complaint not against utilitarianism, but against any standard of morality at all; for certainly no known ethical standard decides an action to be good or bad because it is done by a good or a bad man, still less because done by an amiable, a brave, or a benevolent man, or the contrary. These considerations are relevant, not to the estimation of actions, but of persons and there is nothing in the utilitarian theory inconsistent with the fact that there are other things which interest us in persons besides the rightness and wrongness of their actions. The Stoics, indeed, with the paradoxical misuse of language which was part of their system, and by which they strove to raise themselves above all concern about anything but virtue, were fond of saying that he who has that has everything; that he, and only he, is rich, is beautiful, is a king. But no claim of this description is made for the virtuous man by the utilitarian doctrine. Utilitarians are quite aware that there are other desirable possessions and qualities besides virtue, and are perfectly willing to allow to all of them their full worth. They are also aware that a right action does not necessarily indicate a virtuous character, and that actions which are blamable often proceed from qualities entitled to praise. When this is apparent in any particular case, it modifies their estimation, not certainly of the act, but of the agent. I grant that they are, notwithstanding, of opinion that in the long run the best proof of a good character is good actions; and resolutely refuse to consider any mental disposition as good of which the predominant

tendency is to produce bad conduct. This makes them unpopular with many people, but it is an unpopularity which they must share with everyone who regards the distinction between right and wrong in a serious light; and the reproach is not one which a conscientious utilitarian need be anxious to repel.

If no more be meant by the objection than that many utilitarians look on the morality of actions, as measured by the utilitarian standards, with too exclusive a regard, and do not lay sufficient stress upon the other beauties of character which go toward making a human being lovable or admirable, this may be admitted. Utilitarians who have cultivated their moral feelings, but not their sympathies, nor their artistic perceptions, do fall into this mistake; and so do all other moralists under the same conditions. What can be said in excuse for other moralists is equally available for them, namely, that, if there is to be any error, it is better that it should be on that side. As a matter of fact, we may affirm that among utilitarians, as among adherents of other systems, there is every imaginable degree of rigidity and of laxity in the application of their standards; some are even puritanically rigorous, while others are as indulgent as can possibly be desired by sinner or by sentimentalist. But on the whole, a doctrine which brings prominently forward the interest that mankind have in the repression and prevention of conduct which violates the moral law is likely to be inferior to no other in turning the sanctions of opinion against such violations. It is true, the question "What does violate the moral law?" is one on which those who recognize different standards of morality are likely now and then to differ. But difference of opinion on moral questions was not first introduced into the world by utilitarianism, while that doctrine does supply, if not always an easy, at all events a tangible and intelligible, mode of deciding such differences.

It may not be superfluous to notice a few more of the common misapprehensions of utilitarian ethics, even those which are so obvious and gross that it might appear impossible for any person of candor and intelligence to fall into them; since persons, even of considerable mental endowment, often give themselves so little trouble to understand the bearings of any opinion against which they entertain a prejudice, and men are in general so little conscious of this voluntary ignorance as a defect that the vulgariest misunderstandings of ethical doctrines are continually met with in the deliberate writings of persons of the greatest pretensions both to high principles and to philosophy. We not uncommonly hear the doctrine of utility inveighed against as a *godless* doctrine. If it be necessary to say anything at all against so mere an assumption, we may say that the question depends upon what idea we have formed of the moral character of the Deity. If it be a true belief that God desires, above all things, the happiness of his creatures, and that this was his purpose in their creation, utility is not only not a godless doctrine, but more profoundly religious than any other. If it be meant that utilitarianism does not recognize the revealed will of God as the supreme law of morals, I answer that a utilitarian who believes in the perfect goodness and wisdom of *God* necessarily believes that whatever God has thought fit to reveal on the subject of morals must fulfill the requirements of utility in a supreme degree. But others besides utilitarians have been of opinion that the Christian revelation was intended, and is fitted, to inform the hearts and minds of mankind with a spirit which should enable them to find for themselves what is right, and incline them to do it when found, rather than to tell them, except in a very general way, what it is; and that we need a doctrine of ethics, carefully followed out, to *interpret* to us the will of God. Whether this opinion is correct or not, it is superfluous here to discuss; since whatever aid religion, either natural or revealed, can afford to ethical investigation is as open to the utilitarian moralist as to any other. He can use it as the testimony of God to the usefulness or hurtfulness of any given course of action by as good a right as others can use it for the indication of a transcendental law having no connection with usefulness or with happiness.

Again, utility is often summarily stigmatized as an immoral doctrine by giving it the name of "expediency," and taking advantage of the popular use of that term to contrast it with principle. But that expedient, in the sense in which it is opposed to the right, generally means that which is expedient for the particular interest of the agent himself; as when a minister sacrifices the interests of his country to keep himself in place. When it means anything better than this, it means that which is expedient in a much higher degree. The expedient, in this sense, instead of being the same thing with the useful, is a branch of the hurtful. Thus it would often be expedient, for the purpose of getting over some momentary embarrassment, or attaining some object immediately useful to ourselves or others, to tell a lie. But inasmuch as the cultivation in ourselves of a sensitive feeling on the subject of veracity is one of the must useful, and the enfeeblement of that feeling one of the most hurtful, things to which our

conduct can be instrumental; and inasmuch as any, even unintentional, deviation from truth does that much toward weakening the trustworthiness of human assertion, which is not only the principal support of all present social well-being, but the insufficiency of which does more than any one thing that can be named to keep back civilization, virtue, everything on which human happiness on the largest scale depends—we feel that the violation, for a present advantage, of a rule of such transcendent expediency is not expedient, and that he who, for the sake of convenience to himself or to some other individual, does what depends on him to deprive mankind of the good, and inflict upon them the evil, involved in the greater or less reliance which they can place in each other's word, acts the part of one of their worst enemy. Yet that even this rule, sacred as it is, admits of possible exceptions is acknowledged by all moralists; the chief of which is when the withholding of some fact (as of information from a malefactor, or of bad news from a person dangerously ill) would save an individual (especially an individual other than oneself) from great and unmerited evil, and when the withholding can only be effected by denial. But in order that the exception may not extend itself beyond the need, and may have the least possible effect in weakening reliance on veracity, it ought to be recognized and, if possible, its limits defined; and, if the principle of utility is good for anything, it must be good for weighing these conflicting utilities against one another and marking out the region which one or the other preponderates.

Again, defenders of utility often find themselves called upon to reply to such objections as this—that there is not time, previous to action, for calculating and weighing the effects of any line of conduct on the general happiness. This is exactly as if anyone were to say that it is impossible to guide our conduct by Christianity because there is not time, on every occasion on which anything has to be done, to read through the Old and New Testaments. The answer to the objection is that there has been ample time, namely, the whole past duration of the human species. During all that time mankind have been learning by experience the tendencies of actions; on which experience all the prudence as well as all the morality of life are dependent. People talk as if the commencement of this course of experience had hitherto been put off, and as if, at the moment when some man feels tempted to meddle with the property or life of another, he had to begin considering for the first time whether murder and theft are injurious to human happiness. Even then I do not think that he would find the question very puzzling; but, at all events, the matter is now done to his hand. It is truly a whimsical supposition that, if mankind were agreed in considering utility to be the test of morality, they would remain without any agreement as to what *is* useful, and would take no measures for having their notions on the subject taught to the young and enforced by law and opinion. There is no difficulty in proving any ethical standard whatever to work ill if we suppose universal idiocy to be conjoined with it; but on any hypothesis short of that, mankind must by this time have acquired positive beliefs as to the effects of some actions on their happiness; and the beliefs which have thus come down are the rules of morality for the multitude, and for the philosopher until he has succeeded in finding better. That philosophers might easily do this, even now, on many subjects; that the received code of ethics is by no means of divine right; and that mankind have still much to learn as to the effects of actions on the general happiness, I admit or rather earnestly maintain. The corollaries from the principle of utility, like the precepts of every practical art, admit of indefinite improvement, and, in a progressive state of the human mind, their improvement is perpetually going on. But to consider the rules of morality as improvable is one thing; to pass over the intermediate generalization entirely and endeavor to test each individual action directly by the first principle is another. It is a strange notion that the acknowledgment of a first principle is inconsistent with the admission of secondary ones. To inform a traveler respecting the place of his ultimate destination is not to forbid the use of landmarks and direction-posts on the way. The proposition that happiness is the end and aim of morality does not mean that no road ought to be laid down to that goal, or that persons going thither should not be advised to take one direction rather than another. Men really ought to leave off talking a kind of nonsense on this subject, which they would neither talk nor listen to on other matters of practical concernment. Nobody argues that the art of navigation is not founded on astronomy because sailors cannot wait to calculate the Nautical Almanac. Being rational creatures, they go to sea with it ready calculated; and all rational creatures go out upon the sea of life with their minds made upon the common questions of right and wrong, as well as on many of the far more difficult questions of wise and foolish. And this, as long as foresight is a human quality, it is to be presumed they will continue to do. Whatever we adopt as the fundamental principle of morality, we require sub-ordinate principles to apply it by; the impossibility of doing without them, being common to all systems, can afford no argument against any one in particular; but gravely to argue as if no such secondary principles could be had, and as if mankind had remained till now, and always must remain, without drawing any general conclusions from the experience of human life is as high a pitch, I think, an absurdity has ever reached in philosophical controversy.

The remainder of the stock arguments against utilitarianism mostly consist in laying to its charge the common infirmities of human nature, and the general difficulties which embarrass conscientious persons in shaping their course through life. We are told that a utilitarian will be apt to make his own particular case an exception to moral rules, and, when under temptation, will see a utility in the breach of a rule, greater than he will see in its observance. But is utility the only creed which is able to furnish us with excuses for evil-doing and means of cheating our own conscience? They are afforded in abundance by all doctrines which recognize as a fact in morals the existence of conflicting considerations, which all doctrines do that have been believed by sane persons. It is not the fault of any creed, but of the complicated nature of human affairs, that rules of conduct cannot be so framed as to require no exceptions, and that hardly any kind of action can safely be laid down as either always obligatory or always condemnable. There is no ethical creed which does not temper the rigidity of its laws by giving a certain latitude, under the moral responsibility of the agent, for accommodation to peculiarities of circumstances; and under every creed, at the opening thus made, self-deception and dishonest casuisty get in. There exists no moral system under which there do not arise unequivocal cases of conflicting obligation. These are the real difficulties, the knotty points both in the theory of ethics and in the conscientious guidance of personal conduct. They are overcome practically, with greater or with less success, according to the intellect and virtue of the individual; but it can hardly be pretended that anyone will be the less qualified for dealing with them, from possessing an ultimate standard to which conflicting rights and duties can be referred. If utility is the ultimate source of moral obligations, utility may be invoked to decide between them when their demands are incompatible. Though the application of the standard may be difficult, it is better than none at all; while in other systems, the moral laws all claiming independent authority, there is no common umpire entitled to interfere between them; their claims to precedence one over another rest on little better than sophistry, and, unless determined, as they generally are, by the unacknowledged influence of consideration of utility, afford a free scope for the action of personal desires and partialities. We must remember that only in these cases of conflict between secondary principles is it requisite that first principles should be appealed to. There is no case of moral obligation in which some secondary principle is not involved; and if only one, there can seldom be any real doubt which one it is, in the mind of any person by whom the principle itself is recognized.

John Stuart Mill's "Utilitariansim"

1. According to Mill, the useful is opposed to the agreeable.

    a. True   b. False

2. According to Mill, utility is the foundation of morals.

    a. True   b. False

3. "It is better to be a human being dissatisfied than a pig satisfied; better to be _____

    _____ ."

4. Which of the following is **not** a misconception of Utilitarianism?

    a. Utilitarianism is an ethic of selfishness.
    b. Utilitarianism is an ethic of sensuality.
    c. Utilitarianism is godless system of ethics.
    d. Utilitarianism is a disinterested system of ethics.

5. Explain Mill's argument behind his belief that there is a qualitative difference between pleasures. Do you agree? Why or why not?

John Hick*

GOD HAS MANY NAMES

Let me first thank you for your invitation to deliver this twenty-seventh annual lecture commemorating Claude Goldsmid Montefiore. I always enjoy speaking in a synagogue and to a Jewish audience. And without being in any way an expert on Montefiore's work I have the impression—which some here will not doubt be able either to confirm or to correct—that much at least of what I am going to say would have met with his approval. In speaking of the plurality of ancient religious traditions he said (in the *Jewish Quarterly Review* of 1895), "Many pathways may all lead Godward, and the world is richer for that the paths are not new."

It is these many pathways, and the very fact of their plurality, that I want to think about with you this evening. For I wonder if you have ever considered how much simpler life would be, for everyone dealing in theology and the philosophy of religion, and indeed for every thoughtful religious believer, if there were only one religion. In a sense, from within the ongoing religious life of a particular tradition, we do in fact normally proceed as though there were only one religion, namely our own. But when we stand back from immediate involvement in the life of our own community and look out beyond its borders, it is inescapably evident to us that our own religion is one of several—Buddhism, Islam, Hinduism, Judaism, Christianity, and so on. We have been like a company of people marching down a long valley, singing our own songs, developing over the centuries our own stories and slogans, unaware that over the hill there is another valley, with another great company of people marching in the same direction, but with their own language and songs and stories and ideas; and over another hill yet another marching group—each ignorant of the existence of the others. But then one day they all come out onto the same plain, the plain created by modern global communications, and see each other and wonder what to make of one another. You might think that the different groups would then simply greet one another as fellow companies of pilgrims. But in fact that is made difficult by part of the content of our respective songs and stories. For if we are Christians, we have been singing for centuries that there is no other name given among men, whereby we may be saved, than the name of Jesus. And if we are Jews, we have been singing that we are God's only chosen people, a light to lighten the world. And if we are Muslims, we have been singing that Muhammad (peace be upon him) is the seal of the prophets, bringing God's latest and final revelation. And if we are Buddhists or Hindus, we have been singing yet other songs which imply that we have the highest truth while others have only lesser and partial truths. And having thus referred to the Eastern religions, let me say that in this lecture, in which a member of one of the Semitic or Abrahamic

---

*John Hick (1922–) is one of the foremost living philosophers of religion. Educated at Oxford, he is currently a professor at the University of Birmingham in Great Britain and the Claremont Graduate School in California. His numerous works include *An Interpretation of Religion* and *God Has Many Names,* from which the following selection is taken. Hick is a forceful advocate for a fair-minded openness to the fact of religious pluralism. He maintains that a pluralistic approach, rather than an exclusivistic one, is the most reasonable way to address the issue of religious truth today.

The twenty-seventh Claud Goldsmid Montegiore Lecture, delivered at the Liberal Jewish Synagogue, St. John's Wood, London, on October 16, 1980.

faiths is addressing members of another faith within the same group, I am going to confine myself largely to this more restricted pluralism, with only a brief indication of the way in which my thesis applies to the great religions of the East.

Now it is of course, as we all know, entirely possible to give a naturalistic account of the whole phenomenon of religion, seeing the gods as projections of human hopes and fears. It is possible to hold that man created the gods in his own image; and that this is why different gods are worshiped in different parts of the world. Feuerbach, Marx, and Freud presented alternative versions of this thesis in its relation to Western man; and anthropologists and historians of religion have developed it on a larger scale. Whether the object of a religious worship and contemplation is or is not a creation of the human imagination remains the central question for the philosophy of religion; and I have elsewhere devoted a good deal of time to the discussion of it. But if that question absorbed all one's time, one would never get on to any of the other important issues which also arise. And this evening I would in fact like to assume the religious interpretation of religion, as the human response to a transcendent divine Reality which is other than us, and to try from this point of view to make sense of the fact of religious pluralism. In doing so, I shall be recognizing an important element of truth in the projection theories, but shall be subsuming this truth within an account of our pluralistic human awareness of God.

In assuming the reality of the object of religious worship, religious meditation, religious experience, how are we to refer to that reality? I propose to use the term "the Eternal One." This deliberately draws upon two different sets of associations—on the one hand the ineffable One of the mystical traditions, whether it be the One of Plotinus or the One without a second of the Upanishads, and on the other hand the Holy One of theistic experience, whether it be the Holy One of Israel or of Indian theistic worship. And I am assuming, as is common ground to all the great religious traditions, that the divine reality, the Eternal One, is infinite and is in its fullness beyond the scope of human thought and language and experience; and yet that it impinges upon mankind and is encountered and conceptualized and expressed and responded to in the limited ways which are possible to our finite human nature.

Let us now bring these assumptions to the actual religious history of mankind. Men seem always to have had some dim sense of the divine, expressed in the religious practices of which there is evidence extending back half a million years or more. Indeed it is a reasonable way of defining man to stipulate that the evolving stream of hominid life had become man from the point—wherever this is to be located in the time sequence—at which a religious animal had emerged.

Our fragmentary knowledge of primitive religion is derived partly from archaeological evidence —of burial sites, showing evidence of religious symbolism in connection with death; and of sacred places, marked by stone piles, etc.—and also from the observation, particularly in the last decades of the nineteenth century, of then-surviving "primitive" tribes, mainly in Africa, Australasia and the South Sea Islands, and South America. Early man appears to have lived in very close small communities, each bound together in the kind of group mentality that prevailed prior to the emergence of self-conscious individuality. He was aware of himself as part of the social organism rather than as a separate and autonomous individual. And the group mentality was suffused by an awareness of the supernatural. Men lived in relation to an immense variety of tribal gods and spirits, in many cases personifying the forces of nature; or to ancestors and legendary figures exalted to a divine or quasi-divine status; or to the mysterious numinous power of mana in special places and people; and they were sometimes aware also of a High God, dwelling remotely in the skies, with an implicitly universal domain, though having little connection with the details of men's daily lives. The early forms of consciousness of the Eternal One seem to have been extremely dim and crude in comparison with that expressed in the teachings of any of the great spiritual masters, such as Isaiah or Jesus or Gautama or Muhammad or Kabir or Nanak. Primitive religion seems to have been a sense of an inscrutable environing power to be feared, or of unpredictable and often ruthless beings to be placated, an awareness which evoked a variety of religious practices to take advantage of their goodwill or to avoid their anger. And the moral demand created by this primitive awareness of the Eternal One corresponded to the prevailing level of tribal morality: a god was generally the patron of this tribe over against that, and when the tribes went to war the gods fought for their own, the stronger deity being assumed to prevail. In times of danger the gods could sometimes be propitiated with human sacrifices, so that religion had its terrible and savage aspects, giving vent to the tribe's fears and cruelties as well as celebrating its cohesion and its security. Thus in the earliest stages of religious history the Eternal One was reduced in human awareness to the dimensions of man's own image, so that the gods were, like human kings, often cruel and bloodthirsty; or to the dimensions of the tribe or nation, as the symbol of its unity and power; or again to the more cosmic dimensions of the forces of nature, such as the life-giving and yet burning radiance of the sun, or the destructive power of storm and earthquake, or the mysterious pervasive force of fertility.

Such was the long, slow twilight of what we may call natural religion, or religion without revelation, lasting from the beginnings of human history down to the spiritual dawn which occurred about three millennia ago. We may say of that early twilight period that men had, in virtue of the natural religious tendency of their nature, a dim and crude sense of the Eternal One, an awareness which took what are, from our point of view as Jews or as Christians, at best childish and at worst appallingly brutal and bloodthirsty forms, but which nevertheless constituted the womb out of which the higher religions were to be born. Here, I would say, there was more human projection than divine disclosure. However, the demands which the primitive consciousness of the divine made upon man's life were such as to preserve and promote the existence of human societies, from small drifting groups to large nation-states. Religion was above all a force of social cohesion. There was at this stage no startlingly challenging impact of the Eternal One upon the human spirit, but rather that minimum presence and pressure which was to provide a basis for positive moments of revelation when mankind was ready for them. For the innumerable gods and spirits and demons were essentially projections, made possible by the innate religious character of the human mind. And yet, all this constituted the primitive response to early man's dim sense of the Eternal One. Even the cruelties of primitive religion—the sacrifices of children to appease the gods, the putting to death of chiefs when their powers waned, the slaughter of slaves to be buried with a great king, cannibalism, fearsome austerities—all these expressed, in however degraded and immature a form, men's sense of the claim of a greater reality upon their lives.

Through centuries and millennia the conditions of human life remained essentially the same, and generation after generation lived and died within this prerevelational phase of natural religion. But in the imperceptibly slow evolution of man's life through long periods of time, the conditions gradually formed for the emergence of human individuality. What these conditions were and how they developed are still largely matters of speculation.

But in what Karl Jaspers has identified as the axial period or axial age, from approximately 800 to approximately 200 B.C., significant human individuals appeared through whose free responses to the Eternal One—though always within the existing setting of their own cultures—man's awareness of the divine was immensely enlarged and developed. In China, Confucius lived, and the writer or writers of the *Tao Te Ching;* and thus two great traditions, later to be labeled Confucianism and Taoism, began. In India, Gautama the Buddha, and Mahavira the founder of Jainism, both lived and taught; and the Upanishads were produced and, at the end of this period, the *Bhagavad-Gita.* In Persia, Zoroaster transformed the existing prerevelational religion into what has been called Zoroastrianism—a religion which has since perished as an organized tradition, except for the relatively small Parsi community in India, but which nevertheless exerted a powerful influence upon developing ancient Judaism, and also through Judaism upon Christianity. In Israel, the great Hebrew prophets lived—Jeremiah, the Isaiahs, Amos, Hosea, among others. And in Greece this period produced Phythagoras, Socrates, Plato, and Aristotle. Thus the axial age was a uniquely significant band of time in man's religious history. With certain qualifications one can say that in this period all the major religious options, constituting the different forms of human awareness of the Eternal One, were identified and established, and that nothing of comparably novel significance has happened in the religious life of mankind since. To say this is of course to see Jesus and the rise of Christianity, and again Muhammad and the rise of Islam, as major new developments within the stream of Semitic monotheism that had been formed by the Hebrew prophets. Again it is to see the growth of Mahayana Buddhism (occurring at about the same time as the growth of Christianity) as a development of early Buddhism. At the other end of the axial period there are also certain qualifications to be noted. Judaism may be said to have begun, not with the work of the great prophets, but with the exodus under Moses three or four centuries before the beginning of the axial age; or indeed with the prehistoric figure of Abraham. Nevertheless, while Abraham is the semilegendary patriarch of Judaism and the exodus is its founding event, yet surely the distinctive Jewish understanding of the Eternal One and the relationship in which this understanding was embodied were formed very largely by the great prophets of the axial period. Again, in India the Vedas were written before the axial age; but, while these are foundational scriptures, the transformation of early Vedic religion into the complex of Brahmanism, the Vedanta, and Bhakti, which has constituted what has come to be called Hinduism, occurred during the axial period. Finally, there was, prior to the axial age, a brief moment of pure monotheism in Egypt under the Pharaoh Amenhotep IV; but this was quickly extinguished and left no lasting influence. There are, then, major religious events which occurred shortly before and shortly after the particularly intense concentration of such events which has come to be identified as the axial period. The concept of the axial age is thus not that of a block of time with a sharp beginning and end, nor on the other hand is it so elastic as to be stretched to include everything of significance in mankind's religious history. It is the concept of a concentration of events which, although without precise boundaries, forms a large-scale event in its own right. It differs, however, from other comparable events spread out over a number of generations in being of much wider provenance. Although the Renaissance and the Industrial Revolution, for example, have had worldwide effects, they were relatively local developments, taking place within a single civilization. But the axial period included a series of parallel movements in all the then-existing regions of relatively advanced and stable civilization. We must suppose that it was made possible by a new stage in human development, occurring at much the same time in these different ancient cultures, in which outstanding individuals emerged and were able to be channels of new religious awareness and understanding—in traditional theological terms, of divine revelation. From their work there have flowed what we know today as the great world faiths. The greatest of the spiritual movements stemming from individual founders are the nontheistic religions of Buddhism and Confucianism and the theistic religions of Christianity and Islam. Each of these arose out of a prior tradition of immemorial antiquity—Buddhism coming out of the Hindu stream of religious life; Confucianism (and also Taoism) from the existing Chinese tradition; Christianity out of Jewish religious life and Islam, though less directly, out of the Judeo-Christian tradition. Alongside these there also flows the "primal" religious life of Africa as, arguably, another major world faith.

Let us then think of the Eternal One as pressing in upon the human spirit, seeking to be known and responded to by man, and seeking through man's free responses to create the human animal into (in our Judeo-Christian language) a child of God, or toward a perfected humanity. And let us suppose that in the first millennium B.C. human life had developed to the point at which man was able to receive and respond to a new and much fuller vision of the divine reality and of the claim of that reality upon his life. Such a breakthrough is traditionally called revelation, and the revelation was, as I have pointed out, already plural. But should we not expect there to have been *one* single revelation for all mankind, rather than several different revelations? The answer, I suggest, is no—not if we take seriously into account the actual facts of human life in history. For in that distant period, some two and a half thousand years ago, the civilizations of China, of India, and of the Near East could almost have been located on different planets, so tenuous and slow were the lines of communication between them. A divine revelation intended for all mankind but occurring in China, or in India, or in Israel would have taken many centuries to spread to the other countries. But we are supposing that the source of revelation was always seeking to communicate to mankind, and in new ways to as much of mankind as was living within the higher civilizations that had been developed. From this point of view it seems natural that the revelation should have been plural, occurring separately in the different centers of human culture.

But now let me turn to the epistemology of revelation. Thomas Aquinas stated a profound epistemological truth; which has an even wider application than he realized, when he said that "The thing known is in the knower according to the mode of the knower" (*Summa Theologica,* II/II. Q.1, art. 2). In other words, our awareness of something is the awareness that we are able to have, given our own particular nature and the particular character of our cognitive machinery. This is true of all types of knowledge—sense perception, moral awareness, and religious awareness. In relation to the physical environment, our cognitive machinery, consisting in our sense organs and neurosystem, together with the selecting and organizing function of the mind/ brain, has a twofold function: to make us aware of certain aspects of our environment and at the same time to preserve us from being aware of other aspects of it. We are aware of our physical environment, not as it is in itself, in its virtually infinite complexity, but as it appears to creatures with our particular cognitive machinery. Other forms of animal life presumably experience the same world differently, each in its own way. The point I am making here is that in ordinary sense perception "the thing known" is known "according to the mode of the knower." At this physical level, however, the "mode of the knower" is only to a very slight extent under the control of the knower. We are genetically programmed to experience as we do. For we are all compelled, ultimately on pain of death, to experience the world as it actually is in its relationship to us. Our cognitive freedom is at a minimum at this level.

At the level of moral awareness, however, we have a much greater degree of cognitive freedom, and the correlative of this freedom is responsibility. If we do not want to be conscious of a moral obligation, we are able to rethink the situation and so come to see it in a different light. This is the way in which human wickedness normally operates, namely by self-deception. We do not say to ourselves: This is clearly wrong, but I shall do it nevertheless. We say: Given all the circumstances, this is the necessary and therefore the right thing to do. And this capacity to deceive ourselves is an aspect of our moral freedom. If we were not capable of such subtle self-deception, we would perhaps be more admirable characters, but on the other hand, we would not be the morally free and responsible creatures that we are.

When we now turn to religious awareness we find a yet greater and more crucial degree of cognitive freedom and responsibility, without which we should not be personal beings, capable of a free response to the Eternal One. Let me put the point in explicitly theistic terms. We can imagine finite personal beings created in the immediate presence of God, so that in being conscious of that which is other than themselves they are automatically and unavoidably conscious of God. They are conscious of existing in the presence and under the all-seeing gaze of infinite being, infinite power, infinite wisdom and goodness and love. But how, in that situation, could they have any genuine freedom in relation to their creator? In order to have such freedom must they not exist at a certain distance from him? And so, in creating finite personal life, God has created the space-time universe as a system which functions in accordance with its own inner laws. And man has been produced within and as part of this universe. Because the universe has its own autonomy it is religiously ambiguous—capable of being experienced both religiously and nonreligiously. What we call faith is the interpretative element in the religious way of experiencing the world and our lives within it. And faith is an act of cognitive freedom and responsibility. It reflects the extent to which we are willing, and ready, to exist consciously in the presence of the infinite reality in which being and value are one. In other words, the

thing known—namely the Eternal One—is known according to the mode of the knower; and at this level the cognitive mode of the knower is largely under the knower's own control. He is able to shut out what he does not want, or is not ready, to let in. And so it is that within each of the great streams of religious experience and thought—Judaism and Christianity being two such streams—there are enormous individual variations in the degree of personal response and commitment. There are practicing and nonpracticing, real and nominal, saintly and very unsaintly Jews and Christians.

But I want now to extend the principle that the thing known is known according to the mode of the knower, in order to throw light upon the fact of religious pluralism.

And so we come back to our original question: Why should religious faith take a number of such different forms? Because, I would suggest, religious faith is not an isolated aspect of our lives but is closely bound up with human culture and human history, which are in turn bound up with basic geographical, climatic and economic circumstances. It has been pointed out, for example, that "in nomadic, pastoral, herd-keeping societies the male principle predominates; whereas among agricultural peoples, aware of the fertile earth which brings forth form itself and nourishes its progeny upon its broad bosom, it is the mother-principle which seems important. . . . Among Semitic peoples therefore, whose traditions are those of herdsmen, the sacred is thought of in male terms: God the father. Among Indian peoples whose tradition has been for many centuries, and even millennia, agricultural, it is in female terms that the sacred is understood: God the mother." (Trevor Ling, *A History of Religion, East and West*, p. 146; London: Macmillan & Co., 1968). Again, as has been pointed out by Martin Prozesky, the Canaanites, and other ancient Near Eastern cultures with a comparable mythology, worshiped a sky god (Baal) and an earth goddess (Anath), whereas the ancient Egyptians, in contrast, had a sky goddess (Nut) and an earth god (Geb). Why was Egypt different in this respect? Is it not because Egypt is in the exceptional position that the fertilizing waters, male by analogy, come from the earth, in the form of the river Nile, whereas in the other countries they come from the sky in the form of rain? Now one could, as I mentioned earlier, react to this kind of evidence by concluding that the belief in God is entirely a human projection, guided by cultural influences. But the alternative interpretation is that there is some genuine awareness of the divine, but that the concrete form which it takes is provided by cultural factors. On this view these different human awarenesses of the Eternal One represent different culturally conditioned perceptions of the same infinite divine reality.

To develop this hypothesis, we must, I think, distinguish between the Eternal One in itself, in its eternal self-existent being, beyond relationship to a creation, and the Eternal One in relation to mankind and as perceived from within our different human cultural situations. Man's awareness of the Eternal One—like all our awareness of reality—is focused by concepts. There are in fact two different basic concepts involved in the religious life of mankind. One is the concept of deity, or of the Eternal One as personal, which presides over the theistic modes of religion; and the other is the concept of the Absolute, or of the Eternal One as nonpersonal, which presides over the nontheistic or transtheistic modes of religion. We only have time to be concerned about the theistic modes here. The concept of deity, or of God, takes concrete form, and a "local habitation and a name," in the life of a particular human community and culture as a specific divine *persona* or face or image or icon of the Eternal One. Yahweh of Israel is one such divine *persona*. He exists in relationship with the people of Israel, and cannot be characterized except in that relationship. He has to be described historically as the God of Abraham, of Isaac, and of Jacob, who brought the children of Israel out of bondage in Egypt and led them into their Promised Land. You cannot abstract Yahweh from his historical relationship with this particular people. He is a part of their history and they are a part of his. He is, according to my hypothesis, the divine *persona* in relation to the Jewish people. And as such he represents a genuine, authentic, valid human perception of the Eternal One from within a particular human culture and strand of history. But he is a different divine *persona* from, say, Shiva or from Krishna, who are divine *personae* in relation respectively to the Shaivite and Vaishnavite communities of India. Thus the many gods are not separate and distinct divine beings, but rather different *personae* formed in the interaction of divine presence and human projection. The divine presence is the presence of the Eternal One to our finite human consciousness, and the human projections are the culturally conditioned images and symbols in terms of which we concretize the basic concept of deity.

Summarizing this hypothesis in philosophical terms made possible by the work of Immanuel Kant, we may distinguish between, on the one hand, the single divine noumenon, the Eternal One in itself, transcending the scope of human thought and language, and, on the other hand, the plurality of divine phenomena, the divine *personae* of the theistic religious and the concretizations of the concept of the Absolute in the nontheistic religions. Among the former are Yahweh (or Adonai), and Allah, and the God and Father of Jesus Christ, and Krishna, and Shiva, and many, many more. The principal instances of the latter—the nonpersonal awareness of the Eternal One—are the Brahman of advaitic Hinduism, the Nirvana of Theravada Buddhism, and the Sunyata of Mahayana Buddhism. And each of these forms in which the Eternal One has been perceived by human beings is integral to a complex totality which constitutes what we call a religion, with its distinctive forms of religious experience, its own myths and symbols, its theological systems, its liturgies and its art, its ethics and lifestyles, its scriptures ad traditions—these elements all interacting with and reinforcing one another. And these different totalities constitute varying human responses, within the setting of the different cultures or forms of human life, to the same infinite transcendent divine reality, which we are calling the Eternal One.

Now, finally, let us return to the exclusive claims which each of the great world faiths has developed in the course of its history. Each is accustomed to think of itself as in some important sense superior to all the others; and this thought has usually become welded into its belief system and expressed in its scriptures and liturgies. Is it possible, however, to stand outside these different traditions and to judge their respective merits, and perhaps to conclude that one is in fact superior to the others? Such a judgment might be attempted on either moral or spiritual grounds.

At this point a very important caution is to be observed. Although I have spoken of the different religions as totalities, it has to be added that they are complex, polymorphous, and ever-changing totalities. Thus, for example, Christianity, if we take its entire range throughout its long history, includes many contradictory elements: not only a strong emphasis upon the personal character of God but also a persistent strand of theological and mystical thought in which God is characterized as pure being, or being-itself, or the ground of being, or the depth of being, etc.; again, not only its world-affirming materialism but also its world-denying ascetic, contemplative, and monastic strands; not only, today, pride in modern science as supposedly its own offspring but also earlier vigorous attempts to strangle modern science at birth; not only teaching of unsurpassed power about love of neighbor, and even of enemy, and about forgiveness and peace, but also a long history of persecution and conflict, violence and bloodshed, so that there has been no war involving a Christian nation which has not been supported and blessed by the churches. And each of the other great world religions appears as equally internally complex and multiform and even self-contradictory when we see it spread out along the axis of history. Each has had its periods of spiritual flourishing, its great moments of renewal and reform, its times of cultural creativity and flowering, but also its dark ages, its chauvinistic and regressive moods, and most have had their fits of blind hatred and savage violence. Again, each has produced comparable saints and prophets and thinkers, but also comparable scoundrels and hypocrites and despots and oppressors. Thus the religious totalities are each so complex and various that it is very hard, if not impossible, to make global moral judgments about them. Given a presupposed set of moral criteria, one can point to elements in Christian, or Muslim, or Jewish, or Buddhist history and culture which are admirable and to other elements which are reprehensible. But to weigh all these up together in a common scale and reach an overall moral appraisal is probably impossible. Further, there is the problem that the presupposed set of moral criteria with which one operates will be those of one's own tradition, so that there enters in the whole question, of which we are increasingly conscious today, of the relativity of moral ideas to different cultural and historical circumstances. I really think therefore, that the project of a comparative ethical assessment of the great religious totalities leads into an impossible morass from which nothing useful can emerge.

But if comparative moral judgments about such vast and complex slices of the human story are impossibly difficult to make, what about purely religious and spiritual comparisons? Can we not say, for example, that the awareness of the Eternal One as a personal God is spiritually superior to the awareness of the Eternal One as the Brahman of Hinduism? We can say this, in the sense that many Christians and Jews and Muslims do; but on the other hand many Hindus of the advaitic tradition say the contrary, namely, that the awareness of Brahman as a divine person represents a spiritually lower and cruder form of awareness. How can we hope to resolve such a dispute? We cannot, except simply by confessional assertion. But perhaps we would do better to question the underlying assumption that one major human response to the Eternal

One has to be superior, as a totality, to all others. Why must this be so? May it not rather be that there are several *different* forms of human awareness of and response to the Eternal One, which are each valid and effective in spite of being different? Should we not perhaps reject the assumption of one and only one true religion in favor of the alternative possibility of a genuine religious pluralism?

Let me emphasize at this point that I have been speaking of what we commonly call the great world faiths, not of primitive religion, not of religious movements which have perished, and not of the many new religious movements which are springing up around us all the time. There is a law of the survival of the spiritually fittest which simplifies the religious scene. But when we are confronted by a stream of religious life and thought and experience that has persisted for many centuries, which has produced inspiring scriptures and a rich succession of saints and prophets and profound thinkers, and has provided a spiritual home in which hundreds of millions of human lives have been lived, then I think we have to assume that it represents a genuine awareness of and response to the Eternal One. And I do not believe that we have any objective grounds on which to claim that our own slice of history and tradition is better as a totality than another of the ancient and great traditions. Subjectively, however, each tradition is unique and superior for those who have been spiritually formed by it. For a religion produces in those who have been born and brought up with it souls adapted to that religion, who would accordingly not be at home in any other. It is only when a stream of religious life begins to lose its vitality that some of its population lapse into merely nominal adherence or are attracted away to a different faith. And this is of course the religious situation throughout much of our modern industrialized Western world. But even here the particular religious culture in which we have been formed still has a strong hold. For most Christians in this country Christianity is the religion to which they adhere or against which they rebel; and they are so deeply formed by this tradition, in ways of which they are perhaps often hardly conscious, that not many could become, say, Muslims or Buddhists. Again, not many Muslims or Buddhists could become Christians or Hindus. And I presume that a Jew can hardly imagine not being a Jew, however far he may lapse from Jewish observances. It was a rabbi who said, "Many Jews today do not believe in God, but they nearly all believe that God believes in them!" And, in short, we are so formed by the tradition into which we were born and in which we were raised that it is for us unique and absolute and final. Yet I believe that when we accept the fact of religious pluralism we have to learn to refrain from converting that psychological absoluteness into a claim to the objective absoluteness and superiority of our own faith in comparison with all others.

But to refrain from absolute and exclusive claims is harder for some traditions than for others. For the great business of religion is salvation, the bringing of men and women to fullness of life or perfection of being in relation to the Eternal One. And so religious absolutism takes the form of a claim to be the sole way of salvation. It is not, I would think, too difficult for Judaism to avoid making such a claim. The key concept here is that of God's Chosen People. But this need not mean, and has indeed perhaps never meant, that there is salvation only for Jews. Rather it represents the awareness of a divine vocation to bear witness to God for the good of all mankind. But such an awareness is presumably compatible with others having their own religious vocations. Indeed, every encounter with the Eternal One, when it takes a theistic form, involves a sense of being specifically called, and thus chosen. We are all, I would say, chosen people, though chosen in different ways and for different vocations.

But it is much harder for Christianity to digest the fact of religious pluralism. Here the key concept is that of divine incarnation. There is a direct line of logical entailment from the premise that Jesus was God, in the sense that he was God the Son, the second Person of a divine Trinity, living a human life, to the conclusion that Christianity, and Christianity alone, was founded by God in person; and from this to the further conclusion that God must want all his human children to be related to him through this religion which he has himself founded for us; and then to the final conclusion drawn in the Roman Catholic dogma "Outside the church, no salvation" and its Protestant missionary equivalent, "outside Christianity, no salvation." Today, increasing numbers of Christians find the conclusion unacceptable, because untrue to the evident religious facts. We have, then, to work back up the chain of inference and eventually to question the original premise. This has indeed in any case to be recon-

sidered in the light of the conclusion of so much modern biblical scholarship that the historical Jesus very probably did not claim to be God, or to be God the Son, the second Person of a Trinity, incarnate. The conclusion to which some of us within the Christian fold have come is that the idea of divine incarnation is a metaphorical (or, in technical theological language, a mythological) rather than a literal idea. Incarnation, in the sense of the embodiment of ideas, values, insights in human living, is a basic metaphor. One might say, for example, that in 1940 the spirit of defiance of the British people against Nazi Germany was incarnated in Winston Churchill. Now we want to say of Jesus that he was so vividly conscious of God as the loving heavenly Father, and so startlingly open to God and so fully his servant and instrument, that the divine love was expressed, and in that sense incarnated, in his life. This was not a matter (as it is in official Christian doctrine) of Jesus having two complete natures, one human and the other divine. He was wholly human; but whenever self-giving love in response to the love of God is lived out in a human life, to that extent the divine love has become incarnate on earth. Some such reinterpretation of the idea of incarnation appeals to a number of Christians today, while on the other hand it is resisted by many more; and one cannot at present foresee how this internal Christian debate will eventually go.

But I must be drawing to an end. When I say in a summarizing slogan that God has many names, I mean that the Eternal One is perceived within different human cultures under different forms, both personal and nonpersonal, and that from these different perceptions arise the religious ways of life which we call the great world faiths. The practical upshot of this thesis is that people of the different religious traditions are free to see one another as friends rather than as enemies or rivals. We are members of different households of faith, but households each of which has some precious and distinctive contact with the Eternal One, which others can perhaps learn to share. We should, then, go forward into the new age of growing interreligious dialogue with hope and with positive anticipations and with a sense of pleasurable excitement.

John Hick, "God Has Many Names"

1.   The main issue under discussion here is whether or not religious images are only projections of the human mind.

     a. True   b. False

2.   Hick thinks that religion is the human response to a transcendent divine Reality which is other than us.

     a. True   b. False

3.   The historical period of time in which several religous leaders emerged is called the

     _____ .

4.   Cognitive freedom is at its greatest at the

     a. moral level of awareness.
     b. religious level of awareness.
     c. physical level of awareness.
     d. economic level of awareness.

5.   Identify and evaluate Hick's main argument for religious pluralism.

Sallie McFague*

METAPHORICAL THEOLOGY

There is a God. There is no God. What is the problem? I am quite sure that there is a God in the sense that I am sure my love is no illusion. I am quite sure there is no God in the sense that I am sure there is nothing which resembles what I can conceive when I say that word.[1]

Simone Weil, in her book *Waiting for God,* states the problem of religious language in the classic way. As a religious person, she is certain that her love for God is not an illusion, but she is equally certain that none of her conceptions of the divine resembles God. Her comments are in the great tradition of deeply religious people, and especially the mystics of all religious traditions, who feel conviction at the level of experience, at the level of worship, but great uncertainty at the level of words adequate to express the reality of God.

Augustine, the great Bishop of Hippo, notes that even the person who says the most about God is but "dumb," and yet, he adds, our only alternatives are to speak in halting, inadequate words or to remain silent. The Judeo-Christian tradition, more than many other religious traditions, has chosen not to remain silent. In fact, this tradition and especially Christianity, and within Christianity especially Protestantism, has focused on and at times been obsessed by words, both "the Word of God" and human words about God.

THE PROBLEM OF RELIGIOUS
LANGUAGE

Increasingly, however, religious language is a problem for us, a problem of a somewhat different kind than the classical one. For most of us, it is not a question of being sure of God while being unsure of our language about God. Rather, we are unsure both at the experiential and the expressive levels. We are unsure at the experiential level because we are, even the most religious of us, secular in ways our foremothers and forefathers were not. We do not live in a sacramental universe in which the things of this world, its joys and catastrophes, harvests and famines, births and deaths, are understood as connected to and permeated by divine power and love. Our experience, our daily experience, is for the most part nonreligious. Most of us go through the days accepting our fortunes and explaining our world without direct reference to God. If we experience God at all it tends to be at a private level and in a sporadic way; the natural and public events of our world do not stand for of image God.

Certainly we cannot return to the time of the sacramental universe; but apart from a *religious context* of some kind, religious language becomes both idolatrous and irrelevant. It becomes *idolatrous* because without a sense of awe, wonder, and mystery, we forget the inevitable distance between

---

*Sallie McFague (1933–   ) was eduated at Yale University and is currently Dean of Theology at the Vanderbilt Divinity School. She is the author of numerous books and articles, including *Models of God* and *The Body of God: An Ecological Theory*. The following is excerpted from her *Metaphorical Theology* (1982) in which she challenges literal-minded thesists to grasp the figurative nature of religious language and its implications for the construction of new metaphors for God.

[1]Simone Weil, *Waiting for God* (New York: Harper & Row, 1973), p. 32.

226

our words and the divine reality. It becomes *irrelevant* because without a sense of the immanence of the divine in our lives, we find language about God empty and meaningless. It is no accident, then, that the mystics in all religious traditions have been the most perceptive on the question of religious language. Aware as they are of the transcendence of God, they have not been inclined to identify our words with God; in fact, their tendency is more often to refuse any similarity between our words and the divine reality. Simone Weil stands foursquare in this tradition when she says there is "nothing" which resembles her thoughts about God. The mystics, however, have also been the most imaginative and free in their language about God, finding all sorts of language relevant. As Augustine notes, we must use all the best images available to us in order to say *something* about the divine. The mystics have also not restricted their language about God to biblical or traditional imagery, for the experience of God, the certainty and the immediacy of it, has been the basis for new and powerful religious language.

The *primary context,* then, for any discussion of religious language is worship. Unless one has a sense of the mystery surrounding existence, of the profound inadequacy of all our thoughts and words, one will most likely identify God with our words: God *becomes* father, mother, lover, friend. Unless one has a sense of the nearness of God, the overwhelming sense of the way God pervades and permeates our very being, one will not find religious images significant: the power of the images for God of father, mother, lover, friend will not be appreciated. Apart from a religious context, religious language will inevitably go awry either in the direction of idolatry or irrelevancy or both.

There is, however, another critical context for religious language, one that has not been as central in the classical tradition and that does not surface in the quotation by Weil. In the broadest sense, we could call this the *interpretive context.* It is the context that recognizes that we who attempt to speak about God are social, cultural, and historical beings with particular perspectives influenced by a wide range of factors. The interpretive context within religious faiths has usually been limited to the "tradition," meaning the church or another institution which has set the interpretive precedents for what is proper (orthodox) or improper (heretical) religious language. In the last two hundred years, however, the interpretive context has increased greatly as people have realized the relativity of perspectives. With the introduction of historical criticism of religious texts, we became aware of the relativity of the words and images in sacred Scriptures, that these texts were written by limited people who expressed their experiences of divine reality in the manners and mores of their historical times.

Most recently, we have become conscious, by deepening our awareness of the *plurality* of perspectives, of dimensions of interpretation which had ben largely submerged. That is to say, it is not only our time and place in history that influences our religious language, but also our class, race, and sex; our nationality, education, and family background; our interests, prejudices, and concerns. We have become aware, for instance, of the varying interests that determined the perspectives of New Testament writers. They not only saw their religious experience through the glasses of first-century Palestine but also through the refractions provided by their own individual histories and concerns. Consciousness of the relativity and plurality of interpretations forces us to recognize that religious language is not just the halting attempts by "Christians" to say something appropriate about God, but is the halting attempts by specific individuals: by Paul, a first-century convert from Judaism, who has great empathy with the problems of Jewish Christians but little sympathy for women or slave Christians; by Julian of Norwich, a medieval woman mystic, who spoke of "our tender Mother Jesus"; by Reinhold Niebuhr, a twentieth-century preacher from Detroit, whose experience with American capitalism caused him to see human sinfulness as the basis for political "realism"; by Mary Daly, a twentieth-century, Catholic-educated feminist, who sees the history of the world's religions as an exercise in misogyny. If we lose sight of the relativity and plurality of the interpretive context, our religious language will, as with the loss of the religious context, become idolatrous or irrelevant. It will become idolatrous, for we will absolutize one tradition of images for God; it will become irrelevant, for the experiences of many people will not be included within the canonized tradition.

The issues that emerge, then, from both the worship and the interpretive contexts of religious language, are *idolatry* and *irrelevance:* either we take our language about God literally or we find it meaningless. Another way to phrase these issues is to ask the questions: How does religious language refer to God and which religious images are central? Is there a way of speaking of religious language as referring to God without identifying it with the divine? Are there images which are central to a religious tradition *and* are there revolutionary possibilities within that tradition aiding new images to emerge? These are very complex questions, for they focus on the heart of language—its truth and its meaning. Does religious language refer to anything; if so, to what and how? Does religious language mean anything; if so, what and to whom? Our route to suggesting modest answers to these questions will be slow and indirect, as I believe is appropriate to the subject matter; but a beginning can be made by illustrating the issues of idolatry and irrelevance, truth and meaning, through contemporary movements within our culture that find them especially problematic.

THE IDOLATRY OF RELIGIOUS LANGUAGE

On the issue of the truth of religious language, there are continuing, powerful, conservative religious movements which insist on the literal reference of language to God. Religious conservatism is a widespread tendency within contemporary culture, not restricted to groups which call themselves "evangelicals" or "fundamentalists." This tendency is linked with fear of relativizing Scripture through historical criticism and a refusal to accept a plurality of interpretive perspectives. The Bible, says this movement, *is* the Word of God; the Bible is inerrant or divinely inspired; the words and images of the Bible are the authoritative and appropriate words and images for God. The Bible is a sacred text, different from all other texts, and not relative and pluralistic as are all other human products. The Bible becomes an idol: the fallible, human words of Scripture are understood as referring correctly and literally to God. Even where these sentiments are not expressed clearly or in such extreme fashion, religious literalism remains a powerful current in our society. And it does not stem only from a fear of relativism and plurality. It also derives from the understanding of what counts as "true" in our culture. What is "true" in our positivistic, scientifically oriented society is what corresponds with "reality," with the "facts." Translated into artistic terms, this means realistic art; the "true" painting or sculpture is a copy of what it represents. Translated into religious terms, "true" religious language is also a copy of what it represents; in other words, a literal or realistic representation of God's nature. If the Bible says that God is "father" then God is literally, really, "father"; the word "father" and the associa-

tions of that word truly refer to God's nature. In the same way that the law of gravity refers to the way things really are in the world, so "father" refers to the way God really is.

But there is, I believe, an even deeper reason why religious literalism runs rampant in our time. It is not only that many people have lost the practice of religious contemplation and prayer, which alone is sufficient to keep literalism at bay, or that positivistic scientism has injected a narrow view of truth into our culture. While both are true, it is also the case that we do not think in symbols in the way our forebears did. That is to say, we do not see the things of this world as standing for something else; they are simply what they are. A symbolic sensibility, on the contrary, sees multilayered realities, with the literal level suggestive of meanings beyond itself. While it may have been more justified for people in earlier times to be biblical literalists since they were less conscious of relativity, as symbolic thinkers, they were *not* literalists. From the third century on, the "fourfold method of exegesis"—in which three levels of interpretation followed the literal level—permitted and encouraged the exercise of the imagination in the interpretation of Scripture. While many of the "anagogical" and "tropological" interpretations were fanciful, the abandonment of the four levels in the Protestant Reformation, with the claim that the text was self-explanatory, eventually resulted in literalism.[2] The claim can be made that our time is *more* literalistic than any other time in history. Not only were double, triple, and more meanings once seen in Scripture) and Scripture considered richer as a consequence), but our notion of history as the recording of "facts" is alien to the biblical consciousness. The ancients were less literalistic than we are, aware that truth has many levels and that when one writes the story of an influential person's life, one's perspective will color that story. Ours is a literalistic mentality; theirs was a symbolical mentality. There can be no return to a symbolical mentality in its earlier forms; we no longer believe in four levels of scriptural exegesis or in a three-tiered universe.

Nor can many of us return to a symbolical mentality in its sacramental form; for instance, belief that natural and human objects and events are "figures" of the divine. For a traditional sacramental sensibility, the bread and wine of the Eucharist are symbols of divine nurture; they do not merely "point to" spiritual food, but really and truly *are*

---

[2]See Frank Kermode, *The Classic: Literary Images of Permanence and Change* (New York: Viking Press, 1975).

spiritual food. The things of this world participate in and signify what transcends our world. The sacramental sensibility depends upon a belief that everything is connected, that the beings of this world are analogously related to God (Being-Itself), and hence can be sacramentally related to God. The analogy of being by which all that is *is* because of its radical dependence on God ties everything together in a silent ontological web which reverberates with similarity within dissimilarity out to its farthest reaches. Even a corpse, says Augustine, is like God to the extent that it still has some degree of order left in its decaying flesh and emerging skeleton. In such a universe, everything holds together, everything fits, everything is related.

For a genuine symbolical sensibility such as Dante embraced in his *Divine Comedy,* the symbol—the finite object which signifies the infinite by participating in it—is neither literalized nor spiritualized. It does not become an idol or a mere sign. In our time, however, when there is skepticism concerning the unity of all that is, symbols tend either to be literalized (as in fundamentalism or the doctrine of transubstantiation) or spiritualized (as in Feuerbach or Protestant liberalism).

The medieval sacramental sensibility is not ours, either in theory or practice. Our time is characterized by disunity, by skepticism that anything is related to anything else, and by secularity. If there is to be any fresh understanding of the truth of images as a counter to literalistic truth, it will have to be one that takes seriously the characteristics of the contemporary sensibility.

Before we leave this preliminary overview of literalism and the truth of religious language, it is necessary to add a world for social anthropology about *why* people cling to religious systems with such fervor, especially if they appear threatened by a secularized, relativistic, and pluralistic culture. As Clifford Geertz points out, human beings are "unfinished" at birth and must construct and order their world in ways that no other animals must do. Monkeys and bees are born into a monkey or bee "world" respectively—which is simply there for them. Having to construct our world, we are nec-

essarily (if only subconsciously) protective of it and extremely anxious if it is threatened. We depend, says Geertz, so deeply on our constructions for our most basic sense of sanity that any threat to them is a threat to our very being.[3] Thus, one can conclude that people will be less open, less imaginative, less flexible during times of threat. They will be more literalistic, absolutist, dogmatic when the construction which orders their world is relativized, either through pluralistic perspectives from within the tradition or competing systems from without. Given the pressures against the traditional Christian imagistic system from, for instance, both the liberation theologies and from other world religions, this retreat into literalistic, absolutist hibernation is no surprise.

But literalism will not do. Much of this essay will be devoted to trying to show why it will not do and what the alternative is. Two thoughtful theologians point us in the right direction on the matter of religious language, the first with a straightforward admonition, the second with an analogy of religious language with poetic. British theologian Ian T. Ramsey has written:

> Let us always be cautious of talking about God in straightforward language. Let us never talk as if we had privileged access to the diaries of God's private life . . . so that we may say quite cheerfully why God did what, when and where.[4]

This admonition is never necessary for deeply religious people or persons aware of their own relative and limited perspectives. Old Testament scholar Phyllis Trible has written:

> To appropriate the metaphor of a Zen sutra, poetry is "like a finger pointing to the moon." It is a way to see the light that shines in darkness, a way to participate in transcendent truth and to embrace reality. To equate the finger with the moon or to acknowledge the finger and not perceive the moon is to miss the point.[5]

---

[3]Clifford Geertz, "Religion as a Cultural System," in *Reader in Comparative Religion,* 2nd ed. rev., ed. William Lessa and Evon Vogt (New York: Harper & Row, 1965), p. 209.

[4]Ian T. Ramsey, *Religious Language* (New York: Macmillian Co., 1963), p. 107.

[5]Phyllis Trible, *God and the Rhetoric of Sexuality, Overtures to Biblical Theology* (Philadelphia: Fortress Press, 1978), p. 16.

Or, to rephrase Trible's words for our subject, either to equate human words with the divine reality or to see no relationship between them is inappropriate. Rather, the proper way is "like a finger pointing to the moon." Is *this* the way "to participate in transcendent truth and to embrace reality?" I would agree with Trible that it is; I would call it the "metaphorical" way and will be elaborating on it as the form of religious language.

THE IRRELEVANCE OF RELIGIOUS LANGUAGE

Turning now to the second problem facing religious language in our time—irrelevancy—we note that it also is a widespread phenomenon. In a secularized culture where the practice of regular public and private prayer is not widespread, this is bound to be the case. For many, the images in the Bible have sentimental significance from childhood days and happier times; for some, the biblical language creates a world of its own in sharp distinction from the evil modern world. But for many people, religious language, biblical language, has become, like a creed repeated too many times, boring and repetitious. We are essentially indifferent to it. And this is true despite the fact that biblical imagery is often vivid, powerful, shocking, and revolutionary. But all of the reasons given thus far for the "meaninglessness" of religious language have probably always been current. What distinguishes our time is various groups of people who are saying that traditional religious language is meaningless to them because it excludes them in *special* ways. In a more general sense, religious language in the Judeo-Christian tradition excludes us all, for it is largely biblical language; hence, its assumptions concerning social, political, and cultural matters are not ours. Entering the biblical world for many people is like going into a time warp in which one is transported to a world two thousand years in the past. We are aware of significant connections since both worlds are inhabited by human beings, but the images, problems, issues, and assumptions are different. In one way or another, we are all excluded from the biblical world and the tradition that has been formed from it: few if any of us identify easily or enthusiastically with images of demons, vineyards, Messiah and Son of man, kings, Pharisees, and so on. But the issues are much sharper and more painful for some groups: it is not simply that they do not identify; rather, they feel *specifically* excluded. The indifference and irrelevance that many people feel with regard to religious language is clarified by the critique of the more revolutionary groups, for their particular difficulties with religious language highlight issues that point directly to some of its basic characteristics. The feminist critique of religious language is especially relevant in this regard, for more than any of the other liberation theologies, feminist theology has focused on language, its power and its abuses. Three points in this critique stand out as significant.

First, feminists generally agree that whoever names the world owns the world. The Genesis story, according to the traditional, patriarchal interpretation, sees Adam naming the world without consulting Eve. For many feminists, this is a model of Western culture, including Christianity, which has been and still is a "man's world."[6] The feminist critique of religious language is an extremely sophisticated one, for it is based on a recognition of the fundamental importance of language to human existence. With Ludwig Wittgenstein, feminists would say, "The limits of one's language are the limits of one's world," and with Martin Heidegger, "Language is the house of being." We do not so much use language as we are used by it. Since we are all born into a world which is already linguistic, in which the naming has already taken place, we only own our world to the extent that the naming that has occurred is our naming. Feminist theologians are

---

[6]The following quotation by Carol Christ and Judith Plaskow is an excellent summary of the feminist critique of language and the importance of naming.

Consciousness-raising . . . leads to a critique of culture and to the tasks of transforming or recreating it. Feminists have called their task a "new naming" of self and world. It is through naming that humans progress from childhood to adulthood and learn to understand and shape the world about them. Under patriarchy, men have reserved to themselves the right to name, keeping women in a state of intellectual and spiritual dependency. Mary Daly suggests that the Genesis creation story, in which Adam names the animals and woman, is the paradigm of false naming in Western culture. If the world has been named by Adam without Eve's consultation, then the world has been named from the male point of view. As women begin to name the world for themselves, they will upset the order that has been taken for granted throughout history. They will call themselves and the world into new being. Naming women's experience thus becomes the model not only for personal liberation and growth, but for the feminist transformation of culture and religion (Carol Christ and Judith Plaskow, eds., *Womanspirit Rising: A Feminist Reader in Religion* [New York: Harper & Row, 1979], p. 7).

claiming that the world of Western religion is not their world; it was named by men and excludes women. The world of Western religion can become a world for women only if it is open to their naming. New naming, changes in language, are, however, no minor matters, for if one believes that language and "world" are conterminous, then changes in the one will involve changes in the other, and such changes are often revolutionary. The current resistance to inclusive or unbiased language, for instance, both at the social and religious level, indicates that people know instinctively that a revolution in language means a revolution in one's world.

Second, feminists are saying that the particular problem they have with Western religious language is its patriarchal character. It is not just that "God the father" is a frequent appellation for the divine, but that the entire structure of divine-human and human-human relationships is understood in a patriarchal framework. "God the father," as we shall see, has become a model which serves as a grid or screen through which to see not only the nature of God but also our relations to the divine and with one another. "Patriarchy" then is not just that most of the images of the deity in Western religion are masculine—king, father, husband, lord, master— but it is the Western way of life: it describes patterns of governance at national, ecclesiastical, business, and family levels. We shall investigate this model in some detail at a later time, for it is one of the most prominent in the Judeo-Christian tradition. But the point I am stressing now is the total, overarching character of patriarchalism which contributes to the sense of exclusion on the part of women and hence prompts their criticism of the irrelevance of much of Western religious language to them. They say the model of "God the father" has become an idol. When a model becomes an idol, the hypothetical character of the model is forgotten and what ought to be seen as *one* way to understand our relationship with God has become identified as *the* way. In fact, as happens when a model becomes an idol, the distance between image and reality collapses: "father" becomes God's "name" and patriarchy becomes the proper description of governing relationships at many levels. The transformation of the paternal model into the patriarchal is an important case in point concerning what can happen to models

when *one* dominates. Feminist theologians are insisting that many models of God are necessary, among them feminine models, in order both to avoid idolatry and to include the experience of all peoples in our language about God.

Third, feminist theologians are saying that religious language is not only religious but also human, not only about God but also about us. The tradition says that we were created in the image of God, but the obverse is also the case, for we imagine God in *our* image. And the human images we choose for the divine influence the way we feel about ourselves, for these images are "divinized" and hence raised in status. For instance, earthly kingship gains in importance when the image of king is applied to God.[7] On the contrary, images that are excluded are not legitimated and honored; for instance, as feminists have pointed out, the paucity of feminine imagery for God in the Judeo-Christian tradition means a lower self-image for women in that tradition. The relationship between feminine imagery for the divine and the status of women in a society has been well documented in the history of religions.[8] One of the functions, therefore, of religious language is "naming ourselves" as we "name" God. Those who are conscious of being excluded from a religious tradition are most likely to recognize this important and often forgotten function of religious language.

In a number of ways, then, feminist theologians (and a similar case could be made by black and third world theologians) have shown why religious language is not meaningful in our time. Language which is not our language, models which have become idols, images which exclude our experience are three common failings of religious language, but they are especially evident to groups of people who feel excluded by the classical tradition of a religious faith.

CAN RELIGIOUS LANGUAGE BE REVITALIZED?

If idolatry and irrelevance are the critical issues for religious language in our time, what remedies are possible for revitalization? The crisis is too deep for patchwork solutions, for the problem lies in our most basic sense of "how things hold to-

---

[7]This point is made at length in the classic study by Peter Berger, *The Social Reality of Religion* (London: Faber & Faber, 1969).

[8]See, for example, Rita M. Gross, ed., *Beyond Androcentrism: New Essays on Women and Religion* (Missoula, Mont.: Scholars Press, 1977).

gether." That is, many of us no longer believe in a symbolic, sacramental universe in which the part stands for the whole, the things of this world "figure" another world, and all that is is connected by a web of being. No longer believing in connections of this sort and hence afraid that our images refer to nothing, we literalize them, worshiping the icon in our desperation. Furthermore, we find them irrelevant for they connect us to nothing transcending ourselves: they are "just symbols." The question that looms before us is, I believe, a critical one for religious faith and expression: is it possible to have significant religious language, language that is true and meaningful, without classic sacramentalism? If we can no longer believe in a "figural" world—our world as a whole and in all its parts as a symbol of another world, a microcosm of it—can we still believe that our words about the divine are significant?

Let us consider this question more carefully. What are the characteristics of the classic sacramental perspective? The basis of the sacramental universe within Christianity (and there are similar perspectives in other religions) is the incarnation: the sense of divine immanence in the Hebrew tradition is brought to its apotheosis in the Johannine assertion that "the Word became flesh and dwelt among us." The full presence of God in an otherwise ordinary person, Jesus of Nazareth—as the Chalcedonian statement puts it, "fully God and fully man" —was the basis for a thoroughgoing sacramentalism. If God can be fully present in a particular human being, then all creation has the potential for serving as a symbol of divine immanence. The natural and human orders of creation are not flat but two dimensional: each thing is itself, but as itself, it is also something else—"news of God" as Gerard Manley Hopkins says. The world is alive with the presence of God; it "figures," shows forth, the divine in all its myriad particularity. Sacramentalism of this sort tends to be static and focuses on the natural, not the historical, order. Incarnationalism, as the word indicates, is centered on the body, the flesh, not on human being as restless, moving, growing. The most extreme example of sacramentalism, the eucharistic doctrine of transubstantiation, illustrates clearly both the static and fleshly characteristics of the perspective. The bread and wine *become* the body and blood of Christ: two items of the naturalistic order are changed into what they symbolize. Actually, in this extreme case symbolization gives over to realism; the symbol is consumed by what it represents. But elsewhere in the symbolic perspective, the two dimensions exist in a hierarchical order of macrocosm-microcosm, spirit-body, Christ-church, man-woman, and so on. All is ordered, statically and hierarchically, with the body always "below," but permeated by spirit and capable of expressing and imaging spirit.

In such a universe, of course, the meaning and truth of religious language are no problem. If the entire earthly order is a "figure" of the divine order, if each and every scrap of creation, both natural and human, participates in and signifies the divine order according to its own particularities, its own way of being in the world, then all that is "refers" to Being-Itself and has "meaning," both in itself and as a symbol. Everything is connected hierarchically; hence, everything here below is meaningful both in itself and as a symbol of the divine.

Symbolic sacramentalism received systematic interpretation and ordering in the medieval doctrine of *analogia entis,* the analogy of being. This doctrine says, in essence, that every existing thing participates in Being-Itself, but analogously. That is, being is differentiated absolutely, so that while everything is connected as being immediately and radically dependent on God, each thing has, is, its own act of being and hence is radically particular. The analogy of being does not paint the world all the same color; on the contrary, it stresses the glory of difference. Beneath the distinctions, however, everything is connected and this is the reason why everything in such a universe can be a symbol of everything else and, most especially, of God, who created everything out of the divine plenitude as a mirror and a reflection of the divine self. The analogical way, the symbolic way, rests on a profound *similarity* beneath the surface dissimilarities; what we see and speak of must be the differences, but we rest in the faith that all is empowered by the breath of God, Being-Itself. The vision of God, the goal of all creation, is the belief that one day all of creation shall be one. The many shall return to the One, for the many are in secret one already.

Now, try as we might, many if not most of us cannot work ourselves back into this mentality. If the destiny of religious language rests on a return to the traditional sacramental universe, if the significance of imagistic language depends on a belief that symbols participate in a transcendent reality, the future for religious language is grim. I do not believe either is the case—that we must or can return to such a sacramental universe or that the significance of images rests on symbolic participationism. In fact, we have not had a classic sacramental mentality for a long time (even though it hangs on in many quarters and, improperly understood, is the source of much literalistic realism in religious language). In effect, however, we have not had such a sensibility since at least the Protestant Reformation.

One way to describe what occurred in the Reformation is a profound questioning of the symbolic mentality, a loosening of the connections between symbol and its reference. The eucharistic debate between Luther and the proponents of transubstantiation on the one hand, and between Luther and Zwingli on the other hand, reveals as much. Luther took a mediating position between the bread and wine as one with the body and the blood and these elements as a mere sign recalling them. To Luther, the bread and the wine were still symbols of Christ's body and blood, still participated in that reality, but in a way that I would call "metaphorical," for the assertions "This is my body" and "This is my blood" were not viewed as identity statements, but as including a silent but present negative. One critical difference between symbolic and metaphorical statements is that the latter always contain the whisper, "it is *and it is not.*"

I suggest, therefore, that one of the distinctive characteristics of Protestant thought is its insistence on the "and it is not." It is the iconoclastic tendency in Protestantism, what Paul Tillich calls the "Protestant Principle," the fear of idolatry, the concern lest the finite ever be imagined to be capable of the infinite. We see it in Martin Luther's "masks" of God, that God is revealed and veiled in all symbols; in John Calvin's notion of divine "accommodation" by which God stoops to our level by speaking in signs and images; and in an extreme form in Karl Barth's concept of *analogia fidei,* which insists that our language refers to God only as God from time to time causes our words to conform to the divine being.

The Protestant tradition is, I would suggest, "metaphorical"' the Catholic, "symbolical" (or "analogical" for contemporary Catholicism). I do not mean to suggest a hard and fast distinction here, but only a characteristic sensibility. The Protestant sensibility tends to see dissimilarity, distinction, tension and hence to be skeptical and secular, stressing the transcendence of God and the finitude of creation. The Catholic sensibility tends to see similarity, connection, harmony and, hence, to be believing and religious, stressing the continuity between God and creation. These caricatures are not meant to be directly related to the Protestant and Catholic ecclesiastical institutions or even to the theologies supported by these bodies. Not only are many Protestants "catholic" and many Catholics "protestant," but it is obvious that either tendency without the other would be insupportable. They are complementary. However, a sacramentalism of the medieval sort—the classic Catholic mentality—is not viable today, nor is it supported by most Catholics

who seek a revitalization of this tradition. The most sophisticated revitalization of the symbolic, sacramental tradition interpret it analogically, that is, in a way that stresses many of the characteristics of the metaphorical sensibility: its emphasis on the negativities, on the distance between image and what it represents, on its refusal of easy harmonies. Obversely, a Protestant sensibility which failed to see any connections or unity between God and the world would be totally negative and agnostic. A metaphorical perspective *does* see connections but they are of a tensive, discontinuous, and surprising nature.

One of the interesting and important characteristics of contemporary ecumenical theology is that it is neither traditionally Catholic nor Protestant, emphasizing neither easy continuities nor radical discontinuities, but some form of both. However, as David Tracy points out in his recent book, *The Analogical Imagination,* there are characteristic differences in the Christian community between those for whom experience in the world engenders primarily a sense of wonder and trust and those for whom it engenders primarily a need for healing and transformation. The first moves from an awareness of harmony, taking the negatives into account, while the second moves from an awareness of the negativities, reaching toward a future harmony. They are two "ways," one not necessarily better than the other; it is the contention of this essay, however, that the Protestant sensibility is more characteristic of our time and is the place from which many of us must start. What we seek, then, is a form of theology, a form for our talk about God both at the primary religious level of images and the secondary theological level of concepts, which takes the Protestant sensibility seriously.

METAPHORICAL THEOLOGY

If modernity were the only criterion, our task would be relatively easy. But such is never the case in theology. Christian theology is always an interpretation of the "Gospel" in a particular time and place. So the other task of equal importance is to show that a *metaphorical theology* is indigenous to Christianity, not just in the sense that it is permitted, but is called for. And this I believe is the case. The heart of the Gospel in the New Testament is widely accepted to be the "kingdom of God"; what the kingdom is or means is never expressed but indirectly suggested by the parables of the kingdom. The parables are by no means the only form in the New Testament which deals with the kingdom and we must be cautious lest we make an idol of them.

However, as the dominant genre of Jesus' teaching on the kingdom, they suggest some central, albeit indirect, clues to its reality. As a form of religious language, the parables of the New Testament are very different from symbolic, sacramental language. They do not assume a believing or religious perspective on the part of the listeners to whom they are addressed; they do not assume continuity between our world and a transcendent one; they do not see similarity, connection, and harmony between our ways and the ways of God. On the contrary, they are a secular form of language, telling stories of ordinary people involved in mundane family, business, and social matters; they assume a nonbelieving or secular attitude on the part of their audience; they stress the discontinuity between our ways and the ways of the kingdom; they focus on the dissimilarity, incongruity, and tension between the assumptions and expectations of their characters and another set of assumptions and expectations identified with the kingdom. In other words, they are a form peculiarly suited to what I have called the Protestant sensibility.

They are so suited because they are metaphors, not symbols. They are metaphorical statements about religious matters, about what both transcends and affects us at the deepest level of our existence. What is it about a religious metaphorical statement which makes it more powerful than a symbolical statement? The answer to this question centers on the nature of metaphor and especially of metaphorical statements. To many people "metaphor" is merely a poetic ornament for illustrating an idea or adding rhetorical color to abstract or flat language. It appears to have little to do with ordinary language until one realizes that most ordinary language is composed of "dead metaphors," some obvious, such as "the arm of the chair" and others less obvious, such as "tradition," meaning "to hand over or hand down." Most simply, a metaphor is seeing one thing *as* something else, pretending "this" is "that" because we do not know how to think or talk about "this," so we use "that" as a way of saying something about it. Thinking metaphorically means spotting a thread of similarity between two dissimilar objects, events, or whatever, one of which is better known than the other, and using the better-known one as a way of speaking about the lesser known.

Poets use metaphor all the time because they are constantly speaking about the great unknowns—mortality, love, fear, joy, guilt, hope, and so on. Religious language is deeply metaphorical for the same reason and it is therefore no surprise that Jesus' most characteristic form of teaching, the parables, should be extended metaphors. Less obvious, but of paramount importance, is the fact that metaphorical thinking constitutes the basis of human thought and language. From the time that we are infants we construct our world through metaphor; that is, just as young children learn the meaning of the color red by finding the thread of similarity through many dissimilar objects (red ball, red apple, red cheeks), so we constantly ask when we do not know how to think about something, "What is it like?" Far from being an esoteric or ornamental rhetorical device superimposed *on* ordinary language, metaphor *is* ordinary language. It is the *way* we think. We often make distinctions between ordinary and poetic language, assuming that the first is direct and the second indirect, but actually both are indirect, for we always think by indirection. The difference between the two kinds of language is only that we have grown accustomed to the indirections of ordinary language; they have become conventional. Likewise, conceptual or abstract language is metaphorical in the sense that the ability to generalize depends upon seeing similarity within dissimilarity; a concept is an abstraction of the similar from a sea of dissimilars. Thus, Darwin's theory of survival of the fittest is a high-level metaphorical exercise of recognizing a similar pattern amid an otherwise incredibly diverse set of phenomena.

The primary answer to the question of why religious metaphorical statements are so powerful is that they are in continuity with the way we think ordinarily. We are not usually conscious of the metaphorical character of our thought, of seeing "this" in terms of "that," of finding the thread of similarity amid dissimilars, but it is the only way a child's world can be constructed or our worlds expanded and transformed. Of course, there are important differences between ordinary and religious metaphorical statements which we shall fully note, but the first thing is to insist on their continuity. Symbolic statements, on the other hand, are not so much a way of knowing and speaking as they are sedimentation and solidification of metaphor. For a symbolical or sacramental thought, one does not think of "this" as "that," but "this" as *a part of* "that." The tension of metaphor is absorbed by the harmony of symbol.

Another way to discern tie distinction between metaphorical and sacramental thinking is to say that in metaphorical statements we always make judgments. That is, we make assertions; we say "I am thinking about 'this' in terms of 'that.'" The only times we do not think this way is when we have

234

already accepted a particular way of thinking of something. When we already know something, that is, when we have accepted a perspective on something, then we see and think about it "directly," or so it seems. Actually, it is not the case that anything can be known or thought of directly or literally; rather, we have simply acquired a way of looking at it which is acceptable to us. Even as simple a statement as "this is a chair" means only that I have made a judgment that I will think about this object *as* a chair because there is sufficient similarity between this object and other objects which I have called "chairs" in the past that I believe my assertion is justified. The example may appear ridiculous but it was chosen because it illustrates metaphorical thinking at its most common, continuous, and instantaneous level. It is the same *kind* of thinking as the assertion "Jesus is the savior," inasmuch as here again one is making a decision to think of one thing in terms of another; in both cases, a judgment is involved that similarity is present. The differences between the two statements are vast and important, such as the degree of existential involvement and the much greater ignorance of the subject matter, as well as the novelty of the assertion in the second statement. The point to stress, however, is that human thought is of a piece, it is indirect, and it involves judgments.

We have remarked that metaphor finds the vein of similarity in the midst of dissimilars, while symbol rests on similarity already present and assumed. But the difference is even more marked: metaphor not only lives in the region of dissimilarity, but also in the region of the unconventional and surprising. Both humor and the grotesque are distinctly metaphorical. Humor is the recognition of a *very* unlikely similarity among dissimilars and we laugh because we are surprised to discover that such unlikes are indeed alike in at least one respect. A great many jokes take the form, "How is a _____ like a _____ ?" Likewise, the grotesque forces us to look at radical incongruity, at what is outside, does not fit, is strange and disturbing. Both are extreme metaphorical forms which point up a crucial characteristic of metaphor: good metaphors shock, they bring unlikes together, they upset conventions, they involve tension, and they are implicitly revolutionary. The parables of Jesus are typically metaphorical in this regard, for they bring together dissimilars (lost coins, wayward children, buried treasure, and tardy laborers with the kingdom of God); they

shock and disturb; they upset conventions and expectations and in so doing have revolutionary potential. In this regard, one could characterize symbolic, sacramental thinking as priestly and metaphorical thinking as prophetic. The first assumes an order and unity already present waiting to be realized; the second projects, tentatively, a possible transformed order and unity yet to be realized.[9]

Perhaps the most striking evidence of the revolutionary character of the New Testament parables is the redefinition they give to conventional understandings of the monarchical, hierarchical metaphors of "kingdom" and "rule." God's "kingdom," we discover from the parables, is not like any worldly reign; in fact, its essence is its opposition to the power of the mighty over the lowly, the rich over the poor, the righteous over the unrighteous. It is a *new* rule which is defined by the extraordinary reversal of expectations in the parables as well as in the life and death of Jesus.

The characteristics of metaphorical thinking we have suggested—ordinariness, incongruity, indirection, skepticisms, judgment, unconventionality, surprise, and transformation or revolution—especially as they are realized in Jesus' parables, have persuaded many people to think of Jesus as a parable of God. That is to say, the life and death of Jesus of Nazareth can be understood as itself a "parable" of God; in order to understand the ways of God with us—something unfamiliar and unknown to us, about which we do not know how to think or talk—we look at that life as a metaphor of God. What we see through that "grid" or "screen" is at one level an ordinary, secular story of a human being, but also a story shot through with surprise, unconventionality, and incongruities which not only upset our conventional expectations (for instance, of what a "savior" is and who gets "saved"), but also involve a judgment on our part—"Surely this man is the Christ." In contrast to incarnational christology, however, parabolic christology does not involve an assumption of continuity or identity between the human and the divine; it is not a "Jesusolatry," a form of idolatry. It is, I believe, a christology for the Protestant sensibility and the modern mentality.

All the foregoing comments on metaphor, parable, and Jesus as a parable require considerable elaboration. Perhaps, however, these brief introductory remarks are sufficient for us to attempt to advance a case for a metaphorical theology. If metaphor is the way by which we understand as well as

---

[9]I am indebted to F. W. Dillistone for his distinctive and metaphorical thinking.

enlarge our world and change it—that is, if the only way we have of dealing with the unfamiliar and new is in terms of the familiar and the old, thinking of "this" as "that" although we know the new thing is both like *and* unlike the old—if all this is the case, then it is no surprise that Jesus taught in parables or that many see him as a parable of God. For he introduced a new, strange way of being in the world, a way that could be grasped only through the indirection of stories of familiar life which both "were and were not" the kingdom. And he himself was in the world in a new, strange way which was in many respects an ordinary life but one which also, as with the parables, called the mores and conventions of ordinary life into radical question.

A metaphorical theology, then, starts with the parables of Jesus and with Jesus as a parable of God. This starting place does not involve a belief in the Bible as authoritative in an absolute or closed sense; it does not involve acceptance of a canon or the Bible as "the Word of God." In fact, such a perspective reverses the direction of authority suitable both to Scripture and to the Protestant sensibility. For what we have in the New Testament are confessions of faith by people who, on the basis of their experience of the way their lives were changed by Jesus' Gospel and by Jesus, *gave* authority to him and to the writings about him. The New Testament writings are foundational; they are classics; they are a beginning. But if we take seriously the parables of Jesus and Jesus as a parable of God as our starting point and model, then we cannot say that the Bible is absolute or authoritative in any sense except the way that a "classic" text is authoritative: it continues to speak to us. What must always be kept in mind is that the parables as metaphors and the life of Jesus as a metaphor of God provide characteristics for theology: a theology guided by them is open ended, tentative, indirect, tensive, iconoclastic, transformative. Some of these characteristics appear "negative," in the sense that they qualify any attempts at idolatry, whether this be the idolatry of the Bible, of tradition, of orthodoxy, or of the Church. In such a theology *no* finite thought, product, or creature can be identified with God and this includes Jesus of Nazareth, who as parable of God both "is and is not" God. Against all forms of literalistic realism and idolatry, a metaphorical theology insists that it is not only in keeping with the Protestant sensibility to be open, tentative, and iconoclastic but that these are the characteristics of Jesus' parables and of Jesus' own way of being in the world.

On the other hand, metaphorical theology is not just a modern version of the *via negativa* or an exercise in iconoclasm. It not only says "is not" but

"is," not only no but yes. If the parables of Jesus and Jesus himself as a parable of God are genuine metaphors, then they give license for language about life with God; they point to a real, an assumed similarity between the metaphors and that to which they refer. The many parables of the kingdom tell us something about the rule of God, or what it means to live in the world according to God's way. Jesus as a parable of God tells us actually and concretely (though, of course, indirectly) about God's relationship to us. In other words, a metaphorical theology is "positive" as well as "negative," giving license for speech about God as well as indicating the limits of such speech. Such a theology, as is true of all theologies, must be concerned not only with *how* we speak of God but *what* we say of God. On the question of how we speak of God, a metaphorical theology is firmly opposed to literalism and idolatry of all kinds; on the question of what we say about God, metaphorical theology again turns to the parables and to Jesus as a parable for beginning, foundational clues.

The parables of the New Testament are united by a number of characteristics, of which one of the most outstanding is their concern with *relationships* of various kinds. What is important in the parables is not *who* the characters are (a static notion) but *what they do* (a dynamic one). The plot is always the heart of a parable, what a character or several characters decide in matters having to do with their *relationships with each other*. Whether one thinks of the parable of the Prodigal Son, the Good Samaritan, the Unjust Steward, or the Great Supper, it is relationships and decisions about them that are critical. Just as the central Old Testament religious language is relational—focused on the covenant between God and Israel; so the central New Testament language is relational—focused on persons and their way of being in the world in community. Likewise, if we look at Jesus as a parable of God, we have no alternative but to recognize personal, relational language as the most appropriate language about God. Whatever more one may wish to say about him, he was a person relating to other persons in loving service and transforming power.

I have emphasized the word "person" for two reasons. First, as we were made *in the image of God* (Gen. 3:27), so we now, with the model of Jesus, have further support for imagining God in *our* image, the image of persons. This means that personal, relational images are central in a metaphorical theology—images of God as father, mother, lover, friend, savior, ruler, governor, servant, companion, comrade, liberator, and so on. The Judeo-Christian tradition has always been personalistic and relational in its religious languages. This need not be seen as crude anthropomorphism, but as foundational language, the dominant model, of God-talk. Such language, however, is not the only appropriate religious language: no *one* model can ever be adequate. We find—both in Scripture and in our tradition—naturalistic, impersonal images balancing the relational, personal ones: God as rock, fortress, running stream, power, sun, thunder, First Cause, and so on. The Judeo-Christian tradition has had a decidedly personalistic rather than naturalistic tendency, with appalling consequences for the exploitation of the natural environment. This tradition is personalistic, however, not in an individualistic but in a relational sense, and it is therefore appropriate and required that a revolutionary hermeneutic of this tradition broaden relationship to its widest dimensions, including the entire natural world. In any case, a metaphorical theology will insist that *many* metaphors and models are necessary, that a piling up of images is essential, both to avoid idolatry and to attempt to express the richness and variety of the divine-human relationship.

The second reason for stressing the word "person" is to underscore, in as strong and definitive a way as possible, that it is not patriarchal language which is licensed by Jesus as parable of God. The Christian tradition, and the Jewish as well, have been and still are deeply patriarchal. We will be giving substantial time to this issue, for the profound penetration of the patriarchal model not only in theology but also in the structures of Western culture makes it a critical one for any metaphorical theology to consider. What is stressed in the parables and in Jesus' own life focuses on persons and their relationships; therefore, the dominance of the patriarchal model in the Christian tradition must be seen as a perversion in its hegemony of the field of religious models and its exclusion of other personal, relational models. The dominance of the patriarchal model is idolatrous in its assumption of privileged appropriateness. To put the issue in its simplest form, God's name is not "father" although many Christians use "God" and "father" interchangeably as if "father" were a literal description of God.

A metaphorical theology, then, will emphasize personal, relational categories in its language about God, but not necessarily as the traditional has interpreted these categories. On the contrary, if one looks to the parables and Jesus as a parable to gain some preliminary understanding of what "person" means and what "relationship" means, both applied to us and to God, one finds not a baptizing of conventional hierarchies of relationships, whether these be of class, race, sex, or whatever, but a radical transformation of our expectations. For instance, if are to say "God is father" it is both true *and* untrue, and even where true, it is different from conventional views of patriarchal fatherhood. If we are to call ourselves "children" in relationship to God, this is a limited and in some respects false image. There are personal, relational models which have been suppressed in the Christian tradition because of their social and political consequences; they are, however, as appropriate as the fatherhood model and are necessary both to qualify it and to include the images of personal, relational life of large numbers of people whose experiences have been excluded from traditional Christian language. To mention but two examples in passing, "mother" and "liberator" are metaphors of profound personal relationships with vast potential as models for God. They arise out of the depths of human relational existence and are licensed by the parabolic dimension of the New Testament, not in a literal way (the words do not appear), but in the sense that the characteristics we associate with "mother" and "liberator" fit with (and, of course, also do not fit with) the surprising rule of God as we have it in the parables and the parable of Jesus.

But a metaphorical theology cannot stop with metaphors, with the parables and the life and death of Jesus as extended metaphors of God's rule. Metaphor, parables, and Jesus as parable *fund* theology, but are not theology. If we wish to be precise, we must make a distinction between primary and secondary religious language, between metaphorical and conceptual language. But it is impossible to keep the distinction clear because most primary religious language is implicitly conceptual and most secondary theological language is latently imagistic. The parables of Jesus cry out for interpretation— not for *one* interpretation, but nonetheless for answers to the question, "What does this parable mean?" The richness of imagistic language means that it will always spawn many interpretations. Likewise, the biblical story of Jesus's life and death, an extended metaphor itself and packed with many supporting metaphors (Jesus as Messiah, as Son of man, as Suffering Servant, and so on), is not just a story but is already highly interpreted. What the story *means* is the perspective from which it is told and not something tacked on to pure, unadulterated images. Or if we think of Paul's letters, we see a mixture of images and concepts, the images moving in the direction of concepts in the sense that, for instance, when Paul tells us we are buried with Christ so that we might rise with him, he also tells us what this means (baptism, or the newness of the Christian life). Or if one considers the Nicene

Creed, one sees a mixture of imagistic and conceptual language: the phrase "God of God, Light of Light, Very God of Very God, Begotten not made, Being of one substance with the Father" and so on was deemed necessary to interpret the imagistic language "one Lord Jesus Christ" and "Son of God." Whether the interpretations are good ones, are appropriate, or are still meaningful to us is beside the point. What is critical at the moment is that *some* interpretation is necessary; imagistic language does not just tolerate interpretation but *demands* it.

Thus, metaphorical theology does not stop with metaphors but must deal with the entire gamut of religious/theological language. Robert Funk has noted that it is a tortuous route between Jesus' parables and systematic theology. Indeed it is, but that route must be traversed, for to stop at the level of images, of metaphor, of story is inevitably to give over either to baptizing certain images (usually biblical ones) as alone appropriate or to finding religious images sterile and meaningless. In other words, in terms of the twin issues of idolatry and irrelevance in religious language, *moving beyond* metaphors is necessary both to avoid literalizing them and to attempt significant interpretations of them for our time. It is impossible just to tell "the simple story of Jesus" as it was not told that way in the first place, for the many "stories" of Jesus in the New Testament are each told within several layers of interpretation.

In the continuum of religious language from primary, imagistic to secondary, conceptual, a form emerges which is a mixed type: *the model.* The simplest way to define a model is as a dominant metaphor, a metaphor with staying power. Metaphors are usually the work of an individual, a flash of insight which is often passing. But some metaphors gain wide appeal and become major ways of structuring and ordering experience. Thus, T. S. Eliot's Wasteland or W. H. Auden's Age of Anxiety become perspectives from which modern culture was perceived. There are many kinds of models—scale models, picture models, analogue and theoretical models, as well as root-metaphors which are similar to models but of wider range. For our preliminary purposes, however, the main point is that models are a further step along the route from metaphorical to conceptual language. They are similar to metaphors in that they are images which retain the tension of the "is and is not" and, like religious and poetic metaphors, they have emotional appeal insofar as they suggest ways of understanding our being in the world. The example we

have used before, "God the father," comes readily to mind: it is a metaphor which has become a model. As a model it not only retains characteristics of metaphor but also reaches toward qualities of conceptual thought. It suggests a comprehensive, ordering structure with impressive interpretive potential. As a rich model with many associated commonplaces as well as a host of supporting metaphors, an entire theology can be worked out from this model. Thus, if God is understood on the model of "father," human beings are understood as "children," sin is rebellion against the "father," redemption is sacrifice by the "elder son" on behalf of the "brothers and sisters" for the guilt against the "father" and so on.

Models, as is true of metaphors but in an organic, consistent, and comprehensive manner, give us a way of thinking about the unknown in terms of the known. As Max Black says, a model give us a "grid," "screen," or "filter" which helps us to organize our thoughts about a less familiar subject by means of seeing it in terms of a more familiar one. He gives the example of seeing a military battle in terms of a chess game. The chess model will help to understand tactics and the movement of armies; as he shrewdly notes, however, it also "screens out" certain aspects of battle—for instance, we will not think of blood and death if we use only the chess analogy. Models are necessary, then, for they give us something to think about when we do not know what to think, a way of talking when we do not know how to talk. But they are also dangerous, for they exclude other ways of thinking and talking, and in so doing they can easily become literalized, that is identified as *the* one and only way of understanding a subject. This danger is more prevalent with models that with metaphors because models have a wider range and are more permanent; they tend to object to competition in ways that metaphors do not. In many Old Testament psalms the psalmist will pile up metaphors for God in a riotous *melée,* mixing "rock," "lover," "fortress," "midwife," "fresh water," "judge," "helper," "thunder," and so on in a desperate attempt to express the richness of God's being. But models do not welcome such profusion; even in the case of models of the same *type* (for instance, "God the mother" along with "God the father") there is often great resistance. This is due, in part, to the literalization of models and it is probably the single greatest risk in their use.

It should be evident by now, however, that in all matters except the most conventional (where widely accepted perspectives or models are already operating), thinking by metaphor and hence by models is not optional but necessary. And this is true in the sciences as well as in the humanities. It is sometimes supposed that science deals with its subject matter directly, empirically; science is "factual" whereas poetry and religion are "spiritual, emotional, or imaginative." Unlike them, science does not need the indirection of metaphor but can move inductively from empirical observations to theory and from theory to verification in the "real" world. This positivistic view of science is fortunately no longer the only force in science; rather, what one finds is that much of the most interesting and suggestive work on models is being done by scientists, especially physicists. Relatively little has been written by theologians on models in religion; however, the literature on models in science is enormous, going back a good twenty-five years. As physics comes increasingly to deal with invisibles such as subatomic particles, behaviors of entities that must be imagined rather than observed, it finds itself in a position similar to poetry and religion in that it must attempt to understand the unknown in terms of known models. Also, as more and more conclusions in physics (as well as in many of the other sciences) are expressed in mathematical formulas, models become the only way of connecting scientific knowledge both with ordinary language and with other domains of science. Finally, and most importantly, scientists need models for discovering the new; to think of the new in terms of the old, so long as one does not collapse the two, can often, through the dialectic of similarity and dissimilarity, provide a breakthrough.

There are other uses of models in science as well. But the critical point for our preliminary purposes is to note the widespread acceptance of models in science as well as in many other disciplines. One finds thinking by models in biology, computer science, education theory, political science, ethics, psychology, sociology, and so on. The self-conscious use of models, in regard to both their benefits and their risks, is a common phenomenon in most fields of study. What this means, among other things, is that poetry and religion, the two fields which have always known they must think via metaphor (and as a consequence have been denied by many as dealing in knowledge—truth and meaning), now find that their way of metaphor and indirection is widely accepted as necessary in all creative, constructive thought. A scientist doing a routine experiment does not need models, but a scientist devising an experiment to test a hypothesis may very well need to try out various models in order to locate what is unfamiliar about the present case. And so it is in all creative ventures. What we do not know, we must simulate through models of what we know.

Because of the centrality of models in science and the amount of analysis available on scientific models, we will be looking carefully at some of this material for possible insights into the ways models function in theology. We will discover, for instance, that as interpretive, explanatory devices religious models share structural characteristics with scientific models; but because models in religion emerge from existential experience, they have affectional dimensions as do poetic metaphors. But a metaphorical theology cannot stop at the level of models. To be sure, considerable interpretive activity takes place at such a stage: as dominant metaphors, models manifest priorities within a religious tradition; as organizing networks of images, they are well on the way to systematic thought; as comprehensive ways of envisioning reality, they implicitly raise questions of truth and reference; as metaphors that control the ways people envision both human and divine reality, they cannot avoid the issue of criteria in the choice of certain models and the exclusion of others. A further step of interpretation, however, is called for: conceptual interpretation and criticism.

Concepts and theories arise from metaphors and models; they are an attempt to generalize at the level of abstraction concerning competing and, at times, contradictory metaphors and models. By "concept" we mean an abstract notion; by "theory" we mean a speculative, systematic statement of relationships underlying certain phenomena. A concept is an idea or thought; a theory organizes ideas into an explanatory structure. Concepts, unlike metaphors, do not create new meaning, but rely on conventional, accepted meanings. Theories, unlike models, do not systematize one area in terms of another, but organize concepts into a whole. These definitions are only minimally helpful, however, for they are too neat and compartmentalized for a metaphorical theology. If our thesis holds that *all* though is indirect, then all concepts and theories are metaphorical in the sense that they too are constructions; they are indirect attempts to interpret reality, which never can be dealt with directly. Concepts and theories, however, are at the far end of the continuum and rarely expose their metaphorical roots. These distinctions mainly show the different functions of metaphor, model, and concept or theory in the *one* task of interpreting our being in the world.

Conceptual language tends toward univocity, toward clear and concise meanings for ambiguous, multileveled, imagistic language. In this process something is lost and something is gained: richness and multivalency are sacrificed for precision and consistency. Conceptual thought attempts to find similarities among the models while models insist on dissimilarities among themselves. The relationship, however, is symbiotic. Images "feed" concepts; concepts "discipline" images. Images without concepts are blind; concepts without images are sterile. In a metaphorical theology, there is no suggestion of a hierarchy among metaphors, models, and concepts: concepts are not higher, better, or more necessary than images, or vice versa. Images are never free of the need for interpretation by concepts, their critique of competing images, or their demythologizing of literalized models. Concepts are never free of the need for funding by images, the affectional and existential richness of images, and the qualification against conceptual pretensions supplied by the plurality of images. In no sense can systematic thought be said to *explain* metaphors and models so that they become mere illustrations for concepts; rather the task of conceptual thought is to generalize (often in philosophical language, *the* generalizing language), to criticize images, to raise questions of their meaning and truth in explicit ways.

An example of the movement from parable toward conceptual thought can be illustrated briefly by the career of "the kingdom of God." I would call "the kingdom of God" the root-metaphor of Christianity which is supported and fed by many extended metaphors, the various parables. No *one* parable is adequate as a way of seeing the kingdom, and all the parables together undoubtedly are not either, but they are all that is provided. Many extended metaphors are necessary to give meaning to the model of the kingdom; taken together they display certain common features which are not illustrations of the kingdom so much as exemplifications of it. The process of understanding and interpreting these common features is not deductive or inductive but dialectical: "the rule of God" at this stage *is* all of the parabolic exemplifications. In the hands of Paul and his notion of "justification by faith," however, we move to a higher level of interpretation by a concept generalizing on that rule. Paul Ricoeur points out, and I believe rightly, that Paul's notion is in continuity with the foundational

language of "the kingdom of God" and the underlying parables, but it is less particular, more generalized; less concrete, more abstract; less imagistic, more univocal. Ricoeur calls Paul's concept a "translation language," a semi-conceptual model of discourse which remains under the control of the hermeneutical potential of metaphor *because* it preserves the tension of the foundational language.

For another example of the relationship among metaphors, models, and concepts, one must remember that metaphors and models of God will range widely and have various degrees of dominance within a tradition: person, king, rock, mother, savior, father, fortress, lover, liberator, helper, and many more. We must ask questions of these models. Which ones are dominant? Why should certain ones be dominant? Are they consistent? Are the central models comprehensive? To whom are they significant? To whom are they meaningless or objectionable? Are they fruitful in the sense that they help us to understand our lives better, and are they commensurate with other matters we hold to be important? Do they fit with lived experience or do they have to be rationalized in order to be held? All of these questions and more fall under the heading of the critique of metaphors and models that is the task of conceptual thought.

Systematic thought also tries to organize all the dominant models in a tradition into an overarching system with a key model of its own. For instance, for Paul it was justification by grace through faith; for Augustine, the radical dependance of all that is on God; for Aquinas, the analogy of being whereby each creature participates in and glorifies God through realizing its proper finite end; for Schleiermacher, the feeling of absolute dependence; for Barth, the election of all people to salvation in the election of Jesus Christ before the foundation of the world. Each of these is a radical model, which could be called a "root-metaphor": "a root-metaphor is the most basic assumption about the nature of the world or experience that we can make when we try to give a description of it."[10] Each root-metaphor is a way of seeing "all that is" through a particular key concept. It is also thinking by models and, as is evident, even these root-metaphors are still metaphors: at the highest level of abstraction and generalization one does not escape

[10]The term "root-metaphor" is Stephen Pepper's from his book *World Hypotheses* (Berkeley and Los Angeles: Univ. of California Press, 1942). The quotation is from Earl R. MacCormac, *Metaphor and Myth in Science and Religion* (Durham, N.C.: Duke Univ. Pres, 1976), p. 93.

metaphor (the exceptions are symbolic logic and higher mathematics which do not pretend to refer to reality as lived).

Therefore, we will focus on *models* because, as mediators between metaphors and concepts, they partake of the characteristics of each and are an especially fruitful type of expression to investigate for a metaphorical theology. The aim of a metaphorical theology, as we recall, is to envision ways of talking about the relationship between the divine and the human which are nonidolatrous but relevant: ways which can be said to be true without being literal; ways which are meaningful to all peoples, the traditionally excluded as well as the included. Such a theology, I believe, is appropriate to the Protestant sensibility and I have suggested clues to its character from the parables of Jesus and Jesus as parable. In this framework, moreover, models are critical because models are dominant *metaphors:* they retain the tension of metaphor—its "is and is not" quality which refuses all literalization. Models are also *dominant* metaphors: they are dominant within a tradition both because they have earned that right as "classics" which speak to people across many ages and because they have usurped the right to the false exclusion of other metaphors. Both their right and their usurpation of right must be taken into account.

The tasks of a metaphorical theology will become clear: to understand the centrality of models in religion and the particular models in the Christian tradition; to criticize literalized, exclusive modes; to chart the relationships among metaphors, models, and concepts; and to investigate possibilities for transformative, revolutionary models. The goal of this analysis can then be thought of as an attempt to question the *didactic* tradition of orthodoxy over the more flexible, open, *kerygmatic* point of view epitomized in the parables and Jesus as parable. What must be done in a metaphorical theology is to open up the relationships among metaphor, model, and concept for the purpose both of justifying dominant, founding metaphors as true but not literal *and* of discovering other appropriate dominant metaphors which for cultural, political, and social reasons have been suppressed.

The final task of a metaphorical theology will be a reforming, transforming one. As metaphorical, such theology can never be simply a baptizing of the tradition, for that would mean giving up the *tension* which is at the heart of metaphor. The classic models of the Christian tradition have been and still are hierarchical, authoritarian ones which have been absolutized. As feminist theologians have become increasingly aware, the orthodox tradition did a thorough job of plumbing the depths of one such model, the patriarchal, as a way of being articulate about God. Feminists have become conscious of the profound structural implications of this model as a form of ecclesiastical, social, political, economic, and personal oppression. The problem does not lie with the model itself of "God the father," for it is a profound metaphor and as true as any religious model available, but it has established a hegemony over the Western religious consciousness which it is the task of metaphorical theology to break. The "outsiders" to the mainline Christian tradition— women, blacks, third world people—are questioning the hierarchical, authoritarian, patriarchal models of Western theology. If Christianity is a universal religion (and not a tribal one for white, middle-class males), such voices are legitimate and necessary. As an example of one such voice, we will look at new religious images and models being suggested by women and we will do so in the spirit of openness to the future and to the unity that lies in the future, a spirit appropriate to a metaphorical theology. As Ursula LeGuin, a fantasy and science-fiction writer, says, truth lies in the imagination.[11] This may be only half a truth, but it is the half we most often forget.

---

[11]Ursula K. LeGuin, *The Language of the Night: Essays on Fantasy and Science Fiction,* ed. Susan Wood (New York: G. P. Putnam's Sons, 1979), p. 159.

Sallie McFague, "Metaphorical Theology"

1.   McFague believes that the "Kingdom of God" is the root-metaphor of Christianity.

     a. True   b. False

2.   McFague maintains that our ancestors were more literalistic about language, people, and things than we are today.

     a. True   b. False

3.   McFague holds that Christian theology is always an interpretation of the _____ in a particular time and place.

4.   For McFague, Jesus is

     a. a metaphor for God.
     b. literally the Son of God.
     c. a parable of God.
     d. literally God incarnate.

5.   Explain why McFague is interested in writing a metaphorical theology. Do you agree? Why or why not?

Plato*

AGAINST POETRY

"And, indeed," I said "I also recognize in many other aspects of this city that we were entirely right in the way we founded it, but I say this particularly when reflecting on poetry."

"What about it?" he said.

"In not admitting at all any part of it that is imitative. For that the imitative, more than anything, must not be admitted looks, in my opinion, even more manifest now that the soul's forms have each been separated out."

"How do you mean?"

"Between us—and don't denounce me to the tragic poets and all the other imitators—all such things seem to maim the thought of those who hear them and do not have knowledge of how they really are as a remedy."

"What are you thinking about in saying that?" he said.

"It must be told," I said. "And yet, a certain friendship for Homer, and shame before him, which has possessed me since childhood, prevents me from speaking. For he seems to have been the first teacher and leader of all these fine tragic things. Still and all, a man must not honored before the truth, but, as I say, it must be told."

"Most certainly," he said.

"Then listen, or rather, answer."

"Ask."

"Could you tell me what imitation is general is? For I myself scarcely comprehend what it wants to be."

"Then I," he said, "of course, will comprehend it."

"That wouldn't be anything strange," I said, "since men with duller vision have often, you know, seen things before those who see more sharply."

"That's so," he said. "But with you present I couldn't be very eager to say whatever might occur to me, so look yourself."

"Do you want us to make our consideration according to our customary procedure, beginning from the following point? For we are, presumably, accustomed to set down some one particular form for each of the particular 'manys' to which we apply the same name. Or don't you understand?"

"I do."

"Then let's now set down any one of the 'manys' you please; for example, if you wish, there are surely many couches and tables."

"Of course."

"But as for *ideas* for these furnishings, there are presumably two, one of couch, one of table."

"Yes."

"Aren't we also accustomed to say that it is in looking to the idea of each implement that one craftsman makes the couches and another the chairs we use, and similarly for other things? For presumably none of the craftsmen fabricates the idea itself. How could he?"

"In no way."

"Well, now, see what you call this craftsman here."

"Which one?"

"He who makes everything that each one of the manual artisans makes separately."

"That's a clever and wonderful man you speak of."

---

*See previous biography. In the following selection taken from *The Republic,* Plato discusses the relation of art to truth and the place of art within society. Plato is highly critical of poetry and advocates a regime of strict censorship of it and all of the arts. Again, the main speaker is Socrates.

EXCERPT from THE REPUBLIC OF PLATO (2ND ED.) by ALLAN BLOOM. Copyright © 1991 by Allan Bloom. Reprinted by permission of BasicBooks, a division of HarperCollins Publishers, Inc.

"Not yet. In an instant you'll say that even more. For this same manual artisan is not only able to make all implements but also makes everything that grows naturally from the earth, and he produces all animals—the others and himself too—and, in addition to that, produces earth and heaven and gods and everything in heaven and everything in Hades under the earth."

"That's quite a wonderful sophist you speak of," he said.

"Are you distrustful?" I said. "And tell me, in your opinion could there be altogether no such craftsman; or in a certain way, could a maker of all these things come into being and in a certain way not? Or aren't you aware that you yourself could in a certain way make all these things?"

"And what," he said, "is that way?"

"It's not hard," I said. "You could fabricate them quickly in many ways and most quickly, of course, if you are willing to take a mirror and carry it around everywhere; quickly you will make the sun and the things in the heaven; quickly, the earth; and quickly, yourself and the other animals and implements and plants and everything else that was just now mentioned."

"Yes," he said, "so that they look like they *are*; however, they surely *are* not in truth."

"Fine," I said, "and you attack the argument at just the right place. For I suppose the painter is also one of these craftsmen, isn't he?"

"Of course he is."

"But I suppose you'll say that he doesn't truly make what he makes. And yet in a certain way the painter too does make a couch, doesn't he?"

"Yes," he said, "he too makes what looks like a couch."

"And what about the couchmaker? Weren't you just saying that he doesn't make the form, which is what we, of course, say a couch is, but a certain couch?"

"Yes," he said, "I was saying that."

"Then, if he doesn't make what *is*, he wouldn't make the being but something that is like the being, but is not being. And if someone were to assert that the work of the producer of couches or of any other manual artisan is completely being, he would run the risk of saying what's not true."

"Yes," he said, "at least that would be the opinion of those who spend their time in arguments of this kind."

"Therefore, let's not be surprised if this too turns out to be a dim thing compared to the truth."

"No, let's not."

"Do you," I said, "want us on the basis of these very things to investigate who this imitator is?"

"If you want to," he said.

"There turn out, then, to be these three kinds of couches: one that *is* in nature, which we would say, I suppose, a god produced. Or who else?"

"No one else, I suppose."

"And then one that the carpenter produced."

"Yes," he said.

"And one that the painter produced, isn't that so?"

"Let it be so."

"Then painter, couchmaker, god—these three preside over three forms of couches."

"Yes, three."

"Now, the god, whether he didn't want to or whether some necessity was laid upon him not to produce more than one couch in nature, made only one, that very one which is a couch. And two or more such weren't naturally engendered by the god nor will they be begotten."

"How's that?" he said.

"Because," I said, "if he should make only two, again one would come to light the form of which they in turn would both possess, and that, and not the two, would be the couch that *is*."

"Right," he said.

"Then, I suppose, the god, knowing this and wanting to be a real maker of a couch that really *is* and not a certain couchmaker of a certain couch, begot it as one by nature."

"So it seems."

"Do you want us to address him as its nature-begetter or something of the kind?"

"That's just at any rate," he said, "since by nature he has made both this and everything else."

"And what about the carpenter? Isn't he a craftman of a couch?"

"Yes."

"And is the painter also a craftsman and maker of such a thing?"

"Not at all."

"But what of a couch will you say he is?"

"In my opinion," he said, "he would most sensibly be addressed as an imitator of that of which these others are craftsmen."

"All right," I said, "do you, then, call the man at the third generation from nature an imitator?"

"Most certainly," he said.

"Therefore this will also apply to the maker of tragedy, if he is an imitator; he is naturally as it were third from a king and the truth, as are all the other imitators."

"Probably."

"Then we have agreed about the imitator. Now tell me this about the painter. In your opinion, does he in each case attempt to imitate the thing itself in nature, or the works of the craftsmen?"

"The works of the craftsmen," he said.

"Such as they are or such as they look? For you still have to make that distinction."

"How do you mean?" he said.

"Like this. Does a couch, if you observe it from the side, or from the front, or from anywhere else, differ at all from itself? Or does it not differ at all but only look different, and similarly with the rest?"

"The latter is so," he said. "It looks different, but isn't."

"Now consider this very point. Toward which is painting directed in each case—toward imitation of the being as it is or toward its looking as it looks? Is it imitation of looks or of truth?"

"Of looks," he said.

"Therefore, imitation is surely far from the truth; and, as it seems, it is due to this that it produces everything—because it lays hold of a certain small part of each thing, and that part is itself only a phantom. For example, the painter, we say, will paint for us a shoemaker, a carpenter, and the other craftsmen, although he doesn't understand the arts of any one of them. But, nevertheless, if he is a good painter, by painting a carpenter and is playing him from far off, he would deceive children and foolish human beings into thinking that it is truly a carpenter."

"Of course."

"But, in any event, I suppose, my friend, that this is what must be understood about all such things: when anyone reports to us about someone, saying that he has encountered a human being who knows all the crafts and everything else that single men severally know, and there is nothing that he does not know more precisely than anyone else, it would have to be replied to such a one that he is an innocent human being and that, as it seems, he has encountered some wizard and imitator and been deceived. Because he himself is unable to put knowledge and lack of knowledge and imitation to the test, that man seemed all-wise to him."

"Very true," he said.

"Then, next," I said, "tragedy and its leader, Homer, must be considered, since we hear from some that these men know all arts and all things human that have to do with virtue and vice, and the divine things too. For it is necessary that the good poet, if he is going to make fair poems about the things his poetry concerns, be in possession of knowledge when he makes his poems or not be able to make them. Hence, we must consider whether those who tell us this have encountered these imitators and been deceived; and whether, therefore, seeing their works, they do not recognize that these works are third from what is and are easy to make for the man who doesn't know the truth—for such a man makes what look like beings but are not. Or, again, is there also something to what they say, and do the good poets really know about the things that, in the opinion of the many, they say well?"

"Most certainly," he said, "that must be tested."

"Do you suppose that if a man were able to make both, the thing to be imitated and the phantom, he would permit himself to be serious about the crafting of the phantoms and set this at the head of his own life as the best thing he has?"

"No, I don't."

"But, I suppose, if he were in truth a knower of these things that he also imitates, he would be far more serious about the deeds than the imitations and would try to leave many fair deeds behind as memorials of himself and would be more eager to be the one who is lauded rather than the one who lauds."

"I suppose so," he said. "For the honor and the benefit coming from the two are hardly equal."

"Well, then, about the other things, let's not demand an account from Homer or any other of the poets by asking, if any one of them was a doctor and not only an imitator of medical speeches, who are the men whom any poet, old or new, is said to have made healthy, as Asclepius did; or what students of medicine he left behind as Asclepius did his offspring. Nor, again, will we ask them about the other arts, but we'll let that go. But about the greatest and fairest things of which Homer attempts to speak—about wars and commands of armies and governances of cities, and about the education of a human being—it is surely just to ask him and inquire, 'Dear Homer, if you are not third from the truth about virtue, a craftsman of a phantom, just the one we defined as an imitator, but are also second and able to recognize what sorts of practices make human beings better or worse in private and in public, tell us which of the cities was better governed thanks to you, as Lacedaemon was thanks to Lycurgus, and many others, both great and small, were thanks to many others? What city gives you the credit for having proved a good lawgiver and benefited them? Italy and Sicily do so for Charondas, and we for Solon; now who does it for you?' Will he have any to mention?"

"I don't suppose so," said Glaucon. "At least, the Homeridae themselves do not tell of any."

"Well, is any war in Homer's time remembered that was well fought with his ruling or advice?"

"None."

"Well, then, as is appropriate to the deeds of a wise man, do they tell of many inventions and devices for the arts or any other activities, just as for Thales the Milesian or Anacharsis the Scythian?"

"Not at all; there's nothing of the sort."

"Well, then, if there is nothing in public, it is told that Homer, while he was himself alive, was in private a leader in education for certain men who cherished him for his intercourse and handed down a certain Homeric way of life to those who came after, just as Pythagoras himself was particularly cherished for this reason, and his successors even now still give Pythagoras' name to a way of life that makes them seem somehow outstanding among men."

"Again," he said, "nothing of the sort is said. For Creophylos, Homer's comrade, would, Socrates, perhaps turn out to be even more ridiculous in his education than in his name, if the things said about Homer are true. For it is told that Homer suffered considerable neglect in his own day, when he was alive."

"Yes, that is told," I said. "But, Glaucon, if Homer were really able to educate human beings and make them better because he is in these things capable not of imitating but of knowing, do you suppose that he wouldn't have made many comrades and been honored and cherished by them? But Protagoras, the Abderite, after all, and Prodicus, the Cean, and very many others are able, by private intercourse, to impress upon the men of their time the assurance that they will be able to govern neither home nor city unless they themselves supervise their education, and they are so intensely loved for this wisdom that their comrades do everything but carry them about on their heads. Then do you suppose that if he were able to help human beings toward virtue, the men in Homer's time would have let him or Hesiod go around being rhapsodes and wouldn't have clung to them rather than to their gold? And wouldn't they have compelled these teachers to stay with them at home; or, if they weren't persuaded, wouldn't they themselves have attended them wherever they went, until they had gained an adequate education?"

"In my opinion, Socrates," he said, "what you say is entirely true."

"Shouldn't we set down all those skilled in making, beginning with Homer, as imitators of phantoms of virtue and of the other subjects of their making? They don't lay hold of the truth; rather, as we were just now saying, the painter will make what seems to be a shoemaker to those who understand as little about shoemaking as he understands, but who observe only colors and shapes."

"Most certainly."

"Then, in this way, I suppose we'll claim the poetic man also uses names and phrases to color each of the arts. He himself doesn't understand; but he imitates in such a way as to seem, to men whose condition is like his own and who observe only speeches, to speak very well. He seems to do so when he speaks using meter, rhythm, and harmony, no matter whether the subject is shoemaking, generalship, or anything else. So great is the charm that these things by nature possess. For when the things of the poets are stripped of the colors of the music and are said alone, they themselves, I suppose you know how they look. For you, surely, have seen."

"I have indeed," he said.

"Don't they," I said, "resemble the faces of the boys who are youthful but not fair in what happens to their looks when the bloom has forsaken them?"

"Exactly," he said.

"Come now, reflect on this. The maker of the phantom, the imitator, we say, understands nothing of what *is* but rather of what looks like it *is*. Isn't that so?"

"Yes."

"Well, then, let's not leave it half-said, but let's see it adequately."

"Speak," he said.

"A painter, we say, will paint reins and a bit."

"Yes."

"But a shoemaker and a smith will make them."

"Certainly."

"Then does the painter understand how the reins and the bit must be? Or does even the maker not understand—the smith and the leathercutter—but only he who knows how to use them, the horseman?"

"Very true."

"And won't we say that it is so for everything?"

"How?"

"For each thing there are these three arts—one that will use, one that will make, one that will imitate."

"Yes."

"Aren't the virtue, beauty, and rightness of each implement, animal, and action related to nothing but the use for which each was made, or grew naturally?"

"That's so."

"It's quite necessary, then, that the man who uses each thing be most experienced and that he report to the maker what are the good or bad points, in actual use, of the instrument he uses. For example, about flutes, a flute player surely reports to the flute-maker which ones would serve him in playing, and he will prescribe how they must be made, and the other will serve him."

"Of course."

"Doesn't the man who knows report about good and bad flutes, and won't the other, trusting him, make them?"

"Yes."

"Therefore the maker of the same implement will have right trust concerning its beauty and its badness from being with the man who knows and from being compelled to listen to the man who knows, while the user will have knowledge."

"Certainly."

"And will the imitator from using the things that he paints have knowledge of whether they are fair and right or not, or right opinion due to the necessity of being with the man who knows and receiving prescriptions of how he must paint?"

"Neither."

"Therefore, with respect to beauty and badness, the imitator will neither know nor opine rightly about what he imitates."

"It doesn't seem so."

"The imitator, in his making, would be a charming chap, so far as wisdom about what he makes goes."

"Hardly."

"But all the same, he will imitate, although he doesn't know in what way each thing is bad or good. But as it seems, whatever looks to be fair to the many who don't know anything—that he will imitate."

"Of course he will."

"Then it looks like we are pretty well agreed on these things: the imitator knows nothing worth mentioning about what he imitates; imitation is a kind of play and not serious; and those who take up tragic poetry in iambics and in epics are all imitators in the highest possible degree."

"Most certainly."

"In the name of Zeus," I said, "then, isn't this imitating concerned with something that is third from the truth? Isn't that so?"

"Yes."

"Now, then, on which one of the parts of the human being does it have the power it has?"

"What sort of part do you mean?"

"This sort. The same magnitude surely doesn't look equal to our sight from near and from far."

"No, it doesn't."

"And the same things look bent and straight when seen in water and out of it, and also both concave and convex, due to the sight's being misled by the colors, and every sort of confusion of this kind is plainly in our soul. And, then, it is because they take advantage of this affection in our nature that shadow painting, and puppeteering, and many other tricks of the kind fall nothing short of wizardry."

"True."

"And haven't measuring, counting, and weighing come to light as most charming helpers in these cases? As a result of them, we are not ruled by a thing's looking bigger or smaller or more or heavier; rather we are ruled by that which has calculated, measured, or, if you please, weighed."

"Undeniably."

"But this surely must be the work of the calculating part in a soul."

"Yes, it is the work of that part."

"And to it, when it has measured and indicates that some things are bigger or smaller than others, or equal, often contrary appearances are presented at the same time about the same things."

"Yes."

"Didn't we say that it is impossible for the same thing to opine contraries at the same time about the same things?"

"And what we said is right."

"Therefore, the part of the soul opining contrary to the measures would not be the same as the part that does so in accordance with the measures."

"No, it wouldn't."

"And, further, the part which trusts measure and calculation would be the best part of the soul."

"Of course."

"Therefore, the part opposed to it would be one of the ordinary things in us."

"Necessarily."

"Well, then, it was this I wanted agreed to when I said that painting and imitation as a whole are far from the truth when they produce their work; and that, moreover, imitation keeps company with the part in us that is far from prudence, and is not comrade and friend for any healthy or true purpose."

"Exactly," he said.

"Therefore, imitation, an ordinary thing having intercourse with what is ordinary, produces ordinary offspring."

"It seems so."

"Does this," I said, "apply only to the imitation connected with the sight or also to that connected with the hearing, which we name poetry?"

"It is likely," he said, "that it applies also to this."

"Well, then," I said, "let's not just trust the likelihood based on painting; but let's now go directly to the very part of thought with which poetry's imitation keeps company and see whether it is ordinary or serious."

"We must;"

"Let's present it in this way. Imitation, we say, imitates human beings performing forced or voluntary actions, and, as a result of the action, supposing themselves to have done well or badly, and in all of this experiencing pain or enjoyment. Was there anything else beyond this?"

"Nothing."

"Then, in all this, is a human being of one mind? Or, just as with respect to the sight there was faction and he had contrary opinions in himself at the same time about the same things, is there also faction in him when it comes to deeds and does he do battle with himself? But I am reminded that there's no need for us to come to an agreement about this now. For in the previous arguments we came to sufficient agreement about all this, asserting that our soul teems with ten thousand such oppositions arising at the same time."

"Rightly," he said.

"Yes, it was right," I said. "But what we then left out, it is now necessary to go through, in my opinion."

"What was that?" he said.

"A decent man," I said, "who gets as his share some such chance as losing a son or something else for which he cares particularly, as we were surely saying then, will bear it more easily than other men."

"Certainly."

"Now let's consider whether he won't be grieved at all, or whether this is impossible, but that he will somehow be sensible in the face of pain."

"The latter," he said, "is closer to the truth."

"Now tell me this about him. Do you suppose he'll fight the pain and hold out against it more when he is seen by his peers, or when he is alone by himself in a deserted place?"

"Surely," he said, "he will fight it far more when seen."

"But when left alone, I suppose, he'll dare to utter many things of which he would be ashamed if someone were to hear, and will do many things he would not choose to have anyone see him do."

"That's so," he said.

"Isn't it argument and law that tell him to hold out, while the suffering itself is what draws him to the pain?"

"True."

"When a contradictory tendency arises in a human being about the same thing at the same time, we say that there are necessarily two things in him."

"Undeniably.

"Isn't the one ready to be persuaded in whatever direction the law leads?"

"How so?"

"The law presumably says that it is finest to keep as quiet as possible in misfortunes and not be irritated, since the good and bad in such things aren't plain, nor does taking it hard get one anywhere, nor are any of the human things worthy of great seriousness; and being in pain is an impediment to the coming of that thing the support of which we need as quickly as possible in these cases."

"What do you mean?" he said.

"Deliberation," I said, "about what has happened. One must accept the fall of the dice and settle one's affairs accordingly—in whatever way argument declares would be best. One must not behave like children who have stumbled and who hold on to the hurt place and spend their time in crying out; rather one must always habituate the soul to turn as quickly as possible to curing and setting aright what has fallen and is sick, doing away with lament by medicine."

"That," he said, "at all events, would be the most correct way for a man to face what chance brings."

"And, we say, the best part is willing to follow this calculation—"

"Plainly."

"—whereas the part that leads to reminiscences of the suffering and to complaints and can't get enough of them, won't we say that it is irrational, idle, and a friend of cowardice?"

"Certainly we'll say that."

"Now then, the irritable disposition affords much and varied limitation, while the prudent and quiet character, which is always early equal to itself, is neither easily imitated nor, when imitated, easily understood, especially by a festive assembly where all sorts of human beings are gathered in a theater.

For the imitation is of a condition that is surely alien to them."

"That's entirely certain."

"Then plainly the imitative poet isn't naturally directed toward any such part of the soul, and his wisdom isn't framed for satisfying if—if he's going to get a good reputation among the many—but rather toward the irritable and various disposition, because it is easily imitated."

"Plainly."

"Therefore it would at last be just for us to seize him and set him beside the painter as his antistrophe. For he is like the painter in making things that are ordinary by the standard of truth; and he is also similar in keeping company with a part of the soul that is on the same level and not with the best part. And thus we should at last be justified in not admitting him into a city that is going to be under good laws, because he awakens this part of the soul and nourishes it, and, by making it strong, destroys the calculating part, just as in a city when someone by making wicked men mighty, turns the city over to them and corrupts the superior ones. Similarly, we shall say the imitative poet produces a bad regime in the soul of each private man by making phantoms that are very far removed from the truth and by gratifying the soul's foolish part, which doesn't distinguish big from little, but believes the same things are at one time big and at another little."

"Most certainly."

"However, we haven't yet made the greatest accusation against imitation. For the fact that it succeeds in maiming even the decent men, except for a certain rare few, is surely quite terrible."

"Certainly, if it does indeed do that."

"Listen and consider. When even the best of us hear Homer or any other of the tragic poets imitating one of the heroes in mourning and making quite an extended speech with lamentation, or, if you like, singing and beating his breast, you know that we enjoy it and that we give ourselves over to following the imitation; suffering along with the hero in all seriousness, we praise as a good poet the man who most puts us in this state."

"I know it, of course."

"But when personal sorrow comes to one of us, you are aware that, on, the contrary, we pride ourselves if we are able to keep quiet and bear up, taking this to be the part of a man and what we then praised to be that of a woman."

"I do recognize it," he said.

"Is that a fine way to praise?" I said. "We see a man whom we would not condescend, but would rather blush, to resemble, and, instead of being disgusted, we enjoy it and praise it?"

"No, by Zeus," he said, "that doesn't seem reasonable."

"Yes, it is," I said, "if you consider it in this way."

"In what way?"

"If you are aware that what is then held down by force in our own misfortunes and has hungered for tears and sufficient lament and satisfaction, since it is by nature such as to desire these things, is that which now gets satisfaction and enjoyment from the poets. What is by nature best in us, because it hasn't been adequately educated by argument or habit, relaxes its guard over this mournful part because it sees another's sufferings, and it isn't shameful for it, if some other man who claims to be good laments out of season, to praise and pity him; rather it believes that it gains the pleasure and wouldn't permit itself to be deprived of it by despising the whole poem. I suppose that only a certain few men are capable of calculating that the enjoyment of other people's sufferings has a necessary effect on one's own. For the pitying part, fed strong on these examples, is not easily held down in one's own sufferings."

"Very true," he said.

"Doesn't the same argument also apply to the laughing part? If there are any jokes that you would be ashamed to make yourself, but that you enjoy very much hearing in comic imitation or in private, and you don't hate them as bad, you do the same as with things that evoke pity. For that in you which, wanting to make jokes, you held down by argument, afraid of the reputation of buffoonery, you now release, and, having made it lusty there, have unawares been carried away in your own things so that you become a comic poet."

"Quite so," he said.

"And as for sex, and spiritedness, too, and for all the desires, pains, and pleasures in the soul that we say follow all our action, poetic imitation produces similar results in us. For it fosters and waters them when they ought to be dried up, and sets them up as rulers in us when they ought to be ruled so that we may become better and happier instead of worse and more wretched."

"I can't say otherwise," he said.

"Then, Glaucon," I said, "when you meet praisers of Homer who say that this poet educated Greece, and that in the management and education of human affairs it is worthwhile to take him up for studying and for living, by arranging one's whole life according to this poet, you must love and embrace them as being men who are the best they can be, and agree that Homer is the most poetic and first of the tragic poets; but you must know that only so much of poetry as is hymns to gods or celebration of good men should be admitted into a city. And if you admit the sweetened muse in lyrics or epics, pleasure and pain will jointly be kings in your city instead of law and that argument which in each instance is best in the opinion of the community."

"Very true," he said.

"Well," I said, "since we brought up the subject of poetry again, let it be our apology that it was then fitting for us to send it away from the city on account of its character. The argument determined us. Let us further say to it, lest it convict us for a certain harshness and rusticity, that there is an old quarrel between philosophy and poetry. For that 'yelping bitch shrieking at her master,' and 'great in the empty eloquence of fools,' 'the mob of overwise men holding sway,' and 'the refined thinkers who are really poor and countless others are signs of this old opposition. All the same, let it be said that, if poetry directed to pleasure and imitation have any argument to give showing that they should be in a city with good laws, we should be delighted to receive them back from exile, since we are aware that we ourselves are charmed by them. But it isn't holy to betray what seems to be the truth. Aren't you, too, my friend, charmed by it, especially when you contemplate it through the medium of Homer?"

"Very much so."

"Isn't it just for it to come back in this way—when it has made an apology in lyrics or some other meter?"

"Most certainly."

"And surely we would also give its protectors, those who aren't poets but lovers of poetry, occasion to speak an argument without meter on its behalf, showing that it's not only pleasant but also beneficial to regimes and human life. And we shall listen benevolently. For surely we shall gain if it should turn out to be not only pleasant but also beneficial."

"We would," he said, "undeniably gain."

"But if not, my dear comrade, just like the men who have once fallen in love with someone, and don't believe the love is beneficial, keep away from it even if they have to do violence to themselves; so we too—due to the inborn love of such poetry we owe to our rearing in these fine regimes—we'll be glad if it turns out that it is best and truest. But as long as it's not able to make its apology, when we listen to it, we'll chant this argument we are making to ourselves as a countercharm, taking care against falling back again into this love, which is childish and belongs to the many. We are, at all events, aware that such poetry mustn't be taken seriously as a serious thing laying hold of truth, but that the man who hears it must be careful, fearing for the regime in himself, and must hold what we have said about poetry."

"Entirely," he said. "I join you in saying that."

"For the contest is great, my dear Glaucon," I said, "greater than it seems—this contest that concerns becoming good or bad—so we mustn't be tempted by honor or money or any ruling office or, for that matter, poetry, into thinking that it's worthwhile to neglect justice and the rest of virtue."

"I join you in saying that," he said, "on the basis of what we have gone through. And I suppose anyone else would too."

Plato, "Against Poetry"

1. According to Plato, imitation is the nature of the fine arts.

    a. True   b. False

2. Plato believed a painting of a couch is second removed from reality.

    a. True   b. False

3. Plato believed that the fine arts should be strictly controlled because they _____

    _____

    _____ .

4. Identify the only fit subject for imitation.

Aristotle*

Poetics

DE POETICA
(*Poetics*)

1   Our subject being Poetry, I propose to speak not only of the art in general but also of its species and their respective capacities; of the structure of plot required for a good poem; of the number and nature of the constituent parts of a poem; and likewise of any other matters in the same line of inquiry. Let us follow the natural order and begin with the primary facts.

Epic poetry and Tragedy, as also Comedy, Dithyrambic poetry, and most flute-playing and lyre-playing, are all, viewed as a whole, modes of imitation: But at the same time they differ from one another in three ways, either by a difference of kind in their means, or by differences in the objects, or in the manner of their imitations.

I. Just as colour and form are used as means by some, who (whether by art or constant practice) imitate and portray many things by their aid, and the voice is used by others; so also in the above-mentioned group of arts, the means with them as a whole are rhythm, language, and harmony—used, however, either singly or in certain combinations. A combination of harmony and rhythm alone is the means in flute-playing and lyre-playing, and any other arts there may be of the same description, e.g. imitative piping. Rhythm alone, without harmony, is the means in the dancer's imitations; for even he, by the rhythms of his attitudes, may represent men's characters, as well as what they do and suffer. There is further an art which imitates by language alone, without harmony, in prose or in verse, and if in verse, either in some one or in a plurality of metres.

This form of imitation is to this day without a name. We have no common name for a mime of Sophron or Xenarchus and a Socratic Conversation; and we should still be without one even if the imitation in the two instances were in trimeters or elegiacs or some other kind of verse—though it is the way with people to tack on 'poet' to the name of a metre, and talk of elegiac-poets and epic-poets, thinking that they call them poets not by reason of the imitative nature of their work, but indiscriminately by reason of the metre they write in. Even if a theory of medicine or physical philosophy be put forth in a metrical form, it is usual to describe the writer in this way; Homer and Empedocles, however, have really nothing in common apart from their metre; so that, if the one is to be called a poet, the other should be termed a physicist rather than a poet. We should be in the same position also, if the imitation in these instances were in all the metres, like the *Centaur* (a rhapsody in a medley of all metres) of Chaeremon; and Chaeremon one has to recognize as a poet. So much, then, as to these arts. There are, lastly, certain other arts, which combine all the means enumerated, rhythm, melody, and verse, e.g. Dithyrambic and Nomic poetry, Tragedy and Comedy; with this difference, however, that the three kinds of means are in some of them all employed together, and in others brought in separately, one after the other. These elements of difference in the above arts I term the means of their imitation.

2   II. The objects the imitator represents are actions, with agents who are necessarily either good men or bad—the diversities of human character

*See previous biography. The following selection is taken from Aristotle's *Poetics* and presents his analysis of the nature and importance of tragedy. Aristotle's sympathetic analysis of tragedy contrasts sharply with Plato's hostility.

being nearly always derivative from this primary distinction, since the line between virtue and vice is one dividing the whole of mankind. It follows, therefore, that the agents represented must be either above our own level of goodness, or beneath it, or just such as we are; in the same way as, with the painters, the personages of Plygnotus are better than we are, those of Pauson worse, and those of Dionysius just like ourselves. It is clear that each of the above-mentioned arts will admit of these differences, and that it will become a separate art by representing objects with this point of difference. Even in dancing, flute-playing, and lyre-laying such diversities are possible; and they are also possible in the nameless art that uses language, prose or verse without harmony, as its means; Homer's personages, for instance, are better than we are; Cleophon's are on our own level; and those of Hegemon of Thasos, the first writer of parodies, and Nicochares, the author of the *Diliad,* are beneath it. The same is true of the Dithyramb and the Nome: the personages may be presented in them with the difference exemplified in the . . . of . . . and Argas, and in the Cyclopses of Timotheus and Philoxenus. This difference it is that distinguishes Tragedy and Comedy also; the one would make its personages worse, and the other better, than the men of the present day.

3   III. A third difference in these arts is in the manner in which each kind of object is represented. Given both the same means and the same kind of object for imitation, one may either (1) speak at one moment in narrative and at another in an assumed character, as Homer does; or (2) one may remain the same throughout, without any such change; or (3) the imitators may represent the whole story dramatically, as though they were actually doing the things described.

As we said at the beginning, therefore, the differences in the imitation of these arts come under three heads, their means, their objects, and their manner.

So that as an imitator Sophocles will be on one side akin to Homer, both portraying good men; and on another to Aristophanes, since both present their personages as acting and doing. This in fact, according to some, is the reason for plays being termed dramas, because in a play the personages act the story. Hence too both Tragedy and Comedy are claimed by the Dorians as their discoveries; Comedy by the Megarians—by those in Greece as having arisen when Megara became a democracy, and by the Sicilian Megarians on the ground that the poetry

Epicharmus was of their country, and a good deal earlier than Chionides and Magnes; even Tragedy also is claimed by certain of the Peloponnesian Dorians. In support of this claim they point to the words 'comedy' and 'drama'. Their word for the outlying hamlets, they say, is *comae,* whereas Athenians call them *demes*—thus assuming that comedians got the name not from their *comoe* or revels, but their strolling from hamlet to hamlet, lack of appreciation keeping them out of the city. Their word also for 'to act', they say, is *dran,* whereas Athenians use *prattein.*

So much, then, as to the number and nature of the points of difference in the imitation of these arts.

4   It is clear that the general origin of poetry was due to two causes, each of them part of human nature. Imitation is natural to man from childhood, one of his advantages over the lower animals being this, that he is the most imitative creature in the world, and learns at first by imitation. And it is also natural for all to delight in works of imitation. The truth of this second point is shown by experience: though the objects themselves may be painful to see, we delight to view the most realistic representations of them in art, the forms for example of the lowest animals and of dead bodies. The explanation is to be found in a further fact: to be learning something is the greatest of pleasures not only to the philosopher but also the rest of mankind, however small their capacity for it; the reason of the delight in seeing the picture is that one is at the same time learning—gathering the meaning of things, e.g. that the man there is so-and-so; for if one has not seen the thing before, one's pleasure will not be in the picture as an imitation of it, but will be due to the execution or colouring or some similar cause. Imitation then, being natural to us—as also the sense of harmony and rhythm, the metres being obviously species of rhythms—it was through their original aptitude, and by a series of improvements for the most part gradual on their first efforts, that they created poetry out of their improvisations.

Poetry, however, soon broke up into two kinds according to the differences of character in the individual poets; for the graver among them would represent noble actions, and those of noble personages; and the meaner sort the actions of the ignoble. The latter class produced invectives at first, just as others did hymns and panegyrics. We know of no such poem by any of the pre-Homeric poets, though there were probably many such writers among them; instances, however, may be found from

Homer downwards, e.g. his *Margites,* and the similar poems of others. In this poetry of invective its natural fitness brought an iambic metre into use; hence our present term 'iambic', because it was the metre of their 'iambs' or invectives against one another. The result was that the old poets became some of them writers of heroic and others of iambic verse. Homer's position, however, is peculiar: just as he was in the serious style the poet of poets, standing alone not only through the literary excellence, but also through the dramatic character of his imitations, so too he was the first to outline for us the general forms of Comedy by producing not a dramatic invective, but a dramatic picture of the Ridiculous; his *Margites* in fact stands in the same relation to our comedies as the *Iliad* and *Odyssey* to our tragedies. As soon, however, as Tragedy and Comedy appeared in the field, those naturally drawn to the one line of poetry became writers of comedies instead of iambs, and those naturally drawn to the other, writers of tragedies instead of epics, because these new modes of art were grander and of more esteem than the old.

If it be asked whether Tragedy is now all that it need be in its formative elements, to consider that, and decide it theoretically and in relation to the theatres, is a matter for another inquiry.

It certainly began in improvisations—as did also Comedy; the one originating with the authors of the Dithyramb, the other with those of the phallic songs, which still survive as institutions in many of our cities. And its advance after that was little by little, through their improving on whatever they had before them at each stage. It was in fact only after a long series of changes that the movement of Tragedy stopped on its attaining to its natural form. (1) The number of actors was first increased to two by Aeschylus, who curtailed the business of the Chorus, and made the dialogue, or spoken portion, take the leading part in the play. (2) A third actor and scenery were due to Sophocles. (3) Tragedy acquired also its magnitude. Discarding short stories and a ludicrous diction, through its passing out of its satyric stage, it assumed, though only at a late point in its progress, a tone of dignity; and its metre changed then from trochaic to iambic. The reason for their original use of the trochaic tetrameter was that their poetry was satyric and more connected with dancing than it now is. As soon, however, as a spoken part came in, nature herself found the appropriate metre. The iambic, we know, is the most

speakable of metres, as is shown by the fact that we very often fall into it in conversation, whereas we rarely talk hexameters, and only when we depart from the speaking tone of voice. (4) Another change was a plurality of episodes or acts. As for the remaining matters, the superadded embellishments and the account of their introduction, these must be taken as said, as it would probably be a long piece of work to go through the details.

5   As for Comedy, it is (as has been observed[1]) an imitation of men worse than the average; worse, however, not as regards any and every sort of fault, but only as regards one particular kind, the Ridiculous, which is a species of the Ugly. The Ridiculous may be defined as a mistake or deformity not productive of pain or harm to others; the mask, for instance, that excites laughter, is something ugly and distorted without causing pain.

Though the successive changes in Tragedy and their authors are not unknown, we cannot say the same of Comedy; its early stages passed unnoticed, because it was not as yet taken up in a serious way. It was only at a late point in its progress that a chorus of comedians was officially granted by the archon; they used to be mere volunteers. It had also already certain definite forms at the time when the record of those termed comic poets begins. Who it was who supplied it with masks, or prologues, or a plurality of actors and the like, has remained unknown. The invented Fable, or Plot, however, originated in Sicily with Epicharmus and Phormis; of Athenian poets Crates was the first to drop the Comedy of invective and frame stories of a general and non-personal nature, in other words, Fables or Plots.

Epic poetry, then, has been seen to agree with Tragedy to this extent, that of being an imitation of serious subjects in a grand kind of verse. It differs from it, however, (1) in that it is in one kind of verse and in narrative form; and (2) in its length—which is due to its action having no fixed limit of time, whereas Tragedy endeavours to keep as far as possible within a single circuit of the sun, or something near that. This, I say, is another point of difference between them, though at first the practice in this respect was just the same in tragedies as in epic poems. They differ also (3) in their constituents, some being common to both and others peculiar to Tragedy—hence a judge of good and bad in Tragedy is a judge of that in epic poetry also. All the parts of

---

[1]1448[a] 17: 1448[b] 37.

an epic are included in Tragedy; but those of Tragedy are not all of them to be found in the epic.

6   Reserving hexameter poetry and Comedy for consideration hereafter,[2] let us proceed now to the discussion of Tragedy; before doing so, however, we must gather up the definition resulting from what has been said. A tragedy, then, is the imitation of an action that is serious and also, as having magnitude, complete in itself; in language with pleasurable accessories, each kind brought in separately in the parts of the work; in a dramatic, not in a narrative form; with incidents arousing pity and fear, wherewith to accomplish its catharsis of such emotions. Here by 'language with pleasurable accessories' I mean that with rhythm and harmony or song superadded; and by 'the kinds separately' I mean that some portions are worked out with verse only, and others in turn with song.

I. As they act the stories, it follows that in the first place the Spectacle (or stage-appearance of the actors) must be some part of the whole; and in the second Melody and Diction, these two being the means of their imitation. Here by 'Diction' I mean merely this, the composition of the verses; and by 'Melody', what is too completely understood to require explanation. But further: the subject represented also is an action; and the action involves agents, who must necessarily have their distinctive qualities both of character and thought, since it is from these that we ascribe certain qualities to their actions. There are in the natural order of things, therefore, two causes, Thought and Character, of their actions, and consequently of their success or failure in their lives. Now the action (that which was done) is represented in the play by the Fable or Plot. The Fable, in our present sense of the term, is simply this, the combination of the incidents, or things done in the story; whereas Character is what makes us ascribe certain moral qualities to the agents; and Thought is shown in all they say when proving a particular point or, it may be, enunciating a general truth. There are six parts consequently of every tragedy, as a whole (that is) of such or such quality, viz. a Fable or Plot, Characters, Diction, Thought, Spectacle, and Melody; two of them arising from the means, one from the manner, and three from the objects of the dramatic imitation; and there is nothing else besides these six. Of these, its formative elements, then, not a few of the dramatists have made due use, as every play, one may say, admits of Spectacle, Character, Fable, Diction, Melody, and Thought.

II. The most important of the six is the combination of the incidents of the story. Tragedy is essentially an imitation not of persons but of action and life, of happiness and misery. All human happiness or misery takes the form of action; the end for which we live is a certain kind of activity, not a quality. Character gives us qualities, but it is in our actions—what we do—that we are happy or the reverse. In a play accordingly they do not act in order to portray the Characters; they include the Characters for the sake of the action. So that it is the action in it, i.e. its Fable or Plot, that is the end and purpose of the tragedy; and the end is everywhere the chief thing. Besides this, a tragedy is impossible without action, but there may be one without Character. The tragedies of most of the moderns are characterless—a defect common among poets of all kinds, and with its counterpart in painting in Zeuxis as compared with Polygnotus; for whereas the latter is strong in character, the work of Zeuxis is devoid of it. And again: one may string together a series of characteristic speeches of the utmost finish as regards Diction and Thought, and yet fail to produce the true tragic effect; but one will have much better success with a tragedy which, however inferior in these respects, has a Plot, a combination of incidents, in it. And again: the most powerful elements of attraction in Tragedy, the Peripeties and Discoveries, are parts of the Plot. A further proof is in the fact that beginners succeed earlier with the Diction and Characters than with the construction of a story; and the same maybe said of nearly all the early dramatists. We maintain, therefore, that the first essential, the life and soul, so to speak, of Tragedy is the Plot; and that the Characters come second—compare the parallel in painting, where the most beautiful colours laid on without order will not give one the same pleasure as a simple black-and-white sketch of a portrait. We maintain that Tragedy is primarily an imitation of action, and that it is mainly for the sake of the action that it imitates the personal agents. Third comes the element of Thought, i.e. the power of saying whatever can be said, or what is appropriate to the occasion. This is what, in the speeches in Tragedy, falls under the arts of Politics and Rhetoric; for the older poets make their personages discourse like statesmen, and the modern like rhetoricians. One must not confuse it with Character. Character in a play is that which

---

[2]For hexameter poetry cf. chap. 23 f.; comedy was treated of in the lost Second Book.

reveals the moral purpose of the agents, i.e. the sort of thing they seek or avoid, where that is not obvious—hence there is no room for Character in a speech on a purely indifferent subject. Thought, on the other hand, is shown in all they say when proving or disproving some particular point, or enunciating some universal proposition. Fourth among the literary elements is the Diction of the personages, i.e., as before explained,[3] the expression of their thoughts in words, which is practically the same thing with verse as with prose. As for the two remaining parts, the Melody is the greatest of the pleasurable accessories of Tragedy. The Spectacle, though an attraction, is the least artistic of all the parts, and has least to do with the art of poetry. The tragic effect is quite possible without a public performance and actors; and besides, the getting-up of the Spectacle is more a matter for the costumier than the poet.

7 Having thus distinguished the parts, let us now consider the proper construction of the Fable or Plot, as that is at once the first and the most important thing in Tragedy. We have laid it down that a tragedy is an imitation of an action that is complete in itself, as a whole of some magnitude; for a whole may be of no magnitude to speak of. Now a whole is that which has beginning, middle, and end. A beginning is that which is not itself necessarily after anything else, and which as naturally something else after it; an end is that which is naturally after something itself, either as its necessary or usual consequent, and with nothing else after it; and a middle, that which is by nature after one thing and has also another after it. A well-constructed Plot, therefore, cannot either begin or end at any point one likes; beginning and end in it must be of the forms just described. Again: to be beautiful, a living creature, and every whole made up of parts, must not only present a certain order in its arragement of parts, but also be of a certain definite magnitude. Beauty is a matter of size and order, and therefore impossible either (1) in a very minute creature, since our perception becomes indistinct as it approaches instantaneity; or (2) in a creature of vast size—one, say, 1,000 miles long—as in that case, instead of the object being seen all at once, the unity and wholeness of it is lost to the beholder. Just in the same way, then, as a beautiful whole made up of parts, or a beautiful living creature, must be of some size, but a size to be taken in by the eye, so a story

or Plot must be of some length, but of a length to be taken in by the memory. As for the limit of its length, so far as that is relative to public performances and spectators, it does not fall within the theory of poetry. If they had to perform a hundred tragedies, they would be timed by water-clocks, as they are said to have been at one period. The limit, however, set by the actual nature of the thing is this: the longer the story, consistently with its being comprehensible as a whole, the finer it is by reason of its magnitude. As a rough general formula, 'a length which allows of the hero passing by a series of probable or necessary stages from misfortune to happiness, or from happiness to misfortune', may suffice as a limit for the magnitude of the story.

8 The Unity of a Plot does not consist, as some suppose, in its having one man as its subject. An infinity of things befall that one man, some of which it is impossible to reduce to unity; and in like manner there are many actions of one man which cannot be made to form one action. One sees, therefore, the mistake of all the poets who have written a *Heracleid,* a *Theseid,* or similar poems; they suppose that, because Heracles was one man, the story also of Heracles must be one story. Homer, however, evidently understood this point quite well, whether by art or instinct, just in the same way as he excels the rest in every other respect. In writing an *Odyssey,* he did not make the poem cover all that ever befell his hero—it befell him, for instance, to get wounded on Parnassus and also to feign madness at the time of the call to arms, but the two incidents had no necessary or probable connexion with one another—instead of doing that, he took as the subject of the *Odyssey,* as also of the *Illiad,* an action with a Unity of the kind we are describing. The truth is that, just as in the other imitative arts one imitation is always of one thing, so in poetry the story, as an imitation of action, must represent one action, a complete whole, with its several incidents so closely connected that the transposal or withdrawal of any one of them will disjoin and dislocate the whole. For that which makes no perceptible difference by its presence or absence is no real part of the whole.

9 From what we have said it will be seen that the poet's function is to describe, not the thing that has happened, but a kind of thing that might happen, i.e. what is possible as being probable or necessary.

---

[3] 1449[b] 34.

The distinction between historian and poet is not in the one writing prose and the other verse—you might put the work of Herodotus into verse, and it would still be a species of history; it consists really in this, that the one describes the thing that has been, and the other a kind of thing that might be. Hence poetry is something more philosophic and of graver import than history, since its statements are of the nature rather of universals, whereas those of history are singulars. By a universal statement I mean one as to what such or such a kind of man will probably or necessarily say or do—which is the aim of poetry, though it affixes proper names to the characters; by a singular statement, one as to what, say, Alcibiades did or had done to him. In Comedy this has become clear by this time; it is only when their plot is already made up of probable incidents that they give it a basis of proper names, choosing for the purpose any names that may occur to them, instead of writing like the old iambic poets about particular persons. In Tragedy, however, they still adhere to the historic names; and for this reason: what convinces is the possible; now whereas we are not yet sure as to the possibility of that which has not happened, that which has happened is manifestly possible, else it would not have come to pass. Nevertheless even in Tragedy there are some plays with but one or two known names in them, the rest being inventions; and there are some without a single known name, e.g. Agathon's *Antheius,* in which both incidents and names are of the poet's invention; and it is no less delightful on that account. So that one must not aim at a rigid adherence to the traditional stories on which tragedies are based. It would be absurd, in fact, to do so, as even the known stories are only known to a few, though they are a delight none the less to all.

It is evident from the above that the poet must be more the poet of his stories or Plots than of his verses, inasmuch as he is a poet by virtue of the imitative element in his work, and it is actions that he imitates. And if he should come to take a subject from actual history, he is none the less a poet for that; since some historic occurrences may very well be in the probable and possible order of things; and it is in that aspect of them that he is their poet.

Of simple Plots and actions the episodic are the worst. I call a Plot episodic when there is neither probability nor necessity in the sequence of its episodes. Actions of this sort bad poets construct through their own fault, and good ones on account of the players. His work being for public performance, a good poet often stretches out a plot beyond its capabilities, and is thus obliged to twist the sequence of incident.

Tragedy, however, is an imitation not only of a complete action, but also of incidents arousing pity and fear. Such incidents have the very greatest effect on the mind when they occur unexpectedly and at the same time in consequence of one another; there is more of the marvellous in them then than if they happened of themselves or by mere chance. Even matters of chance seem most marvellous if there is an appearance of design as it were in them; as for instance the statue of Mitys at Argos killed the author of Mitys' death by falling down on him when a looker-on at a public spectacle; for incidents like that we think to be not without a meaning. A Plot, therefore, of this sort is necessarily finer than others.

10 Plots are either simple or complex, since the actions they represent are naturally of this twofold description. The action, proceeding in the way defined, as one continuous whole, I call simple, when the change in the hero's fortunes takes place without Peripety or Discovery; and complex, when it involves one or the other, or both. These should each of them arise out of the structure of the Plot itself, so as to be the consequence, necessary or probably, of the antecedents. There is a great difference between a thing happening *propter hoc* and *post hoc.*

Aristotle, Poetics

1.   Poetry and drama are forms of imitation.

      a. True   b. False

2.   Comedy aims at representing men as better than in actual life; tragedy as worse than in actual life.

      a. True   b. False

3.   Poetry and drama differ according to

      a. medium of imitation.
      b. object of imitation.
      c. manner of imitation.
      d. all of the above.

4.   Why does Aristotle think that poetry is a more philosophical and a higher thing than history?

William Wordsworth*

PREFACE TO LYRICAL BALLADS

Several of my Friends are anxious for the success of these Poems, from a belief, that, if the views, with which they were composed were indeed realised, a class of Poetry would be produced, well adapted to interest mankind permanently, and not unimportant in the quality, and in the multiplicity of its moral relations: and on this account they have advised me to prefix a systematic defence of the theory upon which the Poems were written. But I was unwilling to undertake the task, knowing that on this occasion the Reader would look coldly upon my arguments, since I might be suspected of having been principally influenced by the selfish and foolish hope of *reasoning* him into an approbation of these particular Poems: and I was still more unwilling to undertake the task, because, adequately to display the opinions, and fully to enforce the arguments, would require a space wholly disproportionate to a preface. For, to treat the subject with the clearness and coherence of which it is susceptible, it would be necessary to give a full account of the present state of the public taste in this country, and to determine how far this taste is healthy or depraved; which, again, could not be determined, without pointing out in what manner language and the human mind act and re-act on each other, and without retracing and revolutions, not of literature alone, but likewise of society itself. I have therefore altogether declined to enter regularly upon this defence; yet I am sensible, that there would be something like impropriety in abruptly obtruding upon the Public, without a few words of introduction, Poems so materially different from those upon which general approbation is at present bestowed.

It is supposed, that by the act of writing in verse an Author makes a formal engagement that he will gratify certain known habits of association; that he not only thus apprises the Reader that certain classes of ideas and expressions will be found in his book, but that others will be carefully excluded. This exponent or symbol held forth by metrical language must in different eras of literature have excited very different expectations: for example, in the age of Catullus, Terence, and Lucretius, and that of Statius or Claudian; and in our own country, in the age of Shakspeare and Beaumont and Fletcher, and that of Donne and Cowley, or Dryden, or Pope. I will not take upon me to determine the exact import of the promise which, by the act of writing verse, an Author, in the present day makes to his reader: but it will undoubtedly appear to many persons that I have not fulfilled the terms of an engagement thus voluntarily contracted. They who have been accustomed to the gaudiness and inane phraseology of many modern writers, if they persist in reading this book to its conclusion, will, no doubt, frequently have to struggle with feelings of strangeness and awkwardness: they will look round for poetry, and will be induced to inquire by what species of courtesy these attempts can be permitted to assume that title. I hope therefore the reader will not censure me for attempting to state what I have proposed to myself to perform; and also (as far as the limits of a preface will permit) to explain some of the chief reasons which have determined me in the choice of my purpose: that at least he may be spared any unpleasant feeling of disappointment, and that I myself may be protected from one of the

---

*William Wordsworth (1770–1850) was a leading poet of Romanticism in England. Many of his works are autobiographical and devoted to his perceptions of nature, including *Lyrical Ballads,* of which the following selection is the preface to the second edition (1800). He was particularly concerned about the relation between personal perception, objective truth, and aesthetic value.

most dishonourable accusations which can be brought against an Author; namely, that of an indolence which prevents him from endeavoring to ascertain what is his duty, or, when his duty is ascertained, prevents him from performing it.

The principal object, then, proposed in these Poems was to choose incidents and situations from common life, and to relate and describe them, throughout, as far as was possible in a selection of language really used by men, and, at the same time, to throw over them a certain colouring of imagination, whereby ordinary things should be presented to the mind in an unusual aspect; and, further, and above all, to make these incidents and situations interesting by tracing in them, truly though not ostentatiously, the primary laws of our nature: chiefly, as far as regards the manner in which we associate ideas in a state of excitement. Humble and rustic life was generally chosen, because, in that condition, the essential passions of the heart find a better soil in which they can attain their maturity, are less under restraint, and speak a plainer and more emphatic language; because in that condition of life our elementary feelings co-exist in a state of greater simplicity, and, consequently, may be more accurately contemplated, and more forcibly communicated; because the manners of rural life germinate from those elementary feelings, and, from the necessary character of rural occupations, are more easily comprehended, and are more durable; and, lastly, because in that condition the passions of men are incorporated with the beautiful and permanent forms of nature. The language, too, of these mean has been adopted (purified indeed from what appear to be its real defects, from all lasting and rational causes of dislike or disgust) because such men hourly communicate with the best objects from which the best part of language is originally derived; and because, from their rank in society and the sameness and narrow circle of their intercourse, being less under the influence of social vanity, they convey their feelings and notions in simple and unelaborated expressions. Accordingly, such a language, arising out of repeated experience and regular feelings, is a more permanent, and a far more philosophical language, than that which is frequently substituted for it by Poets, who think that they are conferring honour upon themselves and their art, in proportion as they separate themselves from the sympathies of men, and indulge in arbitrary and capricious habits of expression, in order to furnish food for fickle tastes, and fickle appetites, of their own creation.[1]

I cannot, however, be insensible to the present outcry against the triviality and meanness, both of thought and language, which some of my contemporaries have occasionally introduced into their metrical compositions; and I acknowledge that this defect, where it exists, is more dishonourable to the Writer's own character than false refinement or arbitrary innovation, though I should contend at the same time, that is far less pernicious in the sum of its consequences. From such verses the Poems in these volumes will be found distinguished at least by one mark of difference, that each of them has a worthy *purpose*. Not that I always began to write with a distinct purpose formally conceived; but habits of meditation have, I trust, so prompted and regulated my feelings, that my descriptions of such objects as strongly excite those feelings, will be found to carry along with them a *purpose*. If this opinion be erroneous, I can have little right to the name of a Poet. For all good poetry is the spontaneous overflow of powerful feelings: and though this be true, Poems to which any value can be attached were never produced on any variety of subjects but by a man who, being possessed of more than usual organic sensibility, had also thought long and deeply. For our continued influxes of feeling are modified and directed by our thoughts, which are indeed the representatives of all our past feelings; and, as by contemplating the relation of these general representatives to each other, we discover what is really important to men, so, by the repetition and continuance of this act, our feelings will be connected with important subjects, till at length, if we be originally possessed of much sensibility, such habits of mind will be produced, that, by obeying blindly and mechanically the impulses of those habits, we shall describe objects, and utter sentiments, of such a nature, and in such connection with each other, that the understanding of the Reader must necessarily be in some degree enlightened, and his affections strengthened and purified.

It has been said that each of these poems has a purpose. Another circumstance must be mentioned which distinguishes these Poems from the popular Poetry of the day; it is this, that the feeling

---

[1]It is worth while here to observe, that the affecting parts of Chaucer are amost always expressed in language pure and universally intelligible even to this day.

therein developed gives importance to the action and situation, and not the action and situation to the feeling.

A sense of false modesty shall not prevent me from asserting, that the Reader's attention is pointed to this mark of distinction, far less for the sake of these particular Poems than from the general importance of the subject. The subject is indeed important! For the human mind is capable of being excited without the application of gross and violent stimulants; and he must have a very faint perception of its beauty and dignity who does not know this, and who does not further know, that one being is elevated above another, in proportion as he possesses this capability. It has therefore appeared to me, that to endeavour to produce or enlarge this capability is one of the best services in which, at any period, a Writer can be engaged; but this service, excellent at all times, is especially so at the present day. For a multitude of causes, unknown to former times, are now acting with a combined force to blunt the discriminating powers of the mind, and, unfitting it for all voluntary exertion, to reduce it to a state of almost savage torpor. The most effective of these causes are the great national events which are daily taking place, and the increasing accumulation of men in cities, where the uniformity of their occupations produces a craving for extraordinary incident, which the rapid communication of intelligence hourly gratifies. To this tendency of life and manners the literature and theatrical exhibitions of the country have conformed themselves. The invaluable works of our elder writers, I had almost said the works of Shakspeare and Milton, are driven into neglect by frantic novels, sickly and stupid German Tragedies, and deluges of idle and extravagant stories in verse.—When I think upon this degrading thirst after outrageous stimulation, I am almost ashamed to have spoken of the feeble endeavour made in these volumes to counteract it; and, reflecting upon the magnitude of the general evil, I should be oppressed with no dishonourable melancholy, had I not a deep impression of certain inherent and indestructible qualities of the human mind, and likewise of certain powers in the great and permanent objects that act upon it, which are equally inherent and indestructible; and were there not added to this impression a belief, that the time is approaching when the evil will be systematically opposed, by men of greater powers, and with far more distinguished success.

Having dwelt thus long on the subjects and aims of these Poems, I shall request the Reader's permission to apprise him of a few circumstances related to their *style,* in order, among other reasons, that he may not censure me for not having performed what I never attempted. The Reader will find that personifications of abstract ideas rarely occur in these volumes; and are utterly rejected, as an ordinary device to elevate the style, and raise it above prose. My purpose was to imitate, and, as far as is possible, to adopt the very language of men; and assuredly such personifications do not make any natural or regular part of that language. They are, indeed, a figure of speech occasionally prompted by passion, and I have made use of them as such; but have endeavoured utterly to reject them as a mechanical device of style, or as a family language which Writers in metre seem to lay claim to by prescription. I have wished to keep the Reader in the company of flesh and blood, persuaded that by so doing I shall interest him. Others who pursue a different track will interest him likewise; I do not interfere with their claim, but wish to prefer a claim of my own. There will also be found in these volumes little of what is usually called poetic diction; as much pains has been taken to avoid it as is ordinarily taken to produce it; this has been done for the reason already alleged, to bring my language near to the language of men; and further, because the pleasure which I have proposed to myself to impart, is of a kind very different from that which is supposed by many persons to be the proper object of poetry. Without being culpably particular, I do not know how to give my Reader a more exact notion of the style in which it was my wish and intention to write, than by informing him that I have at all times endeavoured to look steadily at my subject; consequently, there is I hope in these Poems little falsehood of description, and my ideas are expressed in language fitted to their respective importance. Something must have been gained by this practice, as it is friendly to one property of all good poetry, namely, good sense: but it has necessarily cut me off from a large portion of phrases and figures of speech which from father to son have long been regarded as the common inheritance of Poets. I have also thought it expedient to restrict myself still further, having abstained from the use of many expressions, in themselves proper and beautiful, but which have been foolishly repeated by bad Poets, till such feelings of disgust are connected with them as it is scarcely possible by any art of association to overpower.

If in a poem there should be found a series of lines, or even a single line, in which the language, though naturally arranged, and according to the strict laws of metre, does not differ from that of prose, there is a numerous class of critics, who, when they stumble upon these prosaisms, as they call them, imagine that they have made a notable discover, and exult over the Poet as over a man ignorant of his own profession. Now these men would establish a canon of criticism which the Reader will conclude he must utterly reject, if he wishes to be pleased with these volumes. And it would be a most easy task to prove to him, that not only the language of a large portion of every good poem, even of the most elevated character, must necessarily, except with reference to the metre, in nor respect differ from that of good prose, but likewise that some of the most interesting parts of the best poems will be found to be strictly the language of prose when prose is well written. The truth of this assertion might be demonstrated by innumerable passages from almost all the poetical writings, even of Milton himself. To illustrate the subject in a general manner, I will here adduce a short composition of Gray, who was at the head of those who, by their reasonings, have attempted to widen the space of separation betwixt Prose and Metrical composition, and was more than any other man curiously elaborate in the structure of his own poetic diction.

> 'In vain to me the smiling mornings shine,
> And reddening Phoebus lifts his golden fire:
> The birds in vain their amorous descant join,
> Or cheerful fields resume their green attire.
> These ears, alas! For other notes repine;
> *A different object do these eyes require;*
> *My lonely anguish melts no heart but mine;*
> *And in my breast the imperfect joys expire;*
> Yet morning smiles and busy race to cheer,
> And new-born pleasure brings to happier
>   men;
> The fields to all their wonted tribute bear;
> To warm their little loves the birds complain.
> *I fruitless mourn to him that cannot hear,*
> *And weep the more because I weep in vain.'*

It will easily be perceived, that the only part of this Sonnet which is of any value is the lines printed in Italics; it is equally obvious, that, except in the rhyme, and in the use of the single word 'fruitless'

for fruitlessly, which is so far a defect, the language of these lines does in no respect differ from that of prose.

By the foregoing quotation it has been shown that the language of Prose may yet be well adapted to Poetry; and it was previously asserted, that a large portion of the language in every good poem can in no respect differ from that of good Prose. We will go further. It may be safely affirmed, that there neither is, nor can be, any *essential* difference between the language of prose and metrical composition. We are fond of tracing the resemblance between Poetry and Painting, and, accordingly, we call them Sisters: but where shall we find bonds of connection sufficiently strict to typify the affinity betwixt metrical and prose compositions? They both speak by and to the same organs; the bodies in which both of them are clothed may be said to be of the same substance, their affections are kindred, and almost identical, not necessarily differing even in degree; Poetry[2] sheds no tears 'such as Angels weep,' but natural and human tears; she can boast of no celestial ichor that distinguishes her vital juices from those of prose; the same human blood circulates through the veins of them both.

If it be affirmed that rhyme and metrical arrangement of themselves constitute a distinction which overturns what has been said on the strict affinity of metrical language with that of prose, and paves the way for other artificial distinctions which the mind voluntarily admits, I answer that the language of such Poetry as is here recommended is, as far as is possible, a selection of the language really spoken by men; that this selection, wherever it is made with true taste and feeling, will of itself form a distinction far greater than would at first be imagined, and will entirely separate the composition from the vulgarity and meanness of ordinary life; and, if metre be superadded thereto, I believe that a dissimilitude will be produced altogether sufficient for the gratification of a rational mind. What other distinction would we have? Whence is it to come? And where is it to exist? Not, surely, where the Poet speaks through the mouths of his characters: it cannot be necessary here, either for elevation of style, or any of its supposed ornaments: for, if the

---

[2]I here use the word 'Poetry' (though against my own judgment) as opposed to the word Prose, and synonymous with metrical composition. But much confusion has been introduced into criticism by this contradistinction of Poetry and Prose, instead of the more philosophical one of Poetry and Matter of Fact, or Science. The only strict antithesis to Prose is Metre; nor is this, in truth, a *strict* antithesis, because lines and passages of metre so naturally occur in writing prose, that it would be scarcely possible to avoid them, even were it desirable.

Poet's subject be judiciously chosen, it will naturally, and upon fit occasion, lead him to passions the language of which, if selected truly and judiciously, must necessarily be dignified and variegated, and alive with metaphors and figures. I forbear to speak of an incongruity which would shock the intelligent Reader, should the Poet interweave any foreign splendour of his own with that which the passion naturally suggests: it is sufficient to say that such addition is unnecessary. And, surely, it is more probable that those passages, which with propriety abound with metaphors and figures, will have their due effect, if, upon other occasions where the passions are of a milder character, the style also be subdued and temperate.

But, as the pleasure which I hope to give by the Poems now presented to the Reader must depend entirely on just notions upon this subject, and, as it is in itself of high importance to our taste and moral feelings, I cannot content myself with these detached remarks. And if, in what I am about to say, it shall appear to some that my labour is unnecessary, and that I am like a man fighting a battle without enemies, such persons may be reminded, that, whatever be the language outwardly holden by men, a practical faith in the opinions which I am wishing to establish is almost unknown. If my conclusions are admitted, and carried as far as they must be carried if admitted at all, our judgments concerning the works of the greatest Poets both ancient and modern will be far different from what they are at present, both when we praise, and when we censure: and our moral feelings influencing and influenced by these judgments will, I believe, be corrected and purified.

Taking up the subject, then, upon general grounds, let me ask, what is meant by the word Poet? What is a Poet? To whom does he address himself? And what language is to be expected from him?—He is a man speaking to men: a man, it is true, endowed with more lively sensibility, more enthusiasm and tenderness, who has a greater knowledge of human nature, and a more comprehensive soul, than are supposed to be common among mankind; a man pleased with his own passions and volitions, and who rejoices more than other men in the spirit of life that is in him; delighting to contemplate similar volitions and passions as manifested in the goings-on of the Universe, and habitually impelled to create them where he does not find them. To these qualities he has added a disposition to be affected more than other men by absent things as if they were present; an ability of conjuring up in himself passions, which are indeed far from being the same as those produced by real events, yet (especially in those parts of the general sympathy which are pleasing and delightful) do more nearly resemble the passions produced by real events, than anything which, from the motions of their own minds merely, other men are accustomed to feel in themselves:—whence, and from practice, he has acquired a greater readiness and power in expressing what he thinks and feels, and especially those thoughts and feelings which, by his own choice, or from the structure of his own mind, arise in him without immediate external excitement.

But whatever portion of this faculty we may suppose even the greatest Poet to possess, there cannot be a doubt that the language which it will suggest to him, must often, in liveliness and truth, fall short of that which is uttered by men in real life, under the actual pressure of those passions, certain shadows of which the Poet thus produces, or feels to be produced, in himself.

However exalted a notion we would wish to cherish of the character of a Poet, it is obvious, that while he describes and imitates passions, his employment is in some degree mechanical, compared with the freedom and power of real and substantial action and suffering. So that it will be the wish of the Poet to bring his feelings near to those of the persons whose feelings he describes, nay, for short spaces of time, perhaps, to let himself slip into an entire delusion, and even confound and identify his own feelings with theirs; modifying only the language which is thus suggested to him by a consideration that he describes for a particular purpose, that of giving pleasure. Here, then, he will apply the principle of selection which has been already insisted upon. He will depend upon this for removing what would otherwise be painful or disgusting in the passion; he will feel that there is no necessity to trick out or to elevate nature: and, the more industriously he applies this principle, the deeper will be his faith that no words, which *his* fancy or imagination can suggest, will be to be compared with those which are the emanations of reality and truth.

But it may be said by those who do not object to the general spirit of these remarks, that, as it is impossible for the Poet to produce upon all occasions language as exquisitely fitted for the passion as that which the real passion itself suggests, it is proper that he should consider himself as in the situation of a translator, who does not scruple to substitute excellencies of another kind for those which are unattainable by him; and endeavours occasionally to surpass his original, in order to make some amends for the general inferiority to which he feels that he must submit. But this would be to encourage idleness and unmanly despair. Further, it is the language of men who speak of what they do not understand; who talk of Poetry as a matter of amusement and idle pleasure; who will converse with us as gravely about a *taste* for Poetry, as they express it, as if it were a thing as indifferent as a taste for rope-dancing, or Frontiniac or Sherry. Aristotle, I have been told, has said, that Poetry is the most philosophic of all writing: it is so: its object is truth, not individual and local, but general, and operative; not standing upon external testimony, but carried alive into the heart by passion; truth which is its own testimony, which gives competence and confidence to the tribunal to which it appeals, and receives them from the same tribunal. Poetry is the image of man and nature. The obstacles which stand in the way of the fidelity of the Biographer and Historian, and of their consequent utility, are incalculably greater than those which are to be encountered by the Poet who comprehends the dignity of his art. The Poet writes under one restriction only, namely, the necessity of giving immediate pleasure to a human Being possessed of that information which may be expected from him, not as a lawyer, a physician, a mariner, an astronomer, or a natural philosopher, but as a Man. Except this one restriction, there is no object standing between the Poet and the image of things; between this, and the Biographer and Historian, there are a thousand.

Nor let this necessity of producing immediate pleasure be considered as a degradation of the Poet's art. It is far otherwise. It is an acknowledgment of the beauty of the universe, an acknowledgment the more sincere, because not formal, but indirect; it is a task light and easy to him who looks at the world in the spirit of love: further, it is a homage paid to the native and naked dignity of man, to the grand elementary principle of pleasure, by which he knows, and feels, and lives, and moves. We have no sympathy but what is propagated by pleasure: I would not be misunderstood; but wherever we sympathise with pain, it will be found that the sympathy is produced and carried on by subtle combinations with pleasure. We have no knowledge, that is, no general principles drawn from the contemplation of particular facts, but what has been built up by pleasure, and exists in us by pleasure alone. The Man of science, the Chemist and Mathematician, whatever difficulties and disgusts they may have had to struggle with, know and feel this. However painful may be the objects with which the Anatomist's knowledge is connected, he feels that his knowledge is pleasure; and where he has no

pleasure he has no knowledge. What then does the Poet? He considers man the objects that surround him as acting and re-acting upon each other, so as to produce an infinite complexity of pain and pleasure; he considers man in his own nature and in his ordinary life as contemplating this with a certain quantity of immediate knowledge, with certain convictions, intuitions, and deductions, which from habit acquire the quality of intuitions; he considers him as looking upon this complex scene of ideas and sensations, and finding every where objects that immediately excite in him sympathies which, from the necessities of his nature, are accompanied by an overbalance of enjoyment.

To this knowledge which all men carry about with them, and to these sympathies in which, without any other discipline than that of our daily life, we are fitted to take delight, the Poet principally directs his attention. He considers man and nature as essentially adapted to each other, and the mind of man as naturally the mirror of the fairest and most interesting properties of nature. And thus the Poet, prompted by this feeling of pleasure, which accompanies him through the whole course of his studies, converses with general nature, with affections akin to those, which, through labour and length of time, the Man of science has raised up in himself, by conversing with those particular parts of nature which are the objects of his studies. The knowledge both of the Poet and the Man of science is pleasure; but the knowledge of the one cleaves to us as a necessary part of our existence, our natural and unalienable inheritance; the other is a personal and individual acquisition, slow to come to us, and by no habitual and direct sympathy connecting us with our fellow-beings. The Man of science seeks truth as a remote and unknown benefactor; he cherishes and loves it in his solitude: the Poet, singing a song in which all human beings join with him, rejoices in the presence of truth as our visible friend and hourly companion. Poetry is the breath and finer spirit of all knowledge; it is the impassioned expression which is in the countenance of all Science. Emphatically may it be said of the Poet, as Shakspeare hath said of man, 'that he looks before and after.' He is the rock of defence for human nature; an upholder and preserver, carrying everywhere with him relationship and love. In spite of difference of soil and climate, of language and manners, of laws and customs: in spite of things silently gone out of mind, and things violently destroyed; the Poet binds together by passion and knowledge the vast empire of human society, as it is spread over the whole earth, and over all time. The objects of the Poet's thoughts

264

are every where; though the eyes and senses of man are, it is true, his favourite guides, yet he will follow wheresoever he can find an atmosphere of sensation in which to move his wings. Poetry is the first and last of all knowledge—it is as immortal as the heart of man. If the labours of Men of science should ever create any material revolution, direct or indirect, in our condition, and in the impressions which we habitually receive, the Poet will sleep then no more than at present; he will be ready to follow the steps of the Man of science, not only in those general indirect effects, but he will be at his side, carrying sensation into the midst of the objects of the science itself. The remotest discoveries of the Chemist, the Botanist, or Mineralogist, will be as proper objects of the Poet's art as any upon which it can be employed, if the time should ever come when these things shall be familiar to us, and the relations under which they are contemplated by the followers of these respective sciences shall be manifestly and palpably material to us as enjoying and suffering beings. If the time should ever come when what is now called science, thus familiarised to men, shall be ready to put on, as it were, a form of flesh and blood, the Poet will lend his divine spirit to aid the transfiguration, and will welcome the Being thus produced, as a dear and genuine inmate of the household of man.—It is not, then, to be supposed that any one, who holds that sublime notion of Poetry which I have attempted to convey, will break in upon the sanctity and truth of his pictures by transitory and accidental ornaments, and endeavour to excite admiration of himself by arts, the necessity of which must manifestly depend upon the assumed meanness of his subject.

What has been thus far said applies to Poetry in general; but especially to those parts of composition where the Poet speaks through the mouths of his characters; and upon this point it appears to authorise the conclusion that there are few persons of good sense, who would not allow that the dramatic parts of composition are defective, in proportion as they deviate from the real language of nature, and are coloured by a diction of the Poet's own, either peculiar to him as an individual Poet or belonging simply to Poets in general; to a body of men who, from the circumstance of their compositions being in metre, it is expected will employ a particular language.

It is not, then, in the dramatic parts of composition that we look for this distinction of language; but still it may be proper and necessary where the Poet speaks to us in his own person and character. To this I answer by referring the Reader to the description before given of a Poet. Among the qualities there enumerated as principally conducing to form a Poet, is implied nothing differing in kind from other men, but only in degree. The sum of what was said is, that the Poet is chiefly distinguished from other men by a greater promptness to think and feel without immediate external excitement, and a greater power in expressing such thoughts and feelings as are produced in him in that manner. But these passions and thoughts and feelings are the general passions and thoughts and feelings of men. And with what are they connected? Undoubtedly with our moral sentiments and animal sensations, and with the causes which excite these; with the operations of the elements, and the appearances of the visible universe; with storm and sunshine, with the revolutions of the seasons, with cold and heat, with loss of friends and kindred, with injuries and resentments, gratitude and hope, with fear and sorrow. These, and the like, are the sensations and objects which the Poet describes, as they are the sensations of other men, and the objects which interest them. The Poet thinks and feels in the spirit of human passions. How, then, can his language differ in any material degree from that of all other men who feel vividly and see clearly? It might be *proved* that it is impossible. But supposing that this were not the case, the Poet might then be allowed to use a peculiar language when expressing his feelings for his own gratification, or that of men like himself. But Poets do not write for Poets alone, but for men. Unless therefore we are advocates for that admiration which subsists upon ignorance, and that pleasure which arises from hearing what we do not understand, the Poet must descend from his supposed height; and in order to excite rational sympathy, he must express himself as other men express themselves. To this it may be added, that while he is only selecting from the real language of men, or, which amounts to the same thing, composing accurately in the spirit of such selection, he is treading upon safe ground, and we know what we are to expect from him. Our feelings are the same with respect to metre; for, as it may be proper to remind the Reader, the distinction of metre is regular and uniform, and not, like that which is produced by what is usually called POETIC DICTION, arbitrary, and subject to infinite caprices upon which no calculation whatever can be made. In the one case, the Reader is utterly at the mercy of the Poet, respecting what imagery or diction he may choose to connect with the passion; whereas, in the other, the metre obeys certain laws, to which the Poet and Reader both willingly submit because they are certain, and because no interference is made by them with the passion, but such as the concurring testimony of ages has shown to heighten and improve the pleasure which co-exists with it.

It will now be proper to answer an obvious question, namely, Why, professing these opinions, have I written in verse? To this, in addition to such answer as is included in what has been already said, I reply, in the first place, Because, however I may have restricted myself, there is still left open to me what confessedly constitutes the most valuable object of all writing, whether in prose or verse; the great and universal passions of men, the most general and interesting of their occupations, and the entire world of nature before me—to supply endless combinations of forms and imagery. Now, supposing for a moment that whatever is interesting in these objects may be as vividly described in prose, why should I be condemned for attempting to superadd to such description, the charm which, by the consent of all nations, is acknowledged to exist in metrical language? To this, by such as are yet unconvinced, it may be answered that a very small part of the pleasure given by Poetry depends upon the metre, and that it is injudicious to write in metre, unless it be accompanied with the other artificial distinctions of style with which metre is usually accompanied, and that, but such deviation, more will be lost from the shock which will thereby be given to the Reader's associations than will be counterbalanced by any pleasure which he can derive from the general power of numbers. In answer to those who still contend for the necessity of accompanying metre with certain appropriate colours of style in order to the accomplishment of its appropriate end, and who also, in my opinion, greatly under-rate the power of metre in itself, it might, perhaps, as far as relates to these Volumes, have been almost sufficient to observe, that poems are extant, written upon more humble subjects, and in a still more naked and simple style, which have continued to give pleasure from generation to generation. Now, if nakedness and simplicity be a defect, the fact here mentioned affords a strong presumption that poems somewhat less naked and simple are capable of affording pleasure at the present day; and, what I wished *chiefly* to attempt, at present, was to justify myself for having written under the impression of this belief.

But various causes might be pointed out why, when the style is manly, and the subject of some importance, words metrically arranged will long continue to impart such a pleasure to mankind as he who proves the extent of that pleasure will be desirous to impart. The end of Poetry is to produce excitement in co-existence with an overbalance of pleasure; but, by the supposition, excitement is an unusual and irregular state of the mind; ideas and feelings do not, in that state, succeed each other in accustomed order. If the words, however, by which this excitement is produced be in themselves powerful, or the images and feelings have an undue proportion of pain connected with them, there is some danger that the excitement may be carried beyond its proper bounds. Now the co-presence of something regular, something to which the mind has been accustomed in various moods and in a less excited state, cannot but have great efficacy in tempering and restraining the passion by an intertexture of ordinary feeling, and of feeling not strictly and necessarily connected with the passion. This is unquestionably true; and hence, though the opinion will at first appear paradoxical, from the tendency of metre to divest language, in a certain degree, of its reality, and thus to throw a sort of half-consciousness of unsubstantial existence over the whole composition, there can be little doubt but that more pathetic situations and sentiments, that is, those which have a greater proportion of pain connected with them, may be endured in metrical composition, especially in rhyme, than in prose. The metre of the old ballads is very artless; yet they contain many passages which would illustrate this opinion; and, I hope, if the following Poems be attentively perused, similar instances will be found in them. This opinion may be further illustrated by appealing to the Reader's own experience of the reluctance with which he comes to the re-perusal of the distressful parts of Clarissa Harlowe, or the Gamester; while Shakspeare's writings, in the most pathetic scenes, never act upon us, as pathetic, beyond the bounds of pleasure—an effect which, in a much greater degree than might at first be imagined, is to be ascribed to small, but continual and regular impulses of pleasurable surprise from the metrical arrangement. —On the other hand (what it must be allowed will much more frequently happen) if the Poet's words should be incommensurate with the passion, and inadequate to raise the Reader to a height of desirable excitement, then, (unless the Poet's choice of his metre has been grossly injudicious) in the feelings of pleasure which the Reader has been accustomed to connect with metre in general, and in the feeling, whether cheerful of melancholy, which he has been accustomed to connect with that particular movement of metre, there will be found something

266

which will greatly contribute to impart passion to the words, and to effect the complex end which the Poet proposes to himself.

If I had undertaken a SYSTEMATIC defence of the theory here maintained, it would have been my duty to develope the various causes upon which the pleasure received from metrical language depends. Among the chief of these causes is to be reckoned a principle which must be well known to those who have made any of the arts the object of accurate reflection; namely, the pleasure which the mind derives from the perception of similitude in dissimilitude. This principle is the great spring of the activity of our minds, and their chief feeder. From this principle the direction of the sexual appetite, and all the passions connected with it, take their origin: it is the life of our ordinary conversation; and upon the accuracy with which similitude in dissimilitude, and dissimilitude in similitude are perceived, depend our taste and our moral feelings. It would not be a useless employment to apply this principle to the consideration of metre, and to show that metre is hence enabled to afford much pleasure, and to point out in what manner that pleasure is produced. But my limits will not permit me to enter upon this subject, and I must content myself with a general summary.

I have said that poetry is the spontaneous overflow of powerful feelings: it takes its origin from emotion recollected in tranquillity: the emotion is contemplated till, by a species of re-action, the tranquillity gradually disappears, and an emotion, kindred to that which was before the subject of contemplation, is gradually produced, and does itself actually exist in the mind. In this mood successful composition generally begins, and in a mood similar to this it is carried on; but the emotion, of whatever kind, and in whatever degree, from various causes, is qualified by various pleasures, so that in describing any passions whatsoever, which are voluntarily described, the mind will, upon the whole, be in a state of enjoyment. If Nature be thus cautious to preserve in a state of enjoyment a being so employed, the Poet ought to profit by the lesson held forth to him, and ought especially to take care, that, whatever passions he communicates to his Reader, those passions, if his Reader's mind be sound and vigourous, should always be accompanied with an overbalance of pleasure. Now the music of harmonious metrical language, the sense of difficulty overcome, and the blind association of pleasure which has been previously received from works of rhyme or metre of the same or similar construction, an indistinct perception perpetually renewed of language closely resembling that of real life, and yet, in the circumstance of metre, differing from it so widely—all these imperceptibly make up a complex feeling of delight, which is of the most important use in tempering the painful feeling always found intermingled with powerful descriptions of the deeper passions. This effect is always produced in pathetic and impassioned poetry; while, in lighter compositions, the ease and gracefulness with which the Poet manages his numbers are themselves confessedly a principal source of the gratification of the Reader. All that it is *necessary* to say, however, upon this subject, may be effected by affirming, what few persons will deny, that, of two descriptions, either of passions, manners, or characters, each of them equally well executed, the one in prose and the other in verse, the verse will be read a hundred times where the prose is read once.

Having thus explained a few of my reasons for writing in verse, and why I have chosen subjects from common life, and endeavoured to bring my language near to the real language of men, if I have been too minute in pleading my own cause, I have at the same time been treating a subject of general interest; and for this reason a few words shall be added with reference solely to these particular poems, and to some defects which will probably be found in them. I am sensible that my associations must have sometimes been particular instead of general, and that, consequently, giving to things a false importance, I may have sometimes written upon unworthy subjects; but I am less apprehensive on this account, than that my language may frequently have suffered from those arbitrary connections of feelings and ideas with particular words and phrases, from which no man can altogether protect himself. Hence I have not doubt, that, in some instances, feelings, even of the ludicrous, may be given to my Readers by expressions which appeared to me tender and pathetic. Such faulty expressions, were I convinced they were faulty at present, and that they must necessarily continue to be so, I would willingly take all reasonable pains to correct. But it is dangerous to make these alterations on the simple authority of a few individuals, or even of certain classes of men; for where the understanding of an Author is not convinced, or his feelings altered, this cannot be done without great injury to himself: for his own feelings are his stay and support; and, if he set them aside in one instance, he may be induced to repeat this act till his mind shall lose all confidence in itself, and become utterly debilitated. To this it may be added, that the critic ought never to forget that he is himself exposed to the same errors as the Poet, and, perhaps, in a much greater degree: for there can be no presumption in saying of most readers, that it is not probable they will be so well acquainted with the various stages of meaning through which words have passed, or with the fickleness or stability of the relations of particular ideas to each other; and, above all, since they are so much less interested in the subject, they may decide lightly and carelessly.

Long as the Reader has been detained, I hope he will permit me to caution him against a mode of false criticism which has been applied to Poetry, in which the language closely resembles that of life and nature. Such verses have been triumphed over in parodies, of which Dr. Johnson's stanza is a fair specimen: —

'I put my hat upon my head
And walked into the Strand,
And there I met another man
Whose hat was in his hand.'

Immediately under these lines let us place one of the most justly-admired stanzas of the *"Babes in the Wood."*

'These pretty Babes with hand in hand
Went wandering up and down;
But never more they saw the Man
Approaching from the Town.'

In both these stanzas the words, and the order of the words, in no respect differ from the most unimpassioned conversation. There are words in both, for example, 'the Strand,' and 'the Town,' connected with none but the most familiar ideas; yet the one stanza we admit is admirable, and the other as a fair example of the superlatively contemptible. Whence arises this difference? Not from the metre, not from the language, not from the order of the words; but the *matter* expressed in Dr. Johnson's stanza is contemptible. The proper method of treating trivial and simple verses, to which Dr. Johnson's stanza would be a fair parallelism, is not to say, this is a bad kind of poetry, or, this is not poetry; but, this wants sense; it is neither interesting in itself, nor can *lead* to any thing interesting; the images neither originate in the sane state of feeling which arises out of thought, nor can excite thought or feeling in the Reader. This is the only sensible manner of dealing with such verses. Why trouble yourself about the species till you have previously decided upon the genus? Why take pains to prove that an ape is not a Newton, when it is self-evident that he is not a man?

One request I must make of my reader, which is, that in judging these Poems he would decide by his own feelings genuinely, and not by reflection upon what will probably be the judgment of others. How common is it to hear a person say, I myself do not object to this style of composition, or this or that expression, but, to such and such classes of people it will appear mean or ludicrous! This mode of criticism, so destructive of all sound unadulterated judgment, is almost universal: let the Reader then abide, independently, by his own feelings, and, if he finds himself affected, let him not suffer such conjectures to interfere with his pleasure.

If an Author, by any single composition, has impressed us with respect for his talents, it is useful to consider this as affording a presumption, that on other occasions where we have been displeased, he, nevertheless, may not have written ill or absurdly; and further, to give him so much credit for this one composition as may induce us to review what has displeased us, with more care than we should otherwise have bestowed upon it. This is not only an act of justice, but, in our decisions upon poetry especially, may conduce, in a high degree, to the improvement of our own taste; for an *accurate* taste in poetry, and in all the other arts, as Sir Joshua Reynolds has observed, is an *acquired* talent, which can only be produced by thought and a long-continued intercourse with the best models of composition. This is mentioned, not with so ridiculous a purpose as to prevent the most inexperience Reader from judging for himself, (I have already said that I wish him to judge for himself;) but merely to temper the rashness of decision, and to suggest, that, if Poetry be a subject on which much time has not been bestowed, the judgment may be erroneous; and that, in many cases, it necessarily will be so.

Nothing would, I know, have so effectually contributed to further the end which I have in view, as to have shown of what kind the pleasure is, and how that pleasure is produced, which is confessedly produced by metrical composition essentially different from that which I have here endeavoured to recommend: for the Reader will say that he has been pleased by such composition; and what more can be done for him? The power of any art is limited; and he will suspect, that, if it be proposed to furnish him with new friends, that can be only upon condition of his abandoning his old friends. Besides, as I have said, the Reader is himself conscious of the pleasure which he has received from such composition, composition to which he has peculiarly attached the endearing name of Poetry; and all men feel an habitual gratitude, and something of an honourable bigotry, for the objects which have long continued to please them: we not only wish to be pleased, but to be pleased in that particular way in which we have been accustomed to be pleased. There is in these feelings enough to resist a host of arguments; and I should be the less able to combat them successfully, as I am willing to allow, that, in order entirely to enjoy the Poetry which I am recommending, it would be necessary to give up much of what is ordinarily enjoyed. But, would my limits have permitted me to point out how this pleasure is produced, many obstacles might have been removed, and the Reader assisted in perceiving that the powers of language are not so limited as he may suppose; and that it is possible for poetry to give other enjoyments, of a purer, more lasting, and more exquisite nature. This part of the subject has not been altogether neglected, but it has not been so much my present aim to prove, that the interest excited by some other kinds of poetry is less vivid, and less worthy of the nobler powers of the mind, as to offer reasons for presuming, that if my purpose were fulfilled, a species of poetry would be produced, which is genuine poetry; in its nature well adapted to interest mankind permanently, and likewise important in the multiplicity and quality of its moral relations.

From what has been said, and from a perusal of the Poems, the Reader will be able clearly to perceive the object which I had in view: he will determine how far it has been attained; and, what is a much more important question, whether it be worth attaining: and upon the decision of these two questions will rest my claim to the approbation of the Public.

Wordworth, "Preface to the Lyrical Ballads"

Short Answer

1.   What is the significance of pleasure to the making of poetry?

2.   What link does Wordsworth make between poetry and the rural world?

3.   Is the poet different in kind from other human beings? Why or why not?

4.   What, if anything, is non-poetic in human experience? Explain.

5.   What kind of poetic language does Wordsworth seem opposed to? Why?

Northrop Frye*

THE FUNCTION OF CRITICISM
AT THE PRESENT TIME

The subject-matter of literary criticism is an art, and criticism is presumably an art too. This sounds as though criticism were a parasitic form of literary expression, an art based on pre-existing art, a second-hand imitation of creative power. The conception of the critic as a creator *manque* is very popular, especially among artists. Yet the critic has specific jobs to do which the experience of literature has proved to be less ignoble. One obvious function of criticism is to mediate between the artist and his public. Art that tries to do without criticism is apt to get involved in either of two fallacies. One is the attempt to reach the public directly through "popular" art, the assumption being that criticism is artificial and public taste natural. Below this is a further assumption about natural taste which goes back to Rousseau. The opposite fallacy is the conception of art as a mystery, an initiation into an esoteric community. Here criticism is restricted to masonic signs of occult understanding, to significant exclamations and gestures and oblique cryptic comments. This fallacy is like the other one in assuming a rough correlation between the merit of art and the degree of public response to it, though the correlation it assumes is inverse. But art of this kind is cut off from society as a whole, not so much because it retreats from life—the usual charge against it—as because it rejects criticism.

On the other hand, a public that attempts to do without criticism, and asserts that it knows what it likes, brutalizes the arts. Rejection of criticism from the point of view of the public, or its guardians, is involved in all forms of censorship. Art is a continuously emancipating factor in society, and the critic, whose job it is to get as many people in contact with the best that has been and is being thought and said, is, at least ideally, the pioneer of education and the shaper of cultural tradition. There is no immediate correlation either way between the merits of art and its general reception. Shakespeare was more popular than Webster, but not because he was a greater dramatist; W. H. Auden is less popular than Edgar Guest, but not because he is a better poet. But after the critic has been at work for a while, some positive correlation may begin to take shape. Most of Shakespeare's current popularity is due to critical publicity.

Why does criticism have to exist? The best and shortest answer is that it can talk, and all the arts are dumb. In painting, sculpture, or music it is easy enough to see that the art shows forth, and cannot say anything. And, although it sounds like a frantic paradox to say that the poet is inarticulate or speechless, literary works also are, for the critic, mute complexes of facts, like the data of science. Poetry is a *disinterested* use of words: it does not address a reader directly. When it does so, we feel that the poet has a certain distrust in the capacity of readers and critics to interpret his meaning without assistance, and has therefore stopped creating a poem and begun to talk. It is not merely tradition that impels a poet to invoke a Muse and protest that

*Northrop Frye (1912–1993) was a prominent literary theorist who taught at the Universityof Toronto. Frye tried to establish literary criticism as a science in its own right by claiming the literary forms correspond to psychological archetypes. His numerous works include *The Anatomy of Criticism* and *The Great Code,* a study of the literary significance of the Bible. The following article was originally published in the *University of Toronto Quarterly* (1949).

his utterance is involuntary. Nor is it mere paradox that causes Mr. MacLeish, in his famous "Ars Poetica," to apply the words "mute," "dumb," and "wordless" to a poem. The poet, as Mill saw in a wonderful flash of critical insight, is not heard, but overheard. The first assumption of criticism, and the assumption on which the autonomy of criticism rests, is not that the poet does not know what he is talking about, but that he cannot talk about what he knows, any more than the painter or composer can.

The poet may of course have some critical ability of his own, and so interpret his own work; but the Dante who writes a commentary on the first canto of the *Paradiso* is merely one more of Dante's critics. What he says has a peculiar interest, but not a peculiar authority. Poets are too often the most unreliable judges of the value or even the meaning of what they have written. When Ibsen maintains that *Emperor and Galilean* is his greatest play and that certain episodes in *Peer Gynt* are not allegorical, one can only say that Ibsen is an indifferent critic of Ibsen. Wordsworth's Preface to the *Lyrical Ballads* is a remarkable document, but as a piece of Wordsworthian criticism nobody would give it more than about a B plus. Critics of Shakespeare are often supposed to be ridiculed by the assertion that if Shakespeare were to come back form the dead he would not be able to understand their criticism and would accuse them of reading far more meaning into his work than he intended. This, though pure hypothesis, is likely enough: we have very little evidence of Shakespeare's interest in criticism, either of himself or of anyone else. But all that this means is that Shakespeare, though a great dramatist, was not also the greatest Shakespearean critic. Why should he be?

The notion that the poet is necessarily his own best interpreter is indissolubly linked with the conception of the critic as a parasite or jackal of literature. Once we admit that he has a specific field of activity, and that he has autonomy within that field, we are forced to concede that criticism deals with literature in terms of a specific conceptual framework. This framework is not that of literature itself, for this is the parasite theory again, but neither is it something outside literature, for in that case the autonomy of criticism would again disappear, and the whole subject would be assimilated to something else.

Here, however, we have arrived at another conception of criticism which is different from the one we started with. This autonomous organizing of literature may be criticism, but it is not the activity of mediating between the artist and his public which

we at first ascribed to criticism. There is one kind of critic, evidently, who faces the public and another who is still as completely involved in literary values as the poet himself. We may call this latter type the critic proper, and the former the critical reader. It may sound like quibbling to imply such a distinction, but actually the whole question of whether the critic has a real function, independent both of the artist at his most explicit and of the public at its most discriminating, is involved in it.

Our present-day critical traditions are rooted in the age of Hazlitt and Arnold and Sainte-Beuve, who were, in terms of our distinction, critical readers. They represented, not another conceptual framework within literature, but the reading public at its most expert and judicious. They conceive it to be the task of a critic to exemplify how a man of taste uses and evaluates literature, and thus how literature is to be absorbed into society. The nineteenth century has bequeathed to us the conception of the *causerie*, the man of taste's reflections on works of literature, as the normal form of critical expression. I give one example of the difference between a critic and a critical reader which amounts to a head-on collision. In one of his curious, brilliant, scatter-brained footnotes to *Munera Pulveris*, John Ruskin says:

> Of Shakespeare's names I will afterwards speak at more length; they are curiously—often barbarously—mixed out of various traditions and languages. Three of the clearest in meaning have been already noticed. Desdemona—"δυσδαιμονία" miserable fortune—is also plain enough. Othello is, I believe "the careful"; all the calamity of the tragedy arising from the single flaw and error in his magnificently collected strength. Ophelia, "serviceableness," the true, lost wife of Hamlet, is marked as having a Greek name by that of her brother, Laertes; and its signification is once exquisitely alluded to in that brother's last word of her, where her gentle preciousness is opposed to the uselessness of the churlish clergy: "A *ministering* angel shall my sister be, when thou liest howling."

On this passage Matthew Arnold comments as follows:

> Now, really, what a piece of extravagance all that is! I will not say that the meaning of Shakespeare's names (I put aside the question as to the correctness of Mr. Ruskin's etymologies) has no effect at all, may be entirely lost

sight of; but to give it that degree of prominence is to throw the reins to one's whim, to forget all moderation and proportion, to lose the balance of one's mind altogether. It is to show in one's criticism, to the highest excess, the note or provinciality.

Ruskin is a critic, perhaps the only important one that the Victorian age produced, and, whether he is right or wrong, what he is attempting is genuine criticism. He is trying to interpret Shakespeare in terms of a conceptual framework which belongs to the critic alone, and yet relates itself to the plays alone. Arnold is perfectly right in feeling that this is not the sort of material that the public critic can directly use. But he does not suspect the existence of criticism as we have defined it above. Here it is Arnold who is the provincial. Ruskin has learned his trade from the great iconological tradition which comes down through classical and biblical scholarship into Dante and Spenser, both of whom he knew how to read, and which is incorporated in the medieval cathedrals he had pored over in such detail. Arnold is assuming, as a universal law of nature, certain "plain sense" critical assumptions which were hardly heard of before Dryden's time and which can assuredly not survive the age of Freud and Jung and Frazer and Cassirer. What emerges from this is that the critic and critical reader are each better off when they know of one another's existence, and perhaps best off when their work forms different aspects of the same thing.

However, the *causerie* does not, or at least need not, involve any fallacy in the theory of criticism itself. The same cannot be said of the reaction against the *causerie* which has produced the leading twentieth-century substitute for criticism. This is the integrated system of religious, philosophical, and political ideas which takes in, as a matter of course, a critical attitude to literature. Thus Mr. Eliot defines his outlook as classical in literature, royalist in politics, anglo-catholic in religion; and it is clear that the thrid of these has been the spark-plug, the motivating power that drives the other two. Mr. Allen Tate describes his own critical attitude as "reactionary" in a sense intended to include political and philosophical overtones, and the same is true of Hulme's *Speculations,* which are primarily political speculations. Mr. Yvor Winters collects his criticism under the title "In Defence of Reason." What earthly business, one may inquire, has a literary critic to defend reason? He might as well be defending virtue. And so we could go through the list of Marxist, Thomist, Kierkegaardian, Freudian,

Jungian, Spenglerian, or existential critics, all determined to substitute a critical attitude for criticism, all proposing, not to find a conceptual framework for criticism within literature, but to attach criticism to one of a miscellany of frameworks outside it.

The axioms and postulates of criticism have to grow out of the art that the critic is dealing with. The first thing that the literary critic has to do is to read literature, to make an inductive survey of his own field and let his critical principles shape themselves solely out of his knowledge of that field. Critical principles cannot be taken over ready-made from theology, philosophy, politics, science, or any combination of these. Further, an inductive survey of his own field is equally essential for the critic of painting or of mucus, and so each art has its own criticism. Aesthetics, or the consideration of art as a whole, is not a form of criticism but a branch of philosophy. I state all this as dogma, but I think the experience of literature bears me out. To subordinate criticism to a critical attitude is to stereotype certain values in literature which can be related to the extra-literary source of the value-judgment. Mr. Eliot does not mean to say that Dante is a greater poet than Shakespeare or perhaps even Milton; yet he imposes on literature an extra-literary schematism, a sort of religio-political colour-filter, which makes Dante leap into prominence, shows Milton up as dark and faulty, and largely obliterates the outlines of Shakespeare. All that the genuine critic can do with this colour-filter is to murmur politely that it shows things in a new light and is indeed a most stimulating contribution to criticism.

If it is insisted that we cannot criticize literature until we have acquired a coherent philosophy of criticism with its centre of gravity in something else, the existence of criticism as a separate subject is still being denied. But there is one possibility further. If criticism exists, it must be, we have said, an examination of literature in terms of a conceptual framework derivable from an inductive survey of the literary field. The word "inductive" suggests some sort of scientific procedure. What if criticism is a science as well as an art? The writing of history is an art, but no one doubts that scientific principles are involved in the historian's treatment of evidence, and that the presence of this scientific element is what distinguishes history from legend. Is it also a scientific element in criticism which distinguishes it from *causerie* on the one hand, and the superimposed critical attitude on the other? For just as the presence of science changes the character of a subject from the casual to the causal, from the random and intuitive to the systematic, so it also safeguards the integrity of a subject from external invasions. So we may find in science a means of strengthening the fences of criticism against enclosure movements coming not only from religion and philosophy, but from the other sciences as well.

If criticism is a science, it is clearly a social science, which means that it should waste no time in trying to assimilate its methods to those of the natural sciences. Like psychology, it is directly concerned with the human mind, and will only confuse itself with statistical methodologies. I understand that there is a Ph.D. thesis somewhere that displays a list of Hardy's novels in the order of the percentages of gloom that they contain, but one does not feel that that sort of procedure should be encouraged. Yet as the field is narrowed to the social sciences the distinctions must be kept equally sharp. Thus there can be no such thing as a sociological "approach" to literature. There is no reason why a sociologist should not work exclusively on literary material, but if he does he should pay no attention to literary values. In his field Horatio Alger and the writer of the Elsie books are more important than Hawthorne or Melville, and a single issue of the *Ladies' Home Journal* is worth all of Henry James. The literary critic using sociological data is similarly under no obligation to respect sociological values.

It seems absurd to say that there *may* be a scientific element in criticism when there are dozens of learned journals based on the assumption that there is, and thousands of scholars engaged in a scientific procedure related to literary criticism. Either literary criticism is a science, or all these highly trained and intelligent people are wasting their time on a pseudoscience, one to be ranked with phrenology and election forecasting. Yet one is forced to wonder whether scholars as a whole are consciously aware that the assumptions on which their work is based are scientific ones. In the growing complication of secondary sources which constitutes literary scholarship, one misses, for the most part, that sense of systematic progressive consolidation which belongs to a science. Research begins in what is known as "background," and one would expect it, as it goes on, to organize the foreground as well. The digging up of relevant information about a poet should lead to a steady consolidating progress in the criticism of his poetry. One feels a certain failure of nerve in coming out of the background into the foreground, and research seems to prefer to become centrifugal, moving away from the works of art into more and more research projects. I have noticed this particularly in two fields in which I am inter-

ested, Blake and Spenser. For every critic of Spenser who is interested in knowing what, say the fourth book of *The Faerie Queene* actually means as a whole, there are dozens who are interested primarily in how Spenser used Chaucer, Malory, and Ariosto in putting it together. So far as I know there is no book devoted to an analysis of *The Faerie Queene* itself, though there are any number on its sources, and, of course, background. As for Blake, I have read a whole shelf of books on his poetry by critics who did not know what any of his major poems meant. The better ones were distinguishable only by the fact that they did not boast of their ignorance.

The reason for this is that research is ancillary to criticism, but the critic to whom the researcher should entrust his materials hardly exists. What passes for criticism is mainly the work of critical readers or spokesmen of various critical attitudes, and these make, in general, a random and haphazard use of scholarship. Such criticism is therefore often regarded by the researcher as a subjective and regressive dilettantism, interesting in its place, but not real work. On the other hand, the critical reader is apt to treat the researcher as Hamlet did the grave-digger, ignoring everything he throws out except an odd skull that he can pick up and moralize about. Yet unless research consolidates into a criticism which preserves the scientific and systematic element in research, the literary scholar will be debarred by his choice of profession from ever making an immediately significant contribution to culture. The absence of direction in research is, naturally, clearest on the very lowest levels of all, where it is only a spasmodic laying of unfertilized eggs in order to avoid an administrative axe. Here the research is characterized by a kind of desperate tentativeness, an implied hope that some synthesizing critical Messiah of the future will find it useful. A philologist can show the relationship of even the most minute study of dialect to his subject as a whole, because philology is a properly organized science. But the researcher who collects all a poet's references to the sea or God or beautiful women does not know who will find this useful or in what ways it could be used, because he has no theory of imagery.

I am not, obviously, saying that literary scholarship at present is doing the wrong thing or should be doing something else: I am saying that it should be possible to get a clearer and more systematic comprehension of what it is doing. Most literary scholarship could be described as prior criticism (the so-called "lower" criticism of biblical scholarship), the editing of texts and the collecting of relevant facts. Of the posterior (or "higher") criticism that is obviously the final cause of this work we have as yet no theory, no tradition, and above all no systematic organization. We have, of course, a good deal of the thing itself. There is even some good posterior criticism of Spenser, though most of it was written in the eighteenth century. And in every age the great scholar will do the right thing by the instinct of genius. But genius is rare, and scholarship is not.

Sciences normally begin in a state of naïve induction: they come immediately in contact with phenomena and take the things to be explained as their immediate data. Thus physics began by taking the immediate sensations of experience, classified as hot, cold, moist, and dry, as fundamental principles. Eventually physics turned inside out, and discovered that its real function was to explain what heat and moisture were. History began as chronicle; but the difference between the old chronicler and the modern historian is that to the chronicler the events he recorded were also the structure of history, whereas the historian sees these events as historical phenomena, to be explained in terms of a conceptual framework different in shape from them. Similarly each modern science has had to take what Bacon calls (though in another context) an inductive leap, occupying a new vantage ground from which it could see its former principles as new things to be explained. As long as astronomers regarded the movements of heavenly bodies as the structure of astronomy, they were compelled to read their own point of view as fixed. Once they thought of movement as itself an explainable phenomenon, a mathematical theory of movement became the conceptual framework, and so the way was cleared for the heliocentric solar system and the law of gravitation. As long as biology thought of animal and vegetable forms of life as constituting its subject, the different branches of biology were largely effort of cataloguing. As soon as it was the existence of forms of life themselves that had to be explained, the theory of evolution and the conceptions of protoplasm and the cell poured into biology and completely revitalized it.

It occurs to me that literary criticism is now in such a state of naïve induction as we find in a primitive science. Its materials, the masterpieces of literature, are not yet regarded as phenomena to be explained in terms of a conceptual framework which criticism alone possesses. They are still regarded as somehow constituting the framework or form of criticism as well. I suggest that it is time for criticism to leap to a new ground from which it can discover what the organizing or containing forms of its conceptual framework are. And no one can examine the present containing forms of criticism without being depressed by an overwhelming sense of unreality. Let me give one example.

In confronting any work of literature, one obvious containing form is the genre to which it belongs. And criticism, incredible as it may seem, has as yet no coherent conception of genres. The very word sticks out in an English sentence as the unpronounceable and alien thing it is. In poetry, the common-sense Greek division by methods of performance, which distinguishes poetry as lyric, epic, or dramatic according to whether it is sung, spoken, or shown forth, survives vestigially. On the whole it does not fit the facts of Western poetry, though in Joyce's *Portrait* there is an interesting and suggestive attempt made to re-define the terms. So, apart from a drama which belongs equally to prose, a handful of epics recognizable as such only because they are classical imitations, and a number of long poems also called epics because they are long, we are reduced to the ignoble and slovenly practice of calling almost the whole of poetry "lyric" because the Greeks had no other word for it. The Greeks did not need to develop a classification of prose forms: we do, but have never done so. The circulating-library distinction between fiction and non-fiction, between books which are about things admitted not to be true and books which are about everything else, is apparently satisfactory to us. Asked what the forms of prose fiction are, the literary critic can only say, "well, er—the novel." Asked what form of prose fiction *Gulliver's Travels,* which is clearly not a novel, belongs to, there is not one critic in a hundred who could give a definite answer, and not one in a thousand who would regard the answer (which happens to be "Menippean satire") as essential to the critical treatment of the book. Asked what he is working on, the critic will invariably say that he is working on Donne, or Shelley's thought or the period from 1640 to 1660, or give some other answer which implies that history, or philosophy, or literature itself, constitutes the structural basis of criticism. It would never occur to any critic to say, for instance, "I am working on the theory of genres." If he actually were interested in this, he would say that he was working on a "general" topic; and the work he would do would probably show the marks of naïve induction: that is, it would be an effort to classify and pigeon-hole instead of clarifying the tradition of the genre.

If we do not know how to handle even the genre, the most obvious of all critical conceptions, it is hardly likely that subtler instruments will be better understood. In any work of literature the characteristics of the language it is written in form an essential critical conception. To the philologist, literature is a function of language, its works linguistic documents, and to the philologist the phrase "English literature" makes sense. It ought not to make any sense at all to a literary critic. For while the philologist sees English literature as illustrating the organic growth of the English language, the literary critic can only see it as the miscellaneous pile of literary works that happened to get written in English. (I say in English, not in England, for the part of "English literature" that was written in Latin or Norman French has a way of dropping unobtrusively into other departments.) Language is an important secondary aspect of literature, but when magnified into a primary basis of classification it becomes absurdly arbitrary.

Critics, of course, maintain that they know this, and that they keep the linguistic categories only for convenience. But theoretical fictions have a way of becoming practical assumptions, and in no time the meaningless convenience of "English literature" expands into the meaningless inconvenience of the "history of English literature." Now, again, the historian must necessarily regard literature as an historical product and its works as historical documents. It is also quite true that the time a work was written in forms an essential critical conception. But again, to the literary critic, as such, the phrase "history of English literature" ought to mean nothing at all. If he doubts this, let him try writing one, and he will find himself confronted by an insoluble problem of form, or rather by an indissoluble amorphousness. The "history" part of his project is an abstract history, a bald chronicle of names and dates and works and influences, deprived of all the real historical interest that a real historian would give it, however, much enlivened with discussions of "background." This chronicle is periodically interrupted by conventional judgments of value lugged in from another world, which confuse the history and yet are nothing by themselves. The *form* of literary history has not been discovered, and probably does not exist, and every successful one has been either a textbook or a *tour de force*. Linear time is not an exact enough category to catch literature, and all writers whatever are subtly belittled by a purely historical treatment.

Biography, a branch of history, presents a similar fallacy to the critic, for the biographer turns to a different job and a different kind of book when he turns to criticism. Again, the man who wrote the poem is one of the legitimate containing forms of criticism. But here we have to distinguish the poet *qua* poet, whose work is a single imaginative body, from the poet as man, who is something else altogether. The latter involves us in what is known as the personal heresy, or rather the heroic fallacy. For a biographer, poetry is an emanation of a personality; for the literary critic it is not, and the problem is to detach it from the personality and consider it on impersonal merits. The no man's land between biography and criticism, the process by which a poet's impressions of his environment are transmuted into poetry, has to be viewed by biographer and critic from opposite points of view. The process is too complex never to be completely unified, Lowes's *Road to Xanadu* being the kind of exception that goes a long way to prove the rule. In Johnson's *Lives of the Poets* a biographical narrative is followed by a critical analysis, and the break between them is so sharp that it is represented in the text by a space.

In all these cases, the same principle recurs. The critic is surrounded by biography, history, philosophy, and language. No one doubts that he has to familiarize himself with these subjects. But is his job only to be the jackal of the historian, the philologist, and the biographer, or can he use these subjects in his own way? If he is not to sell out to all his neighbours in turn, what is distinctive about his approach to the poet's life, the time when he lived, and the language he wrote? To ask this is to raise one of the problems involved in the whole question of what the containing forms of literature are as they take their place in the conceptual framework of criticism. This confronts me with the challenge to make my criticism of criticism constructive. All I have space to do is to outline what I think the first major steps should be.

We have to see what literature is, and try to distinguish the category of literature among all the books there are in the world. I do not know that criticism has made any serious effort to determine what literature is. Next, as discussed above, we should examine the containing forms of criticism, including the poet's life, his historical context, his language, and his thought, to see whether the critic can impose a unified critical form on these things, without giving place to or turning into a biographer, an historian, a philologist, or a philosopher. Next, we should establish the broad distinctions, such as that between prose and poetry, which are preparatory to working out a comprehensive theory of genres. I do not know that critics have clearly explained what the difference between prose and poetry, for instance, really is. Then we should try to see whether the critic, like his neighbours the historian and the philosopher, lives in his own universe. To the historian there is nothing that cannot be considered historically; to the philosopher nothing that cannot be considered philosophically. Does the critic aspire to contain all things in criticism, and so swallow history and philosophy in his own synthesis, or must he be forever the historian's and philosopher's pupil? If I have shown up Arnold in a poor light, I should say that he is the only one I know who suggests that criticism can be, like history and philosophy, a total attitude to experience. And finally, since criticism may obviously deal with anything in a poem from its superficial texture to its ultimate significance, the question arises whether there are different levels of meaning in literature, and, if so, whether they can be defined and classified.

It follows that arriving at value-judgments is not, as it is so often said to be, part of the immediate tactic of criticism. Criticism is not well enough organized as yet to know what the factors of value in a critical judgment are. For instance, as was indicated above in connection with Blake and Spenser, the question of the quality of a poet's thinking as revealed in the integration of his argument is an essential factor in a value-judgment, but many poets are exhaustively discussed in terms of value without this factor being considered. Contemporary judgments of value come mainly from either the critical reader or from the spokesman of a critical attitude. That is, they must be on the whole either unorganized and tentative, or over-organized and irrelevant. For no one can jump directly from research to a value-judgment. I give one melancholy instance. I recently read a study of the sources of mythological allusions in some of the romantic poets, which showed that for the second part of *Faust* Goethe had used a miscellany of cribs, some of dubious authenticity. "I have now, I hope," said the author triumphantly at the end of his investigation, "given sufficient proof that the second part of *Faust* is not a great work of art." I do not deny the ultimate importance of the value-judgment. I would even consider the suggestion that the value-judgment is precisely what distinguishes the social from the natural science. But the more important it is, the more careful we should be about getting it solidly established.

What literature is may perhaps best be understood by an analogy. We shall have to labour the analogy, but that is due mainly to the novelty of the idea here presented. Mathematics appears to begin in the counting and measuring of objects, as a numerical commentary on the world. But the mathematician does not think of his subject as the counting and measuring of physical objects at all. For him it is an autonomous language, and there is a point at which it becomes in a measure independent of that common field of experience which we think of as the physical world, or as existence, or as reality, according to our mood. Many of its terms, such as irrational numbers, have no direct connection with the common field of experience, but depend for their meaning solely on the interrelations of the subject itself. Irrational numbers in mathematics may be compared to prepositions in verbal languages, which, unlike nouns and verbs, have no external symbolic reference. When we distinguish pure from applied mathematics, we are thinking of the former as a disinterested conception of numerical relationships, concerned more and more with its inner integrity, and less and less with its reference to external criteria.

Where, in that case, is pure mathematics going? We may gain a hint from the final chapter of Sir James Jeans' *Mysterious Universe,* which I choose because it shows some of the characteristics of the imaginative leap to a new conceptual framework already mentioned. There, the author speaks of the failure of physical cosmology in the nineteenth century to conceive of the universe as ultimately mechanical, and suggests that a mathematical approach to it may have better luck. The universe cannot be a machine, but it may be an interlocking set of mathematical formulas. What this means is surely that pure mathematics exists in a mathematical universe which is no longer a commentary on an "outside" world, but contains that world within itself. Mathematics is at first a form of understanding an objective world regarded as its content, but in the end it conceives of the content as being itself mathematical in form, so that when the conception of the mathematical universe is reached, form and content become the same thing.

Jeans was a mathematician, and thought of his mathematical universe as *the* universe. Doubtless it is, but it does not follow that the only way of conceiving it is mathematical. For we think also of literature at first as a commentary on an external "life" or "reality." But just as in mathematics we have to go from three apples to three, and from a square field to a square, so in reading Jane Austen we have to go from the faithful reflection of English

277

society to the novel, and pass from literature as symbol to literature as an autonomous language. And just as mathematics exists in a mathematical universe which is at the circumference of the common field of experience, so literature exists in a verbal universe, which is not a commentary on life or reality, but contains life and reality in a system of verbal relationships. This conception of a verbal universe, in which life and reality are inside literature, and not outside it and being described or represented or approached or symbolized by it, seems to me the first postulate of a properly organized criticism.

It is vulgar for the critic to think of literature as a tiny palace of art looking out upon an inconceivably gigantic "life." "Life" should be for the critic only the seed-plot of literature, a vast mass of potential literary forms, only a few of which will grow up into the greater world of the verbal universe. Similar universes exist for all the arts. "We make to ourselves picture of facts," says Wittgenstein, but by pictures he means representative illustrations, which are not pictures. Pictures as pictures are themselves facts, and exist only in a pictorial universe. It is easy enough to say that while the stars in their courses may form the subject of a poem, they will still remain the stars in their courses, forever outside poetry. But this is pure regression to the common field of experience, and nothing more; for the more strenuously we try to conceive the stars in their courses in non-literary ways, the more assuredly we shall fall into the idioms and conventions of some other mental universe. The conception of a constant external reality acts as a kind of censor principle in the arts. Painting has been much bedevilled by it, and much of the freakishness of modern painting is clearly due to the energy of this revolt against the representational fallacy. Music on the other hand has remained fairly free of it: at least no one, so far as I know, insists that it is flying in the face of common sense for music to do anything but reproduce the sounds heard in external nature. In literature the chief function of representationalism is to neutralize its opposing fallacy of an "inner" or subjective reality.

These different universes are presumably different ways of conceiving the same universe. What we call the common field of experience is a provisional means of unifying them on the level of sense-perception, and it is natural to infer a higher unity, a sort of beatification of common sense. But it is not easy to find any human language capable of reaching such exalted heights. If it is true, as is being increasingly asserted, that metaphysics is a system of verbal constructions with no direct reference to external criteria by means of which its truth or falsehood may be tested, it follows that metaphysics forms part of the verbal universe. Theology postulates an ultimate reality in God, but it does not assume that man is capable of describing it in his own terms, nor does it claim to be itself such a description. In any case, if we assert this final unity too quickly we may injure the integrity of the different means of approaching it. It does not help a poet much to tell him that the function of literature is to empty itself into an ocean of superverbal significance, when the nature of that significance is unknown.

Pure mathematics, we have said, does not relate itself directly to the common field of experience, but indirectly, not to avoid it, but with the ultimate design of swallowing it. It thus presents the appearance of a series of hypothetical possibilities. It by-passes the confirmation from without which is the goal of applied mathematics, and seeks it only from within: its conclusions are related primarily to its own premises. Literature also proceeds by hypothetical possibilities. The poet, said Sidney, never affirmeth. He never says "this is so"; he says "let there be such a situation," and poetic truth, the validity of his conclusion, is to be tested primarily by its coherence with his original postulate. Of course, there is applied literature, just as there is applied mathematics, which we test historically, by its life-likeness, or philosophically, by the cogency of its propositions. Literature, like mathematics, is constantly useful, a word which means having a continuing relationship to the common field of experience. But pure literature, like pure mathematics, is disinterested, or useless: it contains its own meaning. Any attempt to determine the category of literature must start with a distinction between the verbal form which is primarily itself and the verbal form which is primarily related to something else. The former is a complex verbal fact, the latter a complex of verbal symbols.

We have to use the mathematical analogy once more before we leave it. Literature is, of course, dependent on the haphazard and unpredictable appearance of creative genius. So actually is mathematics, but we hardly notice this because in mathematics a steady consolidating process goes on, and the work of its geniuses is absorbed in the evolving and expanding pattern of the mathematical universe. Literature being as yet unorganized by criticism, it still appears as a huge aggregate or miscellaneous pile of creative efforts. The only organizing principle so far discovered in it is chronology, and when we see the miscellaneous pile strung out along a chronological line, some coherence is given to it by the linear factors in tradition. We can trace an epic tradition by virtue of the fact that Virgil succeeded Homer, Dante Virgil, and Milton Dante. But, as already suggested, this is very far from being the best we can do. Criticism has still to develop a theory of literature which will see this aggregate within a verbal universe, as forms integrated within a total form. An epic, besides occurring at a certain point in time, is also something of a definitive statement of the poet's imaginative experience, whereas a lyric is usually a more fragmentary one. This suggests the image of a kind of radiating circle of literary experience in which the lyric is nearer to a periphery and the epic nearer to a centre. It is only an image, but the notion that literature, like any other form of knowledge, possesses a centre and a circumference seems reasonable enough.

If so, then literature is a single body, a vast organically growing form, and, though of course works of art do not improve, yet it may be possible for criticism to see literature as showing a progressive evolution in time, of a kind rather like what Newman postulates for Catholic dogma. One could collect remarks by the dozen from various critics, many of them quite misleading, to show that they are dimly aware, on some level of consciousness, of the possibility of a critical progress toward a total comprehension of literature which no critical history gives any hint of. When Mr. Eliot says that the whole tradition of Western poetry from Homer down ought to exist simultaneously in the poet's mind, the adverb suggests a transcending by criticism of the tyranny of historical categories. I even think that the consolidation of literature by criticism into the verbal universe was one of the things that Matthew Arnold meant by culture. To begin this process seems to me the function of criticism at the present time.

Northrop Frye, "The Function of Criticism at the Present Time"

1.   One obvious function of a literary critic is to mediate between the artist and the public.

      a. True   b. False

2.   Frye holds that the field of literary criticism, as a social science, must be based on the conceptual framework of one of the social sciences.

      a. True   b. False

3.   Frye believes that literary criticism is now in a state of naive _____ as we find in a primitive science.

4.   Which one of the following is **not** a task for the new social science of literary criticism?

      a. to develop a theory of genres
      b. to develop a theory of literature
      c. to distinguish between prose and poetry
      d. to offer value judgments on particular works

5.   Explain what Frye means in saying that literature exists in a verbal universe.

Annette Kolodny*

DANCING THROUGH THE MINEFIELD

During the years that I was in college, from 1958 to 1963, no one thought to ask why so few women poets and novelists appeared on required reading lists or, even less, why women's names were only rarely mentioned when we discussed the "important" or "influential" critics of the day. Where women writers were taught, as in the courses on the history of the English novel, a supposedly exceptional work might be remarked for its "large scope" or "masculine thrust"; but, more often than not, women's novels were applauded for a certain elegance of style, an attention to detail or nuance, and then they were curtly dismissed for their inevitably "feminine" lack of humor, weighty truths, or universal significance. If possible, things were even more dismal in the American literature courses, where Anne Bradstreet was treated as a Puritan anomaly, and Emily Dickinson was presented as a case study who had offered biographer after biographer the occasion to identify the peculiar pathology which *must* explain (or explain away) her otherwise apparently incomprehensible prolific poetic output. These were the years, after all, when no one blinked at Norman Mailer's "terrible confession" that he could not read "any of the talented women who write today," and most nodded in agreement when Theodore Roethke listed among the frequent charges made against women's poetry, its "lack of range—in subject matter, in emotional tone—and a lack of a sense of humor." Elizabeth Janeway has noted that women writers of that period quite properly attempted to reject the label "women's litera-

ture," reacting against the "automatic disparagement of their work" which it implied. For readers as for writers then, as Adrienne Rich recalled, "it seemed to be a given fact that men wrote poems and women frequently inhabited them."

But just beneath the many surface complacencies of the 1950's an anger was brewing. With the radical critiques of American society that emerged in the 1960's there emerged also, though perhaps more slowly, a gradual recognition by women that it was not just the blacks or the other minority groups who were being deprived of their basic civil rights; that women, too, regardless of their class or education, were also, in a real sense, second-class citizens. As this perception was shared, especially in the consciousness-raising groups that marked the beginning of the "new feminism" at the end of the 1960s and the beginning of the 1970s, "the sleepwalkers," as Adrienne Rich called us, began "coming awake"; and, even more important, "for the first time this awakening" took on "a collective reality." By the time I was completing my Ph.D. thesis at the University of California at Berkeley, in 1969, that new collective consciousness had permeated campus study groups and social gatherings sufficiently to make it at least uncomfortable for anyone to merely laugh at or accept as witty Norman Mailer's dismissal of women writers on the grounds "that a good novelist can do without everything but the remnant of his balls." And few of the *women* graduate students, at any rate, were willing to accept without further investigation Roethke's pronounce-

*Annette Kolodny (1941–) is a leading voice of feminist literary criticism in American universities today. Professor Kolodny raises questions about the issue of gender discrimination in the formation of the literary canon and advocates the recovery of women's voices from the silence to which they have traditionally been relegated.

From *Men's Studies Modified*, edited by Dale Spender (1981). Reprinted by permission.

ment that women writers had always contented themselves with 'the embroidering of trivial themes' or shown only "a concern with the mere surfaces of life—that special province of the female talent in prose—hiding from the real agonies of the spirit." That further investigation which began so tentatively at the end of the 1960s became, of course, what we now call "feminist literary criticism."

Had anyone the prescience back then to pose the question of defining a "feminist" literary criticism, she might have been told, after the appearance of Mary Ellmann's *Thinking About Women,* in 1968, that it involved exposing the sexual stereotyping of women in both our literature and our literary criticism and, as well, demonstrating the inadequacy of established critical schools and methods to deal fairly or sensitively with works written by women. And, for the most part, such a prediction would have stood well the test of time. What could not have been anticipated as the 1960s drew to a close, however, was the long-term catalyzing effect of an ideology that, for many of us, had helped to bridge the gap between the world as we found it and the world as we wanted it to be. For those of us who studied literature, a previously unspoken sense of exclusion from authorship, and a painfully personal distress at discovering whores, bitches, muses, and heroines dead in childbirth where we had once hoped to discover ourselves, could now, for the first time, begin to be understood as more than "a set of disconnected, unrealized private emotions." With a renewed courage to make public our otherwise private discontents, what had once been "felt individually as personal insecurity" came at last to be "viewed collectively as structural inconsistency" within the very disciplines we studied. Following unflinchingly the full implications of Ellmann's percipient early observations, and emboldened to do so by the liberating energy of feminist ideology—in all its various forms and guises—feminist criticism very quickly moved beyond merely "expos[ing] sexism in one work of literature after another," and promised, instead, that we might at last "begin to record new choices in a new literary history." So powerful was that impulse that we experienced it, along with Adrienne Rich, as much more than "a chapter in cultural history": it became, rather, "an act of survival." What was at stake was not so much literature or criticism *per se* but the historical, social, and ethical consequences of women's participation in, or exclusion from either enterprise.

The pace of inquiry these last ten years has been fast and furious—especially after Kate Millett's 1970 analysis of the sexual politics of literature added a note of urgency to what had earlier been Ellmann's sardonic anger—while the diversity of that inquiry easily outstripped all efforts to define feminist literary criticism as either a coherent system or a unified set of methodologies. Under this wide umbrella everything has been thrown into question: our established canons, our aesthetic criteria, our interpretive strategies, our reading habits, and, most of all, ourselves as critics and as teachers. To delineate its full scope would require nothing less than a book—a book that would be outdated even as it was being composed. For the sake of brevity, therefore, let me attempt only a summary outline.

Perhaps the most obvious success of this new scholarship has been the return to circulation of previously lost or otherwise ignored works by women writers. Following fast upon the initial success of the Feminist Press in reissuing gems like Rebecca Harding Davis' 1861 novella, *Life in the Iron Mills,* and Charlotte Perkins Gilman's 1892 *The Yellow Wallpaper,* published in 1972 and 1973 respectively, numbers of commercial trade and reprint houses vied with one another in the reprinting of anthologies of lost texts and, in some cases, in the reprinting of whole series. For those of us in American literature especially, the phenomenon promised a radical reshaping of our concepts of literary history and, at the very least, a new chapter in understanding the development of women's literary traditions. So commercially successful were these reprintings, and so attuned were the reprint houses to the political attitudes of the audiences for which they were offered, that many of us found ourselves being wooed to compose critical introductions which would find in the pages of nineteenth-century domestic and sentimental fictions some signs of either muted rebellions or overt radicalism, in anticipation of the current wave of "new feminism." In rereading with our students these previously lost works, we inevitably raised perplexing questions as to the reasons for their disappearance from the canons of "major works," and worried over the aesthetic and critical criteria by which they had been accorded diminished status.

This increased availability of works by women writers led, of course, to an increased interest in what elements, if any, might comprise some sort of unity or connection among them. The possibility that women had developed either a unique, or at least a related tradition of their own, especially intrigued those of us who specialized in one national literature or another, or in historical periods. Nina Baym's *Women's Fiction: A Guide to Novels by and about Women in America, 1820–1870* demonstrates the Americanists' penchant for examining what were once the "best sellers" of their day, the ranks of the popular fiction writers, among which women took a dominant place throughout the nineteenth century, while the feminist studies of British literature emphasized instead the wealth of women writers who have been regarded as worthy of canonization. Not so much building upon one another's work as clarifying, successively, the parameters of the questions to be posed, Sydney Janet Kaplan, Ellen Moer, Patricia Meyer Spacks, and Elaine Showalter, among many others, concentrated their energies on delineating an internally consistent 'body of work' by women which might stand as a female counter-tradition. For Kaplan, in 1975, this entailed examining women writers' various attempts to portray feminine consciousness and self-consciousness not as a psychological category, but as a stylistic or rhetorical device; that same year, arguing essentially that literature publicizes the private, Spacks placed her consideration of a 'female imagination' within social and historical frames, to conclude that, "for readily discernible historical reasons women have characteristically concerned themselves with matters more or less peripheral to male concerns," and attributed to this fact an inevitable difference in the literary emphases and subject matters of female and male writers. The next year, Moer's *Literary Women* focused on the pathway of literary influence that linked the English novel in the hands of women. And, finally, in 1977, Showalter took up the matter of a "female literary tradition in the English novel from the generation of the Brontës to the present day" by arguing that, since women in general constitute a kind of "subculture within the framework of a larger society," the work of women writers, in particular, would thereby demonstrate a unity of "values, conventions, experiences, and behaviors impinging on each individual" as she found her sources of "self-expression relative to a dominant [and, by implication, male] society."

At the same time that women writers were being reconsidered and reread, male writers were similarly subjected to a new feminist scrutiny. The continuing result, to put ten years of difficult analysis into a single sentence, has been nothing less than an acute attentiveness to the ways in which certain power relations—usually those in which males wield various forms of influence over females—are inscribed in the texts (both literary and critical) that we have inherited, not merely as subject matter, but as the unquestioned, often unacknowledged *given* of the culture. Even more important than the new interpretations of individual texts

which such attentiveness has rendered is its probings into the consequences (for women) of the conventions which inform those texts. In surveying selected nineteenth- and early twentieth-century British novels which employ what she calls "the two suitors convention," for example, Jean Kennard sought to understand why and how the structural demands of the convention, even in the hands of women writers, inevitably work to imply "the inferiority and necessary subordination of women." Her 1978 study, *Victims of Convention,* points out that the symbolic nature of the marriage which conventionally concludes such novels "indicates the adjustment of the protagonist to society's values, a condition which is equated with her maturity." Kennard's concern, however, is with the fact that the structural demands of the form too often sacrifice precisely those "virtues of independence and individuality," or in other words, the very "qualities we have been invited to admire in" the heroines. If Kennard appropriately cautions us against drawing from her work any simplistically reductive thesis about the mimetic relations between art and life, her approach does nonetheless suggest that what is important about a fiction is not whether it ends in a death or a marriage, but what the symbolic demands of that particular conventional ending imply about the values and beliefs of the world that engendered it.

Her work thus participates in a growing emphasis in feminist literary study on the fact of literature as a social institution, embedded not only within its own literary traditions but within the particular physical and mental artifacts of the society from which it comes. Adumbrating Millett's 1970 decision to anchor her 'literary reflections' to a preceding analysis of the historical, social, and economic contexts of sexual politics, more recent work—Lillian Robinson's—begins with the premise that the process of artistic creation "consists not of ghostly happenings in the head but of a matching of the states and processes of symbolic models against the states and processes of the wider world." The power relations inscribed in the form of conventions within our literary inheritance, these critics argue, reify the encodings of those same power relations in the culture at large. And the critical examination of rhetorical codes becomes, in their hands, the pursuit of ideological codes, since both embody either value systems or the dialectic of competition between value systems. More often than not, these critics also insist upon examining not only the mirroring of life in art but, as well, the normative impact of art on life. Addressing herself to the popular arts available to working women, for example, Lillian Robinson is interested in understanding not only 'the forms it uses', but, more importantly "the myths it creates, the influence it exerts." "The way art helps people to order, interpret, mythologize, or dispose of their own experience," she declared, may be "complex and often ambiguous, but it is not impossible to define."

Whether its focus be upon the material or the imaginative contexts of literary invention; single texts or entire canons; the relations between authors, genres, or historical circumstances; lost authors or well-known names, the variety and diversity of all feminist literary criticism finally coheres in its stance of almost defensive re-reading. What Adrienne Rich had earlier called "re-vision," that is, "the act of looking back, of seeing with fresh eyes, of entering an old text from a new critical direction," took on a more actively self-protective coloration in 1978, when Judith Fetterley called upon the woman reader to learn to 'resist' the sexist designs a text might make upon her—asking her to identify against herself, so to speak, by manipulating her sympathies on behalf of male heroes, but against female shrew or bitch characters. Underpinning a great deal of this critical re-reading has been the not-unexpected alliance between feminist literary study and those feminist studies in linguistics and language acquisition examined in the chapter by Mercilee Jenkins and Cheris Kramarae. Tillie Olsen's common sense observation of the danger of "perpetuating—by continued usage—entrenched, centuries-old oppressive power realities, early-on incorporated into language," has been given substantive analysis in the writings of feminists who study "language as a symbolic system closely tied to a patriarchal social structure." Taken together, their work demonstrates "the importance of language in establishing, reflecting, and maintaining an asymmetrical relationship between women and men."

To consider what this implies for the fate of women who essay the craft of language is to ascertain, perhaps for the first time, the real dilemma of the poet who finds her most cherished private experience "hedged by taboos, mined with false namings" and, as well, the dilemma of the male reader who, in opening the pages of a woman's book, finds himself entering a strange and unfamiliar world of symbolic significance. For if, as Nelly Furman insists, neither language use nor language acquisition are "gender-neutral," but, instead, are both "imbued with our sex-inflected cultural values" and if, additionally, reading is a process of "sorting out the structures of signification" in any text, then male readers who find themselves outside

of and unfamiliar with the symbolic systems that constitute female experience in women's writings, will necessarily dismiss those systems as undecipherable, meaningless, or trivial. And male professors will find no reason to include such works in the canons of 'major authors'. At the same time, women writers, coming into a tradition of literary language and conventional forms already appropriated, for centuries, to the purposes of male expression, will be forced virtually to 'wrestle' with that language in an effort "to remake it as a language adequate to our conceptual processes." To all of this, feminists concerned with the politics of language and style have been acutely attentive. "Language conceals an invincible adversary," observed French critic Helene Cixous "because it's the language of men and their grammar." But equally insistent, as in the work of Sandra M. Gilbert and Susan Gubar, has been the understanding of the need for *all* readers—male and female alike—to learn to penetrate the otherwise unfamiliar universes of symbolic action that comprise women's writings, past and present.

* * *

To have attempted so many difficult questions and to have accomplished so much—even acknowledging the inevitable false starts, overlapping, and repetition—in so short a time, should certainly, one would imagine, have secured feminist literary criticism full partnership in that academic pursuit which we term, loosely enough, "critical analysis." But, in fact, as the 1979 *Harvard Guide to Contemporary American Writing* makes all too clear, our situation is, at best, ambiguous; at worst, precarious. Boasting that it 'undertakes a critical survey of the most significant writing in the United States between the end of World War II and the end of the 1970s, the *Guide's* Preface promises "first, . . . a survey of intellectual commitments and attitudes during the period" and then "an examination of the theories and practices of literary criticism which have accompanied and to some extent even influenced the writing of these decades." The opening chapter by Alan Trachtenberg on the "Intellectual Background," however, while it pays respectful and often probing attention to the social critics and the 'revolutionary criticism' which marked the 1960s and early 1970s, never mentions what remains as perhaps the most enduring legacy of that critique: the women's liberation movement. Similarly, in his overview of 'American literary criticism since 1945,' A. Walton Litz notes a 'general trend . . . from consensus to diversity,' but he fails to note feminist literary criticism as any contributor to that growing critical diversity. To be sure, the *Guide* includes two chapters by women—Elizabeth Janeway's study of 'Women's Literature' and Josephine Hendin's survey of "Experimental Fiction." And both, in different ways, point to the importance of women writers and the new feminism for current developments in American Literature. That only the women contributors marked this fact, though, suggests the continuing ghettoization of women's interests and demonstrates again how fragile has been the impact of feminist criticism on our non-feminist colleagues and on the academic mainstream in general.

Indeed, for all our effort, instead of being welcomed into that mainstream, we've been forced to negotiate a mine-field. The very energy and diversity of our enterprise has rendered us vulnerable to attack on the grounds that we lack both definition and coherence; while our particular attentiveness to the ways in which literature encodes and disseminates cultural value systems calls down upon us imprecations which echo those heaped upon the Marxist critics of an earlier generation. If we are scholars dedicated to rediscovering a lost body of writings by women, then our finds are questioned on aesthetic grounds. And if we are critics, determined to practice revisionist readings, it is claimed that our focus is too narrow, and our results only distortions or, worse still, polemical misreadings.

The very vehemence of the outcry, coupled with the fact of our total dismissal in some quarters, suggests not our deficiencies, however, but the potential magnitude of our challenge. For what we are asking be scrutinized are nothing less than shared cultural assumptions so deeply rooted and so long ingrained that, for the most part, our critical colleagues have ceased to recognize them as such. In other words, what is really being bewailed in the claims that we distort texts or threaten the disappearance of the great western literary tradition itself is not so much the disappearance of either text or tradition but, instead, the eclipse of that particular *form* of the text, and that particular *shape* of the canon, which previously reified male readers' sense of power and significance in the world. Analogously, by asking whether, as readers, we ought to be 'really satisfied by the marriage of Dorothea Brooke to Will Ladislaw? of Shirley Keeldar to Louis Moore?' or whether, as Jean Kennard suggests, we must reckon with the ways in which "the qualities we have been invited to admire in these heroines [have] been sacrificed to structural neatness," is to raise difficult and profoundly perplexing questions about the ethical implications of our otherwise unquestioned aesthetic pleasures. It is, after all, an imposition of high order to ask the viewer to attend to Ophelia's sufferings in a scene where, before, he'd always so comfortably kept his eye fixed firmly on Hamlet. To understand all this, then, as the real nature of the challenge we have offered and, in consequence, as the motivation for the often overt hostility we've aroused, should help us learn to negotiate the mine-field, if not with grace, then with at least a clearer comprehension of its underlying patterns.

The ways in which objections to our work are usually posed, of course, serve to obscure their deeper motivations. But this may, in part, be due to our own reticence at taking full responsibility for the truly radicalizing premises that lie at the theoretical core of all we have so far accomplished. It may be time, therefore, to redirect discussion, forcing our adversaries to deal with the substantive issues and pushing ourselves into a clearer articulation of what, in fact, we are about. Up until now, I fear, we have only piecemeal dealt with the difficulties inherent in challenging the authority of established canons and then justifying the excellence of women's traditions, sometimes in accord with standards to which they have no intrinsic relation.

At the very point at which we must perforce enter the discourse—that is, claiming excellence or importance for our 'finds'—all discussion has already, we discover, long ago been closed. 'If Kate Chopin were *really* worth reading', an Oxford-trained colleague once assured me, 'she'd have lasted—like Shakespeare'; and he then proceeded to vote against the English Department's crediting a Women's Studies seminar I was offering in American women writers. The canon, for him, conferred excellence; Chopin's exclusion demonstrated only her lesser worth. As far as he was concerned, I could no more justify giving English Department credit for the study of Chopin than I could dare publicly to question Shakespeare's genius. Through hindsight, I've now come to view that discussion as not only having posed fruitless oppositions but as having entirely evaded the much more profound problem lurking just beneath the surface of our disagreement: and that is, that the fact of canonization puts any work beyond questions of establishing its merit and, instead, invites students to offer only increasingly more ingenious readings and interpretations, the purpose of which is to validate the greatness already imputed by canonization.

Had I only understood it for what it was then, into this circular and self-serving set of assumptions I might have interjected some statement of my right to question why *any* text is revered and my need to know what it tells us about "how we live, how we have been living, how we have been led to imagine ourselves, [and] how our language has trapped as well as liberated us." The very fact of our critical training within the strictures imposed by an established canon of major works and authors, however, repeatedly deflects us from such questions; instead, we find ourselves endlessly responding to the *riposte* that the overwhelmingly male presence among canonical authors was only an accident of history— and never intentionally sexist—coupled with claims to the 'obvious' aesthetic merit of those canonized texts. It is, as I say, a fruitless exchange, serving more to obscure than to expose the territory being protected and dragging us, again and again, through the mine-field.

It is my contention that current hostilities might be transformed into a true dialogue with our critics if we at last made explicit what appear, to this observer, to constitute the three crucial propositions to which our special interests inevitably give rise. They are, moreover, propositions which, if handled with care and intelligence, could breathe new life into now moribund areas of our profession:

1. Literary history (and, with that, the historicity of literature) is a fiction;
2. insofar as we are taught how to read, what we engage are not texts but paradigms; and, finally,
3. that since the grounds upon which we assign aesthetic value to texts are never infallible, unchangeable, or universal, we must re-examine not only our aesthetics but, as well, the inherent biases and assumptions informing the critical methods which (in part) shape our aesthetic responses.

For the sake of brevity, I won't attempt to offer the full arguments for each but, rather, only sufficient elaboration to demonstrate what I see as their intrinsic relation to the potential scope of and present challenge implied by feminist literary study:

1. *Literary history (and, with that, the historicity of literature) is a fiction.* To being with, an established canon functions as a model by which to chart the continuities and discontinuities, as well as the influences upon and the interconnections between works, genres, and authors. That model we tend to forget, however, is of our own making. It will take a very different shape, and explain its inclusions and exclusions in very different ways, if the reigning critical ideology believes that new literary forms result from some kind of ongoing internal dialectic within pre-existing styles and traditions or if, by contrast, the ideology declares that literary change is dependent upon societal development and

thereby determined by upheavals in the social and economic organization of the culture at large. Indeed, whenever in the previous century of English and American literary scholarship one alternative replaced the other, we saw dramatic alterations in canonical "wisdom."

This suggests, then, that our sense of a "literary history" and, by extension, our confidence in a so-called historical canon, is rooted not so much in any definite understanding of the past, as in our need to call up and utilize the past on behalf of a better understanding of the present. Thus, to paraphrase David Couzens Hoy, it becomes 'necessary to point out that the understanding of art and literature is such an essential aspect of the present's self-understanding that this self-understanding conditions what even gets taken' as comprising that artistic and literary past. To quote Hoy fully, "this continual reinterpretation of the past goes hand in hand with the continual reinterpretation by the present of itself." In our own time, uncertain as to which, if any, model truly accounts for our canonical choices or accurately explains literary history, and pressured further by the feminists' call for some justification of the criteria by which women's writings were largely excluded from both that canon and history, we suffer what Harold Bloom has called "a remarkable dimming" of "our mutual sense of canonical standards."

Into this apparent impasse feminist literary theorists implicitly introduce the observation that our choices and evaluations of current literature have the effect either of solidifying or of reshaping our sense of the past. The authority of any established canon, after all, is reified by our perception that current work seems to grow, almost inevitably, out of it (even in opposition or rebellion), and is called into question when what we read appears to have little or no relation to what we recognize as coming before. So, were the larger critical community to begin to seriously attend to the recent outpouring of fine literature by women, this would surely be accompanied by a concomitant re-searching of the past, by literary historians, in order to account for the present phenomenon. In that process, literary history would itself be altered: works by seventeenth, eighteenth, or nineteenth century women writers, to which we had not previously attended, for example, might be given new importance as 'precursors' or as prior influences upon present-day authors; while selected male writers might also be granted new prominence as figures whom the women today, or even yesterday, needed to reject. I am arguing, in other words, that the choices we make in the present inevitably alter our sense of the past that led to them.

Related to this is the feminist challenge to that patently mendacious critical fallacy that we read the 'classics' in order to reconstruct the past 'the way it really was', and that we read Shakespeare and Milton in order to apprehend the meanings that they intended. Short of time machines or miraculous resurrections, there is simply no way to know, precisely or surely, what 'really was', what Homer intended when he sang, or Milton when he dictated. Critics more acute than I have already pointed up the impossibility of grounding a reading in the imputation of authorial intention, since the further removed the author is from us, so too must be his or her systems of knowledge and belief, points of view, and structures of vision (artistic and otherwise). (I omit here the difficulty of finally either proving or disproving the imputation of intentionality since, inescapably, the only appropriate authority is unavailable: deceased.) What we have really come to mean when we speak of competence in reading historical texts, therefore, is the ability to recognize literary conventions which have survived through time—so as to remain operational in the mind of the reader—and, where these are lacking, the ability to translate (or perhaps transform?) the text's ciphers into more current and recognizable shapes. But we never really reconstruct the past in its own terms. What we gain when we read the 'classics', then, is neither Homer's Greece nor George Eliot's England *as they knew it* but, rather, an approximation of an already fictively imputed past made available, through our interpretive strategies, for present concerns. Only by understanding this can we put to rest that recurrent delusion that the so-called "continuing relevance" of the classics serves as 'testimony to perennial features of human experience." The only 'perennial feature' to which our ability to read and reread texts written in previous centuries testifies is our inventiveness—in the sense that all of literary history is a fiction which we daily recreate as we reread it. What distinguished feminists in this regard is their desire to alter and extend what we take as historically relevant from out of that vast storehouse of our literary inheritance and, further, their recognition of the storehouse for what it really is: a resource for remodeling our literary history, past, present, and future.

2. *Insofar as we are taught how to read, what we engage are not texts but paradigms.* To pursue the logical consequences of the first proposition leads, however uncomfortably to the conclusion that we appropriate meaning from a text according to what we need (or desire), or, in other words, according to the critical assumptions or predispositions (conscious or not) that we bring to it. And we appropriate different meanings, or report different gleanings, at different times—even from the same text—according to our changed assumptions, circumstances, and requirements. This, in essence, constitutes the heart of the second proposition. For insofar as literature is itself a social institution, so too, reading is a highly socialized—or learned—activity. What makes it so exciting, of course, is that it can be constantly relearned, so as to provide either an individual or an entire reading community, over time, infinite variations of the same text. It *can* provide that; but, I must add, too often it does not. Frequently our reading habits become fixed so that each successive reading experience functions, in effect, normatively, with one particular kind of novel stylizing our expectations of those to follow, the stylistic devices of any favorite author (or group of authors) alerting us to the presence or absence of those devices in the works of others, and so on. 'Once one has read his first poem', Murray Krieger has observed, 'he turns to his second and to the others that will follow thereafter with an increasing series of preconceptions about the sort of activity in which he is indulging. In matters of literary experience, as in other experiences', Krieger concludes, "one is a virgin but once.''

For most readers, this is a fairly unconscious process, and not unnaturally, what we are taught to read well and with pleasure, when we are young, predisposes us to certain specific kinds of adult reading tastes. For the professional literary critic, the process may be no different, but it is at least more conscious. Graduate schools, at their best, are training grounds for competing interpretive paradigms or reading techniques: affective stylistics, structuralism, and semiotic analysis, to name only a few of the more recent entries. The delight we learn to take in the mastery of these interpretive strategies is then often mistakenly construed as our delight in reading specific texts, especially in the case of works that would otherwise be unavailable or even offensive to us. In my own graduate career, for example, with superb teachers to guide me, I learned to take great pleasure in *Paradise Lost,* even though as both a Jew and a feminist, I can subscribe neither to its theology nor to its hierarchy of sexual valuation. If, within its own terms (as I have been taught to understand them), the text manipulates my sensibilities and moves me to pleasure—as I will affirm it does—then, at least in part, that must be because, in spite of my real-world alienation from many of its basic tenets, I have been able to enter that text through interpretive strategies which allow me to displace less comfortable observations with others to which I have been taught pleasurably to attend. Though some of my teachers may have called this process "learning to read the *text* properly', I have now come to see it as learning to effectively manipulate the critical strategies which they taught me so well. Knowing, for example, the poem's debt to epic conventions, I am able to discover in it echoes and reworkings of both lines and situations from Virgil and Homer; placing it within the ongoing Christian debate between Good and Evil, I comprehend both the philosophic and the stylistic significance of Satan's ornate rhetoric as compared to God's majestic simplicity in Book III. But, in each case, an interpretive model, already assumed, had guided my discovery of the evidence of it.

When we consider the implications of these observations for the processes of canon-formation and for the assignment of aesthetic value, we find ourselves locked in a chicken-and-egg dilemma, unable easily to distinguish as primary the importance of *what* we read as opposed to *how* we have learned to read it. For, simply put, we read well, and with pleasure, what we already know how to read; and what we know how to read is to a large extent dependent upon what we have already read (works from which we've developed our expectations and learned our interpretive strategies). What we then choose to read—and, by extension, teach and thereby "canonize"—usually follows upon our previous reading. Radical breaks are tiring, demanding, uncomfortable, and sometimes wholly beyond our comprehension.

Though the argument is not usually couched in precisely these terms, a considerable segment of the most recent feminist rereadings of women writers allows the conclusion that, where those authors have dropped out of sight, the reason may be due not to any lack of merit in the work but, instead, to an incapacity of predominantly male readers to properly interpret and appreciate women's texts— due, in large part, to a lack of prior acquaintance. The fictions which women compose about the worlds they inhabit may owe a debt to prior, influential works by other women or, simply enough, to the daily experience of the writer herself or, more usually, to some combination of the two. The reader coming upon such fiction, with knowledge of neither its informing literary traditions nor its real-world contexts, will thereby find himself hard-pressed, though he recognize the words on the page, to

competently decipher its intended meanings. And this is what makes the recent studies by Spacks, Moer, Showalter, Gilbert and Gubar, and others so crucial: for, by attempting to delineate the connections and inter-relations that make for a female literary tradition, they provide us with invaluable aids for recognizing and understanding the unique literary traditions and sex-related contexts out of which women write.

The (usually male) reader who, both by experience and by reading, has never made acquaintance with those contexts—historically, the lying-in room, the parlor, the nursery, the kitchen, the laundry, and so on—will necessarily lack the capacity to fully interpret the dialogue or action embedded therein; for, as every good novelist knows, the meaning of any character's action or statement is inescapably a function of the specific situation in which it is embedded. Virginia Woolf therefore quite properly anticipated the male reader's disposition to write off what he could not understand, abandoning women's writings as offering "not merely a difference of view, but a view that is weak, or trivial, or sentimental because it differs from his own." Grappling most obviously with the ways in which male writers and male subject matter had already preempted the language of literature, in her essay on 'Women and Fiction', Woolf was also tacitly commenting on the problem of (male) audience and conventional reading expectations when she speculated that the woman writer might well 'find that she is perpetually wishing to alter the established values [in literature]—to make serious what appears insignificant to a man, and trivial what is to him important." "The "competence" necessary for understanding [a] literary message . . . depends upon a great number of codices," after all; as Cesare Segre has pointed out, to be competent, a reader must either share or at least be familiar with, "in addition to the code language . . . the codes of custom, of society, and of conceptions of the world" (what Woolf meant by 'values'). Males ignorant of women's 'values' or conceptions of the world will necessarily, thereby, be poor readers of works that in any sense recapitulate their codes.

The problem is further exacerbated when the language of the literary text is largely dependent upon figuration. For it can be argued, as Ted Cohen has shown, that while "in general, and with some obvious qualifications . . . all literal use of language is accessible to all whose language it is . . . figurative use can be inaccessible to all but those who share information about one another's knowledge, beliefs, intentions, and attitudes." There was nothing

288

fortuitous, for example, in Charlotte Perkins Gilman's decision to situate the progressive mental breakdown and increasing incapacity of the protagonist of *The Yellow Wallpaper* in an upstairs room that had once served as a nursery (with barred windows, no less). But the reader unacquainted with the ways in which women traditionally inhabited a household might not have taken the initial description of the setting as semantically relevant; and the progressive infantilization of the adult protagonist could thereby lose some of its symbolic implications. Analogously, the contemporary poet who declares along with Adrienne Rich, the need for 'a whole new poetry beginning here' is acknowledging the fact that the materials available for symbolization and figuration from women's contexts will necessarily differ from women's contexts will necessarily differ from those that men have traditionally utilized:

Vision begins to happen in such a life
as if a woman quietly walked away
from the argument and jargon in a room
and sitting down in the kitchen, began turning
    in her lap
bits of yarn, calico and velvet scraps,

* * *

pulling the tenets of a life together
with no mere will to mastery,
only care for the many-lived, unending
forms in which she finds herself.[1]

What, then, the fate of the woman writer whose competent reading community is composed only of members of her own sex? And what, then, the response of the male critic who, on first looking into Virginia Woolf or Doris Lessing, finds all of the interpretive strategies at his command inadequate to a full and pleasurable deciphering of their pages? Historically, the result has been the diminished status of women's products and their consequent absence from major canons. Nowadays, however, by pointing out that the act of 'interpreting language is no more sexually neutral than language use or the language system itself', feminist students of language, like Nelly Furman, help us better understand the crucial linkage between our gender and our interpretive, or reading, strategies. Insisting upon "the contribution of the . . . reader [in] the active attribution of significance to formal signifiers," Fur-

man and others promise to shake us all—male and female alike—out of our canonized and conventional aesthetic assumptions.

3. *Since the grounds upon which we assign aesthetic value to texts are never infallible, unchangeable, or universal, we must re-examine not only our aesthetics but, as well, the inherent biases and assumptions informing the critical methods which (in part) shape our aesthetic responses.* I am, on the one hand, arguing that men will be better readers, or appreciators, of women's books when they have read more of them (as women have always been taught to become astute readers of men's texts); on the other hand, it will be noted, the impact of my remarks shifts the act of critical judgment from assigning aesthetic valuations to texts and directs it, instead, to ascertaining the adequacy of any interpretive paradigm to a full reading of both male and female writing. My third proposition—and, I admit, perhaps the most controversial—thus calls into question that recurrent tendency in criticism to establish norms for the evaluation of literary works when we might better serve the cause of literature by developing standards of evaluating the adequacy of our critical methods. This does not mean that I wish to discard aesthetic valuation. The choice, as I see it, is not between retaining or discarding aesthetic values; rather, the choice is between having some awareness of what constitutes (at least in part) the bases of our aesthetic responses and going without such an awareness. For it is my view that insofar as aesthetic responsiveness continues to be an integral aspect of our human response system—in part spontaneous, in part learned and educated—we will inevitably develop theories to help explain, formalize, or even initiate those responses. Indeed, in a sense, this is what criticism is all about.

In challenging the adequacy of received critical opinion or the imputed excellence of established canons, therefore feminist literary critics are essentially seeking to discover how aesthetic value is assigned in the first place, where it resides (in the text or in the reader), and, most importantly, what validity may really be claimed by our so-called aesthetic "judgments." What ends do those judgments serve, the feminist asks; and what conceptions of the world or ideological stances do they (even if unwittingly) help to perpetuate? She confronts, for example, the reader who simply cannot entertain the possibility that women's worlds are

---

[1]Adrienne Rich, "Transcendental Elude" in her *The Dream of a Common Language: Poems 1974–1977* (New York, W. W. Norton & Co., 1978), pp. 76–77.

symbolically rich, the reader who, like the male characters in Susan Glaspell's 1917 short story, "A Jury of Her Peers," has already assumed the innate 'insignificance of kitchen things.'' Such a reader, she knows, will prove himself unable to assign significance to fictions which attend to 'kitchen things'' and will, instead, judge such fictions as trivial and as aesthetically wanting. For her to take useful issue with such a reader, she must make clear that what appears to be a dispute about aesthetic merit is, in reality, a dispute about the *contexts of judgment;* and what is at issue, then, is the adequacy of the prior assumptions and reading habits brought to bear on the text. To put it bluntly: we have had enough pronouncements of aesthetic valuation for a time; it is now our task to evaluate the imputed norms and normative reading patterns that, in part, led to those pronouncements.

By and large, I think I've made my point. Only to clarify it do I add this coda: when feminists turn their attention to the works of male authors which have traditionally been accorded high aesthetic value and, where warranted, follow Tillie Olsen's advice that we assert our "right to say: this is surface, this falsifies reality, this degrades," such statements do not necessarily mean that we will end up with a diminished canon. To question the source of the aesthetic pleasures we've gained from reading Spenser, Shakespeare, Milton, *et al,* does not imply that we must deny those pleasures. It means only that aesthetic response is once more invested with epistemological, ethical, and moral concerns. It means, in other words, that readings of *Paradise Lost* which analyze its complex hierarchal structures but fail to note the implications of gender within that hierarchy; or which insist upon the inherent (or even inspired) perfection of Milton's figurative language but fail to note the consequences, for Eve, of her specifically gender-marked weakness, which, like the flowers to which she attends, requires "propping up"; or which concentrate on the poem's thematic reworking of classical notions of martial and epic prowess into Christian (moral) heroism but fail to note that Eve is stylistically edited out of that process—all such readings, however, useful, will no longer be deemed wholly adequate. The pleasures we had earlier learned to take in the poem will not be diminished thereby; but they will become part of an altered reading attentiveness.

* * *

These three propositions I believe to be at the theoretical core of all current feminist literary crit-

icism, whether acknowledged as such or not. If I am correct in this, then that criticism represents more than a profoundly skeptical stance towards all other pre-existing and contemporaneous schools and methods, and more than an impassioned demand that the variety and variability of women's literary expression be taken into full account, rather than written off as caprice and exception, the irregularity in an otherwise regular design; it represents that locus in literary study where, in unceasing effort, female self-consciousness turns in upon itself, attempting to grasp the deepest conditions of this own unique and multiplicitous realities, in the hope, eventually, of altering the very forms through which the culture perceives, expresses, and knows itself. For, if what the larger women's movement looks for in the future is a transformation of the structures of primarily male power which now order our society, then the feminist literary critic demands that we understand the ways in which those structures have been—and continue to be—reified by our literature and by our literary criticism. Thus, along with other so-called 'radical' critics and critical schools, though our focus remains the power of the word to both structure and mirror human experience, our overriding commitment is to a radical alteration—an improvement, we hope—in the nature of that experience.

What distinguishes our work from those similarly oriented 'social consciousness' critiques, it is said, is its lack of systematic coherence. Pitted against, for example, psychoanalytic or Marxist readings, which owe a decisive share of their persuasiveness to their apparent internal consistency as a system, the aggregate of feminist literary criticism appears woefully deficient in system, and painfully lacking in program. It is, in fact, from all quarters, the most telling defect alleged against us, the most explosive threat in the mine-field. And my own earlier observation that, as of 1976, feminist literary criticism appeared "more like a set of interchangeable strategies than any coherent school or shared goal orientation," has been taken by some as an indictment, by others as a statement of impatience. Neither was intended. I felt then, as I do now, that this would "prove both its strength *and* its weakness," in the sense that the apparent disarray would leave us vulnerable to the kind of objection I've just alluded to, while the fact of our diversity would finally place us securely where, all along, we should have been: camped out, on the far side of the mine-field, with the other pluralists and pluralisms.

In our heart of hearts, of course, most critics are really structuralists (whether or not they accept the label), since what we are seeking are patterns (or structures) that can order and explain the otherwise inchoate; thus, we invent, or believe we discover, relational patternings in the texts we read which promise transcendence from difficulty and perplexity to clarity and coherence. But, as I've tried to argue in these pages, to the imputed 'truth' or 'accuracy' of these findings, the feminist must oppose the painfully obvious truism that what is attended to in a literary work, and hence what is reported about it, is often determined not so much by the work itself as by the critical technique or aesthetic criteria through which it is filtered or, rather, read and decoded. All the feminist is asserting, then, is her own equivalent right to liberate new (and perhaps different) significances from these same texts; and, at the same time, her right to choose which features of a text she takes as relevant since she is, after all, asking new and different questions of it. In the process, she claims neither definitiveness nor structural completeness for her different readings and reading systems, but only their usefulness in recognizing the particular achievements of woman-as-author and their applicability in conscientiously decoding woman-as-sign.

That these alternate foci of critical attentiveness will render alternate readings or interpretations of the same text—even among feminists—should be no cause for alarm. Such developments illustrate only the pluralist contention that, 'in approaching a text of any complexity . . . the reader must choose to emphasize certain aspects which seem to him crucial' and 'in fact, the variety of readings which we have for many works is a function of the selection of crucial aspects made by the variety of readers'. Robert Scholes, from whom I've been quoting, goes so far as to assert that "there is no single 'right' reading for any complex literary work," and, following the Russian formalist school, he observes that "we do not speak of readings that are simply true or false, but of readings that are more or less rich, strategies that are more or less appropriate." The fact that those who share the term 'feminist' nonetheless practice a diversity of critical strategies, leading, in some cases, to quite different readings, requires us to acknowledge among ourselves that sister critics, "having chosen to tell a different story, may in their interpretation identify different aspects of the meanings conveyed by the same passage." In other words, just because we will no longer tolerate the specifically sexist omissions and ignorances of earlier critical schools and methods does not mean that, in their stead, we must establish our own "party lines."

In my view, our purpose is not and should not be the formulation of any single reading method or potentially procrustean set of critical procedures nor, even less, the generation of prescriptive categories for some dreamed-of non-sexist literary canon. Instead, as I see it, our task is to initiate nothing less than a playful pluralism, responsive to the possibilities of multiple critical schools and methods, but captive of none, recognizing that the many tools needed for our work of analysis will necessarily be largely inherited and only partly of our own making. Only by employing a plurality of methods will we protect ourselves from the temptation to so oversimplify any text—and especially those particularly offensive to us—that we render ourselves unresponsive to what Robert Scholes has called "its various systems of meaning and their interaction." Any text we deem worthy of our critical attention is usually, after all, a locus of many and varied kinds of (personal, thematic, stylistic, structural, rhetorical, etc.) relationships. So, whether we tend to treat a text as a *mimesis,* in which words are taken to be recreating or representing viable worlds; or whether we prefer to treat a text as a kind of equation of communication, in which decipherable messages are passed from writers to readers; and whether we locate meaning as inherent in the text, the act of reading, or in some collaboration between reader and text—whatever our predilection, let us generate from it not some strait jacket which limits the scope of possible analysis but, rather, an ongoing dialogue of competing potential possibilities—among feminists and, as well, between feminist and non-feminist critics.

The difficulty of what I describe does not escape me. The very idea of pluralism seems to threaten a kind of chaos for the future of literary inquiry while, at the same time, it seems to deny the hope of establishing some basic conceptual model which can organize all data—the hope which always begins any analytical exercise. My effort here, however, has been to demonstrate the essential delusions which inform such objections: If literary inquiry has historically escaped chaos by establishing canons, then it has only substituted one mode of arbitrary action for another—and, in this case, at the expense of half the population. And if feminists openly acknowledge ourselves as pluralists, then we do not give up the search for patterns of opposition and connection—probably the basis of thinking itself; what we give up is simply the arrogance of claiming that our work is either exhaustive or definitive. (It is, after all, the identical arrogance we are asking our non-feminist colleagues to abandon.)

If this kind of pluralism appears to threaten both the present coherence of and the inherited aesthetic criteria for a canon of 'greats', then, as I have earlier argued, it is precisely that threat which, alone, can free us from the prejudices, the strictures, and the blind-spots of the past. In feminist hands, I would add, it is less a threat than a promise.

What unites and repeatedly reinvigorates feminist literary criticism, then, is neither dogma nor method but, as I have indicated earlier, an acute and impassioned *attentiveness* to the ways in which primarily male structures of power are inscribed (or encoded) within our literary inheritance; the consequences of that encoding for women—as characters, as readers, and as writers; and, with that, a shared analytic *concern* for the implications of that encoding not only for a better understanding of the past, but on behalf of an improved reordering of the present and future as well. If that *concern* identifies feminist literary criticism as one of the many academic arms of the larger women's movement, then that *attentiveness,* within the halls of academe, poses no less a challenge for change, generating, as it does, the three proposition explored here. The critical pluralism which inevitably follows upon those three propositions, however, bears little resemblance to what Lillian Robinson has called "the great bourgeois theme of all, the myth of pluralism with its consequent rejection of ideological commitment as 'too simple' to embrace the (necessarily complex) truth." Only ideological commitment could have gotten us to enter the mine-field, putting in jeopardy our careers and our livelihood. Only the power of ideology to transform our conceptual worlds, and the inspiration of that ideology to liberate long-suppressed energies and emotions, can account for our willingness to take on critical tasks that, in an earlier decade, would have been "abandoned in despair or apathy." The fact of differences among us proves only that, despite our shared commitments, we have nonetheless refused to shy away from complexity, preferring rather to openly disagree than to give up either the intellectual honesty or hard-won insights.

Finally, I would argue, pluralism informs feminist literary inquiry not simply as a description of what already exists but, more importantly, as the only critical stance consistent with the current status of the larger women's movement. Segmented and variously focussed, the different women's organizations, in the United States at least, neither espouse any single system of analysis nor, as a result, express any wholly shared, consistently articulated ideology. The ensuing loss in effective organization and

political clout is a serious one, but it has not been paralyzing; in spite of our differences, we have united to *act* in areas of clear mutual concern (the push for the Equal Rights Amendment, [ERA], is probably the most obvious example). The trade-off, as I see it, has made possible an ongoing and educative dialectic of analysis and preferred solutions, protecting us thereby from the inviting traps of reductionism and dogma. And so long as this dialogue remains active, both our politics and our criticism will be free of dogma—but never, I hope, of feminist ideology, in all its variety. For, whatever else ideologies may be—projections of unacknowledged fear, disguises for ulterior motives, phatic expressions of group solidarity' (and the women's movement, to date, has certainly been all of these, and more)—whatever ideologies express, they are, as Clifford Geertz astutely observes, 'most distinctively, maps of problematic social reality and matrices for the creation of collective conscience. And despite the fact that "ideological advocates . . . tend as much to obscure as to clarify the true nature of the problems involved," as Geertz notes, "they at least call attention to their existence and, by polarizing issues, make continued neglect more difficult. Without Marxist attack, there would have been no labor reform; without Black Nationalists, no deliberate speed"; without Senecca Falls, I would add, no enfranchisement of women, and without 'consciousness raising', no feminist literary criticism nor, even less, Women's Studies.

Ideology, however, only truly manifests its power by ordering the *sum* of our actions. If feminist criticism calls anything into question, it must be that dog-eared myth of intellectual neutrality. For, what I take to be the underlying spirit, or message, of any consciously ideologically-premised criticism —that is, that ideas are important *because* they determine the ways we live, or want to live, in the world—is vitiated by confining those ideas to the study, the classroom, or the pages of our books. To write chapters decrying the sexual stereotyping of women in our literature while closing our eyes to the sexual harassment of our women students and colleagues; to display Katherine Hepburn and Rosalind Russell in our courses on "The Image of the Independent Career Woman in Film," while managing not to notice the paucity of female administrators on our own campus; to study the women who helped make universal enfranchisement a political reality while keeping silent about our activist colleagues who are denied promotion or tenure; to include segments on 'Women in the Labor Movement' in our American Studies or Women's Studies courses while remaining wilfully ignorant of the department secretary fired for her efforts to organize a clerical workers' union; to glory in the delusions of 'merit', 'privilege', and 'status' which accompany campus life in order to insulate ourselves from the millions of women who labor in poverty—all this is not merely hypocritical; it destroys both the spirit and the meaning of what we are about. It puts us, however unwittingly, in the service of those who laid the mine-field in the first place. In my view, it is a fine thing for many of us, individually, to have traversed the mine-field; but that happy circumstance will only prove of lasting importance if, together, we expose it for what it is (the male fear of sharing power and significance with women) and deactivate its components, so that others, after us, may literally dance through the mine-field.

Annette Kolodny's "Dancing Through the Minefield"

Short Answer

1.   How does Kolodny's title relate to her thesis?

2.   What accomplishments does she attribute to feminist criticism?

3.   This article was published in 1981. Do you think she would be as negative today about the success of feminist criticism? Explain.

4.   Do you think Kolodny views literature as something other than literature when she speaks of it as "social text?"

V. HUMANITIES

LIST OF KEY TERMS

imagination:

narrative:

historical evidence:

historical time:

structure

model:

theology:

God:

transcendent:

religious pluralism:

metaphor:

analogy:

Deontological Moral Theory:

Teleological Moral Theory:

Practical Reason:

categorical imperatives:

hypothetical imperatives:

The Categorical Imperative:

First Formulation (Universalizability:)

Second Formulation (Respect for Persons):

autonomy:

Happiness:

The Principle of Utility:

quantitative/qualitative pleasure

The tripartite soul:

the Forms:

catharsis:

plot:

poetry:

Romanticism:

literary criticism:

Feminism:

the canon:

SECTION VI
THE FINE ARTS AND COMMUNICATION

THEME QUESTIONS

1. What is art?

2. What makes a work of art good or bad? What criteria should we use in assessing the value of a work of art?

3. What is the nature of taste? Are there objective standards of taste or is it purely subjective?

4. Where does the creative impulse expressed in the arts come from?

5. What is the relationship between art and truth? Is there such a thing as artistic truth?

6. How does the perspective of the artist influence his or her work?

7. What is the role of art in society?

8. What is the role of mass media in our society?

9. How has the development of electronic mass media affected our perceptions of ourselves and the world we live in?

10. How is communication an art?

Introduction to the Fine Arts and Communication

Lynne Lokensgard

Our pursuit of knowledge reveals a fundamental difference between the sciences and the fine arts. While both the scientist and the fine artist seek to discover knowledge about the experiences of life, the scientist interprets life in order to discover facts, and the fine artist interprets life experiences through the filter of personal perception and feeling. The scientist seeks to provide definite answers about these experiences; the fine artist interprets them through an intuitive process, thereby coloring data by the unique view of an individual. The academic study of the fine arts and communication can be divided into methods of inquiry and theories of art and communication.

Methods of Inquiry

All of the fine arts involve some manner of creative expression and can be divided into two categories: the visual arts and the performing arts. The visual arts usually pertain to the creation of an object to be viewed or the product of a creative thought (the latter exemplified by the recent movement called Conceptual Art). In the performing arts, including theater, dance and music, the artist actually becomes part of the artistic product. The fine artist translates expression through a tool (a medium), which enables its realization. For example, the actor and dancer use the body; the painter uses pigment. Even though the musician uses an instrument, which could be considered a tool, the musical performance is dependent upon active participation of the artist with the medium.

In addition, the fine arts can be studied from a theoretical and historical standpoint. The theoretical standpoint would involve aesthetics and the formal elements. Aesthetics is the philosophical theory of art. The philosophy of art seeks an understanding of the nature of creative expression in the arts and often proposes criteria for good and bad works of art. This understanding does not necessarily depend on the knowledge of facts, for art reflects what is often the unpredictable and inexplicable phenomena of nature and the behavior of human beings. Understanding in the fine arts is possible, but the viewer may need to respond with empathy in order to connect with the artist's intuitive process.

Second, the formal elements are the language—the vocabulary tools employed by the fine artist. This language provides a methodology to help us evaluate the manner in which the fine artist uses his craft. Some of these formal elements in the performing arts are posture, tension and rhythm; in the visual arts we see shape, line, texture and color. Often used interchangeably, we can speak of the painter who expresses rhythm with lines and shapes; colors have tone and pitch; music can have color and nuance. The formal elements serve artistic expression by permitting the artist to communicate his message. We can decipher the fine arts by analyzing these formal elements. However methods of interpreting the vocabulary of the fine arts can and often do vary from culture to culture and between individual artists.

The historical approach involves an analysis of the dynamic interaction between the fine arts and history. The fine arts are the product of a culture and a reflection of its values and beliefs. There is often a close interaction between them; the culture forms the artistic values and determines what is aesthetically pleasing. Studying the values and beliefs of a particular culture provides a sound basis for the interpretation of the art that culture yields. These values and beliefs change greatly throughout history, and as one studies them chronologically, an artistic evolution within a culture and from culture to culture can be discerned. Historically the fine arts evolve toward an increasing complexity of thought and form. Yet the great works of art survive the test of time, and their quality is confirmed by their continuing influence on artists and the inspiration they give to audiences. The goals of the individual artist must also be considered, for from the Renaissance period to the present, most artists have elucidated their personal theories to facilitate the interpretation of their art.

Theories of Art and Communication

Representation is rarely the primary purpose of art. It is not a mirror of nature but an interpretation of it. There is a story about the great Classical Greek sculptor, Polykleitos, a fifth century Athenian, who believed art could improve and uplift mankind. To prove this point, he made two statues of the same male model. One, following the advice of his untrained audience, was visually realistic; the second, according to the rules of art, was modified in proportions to reflect mathematical harmonies. When his viewers were asked to evaluate the two works, they immediately saw the absurdity of the first and the superiority of the second.[1]

An important idea can be taken from this story, for it illustrates that age-old conflict in western culture between the general audience, demanding the representation of reality, and the artist, asserting the superior value of his own creative intuition. Polykleitos believed in the didactic purpose of art to reveal timeless and eternal Truths that are above mere realism. Beauty to the Greeks was the embodiment of harmonious proportions found in the ideal form of man. Believing that man was perfectable, Polykleitos hoped that through proper education, mankind could ascend to a higher level.

Throughout western history, the artist has endeavored to translate subjective experience into the work of art to add meaning to the culture at large. The individual experience of the artist addresses the collective experiences of humanity and is thereby given universal significance. The simple representation of fact and revelation of objective knowledge has rarely satisfied the artist. Creativity is interpretation.

The legacy of Greek idealism is clearly seen in Renaissance art, particularly the theories of Leonardo da Vinci. He confirmed that one knows the world through the careful observation of it, but he idealized all he represented in art, raising the common functions of man to a divine level as did his fellow Florentine, Michelangelo Buonarroti. Leonardo created a dialogue between fact and ideal, for despite all his careful attention to botany, geology and anatomy, he created an ideal world in his painting using his intuitive creative powers (see for example Mona Lisa and Madonna of the Rocks, both in the Louvre Museum in Paris). His disparate scientific studies were united by a smokey atmosphere, called sfumato and dark shadows, called chiaroscuro. Scientific observation was transformed by the veil of Classical idealism, which all Renaissance masters emulated.[2]

In the west the debate between realism and idealism reached a climax in the nineteenth century. The French Revolution and the Industrial Revolution contributed to the emergence of an economically and politically powerful middle class that had a taste for the everyday, given justification by the invention of photography in 1839 by the French scientist, Nicephore Niepce. An obsession for veristic realism affected the official art school (The French Academy of Fine Arts) and its exhibitions (the salons). The French Impressionist style, which dominated the last three decades of the nineteenth century, reflects this attitude in its attempt to faithfully record true outdoor light by optical mix. This belief that the role of art was to reproduce the world as seen, without modifying or sermonizing, is still prevalent among general audiences.

A strong opposition to this attitude, termed Romanticism, emerged during the late eighteenth century. As a movement in literature and the fine arts, it glorified the experience of the individual and forsook cultural values. It thrived in the nineteenth century, attacked the French Academy of Fine Arts and the salon, and is still a vital concept today. The theory of Romanticism contends that the creative artist must explore all the facets of one's emotional being, regardless of the fact that they are nearly impossible to understand or define.

---

[1]Kenneth Clark, *The Nude: A Study in Ideal Form* (New York: Doubleday and Company, Inc., 1956), 63–64.

[2]The late nineteenth century art historian, Heinrich Wolfflin, in 1898, defined the Renaissance style as seeking universals and Beauty in harmonious form, a view that dominated aesthetics in the western world until the nineteenth century. Heinrich Wolfflin, *Classic Art* (London: Phaidon Publications, 1952).

Attempts to apply objective principles to the subjective nature of creativity have nonetheless produced valuable criteria for improved communication in the fine arts. The eighteenth-century philosopher, Edmund Burke, in his essay on taste and beauty, introduced general criteria which could be used in the evaluation of works of art. Similarly, the twentieth-century philosopher, Monroe Beardsley, in his essay, "In Defense of Aesthetic Value" proposes his own criteria for the evaluation of art.

Burke was one of the first aestheticians to attempt to explain the various and mysterious facets of human emotions in the arts. In *A Philosophical Enquiry into the Origin of Our Ideas of the Sublime and the Beautiful*, written in 1756, he identified the sublime as the strongest and most profound emotion that can be expressed in art. He believed that if man could conjure sublime emotions within himself, he could understand his own divine origin. In contradiction to the Classical views of idealism and beauty, that Beauty is a perfect harmony of parts, this view sought to explore the irrational and obscure mechanisms of the human mind. The contemplation of natural forces, particularly awe-inspiring and threatening natural events, could produce sublime emotions. Violent storms—hurricanes, icebergs, mountains and volcanoes, phenomena that both repel and attract—cause ambivalent emotions, such as pleasure/pain. Contradiction and confusion became desirable in the fine arts. This is exemplified by the violent depictions of contemporary events by the French painter, Eugene Delacroix and the Spanish painter, Francisco Goya.

In the fine arts, most twentieth-century styles are based on the expression of diverse human emotions. The great abstract movements (The Blue Rider in Germany, 1911–12 and Abstract Expressionism in the United States, 1945–60) totally eliminate representation of the world as seen to permit the complete and total realization of the world as it is felt by the artist. In his essay, "The Dehumanization of Art," Jose Artega y Gasset shows how a transformation from the depiction of the outside world to the inner world of the artist's imagination occurred gradually over a period of several centuries from the Renaissance to the present.

The process of interiorization (the expression of inner feeling) is central to the visual arts today. The Russian artist, Wassily Kandinsky, founder of the Blue Rider and author of the manual for non-objectivity, Concerning the Spiritual in art explained this process. As early as 1910, he gave justification and meaning to abstractionism by explaining the source of his inspiration as inner need. Rather than copying what is seen by the eyes, he explained, the artist should, through the realization of non-objective form, express more those profound and spiritual ideas felt in the interior world of his mind, particularly the unconscious. Inner need is a driving force within the creative individual. This same process is seen in the monumental gestural paintings of the Abstract Expressionist generation, Jackson Pollock, Franz Kline and Willem de Kooning.

This process of interiorization is also found in the performing arts. Hall Johnson's essay on African American spirituals expresses a similar view in the early slaves' search for freedom through music, and Bruce Baugh's "Aesthetics of Rock Music," urges us to evaluate rock music on the basis of feeling rather than form. While Paul Hindemith supports these views, he also attempts to apply standards to enhance the understanding and evaluation of music. Suzanne Langer's essay, "The Dynamic Image," establishes a definition of dance based on its ability to interpret reality as perceived and expressed by the dancer through the formal elements of the medium.

Study of human communication is almost as old as human civilization. The birth of this area of study can be traced to the first half of the fifth century B.C., when a Sicilian named Corax attempted a systematic examination of communication. He was particularly interested in helping citizens of Athens become more effective in the art of speaking in the courtroom. Since the time of Corax, the study of human communication has undergone many changes. While the art of public speaking has remained an important element in the study of communication, communication researchers today examine a diversity of communication behaviors and contexts. Modern communication scholars may study communication in interpersonal relationships, group interactions, organizations, families, the mass media, politics, the health professions, and intercultural encounters. Communication studies now examines the pervasive role of communication in human affairs and the symbolic processes through which individuals interact with one another, their groups, and their culture. Scholars involved in communication research may employ a variety of methods of inquiry commonly used in scientific, humanistic, or social scientific research. Depending on the issue or question of interest communication researchers use experimentation, historical research, surveys, ethnographic observations, content analysis, legal research, or critical analysis. All communication researchers have an interest in human communication behavior but often taken different approaches to the study of this behavior.

The study of how the mass media affects individuals and society is an important issue in the study of communication. Included in the readings for this section is an article by Raymond Gozzi, Jr., and W. Lance Haynes entitled *Electric Media and Electric Epistemology: Empathy at a Distance.* This article specifically examines how the mass media has changed our ways of knowing and understanding the world. As you read the article think about how the media affects you and how you understand the world. Think about how the electric epistemology has influenced you, your family, and your community.

The art of the Far East has never been restricted by demands for retinal depiction. Zen philosophy, as it influenced Chinese and Japanese aesthetics, stresses the connection between calligraphic writing and representation of objects, and therefore creates a link between symbol and reality. Their written language employs characters which symbolize ideas, thus encouraging abstract thought and training the mind to view the representation of objects and scenes as symbols of grander ideas, not simply mirrors of nature. To the Japanese the vigorous power of the brush strokes in writing and artistic scenes imparts the vital energy of nature and symbolizes a higher truth.

The pursuit of knowledge gives meaning to the world, and the fine arts add resonance to that meaning by exploring the human condition through a creative process. By learning to understanding and empathize with the fine arts, our lives are made richer.

Edmund Burke*

ON TASTE

On a superficial view, we may seem to differ very widely from each other in our reasonings, and no less in our pleasures: but notwithstanding this difference, which I think to be rather apparent than real, it is probable that the standard both of reason and Taste is the same in all human creatures. For if there were not some principles of judgment as well as of sentiment common to all mankind, no hold could possibly be taken either on their reason or their passions, sufficient to maintain the ordinary correspondence of life. It appears indeed to be generally acknowledged, that with regard to truth and falsehood there is something fixed. We find people in their disputes continually appealing to certain tests and standards which are allowed on all sides, and are supposed to be established in our common nature. But there is not the same obvious concurrence in any uniform or settled principles which relate to Taste. It is even commonly supposed that this delicate and aerial faculty, which seems too volatile to endure even the chains of a definition, cannot be properly tried by any test, nor regulated by any standard. There is so continual a call for the exercise of the reasoning faculty, and it is so much strengthened by perpetual contention, that certain maxims of right reason seem to be tacitly settled amongst the most ignorant. The learned have improved on this rude science, and reduced those maxims into a system. If Taste has not been so happily cultivated, it was not that the subject was barren, but that the labourers were few or negligent; for to say the truth, there are not the same interesting motives to impel us to fix the one, which urge us to ascertain the other. And after all, if men differ in their opinion concerning such matters, their difference is not attended with the same important consequences, else I make no doubt but that the logic of Taste, if I may be allowed the expression, might very possibly be as well digested, and we might come to discuss matters of this nature with as much certainty, as those which seem more immediately within the province of mere reason. And indeed it is very necessary at the entrance into such an enquiry, as our present, to make this point as clear as possible; for if Taste has no fixed principles, if the imagination is not affected according to some invariable and certain laws, our labour is like to be employed to very little purpose; as it must be judged an useless, if not an absurd undertaking, to lay down rules for caprice, and to set up for a legislator of whims and fancies.

The term Taste, like all other figurative terms, is not extremely accurate; the thing which we understand by it, is far from a simple and determinate idea in the minds of most men, and it is therefore liable to uncertainty and confusion. I have no great opinion of a definition, the celebrated remedy for the cure of this disorder. For when we define, we seem in danger of circumscribing nature within the bounds of our own notions, which we often take up by hazard, or embrace on trust, or form out of a limited and partial consideration of the object before us, instead of extending our ideas to take in all that nature comprehends, according to her manner

---

*Edmund Burke (1759–97) was a British political theorist and Whig member of Parliament. Though sympathetic to the American colonies' struggle for independence, he reacted with hostility towards the French Revolution and is best known for his defense of tradition and hierarchy in his *Reflections on the Revolution in France,* the first counter-revolutionary tract and starting point of modern conservative thought. In the following excerpt, which is taken from his early *A Philosophical Enquiry Concerning the Sublime and the Beautiful* (1757), Burke argues that there are objective standards of taste.

of combining. We are limited in our enquiry by the strict laws to which we have submitted at our setting out.

—Circa vilem patulumque morabimur orbem
Unde pudor proferre pedem vetat aut operis
lex.

A definition may be very exact, and yet go but a very little way towards informing us of the nature of the thing defined; but let the virtue of a definition be what it will, in the order of things, it seems rather to follow than to precede our enquiry, of which it ought to be considered as the result. It must be acknowledged that the methods of disquisition and teaching may be sometimes different, and on very good reason undoubtedly; but for my part, I am convinced that the method of teaching which approaches most nearly to the method of investigation, is incomparably the best; since not content with serving up a few barren and lifeless truths, it leads to the stock on which they grew; it tends to set the reader himself in the track of invention, and to direct him into those paths in which the author has made his own discoveries, if he should be so happy as to have made any that are valuable.

But to cut off all pretence for cavilling, I mean by the word Taste no more than that faculty, or those faculties of the mind which are affected with, or which form a judgment of the works of imagination and the elegant arts. This is, I think, the most general idea of that word, and what is the least connected with any particular theory. And my point in this enquiry is to find whether there are any principles, on which the imagination is affected, so common to all, so grounded and certain, as to supply the means of reasoning satisfactorily about them. And such principles of Taste, I fancy there are; however paradoxical it may seem to those, who on a superficial view imagine, that there is so great a diversity of Tastes both in kind and degree, that nothing can be more indeterminate.

All the natural powers in man, which I know, that are conversant about external objects, are the Senses; the Imagination; and the Judgment. And first with regard to the senses. We do and we must suppose, that as the conformation of their organs are nearly, or altogether the same in all men, so the manner of perceiving external objects is in all men the same, or with little difference. We are satisfied that what appears to be light to one eye, appears light to another; that what seems sweet to one palate, is sweet to another; that what is dark and bitter to this man, is likewise dark and bitter to that; and we conclude in the same manner of great and little, hard and soft, hot and cold, rough and smooth; and indeed of all the natural qualities and affections of bodies. If we suffer ourselves to imagine, that their senses present to different men different images of things, this sceptical proceeding will make every sort of reasoning on every subject vain and frivolous, even that sceptical reasoning itself, which had persuaded us to entertain a doubt concerning the agreement of our perceptions. But as there will be very little doubt that bodies present similar images to the whole species, it must necessarily be allowed, that the pleasures and the pains which every object excites in one man, it must raise in all mankind, whilst it operates naturally, simply, and by its proper powers only; for if we deny this, we must imagine, that the same cause operating in the same manner, and on subjects of the same kind, will produce different effects, which would be highly absurd. Let us first consider this point in the sense of Taste, as the faculty in question has taken its name from that sense. All men are agreed to call vinegar sour, honey sweet, and aloes bitter; and as they are all agreed in finding these qualities in those objects, they do not in the least differ concerning their effects with regard to pleasure and pain. They all concur in calling sweetness pleasant, and sourness and bitterness unpleasant. Here there is no diversity in their sentiments; and that there is not appears fully from the consent of all men in the metaphors which are taken from the sense of Taste. A sour temper, bitter expressions, bitter curses, a bitter fate, are terms well and strongly understood by all. And we are altogether as well understood when we say, a sweet disposition, a sweet person, a sweet condition, and the like. It is confessed, that custom, and some other causes, have made many deviations from the natural pleasures or pains which belong to these several Tastes; but then the power of distinguishing between the natural and the acquired relish remains to the very last. A man frequently comes to prefer the Taste of tobacco to that of sugar, and the flavour of vinegar to that of milk; but this makes no confusion in Tastes, whilst he is sensible that the tobacco and vinegar are not sweet, and whilst he knows that habit alone has reconciled his palate to these alien pleasures. Even with such a person we may speak, and with sufficient precision, concerning Tastes. But should any man be found who declares, that to him tobacco has a Taste like sugar, and that he cannot distinguish between milk and vinegar; or that tobacco and vinegar are sweet, milk bitter, and sugar sour, we immediately conclude that the organs of this man are out of order, and that his palate is utterly vitiated. We are as far from conferring with such a person upon Tastes, as from reasoning concerning the relations of quantity with one who should deny that all the parts together were equal to the whole. We do not call a man of this kind wrong in his notions, but absolutely mad. Exceptions of this sort in either way, do not at all impeach our general rule, nor make us conclude that men have various principles concerning the relations of quantity, or the Taste of things. So that when it is said, Taste cannot be disputed, it can only mean, that no one can strictly answer what pleasure or pain some particular man may find from the Taste of some particular thing. This indeed cannot be disputed; but we may dispute, and with sufficient clearness too, concerning the things which are naturally pleasing or disagreeable to the sense. But when we talk of any peculiar or acquired relish, then we must know the habits, the prejudices, or the distempers of this particular man, and we must draw our conclusion from those.

This agreement of mankind is not confined to the Taste solely. The principle of pleasure derived from sight is the same in all. Light is more pleasing than darkness. Summer, when the earth is clad in green, when the heavens are serene and bright, is more agreeable than winter, when every thing makes a different appearance. I never remember that any thing beautiful, whether a man, a beast, a bird, or a plant was ever shewn, though it were to an hundred people, that they did not all immediately agree that it was beautiful, though some might have thought that it fell short of their expectation, or that other things were still finer. I believe no man thinks a goose to be more beautiful than a swan, or imagines that what they call a Friezland hen excels a peacock. It must be observed too, that the pleasures of sight are not near so complicated, and confused, and altered by unnatural habits and associations, as the pleasures of the Taste are; because the pleasures of the sight most commonly acquiesce in themselves; and are not so often altered by considerations which are independent of the sight itself. But things do not spontaneously present themselves to the palate as they do to the sight; they are generally applied to it, either as food or as medicine; and from the qualities which they possess for nutritive or medicinal purposes, they often form the palate by degrees, and by force of these associations. Thus opium is pleasing to Turks, on account of the agreeable delirium in produces. Tobacco is the delight of Dutchmen, as it diffuses a torpor and pleasing stupefaction. Fermented spirits please our common people, because they banish care, and all consideration of future or present evils. All of these would

lie absolutely neglected if their properties had originally gone no further than the Taste; but all these, together with tea and coffee, and some other things, have past from the apothecary's shop to our tables, and were taken for health long before they were thought of for pleasure. The effect of the drug has made us use it frequently; and frequent use, combined with the agreeable effect, has made the Taste itself at last agreeable. But this does not in the least perplex our reasoning; because we distinguish to the last the acquired form the natural relish. In describing the Taste of an unknown fruit, you would scarcely say, that it had a sweet and pleasant flavour like tobacco, opium, or garlic, although you spoke to those who were in the constant use of these drugs, and had great pleasure in them. There is in all men a sufficient remembrance of the original natural causes of pleasure, to enable them to bring all things offered to their senses to that standard, and to regulate their feelings and opinions by it. Suppose one who had so vitiated his palate as to take more pleasure in the Taste of opium than in that of butter or honey, to be presented with a bolus of squills; there is hardly any doubt but that he would prefer the butter or honey to this nauseous morsel, or to any other bitter drug to which he had not been accustomed; which proves that his palate was naturally like that of other men in all things, that it is still like the palate of other men in many things, and only vitiated in some particular points. For in judging of any new thing, even of a Taste similar to that which he has been formed by habit to like, he finds his palate affected in the natural manner, and on the common principles. Thus the pleasure of all the senses, of the sight, and even of the Taste, that most ambiguous of the senses, is the same in all, high and low, learned and unlearned.

Besides the ideas, and their annexed pains and pleasures, which are presented by the sense; the mind of man possesses a sort of creative power of its own; either in representing at pleasure the images of things in the order and manner in which they were received by the senses, or in combining those images in a new manner, and according to a different order. This power is called Imagination; and to this belongs whatever is called wit, fancy, invention, and the like. But it must be observed, that this power of the imagination is incapable of producing any thing absolutely new; it can only vary the disposition of those ideas which it has received from the senses. Now the imagination is the most extensive province of pleasure and pain, as it is the region of our fears and our hopes, and of all our passions that are connected with them; and whatever is calculated to affect the imagination with these commanding ideas, by force of any original natural impression, must have the same power pretty equally over all men. For since the imagination is only the representative of the senses, it can only be pleased or displeased with the images from the same principle on which the sense is pleased or displeased with the realities; and consequently there must be just as close an agreement in the imaginations as in the senses of men. A little attention will convince us that this must of necessity be the case.

But in the imagination, besides the pain or pleasure arising from the properties of the natural object, a pleasure is perceived from the resemblance, which the imitation has to the original; the imagination, I conceive, can have no pleasure but what results from one or other of these causes. And these causes operate pretty uniformly upon all men, because they operate by principles in nature, and which are not derived from any particular habits or advantages. Mr. Locke very justly and finely observes of wit, that it is chiefly conversant in tracing resemblances; he remarks at the same time, that the business of judgment is rather in finding differences. It may perhaps appear, on this supposition, that there is no material distinction between the wit and the judgment, as they both seem to result from different operations of the same faculty of *comparing.* But in reality, whether they are or are not dependent on the same power of the mind, they differ so very materially in many respects, that a perfect union of wit and judgment is one of the rarest things in the world. When two distinct objects are unlike to each other, it is only what we expect; things are in their common way; and therefore they make no impression on the imagination: but when two distinct objects have a resemblance, we are struck, we attend to them, and we are pleased. The mind of man has naturally a far greater alacrity and satisfaction in tracing resemblances than in searching for differences; because by making resemblances we produce *new images,* we unite, we create, we enlarge our stock; but in making distinctions we offer no food at all to the imagination; the task itself is more severe and irksome, and what pleasure we derive from it is something of a negative and indirect nature. A piece of news is told me in the morning; thus, merely as a piece of news, as a fact added to my stock, gives me some pleasure. In the evening I find there was nothing in it. What do I gain by this, but the dissatisfaction to find that I had been imposed upon? Hence it is, that men are much more naturally included to belief than to incredulity. And it is upon this principle, that the most

ignorant and barbarous nations have frequently excelled in similitudes, comparisons, metaphors, and allegories, who have been weak and backward in distinguishing and sorting their ideas. And it is for a reason of this kind that Homer and the oriental writers, though very fond of similitudes, and though they often strike out such as are truly admirable, they seldom take care to have them exact; that is, they are taken with the general resemblance, they paint it strongly, and they take no notice of the difference which may be found between the things compared.

Now as the pleasure of resemblance is that which principally flatters the imagination, all men are nearly equal in this point, as far as their knowledge of the things represented or compared extends. The principle of this knowledge is very much accidental, as it depends upon experience and observation, and not on the strength or weakness of any natural faculty; and it is from this difference in knowledge that what we commonly, though with no great exactness, call a difference in Taste proceeds. A man to whom sculpture is new, sees a barber's block, or some ordinary piece of statuary; he is immediately struck and pleased, because he sees something like an human figure; and entirely taken up with this likeness, he does not at all attend to its defects. No person, I believe, at the first time of seeing a piece of imitation ever did. Some time after, we suppose that this novice lights upon a more artificial work of the same nature; he now begins to look with contempt on what he admired at first; not that he admired it even then for its unlikeness to a man, but for the general though inaccurate resemblance which it bore to the human figure. What he admired at different times in these so different figures, is strictly the same; and though his knowledge is improved, his Taste is not altered. Hitherto his mistake was from a want of knowledge in art, and this arose from his inexperience; but he may be still deficient from a want of knowledge in nature. For it is possible that the man in question may stop here, and that the masterpiece of a great hand may please him no more than the middling performance of a vulgar artist; and this not for want of better or higher relish, but because all men do not observe with sufficient accuracy on the human figure to enable them to judge properly of an imitation of it. And that the critical Taste does not depend upon a superior principle in men, but upon superior knowledge, may appear from several instances. The story of the ancient painter and the shoemaker is very well known. The shoemaker set the painter right with regard to some mistakes he had made in the shoe of one of his figures, and which the painter, who had not made such accurate observations on shoes, and was content with a general resemblance, had never observed. But this was no impeachment to the Taste of the painter, it only shewed some want of knowledge in the art of making shoes. Let us imagine, that an anatomist had come into the painter's working room. His piece is in general well done, the figure in question in a good attitude, and the parts well adjusted to their various movements; yet the anatomist, critical in his art, may observe the swell of some muscle not quite just in the peculiar action of the figure. Here the anatomist observes what the painter had not observed, and he passes by what the shoemaker had remarked. But a want of the last critical knowledge in anatomy no more reflected on the natural good Taste of the painter, or of any common observer of his piece, than the want of an exact knowledge in the formation of a shoe. A fine piece of a decollated head of St. John the Baptist was shewn to a Turkish emperor; he praised many things, but he observed one defect; he observed that the skin did not shrink from the wounded part of the neck. The sultan on this occasion, though his observation was very just, discovered no more natural Taste than the painter who executed this piece, or than a thousand European connoisseurs who probably never would have made the same observation. His Turkish majesty had indeed been well acquainted with that terrible spectacle, which the others could only have represented in their imagination. On the subject of their dislike there is a difference between all these people, arising from the different kinds and degrees of their knowledge; but there is something in common to the painter, the shoemaker, the anatomist, and the Turkish emperor, the pleasure arising from a natural object, so far as each perceives it justly imitated; the satisfaction in seeing an agreeable figure; the sympathy proceeding from a striking and affecting incident. So far as Taste is natural, it is nearly common to all.

In poetry, and other pieces of imagination, the same parity may be observed. It is true, that one man is charmed with Don Bellianis, and reads Virgil coldly; whilst another is transported with the Eneid, and leaves Don Bellianis to children. These two men seem to have a Taste very different from each other; but in fact they differ very little. In both these pieces, which inspire such opposite sentiments, a tale exciting admiration is told; both are full of action, both are passionate, in both are voyages, battles, triumphs, and continual changes of fortune. The admirer of Don Bellianis perhaps does not

understand the refined language of the Eneid, who if it was degraded into the style of the Pilgrim's Progress, might feel it in all its energy, on the same principle which made him an admirer of Don Bellianis.

In his favourite author he is not shocked with the continual breaches of probability, the confusion of times, the offenses against manners, the trampling upon geography; for he knows nothing of geography and chronology, and he has never examined the grounds of probability. He perhaps reads of a shipwreck on the coast of Bohemia; wholly taken up with so interesting an event, and only solicitous for the fate of his hero, he is not in the least troubled at this extravagant blunder. For why should he be shocked at a shipwreck on the coast of Bohemia, who does not know but that Bohemia may be an island in the Atlantic ocean? and after all, what reflection is this on the natural good Taste of the person here supposed?

So far then as Taste belongs to the imagination, its principle is the same in all men; there is no difference in the manner of their being affected, nor in the causes of the affection; but in the *degree* there is a difference, which arises from two causes principally; either from a greater degree of natural sensibility, or from a closer and longer attention to the object. To illustrate this by the procedure of the senses in which the same difference is found, let us suppose a very smooth marble table to be set before two men; they both perceive it to be smooth, and they are both pleased with it, because of this quality. So far they agree. But suppose another, and after that another table, and the latter still smoother than the former, to be set before them. It is now very probable that these men, who are so agreed upon what is smooth, and in the pleasure from thence, will disagree when they come to settle which table has the advantage in point of polish. Here is indeed the great difference between Tastes, when men come to compare the excess or diminution of things which are judged by degree and not by measure. Nor is it easy, when such a difference arises, to settle the point, if the excess or diminution be not glaring. If we differ in opinion about two quantities, we can have recourse to a common measure, which may decide the question with the utmost exactness; and this I take it is what gives mathematical knowledge a greater certainty than any other. But in things whose excess is not judged by greater or smaller, as smoothness and roughness, hardness and softness, darkness and light, the shades of colours, all these are very easily distinguished when the difference is any way considerable, but not when it is minute, for want of some common measures which perhaps may never come to be discovered. In these nice cases, supposing the acuteness of the sense equal, the greater attention and habit in such things will have the advantage. In the question about the tables, the marble polisher will unquestionably determine the most accurately. But notwithstanding this want to a common measure for settling many disputes relative to the senses and their representative the imagination, we find that the principles are the same in all, and that there is no disagreement until we come to examine into the preeminence or difference of things, which brings us within the province of the judgment.

So long as we are conversant with the sensible qualities of things, hardly any more than the imagination seems concerned; little more also than the imagination seems concerned when the passions are represented, because by the force of natural sympathy they are felt in all men without any recourse to reasoning, and their justness recognized in every breast. Love, grief, fear, anger, joy, all these passions have in their turns affected every mind; and they do not affect it in an arbitrary or casual manner, but upon certain, natural and uniform principles. But as many of the works of imagination are not confined to the representation of sensible objects, nor to efforts upon the passions, but extend themselves to the manners, and characters, the actions, and designs of men, their relations, their virtues and vices, they come within the province of the judgment, which is improved by attention and by the habit of reasoning. All these make a very considerable part of what are considered as the objects of Taste; and Horace sends us to the schools of philosophy and the world for our instruction in them. Whatever certainty is to be acquired in morality and the science of life; just the same degree of certainty have we in what relates to them in works of imagination. Indeed it is for the most part in our skill in manners, and in the observances of time and place, and of decency in general, which is only to be learned in those schools to which Horace recommends us, that what we called Taste by way of distinction, consists; and which is in reality no other than a more refined judgment. On the whole it appears to me, that what is called Taste, in its most general acceptation, is not a simple idea, but is partly made up of a perception of the primary pleasures of sense, of the secondary pleasures of the imagination, and of the conclusions of the reasoning faculty, concerning the various relations of these, and concerning the human passions, manners and actions. All this is requisite to form Taste, and the ground-work of all these is the same in the human mind; for as the senses are the great originals of all our ideas, and consequently of all our pleasures, if they are not uncertain and arbitrary, the whole ground-work of Taste is common to all, and therefore there is a sufficient foundation for a conclusive reasoning on these matters.

Whilst we consider Taste, merely according to its nature and species, we shall find its principles entirely uniform; but the degree in which these principles prevail in the several individuals of mankind, is altogether as different as the principles themselves are similar. For sensibility and judgment, which are the qualities that compose what we commonly call a *Taste,* vary exceedingly in various people. From a defect in the former of these qualities, arises a want of Taste; a weakness in the latter, constitutes a wrong or a bad one. There are some men formed with feelings so blunt, with tempers so cold and phlegmatic, that they can hardly be said to be awake during the whole course of their lives. Upon such persons, the most striking objects make but a faint and obscure impression. There are others so continually in the agitation of gross and merely sensual pleasures, or so occupied in the low drudgery of avarice, or so heated in the chace of honours and distinction, that their minds, which had been used continually to the storms of these violent and tempestuous passions, can hardly be put in motion by the delicate and refined play of the imagination. These men, though from a different cause, become as stupid and insensible as the former; but whenever either of these happen to be struck with any natural elegance or greatness, or with these qualities in any work of art, they are moved upon the same principle.

The cause of a wrong Taste is a defect of judgment. And this may arise from a natural weakness of understanding (in whatever the strength of that faculty may consist) or, which is much more commonly the case, it may arise from a want of proper and well-directed exercise, which alone can make it strong and ready. Besides that ignorance, inattention, prejudice, rashness, levity, obstinacy, in short, all those passions, and all those vices which pervert the judgment in other matters, prejudice it no less in this its more refined and elegant province. These causes produce different opinions upon every thing which is an object of the understanding, without inducing us to suppose, that there are no settled principles of reason. And indeed on the whole one may observe, that there is rather less difference upon matters of Taste among mankind, than upon most of those which depend upon the naked reason;

and that men are far better agreed on the excellence of a description in Virgil, than on the truth or falsehood of a theory of Aristotle.

A rectitude of judgment in the arts which may be called a good Taste, does in a great measure depend upon sensibility; because if the mind has no bent to the pleasures of the imagination, it will never apply itself sufficiently to works of that species to acquire a competent knowledge in them. But, though a degree of sensibility is requisite to form a good judgment, yet a good judgment does not necessarily arise from a quick sensibility of pleasure; it frequently happens that a very poor judge, merely by force of a greater complexional sensibility, is more affected by a very poor piece, than the best judge by the most perfect; for as every thing new, extraordinary, grand, or passionate is well calculated to affect such a person, and that the faults do not affect him, his pleasure is more pure and unmixed; and as it is merely a pleasure of the imagination, it is much higher than any which is derived from a rectitude of the judgment; the judgment is for the greater part employed in throwing stumbling blocks in the way of the imagination, in dissipating the scenes of its enchantment, and in tying us down to the disagreeable yoke of our reason: for almost the only pleasure that men have in judging better than others, consists in a sort of conscious pride and superiority, which arises from thinking rightly; but then, this is an indirect pleasure, a pleasure which does not immediately result from the object which is under contemplation. In the morning of our days, when the senses are unworn and tender, then the whole man is awake in every part, and the gloss of novelty fresh upon all the objects that surround us, how lively at that time are our sensations, but how false and inaccurate the judgments we form of things? I despair of ever receiving the same degree of pleasure from the most excellent performances of genius which I felt at that age, from pieces which my present judgment regards as trifling and contemptible. Every trivial cause of pleasure is apt to affect the man of too sanguine a complexion: his appetite is too keen to suffer his Taste to be delicate; and he is in all respects what Ovid says of himself in love,

Molle meum levibus cor est violabile telis,
Et semper causa est, cur ego semper amem.

One of this character can never be a refined judge; never what the comic poet calls *elegans formarum, spectator.* The excellence and force of a composition must always be imperfectly estimated from its effect on the minds of any, except we know the temper and character of those minds. The most powerful effects of poetry and music have been displayed, and perhaps are still displayed, where these arts are but in a very low and imperfect state. The rude hearer is affected by the principles which operate in these arts even in their rudest condition; and he is not skilful enough to perceive the defects. But as the arts advance towards their perfection, the science of criticism advances with equal pace, and the pleasure of judges is frequently interrupted by the faults which are discovered in the most finished compositions.

Before I leave this subject I cannot help taking notice of an opinion which many persons entertain, as if the Taste were a separate faculty of the mind, and distinct from the judgment and imagination; a species of instinct by which we are struck naturally, and at the first glance, without any previous reasoning with the excellencies, or the defects of a composition. So far as the imagination and the passions are concerned, I believe it true, that the reason is little consulted; but where disposition, where decorum, where congruity are concerned, in short, wherever the best Taste differs from the worst, I am convinced that the understanding operates and nothing else; and its operation is in reality far from being always sudden, or when it is sudden, it is often far from being right. Men of the best Taste by consideration, come frequently to change these early and precipitate judgments which the mind from its aversion to neutrality and doubt loves to form on the spot. It is known that the Taste (whatever it is) is improved exactly as we improve our judgment by extending our knowledge, by a steady attention to our object, and by frequent exercise. They who have not taken these methods, if their Taste decides quickly, it is always uncertainly; and their quickness is owing to their presumption and rashness, and not to any sudden irradiation that in a moment dispels all darkness from their minds. But they who have cultivated that species of knowledge, which makes the object of Taste, by degrees and habitually attain not only a soundness, but a readiness of judgment, as men do by the same methods on all other occasions. At first they are obliged to spell, but at last they read with ease and with celerity: but this celerity of its operation is no proof, that the Taste is a distinct faculty. Nobody I believe has attended the course of a discussion, which turned upon matters within the sphere of mere naked reason, but must have observed the extreme readiness with which the whole process of the argument is carried on, the grounds discovered, the objects raised and answered, and the conclusions drawn from premises, with a quickness altogether as great as the Taste can be supposed to work with; and yet where nothing but plain reason either is or can be suspected to operate. To multiply principles for every different appearance, is useless, and unphilosophical too in a high degree.

This matter might be pursued much further; but it is not the extent of the subject which must prescribe our bounds, for what subject does not branch out to infinity? it is the nature of our particular scheme, and the single point of view in which we consider it, which ought to put a stop to our researches.

Edmund Burke, On Taste

1.   According to Burke, the reason the objective laws of taste are not readily agreed upon by all is that taste has not been considered a very significant subject of inquiry.

     a.   True   b.   False

2.   Taste is comprised of the faculties of the mind that form a _____
     _____
     _____

3.   How does Burke explain the fact that people have different tastes?

4.   Which one of the following is *not* a way to improve taste?

     a.   improve judgment
     b.   extend knowledge
     c.   steady attention
     d.   rashness
     e.   frequent exercise

Monroe C. Beardsley*

IN DEFENSE OF AESTHETIC VALUE

Although the philosophy of art flourishes in our day as never before, and although the word "aesthetics" is widely accepted as a label for this subject, the *concept* of the aesthetic has grown more problematic with the progress of aesthetics. Some have concluded that the term "aesthetic" marks no distinction, or no distinction of theoretical significance; others have clung to the term but pressed upon us redefinitions that amount to surreptitious substitution of new concepts; still others allow a limited scope for a concept of the aesthetic, but argue that it has nothing to do with art—a view that calls the whole enterprise in question, since it was primarily the existence of artworks that got us into this line of inquiry in the first place.

I should apologize at once for my use of so dubious an expression as "the aesthetic"—a peculiarly philosophic form of nominalization that we have learned to be wary of. It is temporary verbal expedient to postpone debatable commitments, and this particular adjective (which especially calls for caution) will shortly be reunited with familiar nouns.

The problems to which I address myself are created by our inveterate habit of judging artworks as good or poor, better or worse than others. In recent years there has been a certain amount of complaint on this score, both about the judgmental habit itself and about the tendency of aestheticians to concern themselves with it. Now, I am not one to

encourage censoriousness—even in art critics—and I don't doubt that ill-supported, as well as ill-tempered, disparagements of artworks have had deplorable consequences. But since we must select to survive, and must discriminate among degrees of quality in our surroundings in order to lift our lives above the survival level, it is clearly inevitable that we will bring our concern about the better and the worse to artworks, as we do to nearly everything else. It has been wittily suggested[1] that aestheticians' preoccupation with goodness in art has been responsible for a lack of goodness in aesthetics. But even if we grant the alleged deficiencies in the subject, they can hardly be explained by too much thinking, and in any case the remedy is not to be timid in the face of genuine philosophical challenge.

I.

One way of meeting this challenge has developed, over the years, into a well-known account of art appraisals, that is, of judgments about the quality of artworks. This account has roots deep in the past, and we can say that a good many aestheticians have accepted it in general, or substantial parts of it, in one version or another. With some uneasiness, I shall refer to it as the "functional" account of art appraisal (a not very endearing label), which assigns to the art appraiser the task of estimating how well the artworks that fall under his scrutiny fulfill their

---

*Monroe Beardsley (1915–1985) was a professor of philosophy at the University of Pittsburgh and one of the leading aesthetic theorists of the twentieth century. His works include *Aesthetics* and *Aesthetics from Classical Greece to the Present.* The following selection is an address he gave to the American Philosophical Association in 1979 in which he develops the concept of aesthetic value and argues that aesthetic knowledge is possible.

From the PROCEEDINGS AND ADDRESSES OF THE AMERICAN PHILOSOPHICAL ASSOCIATION, Vol. 52 Issue No. 6, pages 723–747. Copyright © by The American Philosophical Association. Reprinted by permission.

[1]By Nelson Goodman, "Merit and Means," in *Art and Philosophy,* ed. Sidney Hook, N.Y. New York University Press, 1966, pp. 56–57; cf. *Languages of Art,* Indianapolis: Bobbs-Merrill, 1968, p. 261.

primary or central purpose. The functional account can be displayed in six stages or steps, which I now propose to call to mind.

It begins with a premise that is well illustrated in a forthright remark by a contemporary writer on literary theory, Lee Lemon:

> We know that "Poor Soul! the center of my sinful earth" is a better poem than "Ozymandias," just as we know that the latter is better than Drayton's "To nothing fitter can I thee compare."[2]

To begin with this exemplary truth takes a good deal for granted. The passage may remind you uncomfortably of a famous sentence of Hume's:

> Whoever would assert an equality of genius and elegance between Ogilby and Milton, or Bunyan and Addison, would be thought to defend no less an extravagance, than if he had maintained a mole-hill to be as high as Teneriffe, or a pond as extensive as the ocean.[3]

Not that the first of Hume's invidious comparisons is likely to excite protest. Although John Ogilby was a pioneer in the printing of road maps (and we are all in his debt), his extant poetical works (largely translations of Vergil and Homer) are held in low esteem by those who have ventured to peruse them. But Bunyan is a different story: he has rightly come to be admired as a prose stylist, and so perhaps a difference of opinion on the comparative merits of his writing and Addison's would strike us as much less unreasonable than Hume's geographical examples. Still, we understand why Bunyan's outcast state prevented his work from receiving, in Hume's day, the unprejudiced judgment required by Hume's own standard of taste. The functional account of art appraisal affirms only that in the case of some artworks we know one to be better than another, and this of course is not precluded by conceding the possibility of error in other cases. It would still be extravagant to equate Michael Drayton's sonnet with Shelley's or Shelley's with Shakespeare's.

Two philosophical tasks naturally present themselves the moment we accede to the first step of the functional account: to explain how one poem, or other artwork, can be better than another; and to explain how we know that this is true of particular pairs of works. I insert a warning here that I am speaking of artworks in a presystematic sense, that is, a sense of anterior to theoretical reflection: they include anything that is a poem or play, or musical composition, or painting, or dance, or sculpture or architectural work, et cetera (the "et cetera" is innocuous, I think, because for my present purpose it doesn't matter who far we carry the list beyond the point which I have left off). In other words, I want to be referring to anything that belongs to some recognized artkind, i.e., it is an artkind instance.

The second step in the development of the functional account is to say that if one artkind-instance can be better than another, there must be some way or manner in which it is better. Two lines of argument, one general and other specific, converge here.

The general argument may be illustrated by a characteristic exchange from the works of P. G. Wodehouse:

> ". . . Of course you have read the Zend Avesta of Zoroaster, Sir Roderick?"
> "I'm afraid not. Is it good?"[4]

The gentle absurdity of the reply points up a feature of such bare ascriptions of goodness to particular things: they are incomplete until we let on what manner of goodness is in question. Even if we say only that the Zend-Avesta is good in some manner or other, we concede that where there is goodness there is a way of being good. If this is not evident for goodness, it must be so for betterness: if someone should claim that the Zend-Avesta is better than the Bagavadgita, it would certainly be in order to inquire in what respect this is, or is believed to be, true. If X is *in no way* better than Y, then X is not better than Y. Here "X" and "Y" stand for individual things. I shall not pause to dispute with those who find intelligibility in more abstract remarks like "Pleasure is good," though I don't myself know how to make very good sense of them.

---

[2]Lee T. Lemon, *The Partial Critics*, N.Y.: Oxford University Press, 1965, p. 223.

[3]David Hume, "Of the Standard of Taste," in *Four Dissertations* (1757).

[4]P. G. Wodehouse, *The Return of Jeeves*, N.Y.: Simon and Schuster, 1954, p. 65.

The specific argument takes off from the observation that a society does assign (no doubt sometimes haphazardly) the role of making such judgments to those who are assumed to have some expertise in making them. We acknowledge that a literary critic, for example, cannot be expected to have the qualifications required for reliable judgment *in* all the respects in which two poems might be compared in quality. I don't suppose, for example, that Lee Lemon, though doubtless equipped to weigh the comparative merits of many literary works, would claim equal authority to discuss the Zend-Avesta of Zoroaster with respect to its theological, ethical, or homiletic quality. So if there is to be such a specialized activity as art criticism, or any branch of it concerned with a particular art, it seems that there must be some limited, discriminable manner of goodness associated with artkind-instances or with their kinds: there must be something that can properly be called "goodness *as* art" or "goodness *as* literature," and so on.

The third step, then, consists in locating and identifying this artistic manner of goodness (waiving the alternative formulations in terms of artkinds). The connection between ways of being good and groups of things that can be judged more or less good has been much and ably explored. We can, I think, set aside here the view (one that seems to have very few current takers) that artkind-instances are themselves intrinsically good. If the special goodness of artkind-instances is, then, extrinsic, and lies in their connections with other things, the procedure for disclosing it seems clear: we inquire what services they offer—that is, what in general (though in varying degrees) they do, or what can be done with them, that is worth doing. It turns out, obviously enough, that artkind-instances are not characteristically to be counted on in enterprises directed toward making physical changes in the world; but they do quite generally give rise to at least temporary psychological changes—and changes for the better—in those who seek them out and make suitable demands on them. In short, their specialty is affording a kind of experience (i.e., inducing an experience specifically by becoming the phenomenally objective apprehended content, or focus of attention, in the experience). What else could artkind-instances be good for, speaking generally and noting especially the salient features of outstanding examples?

But the diversity of experiences is far too great to provide a manageable manner of goodness without one further restriction. We must look for a common feature to mark off the relevant experiences: a certain desirable character, simple or compound, that can be found in many experiences, especially in experiences of artkind-instances, but not only in such experiences; and we require a character that has degree, so that experience may have more or less of it. According to the functional account, there is such a character, and must be one in order to make sense of specifically critical judgments of the quality of artkind-instances. And in casting about for a suitable label for this character, it seizes upon the word "aesthetic." It is hard to see what other word could be more appropriate. It then becomes convenient to say that some experiences have an aesthetic character, but some have a more pronounced or marked aesthetic character than others, and some, indeed, have it in a high degree.

Step four consists in the introduction of one more term that is made available by the concept of aesthetic character. If we suppose that the presence of aesthetic character in an experience confers value on that experience, we may define "aesthetic value" in this way: the aesthetic value of anything is its capacity to impart—*through cognition of it*—a marked aesthetic character to experience. The term "cognition" here refers to an apprehension (but not the *mis*apprehension) of the thing's qualities and relations, including its semantic properties, if any—it covers both perception and interpretive understanding, in a broad sense, even where the art work is a literary text or a conceptual "piece." In equivalent words, to say that X has aesthetic value is to say that X has the capacity to afford, through the cognition of it, an experience that has value on account of its marked aesthetic character. And to say that X has greater aesthetic value than Y is to say that X has the capacity to afford an experience that is more valuable, on account of its more marked aesthetic character, than any experience that Y has the capacity to afford. This pair of definitions does not, of course, define "value," but is designed only to distinguish aesthetic value from other kinds of value.

Step five is to note that the concept of aesthetic value as a distinct kind of value enables us to draw a distinction that is indispensable to the enterprise of art criticism: that is, the distinction between relevant and irrelevant reasons that might be given in support of judgments of artistic goodness. Not everything that can truly be said about artkind-instances has a bearing on their quality as art; but it seems that only in terms of an appropriate theory of value can we tell which true statements support critical judgments and which do not. Putting it briefly, a statement is relevant if and only if it ascribes a property the possession of which makes a difference to the thing's capacity to afford experiences with marked aesthetic character.

Step six may be regarded as optional: it is a suggestion for tying these concepts together more systematically. To get the search for the aesthetic character of experiences under way, we needed the concept of *artkind-instance;* loose as it was, it plainly included many objects that are unchallengeably within the purview of our inquiry. Now we may wonder whether the concepts we have acquired will enable us to frame a more formal definition of "work of art" or "artwork" that will be significant for the purpose of building theory. Now a good many things produced by human beings have been produced at least in part (I mean that this was one motive in the mixture) to satisfy a demand for experiences with aesthetic character—whether in fact they were successful. Even when—as with the most narcissistic self-expressionist or with the most humble Sunday painter—there is no plan to make the work widely available to others, there may be an intention to make it at least *capable* of satisfying such a demand. This must be true of vast numbers of artkind-instances. Moreover, the category seems significant, for these things will play a distinct role in society; they ask to be approached and treated and judged in a special way; their production and reception may require special explanation in psychological and social science, they would presumably have a special relationship to other recurrent and persistent elements of human culture, such as religion and science. So an artwork can be usefully defined as an intentional arrangement of conditions for affording experiences with marked aesthetic character. In other words, if and only if the intention to provide an occasion for experiences of this sort plays a notable part in the production of some object, event, or state of affairs will that thing be a work of art.

The terms "artwork" and "artkind-instance" are not coextensive, since some artkind-instances were not produced with the requisite intention, and some things produced with the requisite intention belong to no established artkind. But the overlap is considerable—as it must be, to keep the proposed definition from being wholly arbitrary. Yet, our definition need not, of course, be strictly bound by prevailing usage, if that exists; its advantage is that it marks an important distinction with reasonable definiteness. The concept of art and the concept of the aesthetic become closely linked; art as a social enterprise is understood in terms of an aesthetic purpose (while allowing that very many artworks

have other purposes as well), just as the judgment of individual artworks is understood in terms of aesthetic success. And this gives us a bearing on the roles that the arts play in culture for, even though these roles go far beyond the provision of aesthetically marked experience, this particular role may nevertheless be both definitive and fundamental to the others.

I noted the detachability of step six from the other elements of the functional account of art appraisal because it meets with so much opposition, which I cannot deal with here—opposition from those who hold that no intention, but only an official institutional endorsement, converts something into an artwork; from those who hold that avant-garde artists have freed the concept of art from any connection with the concept of the aesthetic, and that since they have rightful authority to decide how art is to be defined, their usage is to be followed; from those who hold that general use is authoritative here and that in general use the concept of art is "open" and "essentially contested," so that any attempt to define it is necessarily unfaithful. My view is that the definition of art in terms of aesthetic intention marks an important distinction which the word "art" is best fitted, by its history and widespread current use, to preserve.

II

Despite its plausibility and apparent coherence, the functional account of art appraisal has come under severe attack. It has its weak points which some aestheticians have been industriously trying to shore up, while others shake their heads and certify it as a hopeless case. My aim is to present a fresh brief for the functional account against doubts that have been raised or might sensibly be raised. All six steps have been rejected by someone; but it seems to me that vague expressions of discontent and sweeping condemnations are a good deal more common than cogent refutations or constructive alternatives. So it is up to the defense to secure its own Sixth Amendment rights by trying to articulate the nature of the charges as well as to display and increase the strength of its position.

We may begin by reconsidering step one, the critic's claim to knowledge of artistic goodness. It has been said:

1. that we ought not to judge artworks at all (and if we didn't, then the philosophical problem of justifying such judgments would not arise);
2. that even if we are permitted to judge, there is little or no point in doing so;

3. that even if there is a point in judging, our judgments cannot be true or false;
4. that even if critical judgments are true or false, they cannot be supported by reasons in any standard sense of these terms;
5. that even if these judgments can be supported by reasons, such support can never amount to knowledge.

A thorough discussion of even these preliminary theses could evidently take us far, so my brief reply must have a regrettable air of dogmatism. As to the first charge, I have seen no reason to think that freedom from appraisal is an inalienable right; a plea for exemption must be accompanied by a showing of probable harm. This of course can be done in some situations regarding particularly vulnerable human beings—including some artists.

A pervasive atmosphere in which a highly appraisive attitude prevails, and critics are far more given to judging than to sympathetic understanding, is no doubt an unhealthy one for the arts. It is no part of my aim to defend, much less promote, such a situation; I only say (1) it is generally not judgments as such, but unfair or unreasonable judgments, that threaten artworks, and (2) sometimes we must judge, as well as we can, because sometimes we must choose.

The second charge emerges from some of the essays in recent years that have compared aesthetic judgments of artworks with moral judgments of human actions—often to the disparagement of the former. Two distinct contrasts are unfortunately often confused. The first is between moral judgments and value judgments in general. Here there is such a difference of category that we risk nonsense in comparing them; however, we might want to note, for example, as John Rawls has noted, that value judgments are "advisory" in a way in which moral judgments are not.[5] The second contrast is between aesthetic value judgments and others; and with respect to the charge of pointlessness, I have seen no reason to think that, by their very nature, aesthetic value judgments must be any less useful than others—assuming that we can actually have them. If we can have knowledge of artistic quality, such knowledge is bound to be of use to us on many occasions, as individuals and as citizens—quite apart from its satisfaction of a legitimate curiosity.

In recent years there has been a vigorous advancement of the third objection: that judgments of artistic quality lack truth-value. According to this view—which Joseph Margolis has named "robust relativism" to distinguish it from those forms of relativism which allow truth-value to critical judgments, when properly relativized—other sorts of predicates may properly be applied to critical judgments: they are reasonable, suitable, apt, appropriate, plausible, perhaps, but not true or false.[6] The acceptance of this position would indeed wash away the foundations of the functional account, so it would be good to know of a way to argue against it. I believe we could show at length that to withhold truth-values from critical judgments would be intolerable: we could not manage with what seem to be the clear consequence of such a view, namely, that such judgments could not enter into inductive or deductive reasonings as premises or conclusions. On the inductive side, for example, when some years ago Allen Ginsburg's lurid poem, *Howl*, was tried in a San Francisco court, we should have had to disallow the testimony of those professors of literature who were prepared to swear or affirm that *Howl* was a very good poem, and better than many others. They could not honestly take the required oath if they were robust relativists. But under current constitutional doctrines about obscenity (which, granted, are far from coherent in other respects) such expert testimony concerning literary quality is considered highly germane as evidence of "redeeming social importance." On the deductive side, turning back to the passage from Lee Lemon, it is tempting to say that if he holds that Shakespeare's poem is better than Shelley's and Shelley's than Drayton's, he is logically bound to hold that Shakespeare's is better than Drayton's. This intuition presumes the transitivity of (this kind of) betterness, which can hardly be formulated (as a conditional) unless betterness-propositions have truth-value.

Skepticism of the fourth kind, taking another turn than robust relativism, attacks the very idea of reason-giving in art criticism, again sometimes by invidious comparisons with ethics. Consider, for example, a provocative remark by Gilbert Harman: "It is not appropriate to ask someone who admires

---

[5]*A Theory of Justice,* Cambridge: Harvard University Press, 1971, p. 448.

[6]Joseph Margolis, "Robust Relativism," *Journal of Aesthetics and Art Criticism,* 35 (Fall 1976): 37–46; see especially p. 41.

a painting what his principle is."[7] All right; and it is not appropriate to ask someone who admires Justice Thurgood Marshall what *his* principle is. In these examples, admiring is an attitude. If we are thinking of admiring as an illocutionary act (that is, judging the painting to be good, the Justice to be great), the word is "praising," and there is no absurdity in inquiring about principles on which we praise—in either art or morals. Was Hume confused when he confessed—in a sentence I once chose as an epigraph—"I am uneasy to think I approve of one object, and disapprove of another; call on thing beautiful, and another deform'd; decide concerning truth and falsehood, reason and folly, without knowing upon what principles I proceed?"[8]

If an art appraisal is true or false, its truth-value cannot be utterly unconnected with the truth-value of other propositions that can be independently established and can therefore serve as reasons for accepting or rejecting it. Moreover, if it is true that the painting is a good one, this state of affairs (the painting's being good) invites explanation. Of course *reasons-why* are to be distinguished from *reasons-for-believing,* and (as Gilbert Harman has pointed out) reasons-for-believing something are not always "reasons-for-which-one-believes." But reasons why and reasons for believing appear to be related by a universal principle.[9] Suppose R is a reason why the state of affairs S obtains (that is, R explains that state of affairs, say, painting P's being good); then R will also be a reason for believing that S obtains. Moreover, for someone who does not otherwise know that S obtains, and who possesses certain auxiliary information, R can be a reason *for which* that someone believes that S obtains. I am not summoning up the old questions of the symmetry of explanation and prediction; my thesis is that if we grant that the artistic goodness of a painting is in principle explainable, like other things about it, then we must also grant that belief in its presence could in principle be supported by a reason.

But not everyone will grant the antecedent of this conditional. In the context cited earlier, Gilbert Harman adds: "This is an important difference between morality and aesthetics, since you may think that one melody is good, another banal, without feeling compelled to find aesthetic principles that would distinguish them." "Compelled" needs a gloss here, I think. I cn see how there might not be the same degree of stringency or urgency in the aesthetic as in the moral case—but that is true of value judgments in general. A fairer way of posing the issue would be to ask whether, in the aesthetic case, you would feel some obligation to try to explain, if politely requested, what *makes* one melody better than the other. Whether this explanatory difference, if pointed out, can be erected into a general *principle* would be disputed. I am only urging that artistic superiority must be explainable by reasons-why—and therefore, as I have said, that propositions about it must be supportable by reasons-to-believe.

There remains a fifth charge: that art appraisals, however reasonable, cannot be knowledge. The direct argument here is one that need not detain us: it is simply that the reasons, in the special case of art appraisals, cannot ever provide sufficient justification to transform belief into knowledge. Such a view is, I believe, easily refuted by Hume's method of citing extreme cases: *Paradise Lost* is known to be a better poem than *Howl*. After that, we can concede the multifarious difficulties of getting reliable art appraisals.

The more interesting argument we confront here is the attempt to show an inherent defect in critical judgments that prevents them from being strictly knowable. Claims to knowledge about the goodness of artworks are typically expressed in judgments, and such judgments have often been said (since Kant's Third Critique) to be peculiarly tied to firsthand experience: that is, the illocutionary-act conditions for critical judging are said to include direct acquaintance with the artwork judged (or with a reproduction of it). Thus one who has never heard a musical work can *report* a critic's judgment of it, but not *make* a judgment, and therefore can't be said to *know* that the work is good or poor. Alan Tormey has worked out this view ingeniously: his conclusion is that even the critic's so-called knowledge lacks an essential feature of knowledge, namely transmissibility to others as expressed in Hintikka's formula: "If B knows that A knows that

[7]Gilbert Harman, *The Nature of Morality*, N.Y.: Oxford University Pres, 1977, p. 51.

[8]David Hume, *A Treatise of Human Nature*, I, iv, vii; ed. L. A. Selby-Bigge, Oxford: Clarendon Press, 1888, p. 271.

[9]Gilbert Harman, *Thought,* Princeton: Princeton University Press, 1973, p. 26.

p, then B knows that p."[10] A variation of his argument might be put as follows:

1. Expand the Hintikka formula to this: If A knows that Schubert's string quintet in C is magnificent, and B knows that A knows this, then B knows that the quintet is magnificent.
2. But B *could* know that A knows the quintet is magnificent even if he has never heard the quintet himself. Suppose this possibly is true.
3. Assume that B has never heard the quintet.
4. The B cannot judge, and therefore does not know, that the quintet is magnificent.
5. Then A does not know the quintet is magnificent either, for if he did, his knowledge would be something he could pass on to B.

This argument and its supporting discussion deserve much more attention than I can give them here. My way of escaping its clutches is to concede that here in a sense in which B (who has not heard the music) cannot judge it, but to insist that B can still say that the quintet is magnificent (and this is a judgment in a broader sense), and can justifiably assert this on the authority of A, whom he knows to be an excellent music critic. Thus A's knowledge is transmissible to others, even if the others have to borrow or copy judgments, so to speak, rather than initiate them.

III

We come now to the most direct and serious attack on the functional account, striking at points 2, 3 and 4. It has two parts:

1. Talk of a *kind* of value, in a sense required by the functional account, is not intelligible.
2. Even if there *are* kinds of value, there can be no such thing as aesthetic value, since we cannot isolate a special aesthetic character of experiences.

First as to the genus: how could things that have a value constitute a kind, within which we might mark out subordinate kinds? The most plausible answer can be summarized as follows: Toward anything whatever we may act in a variety of favoring ways, or adopt a variety of positive stances: helping to bring it into existence or to preserve and protect it, seeking it out, choosing or selecting it, making it more accessible to ourselves or others, borrowing or buying, taking advantage of its avail-

ability, etc. To act in any of these ways is to *elect* that thing, and anything that is or could be elected by someone is eligible. An act of electing something at some time may be one for which a justification can be given—i.e., there is an adequate reason for the act. Then we can say that the thing in question has *warranted eligibility*. A plausible view of value in general is that it is warranted eligibility.

This proposal may seem to broad. Couldn't there be an adequate reason for electing something despite its total worthlessness—or even because of it, in a fanciful and somewhat allegorical case? Someone, perhaps in training for sainthood, is instructed by his spiritual mentor to fare forth and return with something that has no value. Which he dutifully does. There *is* an adequate reason for him to bring that object (and we can even say he *has* an adequate reason), so the election is warranted, yet by hypothesis the object lacks value. Or is this hypothesis itself incoherent? I think it is: the task is impossible to perform—it turns out to ba a Koan. Let the object be whatsoever you choose, however humble; it fulfills a purpose, perhaps even carried a message about the last being first or the least being no less precious than the greatest. It has value after all, so it does not defy the concept of value as warranted eligibility.

The question does arise, however, whether this concept can serve as a *definition* of value. In very many cases, at least, the justifying of an election will take the form of showing that the thing makes a contribution (as cause or condition or part of a whole, or in some other way) to the production of a valuable state of affairs. If this is always and necessarily the case, then this justifying procedure is built into the concept of warranted eligibility, which therefore could not without circularity be used in defining value. It is no use to say "X has value" means "The election of X at some time by someone could be justified, because X contributes to the production of a state of affairs with value." The case of the apprentice-saint seems to offer a convenient exception, showing that a reference to value is not a necessary element in the concept of warranted eligibility. But in bringing back the supposedly valueless object, the saint revealed its hitherto unrecognized value—that it could contribute to the realization of that state of affairs which consists in his duty's having been done. The saint's election of the object did not *confer* value on it, but *exploited* its value—which no doubt it shared with many other

---

[10]Alan Tormey, "Critical Judgments," *Theoria* 39 (1973): 35–49.

equally negligible things: it had to be something that at least non-saints, in their blindness, would despise or disdain. The object acquired its value when the duty was imposed, not when the duty was done. Its value is therefore dependent upon, is a consequence of, the rightness of the action. So we could argue that the action is justified by its rightness, and this is one way in which eligibility can be warranted; therefore it would not be circular to define "value" as "warranted eligibility." I leave this question for further consideration elsewhere. In any case the view that value always *involves* warranted eligibility, whether definitory for not, is true and worth stating, because it uncovers a significant feature of the concept of value, and if it is sustained, has certain noteworthy advantages.

For one thing (if to mention this is not thought frivolous), it warms us to our world; it invites us to look about us, at least occasionally, with some pleasure and approval; for very many of those things that fall under our notice or lie within our technological reach either certainly or probably have *some* value. Nor can we ever know the limits to what may later be discovered to be of the value-possessing kind. More appealing from a theoretical point of view, at least to me, is that the procedure of justifying an election seems clearly to involve showing how the thing-to-be-elected fits into a pattern of human activities and natural connections—especially since it is comparative, and requires a showing of superiority to alternatives. Even in the case of the apprentice-saint, we have to see how the act of bringing the object back generates (in Alvin Goldman's sense) an act of doing a duty. Thus it is hard to see how there can be any intrinsic value, since the very process of establishing the existence of value in an object makes that value dependent on the object's connections with other things. But the most important advantage, in the present context, is that the warranted-eligibility concept of value provides a rationale for distinguishing kinds of value. Since nothing has value unless its election sometime by someone could be justified, all value is grounded. If we can classify various grounds on which eligibility might be warranted, we will at the same time be classifying kinds of value—or, for short, *values,* in the plural—since two values will differ in that different kinds of reason are associated with them.

By switching terminology in mid-sentence, I did not mean to slip anything by, so I assert again

that when we speak individually or severally of *a* value, or of this or that value (keeping this locution clearly distinct from talk about valuable *things*), we are referring to a kind of value. But we speak properly of *a* value, I think, only when the kind has been articulated, so to speak—when a classification has been effected and the distinction made explicit. Anything that has value has some kind of value—perhaps several kinds. But for many such kinds we have no handy names and no need for them. When we have sorted out a range of reasons as having to do, say, with the restoration of health (on the assumption that health has a value), we can speak of therapeutic value as *a* value. And since the ground of eligibility is the thing's capacity to contribute in some way to the production of value, we can say that this capacity *is* a value that the thing has.

Thus we see how *a* value is a capacity (to contribute to the production of value), and how it is not circular to offer *this* as a definition, since "value" is not in turn defined by means of "a value."

I see no fatal flaw, then, in the conception of value-kinds. So our problem centers on the proposed species: whether one of these kinds can be *aesthetic* value. And this seems to depend on two things: identifying an aesthetic character in experience on which aesthetic value can be grounded, and showing that the possession of such a character is a valuable feature of such experiences.

IV

It is interesting, I think, that in the most extensive classification and analysis of what he calls the "varieties of goodness," G. H. von Wright finds no clear or secure place for judgments of the goodness of art. The judgment that someone is a good *artist* (painter or musician) is placed in the category of "technical goodness," along with the goodness of plumbers and accountants: the good composer is *good* at composing music.[11] Such a judgment would seem to presuppose another kind of judgment concerning the goodness of the music the good composer composes, but von Wright is silent about this problem. He merely invites his readers, as a kind of exercise, to try to find the proper category for the expression "a good book (work of art)," which he is apparently not prepared to assign to any of his varieties or "forms" of goodness: instrumental,

---

[11]George Henrik von Wright, *The Varieties of Goodness,* N.Y.: Humanities Press, 1963, pp. 38–39.

technical, utilitarian (including the beneficial), hedonic, moral.[12]

I don't attempt any such broad classification here; von Wright's varieties are not, of course, my kinds. But if a place for aesthetic value is found in such a scheme, we must first be clear about the kind. And contemporary aestheticians have reserved much of their sharpest language for casting doubt on the idea that there is a special character of experience that it is the purpose or function of artworks to impart. Artworks are not can-openers that they should be pinned down to a limited task! Both they and the experiences they afford are too varied to allow for the sort of generalization and abstraction required for identifying a function! There can be no restriction on the desiderata we seek in artworks, from moral uplift to entertainment! We must not impose prescriptively a limit on the adventurousness and originality of artists and an end to artistic change! These and similar warnings abound, and of course they are to be heeded. But they do not, in my opinion, rule out the notion of distinctive aesthetic character. Philippa Foot has noted, judiciously, that "We do not . . . use works of literature, or not normally, and could not say that it is by their use that the criteria for their goodness are determined . . ." yet—she adds—"the interest which we have in books and pictures determines the grounds on which their excellence is judged."[13] The objector will be quick to jump on the words "*the* interest," and regale us with a list of various interests that artworks may sustain and satisfy. But of course this is beside the point: we are in search of a value, identified by a distinct character of experience that is worth having—though, of course, part of the justification for calling it "aesthetic" depends on showing that it has a fairly close, regular, dependable relationship to artkind-instances. Those who have doubted or denied the existence of a special aesthetic character rend to rely on two negative arguments: first, that they have not succeeded in finding it, and second, that even its partisans cannot agree on what it is. To the first we may respond with commiseration, to the second with a legitimate excuse. It is fair to plead that to get at the aesthetic character is not necessarily a simple task. It may call for a good deal of subtle phenomenological inquiry, taking into account a wide range of experiences and carefully comparing our introspections with the reports of others. There is a serious problem of finding the right words to discriminate and articulate the noteworthy features of our interaction with outstanding artkind-instances. If there are continuing differences of opinion, or at least in emphasis, as for example about the precise nature of "disinterestedness" and its role in the experience of artworks, the fact is not surprising; and it neither belies the obvious truth that aestheticians have made progress in this direction nor mocks the persistent hope for further progress.

Although I am unready to relinquish more substantial claims concerning the analysis of aesthetic character, I am content here to advance a fairly modest one. Let us treat the aesthetic character as compound and disjunctive. It consists of five discernible features. Experience has an aesthetic character if it has at least four of these five features, including the first one.

1. A willingly accepted guidance over the succession of one's mental states by phenomenally objective properties (qualities and relations) of a perceptual or intentional field on which attention is fixed with a feeling that things are working or have worked themselves out fittingly. Since this awareness is directed *by*, as well as *to*, the object, we may call this feature, for short, *object-directedness.*

2. A sense of freedom, of release from the dominance of some antecedent concerns about past and future, a relaxation and sense of harmony with what is presented or semantically invoked by it or implicitly promised by it, so that what comes has the air of having been freely chosen. For short: *felt freedom.*

3. A sense that the objects of which interest is concentrated are set a little at a distance emotionally—a certain detachment of affect, so that even when we are confronted with dark and terrible things, and feel them sharply, they do not oppress but make us aware of our power to rise above them. For short: *detached affect.*

4. A sense of actively exercising constructive powers of the mind, of being challenged by a variety of potentially conflicting stimuli to try to make them cohere; a keyed-up state amounting to

---

[12]Ibid., p. 11.

[13]Philippa Foot, "Goodness and Choice," *Proceedings of the Aristotelian Society,* Supplementary Vol. 35 (1961), p. 52.

exhilaration in seeing connections between percepts and between meanings, a sense (which may be illusory) of achieved intelligibility. For short: *active discovery*.

5. A sense of integration as a person, of being restored to wholeness from distracting and disruptive impulses (but by inclusive synthesis as well as exclusion), and a corresponding contentment, even, through disturbing feelings, that involves self-acceptance and self-expansion. For short: *a sense of wholeness.*

If I may appropriate—or misappropriate—a colorful term introduced for a contrasting view (which I shall shortly acknowledge), I might call these five properties "symptoms" of the aesthetic in experience.

The limitations of these symptoms, as I have sketched them—object-directedness, felt freedom, detached affect, active discovery, and a sense of wholeness—are perhaps not so obscure that they need to be emphasized by me. (Others will cheerfully accept this labor.) Their vagueness is evident and essential. Yet I believe the descriptions apply to genuine realities, which we find in our experiences of many artworks, as well as other things. The symptoms are common (though not omnipresent) in experience; they are individually often present in play, sport, mathematics, and religion. These activities are sometimes accompanied by experiences with aesthetic character, though this is generally incidental to their central purpose. Here is one aspect of the aesthetic character that has made it difficult to manage—not that it is so rare, but that it turns up so widely, in mild or fleeting forms at least.

Despite their vagueness, these features allow for comparisons of degree among experiences with aesthetic character. The familiar dimensions apply here in usual ways: a feature may be more or less intense, sustained, pervasive, saturating, dominant over other aspects of the experience. More or fewer of the properties may be present, and they may cooperate more or less closely and powerfully. Not all comparisons of aesthetic value that might be attempted can be successful in this pluralistic scheme, so not all possible disputes about aesthetic value can be objectively resolved; but that was never promised. It seems to me, perhaps perversely, a merit of the proposal that it explains the considerable looseness and indeterminacy we actually encounter in the justification of art appraisals. Yet it

remains true that the experience a well-qualified reader of poems obtains under favorable conditions, from reading Shakespeare's "Poor Soul! the center of my sinful earth" will have a decidedly more marked aesthetic character (considered all in all) than the experience that same reader, under similar conditions, will obtain from reading Michael Drayton's "To nothing fitter can I thee compare." That is evidence of greater aesthetic value.

One piece is still missing from the positive case for aesthetic value. Although I have argued that objects possess this value in virtue of their capacity to impart marked aesthetic character to experience, I have so far merely assumed that experiences themselves possess value in virtue of having a capacity that is based on their aesthetic character. It may be evident that it is a good thing for an experience to have an aesthetic character—that this is *one* of the ways in which experiences can be worth having. But the question *why* this character confers value calls for a systematic answer—one that I am afraid is too long for this occasion. It calls for consideration of profoundly difficult questions about the nature of human goodness, what constitutes a good life, happiness, well-being and well-doing, and perhaps the meaning of life—though even if we differ in our answers to these questions, we may be able to agree that it is good for us to experience, at least occasionally, and to a degree seldom made possible except by artworks, the immediate sense (say) of inclusive self-integration and complex harmony with phenomenal objects.

I certainly do not wish to follow some ardent defenders of the aesthetic in their attempt to extend aesthetic value to cover all intrinsic value, to make it the *only* thing that is ultimately good. This idea, I think, derives from Charles Peirce, and it was not one of his better ideas. First, I do not believe there is such a thing as intrinsic value; and second, the attempt can lead to such morally outrageous views as that once stated by David Prall:

It is in their ultimately felt aesthetic quality that men all find such sights [as "the suffering of the poor"] revolting and unendurable . . . . If poverty and disease bore a pleasant aspect to discriminating perception, if injustice were aesthetically and directly satisfying to experience, and to dwell upon, what would there be to condemn it in any rational creature's eyes?[14]

---

[14]David W. Prall, *Aesthetic Judgment*, N.Y.: Thomas Y. Crowell, 1957, p. 349.

Even if an example of injustice had high aesthetic value (and in fact some thoroughly unjust societies have been noted for their elegance or splendor), there would be plenty to condemn it in a rational creature's mind, if not his eyes.

There is an important sense in which the arts, as specialized bearers of aesthetic value, are "non-existential," as Aurel Kolnai has written in an essay on "Aesthetic and Moral Experience": threats to their eligibility do not invoke the moral imperatives of injustice and destitution. Yet, as Dewey always insisted, there is something exemplary in an artwork's way of having worth—it is always a reminder of the possibilities of living fully. If find some wisdom in Kolnai's words, though I would not choose them all:

> If certain churches of certain regions or street corners in certain cities I peculiarly admire and love did not exist, it "wouldn't make much difference." Yet it is in their contemplation and tangible nearness, undoubtedly an *aesthetic* experience, that I seem somehow to become aware of the ineffable goodness of existence more deeply and vividly than in any experience of benefit or thriving, or even of moral virtues.[15]

V

Having displayed, as I hope, some merits of the functional account of art appraisal, I would naturally like to make them stand out by contrasting this accent with available alternatives. There is really only one serious alterative, I think: that put forward by Nelson Goodman. The present argument would be woefully incomplete without at least some attempt to meet his radical challenge.

Nelson Goodman's position rejects aesthetic value, as I have been analyzing and defending it, and proposes instead to base art appraisals on the *cognitive* value of artworks—their capacity to con-tribute to the "creation and comprehension of our worlds."[16] Artworks turn up in this account as characters, or classes of characters, in symbol systems, and like other symbols are to be judged primarily or centrally by their successful functioning as symbols, their "cognitive efficacy." In a memorable passage toward the end of *Languages of Art,* Goodman says that the use of symbols in making and meeting artworks "is for the sake of understanding . . . . What compels is the urge to know, what delights is discovery . . . . The primary purpose is cognition in and for itself."[17] And more recently, in *Ways of Worldmaking,* pursuing a related theme, he adds that "The arts must be taken no less seriously than the sciences as modes of discovery, creation, and enlargement of knowledge in the broad sense of advancement of the understanding."[18] Though, strictly speaking, truth is reserved for verbal claims, a broader category, "rightness of rendering," which involves both construing and constructing worlds, comprises the aims of both arts and sciences.

It is no small part of the debt we owe to *Language of Art*—along with a few other books in recent decades—that we now recognize the extent to which the experience of artworks involves cognitive activities of many sorts—activities which do often in fact eventuate in knowledge and understanding. And much can be said of some arts as "modes of discovery." Yet when we bring together the results of many aesthetic inquiries, especially in our time, we cannot accede to these claims as stated. Instead of saying in general terms of artworks or artkind-instances that "the primary purpose is cognition in and for itself," we ought rather to say that the primary purpose is the aestheticizing of experience. In support of this rebuttal, I sketch three lines of argument.

First, it has not yet been shown, to my satisfaction, that instrumental musical works and nonrepresentational paintings are characters in symbol systems; it has not been adequately explained how they refer to anything.[19] So I think their peculiar

---

[15]Aurel Kolnai, *Ethics, Value, and Reality*, Indianapolis: Hackett, 1978, p. 210.

[16]*Languages of Art*, p. 265.

[17]Ibid., p. 258.

[18]*Ways of Worldmaking*, Indianapolis: Hackett, 1978, p. 102.

[19]Ibid., p. 68.

goodness has to be explained in some other way than by their successful symbol functioning in the service of cognition; what delights may be the discovery of the work itself, but not of other things via the work's reference. It would be temerarious to ascribe the artworks in general a primary purpose that cannot be fulfilled by such large and important subclasses of them.

Second, many natural objects, such as mountains and trees, are not characters in any symbol system, yet they seem to have a value that is closely akin to that of artworks. This kinship can easily be explained in terms of aesthetic value, but hardly in terms of cognitive value.

Third, it is commonplace (but I think well-placed here) that very widely in the arts, where cognitive concern is or could be present, we observe sacrifices in the cognitive dimension for the sake of other ends. Some aestheticians, or course, have tried to show that these apparent retreats are means to greater cognitive achievement (the novelist alters the newspaper facts that inspired his plot only in order to reveal deeper truths of human nature; and Poussin left the Biblical camels out of his famous painting of *Rebecca and Eleazar* the better to portray the essential human situation). This aiming at a "higher" truth certainly occurs in art, and is important; yet there is much that will not explain (including the cases where the novelist changes the facts simply to make a better story—one that is more unified, or dramatic, or ironic, and thus more capable of fulfilling an aesthetic function; and perhaps Poussin found that he could make a better composition without the camels). The longer literature of this controversy supplies many such examples; they argue that cognition is not generally the overriding or dominant purpose of artworks.

And I will even go so far as to suggest—though with appropriate diffidence—that this point is tacitly conceded in Nelson Goodman's theory. It will be recalled that artworks, according to this theory, differ from other symbols basically in that they belong to symbol systems of a special sort, "aesthetic symbol systems." These systems possess one or more of those properties which he calls "symptoms of the aesthetic"—thus he is the victim of my

terminological rip-off a little earlier. The symptoms are (1) syntactic and (2) semantic density, (3) a high degree of repleteness (in that more features of the symbol count), (4) exemplificationality (possession of predicates plus reference to them), and—as he has added in his most recent book—(5) "multiple and complex reference, where a symbol performs several integrated and interacting referential functions."[20] Now on the functional account it is understandable that artists creating artworks should often choose to make them symbols—that some types of symbol are very useful for the purpose of fashioning bearers of aesthetic value. And if we inquire what kinds of symbol lend themselves to this use, there is no better answer than Goodman's. But looking at the matter from within *his* system, it is fair to ask what justifies the selection and classification of these properties as "aesthetic."

To this question Goodman gives significant answers. The first three properties "call for maximum sensitivity of discrimination," since in a dense and replete symbol system minute differences between inscriptions make a difference in what symbols they are and in what they symbolize. Thus (I would suggest) the use of such symbols stimulates and exercises the cognitive faculties connected with perception to the highest degree and makes possible the construction of artworks of great subtlety and refinement, which are open to endless exploration. In an exemplificational symbol the properties referred to or expressed are "shown forth"—vividly presented for concentrated and prolonged affective apprehension.[21] Replete systems and multiple symbols carry complex meanings and compact them, giving an embracing unity to diverse elements of experience. As Goodman says in *Ways of Worldmaking*, "these [aesthetic] properties tend to focus attention on the symbol rather than, or at least along with, what it refers to"[22]—but to the extent that there is a tension here, it seems that our cognitive interests would tend to call for dominant attention to what is referred to, though our aesthetic interests might not. A symbol that attracts attention to itself, and rewards that attention, helps to detach our feelings from that to which it refers. "This emphasis upon the nontransparancy of a work of

---

[20]Ibid.

[21]*Languages of Art*, p. 253.

[22]*Ways of Worldmaking*, p. 69.

art, upon the primacy of the work over what it refers to, far from involving denial or disregard of symbolic functions, derives from certain characteristics of a work as a symbol."[23] That's certainly true, and important. But also perfectly acceptable to anyone who maintains that the meanings and references in artworks are essential to their artistic nature. It is clearly consistent to emphasize the nontransparancy of artworks while insisting on their symbolic character as well; but it is not so clearly consistent to emphasize the nontransparancy of artworks and still insist that the cognitive symbolic function is their *primary* purpose.

It is, I think, some recommendation of aesthetic value (both of its reality and its importance) that the most powerful effort to dispense with it seems, in the end, to be driven back to reliance upon it. But I should not like to conclude with a mere dialectical flourish, even in this serious cause. It is rather the issue itself—underlying as it does so many current and promising controversies, yet, to my mind, still given too little serious discussion—that I wish to emphasize and stir into more active life.[24]

---

[23]Loc cit.

[24]I wish to acknowledge Elizabeth L. Beardsley's very helpful comments on this essay.

Monroe Beardsley, "In Defense of Aesthetic Value"

1.   Identify and briefly explain the six steps of the functional account of the arts.

2.   According to Beardsley, why is it justified to form judgments about works of art?

3.   According to Beardsley, can judgments about the value of works of art be supported with reasons-to-believe? Why or why not?

4.   "Value is warranted eligibility." Explain.

5.   Identify and briefly explain the five features of aesthetic experience.

Paul Hindemith*

THE PHILOSOPHICAL APPROACH

"A composition of everlasting value"—we know of quite a number of musical creations upon which in humility and admiration we bestow this title of reverence. It is our belief in the stability of musical facts that leads us to this and to similar statements. But which musical facts are stable? Certainly not the external body of music in its audible form, although for many people sound seems to be the only factor of importance, perhaps of exclusive validity in their musical experience. An individual piece of music, being many times reborn and going through ever renewed circles of resonant life, through repeated performances, dies as many deaths at the end of each of its phoenixlike resurrections: no stability here, but a stumbling progression from performance to performance. And the totality of this kaleidoscopic picture, all the way from a composition's conception to ultimate death in its last performance is not a stable curve either. Periods of appreciation alternate with periods of neglect; false interpretations, overrating, suppression, nonmusical evaluation—all such uncontrollable circumstances influence the total course of the life of a composition; they shorten, darken, brighten, or lengthen it as they do a human being's life on earth.

Sound, the ever present ingredient of music, is the frailest of its qualities. The sound of a Beethoven symphony, performed by our players on modern instruments, in modern concert halls, is different from the audible form the piece assumed in a performance in Beethoven's time. Attempts to reconstruct the sound which was the ideal of Bach and his contemporaries still encounter many obstacles (and probably always will); and access to the world of musical sound in the Gothic era is almost entirely obscured and obstructed.

It is partly man's own frailty and his unstable conditions of life that forces each new generation to modify its musical aspects and with them the evaluation of compositions; and it is partly the frailty of the musical form itself, which, because it is not built to withstand continual wear and tear, is subject to the musical equivalent of oxidation and decay. Our modern orchestral repertoire rarely includes pieces more than two hundred years old and most likely never will include much music written before 1750, so long as we maintain our manners and places of performance. The more complex the means of reproduction are, the less time-resistant are the pieces they help to represent. Solo pieces, ensemble and choral works of the sixteenth and even the fifteenth century may occasionally appear on programs, and courageous explorers are sometimes apt to dive down to the very beginnings of organized harmonious music.

All this shows that the "everlasting" value of compositions and their potentialities of performance are by no means eternal, and the majesty of the term "everlasting" dims even further when we compare the vigorousness of a musical composition with the thousands of years an architectural creation may last, or with the periods of development in general history and geology.

And yet, there are in music certain values that are not subject to instability. If we want to recognize

---

*Paul Hindemith (1895–1963) was a German composer, musician, and theorist who taught at Yale University, the Berlin School of Music, and the University of Zurich. As a composer, Hindemith sought to overcome the communication gap between the public and 20th century music by using a less dissonant tonality than other contemporary composers. As a theorist, he revived the ancient doctrine that the order of composition should reflect the order of the universe. The following selection comes from his book *A Composer's World* (1952).

Hindemith, Paul, A COMPOSER'S WORLD, Peter Smith Publisher, Inc.; 1969 Gloucester, MA.

and understand such values, we must perceive music not as a mere succession of reasonably arranged acoustical facts; we must extricate it from the sphere of amorphous sound, we must in some way participate, beyond the mere sensual perception of music, in its realization as sound; we must transform our musical impressions into a meaningful possession of our own. How we can do this will be investigated in the following chapters. For the present we will deal merely with philosophical values, the objective of such efforts.

These values, not being tied to the instability of sound or to any other external quality of musical creations, are domiciled in the more esoteric realms of our musical nature. We have to turn to the immaterial, the spiritual aspects of music in order to find them. In our dealings with the ingredients that go into the making of a composition, these values will be of the foremost importance: they will determine the human quality of our music. A musician of culture can hardly be thought of as lacking a strong feeling for, an innate devotion to these values; yet it cannot be the task of a composer untrained in philosophy to analyze them thoroughly. He is not called upon to develop a musical-philosophical system; nor need he, in looking for confirmations of his home-grown philosophy, go systematically through every statement on music ever made in the philosophers' works. Since in venturing into the realm of philosophy we all enjoy freedom of choice, we may concentrate on the works of certain writers and entirely neglect others. We can exercise our prerogative of emphasis or bias without forgetting that our primary concern is, after all, not philosophy, but music.

II

Let me first refer to a book which, more than fifteen hundred years ago, pronounced remarkable postulates concerning eternal musical values; postulates which have only in the most recent development of music philosophy and music psychology regained importance—obviously without due consideration of the earlier appearance. I am talking about Saint Augustine's *De musica libri sex*. In five of these six books the subject of discussion is meter as used in poetry—for us, whose concept of music differs in many respects from that of the ancients, a musically rather unproductive investigation.

In the sixth book, however, the work develops into a most intelligent analysis of musical perception and understanding. According to Augustine, musical impressions are by no means simple reactions to external stimuli. They are, rather, a complex mixture of diverse occurrences. First, there is the mere physical fact of sound. Although sound can exist independent of any listener, it is indispensable as a basic experience before the perception and mental absorption of music can take place. Second, there is our faculty of hearing: the physiological fact that sound waves act upon our ear and by muscular and nervous transmission release reactions in the brain's center of hearing. Third, there is our ability to imagine music mentally without the stimulus of music actually sounded or without recollective reference to a definite former impression. Fourth, there is our ability to uncover previous musical experiences stored in our memory like old keepsakes, to draw them out of their hiding places, revive them mentally, and allow them to impress us with the same intensity as actual music would do, after which they may again be put to rest in the storage chests of our soul. In all these musical happenings both our corporeal and mental nature participate, with the emphasis constantly shifting from one to the other. Fifth, our mental activity must rise to predominance; we must in the moment of actual perception or of soundless concept subject the musical substance to an intellectual examination and judge its musical shape and grade. Thus the mere activity of perceiving or imagining music is combined with the satisfaction we derive from classifying and evaluating it. But we must not become slaves of this enjoyable satisfaction; it deserves as little confidence as a wooden board carrying us through a river's rapids: although we know its ability to float, we would not trust it without reservation. Musical order, as recognized and evaluated by our mind, is not an end in itself. It is an image of a higher order which we are permitted to perceive if we proceed one step further to the sixth degree on our scale of musical assimilation: if we put our enjoyment of such knowledge ("enjoyment, the weight of the soul!") into the side of the balance that tends towards the order of the heavens and towards the unification of our soul with the divine principle.

This sober abstract of an extensive and erudite dialogue cannot give an idea of its truly modern analysis of our faculty of hearing, nor of the profound and enthusiastic treatment of the subject and the conclusions drawn therefrom. Yet these few excerpts will show the lofty heights of psychological and moral clarity reached by musical comprehension in that period. Practical music in the declining Roman Empire had degenerated from a science into a form of agreeable pastime. It impressed people mostly with its entertaining, sensuous qualities, as it does the overwhelming majority of modern listeners. A work like Augustine's *De musica* must, in such circumstances, have appeared as a voice of admonition, and as such cannot have enjoyed a great dissemination. On the other hand, such a musical-philosophical treatise was certainly not the individualistic formulation of an isolated philosopher. It must have expressed the thoughts, feelings, and desires of many a person dissatisfied with the state of music in his time.

Books one to five of the work readily confirm this impression, since they deal with a portion of the classical intellectual heritage that was familiar to any cultured person as part of his education. But the abhorrence of everything pertaining to entertainment, even to professional musicianship is evident in the sixth book; and the conclusions of its final chapters transgress the inherited body of knowledge to a hitherto unexpected degree. However, in their serious attempt to coördinate music with the theses of the Christian creed—thus reinstating this form of art in an elevated community of sciences, a position it had enjoyed in the times of ancient philosophy— the consent of believers who saw in music more than a pleasant play of sounds was assured. They recognized in Augustine's conclusions the best moral, musical, and theological foundation for the development of religious music. True, religious music shows us most clearly the direct effect of the Augustinian attitude, but our secular music also can profit from those venerable ideas—in fact, it cannot exist without their support if it is to be more than entertainment. The tenor of that doctrine is: music has to be converted into moral power. We receive its sounds and forms, but they remain meaningless unless we include them in our own mental activity and use their fermenting quality to turn our soul towards everything noble, superhuman, and ideal. It is our own mind that brings about this conversion; music is but a catalytic agent to this end. The betterment of our soul must be our own achievement, although music is one of those factors which, like religious belief, creates in us most easily a state of willingness towards this betterment. In short, we have to be active; music, like humus in a garden soil, must be dug under in order to become fertile. Composers, performers, teachers, listeners—they all must outgrow the mere registration of musical impressions, the superficial and sentimental attachment to sound.

III

Acknowledging the moral values of the Augustinian attitude and observing its honest scientific foundation, for centuries left unrecognized, we nevertheless may ask whether the serious emphasis on spiritual and even religious aspects is not so grave a burden that its general application will forever remain an unrealizable ideal. Many participants, despite their best intentions, will not have the strength or the knowledge to develop their musical morality above a mediocre level. Can their genuine efforts be considered equal to the experts' more perfect achievements? Can we, furthermore, give full credit to those who after such perfect achievements relapse into periods of idleness? Even the most cultured mind sometimes feels a desire for distracting entertainment, and, as a principle, music for all possible degrees of entertainment ought to be provided. No music philosophy should overlook this fact. There are many methods of creating, distributing, and receiving music, none of which must be excluded from its theses so long as the slightest effort towards stimulating the receiving mind into moral activity is perceptible. The only musical activities to be condemned are those that do not aim at fulfilling such requirements.

Admittedly the dividing line between a devaluated or basically worthless music and a light-weight music of some moral value may not be clearly discernible. Moreover, our Augustinian theorems may not be lenient enough to serve as a guide through this moral-musical no man's land, and there may exist other cases of doubtful musical value in which rigorous decisions may lead to unjust or even entirely false judgments. No wonder, therefore, that many people try to approach the problem of musical responsibility from another angle. Already in medieval times we encounter musical philosophies and theories which oppose Augustinian severity with a more liberal attitude. If on examination we find that these philosophies deal with the problem of musical comprehension with the same devotion and seriousness exhibited in Augustine's work, they will also be accepted as valuable support in our search for clarity.

The most helpful indications of this type can be gathered from Boethius' work *De institutione musica*. It was written in the early sixth century, about one hundred years later than Augustine's *De musica*. Unlike the latter work, it was a well-known book, which throughout the following centuries exerted a strong influence on European musical education. Without this influence the organized technique of composition and its underlying theories, up to about 1700, would probably have taken a course different from the one it actually followed.

The first sentence in Boethius' work can be regarded as the principal thesis of his philosophy. It says: "Music is a part of our human nature; it has the power either to improve or to debase our character." In the relationship of music and the human mind the position of forces has now changed: music has become the active partner; our mind is a passive receiver and is impressed and influenced by the power music exerts. No wonder, then, that music abandons its role as a modest aid to moral growth and assumes gubernatorial rights.

Music itself exists in three different forms, one of which, the so-called *musica humana,* is the principle which unifies the immateriality of our faculty of reasoning with our corporeal existence; which keeps the conscious and rational part of our soul aligned with its instinctive and animalistic feelings; and which brings about the harmonious coherence of our body's members and their smooth and well-tuned synchronization.

The second form of music is *musica instrumentalis,* music as executed by human voices or with the aid of instruments. This meaning of the term "music" coincides with our own modern definition.

The third form, however, acquaints us with the term's most comprehensive meaning. It is *musica mundana,* which governs the heavens, time, and the earth. It causes the planets to revolve in their orbits; its moves the celestial spheres. Without such organizing harmony how would the cohesion of the entire universe be possible?

This definition of music strangely widens the limits of this art, limits which, according to our own concept are drawn by nothing but the possibilities of the musical material and the intellectual abilities of the producing and reproducing participants. It would lose its strangeness if we could, as did the ancients, classify music as part of the quadrivium, that group of four sciences dealing with measurement. Here we would find music united with geometry, which is concerned with the measurement of nonmoving planes and bodies; with astronomy, as the measurer of moving entities; and with arithmetic, in which measurement is sublimated and concentrated into the operation with abstract numbers. The science of music deals with the proportions objects assume in their quantitative and spatial, but also in their biological and spiritual relations. There is no doubt about the existence of these measurements and the importance of their recognition. The only disturbing element to us seems to be the fact that it is music which rules in this field, and that so many great minds clung tenaciously to this concept. They did not doubt the correctness and reliability of music as a science of measurement. The fact that we see so many scientific heroes contribute to the evolution of music

theory seems to provide strong justification for this attitude. The great second-century astronomer Ptolemy, whose concept of the planetary system was generally accepted until the Copernican theory dethroned it some thirteen hundred years later, wrote the major work on Greek music theory; a work that served as a fundamental source of information for many similar books of a later time, including Boethius' *De institutione.* Or we may think of the geometrician Euclid, the physicist Huygens, the mathematician Euler—to mention only one representative of each related science—all of whom wrote on musical-theoretical subjects; or Kepler, whose three basic laws of planetary motion, expounded, at the beginning of the seventeenth century, could perhaps not have been discovered, without a serious backing of music theory. It may well be that the last word concerning the interdependence of music and the exact sciences has not been spoken.

IV

The emphasis Boethius placed on the scientific part of musical experience led him quite naturally to judgments which sometimes sound strange to us. Whereas today we evaluate musicians exclusively with regard to their artistic activities, Boethius classified them according to their intellectual and scientific abilities. For Boethius (as for Augustine before him), singing and playing, especially for the purpose of earning a livelihood, is a low-grade, rather contemptible pursuit. Even a performer of highest vocal or instrumental perfection is far removed from musical insight, is not gifted with scientific enlightenment. How could he be, since all his efforts must be directed towards his technical improvement? Somewhat more elevated than these most sordid of all musicians are those who are given to composing without being totally conscious of the technical and intellectual premises of their actions. They may do their work with talent and conviction, but with them musical instinct is more important than knowledge. It is knowledge—knowledge beyond all craftsmanship and intuition—that dictates the actions of the musician belonging to the third and highest class; "they have the gift of judging everything pertaining to music according to scientific rules," as Boethius says. Let us assume that to the members of this most exalted caste of musicians it was a duty of honor to combine the craft of the two lower classes with their own wisdom. Without this combined insight they could scarcely have possessed the all-embracing power of artistic judgment, as demanded by Boethius, unless we conjecture that even at that time uninformed music judges were already existent.

In his *De institutione* Boethius is by no means an independent author with original ideas. We have already mentioned Ptolemy as his authority, and as further sources for his music theory he frankly adds the names of Aristoxenus, Nicomachus, Archytas, and others. He is, so far as the mere subject matter of his book is concerned, one of numerous compilers of classical learning. Even his book's first sentence, already quoted, which depicts music as the force that influences our souls for good or for evil, is not the result of his own contemplation. This sentence, the intellectual meaning of which is the tenor of the entire work, expresses the idea of musical ethos, so frequently dealt with in Plato's Dialogues. In a social order, as envisaged by Plato, music is neither entertainment nor a stimulus for the moral improvement of the soul. Music's purpose is to aid the government in its attempt at educating its citizens to be better citizens: it is music's ethical power that is summoned up.

Fortunately, Plato's Republic has remained theory. During the past few decades, in which, for the first time in history, governments have influenced the practice of the arts in a grand dictatorial manner, our experiences have been rather discouraging. Theoretically the dictatorship of the philosopher-king and the royal philosopher is demanded, but practically it is without doubt always the greatest musical nitwit with the greatest nonmusical power in whose hands rests the decision on both life and style of a musician.

The idea of musical ethos in its extreme Platonic form is in strict opposition to Augustine's musical attitude. To be sure, they agree in strictly refuting an autocracy of music in the form of shallow and narcotizing entertainment, but Augustine would never grant any worldly power the right to block the individual's musical and spiritual evolution and thus prevent his intellectual apprehension of a supreme divine law. Opponents of the Platonic idea also appeared from the opposite direction. To them it seemed quite inadmissible to couple such sober concepts as state, government, philosophy, and mathematics with music, which in its audible form seemed to be eternally elusive and irrational, and accordingly suspect.

V

A glimpse at the writings of the Roman philosopher Sextus Empiricus (ca. 200 A.D.) will confirm this statement. As a convinced skeptic, invent-

ing arguments against all the sciences practiced during his time, he also scrutinizes music (in Book VI of his treatise *Against the Mathematicians*). He does not believe in any ethical effect of music. Music, as a mere play with tones and forms, can express nothing. It is always our own sentiment that ascribes to the ever-changing combination of tones qualities which correspond with certain trends in our mental disposition. Consequently, music cannot be used as a means of education, and all the stories which are told about the ethical power of music are plain bunk. There is the well-known anecdote of the flute player who plays for a drunk a tune in a certain mode, in order to prevent him from doing mischief. It merely proves that flute players are sometimes more successful educators than are philosophers. Spartan soldiers enter a battle to the accompaniment of music—certainly not because of the exciting effect the tunes have on them, but because of their need of some doping influence which blots out the fear of the horrors to come. Frequently music's salutary effect on animals is mentioned; but have we ever seen a horse react to music the same way an audience does in the theater? Although Sextus' attacks are spiced with similar tidbits, his argumentations are not to be taken too lightly. They contain many sound notions which are important as a regulative against a superemotional or superspiritual evaluation of music. His philosophical system is so well founded that it could serve as a pretty strong justification for our lowest-grade modern entertainment music! Only towards the end of his brisk arguments does one hesitate to follow him. Here he tries to disprove other philosophers with their own logic and demonstrates rather convincingly the nonexistence of melodies and rhythm, and consequently of music altogether.

If Sextus' maxims became our sole guide in the search for musical enlightenment, we would soon be relieved of any worries concerning our musical behavior, for sooner or later music would disappear from our lives. Also Plato's ethos, as recommended and regulated by the government, would be no source of satisfaction, because we do not want to be deprived of our self-determination in respect to music; and so long as no brown, red, or other colored dictatorship sterilizes any individual impulse, we want to be free to produce music, perform it, and listen to it in our own personal ways and to assimilate and interpret it likewise.

It seems that of the different attitudes towards music, as discussed in these pages, our best choice would be either the Augustinian or the Boethian philosophy. Both grant us our own personal and uninhibited decision. There is even, in principle, no third position. The ethos of Plato, the skepticism of Sextus, and many other attitudes, no matter how unrelated they may appear at first sight, are only deviations from, or variations of, our two main trends; or they may represent one of the innumerable middle positions between the two extremes.

Extremes they really are! The Augustinian precept, in which our mind absorbs music and transforms it into moral strength; and the Boethian precept, in which the power of music, its ethos, is brought into action upon our mind. Truly these are basic and unalterable musical values. Either of these philosophies can lead us to the loftiest goals; either enjoys the protectorship of the sciences. Great composers may apply their talent in either direction; the listener may in either way find his most sublime satisfaction. Each individual participant (author, performer, and listener alike) has to decide—and does so, mostly unconsciously—whether he wants to turn to the one side or the other; whether he prefers a half-and-half enjoyment of advantages; or whether eventually, as an unstable wreck without any motion of his own, he merely suffers himself to be tossed around in the ocean of sound.

VI

The ideal conduct would be not a weak compromise of extremes, but their forceful unification in one single act of will power. In other words, although the Augustinian doctrine is silent in respect to the merely technical aspects of music, so that theoretically the highest moral effect could be achieved with music of lowest technical quality, we may assume that music of high quality will at least not be felt to disturb the moral effect. Thus we can imagine that the participant of a high culture, due to his musical taste wants his moral activity incited by only the most perfect music—music that answers the strictest Boethian demands. On the other hand, if we understand the ethical power of music and know how to apply it with maximum efficacy, performers and listeners conscientiously desiring to appreciate such music can do so only by profound devotion to the cause; and once they reach this point of unselfish penetration, the step to the Augustinian ideal of moral assimilation is a slight one. To see the fusion of both doctrines in one single piece of music and its perfect appreciation by performers and listeners who in their noble and understanding fervor do justice to both, we will have to wait for a better world. Here on earth we can do nothing better than strive for the closest possible approach to this idea.

Augustine's musical philosophy, with its decided renunciation of external effects, its inclination towards superhumanity, is never threatened by the danger of degeneration. To many, even to those *bonae voluntatis*, the path to perfection will be too steep; they may feel forced to be satisfied with whatever level they can reach, and some may give up in desperation. Still others, in their craving for the utmost sublimation, may escape the realm of physical music entirely and dwell in a sphere of purest musical spirituality. Boethius' musical philosophy, however, demanding a submission to the ethic power of music (hence implicitly to its sensual allurements as well) easily becomes the subject of degeneration. Its strongly intellectual trend may produce music that in its utter aridity is unpalatable; it may transform the listener into the frequently occurring snob. The emphasis on all facts technical may end in meaningless sound that runs along self-sufficiently without moving the listener's soul. The stress laid upon the outward qualities of the musical material—on sound and form—may in megalomaniacal hypertrophy explode into unartistic noise. The essentially active function of music may force the listener into such a state of passivity that his faculty of musical perception will crave only pieces which offer no resistance whatever, which in every respect satisfy his basest instincts—music which is nothing but a cheap and trashy amenity, an opiate always and everywhere available. Our present era, in which the majority of listeners is constantly subject to this kind of music, has, in my opinion, reached a point below which a further degeneration of the Boethian attitude is impossible.

In spite of this gloomy statement, I do not mean that the situation is hopeless. There still are, and always will be, composers who are more than mere arrangers of sounds. Among the multitude of listeners there exist large groups who demand more from music than a permanent lulling accompaniment to their most banal activities. And not all performers are as godforsaken as many of our virtuosi with their limited repertoire of circus tricks. Finally, in that science which deals with the essence, the effects, and the history of music, one observes a growing tendency to replace the predominantly materialistic methods of the past with ways of research and communication the impulses of which stem from a closer inclination towards an Augustinian interpretation of music and its functions. The durable values of music are not forgotten; they are as alive as they were thousands of years ago, and we as musicians can do nothing better than to accept them as the guiding principles for our work.

Paul Hindemith, "The Philosophical Approach" to Music

1. Briefly explain the Augustinian philosophy of music.

2. Briefly explain "musica humana," "musica instrumentalis," and "musica mundana."

3. Is music more than an entertaining pastime? Explain.

4. The Roman philosopher Sextus Empiricus thought music was more than just delightful arrangements of sound.

    a. True   b. False

5. Hindemith agrees with Empiricus.

    a. True   b. False

Hall Johnson*

NOTES ON THE NEGRO SPIRITUAL [1965]†

The folk-song of the American Negro came to the United States with the first shipload of slaves from Africa. At that time the American settlers had only European music, mostly hymns and social songs of simple construction. They thought of music only for church worship and other special occasions. The Africans, however, came from a long tradition of functional music in daily use in lieu of the written word, songs filled with varied emotions to fit the most dramatic occasions: rituals for worship, birth, death, funeral, wedding, sowing and harvesting, journeying and war—to name a few. The musical instruments of the primitive African tribes were crude and undeveloped so that the songs were dependent on the voices of the singers. Only the drum, in manufacture and performance, left nothing to be desired.

All consideration of music as art is based upon the three elements: rhythm, melody and harmony. The English custom of music for the *ear* only, without any necessary accompaniment of physical motion, tended to develop in the English only the simple static rhythms; but it did give them a feeling for *melody* and *harmony* hitherto unknown to the African slaves. On the other hand, the African had a much more highly developed sense of *rhythm*—

with his constant singing of all types of songs—all punctuated by the insistent beat of the omnipresent drum. Here was a wonderful opportunity to fuse the basic elements of rhythm, melody and harmony into a great American music. Only the Negro slaves, though quite unconsciously, profited by this opportunity. The American settlers had a country to build,—no time to think seriously about music. On the other hand, the slave had no life of his own *except* music,—the making of songs.

Now, no *slave* ever has any *rights:* personal, family, property, time, privacy, freedom of motion, freedom of opinion nor freedom of the physical body. That is the symbolism of the chains. But the only thing that cannot be chained is human thought *unexpressed.* So if you do not want your slave to *speak* freely you should also forbid him to sing,—even without words. The human voice in speech only *releases* the thought; in singing, the same voice gives it wings. But the American master permitted, even *encouraged* his slaves to sing. He got more work done—and, he enjoyed the singing.

So the slaves went on singing in their new home,—at first old homesick songs in their own language,—songs of their lost liberty. But, as the years passed, succeeding generations lost the old

---

*Hall Johnson (1880–1970) was an African-American musician. Trained at the University of Pennsylvania and the Julliard School, he formed the Hall Johnson Choir in New York City in 1926. Johnson dedicated himself to teaching the world to appreciate the tradition of the African-American spiritual.

†Used by permission of the Hall Johnson Estate. Further reproduction of all or any portion of "Notes on the Negro Spiritual" by means of mimeographing, xeroxing, photocopying, or any other means of duplication, may not be performed without the written permission of the Hall Johnson Estate.

memories. The new country, new language, customs and occupations filled their life and gradually obliterated every image of the motherland. But still the slaves continued to sing—even in bondage, indeed, on account of their very chains.

For they found an entirely new subject to sing about. They soon heard the white man's religion, alleviating the woes of this world with the sure hope of eternal freedom in the next. Being unable to read or write, the slaves received these glad tidings at second hand. Every Sunday the coachmen, footmen and body servants sat in the slaves' galleries of the churches and attentively drank up the sermons, prayers, and hymns intended for their masters in the pews. Then the house servants, who worked all day in the "big house," heard, with the master's children, the old Bible stories of prophets, saints and heroes. These privileged ones, when the day's work was over, hurried to the slave quarters to share with the field hands the priceless treasures garnered in the churches, parlors and nurseries of their masters. These second-hand versions were certainly not models of orthodox scriptual prose,—but whatever they may have lacked in authenticity was more than compensated by vivid insight and dramatic fervor.

This new religion of the slaves was no Sunday religion. They needed it every day and every night. The gospel of Jesus, the Son of God, who had lived and died for men, even the lowliest, took hold of their imagination in a strange personal way, difficult to understand for the average Christian of the formal church. For them, He was not only King Jesus but also "Massa Jesus" and even "*my* Jesus." The American Negro slaves literally "embraced" Christianity and, with this powerful spiritual support, life took on new meaning, a new dimension. For now they *knew* with absolute, unshakeable faith, that somewhere, sometime—they would be FREE! And then the slaves began to sing—as they had never sung before.

In fact, the North American Negro slaves were completely satisfied with their new religion,—but not with the *music* that came with it. The songs in the master's church were good enough for the master. He only needed them on Sunday; the other days he had other business to occupy his mind. In a word, he was free,—and the comfortable, roomy hymns of his church services echoed the calm freedom that filled his soul. As for the slave,—he had never heard any music, on land or sea, that could describe his rapture at the very *name* of Jesus. And, after all, from time immemorial, hadn't he always made his own songs? So he opened his mouth and, from a heart bursting with love, faith and adoration, a new song poured forth—and kept pouring and pouring,—renewing his hope in a promised land of Freedom. The American Negro slaves called these religious songs "Spirituals."

The slaves new that their songs were the spiritual guarantee of their personal oneness with life, even in a world that forbade them to live as human beings. What they did not know was that a people who could not write their own names—in any language—were now writing—for all time, one of the grandest pages in the history of the whole world of music.

As time went by, musicians the world over became increasingly aware that a musical miracle was taking place in the southern United States of America. Gradually, through incessant, (though unconscious) study, the slaves had succeeded in grafting onto their own native musical gifts whatever they seemed to need from the western techniques to widen and extend their own creative efforts. The slaves had brought from Africa:—

1. Fine, natural VOICES, developed by centuries of habitual singing out-of-doors.

2. An unerring sense of DRAMATIC VALUES —in words and music—due to the wide variety of their functional songs.

3. A dazzling facility in IMPROVISATION and EMBELLISHMENT.

4. Above all, and underlying all, a supreme understanding of the basic laws of RHYTHM—with all its implications and potentialities as applied to music.

They discovered in the New World:—

1. A more serviceable MUSICAL SCALE—with longer range but smaller intervals.

2. A wider view of musical structure by the use of the METRICAL PHRASE.

3. The sensuous delights of rich HARMONY and exciting COUNTERPOINT.

4. Lastly, the powerful, unifying psychological effects of GOOD PART-SINGING.

The fusion of all these remarkable musical ingredients resulted in far more than just *good* part-singing—with new songs and new singers. This amalgam bore golden fruits.

This musical alchemy soon began to attract the attention of the professional musicians. Organized studies were set up for investigation; books were written; hundreds of melodies were transcribed; but mere ink and paper could not record what was heard—and the phonograph was still to be invented. For the secret magic lay not so much in the fresh wonder of the tunes and words themselves but in the absolutely *new* musical *style of performance* by their creators. For example:

1. The conscious and intentional *alterations* of *pitch* often made in the accepted musical scale;

2. The unconscious, but amazing and bewildering *counterpoint* produced by so many voices in *individual improvisation;*

3. The *absolute insistence* upon the pulsing, *overall rhythm* combining many varying subordinate rhythms.

—to name only a very few effects which defy accurate notation but which are nevertheless essential to the character of the genuine old spirituals. Without these, many of the songs can sound quite trite, although never commonplace.

It must be kept in mind that the Negro Spiritual is essentially a group or choral form—many people singing together. It reached its highest musical peak in the Negro Church during the early years succeeding the abolition of slavery—where large *crowds* sang *freely.* Gradually, with greater *individual* opportunities—economical and educational—the *group* impulse to sing and to make songs began to wane. For the newly emancipated slaves, singing was no longer the sole safety-valve of emotional activity. Freedom of choice brought variety of interest. The spiritual made room for the work-songs, love-songs and "blues", But the racial *singing-style* persisted—and persists to this day. Only the music itself has changed—according to the subject of the song. Still, such was the marvelous vitality inherent in the *old* songs themselves, that they are heard and loved all over the world—in whatever guise or disguise.

The Hall Johnson Negro Choir was organized on September 8, 1925. Its principal aim was not entertainment. We wanted to show how the American Negro slaves—in 250 years of constant practice, self-developed under pressure but equipped with their inborn sense of rhythm and drama (plus their *new religion*)—created, propagated and illuminated an art-form which was, and still is, *unique* in the world of music. The slaves named them "spirituals" to distinguish them from their worldly, "everyday" songs. Also, their musical style of performance was very special. It cannot be accurately notated but must be studied by imitation.

Even then, in 1925, I saw clearly that, with the changing times, in a few years any spirituals remaining would be found only in the libraries—and nobody would know how to sing them. I also knew that I was the only Negro musician born at the right time and in the right place ideally suited for years of study of the Negro musical idiom as expressed in the spirituals. I started right in. I had always been a composer and—here was virgin soil. I assembled a group of enthusiastic and devoted souls and we gave our first public concert on February 26, 1926.

Our earlier singers had no other broad outlet for their native talents—except in the churches. They soon united themselves into a sort of musical family, employing all of their spare time in daily rehearsals. Long years of success only deepened their relationship.

In forty years, the times have changed for Negro singers. Increased living expenses have decreased leisure time. Opportunities have opened up for *individual* Negro singers of talent. These are no longer "chorus-minded." All of these changes have gradually increased our rehearsal difficulties. No matter how fine the voice or how well trained, *every* singer must be in *every* rehearsal to study the old techniques together. In the meanwhile the impossibility of daily rehearsals has effectively put an end to the Hall Johnson Choir. Our last public concert was given in June of 1960.

The last six years have brought me many individual honors, guest-appearances, and citations. For many years, several leading publishers have been distributing my choral and solo arrangements of the old Negro folk-songs. Why not be satisfied to "rest on my laurels"—like an old worn-out prima donna? Why have this definite and desperate sense of having failed in my life-work? It is because the signs I saw forty years ago are coming true. In a few more years, nobody—not even the Negro singers—will know the words and melodies of a dozen spirituals and will be able to sing any one of the dozen properly. Because they will have never heard them. And there ARE NO RECORDINGS!

The Negro Spiritual reached its fullest flowering in the early years of the Emancipation when the ex-slaves gathered in great numbers to sing in their *own* churches—without let or hindrance. But alas! The recording-machine *had not yet been invented!*

In 1938 the RCA Victor Co. recorded a dozen or so songs of the Hall Johnson Choir. A few years later, during the Second World War, the priority on shellac necessitated drastic reductions in the output of the recording companies. The Hall Johnson Choir songs disappeared from the catalogue and have been unavailable ever since.

Of course, all the leading companies would say *their* catalogues are full of Negro songs, even spirituals, and they sincerely believe that. What they really have is a conglomeration of all sorts of modern derivatives sung by soloists or small groups in musical arrangements neither Negro nor spiritual. But they caught the public ear. It is good business and everybody's happy—but me. They don't know any better.

I have no quarrel with the multiple musical progeny of the spiritual: work-songs, game-songs, and later, chaingang-songs, love-songs, ballads, reels, "blues" and, much later, jazz and the "gospel-songs." They have had their uses and evidently will be around for a long time. Only, their musical progenitor has disappeared—the old Negro spiritual.

This amazing literature of folk-song that astonished the musical world came up and flourished under ideal artistic conditions—for two hundred and fifty *slave* years. A singing race, they had the same subject-matter—freedom; the same reason for making and singing their songs—mental release; and unlimited time for practice—even at work! And for crowning inspiration, [they had] an eloquent and unshakable faith in their new religion of *hope*. Why wouldn't they sing!

But after the abolition of slavery, with relative freedom came more individual problems and less spare time. In their own churches the spiritual still held sway. But, gradually, the fierce faith in "my" Jesus began to subside into the quiet trust in the less informal Jesus of the hymn-books. Time and the succeeding generations were closing in. Soon would arrive the various denominations—with vested choirs—and the good old spirituals would have a rest until the midsummer revival meetings—maybe.

So, the old Negro Spiritual is gone. Those who don't believe it never heard it in the first place. Most are too young; others were born in the wrong place. It is nobody's fault. Time ends all things. And because [a thing] is not missed, nobody thinks of making a record of it.

It is not difficult to understand that the spiritual began to wane with the conditions that had given it birth. It was no longer the only safety-valve, and yet the only cement, of the race. It is not indispensable even to the modern Negro. But it is simply irreplaceable in the world of musical history. Neither the Negro nor the United States of America can comprehend the immense value of the appreciation of the whole civilized world for this Negro folk-art, [although] they all agree that is the only authentic, indigenous creative art-form ever to come out of the New World.

It must be kept in mind that the authentic Negro Spiritual is a *choral* form, requiring many voices to color the lush harmonies and bring out the brilliant, syncopated counterpoint so characteristic in the genuine spiritual. No soloist nor small vocal ensemble can hope to produce the necessary effects. The singing of the Hall Johnson Choir in *The Green Pastures* and *Run, Little Chillun* was the only modern example. But, again, [there are] no recordings.

The Ethnic Records in the Library of Congress were collected by northern white researchers. These earnest people, armed with portable recording-machines, went into the rural districts of the South and picked up all kinds of sporadic dribble of Negro folk-singing. All of this is, of course, very interesting but has nothing to do with the grand old spirituals, either in composition or performance.

Of course, many books have been written about the Negro Spiritual and many conscientious attempts made to transcribe the melodies and harmonies. But no printed word can ever describe the actual *sound* of music, and the written score of any song is but a dry skeleton until breathed upon by the living human voice. This is particularly true in the case of the spirituals done in the *true* Negro style. The racial tendency to improvise "between-notes" [and] the great variety of characteristic tone-color and rhythmic accent—all of these Negro techniques simply defy notation in any known system. They must be recorded from the living sound.

Now, I do not claim to be the only human being able to *recognize* the old Negro Spiritual. There is an always-lessening number of people old enough and musical enough to remember it. What I *am* asserting is its *importance* in world history. While the *slaves* were creating immortal melodies like "Swing low, sweet chariot," the *rest* of America had not yet reached its musical adolescence. American composers were still frantically grabbing at the musical apron-strings of Europe. American talent could not be recognized, even by Americans, until stamped and sealed by European approval. Naturally, under those conditions, the fairest flower might escape attention—in *its own* backyard. Significantly enough, the earliest books on the spirituals came from European-trained authors. The American composers came on board just in time to meet granddaughter Jazz. But, no matter the past periods of circumstances, America owes to itself and the rest of the world a definite, musical chronicle of this accidental but durable by-product of slavery-days.

There *must* be *musical recordings* of many of the finest of the old songs, *each* furnished with (1) an interesting program-note; (2) the plain folk-melody—unadorned; (3) then a development-section, along racial lines, showing future possibilities for composition. Such a record-library would not only rescue the grandest American art-form from oblivion, [but] would immeasurably heighten the artistic stature of the United States among the other civilized nations. Also, it would provide an authoritative model for American students. The school-choruses, especially in the West, are especially fond of the spirituals, which they learn as best they can from the sadly-inadequate printed arrangements.

They *really need* records. They [i.e. the recordings] are the future *teachers*.

Now, I wish to prepare the record-library I have described. No one else has spend such a lifetime of study, experience and dedication: Forty years ago, for my experience, I needed nothing but *people* and time—both *free*. But alas! Today I need money—to release both people and the time.

Hall Johnson, "Notes on the Negro Spiritual"

1.   Early European-Americans had a better feel for harmony and melody than the early African slaves.

       a. True   b. False

2.   African slaves embraced Jesus because of the freedom that he represented.

       a. True   b. False

3.   The slaves brought with them a dazzling facility with _____

       _____ .

4.   Which of the following did the slaves not discover in the New World?

       a. Musical Scale
       b. Harmony and Counterpoint
       c. Good part singing
       d. Improvisation

5.   Do you agree with Johnson that the development of the negro spiritual was "one of the grandest pages in the history of the whole world of music." Explain.

Bruce Baugh*

PROLEGOMENA TO ANY AESTHETICS OF ROCK MUSIC

Can there be an aesthetics of rock music? My question is not: Can traditional ways of interpreting and evaluating music be applied to rock music, for clearly they can, with very mixed results. My question is rather: Does rock music have any standards of its own, which uniquely apply to it, or that apply to it in an especially appropriate way? My hunch is that rock music has such standards, that they are implicitly observed by knowledgeable performers and listeners, and that these standards reflect the distinctiveness of rock as a musical genre. Rock music involves a set of practices and a history quite different from those of the European concert hall tradition upon which traditional musical aesthetics have been based. That being so, any attempt to evaluate or understand rock music using traditional aesthetics of music is bound to result in a misunderstanding. It is not that rock music is more modern, since there are many modernist composers in the European tradition, their modernity being precisely a function of their relation to that tradition, which they aim to radicalize and subvert.[1] The difference between rock and "serious" music is that rock belongs to a different tradition, with different concerns and aims. In this paper, I will try to get at the nature of those differences, and in so doing, if only in a negative way, the route that an aesthetics of rock music might take. I will initially make the contrast between rock and European concert music as strong and sharp as possible, which will lead to

some one-sided and simplistic distinctions between the two genres. Nevertheless, even when the distinctions are properly qualified and nuanced, I think the difference remains real and substantial.

If I were to indicated this difference in a preliminary way, I would say that traditional musical aesthetics is concerned with form and composition, whereas rock is concerned with the *matter* of music. Even this way of putting things is misleading, since the form/matter distinction is itself part of traditional aesthetics. But leaving aside the inappropriateness of the term, by "matter" I mean the way music feels to the listener, or the way that it affects the listener's body.

One important material aspect of rock music is the way an individual tone sounds when played or sung in a certain way. Making a tone sound a certain way is a large part of the art of rock music performance, something rock inherits from the performance-oriented traditions from which it springs, particularly the blues. This is obvious in the case of the voice, which is why in rock, as in blues and most jazz, it is the singer and not the song that is important. But it also is true in the case of the electric guitar, an instrument which takes on the expressive function of the voice in much of rock music. The emphasis on the very sound of a musical note as a vehicle of musical expression was summed up in guitarist Eric Clapton's statement that his ideal is to play a single note with such feeling and intensity

---

*Bruce Baugh teaches philosophy at University College of the Cariboo in Kamloops, British Columbia. In this (1993) and other articles, he argues for an approach to rock music that takes it seriously as an art form.

[1]See Theodor W. Adorno, *Philosophy of Modern Music,* trans. Anne G. Mitchell and Wesley V. Blomster (New York: Continuum, 1985).

From THE JOURNAL OF AESTHETICS AND ART CRITICISM 51:1 Winter 1993. Reprinted by permission.

that it would cause listeners to weep (and not, cynics please note, because the music is painfully loud, but because it is painfully beautiful.)

The materiality of tone, or more accurately, of the performance of tones, is only one important material element of rock music. Two others are loudness and rhythm. Both of these are also more properly felt by the body than judged by the mind, as least as far as rock music is concerned, and the proper use of both is crucial to the success for rock music performance, a success which is judged by the feelings the music produces in the listener's body. The fact that rock music aims at arousing and expressing feeling has often been held against it, as if arousing feelings were somehow "cheap," or unworthy of true musical beauty. But the alternative is to look at the material properties of rock music, or those properties correlative to the bodily feelings it arouses, as the key to rock's own criteria of musical excellence. These material or "visceral" properties of rock are registered in the body core, in the gut, and in the muscles and sinews of the arms and legs, rather than in any intellectual faculty of judgment, which is why traditional aesthetics of music either neglects them or derides them as having no musical value.

Classical aesthetics of music explicitly excludes questions concerning how music feels or sounds, and the emotional reactions music provokes, from considerations of musical beauty. This exclusion is argued for in Kant's *Critique of Judgment,* and follows from Kant's definition of "the beautiful" as that which is an object of judgment claiming universal validity.[2] What pleases me because of the sensations it produces in me, says Kant, is merely agreeable. I call something beautiful, by contrast, when I claim that anyone should find its form, or the arrangement of its parts, intrinsically pleasing, not because of the sensations the form arouses or because of its usefulness, but because the form is inherently suitable to being perceived, and so leads to a harmonious free play of the imagination and the understanding. Pleasures and pains based on mere sensation *(Empfindung),* which constitute the "material" part of a perception *(Vorstellung),* are interested and purely subjective. The idiosyncratic responses sensory stimuli produce in me because of my particular dispositions and physical constitution cannot be the basis for a judgment that claims to be valid for all perceiving subjects, since "in these matters, each person rightly consults

his own feelings alone," and these feelings will differ from person to person (Kant, p. 132). The elements of a work of art that produce sensations, then, such as tones or colors, may add charm to the work or provoke emotions, but they add nothing to beauty. When someone speaks, improperly, of a beautiful musical note, this is "the matter of delight passed off for the form" (Kant, pp. 65–66).

Kant does allow (in section 14) that certain tones and colors may be intrinsically beautiful when they are "pure": that is, when they are considered not in their immediacy as mere sensations, but reflectively, as having a determinate form in virtue of the measurable frequency of vibrations of light or air, or the ratio of one frequency to another in the case of juxtaposed tones or colors. Even here, however, the beauty belongs to the *form* of the tone or color (its frequency or ratio), and not to its merely felt or subjective *matter* (see sections 51–52). In any case, too much attention to the individual notes is a dangerous distraction from the proper object of aesthetic regard, compositional form. "The matter of sensation . . . is not essential. Here the aim is merely enjoyment, which . . . renders the soul dull" and the mind dissatisfied (Kant, p. 191). This is a moral fault, and not just an aesthetic one. The hearer who seeks pleasurable or exciting sensations in music forms judgments concerning musical worth that are conditioned by his body and his senses (Kant, p. 132), since they are based on passively experienced pleasures and pains (Kant, p. 149). Such judgments of musical beauty are heteronomous: free, active, judging reason as subordinated to the passive body's involuntary reactions. The beauty of fine art, on the other hand, is not based on sensations, but on the mind's free and autonomous judgment of the suitability of a form for perception (section 44). Consequently music, since so much of its appeal depends on the actual sensations it produces in the listener rather than on composition alone, "has the lowest place among the fine arts" (Kant, p. 195).

Kant, notoriously, was no music lover. Everyone is familiar with his complaint that music lacks urbanity because "it scatters its influence abroad to an uncalled for extent . . . and . . . becomes obtrusive," a remark that contains a grain of truth, especially in an age of powerful stereo systems and "boom boxes," but which does not indicate much appreciation for music. Yet although Kant himself was insensitive to musical beauty, others more

---

[2]Immanuel Kant, *Critique of Judgement,* trans. James Creed Meredith (Oxford: Clarendon Press, 1978); further references given parenthetically in the text.

339

sensitive took up his preoccupation with beauty of form in their aesthetics of music. So Hanslick, who knew music well, made every note of the musical scale "pure" in Kant's sense of having determinate form, and in that each note is "a tone of determinate measurable pitch,"[3] inherently related to every other tone in virtue of the ratios between the pitches, which determine their relation on the scale (Hanslick, p. 95). By making notes "pure" this way, Hanslick partially rescued musical notes from the disreputable position of being merely the cause of conditioned, subjective sensations and pleasures, which could form the basis only of impure and heteronomous aesthetic judgments. This, though, was only a first step in Hanslick's project of elevating music from the position of lowest of the fine arts to the highest and most formal art of all. "Music is unique among the arts," wrote Hanslick, "because its form is its content and . . . its content is its form" (Hanslick, p. 94). In music, unlike painting or literature, there can be no content apart from the form itself, no subject matter independent of the composition or organization of the work. Musical beauty, then, is entirely based on form, that is, on tonal relationships (Hanslick, p. xxiii), and not on any feelings or emotions aroused or expressed by the music (Hanslick, p. 95). By making the matter of music (musical tones) formal, and by making form identical with content, Hanslick made the art Kant regarded as the basest and most material into the highest and most formal.

Of course, the story doesn't stop with Hanslick. The preoccupation with musical form continues on into twentieth century aesthetics, notably in Adorno's philosophy of music, but in a more everyday way, formal concerns predominate in music criticism in general, from journalism to academia.[4]

The obvious rejoinder to this characterization of traditional aesthetics is that it is not *exclusively* formal, but takes into account non-formal or material elements as well. The timbre of a voice or instrument is clearly of great importance to European concert music; if they weren't, top caliber *bel canto* sopranos and Stradivarius violins wouldn't command so much respect and such high prices. Music criticism also takes performance aspects of music into account. But timbre and performance are usually secondary, and are often discussed in terms of the "faithfulness" or "adequacy" of the performance/interpretation to the composition performed or to the composer's "intentions." One justification for playing music on period instruments and in period style is that this better captures what the composition was trying to express, not simply that it sounds better or is more pleasant to listen to. In that case, performance and the notes' sounds are judged in terms of what the composition requires. In classical aesthetics of music, matter is at the service of form, and is always judged in relation to form. Even though traditional aesthetics is not exclusively formal, formal considerations predominate.

When this preoccupation with form and composition is brought to bear on rock music, the chief result is confusion. Usually, rock music is dismissed as insignificant on account of the simplicity of its forms, a simplicity which is real, and not a misperception by those unfamiliar with the genre. Alternatively, more "liberal" critics will try to find significant form where there is very little form at all, and at the expense of neglecting what is really at stake in rock music. This liberal tolerance is a worse mistake than conservative intolerance. In the first place, it is highly condescending to suppose that rock music has value only when it approximates the compositional forms of baroque or romantic music. The Beatles, in particular, were victims of this patronizing attitude. Is "Penny Lane" a better rock song than "Strawberry Fields" because the former contains flourishes of Baroque trumpet and the latter doesn't?[5] Does knowing that "She's Leaving Home" ends on an Aeolian cadence add to our

---

[3]Eduard Hanslick, *On the Musically Beautiful,* trans. Geoffrey Payzant (Indianapolis: Hackett, 1986), p. 71; further references given parenthetically in the text.

[4]In addition to Adorno's *Philosophy of Modern Music,* see his *In Search of Wagner,* translated by Rodney Livingstone (London: New Left Books, 1981), which deals at length with the formal qualities of Wagner's superficially formless music (form as repetition of gestures and *motifs;* harmony, color and sonority as elements in composition, etc.). As did Hanslick, Adorno makes even the apparently *material* aspects of music into formal elements of composition.

[5]Released as the "A-side" and "B-side" respectively of a "single" in 1967; later included in *Magical Mystery Tour,* EMI/Capitol, 1967.

appreciation of it *as a rock song?*[6] I don't think so. Yet for a time, in the late 1960s and early 1970s, critics fawned over complicated works by Yes or Genesis because traditional aesthetics of music could find something to say about their form, never noticing that criteria appropriate to the music of Handel or Boulez might be inappropriate when applied to rock music, and have very little to do with the informal standards of practice and evaluation employed by people who actually perform or listen to rock music on a regular basis.

To the extent that some rock musicians took this sort of criticism seriously, the results were disastrous, producing the embarrassing, pretentious and—in the final analysis—very silly excesses of "art rock." To the extent art rock succeeded, it did so because it was rock, not because it was "art." This was especially notable in the case of the mercifully short-lived subgenre, the "rock opera." The Who's *Tommy*[7] was a good rock opera because it had good rock music and was done tongue-in-cheek (hence its "Underture"), but other attempts were merely bombastic, neither rock nor opera. Rock's borrowings from "classical" music had similar results. Combining a soulful rhythm and blues vocal with a Baroque organ line worked in Procul Harem's "Whiter Shade of Pale,"[8] but in other instances the incorporation of "classical music" (usually this meant a string section) led to rather slight pop songs collapsing under the weight of extraneous instrumentation.[9]

So what standards are appropriate to rock music? I think that the basic principles of an aesthetics of rock can be derived from turning Kantian or formalist aesthetics on its head. Where Kant prized the free and autonomous judgment of reason, and so found beauty in form rather than matter, an aesthetics of rock judges the beauty of the music by its effects on the body, and so is primarily concerned with the "matter" of music. That makes

beauty in rock music to some extent a subjective and personal matter; to the extent that you evaluate a piece on the basis of the way it happens to affect you, you cannot demand that others who are affected differently agree with your assessment. But that does not mean that rock's standards are purely and simply an individual matter of taste. There are certain properties a piece of rock music must have in order to be good, although knowledgeable listeners may disagree concerning whether a given piece of music actually has those properties. In every case, these properties are material rather than formal, and they are based on performance-based standards of evaluation, rather than compositional ones.

The most *obvious* material property of rock is rhythm. Rock music, from its origins in blues and country and folk traditions, is for dancing. It's got a back-beat, you can't lose it. In dance, the connection between the music and the body of the listener is immediate, felt and enacted rather than thought. A bad rock song is one that tries and fails to inspire the body to dance. Good rhythm cannot be achieved through simple formulas; the sign of a bad rock band is that the beat is not quite right, even though the correct time signature and tempo are being observed. A song with beat and rhythm is one that is performed well, not well composed, and this emphasis on performance is one rock shares with other forms of popular music. It is less a matter of tempo than of *timing*, of knowing whether to play on the beat, or slightly ahead of it or behind it, and this is one of those "knacks" that Plato would have refused the status of truly scientific knowledge: it cannot be captured or explained by any stateable principle. It is not accessible to reason.

It might be a bit unfair to claim rhythm and timing as distinctive elements of rock music, since rhythm, beat and timing are important considerations in traditional aesthetics, and are capable of formalization in musical notation. Some classical

---

[6]On the Beatles, *Sgt. Pepper's Lonely Hearts Club Band*, EMI/Capitol, 1967.

[7]Decca, 1969.

[8]Released as a single by A&M records in 1968.

[9]This was the problem with most of Procul Harem's music, at least on their first three albums. In the Beatle's "A Day in the Life" (on *Sgt. Pepper's*), strings were used in an unorthodox and interesting way. In less capable hands, the same technique had awful results; cf. the Buckingham's "Susan" (1967), a song that has mercifully faded into obscurity, where the string passages bear no plausible relation to the song, but are there simply because "A Day in the Life" received critical praise. Rock music does not get any worse than this.

music is based on traditional European dance forms; some music is written expressly for dance, such as ballet; some music is structured primarily around rhythm, rather than tonal sequences. All these forms of music, then, have a prominent relation to the body because of their connection to dance.

Yet the relation is not the same as in the case of rock music. In the first place, the forms of dance that found their way into classical music were already highly formalized versions of what were (perhaps) once folk dances. Whatever their origins, the courtly dances to which Beethoven and Mozart provided the accompaniment were appreciated for their formal qualities (precision and intricacy of movement, order and geometry of patterns), not for their somatic or visceral aspects. On the contrary, in courtly dance, matter and the body are subject to form and the intellect. This was never more true than in Romantic ballet, where the chief effect of the dance consists of the illusion that highly strenuous and athletic movements are effortless, and that the bodies of the dancers are weightless. Here the body is used to negate the body: in ballet, the materiality of the body itself becomes pure form. This is less true of modern music, such as Stravinsky's, but even in this case the music and its performance are regulated by formal structures to which the musicians and dancers must accommodate their motions. In contrast, the effect of the music on the body is of prime importance in rock music and its antecedents (blues, jazz), so that the music is regulated by the dancers: musicians will vary beat, rhythm and tempo until it feels good to dance to. Rock music has no correct tempo, beat or rhythm independent of its effects on the body of the listener or dancer, which is why when non-rock musicians play rock, it often sounds "flat" and feels "dead": it is not that the musicians are playing the wrong tempo, notes or beat, but only that no standard score captures the subtleties or timing and rhythm that a good rock musician can feel. Feeling is the criterion of correctness here, probably because the dance forms on which rock is based do not deny the body's physicality, but emphasize it: feet stomp, bodies gyrate, bodily masses are propelled by masses of sound with insistent and compelling rhythms.

But beat is not the only thing, or the most important. There is a significant body of highly regarded rock music which has no swing, and which you can't dance to because you are not *meant* to dance to it. From the mid-1960s onward, rock music broke out of the rigid confines of verse/chorus/verse

in $\frac{4}{4}$ time. But the significance of this change is not that it made rock more interesting formally. The importance of the change lay rather in the way it called into question some of the boundaries rock set for itself, and opened up new possibilities for expression through the matter of music, through elements other than rhythm. Let me briefly summarize the history of how this transition took place.

In rock music, the voice had always been the main vehicle of expression, and the factor that could make or break a song. One need only compare a Fats Domino original with its pallid Pat Boone "cover" to see that the expressivity of the voice itself, rather than the composition, makes a rock song good. As in blues, it is the performance that counts, and standards of evaluation are based on standards of performance. In this sense, rock music reverses the priorities of European concert hall music, and questions of "faithfulness" to the music rarely arise. The only question is whether the performance/interpretation is convincing, not whether it is "faithful" to some (usually non-existent) score. No one got too upset when Joe Cocker performed the Beatles' "With a Little Help From My Friends" in a way that was not in the least suggested by the original recording. In fact, the originality of Cocker's interpretation was counted a virtue by most. Listeners to European concert hall music are not nearly so tolerant in this regard: they will accept some deviation from the original score, but within limits established by the score itself, rather than by the effectiveness of the performance. Few discerning rock listener's liked Deodato's pop version of Richard Strauss' *Also Sprach Zarathustra*, but they disliked it because it was inane, not because it was a misinterpretation and a "sacrilege." Again, it is a matter of degree, but there is a heavier emphasis on performance, rather than composition, in rock music.

These performance elements of rock music are not easily accounted for by traditional aesthetics. The performance standards for rock vocalists have little to do with the virtuosity of an opera singer or with an ability to hit the note indicated in the composition at the time indicated. Some of the best rock vocalists, from Muddy Waters to Elvis to Lennon to Joplin, are technically quite bad singers. The standards have to do with the amount of feeling conveyed, and with the nuances of feeling expressed. On the other hand, it is not the vocalist who can sing the longest and loudest who is best, either, heavy-metal notwithstanding. A good rock vocalist can insinuate meaning with a growl or a whisper. This does constitute a virtuosity of sort, but one that connects directly with the body, provoking a visceral response which may be complicated and hard to describe, but easy to recognize for those who have experienced it. Still, what the body recognizes may not lend itself to notation or formalization, and it is unlikely that a more adequate form of notation could capture these "material" qualities.

In the 1960s, the modes of expression that had been uniquely associated with the voice were taken up, with various degrees of success, but the instruments themselves, especially by the guitar. I will mention only two fairly striking examples, Cream's performance of the blues song "Spoonful" at the Fillmore Auditorium in 1968,[10] and Jimi Hendrix's "Machine Gun," recorded in concert on New Year's Day, 1970.[11] Neither of these songs, as performed, have much in the way of musical structure, and they do not swing.[12] But they do allow Clapton, with Cream, and Hendrix to explore different ways an electric guitar can sound. Both guitarists have been guilty of virtuosity for its own sake on many occasions, but in these performances, their playing goes beyond mere show-boating. Clapton's playing ranges from droning sitar-like passages to bursts of tightly clustered notes; Hendrix's use of feedback in the central passage *is* the anguish the music conveys, rather than the bald symbolism of his Woodstock performance of "The Star Spangled Banner."[13] In both cases, the guitarists have dropped their "see what I can do with a guitar" pose in favor of "hear what I can say with a guitar." And in both cases, it is a matter of how the tones are played, not the tones themselves, that make the music successful.

In instances like these, rock achieves the expressivity through musical instruments more closely associated with jazz or blues, a use of the guitar far removed from its earlier uses as either a rhythm instrument or a bit of instrumental "filler" between choruses. On the other hand, neither Clapton nor Hendrix, nor any other good rock instrumentalist, takes an intellectualized approach to music. Both play with an intensity that still connects directly with the body, and like good rock singers, both are often not that good technically; they take chances and they make mistakes. Which is why they are unpredictable and exciting in a way that flawless musicians are not. Even when they hit the wrong notes, they do so in interesting and even exciting ways, creating a tension that can add to musical expression. When they hit the right notes, it is not because the notes are right that makes them great guitarists, but the way the notes sound, and the "timing" of the notes.

Part of the intensity of rock performance has to do with an aspect of rock that is often held against it: the sheer volume or loudness of the music. Loudness, in good rock music, is also a vehicle of expression. Obviously, very loud music has an effect on the body, and not just on the ears; you can feel it vibrate in your chest cavity. This can, of course, become simply exhausting and overwhelming, but used properly, it can add to expressivity. The best rock performances, such as the ones discussed here, make extensive use of dynamics, much as a good blues singer does. And just as the blues sometimes must be shouted or hollered to convey the right emotion, so some passages of rock music must be played loud in order to have the proper effect. Bad rock musicians, like any bad musician, take a mechanical or rule-based approach to dynamics and sonority, resulting in derivative and simplistic music. But loudness can be good, if used wisely.[14]

Rhythm, the expressivity of the notes themselves, loudness: These are three material, bodily elements of rock music that would, I submit, constitute its essence, and might form the basis for a genuine aesthetics of rock. Adorno called for the emancipation of dissonance; an aesthetics of rock requires an emancipation of the body, an emancipation of heteronomy. Such an emancipation is also required for the many forms of music centered on

---

[10]On Cream, *Wheels of Fire,* Polydor/Atco, 1968.

[11]On Jimi Hendrix, *Band of Gypsies,* Reprise/Capitol, 1970.

[12]"Spoonful" is based on a descending progression from G to E; all the rest is variation, the point being that the improvised variations are what count here.

[13]On *Woodstock,* Warner-Cotillion, 1970.

[14]The clearest illustration of stupid and derivative rock is the movie, *Spinal Tap.* Unfortunately, the heavy-metal music portrayed there is actually far more laughable than the parody.

the voice and on dance, rather than on compositions and the mind's free judgment of formal beauty. In fact, preoccupation with formal beauty is appropriate to only a very small fragment of the world's music.

I realize that this brief account of rock music leaves out of consideration the question of what makes a good rock *song,* which raises a whole different set of questions, ones where issues of compositional form are clearly relevant, and which would have to deal with the vexed question of the relation of words to music.[15] But my concern here has been with what the knowledgeable listener finds important in rock music, which is almost always performance rather than composition, and the "matter" of the notes rather than the form of the whole. Whatever form the aesthetics of rock will take, it will not be the Kantian one that underlies conventional musical aesthetics. If these *prolegomena* do nothing more than avert the misunderstandings that arise when formalist aesthetics overreaches its proper domain in being applied to rock music, they will have done enough.[16]

---

[15]To my mind, the best essay on this subject remains Robert Christegau's "Rock Lyrics Are Poetry (Maybe): in *The Age of Rock: Sounds of the American Cultural Revolution,* ed. Jonathan Eisen (New York: Random House, 1969), pp. 220–243.

[16]I would like to thank a number of people whose thoughts and comments are incorporated in this essay: Adrian Shepherd, James O. Young, an anonymous referee for the *JAAC,* and Jamie Baugh. None of them are to blame for what appears here.

Bruce Baugh, "Prolegomena to any Future Aesthetics of Rock Music"

1.   What issue does Baugh discuss?

2.   Why does classical aesthetics miss the point of rock music, according to Baugh?

3.   Identify and briefly explain the three material elements of rock music Baugh proposes as a basis for building an aesthetics of rock.

4.   Do you agree with Baugh? Explain. (Give at least one example of a piece of rock music.)

Wassily Kandinsky*

THE SPIRITUAL IN ART

INTRODUCTION

Every work of art is the child of its age and, in many cases, the mother of our emotions. It follows that each period of culture produces an art of its own which can never be repeated. Efforts to revive the art-principles of the past will at best produce an art that is still-born. It is impossible for us to live and feel, as did the ancient Greeks. In the same way those who strive to follow the Greek methods in sculpture achieve only a similarity of form, the work remaining soulless for all time. Such imitation is mere aping. Externally the monkey completely resembles a human being; he will sit holding a book in front of his nose, and turn over the pages with a thoughtful aspect, but his actions have for him no real meaning.

There is, however, in art another kind of external similarity which is founded on a fundamental truth. When there is a similarity of inner tendency in the whole moral and spiritual atmosphere, a similarity of ideals, at first closely pursued but later lost to sight, a similarity in the inner feeling of any one period to that of another, the logical result will be a revival of the external forms which served to express those inner feelings in an earlier age. An example of this today is our sympathy, our spiritual relationship, with the Primitives. Like ourselves, these artists sought to express in their work only internal truths, renouncing in consequence all consideration of external form.

This all-important spark of inner life today is at present only a spark. Our minds, which are even now only just awakening after years of materialism, are infected with the despair of unbelief, of lack of purpose and ideal. The nightmare of materialism, which has turned the life of the universe into an evil, useless game, is not yet past; it holds the awakening soul still in its grip. Only a feeble light glimmers like a tiny star in a vast gulf of darkness. This feeble light is but a presentiment, and the soul, when it sees it, trembles in doubt whether the light is not a dream, and the gulf of darkness reality. This doubt, and the still harsh tyranny of the materialistic philosophy, divide our soul sharply from that of the Primitives. Our soul rings cracked when we seek to play upon it, as does a costly vase, long buried in the earth, which is found to have a flaw when it is dug up once more. For this reason, the Primitive phase, through which we are now passing, with its temporary similarity of form, can only be of short duration.

These two possible resemblances between the art forms of today and those of the past will be at once recognized as diametrically opposed to one another. The first, being purely external, has no future. The second, being internal, contains the seed of the future within itself. After the period of materialist effort, which held the soul in check until it was shaken off as evil, the soul is emerging, purged by trials and sufferings. Shapeless emotions such as fear, joy, grief, etc., which belonged to this time of effort, will no longer greatly attract the

---

*Wassily Kandinsky (1866–1944) was born in Moscow and reared in the Russian Orthodox faith. After a brief stint as a lecturer in law, Kandinsky turned to painting and became an important part of the pre-war *Blaue Reiter,* or Blue Rider, movement in Munich. He later helped to found the Russian Academy of Artistic Sciences and taught at Bauhaus (1922–33). One of the most influential abstract painters of his generation, he is famous for helping to turn the focus of painting away from realistic portrayals of the external world to the expression of the internal world based on the artist's inner need to create. The following piece is excerpted from his classic manifesto on art of the same title (1912).

artist. He will endeavor to awake subtler emotions, as yet unnamed. Living himself a complicated and comparatively subtle life, his work will give to those observers capable of feeling them lofty emotions beyond the reach of words.

The observer of today, however, is seldom capable of feeling such emotions. He seeks in a work of art a mere imitation of nature which can serve some definite purpose (for example a portrait in the ordinary sense) or a presentment of nature according to a certain convention ("impressionist" painting), or some inner feeling expressed in terms of natural form (as we say—a picture with *Stimmung*). All those varieties of picture, when they are really art, fulfil their purpose and feed the spirit. Though this applies to the first case, it applies more strongly to the third, where the spectator does feel a corresponding thrill in himself. Such harmony or even contrast of emotion cannot be superficial or worthless; indeed the *Stimmung* of a picture can deepen and purify that of the spectator. Such works of art at least preserve the soul from coarseness; they "key it up," so to speak, to a certain height, as a turning-key the strings of a musical instrument. But purification, and extension in duration and size of this sympathy of soul, remain one-sided, and the possibilities of the influence of art are not exerted to their utmost.

THE MOVEMENT OF THE TRIANGLE

The life of the spirit may be fairly represented in a diagram as a large acute-angled triangle divided horizontally into unequal parts with the narrowest segment uppermost. The lower the segment the greater it is in breadth, depth, and area.

The whole triangle is moving slowly, almost invisibly forwards and upwards. Where the apex was today the second segment is tomorrow; what today can be understood only by the apex and to the rest of the triangle is incomprehensible gibberish, forms tomorrow the true thought and feeling of the second segment.

At the apex of the top segment stands often one man, and only one. His joyful vision cloaks a fast sorrow. Even those who are nearest to him in sympathy do not understand him. Angrily they abuse him as charlatan or madman. So in his lifetime stood Beethoven, solitary and insulted.[1] How many years will it be before a greater segment of the triangle reaches the spot where he once stood alone? Despite memorials and statues, are they really many who have risen to his level?[2]

In every segment of the triangle are artists. Each one of them who can see beyond the limits of his segment is a prophet to those about him, and helps the advance of the obstinate whole. But those who are blind, or those who retard the movement of the triangle for baser reasons, are fully understood by their fellows and acclaimed for their genius. The greater the segment (which is the same as saying the lower it lies on the triangle) so the greater the number who understand the words of the artist. Every segment hungers consciously or, much more often, unconsciously for their corresponding spiritual food. This food is offered by the artists, and for this food the segment immediately below will tomorrow be stretching out eager hands.

This simile of the triangle cannot be said to express every aspect of the spiritual life. For instance, there is never an absolute shadow-side to the picture, never a piece of unrelieved gloom. Even too often it happens that one level of spiritual food suffices for the nourishment of those who are already in the higher segment. But for them this food is poison; in small quantities it depresses their souls gradually into a lower segment; in large quantities it hurls them suddenly into the depths even lower and lower. Sienkiewicz, in one of his novels, compares the spiritual life to swimming; for the man who does not strive tirelessly, who does not fight continually against sinking, will mentally and morally go under. In this strait a man's talent (again in the biblical sense) becomes a curse—and not only the talent of the artist, but also of those who eat this poisoned food. The artist uses his strength to flatter his lower needs; in an ostensibly artistic form he presents what is impure, draws the weaker elements to him, mixes them with evil, betrays men and helps them to betray themselves, while they convince themselves and others that they are spiritually thirsty, and that from this pure spring they may quench their thirst. Such art does not help the forward movement, but

---

[1] Weber, composer of *Der Freischütz,* said of Beethoven's Seventh Symphony: "The extravagances of genius have reached the limit; Beethoven is now ripe for an asylum." Of the opening phrase, on a reiterated "e," the Abbé Stadler said to his neighbour, when first he heard it: "Always that miserable 'e'; he seems to be deaf to it himself, the idiot!"

[2] Are not many monuments in themselves answers to that question?

hinders it, dragging back those who are striving to press onward, and spreading pestilence abroad.

Such periods, during which art has no noble champion, during which the true spiritual food is wanting, are periods of retrogression in the spiritual world. Ceaselessly souls fall from the higher to the lower segments of the triangle, and the whole seems motionless, or even to move down and backwards. Men attribute to these blind and dumb periods a special value, for they judge them by outward results, thinking only of material well-being. They hail some technical advance, which can help nothing but the body, as a great achievement. Real spiritual gains are at best undervalued, at worst entirely ignored.

The solitary visionaries are despised or regarded as abnormal and eccentric. Those who are not wrapped in lethargy and who feel vague longings for spiritual life and knowledge and progress, cry in harsh chorus, without any to comfort them. The night of the spirit falls more and more darkly. Deeper becomes the misery of these blind and terrified guides, and their followers, tormented and unnerved by fear and doubt, prefer to this gradual darkening the final sudden leap into the blackness.

At such a time art ministers to lower needs, and is used for material ends. She seeks her sustance in hard realities because she knows of nothing nobler. Objects, the reproduction of which is considered her sole aim, remain monotonously the same. The question "what?" disappears from art; only the question "how?" remains. By what method are these material objects to be reproduced? The word becomes a creed. Art has lost her soul.

In the search for method the artist goes still further. Art becomes so specialized as to be comprehensible only to artists, and they complain bitterly of public indifference to their work. For since the artist in such times has no need to *say* much, but only to be notorious for some small originality and consequently lauded by a small group of patrons and connoisseurs (which incidentally is also a very profitable business for him), there arise a crowd of gifted and skilful painters, so easy does the conquest of art appear. In each artistic circle are thousands of such artists, of whom the majority seek only for some new technical manner, and who produce millions of works of art without enthusiasm, with cold hearts and souls asleep.

Competition arises. The wild battle for success becomes more and more material. Small groups who have fought their way to the top of the chaotic world of art and picture-making entrench themselves in the territory they have won. The public, left far behind, looks on bewildered, loses interest and turns away.

But despite all this confusion, this chaos, this wild hunt for notoriety, the spiritual triangle, slowly but surely, with irresistible strength, moves onwards and upwards.

The invisible Moses descends from the mountains and sees the dance round the golden calf. But he brings with him fresh stores of wisdom to man.

First by the artist is heard his voice, the voice that is inaudible to the crowd. Almost unknowingly the artist follows the call. Already in that very question of "how?" lies a hidden seed of renaissance. For when this "how?" remains without any fruitful answer, there is always a possibility that the same "something" (which we call personality today) may be able to see in the objects about it not only what is purely material but also something less solid; something less "bodily" than was seen in the period of realism, which the universal aim was to reproduce anything "as it really is" and without fantastic imagination.[3]

If the emotional power of the artist can overwhelm the "how?" and can give free scope to his finer feelings, then art is on the crest of the road by which she will not fail later on to find the "what" she has lost, the "what" which will show the way to the spiritual food of the newly awakened spiritual life. This "what?" will no longer be the material, objective "what" of the former period, but the internal truth of art, the soul without which the body (*i.e.* the "how") can never be healthy, whether in an individual or in a whole people.

[3]Frequent use is made here of the terms "material" and "non-material," and of the intermediate phrases "more" or "less material." Is everything material? or is *everything* spiritual? Can the distinctions we make between matter and spirit be nothing but relative modifications of one or the other? Thought which, although a product of the spirit, can be defined with positive science, is matter, but of fine and not coarse substance. Is whatever cannot be touched with the hand, spiritual? The discussion lies beyond the scope of this little book; all that matters here is that the boundaries drawn should not be too definite.

This "what" is the internal truth which only art can divine, which only art can express by those means of expression which are hers alone.

ART AND ARTISTS

The work of art is born of the artist in a mysterious and secret way. From him it gains life and being. Nor is its existence casual and inconsequent, but it has a definite and purposeful strength, alike in its material and spiritual life. It exists and has power to create spiritual atmosphere; and from this inner standpoint one judges whether it is a good work of art or a bad one. If its "form" is bad it means that the form is too feeble in meaning to call forth corresponding vibrations of the soul.[4] Therefore a picture is not necessarily "well painted" if it possesses the "values" of which the French so constantly speak. It is only well painted if its spiritual value is complete and satisfying. "Good drawing" is drawing that cannot be altered without destruction of this inner value, quite irrespective of its correctness as anatomy, botany, or any other science. There is no question of a violation of natural form, but only of the need of the artist for such form. Similarly colours are used not because they are true to nature, but because they are necessary to the particular picture. In fact, the artist is not only justified in using, but it is his duty to use only those forms which fulfil his *own need*. Absolute freedom, whether from anatomy or anything of the kind, must be given the artist in his choice of material. Such spiritual freedom is as necessary in art as it is in life.[5]

Note, however, that blind following of scientific precept is less blameworthy than its blind and purposeless rejection. The former produces at least an imitation of material objects which may be of some use.[6] The latter is an artistic betrayal and brings confusion in its train. The former leaves the spiritual atmosphere empty; the latter poisons it.

Painting is an art, and art is not vague production, transitory and isolated, but a power which must be directed to the improvement and refinement of the human soul—to, in fact, the raising of the spiritual triangle.

If art refrains from doing this work, a chasm remains unbridged, for no other power can take the place of art in this activity. And at times when the human soul is gaining greater strength, art will also grow in power, for the two are inextricably connected and complementary one to the other. Conversely, at those times when the soul tends to be choked by material disbelief, art becomes purposeless and talk is heard that art exists for art's sake alone.[7] Then is the bond between the art and the soul, as it were, drugged into unconsciousness. The artist and the spectator drift apart, till finally the latter turns his back on the former or regards him as a juggler whose skill and dexterity are worthy of applause. It is very important for the artist to gauge his position aright, to realize that he has a duty to his art and to himself, that he is not king of the castle but rather a servant of a nobler purpose. He must search deeply into his own soul, develop and tend it, so that his art has something to clothe, and does not remain a glove without a hand.

---

[4]So-called indecent pictures are either incapable of causing vibrations of the soul (in which case they are not art) or they are so capable. In the latter case they are not to be spurned absolutely, even though at the same time they gratify what nowadays we are pleased to call the "lower bodily tastes."

[5]This freedom is man's weapon against the Philistines. It is based on the inner need.

[6]Plainly, an imitation of nature, if made by the hand of an artist, is not a pure reproduction. The voice of the soul will in some degree at least make itself heard. As contrasts one may quote a landscape of Canaletto and those sadly famous heads by Denner.—(Alte Pinakothek, Munich.)

[7]This cry "art for art's sake," is really the best ideal such an age can attain to. It is an unconscious protest against materialism, against the demand that everything should have a use and practical value. It is further proof of the indestructibility of art and of the human soul, which can never be killed but only temporarily smothered.

The artist must have something to say, for mastery over form is not his goal but rather the adapting of form to its inner meaning.[8]

The artist is not born to a life of pleasure. He must not live idle; he has a hard work to perform, and one which often proves a cross to be borne. He must realize that his every deed, feeling, and thought are raw but sure material from which his work is to arise, that he is free in art but not in life.

The artist has a triple responsibility to the non-artists: (1) He must repay the talent which he has; (2) his deeds, feelings, and thoughts, as those of every man, create a spiritual atmosphere which is either pure or poisonous. (3) These deeds and thoughts are materials for his creations, which themselves exercise influence on the spiritual atmosphere. The artist is not only a king, as Peladan says, because he has great power, but also because he has great duties.

If the artist be priest of beauty, nevertheless this beauty is to be sought only according to the principle of the inner need, and can be measured only according to the size and intensity of that need.

That is beautiful which is produced by the inner need, which springs from the soul.

Maeterlinck, one of the first warriors, one of the first modern artists of the soul, says: "There is nothing on earth so curious for beauty or so absorbent of it, as a soul. For that reason few mortal souls withstand the leadership of a soul which gives them beauty."[9]

And this property of the soul is the oil, which facilitates the slow, scarcely visible but irresistible movement of the triangle, onwards and upwards.

---

[8]Naturally this does not mean that the artist is to instill forcibly into his work some deliberate meaning. As has been said the generation of a work of art is a mystery. So long as artistry exists there is no need of theory or logic to direct the painter's action. The inner voice of the soul tells him what form he needs, whether inside or outside nature. Every artist knows, who works with feeling, how suddenly the right form flashes upon him. Böcklin said that a true work of art must be like an inspiration; that actual painting, composition, etc., are not the steps by which the artist reaches self-expression.

[9]*De la beauté intérieure.*

350

Wassily Kandinsky *Spiritual in Art*

1.   Explain Kandinsky's use of the triangle to represent the life of the spirit in artists.

2.   What is the "inner need" of the artist?

3.   Explain the responsibilities of the artist according to Kandinsky.

4.   What does Kandinsky mean when he states that the goal of painting is the adaptation of form to inner meaning?

Jose Ortega y Gassett*

ON POINT OF VIEW IN THE ARTS

When history is what it should be, it is an elaboration of cinema. It is not content to install itself in the successive facts and to view the moral landscape that may be perceived from here; but for this series of static images, each enclosed within itself, history substitutes the image of a movement. "Vistas" which had been discontinuous appear to emerge one from another, each prolonging the other without interruption. Reality, which for one moment seemed an infinity of crystallized facts, frozen in position, liquifies, springs forth, and flows. The true historical reality is not the datum, the fact, the thing, but the evolution formed when these materials melt and fluidify. History moves; the still waters are made swift.

II

In the museum we find the lacquered corpse of an evolution. Here is the flux of that pictorial anxiety which has budded forth from man century after century. To conserve this evolution, it has had to be undone, broken up, converted into fragments again and congealed as in a refrigerator. Each picture is a crystal with unmistakable and rigid edges, separated from the others, a hermetic island.

And, nonetheless, it is a corpse we could easily revive. We would need only to arrange the pictures in a certain order and then move the eye—or the mind's eye—quickly from one to the other. Then, it would become clear that the evolution of painting from Giotto to our own time is a unique and simple action with a beginning and an end. It is surprising that so elementary a law has guided the variations of pictorial art in our western world. Even more curious, and most disturbing, is the analogy of this law with that which has directed the course of European philosophy. This parallel between the two most widely separated disciplines of culture permits us to suspect the existence of an even more general principle which has been active in the entire evolution of the European mind. I am not, however, going to prolong our adventure to this remote arcanum, and will content myself, for the present, with interpreting the visage of six centuries that has been Occidental painting.

III

Movement implies a mover. In the evolution of painting, what is it that moves? Each canvas is an instant in which the mover stands fixed. What is this? Do not look for something very complicated. The thing that varies, the thing that shifts in painting, and which by its shifts produces the diversity of aspects and styles, is simply the painter's point of view.

It is natural enough. An abstract idea is ubiquitous. The isosceles triangle presents the same aspect on Earth as on Sirius. On the other hand, a sensuous image bears the indelible mark of its localization, that is, the image presents something seen from a definite point of view. This localization of the sensible may be strict or vague, but it is inevitable. A church spire, a sail at sea, present themselves to us at a distance that for practical purposes we may estimate with some accuracy. The moon or the blue face of heaven are at a distance

---

*Jose Ortega y Gassett (1883–1955) was a Spanish philosopher who studied and taught at the University of Madrid. Among his numerous works, his most famous are *The Revolt of the Masses* and *The Dehumanization of Art*, from which this reading (1949) is drawn. His existentialist philosophy emphasizes self-creation through the realization of possibilities, and in both art and politics, he tended towards elitism.

essentially imprecise, but quite characteristic in their imprecision. We cannot say that they are so many miles away; their localization in distance is vague, but this vagueness is not indetermination.

Nonetheless, it is not the geodetic *quantity* of distance which decisively influences the painter's point of view, but its optical *quality*. "Near" and "far" are relative, metrically, while to the eye they may have a kind of absolute value. Indeed, the *proximate vision* and the *distant vision* of which physiology speaks are not notions that depend chiefly on measurable factors, but are rather two distinct ways of seeing.

If we take up an object, an earthen jar, for example, and bring it near enough to the eyes, these converge on it. Then, the field of vision assumes a peculiar structure. In the center there is the favored object, fixed by our gaze; its form seems clear, perfectly defined in all its details. Around the object, as far as the limits of the field of vision, there is a zone we do not look at, but which, nevertheless, we see with an indirect, vague, inattentive vision. Everything within this zone seems to be situated behind the object; this is why we call it the "background." But, moreover, this whole background is blurred, hardly identifiable, without accented form, reduced to confused masses of color. If it is not something to which we are accustomed, we cannot say what it is, exactly, that we see in this indirect vision.

The proximate vision, then, organizes the whole field of vision, imposing upon it an optical hierarchy: a privileged central nucleus articulates itself against the surrounding area. The central object is a luminous hero, a protagonist standing out against a "mass," a visual *plebs,* and surrounded by a cosmic chorus.

Compare this with distant vision. Instead of fixing a proximate object, let the eye, passive but free, prolong its line of vision to the limit of the visual field. What do we find then? The structure of our hierarchized elements disappears. The ocular field is homogeneous; we do not see one thing clearly and the rest confusedly, for all are submerged in an optical democracy. Nothing possesses a sharp profile; everything is background, confused, almost formless. On the other hand, the duality of proximate vision is succeeded by a perfect unity of the whole visual field.

IV

To these different modes of seeing, we must add another more important one.

In looking close-up at our earthen jar, the eye-beam strikes the most prominent part of its bulge. Then, as if shattered at this point of contact, the beam is splintered into multiple lines which glide around the sides of the vase and seem to embrace it, to take possession of it, to emphsize its rotundity. Thus the object seen at close range acquires the indefinable corporeality and solidity of filled volume. We see it "in bulk," convexly. But this same object placed farther away, for distant vision, loses this corporeality, this solidity and plentitude. Now it is no longer a compact mass, clearly rotund, with its protuberance and curving flanks; it has lost "bulk," and become, rather, an insubstantial surface, an unbodied spectre composed only of light.

Proximate vision has a tactile quality. What mysterious resonance of touch is preserved by sight when it converges on a nearby object? We shall not now attempt to violate this mystery. It is enough that we recognize this quasi-tactile density possessed by the ocular ray, and which permits it, in effect, to embrace, to touch the earthen jar. As the object is withdrawn, sight loses its tactile power and gradually becomes pure vision. In the same way, things, as they recede, cease to be filled volumes, hard and compact, and become mere chromatic entities, without resistance, mass or convexity. An age-old habit, founded in vital necessity, causes men to consider as "things," in the strict sense, only such objects solid enough to offer resistance to their hands. The rest is more or less illusion. So in passing from proximate to distant vision an object becomes illusory. When the distance is great, there on the confines of a remote horizon—a tree, a castle, a mountain range—all acquire the half-unreal aspect of ghostly apparitions.

V

A final and decisive observation.

When we oppose proximate to distant vision, we do not mean that in the latter the object is farther away. To look means here, speaking narrowly, to focus both ocular rays on a point which, thanks to this, becomes favored, optically privileged. In distant vision we do not fix the gaze on any point, but rather attempt to embrace the whole field, including its boundaries. For this reason, we avoid focusing the eyes as much as possible. And then we are surprised to find that the object just perceived—our entire visual field—is concave. If we are in a house the concavity is bordered by the walls, the roof, the floor. This border or limit is a surface that tends to take the form of a hemisphere viewed from within. But where does the concavity begin? There is no possibility of doubt: it begins at our eyes themselves.

The result is that what we see at a distance is hollow space as such. The content of perception is not strictly the surface in which the hollow space terminates, but rather the whole hollow space itself, from the eyeball to the wall or the horizon.

This fact obliges us to recognize the following paradox: the object of sight is not farther off in distant than in proximate vision, but on the contrary is nearer, since it begins at our cornea. In pure distant vision, our attention, instead of being directed farther away, has drawn back to the absolutely proximate, and the eyebeam, instead of striking the convexity of a solid body and staying fixed on it, penetrates a concave object, glides into a hollow.

VI

Throughout the history of the arts in Europe, then, the painter's point of view has been changing from proximate to distant vision, and painting, correspondingly, which begins with Giotto as painting of bulk, turns into painting of hollow space.

This means there has been nothing capricious in the itinerary followed by the painter's shift of attention. First it is fixed upon the body or volume of an object, then upon what lies between the body of the object and the eye, that is, the hollow space. And since the latter is in front of the object, it follows that the journey of the pictorial gaze is a retrogression from the distant—although close by—toward what is contiguous to the eye.

According to this, the evolution of Western painting would consist in a retraction from the object toward the subject, the painter.

The reader may test for himself this law that governs the movement of pictorial art by a chronological review of the history of painting. In what follows, I limit myself to a few examples that are, as it were, stages on such a journey.

VII. THE QUATTROCENTO

The Flemish and the Italians cultivate with passion the painting of bulk. One would say they paint with their hands. Every object appears unequivocally solid, corporeal, tangible. Covering it is a polished skin, without pores or growth, which seems to delight in asserting its own rounded volume. Objects in the background receive the same treatment as those of the foreground. The artist contents himself with representing the distant as smaller than the proximate, but he paints both in the same way. The distinction of planes is, then,

merely abstract, and is obtained by pure geometrical perspective. Pictorially, everything in these pictures is in one plane, that is, everything is painted from close-up. The smallest figure, there in the distance, is as complete, spherical and detached as the most important. The painter seems to have gone to the distant spot where they are, and from near at hand to have painted them as distant.

But it is impossible to see several objects close-up at the same time. The proximate gaze must shift from one to the other to make each in turn the center of vision. This means that the point of view in a primitive picture is not single, but as many points of view as there are objects represented. The canvas is not painted as a unity, but as a plurality. No part is related to any other; each is perfect and separate. Hence the best means of distinguishing the two tendencies in pictorial art—painting of bulk and painting of hollow space—is to take a portion of the picture and see whether, in isolation, it is enough to represent something fully. On a canvas of Velásquez, each section contains only vague and monstrous forms.

The primitive canvas is, in a certain sense, the sum of many small pictures, each one independent and each painted from the proximate view. The painter has directed an exclusive and analytic gaze at each one of the objects. This accounts for the diverting richness of these Quattrocento catalogues. We never have done with looking at them. We always discover a new little interior picture that we had not observed closely enough. On the other hand, they cannot be seen as a whole. The pupil of our eye has to travel step by step along the canvas, pausing in the same point of view that the painter successively took.

VIII. RENAISSANCE

Proximate vision is exclusive, since it apprehends each object in itself and separates it from the rest. Raphael does not modify this point of view, but introduces in the picture an abstract element that affords it a certain unity; this is composition, or architecture. He continues to paint one object after another, like a primitive; his visual apparatus functions on the same principle. But instead of limiting himself, like the primitive, to paint what he sees as he sees it, he submits everything to an external force: the geometrical idea of unity. Upon the analytic form of objects, there is imperatively fixed the synthetic form of composition, which is not the visible form of an object, but a pure rational schema. (Leonardo, too, for example in his triangular canvases).

Raphael's pictures, then, do not derive from, and cannot be viewed in, a unified field of vision. But there is already in them the rational basis of unification.

IX. TRANSITION

If we pass from the primitive and the Renaissance toward Velásquez, we find in the Venetians, but especially in Tintoretto and El Greco, an intermediate stage. How shall we define it?

In Tintoretto and El Greco two epochs meet. Hence the anxiety, the restlessness that marks the work of both. These are the last representatives of painting in bulk, and they already sense the future problems of painting in hollow space without, however, coming to grips with them.

Venetian art, from the beginning, tends to a distant view of things. In Giorgione and Titian, the bodies seem to wish to lose their hard contours, and float like clouds or some diaphanous fabric. However, the will to abandon the proximate and analytic point of view is still lacking. For a century, there is a struggle between both principles, with victory for neither. Tintoretto is an extreme example of this inner tension, in which distant vision is already on the point of victory. In the canvases of the Escorial he constructs great empty spaces. But in this undertaking he is forced to lean on architectonic perspective as on a crutch. Without those columns and cornices that flee into the background, Tintoretto's brush would fall into the abyss of that hollow space he aspired to create.

El Greco represents something of a regression. I believe that his modernity and his nearness to Velásquez has been exaggerated. El Greco is still chiefly preoccupied with volume. The proof is that he may be accounted the last great foreshortener. He does not seek empty space; in him there remains the intention to capture the corporeal, filled volume. While Velásquez, in *The Ladies in Waiting* and *The Spinners,* groups his human figures at the right and left, leaving the central space more or less free—as if space were the true protagonist—El Greco piles up solid masses over the whole canvas that completely displace the air. His works are usually stuffed with flesh.

However, pictures like *The Resurrection, The Crucified* (Prado) and *Pentecost,* pose the problems of painting in depth with rare power.

But it is a mistake to confuse the painting of depth with that of hollow space or empty concavity. The former is only a more learned way of asserting volume. On the other hand, the latter is a total inversion of pictorial intention.

What we find in El Greco is that the architectonic principle has completely taken over the represented objects and forced these, with unparalleled violence, to submit to its ideal schema. In this way, the analytic vision, which seeks volume by emphasizing each figure for its own sake, is mitigated and neutralized, as it were, by the synthetic intention. The formal dynamic schema that dominates the picture imposes on it a certain unity and fosters the illusion of a single point of view.

Furthermore, there appears already in the work of El Greco another unifying element: chiaroscuro.

X. THE CHIAROSCURISTS

Raphael's composition, El Greco's dynamic schema, are postulates of unity that the artist throws upon his canvas;—but nothing more. Every object in the picture continues as before to assert its volume, and, consequently, its independence and particularism. These unities, then, are of the same abstract lineage as the geometrical perspective of the primitives. Derived from pure reason, they show themselves incapable of giving form to the materials of the picture as a whole; or, in other words, they are not pictorial principles. Each section of the picture is painted without their intervention.

Compared to them, chiaroscuro signified a radical and more profound innovation.

When the eye of the painter seeks the body of things, the objects placed in the painted area will demand, each for itself, an exclusive and privileged point of view. The picture will possess a feudal constitution in which every element will maintain its personal rights. But here, slipping between them, is a new object gifted with a magic power that permits it—even more—obliges it to be ubiquitous and occupy the whole canvas without having to dispossess the others. This magic object is light. It is everywhere single and unique throughout the composition. Here is a principle of unity that is not abstract but real, a thing among other things, not an idea or schema. The unity of illumination or chiaroscuro imposes a unique point of view. The painter must now see his entire work as immersed in the ample element of light.

Thus Ribera, Caravaggio, and the young Velásquez (*The Adoration of the Magi*). They still seek for corporeality according to accepted practice. But this no longer interests them primarily. The object in itself begins to be disregarded and have no other role than to serve as support and background for the light playing upon it. One studies the trajectory of light, emphasizing the fluidity of its passage over the face of volumes, over bulkiness.

Is it not clear what shift in the artist's point of view is implied by this? The Velásquez of *The Adoration of the Magi* no longer fixes his attention upon the object as such but upon its surface, where the light falls and is reflected. There has occurred, then, a retraction of vision, which has stopped being a hand and released its grasp of the rounded body. Now, the visual ray halts at the point where the body begins and light strikes resplendently; from there it seeks another point on another object where the same intensity of illumination is vibrating. The painter has achieved a magic solidarity and unification of all the light elements in contrast to the shadow elements. Things of the most disparate form and condition now become equivalent. The individualistic primacy of objects is finished. They are no longer interesting in themselves, and begin to be only a pretext for something else.

XI. VELÁSQUEZ

Thanks to chiaroscuro, the unity of the picture becomes internal, and not merely obtained by extrinsic means. However, under the light, volumes continue to lurk, the painting of bulk persists through the refulgent veil of light.

To overcome this dualism, art needed a man of disdainful genius, resolved to have no interest in bodies, to deny their pretensions to solidity, to flatten their petulant bulk. This disdainful genius was Velásquez.

The primitive, enamoured of objective shapes, seeks them arduously with his tactile gaze, touches them, embraces them. The chiaroscurist, already less taken with corporeality, lets his ray of vision travel, as along a railway track, with the light ray that migrates from one surface to the next. Velásquez, with formidable audacity, executes the supreme gesture of disdain that calls forth a whole new painting: he halts the pupil of the eye. Nothing more. Such is this gigantic revolution.

Until then, the painter's eye had Ptolemaically revolved about each object, following a servile orbit. Velásquez despotically resolves to fix the one point of view. The entire picture will be born in a single act of vision, and things will have to contrive as best they may to move into the line of vision. It is a Copernican revolution, comparable to that pro-

moted by Descartes, Hume and Kant in philosophic thought. The eye of the artist is established as the center of the plastic Cosmos, around which revolve the forms of objects. Rigidly, the ocular apparatus casts its ray directly forward, without deviating to one side or the other, without preference for any object. When it lights on something, it does not fix upon it, and, consequently, that something is converted, not into a round body, but into a mere surface that intercepts vision.[1]

The point of view has been retracted, has placed itself farther from the object, and we have passed from proximate to distant vision, which, strictly speaking, is the more proximate of the two kinds of vision. Between the eye and the bodies is interposed the most immediate object: hollow space, air. Floating in the air, transformed into chromatic gases, formless pennons, pure reflections, things have lost their solidity and contour. The painter has thrown his head back, half-closed his eyelids, and between them has pulverized the proper form of each object, reducing it to molecules of light, to pure sparks of color. On the other hand, his picture may be viewed from a single point of view, as a whole and at a glance.

Proximate vision dissociates, analyzes, distinguishes—it is feudal. Distant vision synthesizes, combines, throws together—it is democratic. The point of view becomes synopsis. The painting of bulk has been definitively transformed into the painting of hollow space.

XII. IMPRESSIONISM

It is not necessary to remark that, in Velásquez, the moderating principles of the Renaissance persisted. The innovation did not appear in all its radicalism until the Impressionists and Post-Impressionists.

The premises formulated in our first paragraphs may seem to imply that the evolution had terminated when we arrive at the painting of hollow space. The point of view, transforming itself from the multiple and proximate to the single and distant, appears to have exhausted its possible itinerary. Not at all! We shall see that it may retreat even closer to the subject. From 1870 until today, the shift of viewpoint has continued, and these latest stages, precisely because of their surprising and paradoxical character, confirm the fatal law to which I alluded at

---

[1] If we look at an empty sphere from without, we see a solid volume. If we enter the sphere we see about us a surface that limits the interior concavity.

the beginning. The artist, starting from the world about him, ends by withdrawing into himself.

I have said that the gaze of Velásquez, when it falls on an object, converts it into a surface. But, meanwhile, the visual ray has gone along its path, enjoying itself by perforating the air between the cornea and distant things. In *Ladies in Waiting* and *The Spinners,* we see the satisfaction with which the artist has accentuated hollow space as such. Velásquez looks straight to the background; thus, he encounters the enormous mass of air between it and the boundary of his eye. Now, to look at something with the central ray of the eye is what is known as direct vision or vision *in modo recto.* But behind the axial ray the pupil sends out many others at the oblique angles, enabling us to see *in modo obliquo.* The impression of concavity is derived from the *modo recto.* If we eliminate this—for example, by blinking the eyes—we have only oblique vision, those side-views "from the tail of the eye" which represent the height of disdain. Thus, the third dimension disappears and the field of vision tends to convert itself entirely into surface.

This is what the successive impressionisms have done. Velásquez' background has been brought forward, and so of course ceases to be background since it cannot be compared with a foreground. Painting tends to become planimetric, like the canvas on which one paints. One arrives, then, at the elimination of all tactile and corporeal resonance. At the same time, the atomization of things in oblique vision is such that almost nothing remains of them. Figures begin to be unrecognizable. Instead of painting objects as they are seen, one paints the experience of seeing. Instead of an object as impression, that is, a mass of sensations. Art, with this, has withdrawn completely from the world and begins to concern itself with the activity of the subject. Sensations are no longer things in any sense; they are subjective states through which and by means of which things appear.

Let us be sure we understand the extent of this change in the point of view. It would seem that in fixing upon the object nearest the cornea, the point of view is as close as possible to the subject and as far as possible from things. But no—the inexorable retreat continues. Not halting even at the cornea, the point of view crosses the last frontier and penetrates into vision itself, into the subject himself.

XIII. CUBISM

Cézanne, in the midst of his impressionist tradition, discovers volume. Cubes, cylinders, cones begin to emerge on his canvases. A careless observer might have supposed that, with its evolution exhausted, pictorial art had begun all over again and that we had relapsed back to the point of view of Giotto. Not at all! In the history of art there have always been eccentric movements tending toward the archaic. Nevertheless, the main stream flows over them and continues its inevitable course.

The cubism of Cézanne and of those who, in effect, were cubists, that is, stereometrists, is only one step more in the internalizing of painting. Sensations, the theme of impressionism, are subjective states; as such, realities, effective modifications of the subject. But still further within the subject are found the ideas. And ideas, too, are realities present in the individual, but they differ from sensations in that their content—the ideated—is unreal and sometimes even impossible. When I conceive a strictly geometrical cyclinder, my *thought* is an effective act that takes place in me; but the geometric cylinder of which I think is unreal. Ideas, then, are subjective realities that contain virtual objects, a whole specific world of a new sort, distinct from the world revealed by the eye, and which emerges miraculously from the psychic depths.

Clearly, then, there is no connection between the masses evoked by Cézanne and those of Giotto; they are, rather, antagonists. Giotto seeks to render the actual volume of each thing, its immediate and tangible corporeality. Before his time, one knew only the Byzantine two-dimensional image. Cézanne, on the other hand, substitutes for the bodies of things non-existent volumes of his own invention, to which real bodies have only a metaphorical relationship. After Cézanne, painting only paints ideas—which, certainly, are also objects, but ideal objects, immanent to the subject or intrasubjective.

This explains the hodge-podge that, in spite of misleading interpretations, is inscribed on the muddy banner of so-called *cubism.* Together with volumes that seem to accord major emphasis to the rotundity of bodies, Picasso, in his most typical and scandalous pictures, breaks up the closed form of an object and, in pure Euclidian planes, exhibits their fragments—an eyebrow, a mustache, a nose—without any purpose other than to serve as a symbolic cipher for ideas.

This equivocal cubism is only a special manner within contemporary expressionism. In the impression, we reached the minimum of exterior objectivity. A new shift in the point of view was possible only if, leaping behind the retina—a tenuous frontier between the external and internal—painting completely reversed its function and, instead of putting us within what is outside, endeavored to pour out upon the canvas what is within: ideal invented objects. Note how, by a simple advance of the point of view along the same trajectory it has followed from the beginning, it arrives at an inverse result. The eyes, instead of absorbing things, are converted into projectors of private flora and fauna. Before, the real world drained off into them; now, they are reservoirs of irreality.

It is possible that present-day art has little aesthetic value; but he who sees in it only a caprice may be very sure indeed that he has not understood either the new art or the old. Evolution has conducted painting—and art in general inexorably, fatally, to what it is today.

XIV

The guiding law of the great variations in painting is one of disturbing simplicity. First things are painted; then, sensations; finally, ideas. This means that in the beginning the artist's attention was fixed on external reality; then, on the subjective; finally, on the intrasubjective. These three stages are three points on a straight line.

Now, Occidental philosophy has followed an identical route, and this coincidence makes our law even more disturbing.

Let us annotate briefly this strange parallelism.

The painter begins by asking himself what elements of the universe ought to be translated onto canvas, that is, what class of phenomena is pictorially essential. The philosopher, for his part, asks what class of objects is fundamental. A philosophical system is an effort to reconstruct the universe conceptually, taking as a point of departure a certain type of fact considered as the firmest and most secure. Each epoch of philosophy has preferred a distinct type, and upon this has built the rest of the construction.

In the time of Giotto, painter of solid and independent bodies, philosophy believed that the ultimate and definitive reality were individual substances. Examples given of such substances in the schools were: this horse, this man. Why did one believe to have discovered in these the ultimate metaphysical value? Simply because in the practical and natural idea of the world, every horse and every man seems to have an existence of his own, independent of other things and of the mind that contemplates them. The horse lives by himself, complete and perfect, according to his mysterious inner

energy; if we wish to know him, our senses, our understanding must go to him and turn humbly, as it were, in his orbit. This, then, is the substantialist realism of Dante, a twin brother to the painting of bulk initiated by Giotto.

Let us jump to the year 1600, the epoch in which the painting of hollow space began. Philosophy is in the power of Descartes. What is cosmic reality for him? Multiple and independent substances disintegrate. In the foreground of metaphysics there is a single substance—an empty substance—a kind of metaphysical hollow space that now takes on a magical creative power. For Descartes, the *real* is space, as for Velásquez it is hollow space.

After Descartes, the plurality of substance reappears for a moment in Leibniz. These substances are no longer corporeal principles, but quite the reverse: the monads are subjects, and the role of each—a curious symptom—is none other than to represent a *"point de vue."* For the first time in the history of philosophy we hear a formal demand that science be a system which submits the universe to a point of view. The monad does nothing but provide a metaphysical situs for this unity of vision.

In the two centuries that follow, subjectivism becomes increasingly radical, and toward 1880, while the impressionists were putting pure sensations on canvas, the philosophers of extreme positivism were reducing universal reality to pure sensations.

The progressive dis-realization of the world, which began in the philosophy of the Renaissance, reaches its extreme consequences in the radical sensationalism of Avenarius and Mach. How can this continue? What new philosophy is possible? A return to primitive realism is unthinkable; four centuries of criticism, of doubt, of suspicion, have made this attitude forever untenable. To remain in our subjectivism is equally impossible. Where shall we find the material to reconstruct the world?

The philosopher retracts his attention even more and, instead of directing it to the subjective as such, fixes on what up to now has been called "the content of consciousness," that is, the instrasubjective. There may be no corresponding reality to what our ideas project and what our thoughts think; but this does not make them purely subjective. A world of hallucination would not be real, but neither would it fail to be a world, an objective universe, full of sense and perfection. Although the imaginary centaur does not really gallop, tail and mane in the wind, across real prairies, he has a peculiar independence with regard to the subject that imagines him. He is a virtual object, or, as the most recent philosophy expresses it, an ideal object.[2] This is the type of phenomena which the thinker of our times considers most adequate as a basis for his universa l system. Can we fail to be surprised at the coincidence between such a philosophy and its synchronous art, known as expressionism or cubism?

Translated from the Spanish by Paul Snodgress and Joseph Frank

---

[2]The philosophy to which Ortega refers, but which unfortunately he neglects to name, is obviously Husserlian phenomenology. (Translator's Note—J.F.)

Ortega's "On Point of View in the Arts"

1. The main thing that shifts in the history of painting is the painter's point of view.

    a. True   b. False

2. That shift is from distant to proximate vision.

    a. True   b. False

3. Proximate vision has a

    a. visceral quality.
    b. aural quality.
    c. aromatic quality.
    d. tactile quality.

4. Distant vision _____ .

    a. synthesizes.
    b. analyzes.
    c. both a and b
    d. neither a nor b

5. Briefly explain how the history of occidental philosophy parallels the history of western art.

Susanne Langer*

THE DYNAMIC IMAGE: SOME PHILOSOPHICAL REFLECTIONS ON DANCE

Once upon a time a student, paging through a college catalogue, asked me in evident bewilderment: "What is 'philosophy of art'? How in the world can art be philosophical?"

Art is not philosophical at all; philosophy and art are two different things. But there is nothing one cannot philosophize about—that is, there is nothing that does not offer some philosophical problems. Art, in particular, presents hosts of them. Artists do not generally moot such matters explicitly, though they often have fairly good working notions of a philosophical sort—notions that only have to be put into the right words to answer our questions, or at least to move them along toward their answers.

What, exactly, is a philosophical question?

A philosophical question is always a demand for the *meaning* of what we are saying. This makes it different from a scientific question, which is a question of fact; in a question of fact, we take for granted that we know what we mean—that is, what we are talking about. If one asks: "How far from here is the sun?" the answer is a statement of fact, "About ninety million miles." We assume that we know what we mean by "the sun" and by "miles" and "being so-and-so far from here." Even if the answer is wrong—if it fails to state a fact, as it would if you answered "twenty thousand miles"—we till know what we are talking about. We take some

measurements and find out which answer is true. But suppose one asks: "What is space?" "What is meant by 'here'?" "What is meant by 'the distance' from here to somewhere else?" The answer can only be found in thinking—reflecting on what we mean. This is sometimes simple; we analyze our meanings and define each word. But more often we find that we have no clear concepts at all, and the fuzzy ones we have conflict with each other so that as soon as we analyze them, i.e., make them clear, we find them contradictory, senseless, or fantastic. Then logical analysis does not help us; what we need then is the more difficult, but also more interesting part of philosophy, the part that can not be taught by any rule—logical construction. We have to figure out a meaning for our statements, a way to think about the things that interest us. Science is not possible unless we can attach some meaning to "distance" and "point" and "space" and "velocity," and other such familiar but really quite slippery words. To establish those fundamental meanings is philosophical work; and the philosophy of modern science is one of the most brilliant intellectual works of our time.

The philosophy of art is not so well developed, but it is full of life and ferment just now. Both professional philosophers and intellectually gifted artists are asking questions about the meaning of

*Susanne Langer (1895–1985) taught philosophy at Radcliffe and Connecticut Colleges. Under the influence of the German Neo-Kantian Ernst Cassirer, she developed a theory of art that interpreted artistic creations as symbolic expressions of human feeling. The following excerpt is taken from her *Problems of Art: Ten Philosophical Lectures* (1957). She is also well-known for her *Philosophy in a New Key* and *Mind: An Essay on Feeling*.

"art," of "expression," of "artistic truth," "form," "reality," and dozens of other words that they hear and use, but find—to their surprise—they cannot define, because when they analyze what they mean it is not anything coherent and tenable.

The construction of a coherent theory—a set of connected ideas about some whole subject—begins with the solution of a central problem; that is, with the establishing of a key concept. There is no way of knowing, by any general rule, what constitutes a central problem; it is not always the most general or the most fundamental one you can raise. But the best sign that you have broached a central philosophical issue is that in solving it you raise new interesting questions. The concept you construct has *implications,* and by implication builds up further ideas, that illuminate other concepts of the whole subject, to answer other questions, sometimes before you even ask them. A key concept solves more problems than it was designed for.

In philosophy of art one of the most interesting problems—one that proves to be really central—is the meaning of that much-used word, "creation." Why do we say an artist creates a work? He does not create oil pigments or canvas, or the structure of tonal vibrations, or words of a language if he is a poet, or, in the case of a dancer, his body and its mobility. He finds all these things and uses them, as a cook uses eggs and flour and so forth to make a cake, or a manufacturer uses wool to make thread, and thread to make socks. Is it only in a mood of humor or extravagance that we speak of the cake Mother "created." But when it comes to works of art, we earnestly call them creations. This raises the philosophical question: What do we mean by the word? What is created?

If you pursue this issue, it grows into a complex of closely related questions: what is created in art, what for, and how? The answers involve just about all the key concepts for a coherent philosophy of art: such concepts as *apparition,* or the image, *expressiveness, feeling, motif, transformation.* There are others, but they are all interrelated.

It is impossible to talk, in one lecture, about all the arts, and not end with a confusion of principles and illustrations. Since we are particularly concerned, just now, with the dance, let us narrow our discussion and center it about this art. Our first question, then, becomes: What do dancers create?

Obviously, a dance. As I pointed out before, they do not create the materials of the dance—neither their own bodies, nor the cloth that drapes them, nor the floor, nor any of the ambient space, light, musical tone, the forces of gravity, nor any other physical provisions; all these things they *use,*

to create something over and above what is physically there: the dance.

What, then, is the dance?

The dance is an appearance; if you like, an apparition. It springs from what the dancers do, yet is something else. In watching a dance, you do not see what is physically before you—people running around or twisting their bodies; what you see is a display of interacting forces, by which the dance seems to be lifted, driven, drawn, closed, or attenuated, whether it be solo or choric, whirling like the end of a dervish dance, or slow, centered, and single in its motion. One human body may put the whole play of mysterious powers before you. But these powers, these forces that seem to operate in the dance, are not the physical forces of the dancer's muscles, which actually cause the movements taking place. The forces we seem to perceive most directly and convincingly are created for our perception; and they exist only for it.

Anything that exists only for perception, and plays no ordinary, passive part in nature as common objects do, is a virtual entity. It is not unreal; where it confronts you, you really perceive it, you don't dream or imagine that you do. The image in a mirror is a virtual image. A rainbow is a virtual object. It seems to stand on the earth or in the clouds, but it really "stands" nowhere; it is only visible, not tangible. Yet it is a real rainbow, produced by moisture and light for any normal eye looking at it from the right place. We don't just dream that we see it. If, however, we believe it to have the ordinary properties of a physical thing, we are mistaken; it is an appearance, a virtual object, a sun-created image.

What dancers create is a dance; and a dance is an apparition of active powers, a *dynamic image.* Everything a dancer actually does serves to create what we really see; but what we really see is a virtual entity. The physical realities are given: place, gravity, body, muscular strength, muscular control, and secondary assets such as light, sound, or things (usable objects, so-called "properties"). All these are actual. But in the dance, they disappear; the more perfect the dance, the less we see its actualities. What we see, hear, and feel are the virtual realities, the moving forces of the dance, the apparent centers of power and their emanations, their conflicts and resolutions, lift and decline, their rhythmic life. These are the elements of the created apparition, and are themselves not physically given, but artistically created.

Here we have, then, the answer to our first question: what do dancers create? The dynamic image, which is the dance.

This answer leads naturally to the second question: for what is this image created?

Again, there is an obvious answer: for our enjoyment. But what makes us enjoy it as intensely as we do? We do not enjoy every virtual image, just because it is one. A mirage in the desert is intriguing chiefly because it is rare. A mirror image, being common, is not an object of wonder, and in itself, just as an image, does not thrill us. But the dynamic image created in dancing has a different character. It is more than a perceivable entity; this apparition, given to the eye, or to the ear and eye, and through them to our whole responsive sensibility, strikes us as something charged with feeling. Yet this feeling is not necessarily what any or all of the dancers feel. It belongs to the dance itself. A dance, like any other work of art, is a perceptible form that expresses the nature of human feeling—the rhythms and connections, crises and breaks, the complexity and richness of what is sometimes called man's "inner life," the stream of direct experience, life as it feels to the living. Dancing is not a symptom of how the dancer happens to feel; for the dancer's own feelings could not be prescribed or predicted and exhibited upon request. Our own feelings simply occur, and most people do not care to have us express them by sighs or squeals or gesticulation. If that were what dancers really did, there would not be many balletomaniacs to watch them.

What is expressed in a dance is an idea; an idea of the way feelings, emotions, and all other subjective experiences come and go—their rise and growth, their intricate synthesis that gives our inner life unity and personal identity. What we call a person's "inner life" is the inside story of his own history; the way living in the world feels to him. This kind of experience is usually but vaguely known, because most of its components are nameless, and no matter how keen our experience may be, it is hard to form an idea of anything that has no name. It has no handle for the mind. This has led many learned people to believe that feeling is a formless affair, that it has causes which may be determined, and effects that have to be dealt with, but that in itself it is irrational—a disturbance in the organism, with no structure of its own.

Yet subjective existence has a structure; it is not only met from moment to moment, but can be conceptually known, reflected on, imagined and symbolically expressed in detail and to great depth. Only it is not our usual medium, discourse—communication by language—that serves to express what we know of the life of feeling. There are logical reasons why language fails to meet this purpose, reasons I will not try to explain now. The important fact is that what language does not readily do—present the nature and patterns of sensitive and emotional life—is done by works of art. Such works are expressive forms, and what they express is the nature of human feeling.

So we have played our second gambit, answering the second question: What is the work of art for—the dance, the virtual dynamic image? To express its creator's ideas of immediate, felt, emotive life. To set forth directly what feeling is like. A work of art is a composition of tensions and resolutions, balance and unbalance, rhythmic coherence, a precarious yet continuous unity. Life is a natural process of such tensions, balances, rhythms; it is these that we feel, in quietness or emotion, as the pulse of our own living. In the work of art they are expressed, symbolically shown, each aspect of feeling developed as one develops an idea, fitted together for clearest presentation. A dance is not a symptom of a dancer's feeling, but an expression of its composer's knowledge of many feelings.

The third problem on the docket—how is dance created?—is so great that one has to break it down into several questions. Some of these are practical questions of techniques—how to produce this or that effect. They concern many of you but not me, except in so far as solutions of artistic problems always intrigue me. The philosophical question that I would peel out of its many wrappings is: What does it mean to express one's idea of some inward or "subjective" process?

It means to make an outward image of this inward process, for oneself and others to see; that is, to give the subjective events an objective symbol. Every work of art is such an image, whether it be a dance, a statue, a picture, a piece of music, or a work of poetry. It is an outward showing of inward nature, an objective presentation of subjective reality; and the reason that it can symbolize things of the inner life is that it has the same kinds of relations and elements. This is not true of the material structure; the physical materials of a dance do not have any direct similarity to the structure of emotive life; it is the created image that has elements and patterns like the life of feeling. But this image, though it is a created apparition, a pure appearance, is objective; it seems to be charged with feeling because its form expresses the very nature of feeling. Therefore, it is an *objectification* of subjective life, and so is every other work of art.

If works of art are all alike in this fundamental respect, why have we several great domains of art, such as painting and music, poetry and dance? Something makes them so distinct from each other that people with superb talent for one may have none for another. A sensible person would not go to Picasso to learn dancing or to Hindemith to be taught painting. How does dancing, for instance, differ from music or architecture or drama? It has relations with all of them. Yet it is none of them.

What makes the distinction among several great orders of art is another of those problems that arise in their turn, uninvited, once you start from a central question; and the fact that the question of *what is created* leads from one issue to another in this natural and systematic way makes me think it really is central. The distinction between dancing and all of the other great arts—and of those from each other—lies in the stuff of which the virtual image, the expressive form, is made. We cannot go into any discussion of other kinds, but only reflect a little further on our original query: What do dancers create? What is a dance?

As I have said before (so long before that you have probably forgotten), what we see when we watch a dance is a display of interacting forces; not physical forces, like the weight that tips a scale or the push that topples a column of books, but purely apparent forces that seem to move the dance itself. Two people in a *pas de deux* seem to magnetize each other; a group appears to be animated by one single spirit, one Power. The stuff of the dance, the apparition itself, consists of such nonphysical forces, drawing and driving, holding a shaping its life. The actual, physical forces that underlie it disappear. As soon as the beholder sees gymnastics and arrangements, the work of art breaks, the creation fails.

As painting is made purely of spacial volumes—not actual space-filling things but virtual volumes, created solely for the eye—and music is made of passage, movements of time, created by tone—so dance creates a world of powers, made visible by the unbroken fabric of gesture. That is what makes dance a different art from all the others. But as Space, Events, Time, and Powers are all interrelated in reality, so all the arts are linked by intricate relations, different among different ones. That is a big subject.

Another problem which naturally presents itself here is the meaning of *dance gesture;* but we shall have to skip it. We have had enough pursuit of meanings, and I know from experience that if you don't make an end of it, there is no end. But in dropping the curtain on this peep-show of philosophy, I would like to call your attention t one of those unexpected explanations of puzzling facts that sometimes arise from philosophical reflection.

Curt Sachs, who is an eminent historian of music and dance, remarks in his *World History of Dance* that, strange as it may seem, the evolution of dance as a high art belongs to pre-history. At the dawn of civilization, dance had already reached a degree of perfection that no other art or science could match. Societies limited to savage living, primitive sculpture, primitive architecture, and as yet no poetry, quite commonly present the astonished ethnologist with a highly developed tradition of difficult, beautiful dancing. Their music apart from the dance is nothing at all; in the dance it is elaborate. Their worship is dance. They are tribes of dancers.

If you think of the dance as an apparition of interactive Powers, this strange fact loses its strangeness. Every art image is a purified and simplified aspect of the outer world, composed by the laws of the inner world to express its nature. As one objective aspect of the world after another comes to people's notice, the arts arise. Each makes its own image of outward reality to objectify inward reality, subjective life, feeling.

Primitive men live in a world of demonic Powers. Subhuman or superhuman, gods or spooks or impersonal magic forces, good or bad luck that dwells in things like an electric charge, are the most impressive realities of the savage's world. The drive to artistic creation, which seems to be deeply primitive in all human beings, first begets its forms in the images of these all-surrounding Powers. The magic circle around the altar or the totem pole, the holy space inside the Kiwa or the temple, is the natural dance floor. There is nothing unreasonable about that. In a world perceived as a realm of mystic Powers, the first created image is the dynamic image; the first objectification of human nature, the first true art, is Dance.

Susanne Langer "The Dynamic Image: Some Philosophical Reflections on Dance"

1. According to Langer, philosophical questions are questions of fact, while scientific questions are questions of meaning.

    a. True   b. False

2. According to Langer, the best sign that you have broached a central philosophical issue is that in solving it you raise new interesting questions.

    a. True   b. False

3. According to Langer, art is like life in that they both express tensions and resolutions, balances and imbalances, rhythms and feelings.

    a. True   b. False

4. Which of the following statements is false about dance, according to Langer?

    a. Dance is an apparition.
    b. Dance is a virtual entity of active powers, a dynamic image.
    c. Dance has the properties of a physical thing.
    d. Dance expresses the way feelings come and go.

5. Explain how dances express the feeling life of humanity.

Raymond Gozzi, Jr., and W. Lance Haynes*

ELECTRIC MEDIA AND ELECTRIC EPISTEMOLOGY: EMPATHY AT A DISTANCE

The study of epistemology is the study of knowledge about knowledge. This meta-knowledge may be different from what is conventionally thought of as knowledge itself—it may have different forms, be generated in different ways, be subject to different tests. This is particularly the case when we try to comprehend the epistemology of the electric media environment that is so rapidly growing all around us. In such a case, the difference is due to the relationship between knowledge and the media of communication. Thus we leave the secure pathways of established research methods and embark on an effort that is in part speculative and philosophical.

This paper derives from the claim that the major kinds of communication media—oral, writing-based, and electric—carry with them different underlying epistemologies, or ways of knowing. This is not to say that all particular epistemologies rooted in writing-based knowing, for example, are the same; there are demonstrably different shades to be found. However, we claim that dominant media of communication produce sets of assumptions about the knower and the known, and privilege certain warrants for knowledge above others. Thus media set up "zones" of epistemology within which particular ways of knowing are structured.

In oral-based epistemologies, the knower is a functioning participant in the ongoing interactions that produce and sustain knowledge. The known is filtered through the knower's direct experience. Warrants for knowledge come from group experience reflected in the group's oral traditions and from the credibility of group members. Examples of oral-based knowing can be found in the work of Lord (1960), Goody and Watt (1968), Parry (1971), Luria (1976), Ong (1982), Havelock (1986), Olson (1988), and a host of other diverse scholars working in this increasingly promising field of research.

In writing-based epistemologies, the knower is skilled at abstract symbolic manipulation. The known is decoded from the various forms of text (Chesebro 1989), which are objectified for study. Warrants for writing-based knowledge come from tests of credibility that are based on conformity to rules derived from objective examination of fixed texts. Scholars researching oral or electric media epistemologies are confronted with a paradoxical situation because scholarship itself is traditionally a writing-based endeavor. This handicap has been described by McLuhan and Powers (1989) as "tap-dancing in chains" (p. 9). What McLuhan and Powers neglect to note is the degree to which the chains not only confine our knowledge base but string the keys to the academy, tenure, and promotion, as well.

In electric epistemology, the knower appears to experience what we refer to as a distant presence.

---

*Raymond Gozzi, Jr. is Associate Professor of Communication at Bradley University, and W. Lance Haynes is Associate Professor of Speech and Media Studies at the University of Missouri at Rolla. The following article originally appeared in *Critical Studies in Mass Communication* (1992). In it, the authors explore the implications of electronic mass media for the nature of knowledge in the contemporary world.

The known is a compelling simulation, re-created electrically and presented to the knower in what Postman (1988) describes as a "decontextualized" situation. The warrant for knowledge comes from an evoked empathy that is, in some sense, advantaged by the lack of context. "How does it feel?" we want to know, and the answer is increasingly derived purely from the isolated re-creation. This distant presence comes into play not only in the electric mass media but also among the users of telephones and, with rapidly growing importance, in computer-mediated communication networks.

For the sake of clarity, we define knowledge as a program, or set of programs, for perception and/or cognition and/or action. Knowledge programs are storable, transferable, and teachable. Knowledge is the ground that gives meaning to figures, the field upon which arguments are waged, the store from which sense is made of the world.

We define empathy as the capacity for participation in feelings or ideas communicated from elsewhere. Empathy may be positive or negative, depending on whether it evokes agreement or antipathy. Empathy and knowledge suffuse one other: We know with empathy and vice versa. Knowledge stored in books or on magnetic disks need not necessarily be known. Once known, any knowledge generates an affective component in its knower. Conversely, without the affective component, knowledge cannot be known, for participation is not possible without affect.

This paper begins to explore the electric epistemology of empathy at a distance. We first discuss the different "zones" of epistemology that are defined by oral, literate, and electronic media. We demonstrate how our formulation relates to and extends the work of Ong, McLuhan, Postman, and others.

Next we describe the electric "zone" of empathy at a distance in more detail, noting that it places us in a paradoxical relationship to messages: involved emotionally, in the manner of the oral epistemology, but removed physically, in the manner of the literate epistemology. Thus we experience a distant presence and respond, often uncomfortably, with non-involved involvement.

The growth of the zone of electric epistemology will upset existing relationships among epistemologies. We examine some of the consequences of the shifting relationships among zones, as literate institutions lose prestige and power, and institutions of electric communication rise to prominence.

We conclude by discussing changes in the nature of knowledge and wisdom. The paradoxical epistemological situation of a distant presence poses the problem of simulation in an acute form. Knowledge in the electric epistemology will meanwhile be ever more slickly packaged, coming at greater speeds. To cope with this knowledge, we will need a wisdom combining empathy with detachment.

MEDIA AND ZONES OF EPISTEMOLOGY

We are asserting a link between media and epistemology, the study of the nature of knowledge and the validity of knowledge. "How can we know what we (think we) know?" is the eternal epistemic question.

Media of communication are inevitably linked to, implicated with, epistemologies, as pointed out by Postman (1988): "[media] are rather like metaphors, working by unobtrusive but powerful implication to enforce their special definitions of reality" (p. 10). Much of our knowledge comes to us roundabout, through mediation of some sort. The mediation of this second-hand knowledge affects its forms of presentation, encompassing relationships, purposes, and even to some extent content; thus media confine the process of experience itself. A medium of communication structures a certain way of knowing, although it would be imprudent to cast the relationships as a wholly deterministic one. As Ong (1977) notes, "the relationships [of culture and consciousness to the evolution of the word] are varied and complex, with cause and effect often difficult to distinguish" (p. 9).

However, in the broadest sense, we may certainly speak of an underlying epistemology, a particular way of knowing, that is implicit in the interaction between a human being and a particular communication medium. The epistemological form underlying the media-mind relationship can give support to many varied epistemologies, but they will all have a family resemblance if one knows where to look.

The three major communication media we are concerned with here are those that have given their names to three epochs in human communication: oral communication media (to include sounded words, gestures, and the dynamics of face-to-face interactions), written communication media (symbolic recordings and subsequent permeations of spoken language, i.e., writing, stored and transmitted beyond the face-to-face situation), and electric communication media (any of a growing number of media that transmit almost instantaneously from a distance, eclectically combining oral and written forms of mediation with facsimiles of primary sensory encounters, also storeable, and often readily malleable).

To members of contemporary technological societies, each of these communication media forms a "zone" of experience that elicits its own epistemology. The oral zone relies on face-to-face contact, immediate interaction, and a sense of participation. Thus each of us must evolve an oral-based epistemology, a set of cues to look for, a number of feelings to recognize, a series of associations to make, so that we come to recognize situations and define them appropriately. This oral-based way of knowing remains altogether tacit unless objectified by some other way of knowing.

The oral zone of epistemology, for all its power over our direct experience, has been subordinated to another zone of epistemology in most "modern" cultures. The zone of writing-based epistemology permeates the processing of experience within its bounds. It has captured the basic institutions of Western culture—the school system, the governmental and judicial systems, the mainstream churches, newspapers and book publishing, medicine, all scientific research, and, of course, the academy. Writing-based epistemology values abstraction, the separation of the observer from the observed, the subdividing of confusing wholes into comprehensible parts. Literate "logic" proceeds step by step, from explicit grounds to lawfully arrived at conclusions. Writing-based epistemology is about rules, classifications, abstraction, precision, and implied permanence.

Historically, those people who participate only incompletely in the literate epistemology are relegated to less prestigious places in the society. Women, long held out of the educational system; children, incompletely educated; superstitious or mystical people; immigrants from unscientific other cultures—all these groups, mired in one form of oral residue or another, are consigned to an epistemological underclass.

In the twentieth century, however, electronic media have come to challenge the dominance of the literate-based epistemology. The zone of electric epistemology grows as people spend less time reading and more time watching television. The highbrow refusal to own a television set (or a personal computer) is increasingly thought of as anachronistic or even antisocial behavior. The institutions of literate epistemology have become aware of an undermining of their effectiveness but are unable to adequately conceptualize the "effects" of the electric media in terms of their own prior epistemologies. Thus we find various kinds of televised classrooms, computerized card catalogs, electronic journals, and a host of other oxymorons as well as

turbulent "gaps" in historical coherence that follow the pattern predicted by McLuhan and Fiore (1967): "striving to make the new media to the work of the old" (p. 8;1). Schwartz (1981) warns that new media "come into their own only when we stop trying to use them as containers for the old" (p. 41)—because, we contend, along with the electric media comes a new electric epistemology.

ELECTRIC EPISTEMOLOGY: EMPATHY AT A DISTANCE

We are watching television. A politician is defending his or her record to a group of reporters. We hear the words spoken. But we are most impressed by how he or she comes across in total, by our "gut" feelings, by how this politician strikes us personally. This is instant empathy at a distance, a different way of knowing from the old literate focus on the words and the reasoning of the message. This phenomenon has not escaped the notice of modern politics. As Jamieson (1988) notes, "What differentiates Reagan from Truman is Reagan's ability to convey a sense of intimacy, earnestness, candor, and conviction *while delivering a scripted statement* [italics in original]" (p. 173).

We are talking on the telephone. Someone is telling us how much they like person X. Yet we sense something is wrong. We probe. Although the other person will not admit to having problems with person X, we become convinced that all is not as it is being portrayed. Again, this is empathy at a distance. The widened channels of electric media have made available many of the techniques of oral epistemology, which, instead of demanding the conscious reasoning of literacy, relied on the out-of-awareness processes that writing-based thinkers typically lump together as "intuition."

When we are listening to the radio or watching television, the old literate logics do not have the power they once had. Instead, the immediate experience takes over, and we feel and participate in ways reminiscent of the oral epistemology. Yet there is a crucial difference between the oral and the electric: The electric epistemology functions with interactions often distant in both time and space, and the checks and validating experiences available to the face-to-face oral epistemology are not readily applied. We cannot ask the television "Is that a true story?" nor does the answer matter to us in the way it once might have.

Electric media put us in a paradoxical situation, if measured in terms of literate epistemology. We experience a vivid presence, but at a distance.

We are involved, yet we are uninvolved. We are affected, yet we are unaffected. Notice that these apparent paradoxes are a function of the writing-based way we have learned to think about our own interaction, our own humanity.

Electric epistemology, we propose, will produce a new kind of knowledge through instant empathy at a distance. Electric media have widened the channels of communication so that verbal, non-verbal, kinesthetic, and contextual cues can all be transmitted, mimicking the face-to-face contacts of oral epistemology. As the power of simulations grows, participation (in the oral sense) in the electric experience grows also. Such participation also promises to be stimulated by computer-mediated networks. These rapidly developing technologies promise the ability to connect everyone with everyone else, individually or collectively, and to support these connections with the ability to reply, as rapidly as one might in face-to-face conversation, to a marginally objectified product, with the convenience of groups that move slowly but are continually in session.

Thus Ong (1971) describes "secondary orality," in which electric media return us to some aspects of the oral knowledge-generating process—for example, the socializing influences of sound and the use of formulary devices—while still being founded (paradoxically) on "the individualized introversion of the age of writing, print, and rationalism" (pp. 284–286). Our characterization of the zone of electric epistemology is closest to and grows out of Ong's secondary orality.

McLuhan (1964) similarly speaks of the "electric implosion that compels commitment and participation" while rejecting the "partial and specialized character of the viewpoint, however noble," of the "Age of Anxiety" that has been brought on by the move into the environment of the "global village" (p. 5). Paglia ("She Wants Her TV," 1991) relegates the age of anxiety to those born before World War II, who grew up with the novel. The minds of those born after are "formed by TV" and live instead in the "Age of Hollywood" (p. 49).

Postman (1988), somewhat in contrast, condemns television's promotion of irrational, incoherent, show business values and argues that "television's way of knowing is uncompromisingly hostile to typography's way of knowing" (p. 80). Jamieson (1988) openly bemoans the separation of thinking and speaking exemplified by the televised and scripted presidential address (p. 231). Yet both these scholars acknowledge that hope lies only in embracing and mastering the epistemic implications of the new media. Paglia, Postman, and Jamieson reflect the consternation wrought by turbulent gaps in historical coherence brought about as the media shift, while McLuhan and Ong gaze dispassionately beyond. Our effort here builds on all these views by illustrating that what must finally be embraced is indeed paradoxical and thus outside the immediate dictates of writing-based thought.

Electric media carry images from a distance and pose a situation that is ultimately paradoxical in terms of literate epistemology, which relies on the strict conceptual separation of space and time to create full-blown objectification. In contrast to its literate counterpart, the electric media situation is one of distant presence, a blurred objectification that facilitates affective response while largely occluding intellection.

As electric media grow in their ability to simulate people, situations, and environments, these paradoxes will increase. Electric media may start as "extensions" of human nervous systems, as Hall (1977) and McLuhan (1964) have noted. But as the power of simulation passes a certain level, as electric media link up and draw ever more resources together, a reversal seems likely, if not destined, to occur. Human nervous systems will, in effect, become extensions of the electric media.

We can already see this reversal in embryonic form. Take, for example, the telephone. We use it when we wish; the telephone extends our voices as we choose. Yet, we jump when the phone rings and hook ourselves up to the system when it calls us. There is an implicit sense of priority here that is even more vividly in evidence when a cashier or receptionist allows the ringing phone to interrupt an ongoing transaction.

Television, at first, was like attending a movie. Early TV audiences sat in darkened rooms, in silence, giving the set their full attention. The TV was an extension of their desires; it was on because a decision had been made to turn it on. Yet 30 or 40 years later, television has become part of the wallpaper, constantly on in many households, part of the background of life. Notice how it can pull everyone in with a spot announcement, stop conversation with a catchy commercial, draw everyone's attention with a new guest, or strike us quickly with some bright image. Again, these are embryonic moments when we become extensions of the television system.

Thus the electric zone of epistemology is growing, and its associated paradoxes will increasingly engulf us. Distant presence will play an ever-greater role in our lies. We who were first conditioned by writing will more and more be forced to take stances of noninvolved involvement in more and more issues of life.

At its best, the electric epistemology of empathy at a distance will produce a society that is compassionate, humanizing, and generous. We see the beginnings of this in national spontaneous responses to disasters reported on TV, with people donating money, clothes, and supplies to victims. At its worst, the electric epistemology will produce negative empathy, leading to a society that is cynical, distrustful, impulsive, and cruel. We see the germs of this potential in TV programs that urge us to turn our neighbors in to the police and in media-augmented hysterias against certain groups, stigmatized as dope fiends or terrorists. We should remember the role played by radio in magnifying Nazism as well.

SHIFTING ZONES OF EPISTEMOLOGY

We know people are spending more and more time attending to electric media. We also know that electric media are becoming more prominent in the central institutions of our society: banks, the military, government, our very sources of power for everyday life.

As the electric media grow in prominence and as people pay more attention to them, the media will alter the hegemonic relationships of the status quo, in particular among epistemologies. The literate-based epistemologies will discover new sources of power in the electric media. Such American social groups as African-Americans, women, and draft-age youth all discovered new focus in the electric media, giving them more aggressive voices and more attention, allowing them to become more organized than before. The anti-war movements, the civil rights movement, the women's movement, and the counterculture of the 1960s in general all received impetus from electric media, and their ideas received new dignity and importance from the electric epistemology of empathy at a distance (Meyrowitz, 1985).

The social institutions that are based on the electric epistemology—telephone companies, broadcasting networks and stations, cable companies, Hollywood, the utilities, and the various electronic industries, especially those associated with computers—may be expected, in spite of seemingly constant turmoil among themselves, to increasingly challenge and dominate the literate-based institutions. Of special interest here are banks and other financial institutions that had relied on literate epis-

temologies and writing-based media almost exclusively in the past. Now they become increasingly electronic, even planning to eliminate printed currency (literally literate-based) in favor of electronic "funds." Our money will no longer be tangible but will be available to us only if we can access the Electronic Funds Transfer System; it will indeed be distant yet involve us directly. The problems of rational control over spending encountered now by some credit-card holders will grow to threaten the entire population.

Such symptoms of a shift in media may well be ahead of corresponding shifts in epistemology, thus fostering the turbulent gaps in historical coherence where necessary order and control temporarily fail. Perhaps such turbulence facilitated the recent savings and loan debacle, for example. Already hard currency functions largely in transactions too small for magnetically encoded plastic to be used. In a capitalist society where money is so highly prized, the conversion of key institutions to electronic media, with the resulting change in epistemology, will have far-reaching effects.

To take a broader example, consider how the consumer earning-spending cycle, tied tightly to the agricultural year in rural America only a century ago and to the weekly or monthly paycheck much more recently, has now been broadly diffused by the electronic facilitation of credit, of shopping, of household paying and receiving generally. No longer is it customary to wait and save for household needs. Our buying and earning power have been electronically averaged and extended into a future painstakingly predicted and insured by the financial industries themselves. The "hard" transactions of printed currency are relegated increasingly to a petty role in our economic lives.

We may also note that the institutions associated with electric media have been allied with large-scale (continental or worldwide) interests. The transportation industries of shipping and railroads were hosts for the telegraph and radio. Finance was midwife for the telephone and electric utilities. Thus there has been a pressure toward the integration of ever-larger geographical areas with electric media. Now that pressure has pushed electric media into space, with satellites circling the globe and transmitting electric media messages from continent to continent in fractions of a second.

This means that the electric epistemology cannot remain confined to small groups of users, as oral epistemologies have, and cannot remain the property of an educated elite, as literate epistemologies have. Electric epistemologies will have to provide ways of knowing for a planet-wide collection of people, even as electric media are binding together the planet in terms of communication, finance, military and social networks, and governments.

KNOWLEDGE IN ELECTRIC EPISTEMOLOGY

In the ever-encroaching world of electric media, the nature of knowledge is obviously changing. It is important for us to survey those changes and slow them down long enough to get them onto a printed page and to reflect upon them, if only to forestall for our own peculiar media orientations the mass confusion that otherwise looms ahead.

We can already seem some of the key changes in knowledge caused by electric media. The information explosion has seen knowledge accumulate at ever-increasing rates. In the 1980s, scientific knowledge doubled every seven years, according to the World Future Society ("Looking Ahead," 1984), and the pace was increasing. With the advent of desktop technologies, the computer will make electronic publishing and electronic video production accessible to more and more people.

The packaging of knowledge will have to change, emphasizing quick, attractive "bites" of information, much like the "sound bite" on television. Long preambles will disappear. We will have to cut more often to the chase.

The scope of knowledge will become wider, but the depth of knowledge will, in general, become shallower. There will be less time for in-depth study, more necessity for the survey. *Cliffs Notes* will become the exemplar of much "general" education. Professionals will read abstracts, not articles. All that will remain of lengthy books and arguments in the public eye will be a few catch phrases and slogans. McLuhan, for example, is already mainly remembered for one phrase, "The medium is the message," just as Andy Warhol is remembered for his paintings of Campbell's soup cans and, most appropriately, for the phrase, "In the future everyone will be famous for 15 minutes."

The purposes of knowledge will become more varied but also more obscure. Why will we need to know anything in an increasingly automated and automatic environment? Even specialists in repairing that environment will simply need to know how to take one already designed module peg and place it into the proper round hole. We can expect the social distribution of knowledge to become much more varied and idiosyncratic. As computers and databased become available to more people, and

especially if they become located in public libraries, as suggested by Roszak (1986), we will find surprising connections among people and in-depth knowledge about certain narrow topics. Particularly, if automation brings more unemployment, people will have time and incentive to experience more deeply electric knowledge areas of their own choosing.

The structure of knowledge will be obscured behind myriad details. It will only be able to be intuited until some computer graphics program is applied to the problem, and then many elegant equivalent geometric forms will be generated to illustrate the structure of electric knowledge—alas, far too many to permit the firm sense of, say, Britannica's *Propedia*.

The test of knowledge will be empathy. "How does it feel to you?" will be the question. Self-control will require waiting until the morning after, so to speak, and then asking the question again. Yet empathy will have to be united with action. If a person does not act, then he or she will play no part in generating knowledge but will simply absorb the prepared packages coming over the electric media. And so people will have to act, and then ask again, "how does it feel?" It will be all too easy to passively accept the compelling simulations and slick dramatic packagings of knowledge. We can see this problem of passivity emerging already with television viewers, and as more of the work of the brain gets taken over by electric processors, the knower will need to shake himself or herself out of the electrically induced trance state of acceptance and probe the packages coming through.

The forms of knowledge in electric epistemology will increasingly alternate between the romantic and the dramatic, because these are the forms that exert strong emotional affinity. As Haynes (1989) has argued, narrative generally will come to suffuse electric epistemology as it renders plasticity to time and space, enabling the ready transmission of highly abbreviated but richly packed experiences.

We know that the capacity for electric media to simulate people, experiences, and realities is growing. Television is becoming more high-definition and, linked with computers, is rapidly acquiring the capacity to transmit convincing simulations of "real" people doing things they never did, saying things they never said. Beyond television, "simulated realities" are becoming available through direct computer inputs into the nervous system. The "feelies," long predicted by science fiction, are edging closer to embodiment with the development of the hardware to interface with our senses and the software of "virtual reality."

The main problem that we may strive to solve as we embrace the paradoxes of electric epistemology is the problem simulation itself presents. Some tests for the authenticity of information must be developed. Perhaps electronic scanners will be able to screen electric messages for the slight disparities from their contexts that simulated characters must possess. However, the problems of simulation have not been taken seriously enough by those currently functioning within electric epistemology.

For example, the famous "Turing test," posed by the computer pioneer mathematician Alan Turing, tried to show that the question "Can computers think?" is meaningless. Turing proposed allowing a person in one room to pose questions to an entity in another room. The human questioner would receive the answers back in written form. Could the human tell whether he or she was talking to a human or to a computer? The Turing text attempts to say that a simulation of human thought is not different in any important respect from actual human thought. It raises the simulation to the status of the original and claims that if we cannot tell the difference, then it is foolish to think that there may be important differences.

As electric media become more powerful in their abilities to pose convincing simulations, the claim of the Turing test becomes ever more dangerous. Electric epistemology needs to detect simulations to avoid providing destructive and misguided warrants to actions. The authentic must not be allowed to merge conceptually with the simulated. Thus we come to the question of wisdom in electric epistemology.

WISDOM IN ELECTRIC EPISTEMOLOGY

Wisdom in electric epistemology will require empathy, of course, because empathy is the root of this way of knowing. Yet wisdom will require something else: an ironic distance from one's own empathy. It seems that only through such a distance could the Turing test eventually fail. This almost contradictory attitude—to emphasize and yet possess detachment—will undergird wisdom in the electric epistemology.

The appropriate symbol for such wisdom is the oxymoronic phrase. Wisdom in electric epistemology will be humorous yet serious, absurd yet insightful. It must achieve the air of Zen, recognizing that relativity and illusion underlie even the most earnest of pronouncements.

Wisdom must be able to detect electric koans as they are voiced by a noisy electric environment.

Wisdom must be able to accept information and hold it at arms' length. It must be able to reconcile what appear to be opposites in a more literate classificational epistemology.

The wise person on the electric epistemology will possess the ability to discover progressions and to apply patterns to produce understanding, yet must be tolerant of ambiguity and accept incompleteness. The rigid standards of writing, which demand completeness on the fixed page, can no longer hold. The capacity to simulate and detect simulation, to believe and doubt simultaneously, to operate in a universe of only relative fixity, must rise to the call. To tolerate ambiguity will be to accept incompleteness.

As the knowledge environment becomes more dramatic and simulated, so too will behavior emphasize drama and simulation, as people model their behavior on what they know (Gozzi, 1990, pp. 71–81). People will get swept up in the emotions of their current performances and may not reflect upon the consistency of their behavior over time. Thus the question of authenticity versus simulation will reappear in new forms in interpersonal and intrapersonal relations.

The wise person in the electric epistemology will be able likewise to find the individual who is within and behind performances and to emphathize at a distance here too. Identification with the simulation will need to be held to a minimum because simulation is method acting, not mere imitation. The wise person will be able to sight other selves through the refractions of their simulations. Only thus will authentic relationships be possible.

Further, the wise person must be able to step outside the seductive, all-encompassing electric media environment to check on information with other sources. Skills will be needed to "triangulate" information received through electric media by discovering alternative versions, different ideological sources—yes, even print versions. The wise person must be able to navigate the different zones of epistemology with ease and effectiveness.

These are some of the forms wisdom will take in the electric epistemology. Many will get lost, many will find wisdom, and most will bob around in between, occasionally lost, occasionally wise.

Electric media have already cast up for us some models for this kind of wisdom, some "saints" in the pantheon of electric mythology. We have the ironic Johnny Carson, specializing in humor about serious events. We have Woody Allen, who combines insight and absurdity. We had John Lennon, who combined ironic detachment with compassionate involvement. We have Oprah Winfrey, with her sense of compassionate detachment.

The sense of ironic empathy, compassionate detachment, uninvolved involvement, and serious humor embodied in the personas of these electric heroes and heroines is one guide to wisdom in the new electric epistemology. For we must never lose sight of the human being, increasingly decentered in an all-encompassing electric epistemology zone. If empathy is the warrant of knowledge in electric epistemology, this warrant will function correctly only with healthy, aware humans rather than afraid, defensive, disoriented humans. We need to treat others with compassion in order to receive compassion. We must respect everyone.

REFERENCES

Chesebro, J. W. (1989). Text, narration, and media. *Text and Performance Quarterly.* 9(1), 1–23.

Goody, J.,& Watt, I. (1968). The consequences of literacy. In J. Goody (Ed.), *Literacy in traditional societies* (pp. 27–68). Cambridge: Cambridge University Press.

Gozzi, R., Jr. (1990). *New words and a changing American culture.* Columbia, SC: University of South Carolina Press.

Hall, E. T. (1977). *Beyond culture.* Garden City, NY: Anchor.

Havelock, E. A. (1986). *The muse learns to write: Reflections on orality and literacy from antiquity to the present.* New Haven, CT: Yale University Press.

Haynes, W. L. (1989). Shifting media, shifting paradigms, and the growing utility of narrative as metaphor. *Communication Studies, 40*(2), 109–126.

Jamieson, K. H. (1988). *Eloquence in an electronic age: The transformation of political speechmaking.* New York: Oxford University Press.

Looking ahead. (1984, December 26). *Hampshire Gazette,* p. 1.

Lord, A. B. (1960). *The singer of tales.* Cambridge, MA: Harvard University Press.

Luria, A. R. (1976). *Cognitive development: Its cultural and social foundations* (M. Cole, Ed.; M. Lopez-Morillas & L. Solotaroff, Trans.). Cambridge, MA: Harvard University Press.

McLuhan, M. (1964). *Understanding media: The extensions of man* (2nd ed.). New York: Signet.

McLuhan, M., & Fiore, Q. (1967). *The medium is the message.* New York: Bantam Books.

McLuhan, M., & Powers, B. R. (1989). *The global village: Transformations in world life and media in the 21st century.* New York: Oxford University Press.

Meyrowitz, J. (1985). *No sense of place: The impact of electronic media on social behavior.* New York: Oxford University Press.

Olson, D. R. (1988). Mind and media: The epistemic functions of literacy. *Journal of Communication, 38*(3), 27–36.

Ong, W. J. (1971). *Rhetoric, romance, and technology.* Ithaca, NY: Cornell University Press.

Ong, W. J. (1977). *Interfaces of the word.* Ithaca, NY: Cornell University Pres.

Ong, W. J. (1982). *Orality and literacy: the technologizing of the word.* New York: Methuen.

Parry, A. (Ed.). (1971). *The making of homeric verse: The collected papers of Milman Parry.* Oxford: Clarendon Press.

Postman, N. (1988). *Amusing ourselves to death: Public discourse in the age of show business.* New York: Viking/Penguin.

Roszak, T. (1986). *The cult of information: The folklore of computers and the true art of thinking.* New York: Pantheon.

Schwartz, T. (1981). *Media, the second god.* New York: Random House.

She wants her TV! He wants his book: A dinner conversation between Camille Paglia and Neil Postman. (1991, March.) *Harper's Magazine,* pp. 44–55.

Gozzie and Haynes, "Electric Epistemology"

1.   Oral-based cultures have an epistemology based in the credibility of its members, and the known is filtered through the direct experience of the knower.

     a. True   b. False

2.   Written-based cultures have an epistemology based in rules of credibility derived from the examination of texts.

     a. True   b. False

3.   Empathy at a distance is the warrant for knowledge in electric-based cultures because the known is a compelling simulation and is judged according to an overall feeling about it.

     a. True   b. False

4.   An electric epistemology will definitely produce a society that is compassionate, humanizing, and generous.

     a. True   b. False

5.   Briefly explain how electronic media affect our knowledge of the world.

Daisetz Teitaro Suzuki*

ASPECTS OF JAPANESE CULTURE

1

When we look at the development of Japanese culture we find that Zen Buddhism has made many important contributions. The other schools of Buddhism have limited their sphere of influence almost entirely to the spiritual life of the Japanese people; but Zen has gone beyond it. Zen has entered internally into every phase of the cultural life of the people.

In China this was not necessarily the case. Zen united itself to a great extent with Taoist beliefs and practices and with the Confucian teaching of morality, but it did not affect the cultural life of the people so much as it did in Japan. (Is it due to the racial psychology of the Japanese people that they have taken up Zen so intensely and deeply that it has entered intimately into their life?) In China, however, I ought not omit to mention the noteworthy fact that Zen gave great impetus to the development of Chinese philosophy in the Sung dynasty and also to the growth of a certain school of painting. A large number of examples of this school were brought over to Japan beginning with the Kamakura era in the thirteenth century, when Zen monks were constantly traveling between the two neighboring countries. The paintings of Southern Sung thus came to find their ardent admirers on our side of the sea and are now national treasures of Japan, while in China no specimens of this class of painting are to be found.

Before proceeding further, we may make a few general remarks about one of the peculiar features of Japanese art, which is closely related to and finally deducible from the world conception of Zen.

Among things which strongly characterized Japanese artistic talents we may mention the so-called "one-corner" style, which originated with Bayen (Ma Yüan *fl.* 1175–1225), one of the greatest Southern Sung artists. The "one-corner" style is psychologically associated with the Japanese painters' "thrifty brush" tradition of retaining the least possible number of lines or strokes which go to represent forms on silk or paper. Both are very much in accord with the spirit of Zen. A simple fishing boat in the midst of the rippling waters is enough to awaken in the mind of the beholder a sense of the vastness of the sea and at the same time of peace and contentment—the Zen sense of the Alone. Apparently the boat floats helplessly. It is a primitive structure with no mechanical device for stability and for audacious steering over the turbulent waves, with no scientific apparatus for braving all kinds of weather—quite a contrast to the modern ocean liner. But this very helplessness is the virtue of the fishing canoe, in contrast with which we feel the incomprehensibility of the Absolute encompassing the boat and all the world. Again, a solitary bird on a dead branch, in which not a line, not a shade, is wasted, is enough to show us the loneliness of autumn, when days become shorter and nature begins to roll up once more its gorgeous display of

*Daisetz Teitaro Suzuki (1870–1965) was the author of some fifty books on Zen Buddhism, founding editor of *The Eastern Buddhist,* and a member of the Japanese Academy. As one of the foremost practitioners and expositors of Zen Buddhism, Dr. Suzuki sought to make Zen Buddhism comprehensible to Western audiences. The following selection is taken from his book *The Awakening of Zen* (1980) and captures the living experience of enlightenment.

luxurious summer vegetation.[1] It makes one feel somewhat pensive, but it gives one opportunity to withdraw the attention toward the inner life, which, given attention enough, spreads out its rich treasures ungrudgingly before the eyes.

Here we have an appreciation of transcendental aloofness in the midst of multiplicities—which is known as *wabi* in the dictionary of Japanese cultural terms. *Wabi* really means "poverty," or, negatively, "not to be in the fashionable society of the time." To be poor, that is, not to be dependent on things worldly—wealth, power and reputation—and yet to feel inwardly the presence of something of the highest value, above time and social position: this is what essentially constitutes *wabi*. Stated in terms of practical everyday life, *wabi* is to be satisfied with a little hut, a room of two or three *tatami* (mats), like the log cabin of Thoreau, and with a dish of vegetables picked in the neighboring fields, and perhaps to be listening to the pattering of a gentle spring rainfall. The cult of *wabi* has entered deeply into the cultural life of the Japanese people. It is in truth the worshiping of poverty—probably a most appropriate cult in a poor country like ours. Despite the modern Western luxuries and comforts of life which have invaded us, there is still an ineradicable longing in us for the cult of *wabi*. Even in the intellectual life, not richness of ideas, not brilliancy or solemnity in marshaling thoughts and building up a philosophical system, is sought; but just to stay quietly content with the mystical contemplation of Nature and to feel at home with the world is more inspiring to us, at least to some of us.

However "civilized," however much brought up in an artificially contrived environment, we all seem to have an innate longing for primitive simplicity, close to the natural state of living. Hence the city people's pleasure in summer camping in the woods or traveling in the desert or opening up an unbeaten track. We wish to go back once in a while to the bosom of Nature and feel her pulsation directly. Zen's habit of mind, to break through all forms of human artificiality and take firm hold of what lies behind them, has helped the Japanese not to forget 'the soil but to be always friendly with Nature and appreciate her unaffected simplicity. Zen has no taste for complexities that lie on the surface of life. Life itself is simple enough, but when it is surveyed by the analyzing intellect it presents unparalleled intricacies. With all the apparatus of science we have not yet fathomed the mysteries of life. But, once in its current, we seem to be able to understand it, with its apparently endless pluralities and entanglements. Very likely, the most characteristic thing in the temperament of the Eastern people is the ability to grasp life from within and not from without. And Zen has just struck it.

In painting especially, disregard of form results when too much attention or emphasis is given to the all-importance of the spirit. The "one-cornered" style and the economy of brush strokes also help to effect aloofness from conventional rules. Where you would ordinarily expect a line or a mass or a balancing element, you miss it, and yet this very thing awakens in you an unexpected feeling of pleasure. In spite of shortcomings or deficiencies that no doubt are apparent, you do not feel them so; indeed, this imperfection itself becomes a form of perfection. Evidently, beauty does not necessarily spell perfection of form. This has been one of the favorite tricks of Japanese artists—to embody beauty in a form of imperfection or even of ugliness.

When this beauty of imperfection is accompanied by antiquity or primitive uncouthness, we have a glimpse of *sabi*, so prized by Japanese connoisseurs. Antiquity and primitiveness may not be an actuality. If an object of art suggests even·superficially the feeling of a historical period, there is *sabi* in it. *Sabi* consists in rustic unpretentiousness or archaic imperfection, apparent simplicity or effortlessness in execution, and richness in historical associations (which, however, may not always be present); and lastly, it contains inexplicable elements that raise the object in question to the rank of an artistic production. These elements are generally regarded as derived from the appreciation of Zen. The utensils used in the tearoom are mostly of this nature.

The artistic element that goes into the constitution of *sabi*, which literally means "loneliness" or "solitude," is poetically defined by a teamaster thus:

As I come out
To this fishing village,
Late in the autumn day,
No flowers in bloom I see,
Nor any tinted maple leaves.[2]

---

[1]For pictures of a similar nature, see my *Zen Essays*, II and III.

[2]Fujiwara Sadaiye (1162–1241).

Aloneness indeed appeals to contemplation and does not lend itself to spectacular demonstration. It may look most miserable, insignificant, and pitiable, especially when it is put up against the Western or modern setting. To be left alone, with no streamers flying, no fireworks crackling, and this amidst a gorgeous display of infinitely varied forms and endlessly changing colors, is indeed no sight at all. Take one of those *sumiye* sketches, perhaps portraying Kanzan and Jittoku (Hanshan and Shi'h-tê),[3] hang it in a European or an American art gallery, and see what effect it will produce in the minds of the visitors. The idea of aloneness belongs to the East and is at home in the environment of its birth.

It is not only to the fishing village on the autumnal eve that aloneness gives form but also to a patch of green in the early spring—which is in all likelihood even more expressive of the idea of *sabi* or *wabi*. For in the green patch, as we read in the following thirty-one-syllable verse, there is an indication of life impulse amidst the wintry desolation:

To those who only pray for the cherries to
   bloom,
How I wish to show the spring
That gleams from a patch of green
In the midst of the snow-covered mountain-
   village![4]

This is given by one of the old teamasters as thoroughly expressive of *sabi,* which is one of the four principles governing the cult of tea, *cha-no-yu.* Here is just a feeble inception of life power as asserted in the form of a little green patch, but in it he who has an eye can readily discern the spring shooting out from underneath the forbidding snow. It may be said to be a mere suggestion that stirs his mind, but just the same it is life itself and not its feeble indication. To the artist, life is as much here as when the whole field is overlaid with verdure and flowers. One may call this mystic sense of the artist.

Asymmetry is another feature that distinguishes Japanese art. The idea is doubtlessly derived from the "one-corner" style of Bayen. The plainest and boldest example is the plan of Buddhist architecture. The principle structures, such as the Tower Gate, the Dharma Hall, the Buddha Hall, and others, may be laid along one straight line; but

structures of secondary or supplementary importance, sometimes even those of major importance, are not arranged symmetrically as wings along either side of the main line. They may be found irregularly scattered over the grounds in accordance with the topographical peculiarities. You will readily be convinced of this fact if you visit some of the Buddhist temples in the mountains, for example, the Iyeyasu shrine at Nikko. We can say that asymmetry is quite characteristic of Japanese architecture of this class.

This can be demonstrated *par excellence* in the construction of the tearoom and in the tools used in connection with it. Look at the ceiling, which may be constructed in at least three different styles, and at some of the utensils for serving tea, and again at the grouping and laying of the steppingstones or flagstones in the garden. We find so many illustrations of asymmetry, or, in a way, of imperfection, or of the "one-corner" style.

Some Japanese moralists try to explain this liking of the Japanese artists for things asymmetrically formed and counter to the conventional, or rather geometrical, rules of art by the theory that the people have been morally trained not to be obtrusive but always to efface themselves, and that this mental habit of self-annihilation manifests itself accordingly in art—for example, when the artist leaves the important central space unoccupied. But, to my mind, this theory is not quite correct. Would it not be a more plausible explanation to say that the artistic genius of the Japanese people has been inspired by the Zen way of looking at individual things as perfect in themselves and at the same time as embodying the nature of totality which belongs to the One?

The doctrine of ascetic aestheticism is not so fundamental as that of Zen aestheticism. Art impulses are more primitive or more innate than those of morality. The appeal of art goes more directly into human nature. Morality is regulative, art is creative. One is an imposition from without, the other is an irrepressible expression from within. Zen finds its inevitable association with art but not with morality. Zen may remain unmoral but not without art. When the Japanese artists create objects imperfect from the point of view of form, they may even be willing to ascribe their art motive to the current

---

[3]Zen poet-recluses of the T'ang dynasty who have been a favorite subject for Far Eastern painters.

[4]Fujiwara Iyetaka (1158–1237).

notion of moral asceticism; but we need not give too much significance to their own interpretation or to that of the critic. Our consciousness is not after all, a very reliable standard of judgment.

However this may be, asymmetry is certainly characteristic of Japanese art, which is one of the reasons informality or approachability also marks to a certain degree Japanese objects of art. Symmetry inspires a notion of grace, solemnity, and impressiveness, which is again the case with logical formalism or the piling up of abstract ideas. The Japanese are often thought not to be intellectual and philosophical, because their general culture is not thoroughly impregnated with intellectuality. This criticism, I think, results somewhat from the Japanese love of asymmetry. The intellectual primarily aspires to balance, while the Japanese are apt to ignore it and incline strongly toward imbalance.

Imbalance, asymmetry, the "one-corner," poverty, simplification, *sabi* or *wabi*, aloneness, and cognate ideas make up the most conspicuous and characteristic features of Japanese art and culture. All these emanate from one central perception of the truth of Zen, which is "the One in the Many and the Many in the One," or better, "the One remaining as one in the Many individually and collectively."

2

That Zen has helped to stimulate the artistic impulses of the Japanese people and to color their works with ideas characteristic of Zen is due to the following facts: the Zen monasteries were almost exclusively the repositories of learning and art, at least during the Kamakura and the Muromachi eras; the Zen monks had constant opportunities to come in contact with foreign cultures; the monks themselves were artists, scholars, and mystics; they were even encouraged by the political powers of the time to engage in commercial enterprises to bring foreign objects of art and industry to Japan; the aristocrats and the politically influential classes of Japan were patrons of Zen institutions and were willing to submit themselves to the discipline of Zen. Zen thus worked not only directly on the religious life of the Japanese but also most strongly on their general culture.

The Tendai, the Shingon, and the Jōdō[5] contributed greatly to imbue the Japanese with the spirit of Buddhism, and through their iconography to develop their artistic instincts for sculpture, color paintings, architecture, textile fabrics, and metalwork. But the philosophy of Tendai is too abstract and abstruse to be understood by the masses; the ritualism of Shingon is too elaborate and complicated and consequently too expensive for popularity. On the other hand, Shingon and Tendai and Jōdō produced fine sculpture and pictures and artistic utensils to be used in their daily worship. The most highly prized "national treasures" belong to the Tempyō, the Nara, and the Heian periods, when those two schools of Buddhism were in the ascendancy and intimately involved with the cultured classes of the people. The Jōdō teaches the Pure Land in all its magnificence, where the Buddha of Infinite Light is attended by his retinue of Bodhisattvas, and this inspired the artists to paint those splendid pictures of Amida preserved in the various Buddhist temples of Japan. The Nichiren and the Shin are the creation of the Japanese religious mind. The Nichiren gave no specifically artistic and cultural impetus to us; the Shin tended to be somewhat iconoclastic and produced nothing worth mentioning in the arts and literature except the hymns known as *wasan* and the "honorable letters" (*gobunsho* or *ofumi*) chiefly written by Rennyo (1415–99).

Zen came to Japan after Shingon and Tendai and was at once embraced by the military classes. It was more or less by an historical accident that Zen was set against the aristocratic priesthood. The nobility, too, in the beginning felt a certain dislike for it and made use of their political advantage to stir up opposition to Zen. In the beginning of the Japanese history of Zen, therefore, Zen avoided Kyoto and established itself under the patronage of the Hōjō family—Tokiyori, Tokimune, and their successors and retainers.

The Chinese masters brought many artists and objects of art along with them, and the Japanese who came back from China were also bearers of art and literature. Pictures of Kakei (Hsia Kuei, *fl.* (1190–1220), Mokkei (Mu-ch'i, *fl.* c. 1240), Ryōkai (Liang K'ai, *fl.* c. 1210), Bayen (Ma Yüan, *fl.* 1175–1225), and others thus found their way to Japan. Manuscripts of the noted Zen masters of China were also given shelter in the monasteries here. Calligraphy in the Far East is an art just as much as *sumiye* painting, and it was cultivated almost uni-

---

[5]These, with the Shin and the Nichiren, are the principal schools of Buddhism in Japan.

versally among the intellectual classes in olden times. The spirit pervading Zen pictures and calligraphy made a strong impression on them, and Zen was readily taken up and followed. In it there is something virile and unbending. A mild, gentle, and graceful air—almost feminine, one might call it—which prevailed in the periods preceding the Kamakura, is now superseded by an air of masculinity, expressing itself mostly in the sculpture and calligraphy of the period. The rugged virility of the warriors of the Kwanto districts is proverbial, in contrast to the grace and refinement of the courtiers in Kyoto. The soldierly quality, with its mysticism and aloofness from worldly affairs, appeals to the willpower. Zen in this respect walks hand in hand with the spirit of Bushido ("Warriors' Way").

Another factor in the discipline of Zen, or rather in the monastic life in which Zen carries out its scheme of teaching, is this: as the monastery is usually situated in the mountains, its inmates are in the most intimate touch with nature, they are close and sympathetic students of it. They observe plants, birds, animals, rocks, rivers which people of the town would leave unnoticed. And their observation deeply reflects their philosophy, or better, their intuition. It is not that of a mere naturalist. It penetrates into the life itself of the objects that come under the monks' observation. Whatever they may paint of nature will inevitably be expressive of this intuition; the "spirit of the mountains" will be felt softly breathing in their works.

The fundamental intuition the Zen masters gain through their discipline seems to stir up their artistic instincts if they are at all susceptible to art. The intuition that impels the masters to create beautiful things, that is, to express the sense of perfection through things ugly and imperfect, is apparently closely related to the feeling for art. The Zen masters may not make good philosophers, but they are very frequently fine artists. Even their technique is often of the first order, and besides they know how to tell us something unique and original. One such is Musō the National Teacher (1275–1351). He was a fine calligrapher and a great landscape gardener; wherever he resided, at quite a number of places in Japan, he designed splendid gardens, some of which are still in existence and well preserved after so many years of changing times. Among the noted painters of Zen in the fourteenth and fifteenth centuries we may mention Chō Densu (d. 1431),

Kei Shoki (*fl.* 1490), Josetsu (*fl.* 1375–1420), Shūbun (*fl.* 1420–50), Seshū (1421–1506), and others.

Georges Duthuit, the author of *Chinese Mysticism and Modern Painting,* seems to understand the spirit of Zen mysticism. From him we have this: "When the Chinese artist paints, what matters is the concentration of thought and the prompt and vigorous response of the hand to the directing will. Tradition ordains him to see, or rather to feel, as a whole the work to be executed, before embarking on anything. 'If the ideas of a man are confused, he will become the slave of exterior conditions.' . . . He who deliberates and moves his brush intent on making a picture, misses to a still greater extent the art of painting. [This seems like a kind of automatic writing.] Draw bamboos for ten years, become a bamboo, then forget all about bamboos when you are drawing. In possession of an infallible technique, the individual places himself at the mercy of inspiration."

To become a bamboo and to forget that you are one with it while drawing it—this is the Zen of the bamboo, this is the moving with the "rhythmic movement of the spirit" which resides in the bamboo as well as in the artist himself. What is now required of him is to have a firm hold on the spirit and yet not to be conscious of the fact. This is a very difficult task achieved only after long spiritual training.[6] The Eastern people have been taught since the earliest times to subject themselves to this kind of discipline if they want to achieve something in the world of art and religion. Zen, in fact, has given expression to it in the following phrase: "One in All and All in One." When this is thoroughly understood, there is creative genius.

It is of utmost importance here to interpret the phrase in its proper sense. People imagine that it means pantheism, and some students of Zen seem to agree. This is to be regretted, for pantheism is something foreign to Zen and also to the artist's understanding of his world. When the Zen masters declare the One to be in the All and the All in the One, they do not mean that the one is the other and *vice versa*. As the One is in the All, some people suppose that Zen is a pantheistic teaching. Far from it; Zen would never hypostatize the One or the All as a thing to be grasped by the sense. The phrase "One in All and All in One" is to be understood as an expression of absolute Prajñā-intuition and is not to be conceptually analyzed. When we see the

<hr />

[6]Cf. Takuan on "Prajñā Immovable."

moon, we know that it is the moon, and that is enough. Those who proceed to analyze the experience and try to establish a theory of knowledge are not students of Zen. They cease to be so, if they ever were, at the very moment of their procedure as analysts. Zen always upholds its experience as such and refuses to commit itself to any system of philosophy.

Even when Zen indulges in intellection, it never subscribes to a pantheistic interpretation of the world. For one thing, there is no One in Zen. If Zen ever speaks of the One as if it recognized it, this is a kind of condescension to common parlance. To Zen students, the One is the All and the All is the One; and yet the One remains the One and the All the All. "Not two!" may lead the logician to think, "It is One." But the master would go on, saying, "Not One either!" "What then?" we may ask. We here face a blind alley, as far as verbalism is concerned. Therefore, it is said that "If you wish to be in direct communion [with Reality], I tell you 'Not two!' "

The following *mondo*[7] may help to illustrate the point I wish to make in regard to the Zen attitude toward the so-called pantheistic interpretation of nature.

A monk asked Tōsu (T'ou-tzu), a Zen master of the T'ang period: "I understand that all sounds are the voice of the Buddha. Is this right?" The master said, "That is right." The monk then proceeded: "Would not the master please stop making a noise which echoes the sound of a fermenting mass of filth?" The master thereupon struck the monk.

The monk further asked Tōsu: "Am I in the right when I understand the Buddha as asserting that all talk, however trivial or derogatory, belongs to ultimate truth The master said, "Yes, you are in the right." The monk went on, "May I then call you a donkey?" The master thereupon struck him.

It may be necessary to explain these *mondo* in plain language. To conceive every sound, every noise, every utterance one makes as issuing from the fountainhead of one Reality, that is, from one God, is pantheistic, I imagine. For "he giveth to all life, and breath, and all things" (Acts 17:25); and again, "For in him we live, and move, and have our being" (Acts 17:28). If this be the case, a Zen

master's hoarse throat echoes the melodious resonance of the voice flowing from the Buddha's golden mouth, and even when a great teacher is decried as reminding one of an ass, the defamation must be regarded as reflecting something of ultimate truth. All forms of evil must be said somehow to be embodying what is true and good and beautiful, and to be a contribution to the perfection of Reality. To state it more concretely, bad is good, ugly is beautiful, false is true, imperfect is perfect, and also conversely. This is, indeed, the kind of reasoning in which those indulge who conceive the God-nature to be immanent in all things. Let us see how the Zen master treats this problem.

It is remarkable that Tōsu put his foot right down against such intellectualist interpretations and struck his monk. The latter in all probability expected to see the master nonplussed by his statements which logically follow from his first assertion. The masterful Tōsu knew, as all Zen masters do, the uselessness of making any verbal demonstration against such a "logician." For verbalism leads from one complication to another; there is no end to it. The only effective way, perhaps, is to make such a monk as this one realize the falsehood of his conceptual understanding is to strike him and so let him experience within himself the meaning of the statement, "One in All and All in One." The monk was to be awakened from his logical somnambulism. Hence Tōsu's drastic measure.

Secchō here gives his comments in the following lines:

Pity that people without number try to play with the tide;
They are all ultimately swallowed up into it and die!
Let them suddenly awake [from the dead-lock],
And see that all the rivers run backward, swelling and surging.[8]

What is needed here is an abrupt turning or awakening, with which one comes to the realization of the truth of Zen—which is neither transcendentalism nor immanentism nor a combination of the two. The truth is as Tōsu declares in the following:

---

[7]This and what follows are all from the *Hekigan-shu,* case 79.

[8]Seccho (Hsüeh-tou, 980–1052) was one of the great Zen masters of the Sung, noted for his literary accomplishment. The *Hekigan-shu* is based on Seccho's "One Hundred Cases," which he selected out of the annals of Zen.

A monk asks, "What is the Buddha?"
Tōsu answers, "The Buddha."
Monk: "What is the Tao?"
Tōsu: "The Tao."
Monk: "What is Zen?"
Tōsu: "Zen."

The master answers like a parrot, he is echo itself. In fact, there is no other way of illumining the monk's mind than affirming that what is is—which is the final fact of experience.

Another example[9] is given to illustrate the point. A monk asked Jōshu (Chao-chou), of the rang dynasty: "It is stated that the Perfect Way knows no difficulties, only that it abhors discrimination. What is meant by No-discrimination?"

Jōshu said: "Above the heavens and below the heavens, I alone am the Honored One."

The monk suggested, "Still a discrimination."

The master's retort was, "O this worthless fellow! Where is the discrimination?"

By discrimination the Zen masters mean what we have when we refuse to accept Reality as it is or in its suchness, for we then reflect on it and analyze it into concepts, going on with intellection and finally landing on a circulatory reasoning. Jōshu's affirmation is a final one and allows no equivocation, no argumentation. We have simply to take it as it stands and remain satisfied with it. In case we somehow fail to do this, we just leave it alone, and go somewhere else to seek our own enlightenment. The monk could not see where Jōshu was, and he went further on and remarked, "This is still a discrimination!" The discrimination in point of fact is on the monk's side and not on Jōshu's. Hence "the Honored One" now turns into "a worthless follow."

As I said before, the phrase "All in One and One in All" is not to be analyzed first to the concepts "One" and "All," and the preposition is not then to be put between them; no discrimination is to be exercised here, but one is just to accept it and abide with it, which is really no-abiding at all. There is nothing further to do. Hence the master's striking or calling names. He is not indignant, nor is he short-tempered, but he wishes thereby to help his disciples out of the pit which they have dug themselves. No amount of argument avails here, no verbal persuasion. Only the master knows how to turn them away from a logical impasse and how to open a new way for them; let them, therefore, simply follow him. By following him they all come back to their Original Home.

When an intuitive or experiential understanding of Reality is verbally formulated as "All in One and One in All," we have there the fundamental statement as it is taught by all the various schools of Buddhism. In the terminology of the Prajñā school, this is: śūnyatā ("Emptiness") is tathatā ("Suchness"), and tathatā is śūnyatā:śūnyatā is the world of the Absolute, and tathatā the world of particulars. One of the commonest sayings in Zen is "Willows are green and flowers red" or "Bamboos are straight and pine trees are gnarled." Facts of experience are accepted as they are, Zen is not nihilistic, nor is it merely positivistic. Zen would say that just because the bamboo is straight it is of Emptiness, or that just because of Emptiness the bamboo cannot be anything else but a bamboo and not a pine tree. What makes the Zen statements different from mere sense experience, however, is that Zen's intuition grows out of Prajñā and not out of jñā.[10] It is from this point of view that when asked "What is Zen?" the master sometimes answers "Zen" and sometimes "Not-Zen."

We can see now that the principle of sumiye painting is derived from this Zen experience, and that directness, simplicity, movement spirituality, completeness, and other qualities we observe in the sumiye class of Oriental paintings have organic relationship to Zen. There is no pantheism in sumiye as there is none in Zen.

There is another thing I must not forget to mention in this connection, which is perhaps the most important factor in sumiye as well as in Zen. It is creativity. When it is said that sumiye depicts the spirit of an object, or that it gives a form to what has no form, this means that there must be a spirit of creativity moving over the picture. The painter's business thus is not just to copy or imitate nature, but to give to the object something living in its own right. It is the same with the Zen master. When he says that the willow is green and the flower is red, he is not just giving us a description of how nature looks, but something whereby green is green and red is red. This something is what I call the spirit

[9] Hekigan-shu, case 57.

[10] Prajñā may be translated "transcendental wisdom," while jñā or vijñāna is "relative knowledge." For a detailed explanation, see my Studies in Buddhism, pp. 85 ff.

of creativity. *Śūnyatā* is formless, but it is the fountainhead of all possibilities. To turn what is possible into an actuality is an act of creativity. When Tōsu is asked, "What is Dharma?" he answers, "Dharma"; when asked "What is Buddha?" he answers, "Buddha." This is by no means a parrot-like response, a mere echoing, all the answers come out of his creative mind, without which there is no Zen in Tōsu. The understanding of Zen is to understand what kind of mind this is. Yakusan's meeting with Rikō will illustrate this.[11]

Yakusan (Yao-shan, 751–834) was a great master of the T'ang era. When Rikō (Li Ao), governor of the province, heard of his Zen mastership, he sent for him to come to the capital. Yakusan, however, refused to come. This happened several times. Rikō grew impatient and came in person to see the master in his own mountain retreat. Yakusan was reading the *sūtras* and paid no attention whatever to the arrival of the governor. The attendant monk reminded the master of the fact, but he still kept on reading. Rikō felt hurt and remarked,

"Seeing the face is not at all like hearing the name." By this he meant that the person in actuality was not equal to his reputation. Yakusan called out, "O Governor!" Rikō echoed at once, "Yes, Master." The master then said, "Why do you evaluate the hearing over the seeing?" The governor apologized and asked, "What is Tao?" Yakusan pointed up with his hand and then down, and said, "Do you understand?" Rikō said, "No, Master." Thereupon Yakusan remarked, "The clouds are in the sky and water in the jar." It is said that this pleased the governor very much.

Did Rikō really understand what Yakusan meant? Yakusan's is no more than a plain statement of facts as they are, and we may ask, "Where is Tao?" Rikō was a great scholar and philosopher. He must have had some abstract conception of Tao. Could he so readily reconcile his view with Yakusan's? Whatever we may say about this, Yakusan and Tōsu and other Zen masters are all walking the same track. The artists are also required to strike it.

---

[11]*Dentō-roku* ("Transmission of the Lamp") fasc. 14.

D. T. Suzuki's "Aspects of Japanese Culture"

1. "Wabi" really means "poverty" or, negatively, "not to be in the fashionable society of the time."
    a. True   b. False

2. "Sabi" consists in rustic unpretentiousness or archaic imperfection, apparent simplicity or effortlessness in execution.

    a. True   b. False

3. Zen Buddhism united itself to Taoist philosophy in China but had nothing to do with Confucian philosophy.

    a. True   b. False

4. According to Suzuki, which term does not characterize the influence of Zen on Japanese art?

    a. pantheism
    b. solitude
    c. spontaneity
    d. asymmetry

5. Briefly explain how Zen might help an aspiring American artist today.

VI. THE FINE ARTS AND COMMUNICATION

LIST OF KEY TERMS

taste:

aesthetic experience:

aesthetic value:

warranted eligibility:

formal elements:

Classicism:

Romanticism:

abstract expressionism:

point of view:

proximate vision:

distant vision:

virtual reality:

dynamic image:

empathy:

Zen:

VII.
APPENDIX

Introduction to Critical Thinking Through Active Reading

Jon Avery

A significant objective of any core curriculum is to cultivate the foundational skill of critical thinking, which can be defined as active and disciplined reasoning about the meaning and truth of things. It is vital to keep in mind that students who think critically are neither fault finders nor mentally passive, but are actively exercising certain cognitive skills and affective dispositions in search of sound judgment on issues of importance.[1] More specifically, ideal critical thinkers are skilled in the mental processes of **interpretation, analysis, inference, explanation, evaluation, and self-regulation.** Self-regulation is the self-monitoring of one's cognitive acts of analysis, evaluation, inference, explanation, and inference for the purpose of improving them. The ideal critical thinker not only knows how to think critically but also is alert to opportunities to use those skills, for she has developed the disposition to be "habitually inquisitive, well-informed, trustful of reason, open-minded, honest in facing personal biases, willing to reconsider, clear about issues, orderly in complex matters, and persistent in seeking results which are as precise as the subject and the circumstances of inquiry permit."[2]

These skills and dispositions can be exercised while reading, writing, or speaking, but for the purpose of this introduction, let us focus on their application in the process of active reading. Active reading is the conscious exercise of critical thinking skills and dispositions in the activity of reading. There are two main phases to active reading and six steps.[3] The first five steps comprise the first phase of **"analysis"** in which we attempt to understand the author's position. Critical thinking skills in the mental acts of interpretation, inference, and explanation are used in this phase. The last step comprises the second phase of **"evaluation"** in which we decide whether the author succeeded in making his case. A critical thinker relies on a knowledge of the relevant facts and logical reasoning more than just personal opinion when evaluating. Also very useful in this phase of critical thinking are the dispositions of being well-informed, honest in facing personal biases, trust in reason, and being habitually inquisitive. However, these two phases of active reading must be kept distinct, for it is easy for an uncritical reader to evaluate a reading before fully understanding it. The written or spoken summary of active reading is called an abstract, and abstracts are essential to college study because there is so much information to cover and too little time to discuss all of it.

First of all, the active reader identifies the **main point** the author reached in her inquiry, which can usually be succinctly stated in a sentence that summarizes the most important idea, or conclusion, in the article. Second, an active reader becomes aware of the **central issue** the author tried to answer. Since writing is a form of inquiry, any composition is an answer to a question or problem. Incidentally, steps one and two occur almost simultaneously. Step three is the identification of the author's **main argument** in support of that conclusion or thesis, which is discerned by asking why the author believes her main position is true. The author's argument comprises the evidence the author uses to justify her conclusion. Step four is the identification of **key terms,** significant words or phrases around which the author's inquiry and argument revolve. This step helps understand the concepts the author uses to make her arguments. Moreover, these

---

[1]These skills and dispositions are thoroughly described in The Delphi Study, a study commissioned by the American Philosophical Association in which a consensus was reached by forty-six experts from numerous university disciplines about the nature of the ideal critical thinker. Peter A. Facione, *Critical Thinking: A Statement of Expert Consensus for Purposes of Educational Assessment and Instruction,* California State University, Fullerton, CA, 1990.

[2]Facione, 12.

[3]I am grateful to Mortimer Adler and Charles Van Doren for their helpful suggestions on what they call analytical reading in their *How to Read A Book,* (NY: Simon & Schuster, 1940, revised and updated in 1972).

terms could be identified before the question, answer, and evidence if doing so helps understand the author's main points. The fifth step is the identification of **secondary points, issues, and arguments,** which are other points, issues, and arguments the author uses to support or elaborate the main argument. **Evaluation** is the sixth and final step in active reading. An active reader tries to keep personal conclusions for the main issue of an author's article out of the analysis phase of reading, but when the author's points are fully understood, the reader must then decide about the cogency of the author's arguments. This is where the reader's personal reflections on the issue come in.

Here is a summary of directions on how to put an abstract together. Read through each selection, highlighting important and interesting ideas. Put the selection away for awhile. Go back to the highlights and look for only a couple central points the author makes. Try to prioritize those ideas into the main point and the secondary points by using your judgment as to which one is central to the author's overall purpose. You may want to use precise deductive and inductive argument forms to help you formulate the author's arguments as well as your own arguments in the evaluation phase because they are common forms of valid and invalid reasoning. However, this is not necessary. The purpose of giving arguments is to state reasons why a conclusion should be accepted, and precise forms may or may not help in this endeavor.

There are several criteria by which we can evaluate an author's arguments.[4] These criteria are logical criteria that do not depend on our personal preferences, and they may be summarized in the form of questions. Are there any logical fallacies, such as over-generalization, over-simplification, over-looking of alternatives, logical inconsistency, or begging of the question? Are there any inaccurate statements? Are all the terms clearly defined? Are there any questionable assumptions? If all or most of these criteria are met, then whether we like it or not, the author has succeeded in providing a cogent argument. However, if we are not convinced by the argument, and we are to have grounds other than personal preference, then we must explain how the author violates one or more of these criteria. People can very easily be convinced by fallacious arguments, but critical thinkers try to only be convinced by cogent arguments.

Here is a summary of how to write out an evaluation of a reading. First of all, determine if the author has committed any logical fallacies. Review the list of fallacies in any logic textbook. Second, decide whether all of the author's statements in support of the main and secondary conclusions are validated by **observation, memory, expert testimony,** or **logical reasoning.** Third, if the author fails to define all key terms, or defines them in vague or imprecise ways, then note that. Be careful that you do not confuse your inability to comprehend the subject or the inherent difficulty of a subject with the author's failure to provide clear definitions. Then, determine whether the author assumes certain things that are questionable by again consulting observation, memory, expert testimony, or logical reasoning. Last, reach a one sentence conclusion about whether or not the author convinced you of her main point and explain your reasons.

In short, critical thinking skills and dispositions can be nurtured through active reading, but not without effort. In making the effort, though, one can make great strides in intellectual growth and come to a deeper and clearer understanding of things.

---

[4]For further discussion on how to evaluate an author's reasoning see Richard Paul, *Critical Thinking: What Every Person Needs To Survive In A Rapidly Changing World,* edited by A. J. Binker, (Rohnert Park, CA: Center for Critical Thinking and Moral Critique, Sonoma State University, 1990), 51f.

Editor's Note: The following abstract form may be photocopied for use in class at the instructor's discretion.

NAME _____   DATE _____

ABSTRACT

TITLE: _____

1.   Main Point (conclusion/thesis): _____
     _____
     _____
     _____
     _____

2.   Central Issue (question/problem): _____
     _____
     _____

3.   Main Argument (reasons why for conclusion): _____
     _____
     _____
     _____
     _____
     _____

4.   Key Terms (definitions of central words): _____
     _____
     _____
     _____

5.   Secondary conclusion, issue, argument (another important point, question, and reason):
     _____
     _____
     _____
     _____
     _____
     _____
     _____
     _____

6.   Evaluation (convincing/unconvincing and why—fallacies, facts, terms, assumptions, impli-
     cations): _____
     _____
     _____
     _____
     _____
     _____
     _____

Suggestions for Further Reading

Students interested in pursuing further the issues addressed in this book should consider reading the complete works from which the preceding selections are drawn. In addition to those texts, the following books, which range in difficulty from the introductory to the advanced, will also prove useful.

I. PHILOSOPHY

John Dewey, *Reconstruction in Philosophy*.
Ted Honderich, ed., *Philosophy As It Is*.
Abraham Kaplan, *The New World Of Philosophy*.
Julian Marias, *History of Philosophy*.
Jose Ortega y Gassett, *What is Philosophy?*
Bertrand Russell, *The History of Western Philosophy*.
Peter Strawson, *Analysis and Metaphysics*.
Robert Paul Wolff, *About Philosophy*.

II. EPISTEMOLOGY

Bruce Aune, *Rationalism, Empiricism, and Pragmatism*.
A. J. Ayer, *The Problem of Knowledge*.
Roderick Chisholm, *Theory of Knowledge*.
John Dewey, *The Quest for Certainty*.
Immanuel Kant, *Prolegomena to any Future Metaphysics*.
Willard V. O. Quine and James Ullian, *The Web of Belief*.
Bertrand Russell, *Human Knowledge*.

III. MATHEMATICS AND THE NATURAL SCIENCES

Peter Achinstein, ed., *The Concept of Evidence*.
Robert Ackermann, *Data, Instruments, and Theory*.
John D. Barrow, *Theories of Everything: The Quest for Ultimate Explanation*.
Tim Berra, *Evolution and the Myth of Creation*.
Jean Charon, *Cosmology*.
J. B. Conant, *Science and Common Sense*.
Paul Davies, *The Mind of God*.
Richard Dawkins, *The Blind Watchmaker*.
Timothy Ferris, *Coming of Age in the Milky Way*.
Paul Feyerabend, *Against Method*.
Noel R. Hanson, *Patterns of Discovery*.
Stephen Hawking, *A Brief History of Time*.
Carl Hempel, *The Philosophy of Natural Science*.
Phillip Kitcher, *Abusing Science*.
Imre Lakatos and Alan Musgrave, *Criticism and the Growth of Knowledge*.

Ashley Montagu, ed., *Science and Creationism.*
Israel Scheffler, *The Anatomy of Inquiry.*
Dirk Struik, *A Concise History of Mathematics.*
Lewis Thomas, *The Lives of a Cell.*
Stephen Toulmin, *Philosophy of Science.*
James Trefil, *Reading the Mind of God.*

IV. THE SOCIAL SCIENCES

Daniel Bell and Irving Kristol, *The Crisis in Economic Theory.*
Peter Berger, *Invitation to Sociology.*
Peter Berger and Thomas Luckmann, *The Social Construction of Reality.*
Sigmund Freud, *Outline of Psychoanalysis.*
John Kenneth Galbraith, *Economics in Perspective.*
Clifford Geertz, *The Interpretation of Cultures.*
Frank Hahn and Martin Hollis, eds., *Philosophy and Economic Theory.*
Marvin Harris, *Cultural Materialism.*
Robert Heilbroner, *The Worldly Philosophers.*
Claude Levi-Strauss, *Structural Anthropology.*
Seymour Martin Lipset, *Political Man.*
C. Wright Mills, *The Sociological Imagination.*
Lionel Robbins, *The Nature and Significance of Economic Science.*
Alan Ryan, ed., *The Philosophy of Social Explanation.*
B. F. Skinner, *Beyond Freedom and Dignity.*
Max Weber, *The Methodology of the Social Sciences.*

V. HUMANITIES

Wayne Booth, *The Rhetoric of Fiction.*
Arthur Danto, *Narrative and Analysis.*
William Dray, *The Philosophy of History.*
Terry Eagleton, *Literary Theory.*
Mircea Eliade, *The Sacred and the Profane.*
A. C. Ewing, *Ethics.*
William Frankena, *Ethics.*
Northrop Frye, *Anatomy of Criticism.*
Patrick Gardiner, ed., *The Philosophy of History.*
Gilbert Harman, *The Nature of Morality.*
John Hick, ed., *Classical and Contemporary Readings in the Philosophy of Religion.*
John Hick, *The Philosophy of Religion* and *An Interpretation of Religion.*
David Hume, *Dialogues Concerning Natural Religion.*
Immanuel Kant, *Lectures on Philosophical Theology* and *Religion within the Limits of Reason Alone.*
Gordon Kaufman, *The Theological Imagination.*
G. E. Moore, *Ethics.*
Huston Smith, *The World's Religions.*
W. H. Walsh, *Introduction to the Philosophy of History.*

VI. FINE ARTS AND COMMUNICATION

Aristotle, *Rhetoric.*
Monroe Beardsley, *Aesthetics.*
Clive Bell, *Art.*
John Berger, *Ways of Seeing.*
John Dewey, *Art as Experience.*

Simon Frith, *Sound Effects.*
Nelson Goodman, *Languages of Art.*
Richard Hofstadter and Kuhn, eds., *Philosophies of Art and Beauty.*
Leroi Jones, *Blues People.*
Immanuel Kant, *Critique of Judgment.*
Susanne Langer, *Philosophy in a New Key.*
Herbert Marcuse, *The Aesthetic Dimension.*
Marshall McLuhan, *Understanding Media.*
Arthur Schnabel, *Music and the Line of Most Resistance.*
Stephen Toulmin, *The Uses of Argument.*
Ortiz Walton, *Music: Black, White, and Blue.*
Alan Watts, *The Way of Zen.*
Richard Wollheim, *Art and Its Objects.*